The Collected Writings of Frederic Remington

ALSO BY PEGGY AND HAROLD SAMUELS

*The Illustrated Biographical Encyclopedia of
Artists of the American West*

Frederic Remington in 1891. *Authors' wood engraving.*

The Collected Writings of

Edited by

FREDERIC REMINGTON

PEGGY and HAROLD SAMUELS

Illustrated by Frederic Remington

CASTLE

Library of Congress Cataloging in Publication Data

Remington, Frederic, 1861–1909.
The collected writings of Frederic Remington.

Bibliography: p. 630.
I. The West—Collected works.   I.   Samuels, Peggy.
II.   Samuels, Harold.   III.   Title.
PS2695.R72   978   818'.4'08
ISBN 1-55521-1115-1

CONTENTS

viii   *Contents*

x　　*Contents*

LIST OF ILLUSTRATIONS

INTRODUCTION

When Frederic Remington left his neo-Gothic mansion in New Rochelle the end of May 1902 for the simpler eight-bedroom summer cottage on his own Thousand Island, Ingleneuk, he wrote to his friend Owen Wister, "Now that the relaxation has come I despise labor."

Remington might well have thought he was entitled to a rest. At the age of forty, he was one of the most popular artists in the world, and one of the best paid. His sculpture was critically acclaimed, and it sold phenomenally. Remington was the undisputed pictorial arbiter of the American West. As author Emerson Hough complained, if Remington wanted to establish that a Western horse had five legs, he certainly could make it stick.

In addition to satisfying the consuming demands of his art, Remington relished his role as a public figure. He was the friend and confidant of the President of the United States. He belonged to the clubs of the elite and the talented. His companionship was sought after by the leaders of industry and finance who jockeyed to buy key paintings and drawings.

This summer of 1902, though, his message to Wister was a mild deception. Wister had just published his only lasting literary accomplishment, the cowboy novel *The Virginian*. So, when Remington entered his little island studio each morning that summer, his brushes and palette remained hung on the wall. He was composing his answer to

Wister, what he called his long story, the novel *John Ermine of the Yellowstone*.

During the rest of his abbreviated career, Remington thought of himself as an artist, not as an author. As a painter, however, he was never elected a full National Academician, despite the pressure he applied. He was not invited to exhibit with the National Sculpture Society. In contrast, when *The Bookman* about 1905 symbolically divided the country into regions appropriated by individual authors, it accepted Remington into the company of Bret Harte, Joaquin Miller, Longfellow, Mark Twain, Stowe, Riley, Cooper, Irving, and Hawthorne, granting Remington the Southwest as his literary turf. He was one of the 102 authors of the *High Spots of American Literature*.

Remington wrote regularly from 1887 to 1906, creating enough works for a literary lifetime in addition to his painting and sculpture. His articles and stories in magazines comprised 111 appearances, and his one novel, *John Ermine,* written directly for hard-cover publication, was the basis for a play. Remington compiled seven other books to reprint 47 of the magazine pieces into hard cover beginning 1895 with *Pony Tracks*. A few additional articles were reprinted after his death, but 45 of Remington's writings have been generally available only in the original periodicals long out of print. Up until now reading them has called for a visit to the rare book room.

Yet these writings were the prime reason

A Cheyenne Camp. *Painting in authors' collection.*

for the creation of 20 per cent of Remington's paintings and drawings. The art is fine enough to stand on its own, as it has done, but each of the pictures is given dimension and is enhanced by the Remington words. As the Albany *Journal* pointed out in 1898, "Mr. Remington presents a perfect combination when he works with himself . . . picture and text go to form a whole which the reader could not well grasp were it not for the supplemental qualities of each in its bearing on the other."

In short, full appreciation of the art requires the text. Consequently, when Remington is recognized universally as a meaningful historian who recorded on canvas the Western and military genre of his day, his related writings should be given equal value as recorded history. From the article "Artist Wanderings Among the Cheyennes," look at the reproduction of the grisaille oil painting "A Cheyenne Camp."

Then read the portion of the text: "Our buckboard drew gradually nearer the camp of the Cheyennes. A great level prairie of waving green was dotted with the brown toned white canvas lodges, and standing near them were brush 'ramadas,' or sheds, and also wagons. For about ten years they have owned wagons, and now seldom use the travaux. In little groups all over the plain were scattered pony herds, and about the camp could be seen forms wearing bright blankets or wrapped in ghostlike cotton sheets. Little columns of blue smoke rose here and there, and gathered in front of one lodge was squatted a group of men. A young squaw dressed in a bright calico gown stood near a ramada and bandied words with the interpreter while I sketched. Presently she was informed that I had made her picture, when she ran off, laughing at what she considered an unbecoming trick on the part of her entertainer."

This Remington painting is an active triangulated composition pointed with sophistication at the focal squaw, the whole canvas meaningfully employed, and the ethnographic elements in careful array. But consider the text: It prefaces with history, names the objects, adds the color, and in the same breath moves the squaw into the next frame.

For some, the readers, the text above is

superior to the illustration and independent of it. The imagery is visualized in color, the conversation aloud, the young squaw a beauty. Effusively, Theodore Roosevelt wrote Remington December 28, 1897: "You come closer to the real thing with the pen than any other man in the western business. And I include Hough, Grinnell and Wister. Literally innumerable short stories and sketches of cowboys, Indians and soldiers have been, and will be, written. Even if very good they will die like mushrooms, unless they are the very best. Now, I think you are writing this 'very best.' "

It is only fair to note, though, that this nod to Remington preceded Wister's classic, *The Virginian,* about which Roosevelt wrote Wister June 7, 1902, from the White House, "It is a remarkable novel."

The reason Remington wrote for publication was, according to his September 1, 1899, letter to Wister, because it gave him "a chance to use my right as they say in the arena." This was presumably after he had set things up with his left, his illustrations.

The real reason probably related to Remington's constant early need for money as he worked his way out of shared no-studio quarters in Brooklyn. He was a professional illustrator before he was a writer. When Remington sent sketches to *Harper's Weekly* for reproduction in 188(?) he accompanied them with explanatory comments. The Harper copywriter used Remington's prose in preparing the article on the illustration. This is clear in "Soldiering in the Southwest," August 21, 1886, and in "Dragging the Hide," October 27, 1888. These articles are not reprinted here because they are unsigned. By December 1, 1888, in "A Peccary Hunt in Northern Mexico," Remington had a paid and signed article to run with the paid and signed illustration.

E. S. Martin in *Harper's Weekly,* June 23, 1894, explained this as a trend. Time was, Martin said, when illustrators looked on authors with respect. Whereas literature had been the staple of the periodicals, and pictures merely a supplementary attraction,

it began to happen that the pictures became the indispensable thing, and the reading matter only the thread that the pictures were strung on. Writers and illustrators still continued on terms of amicable interdependence, but, alas! through continued association with writers, the illustrators learned to spell. When an artist was too tired to practice art, there was nothing to hinder him from writing. Mr. Remington does not scruple, Martin said, to garnish his horseflesh with narratives of adventure. Little remains, he concluded, except for someone to evolve the theory that the real author of Shakespeare's plays is Mr. Edwin Abbey (who was then illustrating the plays for *Harper's*).

When Remington acted as a reporter, he told a perfectly straightforward story, neatly arranged, without artifice or pretension. His "letterpress" text was unique for its Victorian prissy time, more comparable to the punchy graphic text of the virile 1930s. Helen Card called this a sculptor's prose, terse with its bones showing. In Remington's day, Wister was the larger literary light. In March 1900 Remington with tongue in cheek wrote Wister, "I am only a character man. I'm a snare-drum and you are an organ."

Oddly enough, different eyes have favored different Remington pieces. Roosevelt chose the mood novel *The Way of an Indian,* writing February 20, 1906: "It may be true that no white man ever understood an Indian, but at any rate you convey the impression of understanding him." By July 17, 1907, Roosevelt wrote *Pearson's Magazine* the Remington testimonial: "Nor must we forget the excellent literary work he has done in such pieces as 'Masai's Crooked Trail,' with its peculiar insight into the character of the wildest Indians."

General Nelson Miles acknowledged Remington's descriptive powers as "certainly very good" in "Bear-Chasing in the Rocky Mountains." Remington's severe critic Emerson Hough called "With the Fifth Corps" the best story of the Spanish-American War. C. C. Buel, an editor of

Century, wrote that "With the Fifth Corps" is the only wholly satisfactory article on the Santiago campaign.

Remington himself liked "Black Water and Shallows" of his North Country. A personal choice is the earliest, the twister "Coursing Rabbits on the Plains." "Chasing a Major-General" was quoted by critic Royal Cortissoz as being "an absolutely clear descriptive statement." J. Frank Dobie called Remington a superb reporter for "The Sioux Outbreak in South Dakota." "Indians as Irregular Cavalry" presented an army concept that was debated in Congress and discussed between the President and the War Department. Sculptor Edward Kemeys gave "Shotgun Episode" the dignity of a classic. It is good for the liver, wrote painter Edward Simmons about "Natchez's Pass." Publisher J. Henry Harper noted the stylistic relationship to de Maupassant. George Wharton Edwards, an editor of *Collier's,* wrote: You have hewn John Ermine in bold strokes that remind me irresistibly of the work of Rodin.

There are a dozen Remington pieces that were regarded as classics. There are another dozen that are pedestrian, included here because this is the entire collection of Remington's writings published in magazines and books during his lifetime. Nothing has been edited or deleted.

One word of caution. Frederic Remington was an enormous man with talent to match, but he was emotionally the product of his era. Like Roosevelt and Wister, he was the willing captive of conservative nationalistic jargon. A story like "The Affair of the –th of July," centering around violence by the military against domestic civilians, is incomprehensible unless it is observed that the story appeared in the same February 2, 1895, issue of *Harper's Weekly* as the news reporting the streetcar strike in Brooklyn with the illustration of a soldier shooting a householder who opened a window. What you have is a Remington with his warts on, but a Remington who did not let his personal bias interfere with his objective illustrations.

You also have an artist-correspondent who covered the North American continent, Europe, and Africa while professing to be comfortable only with his own kind, the westerner. Remington himself was at most a qualified westerner, raised in the St. Lawrence River country. He traveled the West at nineteen, as soon as he could get away. He bought a sheep ranch the moment he could afford it, brought his new wife West to live, and returned East only because he could not find a suitable occupation in the West and his wife might otherwise have left him. He refreshed himself in the West through many visits, but he was never a complete westerner in the sense of transplants that took like Charles Russell.

As a final generalization about the writings, it is true that they provide a partial autobiography for Remington. The narrative begins with his experiences raising sheep in Kansas and takes him through his maturation after the Spanish-American War.

His origins clearly indicated a career for Remington as a writer, soldier, or preacher rather than the artist he considered himself. No Remington ancestor back to the days of the Normans in England was a painter. No professional artist of consequence worked in Canton or Ogdensburg during Remington's adolescence.

Robert Taft's genealogical research found a John Remington, the fifth son of an English archdeacon, who emigrated to Massachusetts in 1637. According to Frederic Remington, part of the family moved westward to the Pacific Coast before returning to New England. It was his remote cousins who were the gunmaker Remingtons and the manufacturing Remingtons. Remington was proud of his father's Saxon origin but never mentioned that his mother's family was from Alsace-Lorraine.

Remington's grandfather Seth Williston Remington was born in Vermont in 1807. He became a Universalist minister, moving to Canton, New York, where he was active in raising funds to found St. Lawrence University. Canton, a New England style village of 1,500 with dirt streets and plank walks, was in the "North Country" seventeen miles from the St. Lawrence River at the Canadian border.

Remington's father was Seth Pierre Remington, the fourth child, called Pierre, born in Chautauqua County, New York, in 1834. In 1856 Pierre Remington with a partner started the newspaper *St. Lawrence Plaindealer* as a vehicle for the new Republican party. Pierre Remington was an experienced journalist, ambitious for political recognition, a fiery and excitable editor with firm opinions. He was also an ardent horseman. Remington's mother was Clara Sackrider, the only daughter of Canton's hardware dealer. She was a sturdy retiring figure alongside the romantic Pierre Remington she married in January 1861.

Frederic Sackrider Remington was born October 4, 1861, in Canton in the Court Street clapboard house recorded in the name of his grandmother Maria Pickering Remington. Only seven weeks later, Pierre Remington enrolled to serve three years in Scott's Nine Hundred, the Eleventh New York State Volunteer Cavalry for the Civil War. He helped recruit Company D, was mustered in as captain March 13, 1862, was commissioned a major, and was made colonel by brevet. The colonel was a legitimate war hero, listed as participating in numerous engagements, and cited for gallantry at Douall's Plantation in Louisiana August 4, 1864.

When the colonel returned to Canton in 1865, he found his son a big boy, strong and impetuous, with his own hyperactivity set in the large frame of the Sackriders. The colonel divided his time among his newspaper, Republican politics, and racing standardbred horses. Fred Remington, a "regular boy" with red complexion and sandy hair, adored his father and doted on stories of the war. His outdoor pleasures centered around his father's standardbreds and his own horse that galloped over the hills.

Not precocious and certainly no genius, Fred Remington rebelled from the confinement of school. He was an inattentive student, defacing his books with crude drawings of horses, soldiers, and wild Indians. He began sketching seriously in 1874, after his family moved the twenty miles north to French-Canadian influenced Ogdensburg, where his father had been appointed United States Collector of Customs. The favorite drawing subject was horses.

In the fall of 1875 Remington was sent to Vermont Episcopal Institute, a military school in Burlington. That summer he made his first painting, now in the collection of the Remington Art Museum in Ogdensburg. In the fall of 1876 he transferred to Highland Military Academy in Worcester, Massachusetts. A lazy student, his best subject was English. He was an avid reader of Catlin, Lewis and Clark, Parkman, Gregg, and Irving. This was the year of Custer's fight, heightened for Remington by the obvious similarity between Custer and Remington's father.

After Remington had become a famous artist, the men who had been his classmates at the academy and later at Yale professed to have seen in his sketches the mark of genius. The sketches that have been preserved, however, are cruder than could have been anticipated. In contrast, Remington's gift of phrasing was clear and concise early on. A letter about April 1877 from Remington at the academy to a Maine correspondent is an example: "My hair is short and stiff, and I am about five feet eight inches and weigh one hundred and eighty pounds. There is nothing poetical about me. I live in Ogdensburg, New York, on the banks of the St. Lawrence. I am well instructed in Upton's 'Infantry Tactics,' and have just come off from an hour's drill. I don't swear much, although it is my weak point, and I have to look my letters over carefully to see if there is any cussing in them. I never smoke—only when I can get treated—and I never condescend to the friendly offer of 'Take something, old hoss?' " (The source is Crooker.)

May 27, 1878, Remington wrote from the academy to his uncle Horace Sackrider in the same bantering tone he retained as an adult: "I never intend to do any great amount of labor. I have but one short life and do not aspire to wealth nor fame in a degree which could only be obtained by an extraordinary effort on my part. No, I am going to try and get into Cornell College this coming June and if I succeed will be a Journalist. I mean to study for an artist any how, whether I ever make a success at it or not."

Because the newly established Cornell did not offer an art course, Remington enrolled in the fall of 1878 as one of the thirty students in the Yale University School of Fine Arts. Remington's teacher was Professor John F. Weir, with John Henry Niemeyer the instructor for drawing. Remington became the art school's most famous pupil, but Remington's involvement at Yale was not art. He played forward on the varsity football team captained by the Yale immortal Walter Camp.

When Remington returned to Ogdensburg for Christmas 1879, his father was seriously ill. The colonel died February 18, 1880. Remington never did go back to Yale. His uncle Lamartine Remington had him appointed an executive clerk for the governor of New York, to try to keep him on the family path of writer-politician. This type of employment bored Remington. He went from one job to another.

While visiting in Canton during the summer of 1879, Remington had gone to the County Fair and there met Eva Adele Caten. An unusual young woman for the day in that she was attending college, she reciprocated Remington's love. From the Executive Chamber in Albany August 25, 1880, Remington wrote to Eva Caten's father asking whether the father would consent to an engagement between Remington and Eva Caten, on the basis that Remington had known Eva for a year, that he had a deep affection for her, that he had had "encouragement in all propriety," that she had agreed to the proposal, and that the father

had permitted the courtship. The father said no.

After a year, Remington decided to go West as a fortune hunter. The *St. Lawrence Plaindealer* announced August 10, 1881, that Remington would be departing for Montana that week "to make trial on a ranche." His motivation was the fulfillment of his adolescent dreams, to experience western ways, to observe the young cattle industry, and to visit the new gold fields.

Physically, Remington was heavy-set, not tall but powerful, blondish, strong chin and sensitive mouth. He was familiar with horses, relaxed and friendly in manner, and a "punisher" of food and liquor, as he himself would say. The best afterview of the Montana episode is "A Few Words from Mr. Remington," an article included in this volume. One of the sketches made during this Northwest trip was submitted to *Harper's Weekly,* redrawn by the staff professional W. A. Rogers, and published February 25, 1882, as "Cow-boys of Arizona."

Remington was back clerking in Albany by the middle of October 1881 when he again wrote his uncle Horace Sackrider, this time on the letterhead of the Insurance Department of the State of New York: "I have an appointment to go to New York soon to see George William Curtis of *Harper's Weekly* in order to see if that company will publish some work of mine. Has my saddle come?" If the meeting with Curtis did take place, it does not seem to have been productive.

A year later on his twenty-first birthday, Remington received the balance of his inheritance. A Yale friend wrote Remington that buying a cattle ranch was only for the really rich, like Theodore Roosevelt, but owning a substantial sheep ranch in central Kansas was "the boss business." Remington did spend three quarters of a year raising sheep, gaining the exposure that is comparable to the western experiences of Roosevelt and Wister. This is the point in Remington's life which provided the background for his first published article.

The Collected Writings of Frederic Remington

Coursing Rabbits on the Plains

"Look here, boys, what do you say to running 'jacks' to-morrow?" said Jim, as he brought his chair down from its canted back position against the wall of the room, and, by way of an emphasizer, striking the table a blow with his fist which made the little kerosene lamp dance a jig.

I seconded the motion immediately, but Bob, the owner of the ranch, sat back and reflectively sucked his big pipe, as he thought of the things which ought to be done. The broken fence to the corral down by the creek, dredging the watering holes, the possibilities of trading horses down at Plum Grove and varicus other thrifty plans weighed upon his mind; but Jim continued —"It's nice fall weather now, dry and cold; why, a hoss will jest run hisself to death for fun; that old Bob mule scampered like a four year ole colt all the way to Hoyt's grocery with me today, and, besides, there hain't nothing to do, and the 'jacks' is thicker 'n tumbleweeds on the prairie."

The sporting blood began to mount to Robert's great, contemplative eyes as the arguments went home; so removing his pipe he blew the smoke upwards as sedately as Irving's Dutchmen, shook off his Van Twiller doubts and declared he was an enthusiast, as indeed he was when he had made up his mind.

"That settles it," gleefully shouted Jim, "old Push-Bob (his horse) can have the bit to-morrow. Come here, Peggy, old son." Out from the corner behind the stove sneaked a dog and approached Jim in a delighted, sidelong, apologetic way, which gave the cue to his cur blood.

"I say, Jim, you hain't agoin' to make Peg-Leg run hisself to death over these yar prairies, be you?" came from Phip, the cook, as he put away the supper dishes. "Ha-ha," he laughed; "poor old Peg-Leg: he never seed a jack-rabbit 'cept the rabbit were a' disappearin' down the horizon like a fallin' star. Peg's a right smart good dog to run these yar land turtles with, but Peg hain't much account a' runnin' of jacks."

"Never you mind," replied the chivalric James, whose large nature always went out to the inferior and oppressed, "Peg ain't no sprint-runner fer a fact, but if them spider-dogs (meaning the greyhounds) misses bunny, old Peg gets him before the sun goes down," and patting Peg-Leg encouragingly, "We get there just the same. Well, go lay down and rest yerself; that's a good dog." And Peg-Leg sneaked back to the obscurity of the cook-stove. Peg-Leg was not a greyhound, nor indeed was he a fox-hound, although he was called such by persons not accurate on dog matters. He had lost the symmetry of one forward leg at some time during puphood and had been christened after the Indian fashion from his peculiarity, Peg-Leg. Peg was not a good coursing dog, but after the fashion of his breed, he always caught his rabbit. He ran at a limping gallop, but his nose was a most sensitive organ, and when on a trail he had a tenacity of purpose which was nearly canine insanity. He was, besides, on personal friendly relations with all us boys, and attended our hunts from what I suppose was a sense of duty, as he certainly could not have enjoyed them, considering that he was a long tailing behind the fast hounds and bounding horses; but should the rabbit make a sharp crook and get away in some bad bit of country, we only had to wait until Peg-Leg came up and showed us the way he had gone. The jack-rabbit does not run far at one time, although his break away is indescribable except as a disappearing shadow, but Peg would manage to rout him out again.

The next preliminary was to enlist John S—— in the scheme, for he owned the greyhounds, so I was deputized to go and see Johnnie as I rode on the way to my home down the creek.

"Hark! didn't I hear horses?" ejaculated Phip, as he stopped at the open door after discharging a pan of dish-water into the outer darkness. "Yes, and comin' like mad."

We all went to the door and listened a moment, when James retired to his chair and began to roll a fresh cigarette with the remark, "It's that crazy Englishman; no one but a — fool would ride like that on a dark night." Jim's language was merely figurative, however; for when the clatter, clatter of the horse's hoofs stopped in front of the house and a big red face was thrust into the room with the greeting, "'Ello, bies," one could immediately see that Charlie B—— was not as Jim had described him.

"Come in, Charlie; tie yer hoss to the corral and come in," was Bob's return greeting, whereat Charlie disappeared.

"That chap 'ill go hunting," said the practical Phip, sententiously, as he chuckled away, and poked at the fire; "its a cold day when that Englishman won't go hunting, or anywhere else where there hain't no work ter do." We realized the force of this, and Charlie verified it by declaring that he was delighted with the prospect when he had come in from outside.

Charlie B—— was your typical country Englishman, and the only thing about him

American was the broncho he rode. He was the best fellow in the world, cheery, hearty and ready for a lark at any time of the day or night. He owned a horse ranch seven miles down the creek, and found visiting his neighbors involved considerable riding; but Charlie was a sociable soul, and did not appear to mind that, and he would spend half the night riding over the lonely prairies to drop in on a friend in some neighboring ranch, in consequence of which Charlie's visits were not always timely; but he seemed never to realize that a chap was not in as good condition to visit when awakened from his blanket at three o'clock in the morning as in the twilight hour.

"'Ose going, Bob," he asked.

"Well, let's see;" and Bob surveyed the company. "There's Jim and Fred, and you and myself and Johnnie S——; and Bill Carr will want to go, won't he, Fred?"

"Yes. Bill will want to give old Prince a whirl, and Prince will want to be whirled; for do you know that that old, grey, sleepy plug never wakes up and acts like a horse unless he sees a 'jack' in front of him;" and by way of peroration I added, "He never saw a horse there."

As I had expected, this stirred up the horse question, which commanded all the intellect, the interest, the finer feelings and the subtle jealousies of the cow-camps. The exact running qualities of the horses were debatable, and every new horse that came into the White-water bottoms had to cost its owner a couple of snug bets in order to find out that Prince and Push-Bob could beat him. But whether Prince or Push-Bob was the best was an active subject of conjecture, and one which we never tired of. Jim immediately indulged in some sage doubts on my reflections on Prince, and we all laughed as James began to nerve up for a storm.

"Don't stir up that yar horse question or you'll have Jim a bettin' more money in this ole shanty than the Santa Fé road could put up," came from Phip, who was one of your intellectual horsemen, not given to betting, but taking a more sensible view; "still," he continued, "that 'ar Prince is as good as anybody's horse 'cept fer that heavy for'd leg, but then Push he's a right smart sort of a plug hisself—"

"Hold on, Phip, thought you didn't want the horse question," came from another corner, and Phip laughed, subsided and poked the fire in silence.

"What are you going to ride, Charlie?" was asked.

"The blue mare—the big un's gone lame in 'is stifle of late; think the bloody mules must 'ave landed 'im one on 'is joint; but the little blue mare's a good 'n, she's a good 'oss. I'll show ye fellows a fine pair of 'ind 'oofs to-morrow;" and Charlie slapped his boots with his whip and smiled triumphantly.

"I suppose the little yaller gal will have to take it to-morrow," said Jim, as he gazed humorously at my 180 pounds avoirdupois.

"Yes," I replied; "Terra-Cotta and I'll try and keep up with the procession."

"Bob, there, 'e'll ride that black vagabond of 'is; 'e'll go in partnership with what's 'is name 'ere—Peg-Leg," bantered Charlie.

Bob allowed that if old Jane felt like it, he would distinguish himself, but he added: "I expect she'll get located out there on the prairie and I'll have to send in to the ranch for a pair of mules," referring to a propensity of his favorite mare to balk; "but if she don't, I am not hunting sympathy, fer I won't need it."

So the evening passed pleasantly amid boyish banter, and the horse talk so dear to the stockman's heart. Presently, finding the hour to be late, B—— and I bade the boys on Bob's ranch good night, went out, bestrode our horses and rode off down the creek to our homes. Passing Johnnie S——'s ranch, we pounded a *reveille* on the door, which presently brought the owner to it, rubbing his eyes and inquiring "What the — we wanted in the middle of the night? Oh! it's you, is it, B——? Well, I might know. Say, B——, what's the matter with the daytime for calling on a fellow?"

We explained that our visit would be short, disclosed our plans, and expatiated on the joys of "jack" running, and finally

Johnnie concluded that the interests of his cows required that he run "jacks" on the morrow; so we rode off and left him to his slumbers. Johnnie was an important adjunct, as he owned the greyhounds, but now that his co-operation was assured, everything was ready for the sport. At last I was snug in bed, and B—— was presumably in his somewhat later, though it mattered little as to that, considering his personal habits. Poor B——! later on, his remittances from the old country stopped, and the last I heard of that lump of generous nature he was working for the man who owned his ranch, and keeping better hours in the interest of his employer.

I mention these preliminaries to allow the reader to become interested in the horses which were to do the running, as "jack" coursing is a succession of sharp quarter or half mile dashes, generally run in a clump, and well adapted to the spry little broncho horses, who would cut a sorry figure in a long English fox chase; and then this neat little sport is generally practiced by the ranchmen and farmers of the West, and while not exactly an event in our lives, yet it was a day spent apart from the usual duties, and therefore interesting.

I ate a light breakfast, and indeed the ranch larder helped me to do that; and after a feed of oats, rubbed Terra-Cotta down, and then put a light saddle on in place of my heavy stock saddle weighing some thirty-five pounds. Terra-Cotta was a nervous little half-breed Texas and thoroughbred, of a beautiful light gold-dust color, with a Naples yellow color mane and tail. She always knew that the light saddle meant a sharp run, and her fiery little thoroughbred nature asserted itself. In a moment she was in a te-he, and could scarcely wait for me to mount, but was off in a gallop before I was fully seated. Bill, my ranch-hand, followed me on old Prince, and the gallop across the prairie to Bob's was glorious. The light haze hung over the plains, not yet dissipated by the rising sun. Terra-Cotta's stride was steel springs under me as she swept along, brushing the dew from the grass of the range and taking the bit smartly in her teeth as though to say, "Come on, let's have a run," but I pulled gently and coaxed her to save herself for a later hour. Off to the right we saw another figure going toward Bob's, and in a few moments, by converging, found Johnnie S—— mounted on his big bay and leading one greyhound.

"Good morning, Johnnie, where is the other dog?"

"She thought she would stay at home to-day—you see, the old lady has expectations, and—well, it's good judgment on her part. But here's Daddy, and he's good for all the jack-rabbits on the range."

Later on we came up with Charlie B—— on the blue mare, and rigged out in full English hunting tog, all except a red coat, which is an addition not generally appreciated in the western country.

On over the smiling reach of grass, grown dry and sere in the August suns and hot winds, we galloped four abreast. The boys had on light saddles and snaffle bits, and while Mr. B—— sported a hunting stock, the rest contented themselves with light poles some six feet long, which were to be used as lances, with which to touch the rabbit, a feat most difficult and improbable. We had all discarded our *chaparajos,* and the horses were lightly blanketed. The rise and fall of the perfect lope peculiar to the American broncho was observable in all its ease and beauty. The blue mare looked blue indeed. She was one of those freaks of color which one sees occasionally on the plains. Johnnie's bay horse was a powerful animal, and a pleasant horse to get along with. Johnnie and he had a perfect understanding, and never seemed to clash. It made no difference to the horse on which part of his back Johnnie was, he attended strictly to his own business. Terra is already known, but now glance at Prince. You would not think him a quarter-horse, for he looks like a clumsy, sleepy old plug. Iron grey, with no flesh and big bones, he moves powerfully, steadily, but "where is the

snap?" you will say. Oh, it's there, somewhere, and always comes out on occasion. Many a man associates wealth that is gone with the name of Prince, and many a quarter-horse has found his Waterloo as he has followed old Prince over the scratch; still he is not much of a horse to look at, and that is a strong point, because the other fellows always went their last dollar on appearances.

After a few moments' ride we drew rein in Bob C——'s corral and went into the house, where the boys were eating their breakfasts.

"Do you know, old Phip has got waked up, and thinks he wants to run jacks, so he's going to lower his dignity and take a spurt on Bob," explained Jim.

We all laughed, for we knew Phip was an eminently practical person, who had rarely spared time for trivial things, and had neglected to learn in his studious career to ride a horse. Furthermore, we knew "Bob." "Bob" was a mule, somewhat advanced in years, but with his character as yet unformed, as it were. At least, those who were charitable toward the mule said this, but I think he was bad and malicious. Of course he had spells of goodness, but even a mule must rest from crime; in the main, though, he was sulky, was known to bite, was believed capable of kicking, was grossly given to bucking, and perfectly certain to balk; and the only thing he would not do was to run away, and that is a virtue in a hunting horse. "Bob" had at various times elevated some of the best riders in that part of the country toward the stars, but Phip was incredulous, and had evolved a theory that the base of Bob's character was good, and that all he needed was intelligent handling, etc., all of which will appear later on.

"Jim, do you want to gaunt Peg-Leg for a race, or will you give him his ration?" grinned Phip, as he held up the remains of breakfast on a plate, which Peg-Leg was regarding with fixed and intelligent gaze.

"Oh, give him his grub—he don't exercise violently when he runs; if he don't start on a full stomach he'll starve to death before he can catch a "jack." This brought breakfast and contentment to Peg-Leg.

The horses were saddled, and all being mounted, Phip included, the cavalcade moved out of the corral, across the creek, up the bluffs and on over the range.

"I'm going to watch Push-Bob and Prince to-day to see where the money is," whispered Johnnie to me as we rode ahead. The horses were all fretful and uneasy, except old Prince, whose great good sense always told him when the hour had come. Even old Jane, Bob's mare, condescended to take an interest and manifest a disposition to pound sod, which was exceedingly gratifying to Robert, inasmuch as the condition of Jane's feelings were to be considered as to whether she would go or not. Jane was not a plug, be it understood, but a good American mare, with all the saddle gaits, but she was in the years of discretion, and had multiplied her race in various instances.

"Say, Jim, do you know——"

"There's a jack—take him, Daddy," came a quick cry from Johnnie, and the next moment Johnnie's big bay was off. There goes the rabbit, the dog flies after. "Go on, Terra," I shouted, loosing on the bit, hitting her lightly with a spur, and away we went, all in a ruck. Old Prince was shouldering heavily away on my right, Push-Bob on my quarter, Jane off to the left, and Phip at a stately gallop behind—the blue mare being left at the post as it were.

The horses tore along, blowing great lung-fulls of fresh morning air out in snorts. Our sombreros blew up in front from the rush of air, and our blood leaped with excitement. Away scurried the jack, with his great ears sticking up like two antique bedposts, with Daddy closing the distance rapidly, and our outfit thundering along some eight rods in the rear. Down into a slew of long grass into which the rabbit and dog disappeared we went, with the grass snapping and swishing about the legs of our horses. A dark mass on my left heaves up, and "ho—there goes Bob head over heels."

On we go. "Hope Bob isn't hurt—must have put his foot into a water-hole," are my excited reflections. We are out of the slew, but where is the rabbit and dog?

"Here they go," comes from Phip, who is standing on the edge of the slew, farther down toward the bluffs of the bottoms, where he has gotten as the result of a short cut across.

Phip digs his spurs into the mule, sticks out his elbows and manifests other frantic desires to get there, all of it reminding one strongly of the style of one Ichabod Crane, but as we rush by, it is evident that the mule is debating the question with that assurance born of the consciousness that when the thing is brought to a vote he has a majority in the house. Poor Phip, now for your theories!

Up a rise in the "draw" onto the plain we go helter-skelter, over some stony land and

"The Jack Was Bearing Nearly Onto Me."
New York Public Library.

then a nice level, with Mr. Jack-rabbit twenty rods in the lead and Daddy skimming along in his wake. It is no use running now, he has too much of a start; so I pull in the impetuous Terra and I cut across to the left, hoping bunny will dodge that way, and of course, in the event that he does not, I am out of the race. "Ah, just as I had expected, bunny has dodged," and Daddy whizzed by some two rods before he could feel his rudder and come about. The jack was bearing nearly on to me, with Daddy flying quite far behind. Terra sees it, I think, as I turn her head, shake the rein and whisper, "Go on, girl," and we are off. "Now go on, Terra; what are you good for?" I yelled, lifting her forward. I leaned over and extended my stick, but the jack is by two feet too far. A couple of jumps and —"There, I missed him. Whoa, Terra, you little fool; do you want to run all over the prairie for nothing?"

The rabbit made back for the "draw" or ravine, considering the broken country as better than "a fair field and no favor." He kept doubling and throwing the dog off, for he was evidently old game. The "draw" was rough, stony, and the bed of the dry stream was filled with a thick growth of willows. By some good maneuvering, James got right on to him, and was going straight for the willows. The rabbit and dog shot through, and Jim gallantly followed on Push-Bob, for I verily believe that the horse would have charged a stone wall. As they struck the thick brush, Jim was swept from his seat like a fly from a sugar-bowl, and the horse went on.

After more running about, doubling and twisting, Charlie B—— and Bill C—— started in together, and as I stood in the "draw" dismounted, the rabbit, dog, Charlie and Bill swept over a little hill and full at me, with a regular, reckless "cannon-to-the-right-of-them" swing. I leaped into the saddle as they came. Crash through the willows they went, and there came disaster. The bank was worn away on the other side by a cattle-path just wide enough for one. They were neck and neck, both ambitious to use

the narrow path; so at it they rushed, and any philosopher will anticipate what befel them. They bunted rudely together, upsetting each horse and rider, while I galloped up the path between them with a cheer, leaving them rolling in a cloud of dust, and blaming each other. As accidents seemed to be the rule of the run, I helped out the rule in this wise: The bluffs which overlooked the White-water bottoms lay off to the left some forty rods, and toward them went the dog and rabbit, with me following after pell-mell. I have since explained how it happened in some dozen odd ways, but at this distant day I do not seem to concur in any of my own explanations, so I have ceased laying the blame on Terra Cotta, and taken upon my own shoulders the responsibility of riding full tilt right over the bluffs. When we arrived at the bluff, Terra Cotta could not be stopped. The incline was about 50° and well sodded, though lumpy, and Terra's knees bent under her at the first step downward, and others have said that we made the descent sandwich fashion, though the details are somewhat obscured. I lay on the ground for a moment, expecting to find a bone on a strike, or some blood running, but did not, and so arose to find I was not hurt in the least. Terra got on her feet, shook herself and looked foolish. I took her by the bridle, saying, "Are you hurt, old girl?" As though to say, "Not a bit," she turned about, and every muscle and bone answered its summons. The rabbit got away, and he had almost avenged his race in the ordeal, for upon assembling, Mr. Robert C—— presented himself in a guise which I can only compare to a sketch in plaster. Old Jane had put both forward legs into a slew-hole, and Mr. Robert was dumped in the mud. When we met he still carried a nice coating of slime and blue clay on his person, while old Jane was gradually growing white as the clay dried in the cool air that was blowing. She looked as though she thought her matronly dignity had been trifled with. We did not take these calamities to heart, but thought it a good opening for a day's sport.

Peg-Leg came up and sat down on his haunches near our group, and looked sulkily at the far horizon as much as to say, "That's a nice way to hunt."

"Well, let's try it again! Come along up the 'draw.' Come, Peggy, old boy," said Jim, as he led off at a fox trot. Johnnie had caught the greyhound, and we were ready for another view. We drew up our girths and made up our minds that we would not let the next jack get such a start on us. We kept a sharp lookout, when suddenly Peggy barks and goes limping off across the prairie on what will evidently be a lone hunt, as it is only a trail and no rabbit in sight.

"That's good day for Peg-Leg," laughs Jim. "Peg-Leg is abused, and I'll be hanged if I blame him for bein' disgusted—but he's got a hunt all to hisself now, so good luck to him."

We rode up the "draw" about a quarter of a mile and stopped for Johnnie to fix a *cincha*. He was long about it, and we sat on our horses and chatted. Off to the right about a third of a mile was Peg-Leg, nosing along with an occasional bark. We watched him when he gradually turned toward us.

"Peg's coming this way, and I wouldn't wonder if there was a jack somewhere in the grass, as its long enough to hide one," remarked one.

"Jest mind your eye; I wouldn't wonder if Peg would start one, so look out," went on another, and the words were hardly out of his mouth before a jack of enormous size sprang up from right under Peg's nose, and like a rubber ball came bounding toward us.

"Hi, Johnnie, give Daddy the sight," we yelled.

Daddy got it and was off—we after. The rabbit was evidently only thinking of Peg-Leg, and was running right into the jaws of Daddy.

"There, he got him," we shouted, but, "no," for the jack had passed seemingly right under Daddy's body, was among our horses' feet the next moment, and gone in our rear before we could stop.

Phip, who was galloping in our rear, had his golden opportunity now, and got out his stick to deal the champion stroke, when the mule spying the rabbit coming toward him, shied violently and left Phip sprawling about on the grass. We had swept about with a wheel to the right and left, and were again on the trail. As we passed Phip, he was using some of the strongest parts of the Saxon language with very telling effect. We all laughed and passed on.

After a sharp run, Bill got near enough to the rabbit to deal a violent blow, which started the dust in a shower and broke his stick, but Charlie caught the rabbit on the turn, and with a backhand stroke he knocked what little life was left out of bunny, and Daddy finished him.

Phip caught his mule and came up. He insisted that the mule was perverse beyond all rule and precedent, and passed without discussion some ironical remarks about "riding a horse" which were made by Robert, who was in duty bound to champion his own mule. Peg-Leg was far more disgusted than Phip, and grew melancholy as he reflected on the unfairness of our methods. After being jeered and laughed at a few moments, he started off for the bottoms in a sulk to have a hunt all alone, with no one to gobble his hard-earned glory and meat at the finish.

We proceeded on our way, hoping to find another jack soon, but no jack appeared. Jim's prophecy of the night before fell flat, but still we hoped with the true heroism of the hunter, who should never be discouraged in his search for game. In some respects I consider the hunting field a very good place to test character.

"Do these —— jack-rabbits think we'll 'unt hall day?" queried Charlie, with his rising inflection. We were silent, as we had our doubts as to the jacks having any thoughts in the matter. We were some ten miles from home when we started a jack at last, and took after him, horse, dog and man. Charlie B—— was in the lead, and the rabbit was going toward the ranch and corrals of one John Mitchner, a new arrival in those parts, from somewhere in the Indian Territory. The rabbit made straight for a corral and shot through a wire fence, the dog with a graceful bound went over, and the blue mare seemed to be going through, though Charlie succeeded in stopping her, thus saving himself a good scraping. We lost the rabbit, as it got under a hay-rick and Peg was not about to help us out of our difficulty, he having left in a tiff.

Old John came out of his house smoking a corn-cob pipe, and extended his compliments with a graceful "how-de, boys."

"Hello, John! Come out and hunt rabbits; you have nothing else to do," was the reply.

"Well I reckon as how I'm gettin too ole to be a chasing them nasty little rabbits over these yar prairies, but this yar a runnin' of horses kinder gets me. If I only had that cow-skin horse now what I used ter own back in old Missouri, I'd show——"

"Oh, come off, John; that old cow-skin business is played out," broke in Jim, who had heard old John discourse on the cow-skin racer until he was sick of it. "You will get the world to moving backwards if you keep dinging away about that old hoss. Why, I met a chap from Missouri the other day what allowed as he knew the cow-skin hoss, and he says he's beat him with a mule once back thar in Missouri," went on Jim.

We realized that Jim had evolved this last fabrication on the spot, with no basis of truth, but were content to see old John's cow-skin ghost of discussion annihilated at once.

Old John removed his pipe, his eyes glistened and he replied vehemently, pointing a long, bony finger at Jim—"That feller's a liar, do ye understan'? That feller's a d—— liar, and it's ole John Mitchner as will fill his lyin' hide full of holes ef ye'll jest show him up, do ye understan'? fer I don't allow no Missouri liar to come browsin' about these parts a sayin' as how the cow-skin hoss was ever beat by any critter as wears har—do ye understan', Mr. Jim C——?"

"Oh, yes; I understan', Uncle John. I thought he was a liar at the time, but I did not tell him so, 'cause he had red eyes and was loaded with guns," replied Jim in a conciliatory manner.

"I don't care a peg if he were a man-of-war; you jest allow as I say. I'll make a mineral lead of his carcus if I get a sight on him," added Uncle John, as he grew more resigned, seeming to think the cow-skin stories vindicated by this reckless harangue. "Come, dismount and come in; it's near time fer dinner," said John, as he walked back to the house.

We tied our horses to the fence and followed. "I tell you, boys, if that cow-skin horse ever existed a better horse could have broke old John pretty bad. We'll have to put up a job on old John's sporting blood to-day. You go in, Jim, and run a bluff on him," said Bill to us in a whisper, as we stepped into John's cabin.

We sat about and smoked while old John's boy got a dinner of bacon and eggs. The conversation turned on horses, and with old John in the company, horse talk was a synonym for cow-skin horse talk. At last Jim spoke up, saying, "Say, Uncle John, I don't think you ever owned but one good horse in your life. You hain't any horse in yer corral as could beat a Mexican sheep fer a quarter."

Old John gazed at the stove a few moments and then awoke and began: "Wall, my hoss stock ain't nothin' to brag on now, because I hain't got the money that you fellers down in the creek has got fer to buy 'em with, but I've got a little mare down thar in the corral as I've got a notion ken run some shakes."

"How fast, Uncle John?" queried Jim.

"Well, tol'able fast. I reckon as how she's a smarter horse than is hitched to the fence on the outside of the corral."

"Ha! ha! you don't mean it, Uncle John. Why, my bay Push-Bob or grey Prince would shovel sand into her eyes in great shape at a quarter," provokingly retorted Jim.

"Ye've got a great notion of them 'ar horses of yourn. I'm an old man, and I've got done a racin' of horses, but if your hoss can beat mine you can have the mare," replied John Mitchner, fixedly eyeing Jim.

"It's a go—hoss agin horse," spoke up

Jim, rising. "I'll ride mine and you ride yourn."

"Come on," said John, putting on his hat. We all arose and went out. The boy left the bacon and eggs to burn to a cinder on the cook-stove and followed.

"I'll bet Prince can beat either of you," said Bill, at this stage of the proceedings. "I'll ride him, and we'll all three run, the winner to take both—this yer is going to be a horse race, and it's a good time to see whether Prince or Push-Bob is the better horse."

The offer was accepted, and with this understanding the men began to strip their horses and to remove all their own superfluous clothes, for the quarter-races on the plains are all ridden bareback, and nearly naked. We began to get excited, and finally I provoked old John into betting with me. He wagered a fine mare and colt, which he pointed out in the corral with the remark, "agin yer yaller nag," and continuing, "This yar is a horse race, and I'm a bettin' man when I race horses, which is something I hain't done this ten years." At the last moment, as we had the track paced off on the level prairie, Bob bet his mare against four head of cattle, to be picked from John's herd. The Englishman wanted a hand, and staked the blue mare against a three-year old, said to belong to John Mitchner's boy, and Phip mounted the mule and regarded the proceedings as ominous in an extreme.

"Ye'll get beat sure," he whispered to me; but I sneered, "What, that gray mare beat Push-Bob? Why, Phip, what are you thinking of? She's an old brood mare, and looks as though she had come through in the spring instead of off the grass in the fall."

I was to fire the starting shot with old John's musket, and Charlie and Bob were to judge at the other end along with Mitchner's boy.

The three racers came up to the scratch, Bill and Jim sitting their sleek steeds like centaurs. Old Prince had bristled up and moved with great vim and power. Push-Bob swerved about and stretched his neck on the bit. The boys were bare-footed, with their sleeves rolled up and a handkerchief tied around their heads. Old John came prancing out, stripped to the waist, on his mare, which indeed looked more game when mounted than running loose in the corral. The old man's grey, thin locks were blowing loose in the wind, and he worked his horse up to the scratch in a very knowing way. We all regarded the race as a foregone conclusion and had really begun to pity old John's impoverishment, but still there was the interest in the bout between Prince and Push-Bob. This was the first time the victors of the White-water bottoms had met, and was altogether the greatest race which that country had seen in years. How the boys from the surrounding ranches would have gathered could they have known it, but it is just as well that they did not; for as I fired the gun and the horses scratched away from the mark, Old John went to the front and stayed there to the end, winning by several lengths, while Prince and Push-Bob ran what was called a dead heat, although there was considerable discussion over it for a long time afterwards. There was my dear little Terra gone to the hand of the spoilsman, and the very thought almost broke my heart, as I loved that mare as I shall never love another animal. I went back to the corral, sat down and began to whittle a stick. It took Bob and Charlie a half an hour to walk the quarter of a mile back to the ranch. Bill and John said nothing kept them from flying the country to save their horses but the fact that they had no saddles.

Old John rode up, threw himself from his broncho and drawled out: "Thar now; I've been a layin' fer you fellers ever since I came inter these yar parts and I recon as how I've sort of got ye. If ye'd had more horses with ye, I'd a hade a right smart horse herd arter this race;" and then turning to Jim he added, "Mr. Jim, ye'r a pretty smart feller, don't ye? P'raps ye'l hev more faith in the cow-skin horse stories now, seein' as how this yer grey mare is known back in parts of Missouri as the cow-skin horse, all along of a circumstance the particulars of which I allow p'raps yer don't keer to hear now," whereat he turned his mare into the corral, went and untied Terra Cotta, the black mare, the brown horse and the blue mare, which he also turned loose in his horse corral along with a half-dozen head of his own stock.

"Mr. Jim, will yer be so good as to jest turn that alleged race-horse inter this yar corral, seein' as yer don't own him no more?"

Mr. Jim and Mr. Bill, as old John insisted in calling them in his chilling discourse, did as requested, whereat old John invited us to dinner and turned on his heel. But no one manifested a disposition to dine. We stood leaning over the corral fence, regarding intently the cow-skin horse, as John called her, and wondering at the deceitfulness of appearances. Some one suggested that it was a right good distance home but the walking was good.

"Let's borrow the 'osses," suggested the Englishman.

"I'd walk from here to old Mexico before I'd ask old John fer a horse," replied Bill, and we all declined to solicit John's charity in the matter. So the walk began, and a long, solemn tramp it was over the dry plain. Phip rode the mule, as he was a rather old man and not in shape to walk an odd ten miles, and carried the saddles, and the rest of us trudged along beside.

As we neared home, or Bob's ranch, we begun to feel gaunt, and Phip cheered us by assurances of some tid-bits in the shape of a can of white pears and a cold roast goose which Jim had shot some days previous. As we descended into the bottoms, Peg-Leg greeted us, and as he gazed at our solemn procession, it seems that I could detect a smile of comfort on his canine countenance. The boys on the ranch regarded us curiously and seriously, but it gradually dawned upon them, after numerous questions and evasive answers, what had happened, and they retired to the barn, where I thought I heard discordant sounds for an hour after. Phip set up the can of peaches and we picked the goose clean from a sense of duty.

"Every man in this country will know this inside of two days," regretfully sighed Bob.

"If there war any brush hereabouts I'd take to it," asserted Bill, "but there ain't, and we'll have to go down to Hoyt's grocery to-morrow and face the music—and say, gentlemen, it will be pizen."

Phip was dying to work the "I told you so" business, but he was suppressed by ominous threats of dire resort.

We procured horses of Bob and saddled up to go our various ways. As we started, Jim said—

"Well, boys, how do you like running Jacks?"

We all laughed and parted as goodhumoredly as the circumstances would allow.

That night, Bill and I rode down to Hoyt's grocery and post-office to purchase some necessaries, but through the window in the light of the store we could see old John Mitchner perched on a barrel of sugar and a crowd of the boys around him all convulsed with laughter.

"Bill, let's go home," I remarked, and we trotted off up the road into the darkness.

A Peccary Hunt in Northern Mexico

Having been an ardent sportsman all my life, I was greatly interested in the accounts of the peculiar delights of the pursuit of the peccary, as narrated by a mining engineer of my acquaintance, as we sat conversing in the court of an adobe hotel situated in the Mexican town of Hermosillo, State of Sonora. Upon my expressing a desire to participate in an affair of the sort, my friend invited me to go out into the country and try it with him, a suggestion of which I quickly availed myself. As the train on the Sonora Railroad was about leaving for the north, we drove to the depot and boarded it. We traveled some hours, and then alighted at a station with an unpronounceable name. The Sonora River flows through the country in which we were, on its long journey from the Sierra Madre range to the Gulf of California, with small promise of ever reaching its destination, one would think, for the looks of the hot and thirsty sand through which it found its way. The whole aspect of nature was cruel, with its yellow sparkling sands dotted with cactus, chaparral and other thorny growths, which cut and scratch if you are not wary. No agriculture can be practiced except along the river bottoms, in such places as it is possible to conduct water over the land by ditches or acequias. Around this little lonesome depot, squatted away out there in the desert, was a group of people hanging about to see the train come in and go out. They were very swarthy of skin, and dressed in white, and no doubt had knives under their tunics.

My friend the engineer walked up to an old Mexican who was seated on a box in the shade of the station and shook his hand. I was called up and introduced to Senor Samanego. I could make but poor progress with the Spanish conversation, only comprehending the commonest words and phrases. The old fellow was very polite and dignified, as are all Mexican men, and after the engineer had told him that we had come out to hunt peccaries, he was much amused, and chuckled, and passed some words to two slouch-hatted, cotton shirted vaqueros who stood near gazing stupidly at the Gringos, which is the slang name they apply to the Americans, whereat they mounted their ponies and galloped off through the chaparral in a cloud of dust. After a while they returned, leading two saddle ponies, and the old Mexican motioned us to mount them. My mount was a little drooping, demure beast with fleshless limbs, and a huge saddle with tapaderas on the stirrup which nearly swished on the ground. We rode off again under the guidance of Samanego, followed by the two vaqueros. It was nearing sunset, and was growing cooler as we rode. One could not see far, as the chaparral thickets interposed, but wound and worried through them, stirring up a cloud of dust, until we came to an open space, where we could see the adobe walls of Samanego's rancho. Here we dismounted, and I busied myself with making a sketch of the surrounding objects, which were all so strange to an American like myself. The engineer called loudly to me from a stake-fence corral to come down there, which I did, and to my astonishment he pointed to a small animal which was tied with a rope by one hind leg to a post. "There is a peccary for you, natural as life and twice as ugly," said the engineer, laughing. I gazed at the little beast, for he was typical of what I had come to hunt. A small razor-back hog from Arkansas would not be very unlike him, only he was covered with gray hair, and had three-toed feet, more like a dog than a pig. His eyes were set in a very malevolent fashion as he considered the situation, and his whole aspect was one of belligerency, as much as to say, "If only I could get at you I should take a huge piece out of your leg." They say these peccaries are domesticated at times, but for my part I do not think the game would be worth the candle.

I was aroused early next morning, and found myself in the saddle before I was hardly awake. Again we followed the old Mexican, Samanego, off into the great plain, winding about in the chaparral. We followed down the course of a little stream which was fringed with cotton-wood and palm trees. The engineer said that one of the vaqueros had found peccaries the day before, somewhere below, while he was out looking for stray horses. I will here explain that the method for hunting peccaries, as followed by the Mexican vaqueros or cowboys, is peculiar to them, and consists in roping them by adroitly casting their raeta about their body, much in the same way as they do a steer. In this way they are often taken alive. I had learned to throw a rope in an indifferent fashion during my life on the cattle ranges of the north, and concluded to try my hand with it, instead of using a rifle or six-shooter, as the engineer proposed to do. I felt that the life-long skill of the vaqueros would make my unpracticed efforts contemptuous in comparison; but what of that? The sun came up suddenly from behind the blue line of the far off Sierras, and the terrific glare of another day was to begin. The senor called a halt, and after directing his men to do certain things,

they trotted off into the brush and were lost to sight. I understood that they were to make a detour and strike the creek some distance below, and there beat up the bush toward our position, thus drawing out any peccaries which might be concealed there. We sat down and rolled and smoked cigarettes in a true spirit of appreciation of our Mexican surroundings, for in Mexico everyone smokes cigarettes. The senor explained that the peccary cannot run as fast as a horse, which statement I did not doubt, as I never saw any animal that could. He also added that the little ponies had been trained to run in the chaparral, and could dodge about so quickly to avoid it that an unskilled rider might suddenly find himself on his back in the sand. He further explained that the peccary had a very short and bad temper, and that he was liable to turn the tables arbitrarily at any moment and transform the scene into peccaries hunting a man.

With these instructions, I began to coil my rope, adjust my six-shooter and to tighten my saddle cinchas and girths. We stood at our horses' heads as the old senor looked up at the sun and said it was time the men got back to us. Presently we heard a rustling in some canebrakes down the creek, followed by quick grunts. "Viniendo, senors," whispered Samanego, as he swung himself into his saddle, and looked sharply at his rope. We also mounted, and as I was fairly seated, the patter of the Mexican ponies came to my ears, and amid a cloud of dust I could see the circling reata and the flying hoofs. I also distinguished a little black form scurrying along in front. Circle, circle, circle flowed the long noose of the rope about the cloud of dust, and with a long-drawn sweep it flew forward in graceful coils and settled about the peccary. The pony quickly swerved, the rope straightened, the pony plunged two or three times and made toward us at top speed, dragging the black object behind. "Quando yo salo el dia, estaba mio frio," yelled the Mexican, in great glee, which was a translation of a bit of American slang made by the engineer

A Peccary Hunt in Northern Mexico. *Authors' photoengraving.*

the night before, and taken up by the Mexican in his high spirits. He jerked the little pig about like a football, raising such a cloud of dust around his ears that I had no doubt the little animal would soon want for breath. After this had gone on for a time, and we had admired the graceful horsemanship of the Mexican, the peccary lay still and the Mexican approached him, slowly winding in his rope. He suddenly drew his revolver and shot the prostrate animal. He told the engineer that the beast was shamming death and he shot him for fear he might come to life and make it dangerous for him.

He leaned from his saddle and undid his rope from about the body of the game, again coiled it, and started off at a gallop down the creek. We followed, and could presently hear the cries of the vaqueros, the clatter of the horses' hoofs and could see a cloud of dust coming toward us. One peccary broke cover right in front of us, and then another, until I counted eight. They did not see us until we were nearly onto them, so intent were they on the men behind, and then they swerved. We spurred our horses, and then commenced a mad gallop, with the dust flying and the men yelling. I swung my rope, and aimed to catch a big fellow scurrying along just ahead, when crash I went into a mass of mesquite boughs, which took my hat off and nearly unseated me; but my little pony was in for the hunt, and went along all right, following like a greyhound. The peccaries kept in a bunch, and the old senor was at my side, with the others racing along behind and about us. The senor howled Spanish at me, which I did not understand, but I could see that he was encouraging me to make a cast. I saw my opportunity presently and threw the rope. It settled about my game, but I could not turn my horse as the old Mexican was on my left and I was thus unable to tighten the noose. The peccary, not liking the feeling of the rope in which he was entangling himself at every jump, stopped, and I dashed over him, and just what happened in the dust and confusion that followed I did not keep a strict account of, but I pulled in my pony, dropped my rope, and drew a six-shooter and shot away at the peccary, which was struggling in the sand with the reata more hopelessly entwined about him. The dust settled and I found I had killed a peccary sure enough. The old senor came up shortly and saw my good luck. He dismounted, drew a knife and commenced to skin and cut up the animal on the spot. One of the men was dispatched to where the other dead peccary was, to perform a similar office. These were the only two which we got that day. The old Mexican could easily have gotten another, but he generously gave up his opportunity to me, for which I thanked him. Thus ended a bit of sport which I enjoyed hugely and which I think was quite beyond ordinary methods of hunting.

Horses of the Plains

To men of all ages the horse of northern Africa has been the standard of worth and beauty and speed. It was bred for the purpose of war and reared under the most favorable climatic conditions, and its descendants have infused their blood into all the strains which in our day are regarded as valuable. The Moors stocked Spain with this horse, and the so-called Spanish horse is more Moorish than otherwise. It is fair to presume that the lightly armored cavaliers of the sixteenth century, or during the Spanish conquests in America, rode this animal, which had been so long domesticated in Spain, in preference to the inferior northern horse. To this day the pony of western America shows many points of the Barbary horse to the exclusion of all other breeding. His head has the same facial line; and that is a prime point in deciding ancestry in horses. Observe, for instance, the great dissimilarity in profile displayed by old plates of the Godolphin Arabian and the Darley Arabian, two famous sires, kings of their races, the one a Barb and the other an Arabian.

In contemplating the development of the horse, or rather his gradual adjustment to his environment, no period more commends itself than that of the time from the Spanish invasion of Mexico to the present day. The lapse of nearly four centuries and the great variety of dissimilar conditions have so changed the American "bronco" from his Spanish ancestor that he now enjoys a distinctive individuality. This individuality is also subdivided; and as all types come from a common ancestry, the reasons for this varied development are sought with interest, though I fear not always with accuracy. Cortes left Cuba on his famous expedition with "sixteen horses," which were procured from the plantations of that island at great expense.

As a matter of course these horses did not contribute to the stocking of the conquered country, for they all laid down their lives to make another page of military history in the annals of the Barbary horse. Subsequent importations must have replenished the race. Possibly the dangers and expense attendant on importation did not bring a very high grade of horses from Spain, though I am quite sure that no sane don would have preferred a coarse-jointed great Flemish weight-carrier for use on the hot sands of Mexico to a light and supple Barb, which would recognize in the sand and heat of his new-world home an exact counterpart of his African hills. As the Spaniards worked north in their explorations, they lost horses by the adverse fortunes of war and by their straying and being captured by Indians. At a very early date the wild horse was encountered on the plains of Mexico, but a long time elapsed before the horse was found in the north. La Salle found the Comanches with Spanish goods and also horses in their possession, but on his journey to Canada it was with great difficulty that he procured horses from the Indians farther north. In 1680, or contemporaneously with La Salle's experience in the south, Father Hennepin lived with the Sioux and marched and hunted the buffalo on foot. At a much later day a traveler heard the Comanches boast that they "remembered when the Arapahoes to the north used dogs as beasts of burden." That horses were lost by the Spaniards and ran in a wild state over the high, dry plains of Mexico and Texas at an early day is certain; and as the conditions of life were favorable, they must have increased rapidly. How many years elapsed before the northern Indians procured these animals, with which they are so thoroughly identified, is not easily ascertainable. Cheyenne Indians who were well versed in that tribal legend which is rehearsed by the lodge fire in the long winter nights have told me gravely that they always have had horses. I suspect that this assertion has its foundation in the vanity of their cavalier souls, for the Cheyenne legend runs very smoothly, and has paleface corroboration back to a period when we know that they could not have had horses.

Only on the plains has the horse reached his most typical American development. The range afforded good grass and they bred indiscriminately, both in the wild state and in the hands of the Indians, who never used any discretion in the matter of coupling the best specimens, as did the Indians of the mountains, because of the constant danger of their being lost or stolen, thus making it unprofitable. Wild stallions continually herded off the droves of the Indians of the southern plains, thus thwarting any endeavor to improve the stock by breeding. It is often a question whether the "pinto,"* or painted pony of Texas, is the result of a pinto ancestry, or of a general coupling of horses of all colors. The latter, I think, is the case, for the Barb was a one-color horse, and the modern horsebreeder in his science finds no difficulty in producing that color which he deems the best. The Comanches, Wichitas, and Kiowas hold that stallion in high esteem which is most bedecked and flared by blotches of white hair

* Parti-colored "calico," as sometimes called.

on the normal color of his hide. The so-called Spanish horse of northern Mexico is less apt to show this tendency towards a parti-colored coat, and his size, bone, and general development stamp him as the best among his kind, all of which qualities are the result of some consideration on the part of man with a view to improve the stock. The Mexicans on their Indian-infested frontier kept their horses close herded; for they lived where they had located their ranches, desired good horses, and took pains to produce them. The sires were well selected, and the growing animals were not subjected to the fearful setbacks attendant on passing a winter on the cold plains, which is one of the reasons why all wild horses are stunted in size. Therefore we must look to the Spanish horse of northern Mexico for the nearest type to the progenitors of the American bronco. The good representatives of this division are about fourteen and a half hands in stature; of large bone, with a slight tendency to roughness; generally bay in color; flat-ribbed, and of great muscular development; and, like all the rest, have the Barbary head, with the slightly oval face and fine muzzle.

Nearly identical with this beast is the mustang of the Pacific coast—a misnomer, by the bye, which for a generation has been universally applied by fanciful people to any horse bearing a brand. This particular race of horses, reared under slightly less advantageous circumstances than the Spanish horse of old Mexico, was famous in early days; but they are now so mixed with American stock as to lose the identity which in the days of the Argonauts was their pride.

The most inexperienced horseman will not have to walk around the animal twice in order to tell a Texas pony; that is, one which is full bred, with no admixture. He has fine deer-like legs, a very long body, with a pronounced roach just forward of the coupling, and possibly a "glass eye" and a pinto hide. Any old cowboy will point him out as the only creature suitable for his purposes. Hard to break, because he has any amount of latent devil in his disposition, he does not break his legs or fall over backwards in the "pitching" process as does the "cayuse" of the North-west. I think he is small and shriveled up like a Mexican because of his dry, hot habitat, over which he has to walk many miles to get his dinner. But, in compensation, he can cover leagues of his native plains, bearing a seemingly disproportionately large man, with an ease both to himself and to his rider which is little short of miraculous. I tried on one occasion to regenerate a fine specimen of the southern plains sort, and to make a pretty little cob of the wild, scared bundle of nerves and bones which I had picked out of a herd. I roached his mane and docked his tail, and put him in a warm stall with half a foot of straw underneath. I meted out a ration of corn and hay which was enough for a twelve-hundred work-horse in the neighboring stall. I had him combed and brushed and wiped by a good-natured man, who regarded the proceeding with as much awe as did the pony. After the animal found out that the corn was meant to be eaten, he always ate it; but after many days he was led out, and, to my utter despair, he stood there the same shy, perverse brute which he always had been. His paunch was distended to frightful proportions, but his cat hams, ewe neck, and thin little shoulders were as dry and hard as ever. Mentally he never seemed to make any discrimination between his newly found masters and the big timber wolves that used to surround him and keep him standing all night in a bunch of fellows. On the whole it was laughable, for in his perversity he resisted the regenerating process much as any other wild beast might. For all that, these animals are "all sorts of a horse" in their own particular field of usefulness, though they lack the power of the Spanish horse. Once in Arizona I rode one of the latter animals, belonging to Chief Ascension Rios of the Papagoes, at a very rapid gallop for twenty-four miles, during the middle of the day, through the desert sand. The thermometer stood as high as you please in the shade, and the hot sun on the white sand made the heat something frightful; and personally I am not noted for any of the physical characteristics which distinguish a fairy. At the end of the journey I was confirmed in the suspicion that he was a most magnificent piece of horse-flesh for a ride like that, and I never expect to see another horse which can make the trip and take it so lightly to heart. He stood there like a rock, and was good as at starting, having sweat only a normal amount. The best test of a horse is, not what he can do, but how easily he can do it. Some of the best specimens of the horse and rider which I have ever had occasion to admire were Mexican *vaqueros,* and I have often thought the horses were more worthy than the men.

The golden age of the bronco was ended some twenty years ago when the great tidal wave of Saxonism reached his grassy plains. He was rounded up and brought under the yoke by the thousand, and his glories departed. Here and there a small band fled before man, but their freedom was hopeless. The act of subjugation was more implied than real, and to this day, as the cowboy goes out and drives up a herd of broncos to the corral, there is little difference between the wild horse of old and his enslaved progeny. Of course the wild stallion is always eliminated, and he alone was responsible for the awe which a wild horse inspired. As I have before remarked, the home of the Simon-pure wild horse is on the southern plains, and when he appears elsewhere he has been tranported there by man and found his freedom later on. I have found food for reflection in tracing the causes of the varied development of these broncos under different conditions. A great many of the speculations in which I indulge may be faulty, as they deal with a subject not widely investigated by any more learned savants than one is apt to find about the fires of the cow-camps in the far West. One must not forget, also, that the difficulty increases as years pass, because the horses are driven about from one section to another, and thus crossed with the stock of the country until in a very few years they became a homogeneous type. The solutions to these problems must always be personal views, and in no sense final. One thing is certain: of all the monuments which the Spaniard has left to glorify his reign in America there will be none more worthy than his horse. This proposition I have heard combated, however, by a person who had just been "bucked" violently from the back of a descendant of the Barbs. He insisted that the Spaniards had left little to glorify their reign in America, least of all their miserable scrubby ponies. Nevertheless, the Spaniard's horses may be found to-day in countless thousands, from the city of the Montezumas to the regions of perpetual snow; they are grafted into our equine wealth and make an important impression on the horse of the country.

There is a horse in the Indian Territory, Arkansas, and Missouri, called the Cherokee pony, which is a peculiar animal. Of low stature, he is generally piebald, with a great profusion of mane and tail. He is close set, with head and legs not at all of the bronco type, and I know that his derivation is from the East, though some insist on classing him with our Western ponies; but he is a handsome little beast, easily adapts himself to surroundings, and is in much favor in the Eastern markets as a saddle pony for boys and for ladies' carts.

The most favorable place to study the pony is in an Indian camp, as the Indians rarely defeat the ends of nature in the matter of natural selection; and further, the ponies are allowed to eat the very greenest grass they can find in the summer time, and to chew on a cotton-wood saw-log during the winter, with perfect indifference on the part of their owners. The pony is thus a reflex of nature, and, coupled with his surroundings, is of quite as much interest as the stretch of prairie grass, the white lodges, and the blanketed forms. The savage red man in his great contest with nature has learned, not to combat nature, but to observe her moods and to prepare a simple means of escape. He puts up no fodder for the winter, but relies on the bark of the cotton-wood. Often he is driven to dire extremity to bring his stock through the winter. I have been told that in the Canadian North-west the Blackfeet have bought grain for their ponies during a bad spell of weather, which act implies marvelous self-denial, as the cost of a bushel of oats would bring financial ruin on any of the tribe. Before the early grass starts in the spring the emaciated appearance of one of these little ponies in the far North-west will sorely try the feelings of an equine philanthropist should he look along the humpy ribs and withered quarters. But alack! when the young grass does shoot, the pony scours the trash which composes his winter diet, sheds his matted hair, and shines forth another horse. In a month "Richard's himself again," ready to fly over the grassy sward with his savage master or to drag the *travaux* and pack the buxom squaw. Yet do not think that at this time the Indian pony is the bounding steed of romance; do not be deluded into expecting the arched neck, the graceful lines, and the magnificent limbs of the English hunter, for, alas! they are not here. They have existed only on paper. He may be all that the wildest enthusiast may claim in point of hardihood and power, as indeed he is, but he is not beautiful. His head and neck join like the two parts of a hammer, his legs are as fine as a deer's, though not with the flat knee-cap and broad cannon-bone of the English ideal. His barrel is a veritable tun, made so by the bushels of grass which he consumes in order to satisfy nature. His quarters are apt to run suddenly back from the hips, and the rear view is decidedly mulish about the hocks. The mane and the tail are apt to be light, and I find that the currycomb of the groom has a good deal to do in deciding on which side of the horse's neck the mane shall fall; for on an Indian pony it is apt to drop on the right and the left, or stand up in the middle in perfect indecision. The Indian never devotes any stable-work to his mount, although at times the pony is bedecked in savage splendor. Once I saw the equipment of a Blackfoot war pony, composed of a mask and bonnet gorgeous with red flannel, brass-headed tacks, silver plates, and feathers, which was art in its way.

As we go very far into the Canadian North-west we find that the interminable cold of the winters has had its effect, and the pony is small and scraggy, with a disposition to run to hair that would be the envy of a goat. These little fellows seem to be sadly out of their reckoning, as the great northern wastes were surely not made for horses; however, the reverse of the proposition is true, for the horses thrive after a fashion and demonstrate the toughness of the race. Unless he be tied up to a post, no one ever knew an Indian pony to die of the cold. With his front feet he will paw away the snow to an astonishing depth in order to get at the dry herbage, and by hook or by crook he will manage to come through the winter despite the wildest prophecies on the part of the uninitiated that he cannot live ten days in such a storm. The Indian pony often finds to his sorrow that he is useful for other purposes than as a beast of burden, for his wild masters of the Rocky Mountains think him excellent eating. To the Shoshonees the particular use of a horse was for the steaks and the stews that were in him; but the Indian of the plains had the buffalo, and could afford, except in extreme cases, to let his means of transportation live. The Apaches were never "horse Indians," and always readily abandoned their stock to follow the mountains on foot. In early times their stock-stealing raids into Mexico were simply foraging expeditions, as they ate horses, mules, cattle, and sheep alike. In the grassy valleys of the northern Rocky Mountains, walled in as they are by the mountain ranges, horse-breeding was productive of good, and was followed. Thus the "cayuse," a fine strain of pony stock,

A "Cayuse." *Authors' wood engraving.*

took its name from a tribe, though it became disseminated over all that country. As it was nearly impossible for the Indians to steal each other's horses on every occasion, the people were encouraged to perpetuate the good qualities of their favorite mounts.

The cayuse is generally roan in color, with always a tendency this way, no matter how slight. He is strongly built, heavily muscled, and the only bronco which possesses square quarters. In height he is about fourteen hands; and while not possessed of the activity of the Texas horse, he has much more power. This native stock was a splendid foundation for the horse-breeders of Montana and the North-west to work on, and the Montana horse of commerce rates very high. This condition is not, however, all to the credit of the cayuse, but to a strain of horses early imported into Montana from the West and known as the Oregon horse, which breed had its foundation in the mustang.

In summing up for the bronco I will say that he is destined to become a distinguished element in the future horse of the continent, if for no other reason except that of his numbers. All over the West he is bred into the stock of the country, and of course always from the side of the dam. The first one or two crosses from this stock are not very encouraging, as the blood is strong, having been bred in and in for so many generations. But presently we find an animal of the average size, as fine almost as a thoroughbred, with his structural points corrected, and fit for many purposes. He has about the general balance of the French ponies of Canada or perhaps a Morgan, which for practical purposes were the best horses ever developed in America. At this stage of the development of the bronco he is no longer the little narrow-shouldered, cat-hammed brute of his native plains, but as round and square and arched as "anybody's horse," as a Texan would express it. In this shape I see him ridden in Central Park, and fail to see but that he carries himself as gallantly as though his name were in the "Stud-Book." I often see a pair of these

horses dragging a delivery wagon about on the pavements, and note the ease with which they travel over many miles of stone-set road in a day. I have also a particular fad which I would like to demonstrate, but will simply say that this horse is the *ne plus ultra* for light cavalry purposes. In the Department of Arizona they have used many Californian horses, and while some officers claim that they are not as desirable as pure American stock, I venture to think that they would be if they were used by light cavalry and not by dragoons.

In intelligence the bronco has no equal, unless it is the mule, though this comparison is inapt, as that hybrid has an extra endowment of brains, as though in compensation for the beauty which he lacks. I think that the wild state may have sharpened the senses of the bronco, while in domestication he is remarkably docile. It would be quite unfair to his fellows to institute anything like a comparison without putting in evidence the peculiar method of defense to which he resorts when he struggles with man for the mastery. Every one knows that he "bucks," and familiarity with that characteristic never breeds contempt. Only those who have ridden a bronco the first time it was saddled, or have lived through a railroad accident, can form any conception of the solemnity of such experiences. Few Eastern people appreciate the sky-rocket bounds, and grunts, and stiff-legged striking, because the "bucking" process is entered into with great spirit by the pony but once, and that is when he is first under the saddle-tree. If that "scrape" is "ridden out" by his master the bronco's spirit is broken; and while he may afterwards plunge about, he has intelligence enough not to "kick against the pricks."

His greatest good quality is the ease with which he stands any amount of hard riding over the trail; and this is not because of any particular power which he has over the thoroughbred, for instance, but because of his "hard stomach." He eats no grain in the growing stages of his life, and his stomach has not been forced artificially to supply a system taxed beyond the power of the stomach to fill. The same general difference is noted between an Indian and a white man. You may gallop the pony until your thoroughbred would "heave and thump" and "go wrong" in a dozen vital places, and the bronco will cool off and come through little the worse for the experience.

Some years ago I drove up to a stage station in the San Pedro Valley in Arizona, and the Mexican stock tender had had a hard time in rounding up his stage stock. His herd pony had been run until, as he stood there under the shade of a brush corral, covered with foam and dust, with his belly drawn up almost to his spine and gasping occasionally as though it was his last, I felt sure I should see him die before I left the station. I was afterwards told by the stage boss in a bluff, matter-of-course way, in answer to my inquiry, that he had "pulled through all right: you can't kill them critters"; and now I am perfectly positive that you cannot.

As a saddle animal simply, the bronco has no superior. The "lope" is a term which should never be applied to that motion in any other breed of horses. I have watched a herd of cow-ponies being driven over the prairie where the undulations of the backs in the moving throng were as regular and easy as the rise and fall of the watery waves. The fox-trot, which is the habitual gait of all plainsmen, cowboys, and Indians, is easily cultivated in him, and his light, supple frame accommodates itself naturally to the motion.

This particular American horse lays claim to another quality, which in my estimation is not least, and that is his wonderful picturesqueness. He graces the Western landscape, not because he reminds us of the equine ideal, but because he comes of the soil, and has borne the heat and burden and the vicissitudes of all that pale of romance which will cling about the Western frontier. As we see him hitched to the plow or the wagon he seems a living protest against utilitarianism; but, unlike his red master, he will not go. He has borne the Moor, the Spanish conqueror, the red Indian, the mountain-man, and the vaquero through all the glories of their careers; but they will soon be gone, with all their heritage of gallant deeds. The pony must meekly enter the new régime. He must wear the collar of the new civilization and earn his oats by the sweat of his flank. There are no more worlds for him to conquer; now he must till the ground.

A Scout with the Buffalo-Soldiers

I sat smoking in the quarters of an army friend at Fort Grant, and through a green lattice-work was watching the dusty parade and congratulating myself on the possession of this spot of comfort in such a disagreeably hot climate as Arizona Territory offers in the summer, when in strode my friend the lieutenant, who threw his cap on the table and began to roll a cigarette.

"Well," he said, "the K. O. has ordered me out for a two-weeks' scouting up the San Carlos way, and I'm off in the morning. Would you like to go with me?" He lighted the cigarette and paused for my reply.

I was very comfortable at that moment, and knew from some past experiences that marching under the summer sun of Arizona was real suffering and not to be considered by one on pleasure bent; and I was also aware that my friend the lieutenant had a reputation as a hard rider, and would in this case select a few picked and seasoned cavalrymen and rush over the worst possible country in the least possible time. I had no reputation as a hard rider to sustain, and, moreover, had not backed a horse for the year past. I knew too that Uncle Sam's beans, black coffee, and the bacon which every old soldier will tell you about would fall to the lot of any one who scouted with the 10th Dragoons. Still, I very much desired to travel through the country to the north, and in a rash moment said, "I'll go."

"You quite understand that you are amenable to discipline," continued the lieutenant with mock seriousness, as he regarded me with that soldier's contempt for a citizen which is not openly expressed but is tacitly felt.

"I do," I answered meekly.

"Put you afoot, citizen; put you afoot, sir, at the slightest provocation, understand," pursued the officer in his sharp manner of giving commands.

I suggested that after I had chafed a Government saddle for a day or two I should undoubtedly beg to be put afoot, and, far from being a punishment, it might be a real mercy.

"That being settled, will you go down to stable-call and pick out a mount? You are one of the heavies, but I think we can outfit you," he said; and together we strolled down to where the bugle was blaring.

At the adobe corral the faded coats of the horses were being groomed by black troopers in white frocks; for the 10th United States Cavalry is composed of colored men. The fine alkaline dust of that country is continually sifting over all exposed objects, so that grooming becomes almost as hopeless a task as sweeping back the sea with a house-broom. A fine old veteran cavalry-horse, detailed for a sergeant of the troop, was selected to bear me on the trip. He was a large horse of a pony build, both strong and sound except that he bore a healed-up saddle-gall, gotten, probably, during some old march upon an endless Apache trail. His temper had been ruined, and a grinning soldier said, as he stood at a respectful distance, "Leouk out, sah. Dat ole hoss shore kick youh head off, sah."

The lieutenant assured me that if I could ride that animal through and not start the old gall I should be covered with glory; and as to the rest, "What you don't know about cross-country riding in these parts that horse does. It's lucky there isn't a hole in the ground where his hoofs trod, for he's pounded up and down across this Territory for the last five years."

Well satisfied with my mount, I departed. That evening numbers of rubber-muscled cavalry officers called and drew all sorts of horrible pictures for my fancy, which greatly amused them and duly filled me with dismal forebodings. "A man from New York comes out here to trifle with the dragoon," said one facetious chap, addressing my lieutenant; "so now, old boy, you don't want to let him get away with the impression that the cavalry don't ride." I caught the suggestion that it was the purpose of those fellows to see that I was "ridden down" on the trip; and though I got my resolution to the sticking-point, I knew that "a pillory can outpreach a parson," and that my resolutions might not avail against the hard saddle.

On the following morning I was awakened by the lieutenant's dog-rubber,* and got up to array myself in my field costume. My old troop-horse was at the door, and he eyed his citizen rider with malevolent gaze. Even the dumb beasts of the army share that quiet contempt for the citizen which is one manifestation of military spirit, born of strength, and as old as when the first man went forth with purpose to conquer his neighbor man.

Down in front of the post-trader's was gathered the scouting party. A tall sergeant, grown old in the service, scarred on battlefields, hardened by long marches,—in short, a product of the camp,—stood by his horse's head. Four enlisted men, picturesquely clad in the cavalry soldier's field costume, and two packers, mounted on diminutive bronco mules, were in charge of

* Soldier detailed as officer's servant.

four pack-mules loaded with *apperajos* and packs. This was our party. Presently the lieutenant issued from the headquarters' office and joined us. An orderly led up his horse. "Mount," said the lieutenant; and swinging himself into his saddle he started off up to the road. Out past the groups of adobe houses which constitute a frontier military village or post we rode, stopping to water our horses at the little creek, now nearly dry,—the last water for many miles on our trail,—and presently emerged upon the great desert. Together at the head of the little cavalcade rode the lieutenant and I, while behind, in single file, came the five troopers, sitting loosely in their saddles with the long stirrup of the United States cavalry seat, forage-hats set well over the eyes, and carbines, slickers, canteens, saddle-pockets, and lariats rattling at their sides. Strung out behind were the four pack-mules, now trotting demurely along, now stopping to feed, and occasionally making a solemn and evidently well-considered attempt to get out of line and regain the post which we were leaving behind. The packers brought up the rear, swinging their "blinds" and shouting at the lagging mules in a manner which evinced a close acquaintance with the character and peculiarities of each beast.

The sun was getting higher in the heavens and began to assert its full strength. The yellow dust rose about our horses' hoofs and settled again over the dry grass and mesquite bush. Stretching away on our right was the purple line of the Sierra Bonitas, growing bluer and bluer until lost in the hot scintillating atmosphere of the desert horizon. Overhead stretched the deep blue of the cloudless sky. Presently we halted and dismounted to tighten the packs, which work loose after the first hour. One by one the packers caught the little mules, threw a blind over their eyes, and "Now, Whitey! Ready! eve-e-e-e—gimme that loop," came from the men as they heaved and tossed the circling ropes in the mystic movements of the diamond hitch. "All fast, Lieutenant," cries a packer, and mounting we move on up the long slope of the mesa towards the

Sierras. We enter a break in the foothills, and the grade becomes steeper and steeper, until at last it rises at an astonishing angle.

The lieutenant shouts the command to dismount, and we obey. The bridle-reins are tossed over the horses' heads, the carbines thrown butt upwards over the backs of the troopers, a long drink is taken from the canteens, and I observe that each man pulls a plug of tobacco about a foot long from one of the capacious legs of his troop-boots and wrenches off a chew. This greatly amused me, and as I laughed I pondered over the fertility of the soldier mind; and while I do not think that the original official military board which evolved the United States troop-boot had this idea in mind, the adap-

Trooper in Tow. *Authors' wood engraving.*

tation of means to an end reflects great credit on the intelligence of some one.

Up the ascent of the mountain we toiled, now winding among trees and brush, scrambling up precipitous slopes, picking a way across a field of shattered rock, or steadying our horses over the smooth surface of some bowlder, till it seemed to my uninitiated mind that cavalry was not equal to the emergencies of such a country. In the light of subsequent experiences, however, I feel confident that any cavalry officer who has ever chased Apaches would not hesitate a moment to lead a command up the Bunker Hill Monument. The slopes of the Sierra Bonitas are very steep, and as the air became more rarified as we toiled upward I found that I was panting for breath. My horse—a veteran mountaineer—grunted in his efforts and drew his breath in a long and labored blowing; consequently I felt as though I was not doing anything unusual in puffing and blowing myself. The resolutions of the previous night needed considerable nursing, and though they were kept alive, at times I reviled myself for being such a fool as to do this sort of thing under the delusion that it was an enjoyable experience. On the trail ahead I saw the lieutenant throw himself on the ground. I followed his example, for I was nearly "done for." I never had felt a rock that was as soft as the one I sat on. It was literally downy. The old troop-horse heaved a great sigh, and dropping his head went fast asleep, as every good soldier should do when he finds the opportunity. The lieutenant and I discussed the climb, and my voice was rather loud in pronouncing it "beastly." My companion gave me no comfort, for he was "a soldier, and unapt to weep," though I thought he might have used his official prerogative to grumble. The negro troopers sat about, their black skins shining with perspiration, and took no interest in the matter in hand. They occupied such time in joking and in merriment as seemed fitted for growling. They may be tired and they may be hungry, but they do not see fit to augment their misery by finding fault with everybody and everything. In this particular they are charming men with whom to serve. Officers have often confessed to me that when they are on long and monotonous field service and are troubled with a depression of spirits, they have only to go about the campfires of the negro soldier in order to be amused and cheered by the clever absurdities of the men. Personal relations can be much closer between white officers and colored soldiers than in the white regiments without breaking the barriers which are necessary to army discipline. The men look up to a good officer, rely on him in trouble, and even seek him for advice in their small personal affairs. In barracks no soldier is allowed by his fellows to "cuss out" a just and respected superior. As to their bravery, I am often asked, "Will they fight?" That is easily answered. They have fought many, many times. The old sergeant sitting near me, as calm of feature as a bronze statue, once deliberately walked over a Cheyenne rifle-pit and killed his man. One little fellow near him once took charge of a lot of stampeded cavalry-horses when Apache bullets were flying loose and no one knew from what point to expect them next. These little episodes prove the sometimes doubted self-reliance of the negro.

After a most frugal lunch we resumed our journey towards the clouds. Climbing many weary hours, we at last stood on the sharp ridge of the Sierra. Behind us we could see the great yellow plain of the Sulphur Spring Valley, and in front, stretching away, was that of the Gila, looking like the bed of a sea with the water gone. Here the lieutenant took observations and busied himself in making an itinerary of the trail. In obedience to an order of the department commander, General Miles, scouting parties like ours are constantly being sent out from the chain of forts which surround the great San Carlos reservation. The purpose is to make provision against Apache outbreaks, which are momentarily expected, by familiarizing officers and soldiers with the vast solitude of mountain and desert. New trails for the movement of cavalry columns across the mountains are threaded out, waterholes of which the soldiers have no previous knowledge are discovered, and an Apache band is at all times liable to meet a cavalry command in out-of-the-way places. A salutary effect on the savage mind is then produced.

Here we had a needed rest, and then began the descent on the other side. This was a new experience. The prospect of being suddenly overwhelmed by an avalanche of horseflesh as the result of some unlucky stumble makes the recruit constantly apprehensive. But the trained horses are sure of foot, understand the business, and seldom stumble except when treacherous ground gives way. On the crest the prospect was very pleasant, as the pines there obscured the hot sun; but we suddenly left them for the scrub mesquite which bars your passage and reaches forth for you with its thorns when you attempt to go around.

We wound downward among the masses of rock for some time, when we suddenly found ourselves on a shelf of rock. We sought to avoid it by going up and around, but after a tiresome march we were still confronted by a drop of about a hundred feet. I gave up in despair; but the lieutenant, after gazing at the unknown depths which were masked at the bottom by a thick growth of brush, said, "This is a good place to go down." I agreed that it was if you once got started; but personally I did not care to take the tumble.

Taking his horse by the bits, the young officer began the descent. The slope was at an angle of at least sixty degrees, and was covered with loose dirt and bowlders, with the mask of brush at the bottom concealing awful possibilities of what might be beneath. The horse hesitated a moment, then cautiously put his head down and his leg forward and started. The loose earth crumbled, a great stone was precipitated to the bottom with a crash, the horse slid and floundered along. Had the situation not been so serious it would have been funny, because the angle of the incline was so great that the horse actually sat on his haunches like a dog. "Come on!" shouted the redoubtable man of war; and as I was next on the ledge and could not go back or let any one pass me, I remembered my resolutions. They prevailed against my better judgment, and I started. My old horse took it unconcernedly, and we came down all right, bringing our share of dirt and stones and plunging through the wall of brush at the bottom to find our friend safe on the lower side. The men came along without so much as a look of interest in the proceeding, and then I watched the mules. I had confidence in the reasoning powers of a pack-mule, and thought that he might show some trepidation when he calculated the chances; but not so. Down came the mules, without turning an ear, and then followed the packers, who, to my astonishment, rode down. I watched them do it, and know not whether I was more lost in admiration or eager in the hope that they would meet with enough difficulty to verify my predictions.

We then continued our journey down the mountains through a box-cañon. Suffice it to say that, as it is a cavalry axiom that a horse can go wherever a man can if the man will not use his hands, we made a safe transit.

Our camp was pitched by a little mountain stream near a grassy hillside. The saddles, packs, and *apperajos* were laid on the ground and the horses and mules herded on the side of the hill by a trooper, who sat perched on a rock above them, carbine in hand. I was thoroughly tired and hungry, and did my share in creating the famine which it was clearly seen would reign in that camp ere long. We sat about the fire and talked. The genial glow seems to possess an occult quality: it warms the self-confidence of a man; it lulls his moral nature; and the stories which circulate about a campfire are always more interesting than authentic. One old packer possessed a wild imagination, backed by a fund of experiences gathered in a life spent in knocking about everywhere between the Yukon River and the City of Mexico, and he rehearsed tales which would have staggered the Baron. The men got out a pack of Mexican cards and gambled at a game called "Coon-can" for a few nickels and dimes and that other soldier currency—

tobacco. Quaint expressions came from the card party. "Now I'se a-goin' to scare de life outen you when I show down dis han'," said one man after a deal. The player addressed looked at his hand carefully and quietly rejoined, "You might scare *me,* pard, but you can't scare de fixin's I'se got yere." The utmost good-nature seemed to prevail. They discussed the little things which make their lives. One man suggested that "De big jack mule, he behavin' hisself pretty well dis trip; he hain't done kick nobody yet." Pipes were filled, smoked, and returned to that cavalryman's grip-sack, the boot-leg, and the game progressed until the fire no longer gave sufficient light. Soldiers have no tents in that country, and we rolled ourselves in our blankets and, gazing up, saw the weird figure of the sentinel against the last red gleam of the sunset, and beyond that the great dome of the sky, set with stars. Then we fell asleep.

When I awoke the next morning the hill across the cañon wall was flooded with a golden light, while the gray tints of our camp were steadily warming up. The soldiers had the two black camp-pails over the fire and were grooming the horses. Every one was good-natured, as befits the beginning of the day. The tall sergeant was meditatively combing his hair with a currycomb; such delightful little unconventionalities are constantly observed about the camp. The coffee steamed up in our nostrils, and after a rub in the brook I pulled myself together and declared to my comrade that I felt as good as new. This was a palpable falsehood, as my labored movements revealed to the hard-sided cavalryman the sad evidence of the effeminacy of the studio. But our respite was brief, for almost before I knew it I was again on my horse, following down the cañon after the black charger bestrided by the junior lieutenant of K troop. Over piles of rocks fit only for the touch and go of a goat, through the thick mesquite which threatened to wipe our hats off or to swish us from the saddle, with the air warming up and growing denser, we rode along. A great stretch of sandy desert could be seen, and I foresaw hot work.

In about an hour we were clear of the descent and could ride along together, so that conversation made the way more interesting. We dismounted to go down a steep drop from the high mesa into the valley of the Gila, and then began a day warmer even than imagination had anticipated. The awful glare of the sun on the desert, the clouds of white alkaline dust which drifted up until lost above, seemingly too fine to settle again, and the great heat cooking the ambition out of us, made the conversation lag and finally drop altogether. The water in my canteen was hot and tasteless, and the barrel of my carbine, which I touched with my ungloved hand, was so heated that I quickly withdrew it. Across the hot-air waves which made the horizon rise and fall like the bosom of the ocean we could see a whirlwind or sand-storm winding up a tall spiral until it was lost in the deep blue of the sky above. Lizards started here and there; a snake hissed a moment beside the trail, then sought the cover of a dry bush; the horses moved along the downcast heads and drooping ears. The men wore a solemn look as they rode along, and now and then one would nod as though giving over to sleep. The pack-mules no longer sought fresh feed along the way, but attended strictly to business. A short halt was made, and I alighted. Upon remounting I threw myself violently from the saddle, and upon examination found that I had brushed up against a cactus and gotten my corduroys filled with thorns. The soldiers were overcome with great glee at this episode, but they volunteered to help me pick them from my dress. Thus we marched all day, and with canteens empty we "pulled into" Fort Thomas that afternoon. I will add that forageless cavalry commands with pack-animals do not halt until a full day's march is completed, as the mules cannot be kept too long under their burdens.

At the fort we enjoyed that hospitality which is a kind of freemasonry among army officers. The colonel made a delicious concoction of I know not what, and provided a hammock in a cool place while we drank it. Lieutenant F—— got cigars that were past praise, and another officer had provided a bath. Captain B—— turned himself out of doors to give us quarters, which graciousness we accepted while our consciences pricked. But for all that Fort Thomas is an awful spot, hotter than any other place on the crust of the earth. The siroccos continually chase each other over the desert, the convalescent wait upon the sick, and the thermometer persistently reposes at the figures 125° F. Soldiers are kept in the Gila Valley posts for only six months at a time before they are relieved, and they count the days.

On the following morning at an early hour we waved adieus to our kind friends and took our way down the valley. I feel enough interested in the discomforts of that march to tell about it, but I find that there are not resources in any vocabulary. If the impression is abroad that a cavalry soldier's life in the South-west has any of the lawn-party element in it, I think the impression could be effaced by doing a march like that. The great clouds of dust choke you and settle over horse, soldier, and accouterments until all local color is lost and black man and white man wear a common hue. The "chug, chug, chug" of your tired horse as he marches along becomes infinitely tiresome, and cavalry soldiers never ease themselves in the saddle. That is an army axiom. I do not know what would happen to a man who "hitched" in his saddle, but it is carefully instilled into their minds that they must "ride the horse" at all times and not lounge on his back. No pains are spared to prolong the usefulness of an army horse, and every old soldier knows that his good care will tell when the long forced march comes some day, and when to be put afoot by a poor mount means great danger in Indian warfare. The soldier will steal for his horse, will share his camp bread, and will moisten the horse's nostrils and lips with the precious water in the canteen. In garrison the troop-horses lead a life of ease and plenty; but it is varied at times by a pursuit of hostiles, when they are forced over the hot sands and up over the perilous mountains all day long, only to see the sun go down with the rider still spurring them on amid the quiet of the long night.

Through a little opening in the trees we see a camp and stop in front of it. A few mesquite trees, two tents, and some sheds made of boughs beside an *acequia* make up the background. By the cooking-fire lounge two or three rough frontiersmen, veritable pirates in appearance, with rough flannel shirts, slouch hats, brown canvas overalls, and an unkempt air; but suddenly, to my intense astonishment, they rise, stand in their tracks as immovable as graven images, and salute the lieutenant in the most approved manner of Upton. Shades of that sacred book the "Army Regulations," then these men were soldiers! It was a camp of instruction for Indians and a post of observation. They were nice fellows, and did everything in their power to entertain the cavalry. We were given a tent, and one man cooked the army rations in such strange shapes and mysterious ways that we marveled as we ate. After dinner we lay on our blankets watching the groups of San Carlos Apaches who came to look at us. Some of them knew the lieutenant, with whom they had served and whom they now addressed as "Young Chief." They would point him out to others with great zest, and babble in their own language. Great excitement prevailed when it was discovered that I was using a sketch-book, and I was forced to disclose the half-finished visage of one villainous face to their gaze. It was straightway torn up, and I was requested, with many scowls and grunts, to discontinue that pastime, for Apaches more than any other Indians dislike to have portraits made. That night the "hi-ya-ya-hi-ya-hi-yo-o-o-o" and the beating of the tom-toms came from all parts of the hills, and we sank to sleep with this grewsome lullaby.

The following day, as we rode, we were never out of sight of the brush huts of the Indians. We observed the simple domestic processes of their lives. One naked savage got up suddenly from behind a mesquite bush, which so startled the horses that quicker than thought every animal made a violent plunge to one side. No one of the trained riders seemed to mind this unlooked-for movement in the least beyond displaying a gleam of grinning ivories. I am inclined to think that it would have let daylight upon some of the "English hunting-seats" one sees in Central Park.

All along the Gila Valley can be seen the courses of stone which were the foundations of the houses of a dense population long since passed away. The lines of old irrigating ditches were easily traced, and one is forced to wonder at the changes in Nature, for at the present time there is not water sufficient to irrigate land necessary for the support of as large a population as probably existed at some remote period. We "raised" some foothills, and could see in the far distance the great flat plain, the buildings of the San Carlos agency, and the white canvas of the cantonment. At the ford of the Gila we saw a company of "doughboys" wade through the stream as our own troop-horses splashed across. Nearer and nearer shone the white lines of tents until we drew rein in the square where officers crowded around to greet us. The jolly post-commander, the senior captain of the 10th, insisted upon my accepting the hospitalities of his "large hotel," as he called his field tent, on the ground that I too was a New Yorker. Right glad have I been ever since that I accepted his courtesy, for he entertained me in the true frontier style.

Being now out of the range of country known to our command, a lieutenant in the same regiment was detailed to accompany us beyond. This gentleman was a character. The best part of his life had been spent in this rough country, and he had so long associated with Apache scouts that his habits while on a trail were exactly those of an Indian. He had acquired their methods and also that instinct of locality so peculiar to red men. I jocosely insisted that Lieutenant Jim only needed breech-clout and long hair in order to draw rations at the agency. In the morning, as we started under his guidance, he was a spectacle. He wore shoes and a white shirt, and carried absolutely nothing in the shape of canteens and other "plunder" which usually constitute a cavalryman's kit. He was mounted on a little runt of a pony so thin and woe-begone as to be remarkable among his kind. It was insufferably hot as we followed our queer guide up a dry cañon, which cut off the breeze from all sides and was a veritable human frying-pan. I marched next behind our leader, and all day long the patter, patter of that Indian pony, bearing his tireless rider, made an aggravating display of insensibility to fatigue, heat, dust, and climbing. On we marched over the rolling hills, dry, parched, desolate, covered with cactus and loose stones. It was Nature in one of her cruel moods, and the great silence over all the land displayed her mastery over man. When we reached water and camp that night our ascetic leader had his first drink. It was a long one and a strong one, but at last he arose from the pool and with a smile remarked that his "canteens were full." Officers in the regiment say that no one will give Lieutenant Jim a drink from his canteen, but this does not change his habit of not carrying one; nevertheless, by the exercise of self-denial, which is at times heroic, he manages to pull through. They say that he sometimes fills an old meat-tin with water in anticipation of a long march, and stories which try credulity are told of the amount of water he has drunk at times.

Yuma Apaches, miserable wretches, come into camp, shake hands gravely with every one, and then in their Indian way begin the inevitable inquiries as to how the coffee and flour are holding out. The campfire darts and crackles, the soldiers gather around it, eat, joke, and bring out the greasy pack of cards. The officers gossip of army affairs, while I lie on my blankets, smoking and trying to establish relations with a very small and very dirty little Yuma Apache, who sits near me and gazes with sparkling eyes at the strange object which I undoubtedly seem to him. That "patroness of rogues," the full moon, rises slowly over the great hill while I look into her honest face and lose myself in reflections. It seems but an instant before a glare of sun strikes

my eyes and I am awake for another day. I am mentally quarreling with that insane desire to march which I know possesses Lieutenant Jim; but it is useless to expostulate, and before many hours the little pony constantly moving along ahead of me becomes a part of my life. There he goes. I can see him now—always moving briskly along, pattering over the level, trotting up the dry bed of a stream, disappearing into the dense chapparal thicket that covers a steep hillside, jumping rocks, and doing everything but "halt."

We are now in the high hills, and the air is cooler. The chapparal is thicker, the ground is broken into a succession of ridges, and the volcanic bowlders pile up in formidable shapes. My girth loosens and I dismount to fix it, remembering that old saddle-gall. The command moves on and is lost to sight in a deep ravine. Presently I resume my journey, and in the meshwork of ravines I find that I no longer see the trail of the column. I retrace and climb and slide down hill, forcing my way through chapparal, and after a long time I see the pack-mules go out of sight far away on a mountain slope. The blue peaks of the Pinals tower away on my left, and I begin to indulge in mean thoughts concerning the indomitable spirit of Lieutenant Jim, for I know he will take us clear over the top of that pale blue line of far-distant mountains. I presume I have it in my power to place myself in a more heroic light, but this kind of candor is good for the soul.

In course of time I came up with the command, which had stopped at a ledge so steep that it had daunted even these mountaineers. It was only a hundred-foot drop, and they presently found a place to go down, where, as one soldier suggested, "there is n't footing for a lizard." On, on we go, when suddenly with a great crash some sandy ground gives way, and a collection of hoofs, troop-boots, ropes, canteens, and flying stirrups goes rolling over in a cloud of dust and finds a lodgment in the bottom of a dry watercourse. The dust settles and discloses a soldier and his horse. They rise to their feet and appear astonished, but as the soldier mounts and follows on we know he is unhurt. Now a coyote, surprised by our cavalcade and unable to get up the ledge, runs along the opposite side of the cañon wall. "Pop, pop, pop, pop" go the six-shooters, and then follow explanations by each marksman of the particular thing which made him miss.

That night we were forced to make a "dry camp"; that is, one where no water is to be found. There is such an amount of misery locked up in the thought of a dry camp that I refuse to dwell upon it. We were glad enough to get upon the trail in the morning, and in time found a nice running mountain-brook. The command wallowed in it. We drank as much as we could hold and then sat down. We arose and drank some more, and yet we drank again, and still once more, until we were literally water-logged. Lieutenant Jim became uneasy, so we took up our march. We were always resuming the march when all nature called aloud for rest. We climbed straight up impossible places. The air grew chill, and in a gorge a cold wind blew briskly down to supply the hot air rising from sands of the mesa far below. That night we made a camp, and the only place where I could make my bed was on a great flat rock. We were now among the pines, which towered above us. The horses were constantly losing one another in the timber in their search for grass, in consequence of which they whinnied, while the mules brayed, and made the mountain hideous with sound.

By another long climb we reached the extreme peaks of the Pinal range, and there before us was spread a view which was grand enough to compensate us for the labor. Beginning in "gray reds," range after range of mountains, overlapping each other, grow purple and finally lose themselves in pale blues. We sat on a ledge and gazed. The soldiers were interested, though their remarks about the scenery somehow did not seem to express an appreciation of the grandeur of the view which impressed itself strongly upon us. Finally one fellow, less æsthetic than his mates, broke the spell by a request for chewing-tobacco, so we left off dreaming and started on.

That day Lieutenant Jim lost his bearings, and called upon that instinct which he had acquired in his life among the Indians. He "cut the signs" of old Indian trails and felt the course to be in a certain direction—which was undoubtedly correct, but it took us over the highest points of the Mescal range. My shoes were beginning to give out, and the troop-boots of several soldiers threatened to disintegrate. One soldier, more ingenious than the rest, took out some horse-shoe nails and cleverly mended his boot-gear. At times we wound around great slopes where a loose stone or the giving way of bad ground would have precipitated horse and rider a thousand feet below. Only the courage of the horses brings one safely through. The mules suffered badly, and our weary horses punched very hard with their foreparts as they went down hill. We made the descent of the Mescals through a long cañon where the sun gets one in chancery, as it were. At last we reached the Gila, and nearly drowned a pack-mule and two troopers in a quicksand. We began to pass Indian huts, and saw them gathering wheat in the river bottoms, while they paused to gaze at us and doubtless wondered for what purpose the buffalo-soldiers were abroad in the land. The cantonment appeared, and I was duly gratified when we reached it. I hobbled up to the "Grand Hotel" of my host the captain, who laughed heartily at my floundering movements and observed my nose and cheeks, from which the sun had peeled the skin, with evident relish at the thought of how I had been used by his lieutenant. At his suggestion I was made an honorary member of the cavalry, and duly admonished "not to trifle again with the 10th Nubian Horse if I expected any mercy."

In due time the march continued without particular incident, and at last the scout "pulled in" to the home post, and I again sat in my easy-chair behind the lattice-work, firm in the conviction that soldiers, like other men, find more hard work than glory in their calling.

On the Indian Reservations

I was camping with a couple of prospectors one night some years ago on the south side of the Pinal Range in Arizona Territory. We were seated beside our little cooking fire about 9 o'clock in the evening engaged in smoking and drowsily discussing the celerity of movement displayed by Geronimo, who had at last been heard of down in Sonora, and might be already far away from there, even in our neighborhood. Conversation lapsed at last, and puffing our pipes and lying on our backs we looked up into the dark branches of the trees above. I think I was making a sluggish calculation of the time necessary for the passage of a far-off star behind the black trunk of an adjacent tree when I felt moved to sit up. My breath went with the look I gave, for, to my unbounded astonishment and consternation, there sat three Apaches on the opposite side of our fire with their rifles across their laps. My comrades also saw them, and, old, hardened frontiersmen as they were, they positively gasped in amazement.

"Heap hungry," ejaculated one of the savage apparitions, and again relapsed into silence.

As we were not familiar with Mr. Geronimo's countenance we thought we could see the old villain's features in our interlocutor's, and we began to get our artillery into shape.

The savages, in order to allay the disturbance which they had very plainly created, now explained.

"We White Mountain. No want fight—want flour."

They got the flour in generous quantities, it is needless to add, and although we had previously been very sleepy, we now sat up and entertained our guests until they stretched themselves out and went to sleep. We pretended to do the same. During that night I never closed my eyes, but watched, momentarily expecting to see more visitors come gliding out of the darkness. I should not have been surprised even to see an Apache drop from a branch above me.

They left us in the morning, with a blessing couched in the style of forcible speech that my Rocky Mountain friends affected on unusual occasions. I mused over the occurrence; for while it brought no more serious consequences than the loss of some odd pounds of bacon and flour, yet there was a warning in the way those Apaches could usurp the prerogatives of ghosts, and ever after that I used to mingle undue proportions of discretion with my valor.

Apaches are wont to lurk about in the rocks and *chaparral* with the stealth of coyotes, and they have always been the most dangerous of all the Indians of the Western country. They are not at all valorous in their methods of war, but are none the less effective. In the hot desert and vast rocky ranges of their country no white man can ever catch them by direct pursuit. Since railroads and the telegraph have entered their territory, and military posts have been thoroughly established, a very rigorous military system has kept them in the confines of the San Carlos reservation, and there is no longer the same fear that the next dispatches may bring news of another outbreak. But the troopers under General Miles always had their cartridge-belts filled and their saddle-pockets packed, ready at any hour of the day to jump out on a hostile trail.

The affairs of the San Carlos agency are administered at present by an army officer, Captain Bullis of the Twenty-fourth Infantry. As I have observed him in the discharge of his duties I have had no doubt that he pays high life insurance premiums. He does not seem to fear the beetle-browed pack of murderers with whom he has to deal, for he has spent his life in command of Indian scouts, and not only understands their character, but has gotten out of the habit of fearing anything. If the deeds of this officer had been done on civilized battlefields instead of in silently leading a pack of savages over the desert waste of the Rio Grande or the Staked Plain, they would have gotten him his niche in the temple of fame. Alas! they are locked up in the gossip of the army mess-room, and end in the soldiers' matter-of-fact joke about how Bullis used to eat his provisions in the field, opening one can a day from the packs, and, whether it was peaches or corned-beef, making it suffice. The Indians regard him as almost supernatural, and speak of the "Whirlwind" with many grunts of admiration as they narrate his wonderful achievements.

The San Carlos reservation, over which he has supervision, is a vast tract of desert and mountain, and near the center of it, on the Gila River, is a great flat plain where the long, low adobe buildings of the agency are built. Lines of white tents belonging to the cantonment form a square to the north. I arrived at this place one evening, after a hot and tiresome march, in company with a cavalry command. I found a good bunk in the tent of an army officer whose heart went out to the man in search of the picturesque, and I was invited to destroy my rations that evening at the long table of the officers' mess, wondering much at the culinary miracles performed by the Chinamen who presided over its destinies. The San Carlos is a

hotter place than I ever intend to visit again. A man who is used to breathing the fresh air of New York Bay is in no condition to enjoy at one and the same time the dinner and the Turkish bath which accompanies it. However, army officers are as entertaining in their way as poets, and I managed to be both stoical and appreciative.

On the following morning I got out my sketch-book, and taking my host into my confidence, I explained my plans for action. The captain discontinued brushing his hair and looked me over with a humorous twinkle in his eyes. "Young man," he said, "if you desire to wear a long, gray beard you must make away with the idea that you are in Venice."

I remembered that the year before a Blackfoot upon the Bow River had shown a desire to tomahawk me because I was endeavoring to immortalize him. After a long and tedious course of diplomacy it is at times possible to get one of these people to gaze in a defiant and fearful way down the mouth of a camera; but to stand still until a man draws his picture on paper or canvas is a proposition which no Apache will entertain for a moment. With the help of two officers, who stood up close to me, I was enabled to make rapid sketches of the scenes and people; but my manner at last aroused suspicion, and my game would vanish like a covey of quail. From the parade in front of our tent I could see the long lines of horses, mules, and burros trooping into the agency from all quarters. Here was my feast. Ordinarily the Indians are scattered for forty miles in every direction; but this was ration-day, and they all were together. After breakfast we walked down. Hundreds of ponies, caparisoned in all sorts of fantastic ways, were standing around. Young girls of the San Carlos tribe flitted about, attracting my attention by the queer ornaments which, in token of their virginity, they wear in their hair. Tall Yuma bucks galloped past with their long hair flying out behind. The squaws crowded around the exit and received the great chunks of beef which a native butcher threw to them. Indian scouts in military coats and armed with rifles stood about to preserve order. Groups of old women sat on the hot ground and gossiped. An old chief, with a very respectable amount of adipose under his cartridge-belt, galloped up to our group and was introduced as Esquimezeu. We shook hands.

These Indians have natural dignity, and it takes very little knowledge of manners for them to appear well. The Apaches have no expression for a good-bye or a greeting, and they never shake hands among themselves; but they consider handshaking an important ceremony among white men, and in their intercourse with them attach great importance to it. I heard an officer say that he had once seen an Apache come home after an absence of months: he simply stepped into the jicail, sat down without a word, and began rolling a cigarette.

The day was very hot, and we retired to the shade of Captain Bullis's office. He sat there with a big sombrero pulled over his eyes and listened to the complaints of the Indians against one another. He relegated certain offenders to the guard-house, granted absolute divorces, and probated wills with a bewildering rapidity. The interpreter struggled with his English; the parties at law eyed one another with villainous hate, and knives and rifles glistened about in a manner suggestive of the fact that the court of last resort was always in session. Among these people men are constantly killing one another, women are carried off, and feuds are active at all times. Few of these cases come before the agent if the parties think they can better adjust their own difficulties by the blood-atonement process, but the weak and the helpless often appeal.

After leaving the office and going some distance we were startled by a gun-shot from the direction of the room we had just left. We started back. The negro soldiers of the guard came running past; the Indians became excited; and every one was armed in a minute. A gaint officer of infantry, with a white helmet on his head, towered above the throng as he forced his way through the gathering mass of Indians. Every voice was hushed, and every one expected anything imaginable to happen. The Indians began to come out of the room, the smoke eddying over their heads, and presently the big red face and white helmet of the infantry officer appeared. "It's nothing, boys—only an accidental discharge of a gun." In three minutes things were going on as quietly as before.

Captain Bullis sauntered up to us, and tipping his hat on one side meditatively scratched his head as he pointed to an old wretch who sat wrapped in a sheet against the mud wall of the agency.

"There's a problem. That old fellow's people won't take care of him any longer, and they steal his rations. He's blind and old and can't take care of himself." We walked up and regarded the aged being, whose parchment skin reminded us of a mummy. We recoiled at the filth, we shuddered at his helplessness, and we pitied this savage old man so steeped in misery; but we could do nothing. I know not how the captain solved his problem. Physical suffering and the anguish of cast-off old age are the compensations for the self-reliant savage warrior who dozes and dreams away his younger days and relegates the toil to those within his power.

We strolled among the horses and mules. They would let me sketch them, though I thought the half-wild beasts also shrunk away from the baleful gaze of the white man with his bit of paper. Broncos, mules, and burros stood about, with bags of flour tied on their saddles and great chunks of meat dripping blood over their unkempt sides. These woe-begone beasts find scant pasture in their desert home, and are banged about by their savage masters until ever-present evils triumph over equine philosophy. Fine navy blankets and articles of Mexican manufacture were stretched over some of the saddles, the latter probably obtained in a manner not countenanced by international law.

The Apaches have very little native manufacture. They rely on their foraging into Mexico for saddlery, serapes, and many other things; but their squaws make wicker-work, some of which I have never seen surpassed. *Allas,* or water-jars, of beautiful mold and unique design, are sold to any one who desires to buy them at a price which seems absurdly mean when the great labor expended on them is considered. But Apache labor is cheap when Apaches will work at all. The women bring into the cantonment great loads of hay on their backs, which is sold to the cavalry. It is all cut with a knife from bunches which grow about six inches apart, and is then bound up like wheat and carried for miles.

By evening all the Indians had betaken themselves to their own rancherias, and the agency was comparatively deserted for another week.

I paused for a day on the Gila, some miles from the agency, to observe the methods of agriculture practiced by the San Carlos Indian tribe. The Gila River bottoms are bounded on each side by bluffs, and on these the Indians build their brush jicails. High above the stifling heat of the low ground the hot winds from the desert blow through the leafy bowers which they inhabit. As they wear no clothing except breech-cloth and moccasins, they enjoy comparative comfort. The squaws go back and forth between their jicails and the river carrying wicker allas filled with muddy water, and the whole people seek the river and the system of irrigating ditches at evening time to turn the water over the parched ground and nourish the corn, wheat, and vegetables which grow there. Far up the valley the distant *stump* of a musket-shot reaches our ears; then another comes from a nearer point, and still another. Two or three women begin to take away the boards of an acequia dam near as the water rises to their knees, and with a final tug the deepening water rushes through. "Bang!" goes the Springfield carbine of an Indian standing at my elbow, and after some moments another gun-shot comes to our ears from below. As the minutes pass the reports come fainter and fainter, until we are just conscious of the sounds far off down the valley.

The pile of straw round which a mounted Indian has been driving half a dozen horses all day in order to stamp out the grain has lowered now until he will have but an hour's work more in the morning. He stops his beasts and herds them off to the hills to graze. The procession of barefooted men and of women bearing jars comes winding over the fields towards their humble habitations on the bluffs. The sun sinks behind the distant Sierras, and the beautiful quiet tones of the afterglow spread over the fields and the water. As I stand there watching the scene I can almost imagine that I see Millet's peasants; but, alas! I know too well the difference.

My companion, a lieutenant of cavalry, and I bethink ourselves to go back to the camps of these people to spend an evening; so, leaving the troopers about their fires, we take our way in company with an old Government Indian scout to his own jicail. The frugal evening meal was soon disposed of, and taking our cigarettes we sat on the bluffs and smoked. A traveler in the valley looking up at the squatting forms of men against the sky would have remembered the great strength of chiaroscuro in some of Doré's drawings and to himself have said that this was very like it.

I doubt if he would have discerned the difference between the two white men who came from the bustling world so far away and the dark-skinned savages who seemed a sympathetic part of nature there, as mute as any of its rocks and as incomprehensible to the white man's mind as any beast which roams its barren wastes.

It grew dark, and we forbore to talk. Presently, as though to complete the strangeness of the situation, the measured "thump, thump, thump" of the tom-tom came from the vicinity of a fire some short distance away. One wild voice raised itself in strange discordant sounds, dropped low, and then rose again, swelling into shrill yelps, in which others joined. We listened, and the wild sounds to our accustomed ears became almost tuneful and harmonious. We drew nearer, and by the little flickering light of the fire discerned half-naked forms huddled with uplifted faces in a small circle around the tom-tom. The fire cut queer lights on their rugged outlines, the waves of sound rose and fell, and the "thump, thump, thump, thump" of the tom-tom kept a binding time. We grew in sympathy with the strange concert, and sat down some distance off and listened for hours. It was more enjoyable in its way than any trained chorus I have ever heard.

The performers were engaged in making medicine for the growing crops, and the concert was a religious rite, which, however crude to us, was entered into with a faith that was attested by the vigor of the performance. All savages seem imbued with the religious feeling, and everything in nature that they do not comprehend is supernatural. Yet they know so much about her that one often wonders why they cannot reason further.

The one thing about our aborigines which interests me most is their peculiar method of thought. With all due deference to much scientific investigation which has been lavished upon them, I believe that no white man can ever penetrate the mystery of their mind or explain the reason of their acts.

The red man is a mass of glaring incongruities. He loves and hates in such strange fashions, and is constant and inconstant at such unusual times, that I often think he has no mental process, but is the creature of impulse. The searching of the ethnologist must not penetrate his thoughts too rapidly, or he will find that he is reasoning for the Indian, and not with him.

THE COMANCHES.

After coming from the burning sands of Arizona the green stretches of grass and the cloud-flecked sky of northern Texas were very agreeable. At a little town called Henrietta I had entered into negotiations with a Texas cowboy to drive me over certain parts of the Indian Territory. He rattled up to my quarters in the early morning with a covered spring-wagon drawn by two broncos so thin and small and ugly that my

sympathies were aroused, and I protested that they were not able to do the work.

The driver, a smart young fellow with his hat brim knocked jauntily back in front, assured me that "They can pull your freight, and you can bet on it." I have learned not to trust to appearances regarding Western ponies, and so I clambered in and we took up our way.

The country was a beautiful rolling plain, covered with rank, green grass and dotted with dried flowers. Heavily timbered creeks interlaced the view and lessened its monotony. The sun was hot, and the driver would nod, go fast asleep, and nearly fall out of the wagon. The broncos would quiet down to a walk, when he would suddenly awake, get out his black snake whip, and roar "mule language" at the lazy creatures. He was a good fellow and full of interest, had made the Montana trail three times with the Hash Knife outfit, and was full of the quaint expressions and pointed methods of reasoning peculiar to Western Americans. He gave me volumes of information concerning Comanches and Indians in general; and while his point of view was too close for a philosophical treatment of the case, he had a knowledge of details which carried him through. Speaking of their diet, he "allowed anything's grub to an Injun, jus' so it hain't pisen."

We came at last to the Red River, and I then appreciated why it was called red, for its water is absolutely the reddest thing I ever saw in nature. The soil thereabouts is red, and the water is colored by it. We forded the river, and the little horses came so near sticking fast in the middle that my cowboy jumped out up to his waist and calmly requested me to do the same. I did, but to the ruin of a pair of white corduroys. We got through, however, and were in the Territory. Great quantities of plums, which the Indians gather, grow near the river.

In due course of time we came in sight of Fort Sill, which is built of stone, in a square around a parade of grass, and perched on rising ground. The plains about were dotted with the skulls of cattle killed for ration day. Sheds of poles covered with branches dotted the plains, and on our right the "big timber" of Catch Creek looked invitingly cool.

At Fort Sill I became acquainted with Mr. Horace P. Jones the Comanche interpreter, who has lived with that tribe for thirty-one years. He is an authority on the subject of Indians, and I tried to profit by his knowledge. He spoke of one strange characteristic of the Comanche language which makes their speech almost impossible to acquire. Nearly all Comanches are named after some object in nature, and when one dies the name of the object after which he was named is changed and the old word is never spoken again. Mr. Jones often uses one of the words which a recent death has made obsolete, and is met with muttered protestations from his Indian hearers. He therefore has to skirmish round and find the substitute for the outlawed word.

The Comanches are great travelers, and wander more than any other tribe. Mr. Jones has known Comanches to go to California, and as far south as Central America, on trips extending over years. They are a jolly, round-faced people who speak Spanish, and often have Mexican blood in their veins—the result of stolen Mexican women, who have been ingrafted into the tribe.

The Comanches are less superstitious than Indians are generally. They apply an amount of good sense to their handling of horses which I have never seen among Indians elsewhere. They breed intelligently, and produce some of the most beautiful "painted" ponies imaginable. They take very good care of them, and in buying and selling have no lessons to learn from Yankee horse-traders. They still live in lodges, but will occupy a good house if they can obtain one. About this thing they reason rather well; for in their visits to the Caddoes and the Shawnees they observe the squalid huts in the damp woods, with razor-back hogs contesting the rights of occupancy with their masters, and they say that the tepee is cleaner, and argue that if the Shawnees represent civilization, their own barbarism is the better condition of the two. However, they see the good in civilization and purchase umbrellas, baby-carriages, and hats, and of late years leave the Winchester at home; although, like the Texan, a Comanche does not feel well dressed without a large Colt strapped about his waist. Personal effects are all sacrificed at the death of their owners, though these Indians no longer destroy the horses, and they question whether the houses which are built for them by the Government should be burned upon the death of the tenant. Three or four have been allowed to stand, and if no dire results follow the matter will regulate itself.

The usual corps of Indian scouts is camped under the walls of Fort Sill, and is equally divided between the Comanches and the Kiowas. They are paid, rationed, and armed by the Government, and are used to hunt up stray Government horses, carry messages, make arrests among their own people, and follow the predatory Texas cowboy who comes into the Territory to build up his fortunes by driving off horses and selling corn-juice to the Indians.

The Comanches are beginning to submit to arrests without the regulation exchange of fusillade; but they have got the worst of Texas law so long that one cannot blame them for being suspicious of the magistracy. The first question a Comanche asks of a white stranger is, "Maybe so you Texas cowboy?" to which I always assure them that I am a Kansas man, which makes our relations easy. To a Comanche all bad men are "Texas cowboys," and all good people are "Kansas men."

At the scout camp I was allowed to sketch to my heart's content, and the people displayed great interest in the proceedings.

The morning of the Fourth of July found Mr. Jones and me in the saddle and on the way to the regulation celebration at the agency below the post. The Fourth of July and Christmas are the "white man's big Sundays" to the Indians, and they always expect the regular horse-race appropriations. The Indians run their ponies. Extra beeves are killed, and the red men have always a great regard for the "big Sundays."

As we approach the agency it is the hour for the race, and the throng moves to some level plain near, where a large ring is formed by the Indians on horseback.

An elderly Indian of great dignity of presence steps into the ring, and with a graceful movement throws his long red blanket to the ground and drops on his knees before it, to receive the wagers of such as desire to make them. Men walk up and throw in silver dollars and every sort of personal property imaginable. A Winchester rifle and a large nickel-plated Colt's revolver are laid on the grass near me by a cowboy and an Indian, and then each goes away. It was a wager, and I thought they might well have confidence in their stakeholder—mother earth. Two ponies, tied head and head, were led aside and left, horse against horse. No excitement seemed to prevail. Near me a little half-Mexican Comanche boy began to

disrobe until he stood clad only in shirt and breech-cloth. His father addressed some whispered admonition and then led up a roan pony, prancing with impatience and evidently fully conscious of the work cut out for him that day. With a bound the little fellow landed on the neck of the pony only half way up; but his toes caught on the upper muscles of the pony's leg, and like a monkey he clambered up and was in his seat. The pony was as bare as a wild horse except for a bridle, and loped away with his graceful little rider sitting like a rock. No, not like a rock, but limp and unconcerned, and as full of the motion of the horse as the horse's tail or any other part of him.

A Kiowa with loose hair and great coarse face broke away from the group and galloped up the prairie until he stopped at what was to be the starting-point, at the usual distance of "two arrow flights and a pitch." He was followed by half a dozen ponies at an easy lope, bearing their half-

In the Betting Ring. *Painting in IBM Collection.*

naked jockeys. The Indian spectators sat about on their ponies, as unmoved in countenance as oysters, being natural gamblers, and stoical as such should be, while the cowboys whispered among themselves.

"That's the bay stallion there," said one man to me, as he pointed to a racer, "and he's never been beaten. It's his walk-over, and I've got my gun up on him with an Injun."

It was to be a flying start, and they jockeyed a good deal and could not seem to get off. But presently a puff of smoke came from the rifle held aloft by the Kiowa starter, and his horse reared. The report reached us, and with a scurry the five ponies came away from the scratch, followed by a cloud of dust. The *quirts* flew through the air at every jump. The ponies bunched and pattered away at a nameless rate, for the quarter-race pony is quick of stride. Nearer and nearer they came, the riders lying low on their horses' necks, whipping and ki-yi-yi-ing. The dust in their wake swept backward and upward, and with a rush they came over the scratch, with the roan pony ahead and my little Mexican fellow holding his quirt aloft, and his little eyes snapping with the nervous excitement of the great event. He had beaten the invincible bay stallion, the pride of this Comanche tribe, and as he rode back to his father his face had the settled calm which nothing could penetrate, and which befitted his dignity as a young runner.

Far be it from these quaint people ever to lose their blankets, their horses, their heroism, in order to stalk behind a plow in a pair of canvas overalls and a battered silk hat. Now they are great in their way; but then, how miserable! But I have confidence that they will not retrograde. They can live and be successful as a pastoral people, but not as sheep herders, as some great Indian department reformer once thought when he placed some thousands of these woolly idiots at their disposal.

The Comanches travel about too much and move too fast for sheep; but horses and cattle they do have and can have so long as they retain possession of their lands. But if the Government sees fit to consecrate their lands to the "man with the hoe," then, alas! good-bye to all their greatness.

Bidding adieu to my friends at Fort Sill, I "pulled out" for Anadarko on the Washita, where the head agency of the Comanches, Kiowas, and Wichitas is located. The little ponies made bad work of the sandy roads. Kiowa houses became more numerous along the road, and there is evidence that they farm more than the brother tribe, but they are not so attractive a people. Of course the tepee is pitched in the front yard and the house is used as a kind of out-building. The medicine-bags were hanging from the tripod of poles near by, and an occasional buck was lying on his back "smoking his medicine"— a very comfortable form of devotion.

We saw the grass houses of the Wichitas, which might be taken for ordinary haystacks. As they stand out on the prairie surrounded by wagons, agricultural implements, and cattle, one is caught wondering where is the remainder of the farm which goes with this farm-yard.

These Territory Apaches are very different from their brothers of the mountains. They are good-looking, but are regarded contemptuously by other Indians and also by the traders. They are treacherous, violent, and most cunning liars and thieves. I spent an evening in one of their tepees watching a game of monte, and the gambling passion was developed almost to insanity. They sat and glared at the cards, their dark faces gleaming with avarice, cunning, and excitement. I thought then that the good white men who would undertake to make Christian gentlemen and honest tillers of the soil out of this material would contract for a job to subvert the process of nature.

Our little ponies, recuperated by some grain and rest, were once more hooked up, and the cowboy and I started for Fort Reno to see the Arrapahoes and the Cheyennes, hoping to meet them far along on "the white man's road."

Artist Wanderings Among the Cheyennes

After a hard pull we came to a beautiful creek heavily timbered with post-oak, black-jack, and pecan trees. Taking our well-worn ponies from the pole we fed and curried them, hoping that by careful nursing they might be gotten through to Fort Reno. I wasted some anxiety on myself as I discovered that my cowboy driver unrolled from a greasy newspaper the provisions which he had assured me before starting was a matter which had been attended to. It was "poor picking" enough, and I did not enjoy my after-dinner smoke when I realized that the situation was complicated by the fact that we had eaten everything for dinner and were then miles from Reno, with a pair of played-out ponies.

Hooking up again, we started on. On a little hill one jaded beast "set back in the breeching" and we dismounted to push the wagon and coax him along. The road was heavy with sand and we lost a parallel trail made by the passage of the Eighth Cavalry some weeks before. We hoped to discover the "breaks"* of the South Canadian River before darkness set in; but the land rose steadily away in front, and we realized that something must be done. At last coming suddenly upon a group of miserable pole cabins, we saw two Caddoes reclining on a framework of poles. I conceived the idea of hiring one of these to guide us through in the darkness. The wretches refused to un-

* The lowering of the land, cut by streams tending towards the basin of a large river.

derstand us, talk English, sign language; or what we would. But after a hard bargain one saddled his pony and consented to lead the way through the darkness. On we traveled, our valuable guide riding so far ahead that we could not see him, and at last we came suddenly in sight of the bright surface of the South Canadian. The sun was fast sinking, and by the time we had crossed the wide sand-bars and the shallow water of the river bottom a great red gleam was all that remained on the western horizon. About a mile to the left flickered the camp-fires about a group of lodges of Arapahoes. We fed our team and then ourselves crunched kernels of "horse-trough corn" which were extracted from the feed box. Our Caddo sat on his horse while we lay stretched on the grassy bank above the sand flats. A dark-skinned old Arapaho rode up, and our Caddo saluted him. They began to converse in the sign language as they sat on their ponies, and we watched them with great interest. With graceful gestures they made the signs and seemed immediately and fully to comprehend each other. As the old Arapaho's face cut dark against the sunset I thought it the finest Indian profile I had ever seen. He was arrayed in the full wild Indian costume of these latter days, with leggings, beaded moccasins, and a sheet wrapped about his waist and thighs. The Caddo, on the contrary, was a progressive man. His hair was cropped in Cossack style; he wore a hat, boots, and a great "slicker," or cowboy's oil-skin coat. For the space of half an hour they thus interested each other. We speculated on the meaning of the signs, and could often follow them; but they abbreviated so much and did it all so fast that we missed the full meaning of their conversation. Among other things the Caddo told the Arapaho who we were, and also made arrangements to meet him at the same place at about 10 o'clock on the following day.

Darkness now set in, and as we plunged into the timber after the disappearing form of our guide I could not see my companions on the seat beside me. I think horses can make out things better than men can under circumstances like these; and as the land lay flat before us, I had none of the fears which one who journeys in the mountains often feels.

The patter of horses' hoofs in the darkness behind us was followed by a hailing cry in the guttural tone of an Indian. I could just make out a mounted man with a led horse beside the wagon, and we exchanged inquiries in English and found him to be an acquaintance of the morning, in the person of a young Cheyenne scout from Fort Reno who had been down to buy a horse of a Caddo. He had lived at the Carlisle school, and although he had been back in the tribe long enough to let his hair grow, he had not yet forgotten all his English. As he was going through to the post, we dismissed our Caddo and followed him.

Far ahead in the gloom could be seen two of the post lights, and we were encouraged. The little ponies traveled faster and with more spirit in the night, as indeed do all horses. The lights did not come nearer, but kept at the indefinite distance peculiar to lights on a dark night. We plunged into holes, and the old wagon pitched and tipped in a style which insured keeping its sleepy occupants awake. But there is an end to all things, and our tedious trail brought us into Fort Reno at last. A sleepy boy with a lamp came to the door of the post-trader's and wanted to know if I was trying to break the house down, which was a natural conclusion on his part, as sundry dents in a certain door of the place will bear witness to this day.

On the following morning I appeared at the headquarters office, credentials in hand. A smart, well-gotten up "non-com." gave me a chair and discreetly kept an eye on the articles of value in the room, for the hard usage of my recent travels had so worn and soiled my clothing that I was more picturesque than assuring in appearance. The colonel came soon, and he too eyed me with suspicious glances until he made out that I was not a Texas horse thief nor an Oklahoma boomer. After finding that I desired to see his protégés of the prairie, he sent for the interpreter, Mr. Ben. Clark, and said, "Seek no farther; here is the best Cheyenne in the country."

Mr. Clark I found to be all that the colonel had recommended, except that he did not look like a Cheyenne, being a perfect type of the frontier scout, only lacking the long hair, which to his practical mind a white man did not seem to require. A pair of mules and a buckboard were provided at the quartermaster's corral, and Mr. Clark and I started on a tour of observation.

We met many Cheyennes riding to some place or another. They were almost invariably tall men with fine Indian features. They wore the hair caught by braids very low on the shoulders, making a black mass about the ears, which at a distance is not unlike the aspect of an Apache. All the Indians now use light "cow-saddles," and ride with the long stirrups peculiar to Western Americans, instead of "trees" of their own construction with the short stirrup of the old days. In summer, instead of a blanket, a white sheet is generally worn, which becomes dirty and assumes a very mellow tone of color. Under the saddle the bright blue or red Government cloth blanket is worn, and the sheet is caught around the waist, giving the appearance of Zouave trousers. The variety of shapes which an Indian can produce with a blanket, the great difference in wearing it, and the grace and naturalism of its adjustment, are subjects one never tires of watching. The only criticism of the riding of modern Indians one can make is the incessant thumping of the horse's ribs, as though using a spur. Outside of the far South-west, I have never seen Indians use spurs. With the awkward old "trees" formerly made by the Indians, and with the abnormally short stirrup, an Indian was anything but graceful on horseback, although I have never heard any one with enough temerity to question his ability. I always like to dwell on this subject of riding, and I have an admiration for a really good rider which is altogether beyond his deserts in the light of philosophy. In the Eastern States the European riding-master has proselyted to such an extent that it is rather a fashionable fad to question the utility of the Western method. When we consider that for generations these races of men who ride on the plains and in the Rocky Mountains have been literally bred on a horse's back, it seems reasonable to suppose they ought to be riders; and when one sees an Indian or a cowboy riding up precipices where no horses ought to be made to go, or assuming on horseback some of the grotesque positions they at times affect, one needs no assurance that they do ride splendidly.

As we rattled along in the buckboard, Mr. Clark proved very interesting. For thirty odd years he has been in contact with the Cheyennes. He speaks the language fluently, and has discovered in a trip to the far North that the Crees use almost identically the same tongue. Originally the Cheyennes came from the far North, and they are Algonquin in origin. Though their legend of the famous "medicine arrow" is not a recent discovery, I cannot forbear to give it here.

A long time ago, perhaps about the year 1640, the Cheyennes were fighting a race of men who had guns. The fighting was in the vicinity of the Devil's Lake country, and the Cheyennes had been repeatedly worsted in combat and were in dire distress. A young Horatius of the tribe determined to sacrifice himself for the common weal, and so wandered away. After a time he met an old man, a mythical personage, who took pity on him. Together they entered a great cave, and the old man gave him various articles of "medicine" to choose from, and the young man selected the "medicine arrows."

After the old man had performed the proper incantations, the hero went forth with his potent fetish and rejoined the tribe. The people regained courage, and in the fight which soon followed they conquered and obtained guns for the first time. Ever since the tribe has kept the medicine arrows, and they are now in the Indian Territory in the possession of the southern Cheyennes. Years ago the Pawnees captured the arrows and in ransom got vast numbers of ponies, although they never gave back all of the arrows, and the Cheyennes attribute all their hard experiences of later days to this loss. Once a year, and oftener should a situation demand it, the ceremony of the arrows takes place. No one has ever witnessed it except the initiated priests.

The tribal traditions are not known thoroughly by all, and of late years only a very few old men can tell perfectly the tribal stories. Why this is so no one seems to know, unless the Indians have seen and heard so much through the white men that their faith is shaken.

Our buckboard drew gradually nearer the camp of the Cheyennes. A great level prairie of waving green was dotted with the brown toned white canvas lodges, and standing near them were brush "ramadas," or sheds, and also wagons. For about ten years they have owned wagons, and now seldom use the *travaux*. In little groups all over the plain were scattered pony herds, and about the camp could be seen forms wearing bright blankets or wrapped in ghostlike cotton sheets. Little columns of blue smoke rose here and there, and gathered in front of one lodge was squatted a group of men. A young squaw dressed in a bright calico gown stood near a ramada and bandied words with the interpreter while I sketched. Presently she was informed that I had made her picture, when she ran off, laughing at what she considered an unbecoming trick on the part of her entertainer. The women of this tribe are the only squaws I have ever met, except in some of the tribes of the northern plains, who have any claim to be considered good looking. Indeed, some of them are quite as I imagine Pocahontas,

Minnehaha, and the rest of the heroines of the race appeared. The female names are conventional, and have been borne by the women ever since the oldest man can remember. Some of them have the pleasant sound which we occasionally find in the Indian tongues: "Mut-say-yo," "Wau-hi-yo," "Mo-ka-is," "Jok-ko-ko-me-yo," for instance, are examples; and with the soft guttural of their Indian pronunciation I found them charming. As we entered the camp all the elements which make that sort of scene interesting were about. A medicine-man was at work over a sick fellow. We watched him through the opening of a lodge and our sympathies were not aroused, as the patient was a young buck who seemed in no need of them. A group of young men were preparing for a clan dance. Two young fellows lay stretched on the grass in graceful attitudes. They were what we call "chums." Children were playing with dogs; women were beading moccasins; a group of men lay under a wagon playing monte; a very old man, who was quite naked, tottered up to our vehicle and talked with Mr. Clark. His name was Bull Bear, and he was a strange object with his many wrinkles, gray hair, and toothless jaws.

From a passing horseman I procured an old "buck saddle" made of elk horn. They are now very rare. Indian saddlery is interesting, as all the tribes had a different model, and the women used one differing from that of the men.

We dismounted at the lodge of Whirlwind, a fine old type who now enjoys the prestige of head chief. He was dignified and reserved, and greeted us cordially as he invited us to a seat under the ramada. He refused a cigar, as will nearly all Indians, and produced his own cigarettes.

Through the interpreter we were enabled to converse freely. I have a suspicion that the old man had an impression that I was in some way connected with the Government. All Indians somehow divide the white race into three parts. One is either a soldier, a Texas cowboy, or a "big chief from Washington," which latter distinction I enjoyed. I

explained that I was not a "big chief," but an artist, the significance of which he did not grasp. He was requested to put on his plumage, and I then proceeded to make a drawing of him. He looked it over in a coldly critical way, grunted several times, and seemed more mystified than ever; but I do not think I diminished in his estimation. In his younger days Whirlwind had been a war chief; but he traveled to Washington and there saw the power and numbers of the white man. He advised for peace after that, and did not take the warpath in the last great outbreak. His people were defeated, as he said they would be, and confidence in his judgment was restored. I asked him all sorts of questions to draw on his reminiscences of the old Indian life before the conquest, all of which were answered gravely and without boasting. It was on his statesmanlike mind, however, to make clear to me the condition of his people, and I heard him through. Though not versed in the science of government, I was interested in the old man's talk. He had just returned from a conference of the tribes which had been held in the Cherokee country, and was full of the importance of the conclusions there evolved. The Indians all fear that they will lose their land, and the council advised all Indians to do nothing which would interfere with their tenure of the land now held by them. He told with pride of the speech he made while there and of the admiration with which he was regarded as he stood, dressed in the garb of the wild Indian, with his tomahawk in hand. However, he is a very progressive man, and explained that while he was too old to give up the methods of life which he had always observed, yet his son would be as the civilized Cherokees are. The son was squatted near, and I believed his statement, as the boy was large of stature and bright of mind, having enjoyed some three years' schooling at a place which I have now forgotten. He wore white men's clothes and had just been discharged from the corps of scouts at Reno. When I asked the boy why he did not plow and sow and reap, he simply shrugged his shoulders at my ignorance, which, in justice to myself, I must explain was only a leading question, for I know that corn cannot be raised on this reservation with sufficient regularity to warrant the attempt. The rainfall is not enough; and where white men despair, I, for one, do not expect wild Indians to continue. They have tried it and have failed, and are now very properly discouraged. Stock-raising is the natural industry of the country, and that is the proper pursuit of these people. They are only now recovering by natural increase from the reverses which they suffered in their last outbreak. It is hard for them to start cattle herds, as their ration is insufficient, and one scarcely can expect a hungry man to herd cattle when he needs the beef to appease his hunger. Nevertheless, some men have respectable herds and can afford to kill an animal occasionally without taking the stock cattle. In this particular they display wonderful forbearance, and were they properly rationed for a time and given stock cattle, there is not a doubt but in time they would become self-supporting. The present scheme of taking a few boys and girls away from the camps to put them in school where they are taught English, morals, and trades has nothing reprehensible about it, except that it is absolutely of no consequence so far as solving the Indian problem is concerned. The few boys return to the camps with their English, their school clothes, and their short hair. They know a trade also, but have no opportunity to be employed in it. They loaf about the forts for a time with nothing to do, and the white men talk pigeon English to them and the wild Indians sneer at them. Their virtues are unappreciated, and, as a natural consequence, the thousands of years of barbarism which is bred in their nature overcome the three little seasons of school training. They go to the camps, go back to the blanket, let their hair grow, and forget their English. In a year one cannot tell a schoolboy from any other little savage, and in the whole proceeding I see nothing at all strange.

The camp will not rise to the school-boy,

and so Mahomet goes to the mountain. If it comes to pass that the white race desires to aid these Indians to become a part of our social system instead of slowly crushing them out of it, there is only one way to do it. The so-called Indian problem is no problem at all in reality, only that it has been made one by a long succession of acts which were masterly in their imbecility and were fostered by political avarice. The sentiment of this nation is in favor of no longer regarding the aborigines of this country as a conquered race; and except that the great body of our citizens are apathetic of things so remote as these wards of the Government, the people who have the administration of their destinies would be called to account. No one not directly interested ever questioned that the Indian Department should have been attached to the War Department; but that is too patent a fact to discuss. Now the Indian affairs are in so hopeless a state of dry-rot that practical men, in political or in military circles, hesitate to attempt the rôle of reformers. The views which I have on the subject are not original, but are very old and very well understood by all men who live in the Indian countries. They are current among army officers who have spent their whole lives on the Indian frontier of the far West, but are not often spoken, because all men realize the impotency of any attempt to overcome the active work of certain political circles backed by public apathy and a lot of theoretical Indian regenerators. If anything is done to relieve the condition of the Indian tribes it must be a scheme which begins at the bottom and takes the "whole outfit," as a Western man would say, in its scope. If these measures of relief are at all tardy, before we realize it the wild Indian tribes will be, as some writer has said, "loafers and outcasts, contending with the dogs for kitchen scraps in Western villages." They have all raised stock successfully when not interfered with or not forced by insufficient rations to eat up their stock cattle to appease their hunger, and I have never heard that Indians were not made of soldier stuff.

The Branding Chute at the Beef Issue. *Painting in George F. Harding Museum, Chicago.*

A great many Western garrisons have their corps of Indian scouts. In every case they prove efficient. They are naturally the finest irregular cavalry on the face of this globe, and with an organization similar to the Russian Cossacks they would do the United States great good and become themselves gradually civilized. An irregular cavalry is every year a more and more important branch of the service. Any good cavalry officer, I believe, could take a command of Indians and ride around the world without having a piece of bacon, or a cartridge, or a horse issued by his Government. So far as effective police work in the West is concerned, the corps of Indian scouts do nearly all of that service now. They all like to be enlisted in the service, universally obey or-

ders, and are never disloyal. But nothing will be done; so why continue this?

For hours we sat in the ramada of the old chief and conversed, and when we started to go I was much impressed by the discovery that the old Indian knew more about Indians, Indian policy, and the tendencies and impulses of the white men concerning his race than any other person I had ever met.

The glories of the reign of an Indian chieftain are past. As his people become more and more dependent on the Government his prestige wanes. For instance, at the time of our visit to this camp the people were at loggerheads regarding the locality where the great annual Sun Dance, or, more literally, "The Big Medicine," should be held. The men of the camp that I visited wanted it at one place, and those of the "upper camp" wanted it at another. The chief could not arrange the matter, and so the solution of the difficulty was placed in the hands of the agent.

The Cheyenne agency buildings are situated about a mile and a half from Fort Sill. The great brick building is imposing. A group of stores and little white dwelling-houses surround it, giving much the effect of a New England village. Wagons, saddled ponies, and Indians are generally disposed about the vicinity and give life to the scene. Fifteen native policemen in the employ of the agency do the work and take care of the place. They are uniformed in cadet gray, and with their beaded white moccasins and their revolvers are neat and soldierly looking. A son of old Bent, the famous frontiersman, and an educated Indian do the clerical work, so that the agent is about the only white man in the place. The goods which are issued to the Indians have changed greatly in character as their needs have become more civilized. The hatchets and similar articles of the old traders are not given out, on the ground that they are barbarous. Gay colored clothes still seem to suit the esthetic sense of the people, and the general effect of a body of modern Indians is exceeding brilliant. Arabs could not surpass them in this respect.

They receive flour, sugar, and coffee at the great agency building, but the beef is issued from a corral situated out on the plain at some distance away. The distribution is a very thrilling sight, and I made arrangements to see it by procuring a cavalry horse from Colonel Wade at the fort and by following the ambulance containing an army officer who was detailed as inspector. We left the post in the early morning, and the driver "poured his lash into the mules" until they scurried along at a speed which kept the old troop-horse at a neat pace.

The heavy dew was on the grass, and clouds lay in great rolls across the sky, obscuring the sun. From the direction of the target range the "stump" of the Springfields came to our ears, showing that the soldiers were hard at their devotions. In twos, and threes, and groups, and crowds, came Indians, converging on the beef corral. The corral is a great ragged fence made of an assortment of boards, poles, scantling, planks, old wagons, and attached to this is a little house near which the weighing scales are placed. The crowd collected in a great mass near the gate and branding-chute. A fire was burning, and the cattle contractors (cowboys) were heating their branding-irons to mark the "I. D." on the cattle distributed, so that any Indian having subsequently a hide in his possession would be enabled to satisfy roving cattle inspectors that they were not to be suspected of killing stock.

The agent came to the corral and together with the army officer inspected the cattle to be given out. With loud cries the cowboys in the corral forced the steers into the chute, and crowding and clashing they came through into the scales. The gate of the scales was opened and a half-dozen frightened steers crowded down the chute and packed themselves in an unyielding mass at the other end. A tall Arapaho policeman seized a branding-iron, and mounting the platform of the chute poised his iron and with a quick motion forced it on the back of the living beast. With a wild but useless plunge and a loud bellow of pain the steer shrunk from the hot contact; but it was all over, and a long black "I. D." disfigured the surface of the skin.

Opposite the branding-chute were drawn up thirty young bucks on their ponies, with their rifles and revolvers in hand. The agent shouted the Indian names from his book, and a very engaging lot of cognomens they were. A policeman on the platform designated a particular steer which was to be the property of each man as his name was called. The Indian came forward and marked his steer by reaching over the fence and cutting off an ear with a sharp knife, by severing the tail, or by tying some old rag to some part of the animal. The cold-blooded mutilation was perfectly shocking, and I turned away in sickened disgust. After all had been marked, the terrified brutes found the gate at the end of the chute suddenly opened by the police guard; but before this had been done a frantic steer had put his head half through the gate, and in order to force him back a red-hot branding-iron was pushed into his face, burning it horribly. The worst was over; the gates flew wide, and the maddened brutes poured forth, charging swiftly away in a wild impulse to escape the vicinity of the crowd of humanity. The young bucks in the group broke away, and each one, singling out his steer, followed at top speed, with rifle or six-shooter in hand. I desired to see the whole proceeding, and mounting my cavalry horse followed two young savages who seemed to have a steer possessed of unusual speed. The lieutenant had previously told me that the shooting at the steers was often wild and reckless, and advised me to look sharp or I might have to "pack a bullet." Puffs of smoke and the "pop! pop!" of the guns came from all over the plain. Now a steer would drop, stricken by some lucky shot. It was buffalo-hunting over again, and was evidently greatly enjoyed by the young men. My two fellows headed their steer up the hill on the right, and when they had gotten him far enough away they "turned loose," as we say. My old cavalry horse began to exhibit a lively interest in the smell of gunpowder, and plunged away until he had me up and in front of the steer and the Indians, who rode on each side. They blazed away at the steer's head, and I could hear a misdirected bullet "sing" by uncomfortably near. Seeing me in front, the steer dodged off to one side, and the young fellow who was in his way, by a very clever piece of horsemanship, avoided being run over. The whole affair demonstrated to me that the Indian boys could not handle the revolver well, for they shot a dozen rounds before they killed the poor beast. Under

their philosophic outward calm I thought I could see that they were not proud of the exhibition they had made. After the killing, the squaws followed the wagons and proceeded to cut up the meat. After it had been divided among themselves, by some arrangement which they seemed to understand, they cut it into very thin pieces and started back to their camps.

Peace and contentment reign while the beef holds out, which is not long, as the ration is insufficient. This is purposely so, as it is expected that the Indians will seek to increase a scant food supply by raising corn. It does not have that effect, however. By selling ponies, which they have in great numbers, they manage to get money; but the financial future of the Cheyennes is not flattering.

Enlistment in the scouting corps at Reno is a method of obtaining employment much sought after by the young men. The camp is on a hill opposite the post, where the white tepees are arranged in a long line. A wall tent at the end is occupied by two soldiers who do the clerical work. The scouts wear the uniform of the United States army, and some of them are strikingly handsome in the garb. They are lithe and naturally "well set up," as the soldiers phrase it. They perform all the duties of soldiers; but at some of the irksome tasks, like standing sentry, they do not come out strong. They are not often used for that purpose, however, it being found that Indians do not appreciate military forms and ceremonies.

Having seen all that I desired, I procured passage in the stage to a station on the Santa Fe Railroad. In the far distance the train came rushing up the track, and as it stopped I boarded it. As I settled back in the soft cushions of the sleeping-car I looked at my dirty clothes and did not blame the negro porter for regarding me with the haughty spirit of his class.

Two Gallant Young Cavalrymen

A small band of renegade Apache Indians recently murdered and plundered a freighter in Arizona. Troops, under Lieutenant James M. Watson and Powhatan H. Clarke, were put on the trail, and, with the aid of Indian scouts from the San Carlos "scout camp," followed it at a terrific pace for over three hundred miles through the deserts and rocky ranges of the country until they struck the hostiles in an almost inaccessible position. After the first shots were exchanged the Indians took to the rocks and continued the firing, evidently determined to sell their lives as dearly as possible. The colored troops and Indian scouts, although exposing themselves heroically, escaped all casualties, but finally succeeded in killing two of the hostiles. After another had been wounded the remainder surrendered.

Two horses which the Indians had stolen were almost fagged to death after the hard pushing which the troops had given them. The prisoners were taken to the guardhouse at San Carlos, to be subsequently turned over to the civil authorities for trial. It is safe to predict that the days of the revolting crimes of this particular lot of Apaches have passed away. "There is no doubt that the prisoners will be hanged," says the press despatch. The writer of this does not think it safe to say that the revolting crimes of Apaches will pass away until Apaches are no more; but they will undoubtedly be hanged, as the press man says.

The régime of General Miles in the De-partment of Arizona is frequently vindicated nowadays, but no better example of the running down of Apache murderers has occurred than this last, and the young officers who conducted it are entitled to praise. Since the long race after Geronimo, which General Miles inaugurated and brought to a successful termination, there have been several other outbreaks, but the young men of the Tenth and Fourth Cavalry have learned how to ride a long race, and have been successful in nipping in the bud what might be another reign of terror in Sonora, Arizona, and New Mexico.

Every autumn the troops in the department have a series of manœuvres which is largely based on the idea of chasing and fighting Indians. They are all familiar with the vast expanse of mountain and desert; they can thread the perilous trails of the Sierras, and go straight to the water-holes. They can ride long distances on the trail of the "foe which is ever ahead," and fight him after his own fashion should the opportunity offer. The troops in the chain of forts which surround the San Carlos Indian Reservation are at all times ready to take the field inside of thirty minutes, which soldiers will understand is a very short time indeed; and it is this taste of warlike efficiency that makes it rather discouraging for Apaches to pursue their natural tendencies. Force and efficiency are things which an Indian can comprehend in our civilization.

The moral of all this soldiering in the Southwest is that General Miles has suc-

Lieutenant Powhatan H. Clarke, Tenth Cavalry. *Authors' photoengraving.*

ceeded in making it possible for a white man to live in that country and pursue his calling without absolute certainty of being shot down like a wild beast; for until he took command an Apache Indian never had much discrimination between a white man and an antelope when he was abroad with a gun. But beyond the great purpose of this military scheme of police protection there is another which must be taken into account, and that is the development of a race of cavalrymen and officers who will start eventually a "new school," as the critics say, in the cavalry work. The country is about the toughest piece of landscape gardening that the Creator ever constructed, and cavalrymen who have chased Apaches would not hesitate to follow a bunch of canvas-back ducks in their wanderings. They learn to go light, to work off from a base of supplies, and I venture to say that if the bacon and crackers were low in the packs and the

"trail hot," that Lieutenant Jim Watson would pay more attention to the trail than the crackers.

The writer of this has had occasion to observe the two heroes of the illustrations, Mr. Clarke and Mr. Watson, and he will use great caution in his movements in the future so that he will not be compelled to see more of them. Both of the gentlemen are fine fellows in barracks, but by long study and thought they have contracted a species of insanity peculiar to enterprising young cavalry officers, and when in the field they make it tedious for any one who follows their lead. Nothing more delights these men than to come into possession of a tenderfoot guest from the East, or an officer from some of the European armies, with orders to show him some of their work. They shake hands with the victim, say a pleasant thing or two, and then go outside the door and smile large smiles, like an ogre of old, as they think what a fine possibility the guest is for a physical wreck. They are both made of whalebone and rubber, and are inured to any heat which a Turkish bath might supply. Clarke is considered one of the finest riders in the army, and can do things on a horse's back which is the perfection of what a West Point cadet thinks he can do. I have a theory, born of some observation, that there are young cavalry officers in the United States service who can ride better than any other class of men in the world. I have no idea that every one will agree with me in this matter, but I hold my faith with the placid calm of a man who has ceased to argue. The little "cherub who sits up aloft" has his hands full to look after Lieutenant Clarke and keep him from breaking his neck, but I am quite sure he was not intended for that form of death.

Lieutenant Watson is possessed of an idea that a cavalryman ought to be able to take a horse and a tooth-brush and ride to the moon. He has an Apache fondness for "bald peaks," and his trail generally leads up the highest elevations in the neighborhood. He rides light, not even carrying canteens in the desert country where he operates. There is a standing joke in the army on the last man to join from West Point. It is that Lieutenant Watson will ride up to him in the middle of some particularly hard, dry march, and suavely beg a drink from his canteen. This favor is granted, and the Lieutenant presently returns the canteen emptied of its contents, with a bland "Thank you, sir." He never is able to borrow a canteen from that gentleman again. In fact, no one will share his water with Watson; but that does not change his habit of not carrying one. He once tried this little pleasantry on your humble servant, but a kindly disposed person had explained the thing beforehand, and I did not respond. The Lieutenant has served so long with Indian scouts that he has acquired many of their methods, until he is a kind of "split the difference" between a cultivated gentleman and a wild Indian. He has that aboriginal instinct of locality developed in a high degree, and can always point, like the hand of a compass, to the particular "jacal" where he belongs. In a case of civilized war, I imagine that Lieutenant Watson could keep quite a body of the enemy's horse engaged in guessing his whereabouts.

Lieutenant Clarke is a Virginian, but with Louisiana French in his blood. He is adored by his men, and universally popular. He rides the horses which no one else can, and chases the festive jack-rabbit with his pack of hounds right into the parade; but to the stranger's inquiry as to these wild proceedings the by-standers only explain, "Oh, that's Clarke!" Altogether one of those old-time kind of "ride into battle with his life on

his sleeve" soldiers, and one not to be particularly commended for bravery, since trepidation would be quite a novel experience for him. He once pulled a wounded corporal under cover from Apache bullets at some little personal risk, since they fired some fifty shots at him, and replied to some admiring friends concerning it, "Well, what else could I do?" Of course it is really seen that he could do nothing else, although most other men would be fertile enough in expedients to devise a way for not doing the thing at all. Some of the old commanders in the department regard Clarke as a "broncho" in barracks, but they all have a kindly regard for the soldierly qualities of the young man, which he generously reciprocates. For instance, he has a particular admiration for General Merritt, ostensibly based on the fine military record and writings of that officer, although I think his acquaintance with the virtues of the general dates from a ten days in the guard-house at the instigation of the latter. Ordinarily a civilian would not appreciate an attention of that sort, but that merely goes to show that a soldier is built on different lines.

With all their faults and propensities for making life a burden to their guests who come down for a ride or a scout with them, I still bear no malice, and in all seriousness I feel impelled to declare that the country can feel sure that it has men in its calvary service who are young, hardy, enterprising, and, above all, intelligent. They will do their part, if Uncle Sam needs them, in a more glorious field than chasing Apaches over the rocks, and do it just as well.

Chasing a Major-General

The car had been side-tracked at Fort Keough, and on the following morning the porter shook me, and announced that it was five o'clock. An hour later I stepped out on the rear platform, and observed that the sun would rise shortly, but that meanwhile the air was chill, and that the bald, square-topped hills of the "bad lands" cut rather hard against the gray of the morning. Presently a trooper galloped up with three led horses, which he tied to a stake. I inspected them, and saw that one had a "cow saddle," which I recognized as an experiment suggested by the general. The animal bearing it had a threatening look, and I expected a repetition of a performance of a few days before, when I had chased the general for over three hours, making in all twenty-eight miles.

Before accepting an invitation to accompany an Indian commission into the Northwest I had asked the general quietly if this was a "horseback" or a "wagon outfit." He had assured me that he was not a "wagon man," and I indeed had heard before that he was not. There is always a distinction in the army between wagon men and men who go without wagons by transporting their supplies on pack animals. The wagon men have always acquired more reputation as travellers than Indian fighters. In a trip to the Pine Ridge Agency I had discovered that General Miles was not committed to any strained theory of how mounted men should be moved. Any settled purpose he might have about his movements were all

locked up in a desperate desire to "get thar." Being a little late in leaving a point on the railroad, I rode along with Lieutenant Guilfoil, of the Ninth, and we moved at a gentle trot. Presently we met a citizen in a wagon, and he, upon observing the lieutenant in uniform, pulled up his team and excitedly inquired,

"What's the matter, Mr. Soldier?"

Guilfoil said nothing was the matter that he knew of.

"Who be you uns after?"

"No one," replied the lieutenant.

"Well, I just saw a man go whirling up this 'ere valley with a soldier tearin' after him fit to kill" (that was the general's orderly), "and then comes a lot more soldiers just a-smokin', and I sort of wondered what the man had done."

We laughed, and remarked that the general must be riding pretty hard. Other citizens we met inquired if that man was a lunatic or a criminal. The idea of the soldiers pursuing a man in citizen's clothes furthered the idea, but we assured them that it was only General Miles going somewhere.

All of these episodes opened my eyes to the fact that if I followed General Miles I would have to do some riding such as I had rarely done before. In coming back to the railroad we left the Pine Ridge Agency in the evening without supper, and I was careful to get an even start. My horse teetered and wanted to gallop, but I knew that the twenty-eight miles would have to be done at full speed, so I tried to get him down to a

fast trot, which gait I knew would last better; but in the process of calming him down
to a trot I lost sight of the general and his
orderly as they went tearing like mad over a
hill against the last gleam of the sunset. I
rode at a very rapid trot over the hills in the
moonlight for over three hours, but I never
saw the general again until I met him at dinner. Then I further concluded that if I followed the general I would have no time to
regait my horses, but must take them as I
found them, gallop or trot. So on this cool
morning at Keough I took observations of
the horses which were tied to the post, with
my mind full of misgivings.

Patter, patter, patter—clank, clank,
clank; up comes the company of Cheyenne
scouts who are to escort the general—fine-
looking, tall young men, with long hair, and
mounted on small Indian ponies. They were
dressed and accoutred as United States soldiers, and they fill the eye of a military man
until nothing is lacking. Now the general
steps out of the car and hands the commission into a six-mule ambulance. I am given
a horse, and, mounting, we move off over
the plain and into the hills. The sun comes
streaming over the landscape, and the general is thinking about this old trail, and how
years before he had ploughed his way
through the blinding snow to the Lame
Deer fight. I am secretly wishing that it
would occupy his mind more fully, so that
my breakfast might settle at the gentle gait
we are going, but shortly he says, "It's sixty
miles, and we must move along." We break
into a gallop. The landscape is gilded by the
morning sun, and the cool of the October air
makes it a perfect thing, but there are elements in the affair which complicate its perfection. The "bad lands" are rough, and the
general goes down a hill with even more rapidity than up it. The horses are not the
perfect animals of the bridle-path, but poor
old cavalry brutes, procured by the government under the old contract system, by
which the government pays something like
$125 for a $60 horse. This could be remedied by allowing the officers of each regiment to buy their own horses; but in our

army nothing is remedied, because a lot of
nice old gentlemen in Washington are too
conservative to do anything but eat and
sleep. There is a bit of human nature at the
bottom of our army organization, and
where is the man who can change that?
Men who were the very jewels of the profession years ago have reached in due time the
upper grades of rank, and occupy the bureaus of the department. These men who
have acquired rank, years, and discretion
naturally do nothing, and with sedate gravity insist that no one else shall do anything.
The ambitious young men have to wait patiently for their retirement, and in process
of waiting they, too, become old and conservative. Old soldiers are pardonable rubbish, since soldiers, like other men, must
age and decay, the only distinction being
that youthful vigor is of prime importance
to a soldier, while in the case of the citizen
any abatement of vigor is rewarded by
being shelved. What to do with old soldiers
is a problem which I will hand over to the
economists as being beyond my depth. But
to return to the going downhill. General
Miles has acquired his knowledge of riding
from wild Indians, and wild Indians go
uphill and downhill as a matter of course at
whatever gait they happen to be travelling.
He would make his horse climb a tree with
equal gravity if he was bound that way. The
general has known Indians to ride for two
days and a night at a rapid gallop, and it
never occurs to him that he cannot do anything which any one else can; so he spurs
along, and we go cutting around the *coulies*
and bluffs like frightened antelopes or mad
creatures. The escort strings out behind.
This is observed with a grim humor by the
general, who desires nothing so much as to
leave his escort far in the rear. He turns in
his saddle, and seeing the dust of the escort
far behind, says: "Shake up the young men
a little; do 'em good. They get sleepy;" and
away we go.

It is over thirty miles to the first relay station, or courier's camp, and another problem looms up. The general's weight is over
two hundred pounds, and I confess to two

hundred and fifteen avoirdupois, and, as I
have before remarked, my horse was not an
Irish hunter, so my musing took a serious
vein. It is all very well for a major-general
to ride down a cavalry horse, but if such an
accident were to happen to me, then my
friends in the cavalry would crown me with
thorns. Two hundred and fifteen pounds
requires a great deal more careful attention
than a one-hundred-and-forty-pound wasp-
waisted cavalryman. What the latter can do
with impunity would put me on foot—a
thing that happened some ten years since in
this very State of Montana, and a thing I
have treasured in mind, and will not have
repeated. So I brought the old horse down
to a trot, and a good round trot eats up a
road in short order. Your galloper draws
away from you, but if the road is long
enough, you find that you are at his heels.

After a good day's ride of something like
sixty miles, we met a troop of the Eighth
Cavalry near its camp on the Tongue River,
and the general is escorted in. The escorts
draw into line, salute, and the general is
duly deposited in a big Sibley tent; and I go
away on the arms of some "cavalry kids"
(as young lieutenants are called) to a hole
in the ground (a dugout) where they are
quartered. On the following morning I am
duly admonished that if my whereabouts
could have been ascertained on the previous
evening, the expedition would have continued to the camp of the First Cavalry. I do
not think the general was unduly severe, desiring simply to shift the responsibility of
the procrastination on to other shoulders,
and meanwhile being content to have things
as they were. I was privately thanked by the
citizen members of the commission for the
delay I had caused, since they had a well-
grounded conviction that sixty miles a day
in an army ambulance was trouble enough.
After some sarcasm by a jolly young sub, to
the effect that "if one wants to call a citizen
out of a tent, one must ring a dinner-bell,"
we were again mounted and on the way. I
was badly mounted that day, but able to
participate in the wild charge of forty-five
miles to the Lame Deer camp, near the
Cheyenne Agency. The fifty Cheyenne
scouts and a troop of the Eighth were in escort.

By a happy combination I was able to
add greatly to my equestrian knowledge on
this ride. It happened in this way; but I
must explain. Some years ago I had occasion to ride a stock saddle (the cowboy article), and with all the positiveness of imma-
ture years, I held all other trees and all
other methods of riding in a magnificent
contempt. Later on I had to be convinced
that a great many young cavalry officers in
our service were the most daring and perfect riders, and that the McClelland saddle
was the proper thing. I even elaborated a
theory in explanation of all this, which I
had duly shattered for me when I came East
and frequented a New York riding-
academy, where a smiling professor of the
art assured me that cowboys and soldiers
were the worst possible riders. Indeed, the
sneers of the polite European were so su-
perlative that I dared not even doubt his
statements. Of course I never quite understood how my old champions of the cattle
range and the war trail could pick things off
the ground while in full career, or ride like
mad over the cut banks and bowlders, if
they were such desperately bad riders; and I
was never able to completely understand
why my European master could hardly turn
in his saddle without tumbling off. But still
he reduced me to submission, and I ceased
even to doubt. I changed my style of riding,
in deference to a public sentiment, and got
my legs tucked up under my chin, and
learned to loose my seat at every alternate
footfall, and in time acquired a balance
which was as secure as a pumpkin on the
side of a barrel. Thus equipped with all this
knowledge and my own saddle, I went out
to the Northwest with the purpose of introducing a little revolution in cavalry riding.
Things went swimmingly for a time. The interpreters and scouts watched my riding
with mingled pity and scorn, but I knew
they were unenlightened, and in no way to
be regarded seriously. The general was duly
amused by my teetering, and suggested to

the smiling escort officers that "he has lived so long abroad, you know," etc., all of which I did not mind, for my faith in the eternal art of the thing was complete. Now to tell how I discovered that I was riding a seat which was no seat at all, and was only retained by a series of happy accidents, I will continue. While at the head of the column, where I could see the deep ruts in the road and the bowlders, and could dodge the prairie-dog holes, it was simple enough; but my horse being a very clumsy galloper, and beginning to blow under the pace, I began to pull up, calculating to get a sharp trot, and overhaul the column when it slowed down. The column of soldiers dashed by, and the great cloud of dust rose up behind them which always follows a herd of animals in the West. Being no longer able to see, the only thing to do under the circumstances was to give my horse his head, and resign myself to the chances of a gopher hole, if it was foreordained that my horse should find one. True to his instincts, my old cavalry horse plunged into the ranks. You cannot keep a troop horse out of the ranks. They know their place, and seek it with the exactitude of water. If the cavalry tactics are ever changed, the present race of horses will have to be sold, because, while you can teach a horse anything, you cannot unteach him.

In front I could see two silhouettes of soldiers tearing along, and behind could hear the heavy pounding of the troop horses, the clank of arms, the snorts and heavy breathings. I could hardly see my horse's head, to say nothing of the ground in front. Here is where the perfect grip with the thighs is wanted, and here is where the man who is bundled up like a ball on his horse's back is in imminent danger of breaking his neck. I felt like a pack on a government mule, and only wished I had some one to "throw the diamond hitch over me." The inequalities of the road make your horse plunge and go staggering sidewise, or down on his knees, and it is not at all an unusual thing for a cavalryman to upset entirely, though nothing short of a total turn-over will separate a veteran soldier from his horse. After a few miles of these vicissitudes I gained the head of the column, and when the pace slackened I turned the whole thing over in my mind, and a great light seemed to shine though the whole subject. For a smooth road and a trotting horse, that European riding-master was right; but when you put a man in the dust or smoke, over the rocks and cut banks, on the "bucking" horse, or where he must handle his weapons or his *vieta,* he must have a seat on his mount as tight as a stamp on an envelope, and not go washing around like a shot in a bottle. In a park or on a country road, where a man has nothing to do but give his undivided attention to sticking on his saddle, it has its advantages. An Indian or a cowboy could take the average park rider off from his horse, scalp him, hang him on a bush, and never break a gallop. I do not wish to seem intolerant, because I will say that the most beautiful horse and the most perfect horseman I have ever seen was the bay gelding Partisan and his rider in the high-school class at the recent Horse Show in New York; but I do insist that no one shall for a moment imagine that the American style of riding is not the firmest of all seats.

With a repetition of the military forms, we reached the cavalry camp on the Lame Deer Creek. This is an old battle-ground of the general's—his last fight with the Cheyennes, where, as the general puts it, we "kicked them out of their blankets in the early morning." These Indians recognize him as their conqueror, and were allied with him in the Nez Percé campaign. One old chief pointed to the stars on his shoulder-strap, and charged him to remember that they helped to put them there.

That night was very cold, and I slept badly, so at an early hour I rolled out of my blankets and crawled into my clothes. I stepped out of my tent, and saw that the stars were yet visible and the light of the morning warming up to chase the gray shadows over the western hills. Three tight little cavalry soldiers came out on the parade, and blew three bugles as hard as ever they could to an unappreciative audience of sleepy soldiers and solemn hills. I walked down past the officers' row, and shook the kinks out of my stiffened knees. Everything was as quietly dismal as only a sleeping camp can be. The Sibley containing General Miles showed no signs of life, and until he arose this little military solar system would not revolve. I bethought me of the irregulars. They were down in the river bottom—Lieutenant Casey and his Indian scouts. I knew that Casey had commanded Indian scouts until his temper was as refined as beaten gold, so I thought it safer to arouse him than any one else, and, walking down, I scratched at his tent—which is equivalent to knocking—and received a rather loud and surly inquiry as to what I wanted. My sensitive nature was so shocked by this that, like the bad actor, I had hopes for no more generous gift than a cigarette. I was let into the Sibley, and saw the ground covered with blanketed forms. One of the swathed forms sat up, and the captain allowed he wanted to get up in the night, but that ever since Lieutenant Blank had shot at the orderly he was afraid to move about in the gloom. Lieutenant B. sat up and denied the impeachment. Another officer arose and made some extended remarks on the unseemly disturbance at this unseasonable hour. To pass over these inequalities of life, I will say that the military process of stiffening a man's backbone and reducing his mind to a logarithm breeds a homogeneous class whom we all know. They have small waists, and their clothes fit them; they are punctilious; they respect forms, and always do the dignified and proper thing at the particular instant, and never display their individuality except on two occasions: one is the field of battle and the other is before breakfast. Some bright fellow will one day tell in print the droll stock anecdotes of the United States army, and you'll all agree that they are good. They are better, though, if you sit in a Sibley on a cold morning while the orderly boils the coffee; and are more fortunate if you have Ned Casey to embellish

what he calls the international complications which arose from the bombardment of Canada with paving-stones by a drunken recruit at Detroit.

After the commission had talked to a ring of drowsy old chiefs, and the general had reminded them that he had thrashed them once, and was perfectly willing to do it again if they did not keep in the middle of the big road, the commission was loaded into the ambulances. The driver clucked and whistled and snapped his whip as a preliminary which always precedes the concerted movement of six mules, and we started. This time I found that I had a mount that was "a horse from the ground up," as they phrase it in the red-blooded West. Well it was so, for at the relay camp I had issued to me a sorrel ruin which in the pristine vigor of its fifth year would not have commanded the value of a tin cup. After doing a mile of song and dance on this poor beast I dismounted, and shifting my saddle back to my led horse of the morning, which was led by a Crow scout, made the sixty-mile march of that day on the noble animal. Poor old chap, fit for a king, good for all day and the next, would bring six hundred dollars in the New York Horse Exchange, but condemned to pack a trooper in the ranks until a penurious government condemns and sells him to a man who, nine times out of ten, by the law of God, ought not to be intrusted with the keeping of the meanest of his creatures, to say nothing of his noblest work—a horse. "Such is life," is the salve a good soldier puts on his wounds.

During the day we went all over the battle-field of the Little Big Horn. I heard a good deal of professional criticism, and it is my settled conviction that had Reno and Benteen gone in and fought as hard as they were commanded to do, Custer would have won his fight, and to-day be a major-general. The military moral of that affair for young soldiers is that when in doubt about what to do it is always safe to go in and fight "till you drop," remembering that,

Troopers Singing the Indian Medicine Song. *Engraving in authors' collection.*

however a citizen may regard the proposition, a soldier cannot afford to be anything else than a "dead lion."

We were nearing the Crow Agency and Fort Custer, and it is against all my better impulses, and with trepidation at the impropriety of unveiling the truth, that I disclose the fact that the general would halt the column at a convenient distance from a post, and would then exchange his travel-worn garb for glittering niceties of a major-general's uniform. The command then advanced into the fort. The guns bellowed and the cavalry swung into line, while numerous officers gathered, in all the perfection of neat-fitting uniforms, to receive him. At this time the writer eliminated himself from the ceremonial, and from some point of vantage proceeded to pull up his boots so as to cover as much as possible the gaping wounds in his riding-trousers, and tried vainly to make a shooting-jacket fit like an officer's blouse, while he dealt his hat sundry thumps in a vain endeavor to give it a more rakish appearance. He was then introduced and apologized for in turn. To this day he hopes the mantle of charity was broad enough to cover his case.

What a contrast between soldiers in field and soldiers in garrison! Natty and trim—as straight as a sapling, with few words and no gestures—quite unlike those of two days, or rather nights, ago, when the cold froze them out of their blankets, and they sat around the camp-fires pounding tin cans and singing the Indian medicine song with a good Irish accent. Very funny that affair—the mixture of Cheyenne and Donnybrook is a strange noise.

The last stage from Custer to the railroad is thirty-five miles and a half, which we did with two relays, the latter half of it in the night. There was no escort—only two orderlies and the general—and I pattered along through the gloom. The clouds hung over the earth in a dense blanket, and the road was as dim as a Florentine fresco; but night nor cold nor heat can bring General Miles to a walk, and the wild charge in the dark was, as an experience, a complete thing. You cannot see; you whirl through a cañon cut in the mud; you plough through the sage-brush and over the rocks clatter and bang. The general is certainly a grim old fellow—one of the kind that make sparks fly when he strikes an obstacle. I could well believe the old Fifth Infantryman who said "he's put many a corn on a dough-boy's foot," and it's a red-letter day for any one else that keeps at his horse's heels. You may ride into a hole, over a precipice, to perdition, if it's your luck on this night, but is not the general in front? You follow the general—that's the grand idea—that is the military idea. If the United States army was strung out in line with its general ahead, and if he should ride out into the broad Atlantic and swim to sea, the whole United States army would follow along, for that's the idea, you know.

But for the headlong plunge of an or-derly, we passed through all right, with due thankfulness on my part, and got to our car at the siding, much to the gratification of the Chicago colored man in charge, who found life at Custer Station a horrid blank. Two hundred and forty-eight miles in thirty-six hours and a half, and sixty miles of it on one horse, was not bad riding, considering everything. Not enough to make a man famous or lame, but enough for the time being.

The Art of War and Newspaper Men

Less than two weeks ago I passed over the trail from Rushville, Nebraska, to the Pine Ridge Agency behind Major-General Nelson A. Miles. To-night the moon is shining as it did then, but it will go down in the middle of the night, and I can see in my mind's eye the Second Infantry and the Ninth Troopers, with their trains of wagons, plodding along in the dark. The distance is twenty-eight miles, and at four o'clock in the morning they will arrive. When the Ogallalas view the pine-clad bluffs they will see in the immediate foreground a large number of Sibley tents, and being warriors, they will know that each Sibley has eighteen men in it. They will be much surprised. They will hold little impromptu councils, and will probably seek for the motive of this concentration of troops. And some man will say: "Well, the soldiers are here, and if your people don't keep quiet— Well, you know what soldiers are for." The Ogallalas will understand why the soldiers are there without any further explanation. There may be and probably will be some white friend of the Indians who can tell them something they do not know. A little thing has happened since the Ogallalas laid their arms

Infantry on the March. *Authors' photoengraving.*

down, and that is that the bluecoats in the Second Infantry can put a bullet into the anatomy of an Ogallala at one thousand yards' range with almost absolute certainty if the light is fair and the wind not too strong.

I must not try to prophesy what the Ogallalas will do when they see the Sibleys, but I hope the friend will be there to tell them what a regular soldier and a Long Tom can do. The days when they could circle like hawks about a rabbit are gone. The modern United States soldier can pile a pony up in a heap before its rider can go one hundred yards. I realize that before this matter is printed the biggest Indian war since 1758 will be in progress, or that the display of military force will have accomplished its object, and the trouble gone.

The thing that is most remarkable about this concentration of troops is that the white people of the country read it in the evening papers, and with the first rays of to-morrow's sun the Ogallalas, the Cheyennes, and the Sitting Bull people will see it with their own eyes. Why did not the white people know it before? It must have occupied the military authorities for some days. The reason is this: not until late years could the Indians read English, but now the school-boys and squaw men can, and I have picked up copies of the New York and Chicago papers on the counters of an Indian trader's store, where a room was full of Indians, three or four of whom could probably read as well as most men. The cause of the secrecy is at once apparent. If an Omaha paper had printed a despatch saying that General Miles was suddenly to concentrate troops at Pine Ridge Agency in three days' time, that paper would be on the counter in a trader's store inside of a day and a half, and the Ogallalas, in all probability, would be scampering over the plains on the way to meet the northern Cheyennes and join issue with Uncle Sam's troops. Now they awake some fine morning and see the Sibleys, and if a turbulent disposition is displayed, the ringleaders are arrested, and the thing stopped. Hundreds of settlers' lives will be saved, thousands of dollars' worth of horses and cattle are left untouched, and the general government escapes the expenses of a war which would run into the millions. Meanwhile you and I read our papers; and find we are reading news which is fresh, only it might have been printed three days before.

In these days a military officer has to conduct his operations as secretly in Indian war as he would in a civilized case, all of which is very different from the days when expeditions were fitting out for months, and every man knew of it. The Interior Department, a few old medicine men, and the most desperate of the old war chiefs must divide the blame for the whole business.

Indians as Irregular Cavalry

The lowest type of Italian or Hungarian immigrant has little or no comprehension of American government or civilization. Most of them could not tell the difference between the Constitution and a coal-scuttle. The Indians are most enlightened, for they have at least one distinct impression regarding the government. They know that it never keeps its word. Any old chief will tell you that white men are all liars, and if you press him regarding it, he will prove it, and the only exception he will make is the white soldier. This class of men has formed a decided respect for the Indians, on the principle of that strange liking you have for a man after you have fought with him. Every young West-Pointer learns very early in his career never to speak anything but the exact truth to an Indian. This code of morals was acquired from a savage race. Think of it! Buffalo hump seems to feed moral character better than *pâté de foie gras*. I have heard Indian commissions talk to a ring of chiefs about their land titles, and the Indians could no more understand the white man's legal talk than the white man can smell a camp fire a mile away as an Indian can. Their title to their lands is clear in their minds, because some representative of the government has told them it was, and that ought to be reason enough, they think.

After we regard Indians as children in their relation to us, we must understand another thing, and that is that they are only second to the Norsemen of old as savage warriors. They possess all the virtues and some of the weaknesses of that condition. About a year ago a Portuguese newspaper intimated that the English nation were simply Norse pirates, notwithstanding they were supposed to have progressed somewhat in a thousand years. Twenty-five years has not made a plodding, praying man out of the befeathered brave of the Great Plains, and twenty-five years more will not either.

Above wealth, wives, children, and civil renown, there is one thing an Indian holds next to his God, and around their mind is emblazoned the halo of him who can fight and die. A soldier—that is the man whose image fills an Indian's eye. The bow and the lance were the emblems of all that was noble in the old days, and a little man in a blue uniform is the only thing good about the white people which an Indian ever saw. He represents courage, justice, and truth; and while the civil agents sent from Washington to dole out bad and insufficient rations to a conquered race may receive the homage, they can never command the respect of the wild tribes.

After two centuries of civil administration, with its agents, its treachery, its inefficiency, and at times its horrible corruption, where are the Indians? Such as survived the flood of white immigration are living in poverty and ignorance. They have never attained even an ordinary state of industrial progress. The Indians now living on reservations in the State of New York have

One of the Fort Keogh Cheyenne Scout Corps, Commanded by Lieut. Casey. *Authors' photoengraving.*

had two hundred years of civil agents, and have had their morals looked after by the Christian Church, and yet I could never see that they had any mission in life beyond waiting for death. The Cherokees and isolated individual instances which might be quoted to the contrary are half white in their blood, which will account for their progress. It must also be borne firmly in mind that all these Eastern Indians were corn planters from remote times. The wild buffalo-eating Indians are steadily retrograding. With the healthy occupations of the hunter gone, they draw their rations list-

lessly, which having eaten, they starve, and in idleness their minds, morals, and bodies degenerate from lack of use. It seems that no amount of explaining will ever suppress that inevitable question of "Why do they not farm?" But to treat the thing seriously, I will explain that a part of the Indian Territory is a fine farming country, and is inhabited by the remnants of the Eastern tribes, who do farm to some extent. The Cheyennes, Comanches, Kiowas, and Arapahoes live west of the rain belt, and it is exceptional when a corn crop can be raised once in four years. That seems to be reason enough to deter white men from farming there, and it ought to at least account for the Indians' lack of success. Those parts of Kansas and Texas lying north and south of these reservations are not regarded as farming countries. On certain parts of the Sioux reserve crops might be raised, but on the greater area of it no results can be attained without irrigation. The northern Cheyennes could not farm for the same reason, though the Crows are more fortunately situated, as the broad bottoms of the Little Big Horn can be irrigated at a trifling expense. A curious fact might be mentioned in confirmation of all this, which is that there are less white people on the high plains of the Northwest now than there were ten years ago, and there will probably be less in ten years more than there are now, unless the country is reclaimed by irrigation, which could only be done by a system of water storage made possible after a vast outlay of labor and capital. Knowing these facts, it is serious ignorance when one hears this talk about farming on the old buffalo range. Any stockman will tell you that it is a question, and most of them will decide in the negative, when you ask if the high plains of the Northwest are a cattle country, to say nothing of agriculture. All these reports of Indian agents to their department about the industrial, and especially the agricultural, progress of their wards are gilded, to say the least; and in a great many instances you can rub off the gilt and disclose simple commonplace lies, with no foundation whatever in fact. But the Indian agents are simply men who are occupying a political appointment for a brief term, and they do many things which are not high-minded. It does not seem necessary for me to go on to prove that the Indian Department is not a joy forever. Very few people think it is, and most of those who do have a finger in the pie. They have never been distinguished for anything except Indian wars, and for almost every affair of the kind they are entirely responsible. The Northwest is dotted over with soldiers sleeping out in the snows of this winter because of this mismanagement

of the Indian Bureau. With an instance of this incompetency before their eyes nearly half of the time, people in the East ought to understand, and every man who in the West comes near enough to get the stench cannot but know its rottenness. It's unchristian, it's inhuman, it's vile. It is the constantly recurring old story—a gross case of mismanagement. And then the army is called in to be responsible—to protect the lives of the settlers, and in these days to shoot down a people who have the entire sympathy of every soldier in the ranks.

Of course I know as well as any one else what will be done in this matter. The dishonor will continue, and I only hope for pardon when I oppose the laws of nature. The Saxon race is not in a habit of dividing the spoils with a conquered one. It never has, and the millennium is yet a long way off. Many generations from now posterity will apologize for their rude ancestry, much as we do for the enterprising fur traders, whose hands weighed a pound in a beaver-skin transaction. The only excuse I have for not being absurd in this matter, when I argue that the wild Indian tribes can be allowed to live, is that their lands are so worthless that we do not want them, and that, secondly, they can be made useful to us—two reasons selfish enough for us to entertain. To touch ancient history for a sentimental reason, we all know that the hatred of the Six Nations for the Canadas made the English occupation of this continent possible, which would have been questionable in its contest with the French régime, backed by its Church and State. To come to our own generations, we recognize that Indians have co-operated with our troops in every contest for the acquisition of the Great West. Delawares guided our columns to Mexico in '47. Friendly Cheyennes led Mackenzie into his fight on the Big Horn Mountains against their own tribe. General Crook was guided to every hidden stronghold of the Apaches by Apaches who were not disaffected. I do not, of course, mean to say that these acts were inspired by true loyalty to the old flag, but I do think it demonstrates that experienced United States army officers can handle these people under any and all conditions. One thing is certain —the wild tribes are steadily retrograding under Interior Department management. I do not for a moment want to be understood as censuring the present administration in particular. It was as true of the last administration as it is of this one, and it will be as true of the next as it was of the last. It is the system which is responsible. We are year after year oppressing a conquered people, until it is now assuming the magnitude of a crime. Any administration which will change this order of things will have one claim on immortality.

There is at present a disposition to recognize that things are not as they should be, and this last Sioux Indian affair has demonstrated that the Indian Bureau is inefficient, and has near cost us a bloody war. Its continued management of Indian affairs is liable at any time to send wild Indians on the war-path. Every man in the United States knows that this is so if he takes pains to investigate, and yet the thing goes on. In the case of the Apaches, they were self-supporting for years after their early conquest by General Crook, and were then turned over to the Indian Department. The result was a series of bloody outbreaks, which came near depopulating Arizona, New Mexico, and Sonora. The northern Cheyennes, after they surrendered to General Miles, irrigated and raised crops at the mouth of Tongue River for two years, and almost immediately sank into poverty and sloth when given the Interior Department ration, for which they did not have to work in order to procure. These are cases in hand. Efforts have been made and thousands of dollars expended at the Cheyenne Agency, on the Lame Deer Creek, to make the Indians farm. I did not see an acre of ploughed ground while there, although there may be some hidden away for all I know. The short ration which is issued to them keeps them in dire hunger, and if starving savages kill ranchmen's cattle I do not blame them. I would do the same under similar circumstances. Recently

I see that some gentleman in Congress proposed to make Indians pay the penalty of their violent protests against starvation by seizing their own property. When a man thinks about the property of the northern Cheyennes, he laughs at the idea. The average Cheyenne buck could very readily get his entire earthly possessions on four or five ponies. People are prone to think that since the buffalo are gone the Indian cannot wage war. Error of errors! They were at a great disadvantage in those days, because they had to stop fighting and go out hunting, while now they can find a herd of domestic cattle in a day's ride in any direction either east or west of the Rocky Mountains, and a hay-stack, often enough to recuperate their ponies for the winter war-path. They have arms and ammunition, and I marvel only at their moderation. Chief Joseph demonstrated what a few desperate Indians can do when driven to it.

Now we will suppose that the American people desire to do justice to the wild Indians; we will suppose that they want to avert these interminable Indian outbreaks; and we will assume that they have the best interests of the American army at heart; and then we will turn them all over to the War Department. Since the Indian ring found the Apaches unprofitable, and they passed to the War Department, you do not hear of outbreaks among them. It was only through the statements of a general in the United States army that the United States Senate learned that the Sioux were being starved. The army people would like to take the Indians, as they do not doubt their own ability to handle them; and the thing farthest from their minds would be to precipitate hostilities with the red men, since the War Department does not regard Indian campaigning as war. The War Department could then organize them into a semi-industrial military force, much after the fashion of the Cossacks, whose company chief is responsible for their operations in peace and their deeds in war. He is both the head of the village and the war chief. Four or five irregular cavalry regiments could be organized, at the discretion of the war-office officials, and then the separate troop formations could be 100 men each. We might say, for instance, that is A Troop of the First Irregular Cavalry—they are Crows; and that is K Troop of the same regiment—they are Cheyennes. Each company should have its own permanent village, situated near its agricultural or stock-raising operations, and let the captain of the company be the head of the village. He has judicial and administrative powers, and is responsible to his superior in a military way. These officers should come from the regular army, and they may apply for the appointments after their experience and natural capacity are considered. Under this arrangement pride of company is inculcated, and emulation is natural between the troops and their commander. Each officer would then be given an opportunity to apply his theories, and by experience much might be developed. There can be issued the regular clothing and pay of a soldier, and a ration for themselves and families such as is sufficient. This ration in time might be decreased if they attained to agricultural success. Each man should be required to have at least two good serviceable ponies, and each company should have a complete pack train. This would cost a little more than under the Interior Department, but when we figure on the attendant Indian wars, it would be as nothing. In time the regiments of the regular army could be withdrawn from the small posts, and concentrated by brigades, with great good to themselves from every point of view.

All this has been suggested in times past, and found fault with by a certain class of politicians "who are not in with the deal," and by a good many estimable people belonging to Indian societies, who are in a habit of congregating with the purpose of harrowing up each other's feelings over the wrongs of the red men. I am happy to say that the above suggestion is no longer an experiment, but has been tried thoroughly, with results which are so astonishingly successful that they should be seen to be appreciated. There is a corps of Apache scouts at

San Carlos, and they are doing very well, but need experienced men to deal with them. I would not recommend that they be brought under this régime at present. They live in a very difficult country, and are yet wild, having had very little contact with white people, and having been lately at war with the United States troops. Their present management is the best one for a considerable period in the future. There is a small but efficient corps of Comanche and Kiowa scouts at Fort Sill, whose main business is to keep individual Texans in a realizing state of mind when they covet their neighbor's horse or his ox. They are good material for soldiers; and so are their neighbors, the southern Cheyennes and the Arapahoes, although these latter are undergoing the operation of being starved into farming, and regard the whole process with ill-concealed disgust. There is a very fine corps of Cheyennes at Fort Reno, and they were the first perfectly uniformed and organized troop of Indians I had ever seen; and I talked with some Carlisle school-boys who had lately been discharged from the corps in order to make room for others of the tribe, and they were full of regrets, as they had liked soldiering, and now had nothing to do but draw rations at the agency. They were very bright young fellows, fairly educated, and each had a trade, I believe. There was no possible way for them to earn a living. They were not allowed off the reservation, and so they must sit calmly down and do nothing. Idleness is fully as bad for an Indian as a white man, and is always the godfather of folly and crime. At Reno I saw young scouts who would make a West Point drill-master's mouth water. They were "set up" until they had completely lost the habitual slouch of an Indian, and strode about as straight and proud as a drill-sergeant. Indeed, it was this little corps which first impressed me with the possibilities of the whole scheme. Their pride in being soldiers was the noticeable feature. A young scout passed through the garrison, and no man about the post held his head up higher or put his foot down firmer than that young chap, who would, in his blanket, have sneaked along under the gutters of the buildings like a coyote under a cut bank. They were well dressed, well fed, full of pride in their business, and full of respect for their superiors. The same man, if he were ploughing a field would ill conceal his mortification at doing a thing which he had been taught for generations was low-spirited, degrading, and which he had always found profitless.

The Indian tribes are yet warriors; they have not lost their instincts or respect for the trade of war; but an Indian will do the most arduous and laborious work if he has a cavalry uniform on, when he would not lift his little finger to the task if dressed in his bright blanket and bead-work, both of which are emblematic of a thousand years of glorious deeds of arms. He sees the white soldiers work, and makes as great a distinction between the laboring soldier and his agricultural brother, as you would between a farm hand and a gentleman cultivating orchids in his conservatory. I had become aware that the government was trying the experiment at Fort Keogh. When at that place I was driven out to the little village of Lieutenant E. W. Casey's Cheyenne scouts. I saw a long line of well-constructed log buildings, corrals, and stables, also a large garden fenced and cultivated. I entered the houses and saw comfort and cleanliness. I saw smiling faces and laughing children. I saw perfectly kept cavalry arms and accoutrements, and fine Indian soldiers, who stood like bronze statues, and saluted in the best possible form, while never a muscle of their stern faces twitched, and they looked a soldier, and felt a soldier, and were in fact the finest I had ever seen. I saw them mount and fall in and drill in admirable shape, all by a sign of Lieutenant Casey's right hand, because they do not understand English well enough. I admired the indomitable zeal of Lieutenant Casey, and hoped his work would lead to greater things. Indeed, if he were properly supported, why could not Fort Keogh be abandoned at some future day, and why could not Casey and his com-

pany of the First Irregular Cavalry do the work of the garrison, and let the Eighth Cavalry and the Twenty-second Infantry go to Fort Snelling, and there perfect themselves, so that when we call for the skeleton of our army organization in time of war, we will find it worthy to be built on to.

Six months before, all these men were down at the Lame Deer Agency doing nothing, unless to go out gunning for a ranchman's cattle. Lieutenant Casey brought them up to the mouth of the Tongue River, uniformed and equipped them, and ploughed and made a garden after irrigating the land. He then took them up the Yellowstone, and—it is almost beyond belief—he gave them axes, with which they mauled logs, and with the help of their ponies they tugged them out to the river, and drove them down to the fort. They then hewed the logs, and built cabins as good as any ranchman's in the country. Lieutenant Casey and his interpreter (an old Fifth Infantry soldier who has been in battle against Cheyennes) were the only white men along. Beyond doing all this work, they are well drilled, and all in six months. We keep army recruits four months at a depot before we forward them. I should not be surprised if Lieutenant Casey had his Indians herding sheep in course of time, and that is the particular thing that an Indian will not do.

What did I see at the Lame Deer Agency? A lot of shrouded creatures lying about or darting over the hills, as purposeless and mysterious as creatures out of Dante's "Inferno." Later on in my travels a lot of dark-skinned soldiers were drawn up to escort a major-general. They were the Crow Scout Corps of Fort Custer, under command of Lieutenant S. C. Robertson, of the First Cavalry, another zealous young man with a fiery purpose to have the best scout corps on the crust of the earth. His methods are different from Casey's. He wastes no time on industrial affairs, but goes in for the purely military standard. He is a West-Pointer and a graduate of the French School of Cavalry, talks the sign language, and is rapidly mastering the Crow tongue. Lieutenant Casey is a West-Pointer, an old soldier who has fought with Indian scouts under him, and has seen much of their people. Here are young men as types. They are educated; they are brave; they are soldiers for life. They can have no success in life beyond what their military accomplishments bring them. They know that the least indiscretion on their part would cost them their commissions. This is the sort of man who should take the place of the ha'-penny politician who has been nurtured in the belief that to plunder the Indians is a natural reward for good service in his political district. As we rode along with these active warriors they would put their ponies at top speed down very steep hills; they were far ahead and on the flanks. It was the most perfect piece of escort duty that I ever saw. They wore leather leggins instead of cavalry boots, as did Casey's men, and they had no saddle pockets or rope lariats. Instead of this latter, they carried their own hair rope, lighter and stronger than the great piece of hemp of the cavalry. An Indian is the best possible light irregular cavalryman, and his methods cannot be improved by introducing ours, and he can learn little indeed from a white trooper.

Major-General Miles having had a vast experience with Indians, I agree with him when he says we should not be over-hasty in arming a people who may at any time be our opponents. We must not forget, though, that it is impossible to keep the Sioux disarmed and still allow them their liberty. We must also remember that Indian police and scouts, in the service both of the army and the agents, have never proved untrustworthy, or attended the ghost dances of the last year. If a large Indian military establishment were maintained, one tribe could be made to fight another as readily as it has been done in times past. But under a just administration of their affairs there would be no more chances of the Indians breaking out than there would be of the people of Deadwood or Helena. Industry and proper care will do completely away with all the turbulence which at times characterizes the present administration of affairs. As scouts they are used constantly on detached service. They are perfect marvels as couriers, and can trail stray horses, scout the country, arrest deserters, and guide troops about. When the government starts its great horse-breeding farm, which it must do shortly or have its cavalry mounted on brewery horses, they would be of great use as herders. They could raise crops in summer, and, in short, be made to work systematically, as Lieutenant Casey has demonstrated. The small scout corps as at present organized have their time fully taken up with duties of a purely military character, but under the Cossack organization they would be a semi-industrial military class, who in time would become self-supporting.

There are many views as to their proper organization and equipment among practical and experienced army officers, but all this is a small matter which could be changed from time to time in the light of experience. General Miles would have them armed only with the revolver, and accoutred as lightly as possible, in order that they might ride with great rapidity and endure long. This would be proper as mere scouts, but as irregular cavalry they should have the carbine. It would be a pity to equip and handle Indian soldiers in any manner calculated to eradicate their primitive traits. A little thing, for instance, is this: by long moving in the solid ranks a cavalry horse cannot be forced out of them. In the battle of the Little Big Horn General Custer's horses stampeded over the field in solid troop formations. This is not a grave defect in dragoon cavalry operations, but would be fatal to light cavalry. The Indian and his pony must be the unit, not the company. Indians should be allowed to scatter out on the march, and not be kept in the column. It is a curious fact that on the plains you can tell two cow-boys from two Indians at a great distance. The cow-boys will ride abreast, and the Indians will trail after each other. As to the uniform of these bodies, I suggest one in my drawings which is light, inexpensive, and which preserves as much of the local color of the Indian as possible. I believe in building the little log village. Some commanders will not agree with this, saying that it softens the men; let them live in the tepee, and retain the hardihood of the hunter state. We must remember that the organization I speak of is semi-industrial as well, and in process of time would lose much of its military character. If the Crows, Cheyennes, and Sioux become wealthy, industrious, and contented, the First Cavalry will not be at Fort Custer, but in New York, Leavenworth, or Chicago. In the case of a light scouting corps, I admit you must nurse the savage.

There is one thing that cannot be urged too strongly—a wagon should form no part of a light cavalry outfit. A scout corps which is tied up to some wagons is about as useless as a sprint runner with a cork leg. Pack trains of large broncho horses to each troop should be issued, and there should be enough of them so that they might be loaded lightly, and thus be able to pass over the country as rapidly as the exigencies of the case might require. In the winter oil-tanned cow-skin moccasins should be issued. A system of tactics should be gotten up for the Indian soldiers, vast simplicity being the consideration, and preserving all the signs and movements peculiar to their old warrior days.

As to the efficiency of these people on light cavalry duties there can be no question. Lieutenant Carter Johnson told me that he thought he could take a command of Apaches and ride from Arizona to Washington without losing all of his command, and judging from some of that officer's exploits, I am inclined to think he could. As to their faithfulness, an officer recently sent a Crow scout with a message, and inadvertently said, "Go quick!" The Crow, thinking the thing was vital, rode a hundred miles and killed his horse (his own property) to deliver the message. A Crow scout also rode for three days after a stray horse, covering an enormous distance, which I have forgotten. Lieutenant Casey's scouts will fell trees and build houses. In short, experienced officers can do anything with these men, and the Indians like it. The dearest dream of any Indian is that some day he may be a government scout. And when he thinks of being a pure and simple farmer it chills his soul, and he welcomes the ghost dance, and would welcome anything else which would take him from the lazy starvation of the agency.

Let these people who claim to be friends of the Indian cease their chatter, and help this or some other practical scheme of regeneration. Let some statesman have the courage to curb this restless thirst for spoil in land which characterizes our frontier population, and teach them to value the solemn obligations of this government as they would a copper cent at least. Let our army have the fruits of its work; and let us preserve the native American race, which is following the buffalo into painted pictures and printed books.

The Sioux Outbreak in South Dakota

We discussed the vague reports of the Wounded Knee fight in the upper camps of the cordon, and old hands said it could be no ordinary affair because of the large casualty. Two days after I rode into the Pine Ridge Agency, very hungry and nearly frozen to death, having ridden with Captain Baldwin, of the staff, and a Mr. Miller all night long. I had to look after a poor horse, and see that he was groomed and fed, which require considerable tact and "hustling" in a busy camp. Then came my breakfast. That struck me as a serious matter at the time. There were wagons and soldiers—the burial party going to the Wounded Knee to do its solemn duty. I wanted to go very much. I stopped to think; in short, I hesitated, and of course was "lost," for after breakfast they had gone. Why did I not follow them? Well, my natural prudence had been considerably strengthened a few days previously by a half-hour's interview with six painted Brulé Sioux, who seemed to be in command of the situation. To briefly end the matter, the burial party was fired on, and my confidence in my own good judgment was vindicated to my own satisfaction.

I rode over to the camp of the Seventh United States Cavalry, and met all the officers, both wounded and well, and a great many of the men. They told me their stories in that inimitable way which is studied art with warriors. To appreciate brevity you must go to a soldier. He shrugs his shoulders, and points to the bridge of his nose, which has had a piece cut out by a bullet, and says, "Rather close, but don't amount to much." An inch more, and some youngster would have had his promotion.

I shall not here tell the story of the Seventh Cavalry fight with Big Foot's band of Sioux on the Wounded Knee; that has been done in the daily papers; but I will recount some small-talk current in the Sibley tepees, or the "white man's war tents," as the Indians call them.

Lying on his back, with a bullet through the body, Lieutenant Mann grew stern when he got to the critical point in his story. "I saw three or four young bucks drop their blankets, and I saw that they were armed. 'Be ready to fire, men; there is trouble.' There was an instant, and then we heard sounds of firing in the centre of the Indians. 'Fire!' I shouted, and we poured it into them."

"Oh yes, Mann, but the trouble began when the old medicine-man threw the dust in the air. That is the old Indian signal of 'defiance,' and no sooner had he done that act than those bucks stripped and went into action. Just before that some one told me that if we didn't stop that old man's talk he would make trouble. He said that the white men's bullets would not go through the ghost shirts."

Said another officer, "The way those Sioux worked those Winchesters was beautiful." Which criticism, you can see, was professional.

Added another, "One man was hit early in the firing, but he continued to pump his

Winchester; but growing weaker and weaker, and sinking down gradually, his shots went higher and higher, until his last went straight up in the air."

"Those Indians were plumb crazy. Now, for instance, did you notice that before they fired they raised their arms to heaven? That was devotional."

"Yes, captain, but they got over their devotional mood after the shooting was over," remonstrated a cynic. "When I passed over the field after the fight one young warrior who was near to his death

The Medicine-Man's Signal: Throwing Dust in the Air—Then the Firing Began. *Authors' photoengraving.*

asked me to take him over to the medicine-man's side, that he might die with his knife in the old conjurer's heart. He had seen that the medicine was bad, and his faith in the ghost shirt had vanished. There was no doubt but that every buck there thought that no bullet could touch him."

"Well," said an officer, whose pipe was working into a reflective mood, "there is one thing which I learned, and that is that you can bet that the private soldier in the United States army will fight. He'll fight from the drop of the hat anywhere and in any place, and he'll fight till you call *time*. I never in my life saw Springfield carbines worked so industriously as at that place. I noticed one young fellow, and his gun seemed to just blaze all the while. Poor chap! he's mustered out for good."

I saw the scout who had his nose cut off. He came in to get shaved. His face was covered with strips of courtplaster, and when informed that it would be better for him to forego the pleasure of a shave, he reluctantly consented. He had ridden all day and been in the second day's fight with his nose held on by a few strips of plaster, and he did not see just why he could not be shaved; but after being talked to earnestly by a half-dozen friends he succumbed.

"What became of the man who did that?" I asked of him.

He tapped his Winchester and said, "Oh, I got him all right!"

I went into the hospital tents and saw the poor fellows lying on the cots, a little pale in the face, and with a drawn look about the mouth and eyes. That is the serious part of soldiering. No excitement, no crowd of cheering comrades, no shots and yells and din of battle. A few watchful doctors and Red Cross stewards with bottles and bandages, and the grim spectre of the universal enemy hovering over all, and ready to dart down on any man on the cots who lay quieter and whose face was more pale than his fellows.

I saw the Red Cross ambulances draw up in line, and watched the wounded being loaded into them. I saw poor Garlington.

His blond mustache twitched under the process of moving, and he looked like a man whose mustache wouldn't twitch unnecessarily. Lieutenant Hawthorne, who was desperately shot in the groin while working the little Hotchkiss cannon, turned his eyes as they moved Garlington from the next cot, and then waited patiently for his own turn.

I was talking with old Captain Capron, who commanded the battery at the fight—a grim old fellow, with a red-lined cape overcoat, and nerve enough for a hundred-ton gun. He said: "When Hawthorne was shot the gun was worked by Corporal Weimert, while Private Hertzog carried Hawthorne from the field and then returned to his gun. The Indians redoubled their fire on the men at the gun, but it seemed only to inspire the corporal to renewed efforts. Oh, my battery was well served," continued the captain, as he put his hands behind his back and looked far away.

This professional interest in the military process of killing men sometimes rasps a citizen's nerves. To the captain everything else was a side note of little consequence so long as his guns had been worked to his entire satisfaction. That was the point.

At the mention of the name of Captain Wallace, the Sibley became so quiet that you could hear the stove draw and the wind wail about the little canvas town. It was always "Poor Wallace!" and "He died like a soldier, with his empty six-shooter in his right hand, shot through the body, and with two jagged wounds in his head."

I accosted a soldier who was leaning on a crutch while he carried a little bundle in his right hand. "You bet I'm glad to get out in the sunlight; that old hospital tent was getting mighty tiresome."

"Where was I shot?" He pointed to his hip. "Only a flesh wound; this is my third wound. My time is out in a few days; but I'm going to re-enlist, and I hope I'll get back here before this trouble is over. I want to get square with these Injuns." You see, there was considerable human nature in this man's composition.

The ambulance went off down the road, and the burial party came back. The dead were for the time forgotten, and the wounded were left to fight their own battles with stitches and fevers and suppuration. The living toiled in the trenches, or stood out their long term on the pickets, where the moon looked down on the frosty landscape, and the cold wind from the north searched for the crevices in their blankets.

Lieutenant Casey's Last Scout

ON THE HOSTILE FLANKS WITH THE CHIS-CHIS-CHASH

The train bearing the Cheyenne scout corps pulled into Rapid City somewhat late. It is possible you may think that it was a train of Pullman palace cars, but you would be mistaken, for it was a freight train, with the horses in tight box-cars, the bacon and Chis-chis-chash* on flat gravel cars, and Lieutenants Casey and Getty in the caboose. Evidently the element of haste was woven into this movement. We were glad to meet again. Expansive smiles lit up the brown features of the Indian scouts as they recognized me. Old Wolf-Voice came around in his large, patronizing way and said, "How? —what you do out here?" Wolf-Voice was a magnificent type of the Indian, with a grand face, a tremendous physique, and enough self-containment for a High-Church bishop. High-Walking nudged Stump-Horn and whispered in his ear, and they both smiled as they looked at me. Lieutenant Casey walked out in the road and talked with General Miles, who sat on his beautiful sorrel horse, while two scouts and a young "horse-pusher"† from St. Louis helped me to load one strawberry-roan horse, branded "52" on the nigh front foot, into a box-car with a scrawny lot of little ponies, who showed the hard scouting of the last month in their lank quarters.

The quartermaster came down and asked Lieutenant Casey for a memorandum of his outfit, which was "70 horses, 49 Indian scouts, 1 interpreter, 2 white officers, 1000

* The name the Cheyennes apply to themselves.
† Boy who travels with horses on the cars.

pounds of bacon, so many crackers, 2000 pounds forage, 5 Sibley tents, and 1 citizen," all of which the quartermaster put down in a little book. You are not allowed by United States quartermasters to have an exaggerated estimate of your own importance. Bacon and forage and citizens all go down in the same column, with the only distinction that the bacon and forage outnumber you.

We were pulled down the road a few miles to the town of Hermoso, and there, in the moonlight, the baggage was unloaded and the wild little ponies frightened out of the cars, down a chute, into the stock corrals. The Sibleys were pitched, and a crowd of curious citizens, who came down to feast their eyes on the Chis-chis-chash, were dissipated when a rather frugal dinner was prepared. This was Christmas night, and rather a cheerless one, since, in the haste of departure, the Sibley stoves had been forgotten. We never had stoves again until the gallant Leavenworth battalion came to the rescue with their surplus, and in the cold, frosty nights in the foot-hills there can be no personal happiness where there are no stoves. We brewed a little mess of hot stuff in a soldier's tin cup, and, in the words of Private Mulvaney, we drank to the occasion, "three fingers—standing up!"

The good that comes in the ill wind where stoves are lacking is that you can get men up in the morning. Sun-worship must have originated in circumstances of this kind. The feeling of thankfulness at the sight of the golden rays permeates your soul, and your very bones are made glad.

A few ounces of bacon, some of those accursed crackers which are made to withstand fire, water, and weevil, a quart of coffee blacker than evil, then down come the Sibleys, the blankets are rolled and the saddles adjusted, and bidding *adios* to the First Infantry (which came in during the night), we trot off down the road.

These, then, are the Cheyenne scouts. Well, I am glad I know the fact, but I never can reconcile the trim-looking scout corps of Keogh with these strange-looking objects. Erstwhile their ponies were fat, and cavorted around when falling in ranks; now they paddle along in the humblest kind of a business-like jog-trot. The new overcoats of the corps metamorphose the scouts into something between Russian Cossacks and Black Crooks. Saddle pockets bulge out, and a thousand and one little alterations in accoutrement grow up in the field which are frowned down in garrison. The men have scouted hard for a month, and have lost two nights sleep, so at the halts for the wagons they lop down in the dust of the road, and sleep, while the little ponies stand over them, ears down, heads hanging, eyes shut, and one hind foot drawn up on its toe. Nothing can look so dejected as a pony, and doubtless few things have more reason to feel so. A short march of twenty-five miles passes us through the Seventeenth Infantry camp under Colonel Offley, and down to the Cheyenne River, where we camp for the night. There is another corps of Cheyenne scouts somewhere here on the river, under Lieutenant L. H. Struthers, of the First Infantry, and we expect to join them. On the other side of the Cheyenne rise the tangled masses of the famous Bad Lands—seamed and serrated, gray here, the golden sunset flashing there, with dark recesses giving back a frightful gloom—a place for stratagem and murder, with nothing to witness its mysteries but the cold blue winter sky. Yet we are going there. It is full of savage Sioux. The sun goes down. I am glad to cease thinking about it.

It is such a mere detail that I will not waste time on it, but this freezing out of your blankets four or five times every night, and this having to go out and coax a cooking fire into a cheerful spirit, can occupy a man's mind so that any words not depraved do not seem of any consequence. During one of the early hours I happened to sleep, and in this interval Mr. Struthers came into our tepee. He had been on a night's ride to the colonel for orders, and in passing, dropped in for a chat with Casey. When about to go, he said.

"Oh, by-the-way, I met Remington."

"Do you want to renew the acquaintance?" replied Casey.

"Why—how—why—yes."

"Well, he's there, on the other side of this tent." And Mr. Struthers passed out in the gloom, and his muttered expressions of astonishment were presently lost in the distance. I had ridden and camped with Mr. Struthers a few days since in the up country, while on the way to "the galloping Sixth."

The next day we passed down the river, and soon saw what to inexperienced eyes might be dark gray rocks on the top of yellow hills. They were the pickets of the Cheyennes, and presently we saw the tepees and the ponies, and then we rode into camp. The men from Tongue River greeted the men from Pine Ridge—the relatives and friends—with *ki-yis* of delight. The corps from Pine Ridge was organized from the Cheyennes on that reservation, and was as yet only partially disciplined, and in no way to be compared with Casey's Old Guard from Tongue River. Some two nights before, the Sioux had fired into their camp, and they had skirmished with the enemy. The vermilion of the war-path was on every countenance, and, through sympathy, I saw that our men too had gone into this style of decorative art; for faces which had previously been fresh and clean now passed my vision streaked and daubed into preternatural ferocity.

It grew late and later, and yet Lieutenant Struthers did not return from his scouting of the day. We were alarmed, and wondered and hoped; for scouting through the Bad Lands to the stronghold was dangerous, to state it mildly. A few shots would not be heard twelve miles away in the hills. We pictured black objects lying prone on the sand as we scouted next day—little masses of clay which had been men and horses, but would then be as silent as the bare hillocks about them.

"Ki-yi-yip—a-ou!" and a patter in the gloom.

"That's Struthers." We fall over each other as we pile out of the hole in the Sibley, and find Struthers and Lieutenant Byrom, of the Eighth Cavalry, all safe and sound.

"We have been on the stronghold; they are all gone; rustle some coffee," are words in the darkness; and we crawl back into the tent, where presently the big, honest, jolly eyes of Mr. Struthers look over a quart cup, and we are happy. Byrom was a fine little cavalryman, and I have good reason to know that for impudent daring of that desperately quiet kind he is distinguished in places where all men are brave.

Away goes the courier to the colonel for orders, and after a time back he comes—a wild dash of twelve miles in the dark, and of little moment here, but a life memory to an unaccustomed one.

"We go on the stronghold in the morning," says Casey; "and now to bed." A bed consists of two blankets spread on the ground, and all the personal property not otherwise appropriated piled on top. A luxury, mind you, is this; later it was much more simple, consisting of earth for a mattress and the sky for a counterpane.

The sun is not up when in comes the horse herd. My strawberry roan goes sneaking about in the frosty willows, and after sundry well-studied manœuvres I get a grip on the lariat, and am lugged and jerked over the brush until "52 on the nigh front foot" consents to stand still. I saddle up, but have lost my gun. I entreat Mr. Thompson, the interpreter, to help me find it. Mr. Thompson is a man who began fighting for the Union in East Tennessee about thirty years long gone, and he has continued to

engage in that work up to date. Mr. Thompson has formed a character which is not as round as a ball, but much more the shape of horn-silver in its native state. He is humorous by turns, and early in my acquaintance he undertook the cultivation of my mind in the art of war as practised on the frontier. On this occasion he at last found my Springfield, and handed it to me with the admonition "that in times like these one warrior can't look after another warrior's gun."

The wagons were to go—well, I never knew where, but they went off over the hills, and I never saw them again for some miserable days and dreary nights. Five Pine Ridge Cheyennes and Mr. Wolf-Voice were my party, and we filed away. At Battle Creek we watered, and crossed the Cheyenne a mile above. My horse was smooth shod, and the river frozen half-way over, so we slid around on the ice, and jumped into the icy waters, got wet, crawled out, slid around some more, and finally landed. Mr. Wolf-Voice looked me over, and smilingly said, "Me think you no like 'em"; wherein his conclusion was eminently correct. Who does like to have a mass of ice freeze on him when naturally the weather is cold enough to satisfy a walrus?

It was twelve miles through the defiles of the Bad Lands to the blue ridge of the high mesa where the hostiles had lived. The trail was strewn with dead cattle, some of them having never been touched with a knife. Here and there a dead pony, ridden to a stand-still and left nerveless on the trail. No words of mine can describe these Bad Lands. They are somewhat as Doré pictured hell. One set of buttes, with cones and minarets, gives place in the next mile to natural freaks of a different variety, never dreamed of by mortal man. It is the action of water on clay; there are ashes, or what looks like them. The painter's whole palette is in one bluff. A year's study of these colors by Mr. Bierstadt, Professor Marsh, and Mr. Notman might possibly convey to the Eastern mind an idea; so we'll amble along after Mr. Wolf-Voice, and leave that subject intact.

"Hark!" My little party stops suddenly, and we all listen. I feel stupid.

"You hear 'em?" says Wolf-Voice, in a stage-whisper.

"Hear what?" I say.

"Shots."

Then we all get out our guns and go galloping like mad. I can't imagine why, but I spur my horse and perform equestrian feats which in an ordinary frame of mind I should regard as insane. Down a narrow trail we go, with the gravel flying, and through a *coulée,* up a little hill, on top of which we stop to listen, and then away we go. The blue wall grows nearer, and at last we are under it. A few cotton-wood trees, some frozen water, a little cleft on the bluffs, and I see a trail winding upward. I know these warriors are going up there, but I can't understand precisely how. It is not the first perilous trail I have contemplated; but there are dead cattle lying at the bottom which had fallen off and been killed in the ascent. We dismount and start up. It tells on your wind, and tries the leg muscles. Up a steep place a horse wants to go fast, and you have to keep him from running over you. A bend in the trail where the running water has frozen seems impassable. I jump across it, and then pull the bridle and say, "Come on, boy!" If I were the horse I would balk, but the noble animal will try it. A leap, a plunging, and with a terrible scrabble we are all right. Farther up, and the incline is certainly eighty-five degrees. My horse looses his front feet, but a jerk at the headstall brings him down, and he plunges past me to be caught by an Indian at the top of the trail. For a moment we breathe, and then mount.

Before us is a great flat plain blackened by fire, and with the grass still burning. Away in the distance, in the shimmer of the air waves, are figures.

"Maybe so dey Sioux," says Wolf-Voice. And we gallop towards them.

"What will you do if they are?" I ask.

"Stand 'em off," replies the war-dog.

Half an hour's ride showed them to be some of our Cheyennes. All about the plain were strewn the remains of dead cattle (heads and horns, half-butchered carcasses, and withal a rather impressive smell), coyotes, and ravens—all very like war. These Brulés must have lived well. There were lodge poles, old fires, and a series of rifle pits across the neck of land which the Sioux had proposed to defend; medicine poles, and near them the sacrifices, among which was food dedicated to the Great Spirit, but eventually consumed by the less exalted members of Casey's command. I vandalized a stone pipe and a rawhide stirrup.

The less curious members of our band had gone south, and Wolf-Voice and I rode along together. We discussed war, and I remember two of Wolf-Voice's opinions. Speaking of infantry and their method of fighting, he said:

"Dese walk-a-heap soldiers dey dig hole —get in—shoot heap—Injun can't do nothin' wid 'em—can't kill 'em—can't do nothin' but jes go 'way."

Then, explaining why the Sioux had shown bad generalship in selecting their position, he turned in his saddle, and said, "De big guns he knock 'em rifle pit, den de calavy lun pas' in column—Injun no stop calavy—kill 'em heap, but no stop 'em— den de walk-a-heap dey come too, and de Sioux dey go ober de bluffs." And with wild enthusiasm he added, "De Sioux dey go to hell!" That prospect seemed to delight Mr. Wolf-Voice immensely.

It was a weary ride over the black and smoking plain. A queer mirage was said by my Indian to be the Cheyenne scouts coming after us. Black figures of animals walking slowly along were "starving bronchos abandoned by the hostiles."

"Cowboy he catch 'em," said Wolf-Voice.

I explained that Colonel Offley had orders not to allow any citizens to cross the Cheyenne River.

"Cowboy he go give um dam; he come alle samee."

And I thought Wolf-Voice was probably right.

On the southern edge of the bluffs of the mesa we halted, and found water for man and beast. The command gradually concentrated, and for half an hour we stood on the high points scanning the great flats below, and located the dust of the retiring hostile column and the back lying scouts. Lieutenant Casey had positive orders not to bring on an engagement, and only desired to hang on their flanks, so as to keep Miles familiar with the hostile movements. A courier started on his lonely ride back with a note for the major-general. Our scouts were flying about far down the valley, and we filed off after them. Presently a little column of dust follows a flying horseman towards us. On, on he comes. The scouts grow uneasy; wild creatures they are, with the suspicion of a red deer and the stealth of a panther.

The Sioux have fired on our scouts. Off we go at a trot, scattering out, unslinging our guns, and the air full of fight. I ride by Casey, and see he is troubled. The orders in his pocket do not call for a fight. Can he hold these wild warriors?

"Struthers, we have got to hold these men," said Casey, in a tone of voice which was full of meaning. To shorten the story, our men were at last gotten into ranks, and details made to cover the advance. The hostiles were evidently much excited. Little clouds of dust whirling hither and thither showed where the opposing scouts were shadowing each other. The sun was waning, and yet we spurred our weary horses on towards the enemy. Poor beasts! no food and too much exercise since daylight.

The Cheyennes were uneasy, and not at all pleased with this scheme of action. What could they know about the orders in Lieutenant Casey's pocket, prompted by a commanding general thinking of a thousand and one interests, and with telegrams from Washington directing the avoidance of an Indian war?

Old-soldier Thompson even, with all his intelligence and knowledge of things, felt the wild Berserker battle valor, which he smothered with difficulty, and confined himself to potent remarks and spurring of old Piegan. He said: "This is a new kind of war. Them Injuns don't understand it, and

to tell you the truth, I don't nuther. The Injuns say they have come all the way from Tongue River, and are going back poor. Can't get Sioux horses, can't kill Sioux," and in peroration he confirmed his old impression that "this is a new kind of war"; and then relapsed into reveries of what things used to be before General Miles invented this new kind of war.

In our immediate front was a heavy body of Sioux scouts. Lieutenant Casey was ahead. Men broke from our ranks, but were held with difficulty by Struthers and Getty. Back comes Casey at a gallop. He sees the crisis, and with his hand on his six-shooter, says, "I will shoot the first man through the head who falls out of the ranks." A mutiny is imminent in the Pine Ridge contingent, but the diplomat Struthers brings order at last, and we file off down the hills to the left, and stop by a stream, while Casey goes back and meets a body of Sioux on a high hill for a powwow. I watched through a glass, and the sun went down as they talked. We had orders not to remove our saddles, and stood in the line nervously expecting anything imaginable to happen. The daring of Casey in this case is simply an instance of a hundred such, and the last one cost him his life. By his prompt measures with his own men, and by his courage in going among the Sioux to powwow, he averted a bloody battle, and obeyed his orders. There was one man between two banks of savage warriors who were fairly frothing at the mouth—a soldier; the sun will never shine upon a better.

At last, after an interminable time, he came away. Far away to the right are two of our scouts driving two beeves. We see the bright blaze of the six-shooters, the steers tumble, and hunger is no longer one of our woes.

The tired horses are unsaddled, to eat and drink and roll. We lay dry cotton-wood limbs on the fires, heavy pickets are told off, and our "bull meat" is cooked in the primitive style. Old Wolf-Voice and another scout are swinging six ribs on a piece of rawhide over a fire, and later he brings me a rib and a little bit of coffee from a roll in his handkerchief. I thought him a "brick," and mystified him by telling him so.

Three or four Brulés are let in through our pickets, and come "wagging their tails," as Two-Moons says, but adding, "Don't you trust the Sioux." They protest their good intentions, borrow tobacco, and say Lieutenant Casey can send in a wagon for commissaries to Pine Ridge, and also that I can go through their lines with it. Were there ever greater liars on earth?

I sat near the fire and looked intently at one human brute opposite, a perfect animal, so far as I could see. Never was there a face so replete with human depravity, stolid, ferocious, arrogant, and all the rest—ghost-shirt, war-paint, feathers, and arms. As a picture, perfect; as a reality, horrible. Presently they go away, and we prepare for the night. This preparing for the night is a rather simple process. I have stolen my saddle blanket from my poor horse, and, with this laid on the ground, I try my saddle in four or five different positions in its capacity of pillow. The inventor of the Whitman tree never considered this possible use of his handiwork, or he might have done better. I next button the lower three buttons of my overcoat, and thus wrapped "I lie down to pleasant dreams"—of rheumatism.

An hour later and the fires go down. Black forms pass like uneasy spirits, and presently you find yourself thrashing around in the underbrush across the river after branches to feed that insatiable fire. One comrade breaks through the ice and gets wet, and inelegant remarks come from the shadowy blackness under the river-banks. I think a man shouldn't use such language even under such circumstances, but I also think very few men wouldn't. A chilling wind now adds to the misery of the situation, and the heat of the fire goes off in a cloud of sparks to the No Man's Land across the river. After smoking a pipe for two hours your mouth is raw and your nervous system shattered, so nothing is left but to sit calmly down and just suffer. You can hate the Chinese on the other side of the world, who are now enjoying the rays of the sun.

And morning finds you in the saddle. It always does. I don't know how it is—a habit of life, I suppose. Mornings ought to find me cosily ensconced in a good bed, but in retrospect they seem always to be in the saddle, with a good prospect of all day ahead, and evening finds me with a chunk of bull meat and without blankets, until one fine day we come to our wagons, our Sibleys, and the little luxuries of the mess chest.

The next morning I announced my intention of going to Pine Ridge Agency, which is twenty-five miles away. Mr. Thompson, two scouts, and a Swedish teamster are to go in for provisions and messages. Mr. Thompson got in the wagon. I expressed my astonishment at this and the fact that he had no carbines, as we expected to go through the hostile pickets and camp. He said, "If I can't talk them Injuns out of killin' me, I reckon I'll have to go." I trotted along with Red-Bear and Hairy-Arm, and a mile and a half ahead went the courier, Wells. Poor man! in two hours he lay bleeding in the road, with a bullet through the hips, and called two days for water before he "struck the long trail to the kingdom come," as the cowboys phrase it.

We could see two black columns of smoke, which we did not understand. After we had gone eight or ten miles, and were just crossing a ravine, we saw a Sioux buck on a little hill just ahead, out of pistol-shot. He immediately rode the "danger signal." Red-Bear turned his horse in the "peace sign," and advanced. We drove over the ravine, and halted. I dismounted. Six young Brulé Sioux rose out of the ground, and rode up to Red-Bear, and the hills were full of pickets to the right and left. We waited to hear the result of Red-Bear's conversation, when he presently came back and spoke to Thompson in Cheyenne. I looked at him; his eyes were snapping, and his facial muscles twitched frightfully. This was unusual, and I knew that things were not well.

"Red-Bear says we will have to go back,"

explained Thompson; and turning to Red-Bear he requested that two Sioux might come closer, and talk with us. Things looked ominous to me, not understanding Cheyenne, which was being talked. "This is a bad hole, and I reckon our cake is dough right here," said Thompson.

Hairy-Arm's face was impassive, but his dark eyes wandered from Brulé to Brulé with devilish calculation. Two young bucks came up, and one asked Thompson for tobacco, whereat he was handed a package of Durham by Thompson, which was not returned.

"It's lucky for me that tobacco ain't a million dollars," sighed Thompson.

Another little buck slipped up behind me, whereat Mr. Thompson gave me a warning look. Turning, I advanced on him quickly (I wanted to be as near as possible, not being armed), and holding out my hand, said, "How colah?" He did not like to take it, but he did, and I was saved the trouble of further action.

"We'll never get this wagon turned around," suggested Mr. Thompson, as the teamster whipped up; but we did. And as we commenced our movement on Casey's camp, Mr. Thompson said, "Go slow now; don't run, or they'll sure shoot."

"Gemme gun," said the little scout Red-Bear, and we all got our arms from the wagon.

There was no suspense now. Things had begun to happen. A little faster, yet faster, we go up the little banks of the *coulée,* and, ye gods! what!—five fully armed, well-mounted cowboys—a regular rescue scene from Buffalo Bill's show.

"Go back!" shouted Thompson.

Bang! bang! bang! and the bullets whistle around and kick up the dust. Away we go.

Four bucks start over the hills to our right to flank us. Red-Bear talked loudly in Cheyenne.

Thompson repeated, "Red-Bear says if any one is hit, get off in the grass and lie down; we must all hang together."

We all yelled, "We will."

A well-mounted man rode like mad ahead of the laboring team horses to carry the news to the scout camp. The cowboys, being well mounted, could easily have gotten away, but they stuck like true blues.

Here is where the great beauty of American character comes out. Nothing can be taken seriously by men used to danger. Above the pounding of the horses and the rattle of the wagon and through the dust came the cowboy song from the lips of Mr. Thompson:

> "Roll your tail,
> And roll her high;
> We'll all be angels
> By-and-by."

We deployed the flanks of the wagon so that the team horses might not be shot, which would have stopped the whole outfit, and we did ten miles at a record-breaking gallop. We struck the scout camp in a blaze of excitement. The Cheyennes were in war-paint, and the ponies' tails were tied up and full of feathers. Had the Sioux materialized at that time, Mr. Casey would have had his orders broken right there.

After a lull in the proceedings, Mr. Thompson confided to me that "the next time I go to war in a wagon it will put the drinks on me"; and he saddled Piegan, and patted his neck in a way which showed his gratification at the change in transport. We pulled out again for the lower country, and as our scouts had seen the dust of Colonel Sanford's command, we presently joined them.

Any remarks made to Mr. Thompson on the tobacco subject are taken seriously, and he has intimated to me a quiet yearning for a shot at "the particular slit-mouthed Brulé who got away with that Durham."

How we awoke next morning with the sleet freezing in our faces, and how we made camp in the blizzard, and borrowed Sibley stoves of the soldiers, and how we were at last comfortable, and spent New-Year's Eve in a proper manner, is of little interest.

I was awakened at a late hour that night

by Captain Baldwin, of General Miles's staff, and told to saddle up for a night ride to Pine Ridge. This was the end of my experience with Lieutenant Casey and his gallant corps. We shook hands cheerily in the dim candle-light of the tepee, and agreeing to meet in New York at some not distant day, I stepped out from the Sibley, mounted, and rode away in the night.

Three days later I had eaten my breakfast on the dining-car, and had settled down to a cigar and a Chicago morning paper. The big leads at the top of the column said, "Lieutenant E. W. Casey Shot." Casey shot! I look again. Yes; despatches from headquarters—a fact beyond question.

A nasty little Brulé Sioux had made his *coup*, and shot away the life of a man who would have gained his stars in modern war as naturally as most of his fellows would their eagles. He had shot away the life of an accomplished man; the best friend the Indians had; a man who did not know "fear"; a young man beloved by his comrades, respected by his generals and by the Secretary of War. The squaws of another race will sing the death-song of their benefactor, and woe to the Sioux if the Northern Cheyennes get a chance to *coup!*

"Try to avoid bloodshed," comes over the wires from Washington. "Poor savages!" comes the plaintive wail of the sentimentalist from his place of security; but who is to weep for the men who hold up a row of brass buttons for any hater of the United States to fire a gun at? Are the squaws of another race to do the mourning for American soldiers? Are the men of another race to hope for vengeance? Bah!

I sometimes think Americans lack a virtue which the military races of Europe possess. Possibly they may never need it. I hope not. American soldiers of our frontier days have learned not to expect sympathy in the East, but where one like Casey goes down there are many places where Sorrow will spread his dusky pinions and the light grow dim.

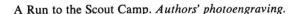

A Run to the Scout Camp. *Authors' photoengraving.*

General Miles's Review of the Mexican Army

By seven o'clock the chargers were at the door of the Hotel of the Garden, and the passing crowd ceased for a time to toil and spin, and were all eyes for the American soldiers who were mounting. I confessed to an interest in the sight myself, since nearly all the United States soldiers I have seen had left their plumage in some fort, and were to be only considered from the utili-tarian stand-point. The appearance of General Miles and Captain Maus, of his staff, seemed to thoroughly satisfy a crowd who were well used to military gorgeousness. It is simply marvellous how much gold cord comes into the possession of an aide-de-camp on the staff, and the metamorphoment of Captain Maus, the erstwhile chief of Indian scouts, into the glitter of the full rig

General Miles Reviewing the Mexican Army. *Authors' photoengraving.*

was like to upset the dignity of a less heroic character.

It is well known that of all "landlubbers," to a sailor's eye, the worst ones are the soldiers. It is also seldom that a soldier can get his naval brother into a precarious situation; but in order to be properly represented at the review, it was necessary for Lieutenant A. C. Baker, of the United States navy, to mount a horse, and then was unfolded to the sight of men the fearful and marvellous phenomenon of a sailor on horseback. To his eternal credit be it said that the steed's cargo did not "list," and the "tiller-ropes" worked perfectly.

The Mexican general and his staff, accompanied by a gendarme escort, rode with the American officers to the great plain of the Viga. For military purposes the grounds are magnificent, stretching away for miles, and able to accommodate all the men who are liable to be concentrated there.

The brigade was formed, and the staff rode away down the lines in a cloud of dust. Some evolutions were accomplished, and then the "marchpast" began.

Solid ranks of infantry scuttled along, headed by their big brass bands and heavy drumcorps. They march loosely, with a lack of precision, but they move much faster than our soldiers. Some of the young line officers, lately from the school of Chapultepec, were fine young fellows, and gave their commands and salutes with great spirit. The men were in heavy marching order, which is as it should be. They looked business-like, and not as though they were going out to play tennis.

The battery rumbled along with its four-inch De Banque cannon drawn by mules. I was forced to wonder how those mules would act under fire, but there is no doubt but that they could draw the heavy guns through the burning sands of their country better than horses.

Then came the Seventh Mexican Cavalry, the crack regiment of the army, and it is my belief that a better cavalry regiment would be hard to find.

The tough, well-conditioned bronco horses were of fair size, and the Mexican cavalry accoutrement is lighter and better than our own. The swarthy Indian soldiers rode beautifully, and the alignment showed the good work of the drill-ground.

As the last file-closer went by, the American soldiers rode away with an increased respect for their fellows of the sister republic. The Mexican people have bitter memories of two foreign invasions, and they have built a service which, if ever called to oppose an enemy again, will fill that enemy with bullets and favorable opinions, and it will not be dissipated by a defeat or two, as it was before it was reorganized—or, better, created—by the soldier-statesman, President Diaz.

A Day with the Seventh Regiment

I have seen various kinds of soldiers, and I ran up to the State camp at Peekskill when the famous Seventh Regiment was in camp, in the expectation of seeing yet another kind. In this I was disappointed, for whatever the men of the Seventh may be in citizens' clothes, they are much like other men in the uniform. I do not mean in their full-dress uniform; in that they are like the lilies of the field in their gorgeousness, but I must say, and it is a heresy which will damn one, that the full dress is more capable of destroying all semblance of the Creator's image than anything except a bishop's robe or a butcher's linen.

Of course it was obvious that they were all gentlemen, but I do not know as that is a distinction, since in this age most men are, and when you think of it, it will occur that it takes much more natural capacity and a longer training to be a buccaneer than a gentleman.

One does not expect to find the reckless abandon of a frontier wardog in a man who fumbles money in a metropolitan bank all the remainder of the year, and when one sees a whole regiment without a well-used guard-house, it makes you think a second time. The intelligence of the rank and file is what marks the Seventh, and when one thousand young men are keyed to concert pitch in a frantic endeavor to do the whole thing in the most perfect manner, and where the admonition that "you are a disgrace to your company, sir," is the equivalent of ten days in the guard-house, one begins to understand the Seventh. I sought for effemi-

nacy, and found it not. The individuals of the Seventh are sturdy young men, with no thought of being anything but a soldier while acting in that capacity, and they are as fit to campaign on bacon and beans as people who like that diet. The Seventh Regiment particularly interests military men in that it is pre-eminently an officers' school. I do not attempt to say how many men it could turn out in a great emergency as line officers. During the civil war it did remarkably in this respect, but, of course, the standard nowadays is much higher than it was in '61. The proud Colonel will tell you, "One thousand line officers, sir, without question, sir," and he would not expect you to believe it could do much better than two hundred and fifty, although you will say to yourself, "It can turn out one rattling good Colonel, at any rate." The Seventh is as proud of its Colonel as he is of them, and a glance at his gaunt frame and square jaw and the mental snap and quick jerky talk will assure you that he would be a "blood-letter" if the Seventh ever saw service. The Seventh's record is a proud one, but I would risk my reputation as a prophet on that Colonel of theirs if he ever had a chance to "put his regiment in." There would be dead soldiers "a plenty," and that's what they are for. If I were to allow myself to criticise the honorable Colonel, I should say that he was badly mounted for a Colonel. His charger was about fit for a contract wagon boss, but as I understand it, the State is in some way responsible for this loss of dignity on his part.

It is a curious thing, but suppose you had

to go looking up and down the earth for an ideal cavalryman, would you go last to a "hinfantry hadjutant"; and yet, if you were me, you would go to the Seventh Regiment first, and there find your ideal.

The camp was clean, of course. I never saw such neat police-work, it being what they call "nasty particular," in contradistinction to the thing. This is well, but then you expect it. There is, though, an element of interest in seeing a young man reputed to have more money than some people have hay go about wheeling a barrow and picking up refuse, like an Italian on Broadway. It is certainly a good training for a proud and stiff-necked generation.

The battalion drills—but why speak of them? The blaze of glory which always follows the faultless line of the marching Seventh was there, if the admiring throngs of young women were not. This thing is the militiaman's pride; but it is not war; it is not even military in this day; it's obsolete; it interests women and children.

Old Frederick the Great was a proper soldier in his day, but he did not know about smokeless powder and magazine-guns and rapid-fire rifle cannon, or he would have done differently. Napoleon's maxim was that to hold superiority a people must change its tactics every ten years. A general officer on the French staff, who is authority on military matters all over the world, says, "Progress is life and the *status quo* is the death of armies and, what is worse, of nations. Tactics must change in form age to age and at epochs relatively near."

The Seventh Regiment is not expected to institute any startling innovations in tactics naturally, but since Upton will go the way of all things very soon, it is not well to bear down on his solid formations to the neglect of the skirmish drill, which will have relatively more importance in this day than ever before. There are three things that a modern soldier must know: he must shoot like no one else in the world, but much better; he must know all the evolutions, and be familiar with all the possibilities of the skirmish drill; and he must be acquainted with every conceivable condition which may happen on the outposts. This is what he will have to do, and the faultless line, the perfect tread, and the absolute trail to the rifles are as nothing compared to it. To break down the traditions which have appertained since Gustavus Adolphus is desperate work, and in doing it one is apt to say more than he means; but soldiers are progressing in this age, true to the spirit of it, and humiliation will come to him who goes in for traditions. The solid wall of men will not go into the "fringe of fire" as though at a marchpast any more. The best, or rather the most stolid, troops of Europe, under the greatest leader, tried that at Plevna, and the Martini-Henry made old clothes and fertilizer of them. We should remember that our Remington and Springfield guns are as obsolete as a flint-lock Brown Bess. Possibly no more men will be killed, in proportion to numbers engaged, with Lebel rifles than with Brown Besses, but it will be done differently. In the camps in the Sioux coun-

In Firing Position. *Authors' wood engraving.*

try this winter, I was talking to the best shot in the United States army, and we saw a horseman far away. He was a speck. I asked him if he could hit him. He replied, "I could kill him sure if he would not run until I got his range, and if I waited until he came within a known range, I could be sure of him." It was perfectly startling. I was once riding with a little troop of cavalry, and the officer and I were talking about shooting. To elucidate an idea, he turned and suddenly dismounted three men, telling them to fire five rounds apiece at a black object across the cañon, and to do it quickly. The men dropped on the ground, and poured fifteen shots into the rock or stump, whatever it was, at an unknown distance, and they hit it over and over again. I think it was about seven hundred yards, and we could see the bullets strike in the sand. The frightful possibilities of a modern rifle in the hands of experts are not too well understood. Add to that the thin mist of the smokeless powder and the ceaseless crash of the magazine, and then think twice about your battalion drills.

Soldiers have always needed a good pair of legs, but I have an idea that they must yet be improved upon by modern soldiers. The "get there quickest with the most men" will be more imperative now than ever before, since it will be the constant endeavor to get round the flanks, and not oppose the solid force in front, made little short of immovable, with modern rifles and cannon.

I saw the Seventh at company skirmish. It was on the plain near the camp, and was all done without hesitation; and the fire was rapid, and, of course, I suppose would have been well delivered if with ball-cartridge. I was disappointed not to have seen the battalion pushed over the hill in skirmish line. It is half unlikely that men would be pushed over a small plain like that at the camp in actual warfare. In the woods and among the rocks the officers could instruct the young men in the real efficiency of a soldier on the line—how best to advance under the cover of natural objects; how to lose distance and regain it in seeking cover, or when an open space is encountered. When in the thick trees, where you see but two or three men

on your line, you find it more difficult to keep your proper position. The skirmish drill is full of individualisms, and the young soldier must study the ground in front. The hard school of war would soon teach its lessons, but there would be many a fine youngster laid out on his back in the process of learning, when a little drill will do fairly well in the place thereof. The mere details of the drill are not hard to learn, but the application of it is quite another thing. It is like unto the bayonet exercise of Upton, for it is only when you "engage" that you begin to be alive to the complications of the same. The moral quality which will come to the young soldier in this sort of practice is the idea that he must be effective and deadly, he must do damage, and receive as little as possible in return. Young men in the Guard are too much impressed with the "pipe-clay" and "stand up straight" ideas, which are matters of course, and have nothing to do with effectiveness in a soldier. The science of war, or "murder made perfect," is brought to their attention principally by the crash of the battalion volley, and they have that good, comfortable touch of elbow which is a thing white men do not have to be taught, since in every little slaughter of troops in our Indian wars the tendency has been to bunch up, whereas in nine times out of ten a loose formation would have served better.

I have only just now begun to realize that I have placed myself on a pedestal, that I am developing into a critic, and that is not to my liking. If the people of this world had to dispense with some one of its possessions, that to be anything from cold boiled cabbage up to a locomotive, I think they would select a critic; but I will excuse myself on the ground that this is an idea and not a criticism. I have made bold simply to state certain impressions of my own, and since one man is as liable to preach good doctrine as another, any one to whom my words do not commend themselves can dismiss them.

With men such as compose the Seventh Regiment, and with men who take pride in their corps which they do, anything is possible. They can be sent to college, as it were, long before an average recruit is out of the depot. The new tactics will soon come in vogue; it has not ceased to be a hope among military men that the army and the Guard will one day have a good modern rifle, and then Guardsmen can go in for the death-dealing, and sort of "let up" on the "toes depressed" business.

Our National Guard should be furnished with intrenching tools, and be taught in the use of them at the State camp. The rifle and the trowel are twin-brothers, and one is as necessary as the other. The far-reaching fire of modern rifle cannon will meet every infantry regiment as it moves forward, and it may be necessary to lie under that fire for a time; and a man will lie more composedly in a little hole than on top of the ground; and besides that, a soldier might want to cut a little wood to boil some coffee if the wagons didn't come up—and you know that wagons do not always come when they ought to.

I am tempted to speak of a neat little invention which is on trial in I Company of the Seventh Regiment, and it is the little leggin. It is of black leather, and very much like the British affair. There has always been a complaint against the leggin in use in the regular army, because it falls down over the foot, and picks up mud and snow. This thing has commended itself, and it would be well if generally adopted.

Ordnance boards have been distinguished in America on many occasions, and it is not for their intelligence either. The most startling adoption which I ever saw tied on to a soldier is the cartridge-box of the National Guard. It is a fearful and wonderful contrivance. It carries about enough ammunition for a soldier's salute at a funeral. A regiment of the Guard would be spectators in a fight before it had fairly opened. Think how regular soldiers load up with cartridges when the "weather is thick ahead." They fill nose-bags and pockets and belts. This is seemingly a very small matter, but many a fine regiment has been hopelessly disgraced before now in consequence of empty cartridge-boxes.

I had one very good impression at the State camp among all these cranky observations, and that is that the men worked hard. They were at it early and late, and without grumbling. No one should have the impression that there is any picnicking at the State camp, but, on the other hand, lots of zealous work, and a general idea of improvement. Young men such as compose the Guard can be relied on to extract a due proportion of amusement out of life, and it is well seen to that their lives are not monotonous. It is unlikely that the men of this generation in America will ever "seek the bubble reputation at the cannon's mouth"; and if we are to slip into the other stage, let us be able to tell the boys that we only lacked the opportunity, as, for that matter, we were good men in our day. Let us not have to make statements to the boys that are not founded on fact, for some bright youngster might say, "Oh, your ideas of fighting had the dust of countless generations on them," for it would be then that we would realize that we had lived in vain.

Universal peace was thought to be at hand a long time since, and there will always be a small army of refined minds who are firm in the hope that because they do not like fighting, all other men will be of the same mind shortly; but I have never been able to discover that human nature in the aggregate underwent any alteration. When the canine teeth in man become square, and not pointed, I shall begin to see that he is changing; but the most diligent research will not give you any clew to a difference between a modern man and the fellow of the stone age. A little more hair on his body had the latter man, but I would wager he could be thrashed by a modern prize-fighter. It is well enough to keep a little of the military seed corn in a country, if only for your mobs, which "ye have always with you." As an eccentric old fighting colonel of the regular army once said to me as we stood looking at his men, "They need a little killing; can't have soldiers without fighting." And of course the mobs are useful in filling that want.

Training Cavalry Horses to Jump Obstacles

One would suppose that a small army like our own would be perfection, but since that means a great deal, it is not at all surprising that it fails to realize it. Its sins are all of omission, and its training of cavalry horses is its great crime. The riding of United States cavalrymen has always gladdened the heart of witnesses. They began in a great and desperate war, and since those days they have been environed by the best native riders on earth, namely, Indians and cowboys, so it is not surprising that they sit horses well under any circumstances; but having been doing active fieldwork in a pioneer sort of a way for a generation, they have had no riding halls, and very little incentive to do the *haute école*. This condition is changing from year to year, and since Uncle Sam is no longer building army posts, the cavalryman can devote himself more to the niceties of his profession than he has in the past. The "chopping and digging" stage has gone, and the horses furnished the army are better than of old, thanks to the efforts of certain cavalry officers and to a slight increase in civil official morality, although horses bought under the contract system will always be obtained by regarding their price instead of their quality.

Another reason why this thing is not of more importance in our cavalry is that they have campaigned on the vast stretches of the great plains and in the mountains, and have had to do with long hard marches rather than short sharp work in a fenced and ditched country. It is true that I have seen a whole column of United States cavalry go up and down bad mountain country in places so perilous that a horse not accustomed to it would fairly faint with fright, but all that was born of the necessity, the lack of which is felt when we speak of training cavalry horses after the methods of the European cavalryman.

That this necessity now exists I do not mean, only now that officers have more time at their disposal they can continue to cultivate that part of their profession, which is no small part. I know a great many instances personally where cavalry officers have applied themselves in this way, and have done creditable work. Lieutenant S. C. Robertson, of the First Plungers, has been through the mill of the foreign horse schools, and his knowledge does not come amiss.

Lieutenants Clark and Smith, of the Tenth Cavalry, have conducted a series of experiments, the subject of which forms my page of sketches. The use of natural obstacles, which can readily be found in any country, was the idea, and thus the dry work of mere hurdles avoided, although, of course, a little hurdle to begin with. They use a dead steer when one can be found, which is a not unusual thing on the "cow range." I saw a troop of cavalry fairly disorganized by a dead beef on the San Carlos post-road, and the school of cavalry practice which was immediately instituted right there was one of the gayest scenes I have

Training Horses to Leap Obstacles, Tenth United States Cavalry. *Painting from the Warner Collection of Gulf States Paper Corporation, Tuscaloosa, Alabama.*

ever had the fortune to witness. If a man had come suddenly upon the bluffs of the Gila, he would have said, "There is a desperate cavalry battle going on down in the bottom." But it was only the troopers trying to get their horses over a steer, which, in the words of the wild cowboy, was "too dead to skin." The result was finally accomplished, and now that detachment might be relied on to at least charge a dead body, which, by-the-way, is not so simple a thing for a horse as one might think. I knew very intimately a man who was peacefully riding along the highway in Westchester County, when he suddenly espied a dead horse at the roadside. Presently his horse also perceived, and the scenes that ensued were highly gratifying to the small boys who gathered about. He first went bodily over a steep drop from the road into a pile of rocks, after that he climbed up a high terrace owned by a gentleman, and after a long time the live horse

had his front feet on the body of the dead horse, and peace reigned.

There are three things that a good cavalry officer must know. He must ride well himself, which is the least of all these things, and he almost universally does. He should be able to train any horse to the full extent of the horse's ability, either in the high school or the jumping, and that is not a very difficult thing for an active, patient, and intelligent man to do. Lastly, he should know what comparatively few of them do, and that is, all about a horse; in short, that knowledge one finds in the racing stable—horsy knowledge—about the physical construction, the temperament, the intelligence, of the brutes, and how this one should be bitted, and this one be worked a great deal in one way, while another horse is schooled in another. One horse may need a vast amount of exercise, while another may get along with very little; one horse may be ridden by a recruit at the risk of spoiling his gaits, while some other horse may have so good a gait that the recruit cannot spoil it. These cases are only a few out of the three or four million which are a part of the make-up of horse knowledge. Some cavalry officers do not care about all these things, but they are simply a disgrace to their profession, and so not to be considered except with scorn. The most remarkable case of this knowledge and judgment regarding horses in a cavalryman was that of Captain Montgomery, of the Fifth Cavalry, as told by Captain Charles King, in his *Campaigning with Crook,* which I quote: "In horseflesh and equipments the gaps were appalling. Some companies of the Fifth were very much reduced, and, of course, when the horse dropped exhausted on the trail there was no transportation for the 'kit.' It often happened that for days the soldier led his horse along the flanks of the column or in the rear of the regiment, striving hard to nurse his failing strength, hunting eagerly for every little bunch of grass that might eke out his meagre subsistence. In all the array of company losses there was one, and only one, shining contrast—Montgomery, of Company B—the Greys cavalry submitted a clear 'bill of health'; he had not lost a single horse. The fact that Captain Montgomery paraded every horse with which he started is due to the unerring judgment and ceaseless vigilance with which he noted every symptom of weakness in any and every animal in his troop, and cared for it accordingly."

From a purely professional standpoint I think this feat was probably as noted an achievement as any cavalryman could well ask for. It towers over the man who can pick a cracker off the ground at a gallop off a sixteen-hand horse, and the *passage* and *pirouette* are as nothing compared; but if Captain Montgomery can pick up the cracker, and do the *passage,* he should have a marble monument at West Point, and every cadet should be made to go out twice a day and sing a pæan before it.

The United States trooper knows enough by the time he has served one enlistment, but his horse, which has as great a capacity for war as the recruit, comes out with little to his credit. Why should he not be educated? Well, let us hope he may be.

Coolies Coaling a Ward Liner—Havana

The big Ward Line steamer was lying at her anchors in the quiet harbor of Havana awaiting her cargo and coal to the port of New York. Her people were watching the great white men-of-war, the black liners to France and the tight island, and the dozens of lesser craft bound to here and there and everywhere. They saw the strange lighters peculiar to the Spanish American ports bearing their loads of fruit and tobacco to our hold: and they watched the clean-limbed, warm brown creoles as they worked at the bale hooks, and they thought, they are not white, but possibly a better color; they are a more solid color; a color produced by the sun pouring on to human flesh, and a natural result, while we—we are white, pale, will I say an unnatural color; it seems that to all people who are brown or black; but, of course, we are, as the base-ball folks say, "the people," and why quibble.

The folks on the *Orizaba* saw the coal-lighters coming out in tow with the car-

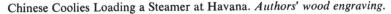

Chinese Coolies Loading a Steamer at Havana. *Authors' wood engraving.*

bonaceous matter calculated on by arithmetical folks to take the *Orizaba* to New York. Naturally, coal-barges are infinitely commonplace. Why watch a coal-barge? No one will, and no one did; but the people on the coal-barge seemed strange; Chinese evidently. Chinese are grotesque; but the people on these coal-barges out-Chinesed the Celestials. They were comic opera at a hundred yards; but at close range one forgot the soldier caps, the foot-ball jackets, the Canadian lumber-camp mackinaws, and the rest of the world, and was gratified by a most astonishing array of physiognomy.

"Canton River coolies," explained the chief engineer to me; and he was one of those old sailors who have been everywhere, and who know everything except how to localize themselves. The coal-barge came alongside, and I went down to look over a line of costume and physiognomy which would be a boiling down of ten years' experience in the sketch class at the Art Students' League.

As to physiognomy, volumes, years, nothing, could convey the idea. Some had noses —of course most of them did, but then, again, some did not—likewise ears, and so on through the list of human parts, bar brains, which were wholly lacking. I went down to the port-hole of the lower deck, and contemplated this so-called humanity. Nothing that I had ever seen compared with it. The mutilated body of the red Indian's atrocity, the starved and frozen steer, the white corpse on the marble of the dissecting-table, the damned and forsaken of a great city, nothing to compare—it was a climax. Dante and Doré would have stopped short; but I must go on to say that here was a new genus—a God-forsaken, a man-abhorred creature, a drug-racked, leprosy-eaten thing, devoid of mentality, and of every other thing which distinguishes man from animals, and if in my vocabulary I knew of a better word than animals, I would not use that word, since I mean a thing lower than that. I experienced every thrill, every shudder, every horrible emotion of which I am capable. Even pity was ab-

sent. It was usurped by self-preservation. I saw the terrible man—a thing which might taint my people; a thing which I knew that the political machinery of my country could not keep at a distance. I felt a fear, a desire to get away, as from a savage or a bear or something absolutely inimical to decent clean life. Such an array of filth and vermin, of unclean morals, and ghastly eaten sodden human flesh I had never suspected. The sloughed-off sore of a despotism so ancient that the mind dulls in contemplation of its age was to be met by my kind of men—nay, mingled with. They were in Havana, why not in New York? I never saw them; they may not be outside of Havana. We hope? Yes, but we do nothing.

These coolies pass coal, and they serve up a moral sermon, a frightful picture, and a political lesson to any one who will stop and look.

I am told that these things come into the United States by the hundreds every year. I am willing to be told that the great mass of our Chinese immigrants are clean and industrious, and I have had the experience of travelling our whole Canadian border with Mr. Julian Ralph, who was sent to investigate this thing, and yet if the people of America, who are clean, wholesome, and industrious, could see the reeking sore which sloughs off the Chinese Empire; if they could understand the half-dozen things which I cannot tell, because it would not be printed in a decent journal—they would understand.

Americans are a strange people; at once the most generally intelligent, and, because of their great variety of interests, the most neglectful of their own good ends in the world. These Chinese will come, and we will see a quarter column in the papers every other morning, and yet a great national evil is overshadowed by the little nothingness of a local campaign. The Asiatic leprosy, the drug, the immoral sore of China, is broadcast in this land, and we like it too. Go to Havana, and, if you inquire, you may find it more adjacent.

A Merry Christmas in a Sibley Tepee

"Eat, drink, and be merry, for to-morrow we die." Not a good excuse, but it has been sufficient on many occasions to be true. The soldier on campaign passes life easily. He holds it in no strong grip, and the Merry Christmas evening is as liable to be spent in the saddle in fierce contact with the blizzard as in his cosey tepee with his comrades and his scant cheer. The jug containing the spirits of the occasion may have been gotten from a town fifty miles away on the rail-road. It is certainly not the distillation of the summer sunlight, and is probably "tough" enough stuff to mingle naturally with its surroundings; but if one "drinks no more than a sponge" he may not have the jaded, retrospective feeling and the moral mending on the day to come. To sit on a camp chest, and to try and forget that the soldier's quart cup is not filled with best in the market, and then to enter into the full appreciation of the picturesque occasion, is to forget that long marches, "bull meat," and sleepless, freezing nights are in the background. Pleasant hours sit so nicely in their complemental surrounding of hard

Merry Christmas in a Sibley Tepee. *Painting in "21" Club Collection—Peter Kriendler, President.*

ones, since everything in the world is relative. As to the eating in a cavalry camp on campaign, it is not overdone, for beans and coffee and bacon and bacon and coffee and beans come round with sufficient regularity to forestall all gormandizing. The drinking is not the prominent feature either, but helps to soften the asperities of a Dakota blizzard which is raging on the other side of the "ducking."

The Sibley tent weaves and moans and tugs frantically at its pegs. The Sibley stove sighs like a furnace while the cruel wind seeks out the holes and crevices. The soldiers sit in their camp drawing-room buttoned up to the chin in their big canvas overcoats, and the muskrat caps are not removed. The freemasonry of the army makes strong friendships, and soldiers are all good fellows, that being a part of their business. There are just enough exceptions to prove the rule. The cold, bloodless, compound-interest snarler is not in the army, and if he were he would be as cheerless on a damp evening as he would in a fight. One man is from Arizona, another from Washington, and the rest from the other corners of Uncle Sam's tract of land. They have met before, and memory after memory comes up with its laughter and pathos of the old campaigns. One by one the "shoulder-straps" crawl in through the hole in the tepee. And, mind you, they do not walk in like a stage hero, with dash and abandon and head in the air; they prostrate themselves like a Turk at prayer, and come crawling. If they raise the flap ever so much, and bring company of the Dakota winds, they are met with a howl of protests. After gaining erectness, they brush the snow from their clothes, borrow a tin cup, and say, "How! how!"

The chief of scouts buttons up to his eyes, and must go look after his "Inguns"; the officer of the day comes in to make his papers, and if he keeps the flying jokes out of his statistics, he does well enough. The second lieutenant, fresh from West Point, doesn't hesitate to address the grizzled colonel of twenty campaigns—nay, he may even

deign to advise him on the art of war; but that is unsatisfactory—the advising of colonels—because the colonel's advice to the sub has always to be acted upon, whereas the sub's advice to the colonel is mostly nullified by the great powers of discretion which are vested in the superior rank. The life-study of a sub should be to appear like the cuckoo-bird in a German clock—at the proper moment; and when he appears at wrong intervals, he is repaired. Colonels are terrible creatures, with vast powers for promoting happiness or inflicting misery. If he will lend the moderating influence of his presence, it is well; but if he sends his man around to "present his compliments, and say that the d—— row will immediately cease," his wishes if not his personality are generally respected.

It is never a late evening, such a one as this; it's just a few stolen moments from the "demnition grind." The last arrival may be a youngster just in from patrol, who explains that he just "cut the trail of forty or fifty Sioux five miles below, on the crossing of the White River;" and you may hear the bugle, and the bugle may blow quick and often, and if the bugle does mingle its notes with the howling of the blizzard, you will discover that the occasion is not one of merriment. But let us hope that it will not blow.

The toasts go around, and you use your tobacco in a miserly way, because you can't get any more, since only to-day you have offered a dollar for a small plug to a trooper, and he had refused to negotiate, although he had pared off a small piece as a gift, and intimated that generosity could go no further. Then you go to your tepee, half a mile down the creek at the scout camp, and you stumble through the snow-laden willows and face the cutting blast, while the clash and "Halt!" of the sentinel stop you here and there. You pull off your boots and crawl into your blankets quickly before the infernal Sibley stove gives its sigh as the last departing spark goes up the chimney, and leaves the winds and drifting snows to bellow and scream over the wild wastes.

The Galloping Sixth

I once knew a man, whose judgment had been softened by years and experience, who said that "the two most desirable positions in the world are the editorship of a great metropolitan newspaper and the colonelcy of a cavalry regiment." I can only partially imagine what the editor thinks about or what his troubles and cares may be, and I had always supposed that a colonel of cavalry went around in a state of mind wherein the romantic dash and whirl of a thousand moving horses passed in cyclorama before his appreciative senses. I have discovered that to be precisely the idea that never enters his head. I was a guest of General Carr, the colonel commanding the "Galloping Sixth" Regiment of United States Cavalry, at its camp on the Cheyenne River, and I assure you that he thought of nothing but "bacon and forage." No tramp of steeled hoofs, no floating guidons, no gallant men or plumes or flashing sabres; nothing but "bacon and forage."

In the quiet hours of the night there was a stir in the great headquarters tent. Orderlies ran to awaken a half-dozen officers. They came in hot haste. I was somewhat startled by these precipitous proceedings. Visions of enemy and the clash of arms played through my fancy.

"You will report immediately how many days' rations of bacon there are at our disposal," said the Colonel; whereupon he returned to his couch.

Off ran the officers, and commissary sergeants by the dozen were lugged out of their blankets. A wild scurrying, a flashing of lanterns, a host of men tumbling over packages in the dark. After an elaborate investigation the Colonel was awakened, and report made that there were "so many pounds of bacon, sir!" whereat quiet was allowed to resume its sway.

Being somewhat amused by this unwonted interest in bacon, I provoked an explanation in the morning from the Colonel.

"Sir, the most important things about a cavalry regiment are the stomachs of the men and horses."

The fighting is a mere detail, but the bacon and forage weigh with crushing force on the mind of the commander. It is thus demonstrated that the editor is the more enviable person, and yet there are minor reasons why one should still desire to be a colonel of cavalry.

Poor Czar of All the Russias! he is a citizen of a republic compared to the autocrat of the cavalry camp. A thousand horses stand on the picket lines ready to gallop at his wish; a thousand gallant little men become deathly rigid at his approach; even the mules tied at the tail-boards of the wagons dare hardly wiggle their stumpy tails without an order from the commanding officer. One might suppose that this environment might produce a peculiar man in the person of the Colonel, and it does. It is not at the first meeting that one can separate the physiology of the Colonel and the man. From always being the hub of the wheel, the Colonel rather makes a citizen feel as though he

Cooking in Camp. *Authors' photoengraving.*

ought to get in among the spokes and revolve in his turn.

Next in importance in the little military
village is the Adjutant. He is generally a
prefunctory individual, with a greater interest in having things run smoothly than any
one else, since he must first feel the Colonel's displeasure. A visitor should establish
relations with the Adjutant, and then if he
happens to transgress the proprieties of the
camp, it is within the power of the Adjutant
to dull the sharpness of the thorns in the
bed he must lie on.

It is better not to bother the busy Colonel
too much, so leave him to his bacon and
forage, and go look at the private. He certainly takes on a character all his own. Personally reckless, desperately improvident,
and with little on his mind but his hat and
hair, he is given to grumbling, and will
d—— his own eyes as quick as the Colonel's; he is full of soldier expressions, and
the adaptability of the average United States
soldier to any condition which may arise is
always astonishing. There are several hundred thousand little methods of producing
comfort in unpleasant places which are traditions in the army, and have been handed
down from the army in Flanders to the last
recruit from Jefferson Barracks.

If it were possible to enumerate the many
ways in which hardtack can be served, I
would do so. The sparks from the conical
stove burn holes in the canvas of the Sibley
tent. The way to repair these holes was not
discovered at once, but by process of evolution one man has learned to stoop down
while a comrade climbs on his back, and is
thus enabled to reach up and stuff grass in
the holes.

After about a year's service every recruit
discovers that his mission in life is to keep
the inside of his particular horse stuffed as
full of hay and grain as circumstances and
the horse will admit. He estimates its capacity to be equal to what he can lay his hands
on. It is only the strict methods of issue
which prevent cavalry horses from acquir-
ing a founder. Men who are perfectly honest in every other particular will steal forage
for their horses. They are such persistent
and accomplished grain thieves that it is
necessary in times of scarcity to stand by
your horse until he has eaten the last kernel,
or it will be abstracted from his nose-bag
and fed to some other beast.

Why soldiers have the millions of dogs I
never knew until an officer said: "Simply
something on which to lavish affection; it's
a ground-cropping of human nature. We

used to try to get rid of the dogs at our garrison, but found it impossible. When we changed our station we thought to solve the difficulty. Orders were issued to take no dogs. While *en route* to this place I heard strange noises at times, and discovered that every nose-bag contained a pup, and by express and every imaginable means the dogs came along, until in a week's time I recognized that no single dog from our post in Arizona was missing in Dakota."

This soldier man's relations with his comrades are peculiar. There seems to be no suggestion of domestic bliss, and yet beyond frequent reminders that the one addressed is held in abject contempt by the speaker, they seem to worry along. They come to know each other very intimately, and the bright vermilion hue of the English which they exchange passes unheeded as the winds, while to the uninitiated the awful directness of the sentence a soldier uses when he requests his comrade to "move along a little" fairly chills you.

Now the Lieutenant, when he requires anything, will send "his compliments and the request," but when the first sergeant speaks, hell yawns for the heedless.

An Appeal for Justice

Not long ago the press despatches said that shyster lawyers in the Indian Territory were making legal raids on the Cheyennes. The Indians now have their lands in severalty, and a new assortment of trouble and care with them. The famine, the small pox, the pneumonia, the strong-water, and the Texas cowboy had nearly done for them; but now the frontier lawyer gets in his talons, and the end is nigh. The Indians did what Indians always do in these latter days, head straight for a United States army officer and pour out their tale of woe. The army officer protests that he can do nothing; but he sets the complaint going "through military channels," and finally it comes plump up against the solid wall of divided authority in Washington, and as a living subject ceases to exist. It is henceforth history—one of the pages of a dead and forgotten past.

Meanwhile the wronged Indian goes back

An Appeal for Justice. *Authors' photoengraving.*

to his tepee and waits. White people try to explain the process of common law to him, and, of course, every one starts in by admitting that he has "gotten the worst of it." The Indian does not submit readily, that being a virtue only developed by the highest evolution of civilization. To the Indian it does not matter whether it is constitutional or unconstitutional. The common law mixes things hopelessly when it subverts his natural rights, and the application of statutes which puts sharp stones in his path simply cap the climax. Then his agent, if he has his ward's interest at heart, does what he can; but civil bureaus do things in such a roundabout, day-after-to-morrow new ruling, red-tape and pigeon-hole way that the relief comes tardily, if at all. What the Indian wants is simply one white man in the whole white race who can say to him, "you can do this," or "you can do that," and who will not habitually lie to him. The agent refers to Washington, and the matter referred is given a decent burial. The white soldier raises his right hand ever so little, speaks short and sharp, and the thing is done. The Indian appreciates the difference, but cannot understand why General Nelson Miles cannot straighten out whatever is crooked in his whole world of woes.

The land-in-severalty scheme is a very good scheme, but under the law and shiftless civil administration it will open up a new field of trouble for our red brother beside which the predatory cowboy, the whiskey-peddler, and the misappropriated beef issue were as nothing. He will now have to deal with the frontier lawyer and the trafficking person who is "not there for his health," and when he encounters their diabolical cunning and matchless imposture, he will come out of the tussel with, it is to be hoped, the primitive fig-leaf at least. The white man's "forever" will grow to a very much shorter time, and he will come to recognize in the law of the land an enemy whose armor he cannot pierce.

The soldier says nothing, but he lives with the Indian, and he thinks what fine soldiers they make, and how well we succeed with him when we get a chance. The soldier never tells him what is not so, or promises what he cannot fulfil. When Mr. Lo gets in trouble he appears at headquarters and states his case. When Mr. Lo troubles any one else, the soldier slips a 45 into his Springfield, and subsequently slips it into the hide of Mr. Lo. Both of these proceedings inspire respect in the mind of the Indian, who is by no means a fool, and readily appreciates when he is treated properly and with justice.

The Sioux and Apaches were always more intelligent in their dealings with the white race than any of the other tribes. When too much constitutionality and law and statutes were run in on them by the white men, they just saddled up the big pony and got out their Winchesters and left a smoking waste and heaps of white carrion in their wake. Then the commission which came out to fix the thing up and save an administration an Indian war, approached the subject in a fair and liberal way, and generally did what it said it would.

Buffalo Bill in London

The Tower, the Parliament, and Westminster are older institutions in London than Buffalo Bill's show, but when the New-Zealander sits on the London Bridge and looks over his ancient manuscripts of Murray's Guide-book, he is going to turn first to the Wild West. At present everyone knows where it is, from the gentleman on Piccadilly to the dirtiest coster in the remotest slum of Whitechapel. The cabman may have to scratch his head to recall places where the traveller desires to go, but when the "Wild West" is asked for he gathers his reins and uncoils his whip without ceremony. One should no longer ride the deserts of Texas or the rugged uplands of Wyoming to see the Indians and the pioneers, but should go to London. It is also quite unnecessary to brave the fleas and the police of the Czar to see the Cossack, or to tempt the waves which roll between New York and far-off Argentine to study the "guachos." It is all in London. The Cossacks and the "guachos" are the latest addition, and they nearly complete the array of wild riders. There you can sit on a bench and institute comparisons. The Cossacks will charge you with drawn sabres in a most genuine way, will hover over you like buzzards on a battle-field—they soar and whirl about in graceful curves, giving an uncanny impression, which has doubtless been felt by many a poor Russian soldier from the wheat fields of Central Europe as he lay with a bullet in him on some distant field. They march slowly around over imaginary steppes, singing in a most dolorous way—looking as they did in Joseph Brandt's paintings. They dance over swords in a light-footed and crazy way, and do feats on their running horses which brings the hand clapping. They stand on their heads, vault on and off, chase each other in a game called "chasing the handkerchief," and they reach down at top speed and mark the ground with a stick. Their long coat-tails flap out behind like an animated rag-bag, while their legs and arms are visible by turns. Their grip on the horse is maintained by a clever use of these stirrups, which are twisted and crossed at will. They are armed like "pin-cushions," and ride on a big leather bag which makes their seat abnormally high.

The "guachos" are dressed in a sort of Spanish costume, with tremendous pantaloons of cotton and boots made of a colt's skin, which in their construction are very like Apache moccasins. They carry a knife at their back which would make a hole which a doctor couldn't sew up with less than five stitches, if indeed he was troubled at all. They ride a saddle which one of the American cowboys designated as a "— — feather bed," and they talk Spanish which would floor a Castilian at once. They ride bucking horses by pairs, and amuse the audience by falling off at intervals.

The great interest which attaches to the whole show is that it enables the audience to take sides on the question of which people ride best and have the best saddle. The whole thing is put in such tangible shape as

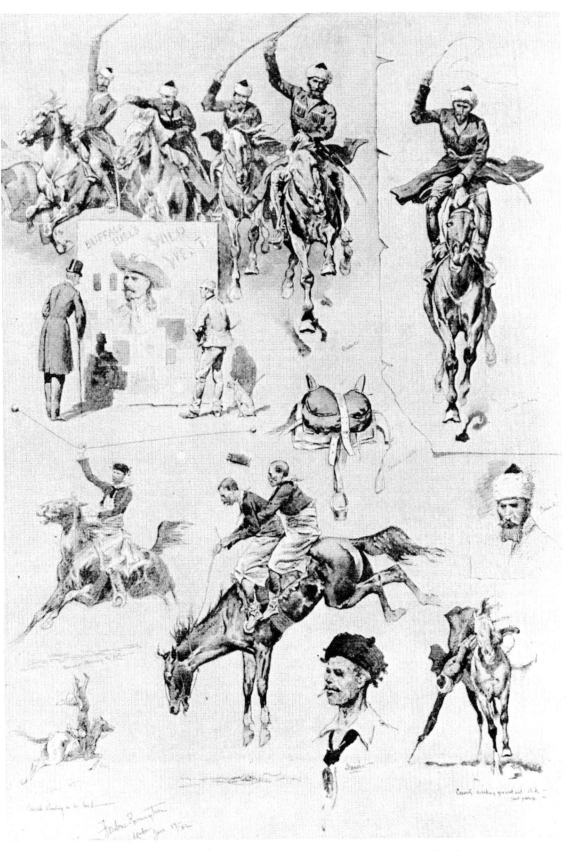

Buffalo Bill's Wild West Show in London—The Cossacks and Guachos.
Authors' photoengraving.

to be a regular challenge to debate to lookers on. I for one formed my opinion, and have sacrificed two or three friends on the altar of my convictions. There is also a man in a pink coat who rides a hunting seat in competition with a yellow savage on a clear horse, and if our Englishman is not wedded to his ideals he must receive a very bad shock at beholding.

As you walk through the camp you see a Mexican, an Ogallala, and a "guacho" swapping lies and cigarettes while you reflect on the size of the earth. The manager, Major Burke, will tell you that you must not imagine that it is a simple job to handle this aggregated wild humanity from the waste places, because when a savage gets an idea into his head it takes enough debating to pass the home-rule for Ireland bill to get it out again. The Indians smell the choice meat which is being cooked for Colonel Cody's private tepee, and in their simple, unostentatious way they will come around and demand a rib. The Major says that the Indians eat too much for the good of their health, as they are constantly coming around to the cook asking for meat between meals. I have known of Indian scouts consuming ten days' rations in one day, but they kept their general good health by going without eating for the next week following; but in London it is different. The Major has to fine the cowboys for standing on their heads in the ring after the Cossack manner, all of which interferes with the eternal fitness of things. He will tell you that the Cossack saddle "sores the backs" of the horses, and gives the stablemen no end of trouble. The Major will conclude that the management of a light-opera company on the road is a mere beginner's work beside the people with the Wild West show, because they are all schooled in the theory that it is the proper thing to run a ten-inch knife into the anatomy of any one who does not agree with "their peculiar whim."

The remote effect of the whole thing will be that cattlemen out West will have little boys with cockney accents wanting to hire out as "cow-punchers," and the Sioux will have to "roost high" when this new generation of Indian fighters grows up in London, for it will last after the Sioux are raising one hundred bushels of corn to the acre.

Next year the whole outfit is coming over to the World's Fair with the rest of Europe, and they are going to bring specimens of all the continental cavalry. The Sioux will talk German, the cowboys already have an English accent, and the "guachos" will be dressed in good English form.

The Wild West show is an evolution of a great idea. It is becoming as great an educator as P. T. Barnum's, and, with its aggregate of wonders from the out-of-the-way places, it will represent a poetical and harmless protest against the Derby hat and the starched linen—those horrible badges of the slavery of our modern social system, when men are physical lay figures, and mental and moral cog-wheels and wastes of uniformity—where the greatest crime is to be individual, and the unpardonable sin to be out of the fashion.

Military Athletics at Aldershot

It is not necessary to account for the fact that the people of the British Isles are the best racers physically on the earth, but I supposed it could be done. The long twilights in summer make games possible, and in winter every one who is not physically perfect must die. There are other reasons, but these are the chief ones. The serious business of John Bull's life is on the cricket or tennis ground, and Parliament adjourns for the races. Men never become so old that they quite give up these things, and then you know that when Mr. Jorrocks makes his pile of flesh and money he "rides to hounds." The "costers" all like a "go" with or without the gloves, and the greatest English reputations—I mean those which shall live with Milton and Shakespeare—were made in a 24-foot ring. The art stores in London have nothing but "sporting plates" in the windows for sale, although they make a concession to art conventions occasionally by keeping a picture of a Greek woman lying around in the lackadaisical "posy" manner affected by artists' models.

So when John Bull becomes "Tommy Atkins" he naturally joins the British Military Athletic Association, and when he is not drilling or drinking beer he is cultivating his latent talents for doing some one thing in athletics which shall win him a prize at the tournaments. He will journey all the way from Scotland or Ireland to Aldershot, and be hammered almost to death, for the everlasting distinction and honor of the Scotch Grays or Enniskillens.

The games continue for two or three days, and there are a tremendous lot of entries. The barracks and the line are deserted, and officers and men take a hand. The women all go too, and the ladies sit under a big canvas awning, and the women who are not ladies do the best they can. The color and cut of many brilliant uniforms enliven the scene, and if ever John Bull betrays any emotion he does it then.

The 24-foot ring has the greatest fascination for Tommy Atkins, and he sits on the ground in great rings which widen away from the stakes and ropes as does the water of a quiet pool when an angler's fly strikes it. There is no mystery about the proceedings of a "go" to Tommy. The thing is not so new to him that he indulges in superficialities concerning the bout. He passes his remarks in terse and strongly shaded sentences, and "bets his sesterces upon their blood." The pale young recruit is there with his new uniform: the dull light of the factory has bleached his skin. The tall guardsman strides about with his neat clothes and grand air. You find Ortheris and Mulvaney in plenty. They have come all the way from India. They are no longer white men, but the sun has eaten and burned into their skin until their red coat is a quiet note of color in the contrast. Taken altogether Tommy is a fighter. He likes his beer and his girl, but the great, overpowering dissipation is a fight. He would rather put up the fight himself, but if that is inconvenient or not at hand he likes to watch

An Athletic Tournament of the British Army at Aldershot. *Authors' photoengraving.*

others fight; and if a British officer desires the approbation of his men, he can gain renown by winning a game at Aldershot, which shall make his star to shine until a brilliant Engmer or the best light in the Intelligence Office shall be of an invisible magnitude.

In these days when all Europe has gone back to the lance as a cavalry arm, that weapon has the stage. A light bridle hand and a clever whirling of the pole as it searches out the life of the opponent make pretty work. It is a great pity that the pitiless, all-penetrating, rapid-firing rifle cannot be traded for the "gray goose's wing," and all these miserable machinating staff and ordnance officers and inventors be relegated to the devil, when once again war and fight-ing should make men glad and death easy. Oh, sorry the day—of steamships and box-cars and Nordenfelts and British interests! If again could come the times when the "tall fellows of England" could drop over the Channel and "spit" a few French, or follow one lord to conclusions against his neighbor lord!—when, as Philippe de Co-mines said, "it presented the rare spectacle of a land where there are no buildings de-stroyed or demolished by war, and where the mischief of it falls on those who make the war." But we fear for the future: a few more "boxes of tricks," say balloons and dynamite in conjunction, and it will become necessary to give over fighting altogether. What will take the place of fighting? Talk and subterfuge, more international law, and men trained from boyhood to lie and dissemble. I suppose this will be it. Then cowards will be even more respected than they are now, and the fittest to survive will not be the ones with the strong backs, the perfect nerve force, and the "red blood in their necks." The Orientals may "come again" in those days. But meanwhile England is hardening and supplying her loins and biceps to push her lances and bayonets; and if Mr. Edison and his fellows will only confine themselves to inventions of civil importance there is yet hope that the rapid-fire guns will get out of order, that the machinery in the big ships will not work properly in action, and that the balloon may be carried out of its course by the wind. If you happen in the mean time to be in London in June, take a run down to Aldershot and see Tommy at his very best.

The Uprising in Chihuahua

Press despatches report an insurrection in Chihuahua, and it is not at all surprising. Having just returned from that country, I saw and associated with the people who are now in the attitude of insurgents. Amalla I have never heard of, but Santaana, whose picture I reproduce, was the man who was second in command of the Mexican force that killed Captain Crawford in '85, and who succeeded to the leadership when

The Uprising in Chihuahua. *Authors' photoengraving.*

Chato, the Apache, shot the chief of the Mexicans. He is a subsidized outlaw, hired by the government to fight in the mountains, but when recently called upon to bring in his people to help take the town of Temochicu—where the fight occurred in the church, and where eighty-five men killed three hundred and fifty soldiers before they were cleaned up—he refused to act against the insurgents. The authorities in Guerrero, which is the important town of the district, tried to disarm him and his forces. The latter took position in an old adobe bull-ring, held off the government forces until nightfall, and then escaped. He was shot in the knee, and was lame when I saw him. One of his men, in describing their escape to me, said, "When we were three miles down the road we could still hear the troops firing into the bull-ring." He was then proscribed. He lives in Rincon, a little mud town lying at the foot of a pass into the mountains, and that pass was fortified with rifle-pits, and will be held by these people later to cover their retreat into the Sierra Madre.

The whole country is in a state of famine as the result of crop failures. Beans are worth fourteen dollars a bushel. But this year they will raise good crops, since they have had good rainfalls. There are a great many men who are out in the mountains or declared banditti by the government. The town of Tejolochachic is the headquarters for a band of outlaws, and three men were killed in a terrific fight right across the street from where we staid the first night in town. The head politico and other leading men are terrorized, and dare not leave their doors. They have been repeatedly shot at, and the doorway of the head politico in question is all bullet-marked. The people of this country have risen in rebellion many times in the old days, and have repeatedly captured the city of Chihuahua, and unless President Diaz sends two regiments of cavalry, two regiments of infantry, and a battery immediately to cope with the insurgent forces, they will grow in strength until a revolution of great consequence will develop.

The people are brave mountaineers who love fighting, and they are very much dissatisfied. They are all armed with Winchesters and Colts, well mounted, and with the vast mountain wilderness of the Sierra Madre as a base. They are poor and short of cartridges, which is their only handicap.

The revolutionists will, however, fail, for in all probability a large force will be sent against them. A battle will follow, and when the smoke clears away, if the federal troops are victorious, there will not be anything left of Santa Tomas, Tejolochachic, and Rincon except little piles of mud, for such is the resolute way in which Mexican officers treat the people who "go out."

Black Water and Shallows

The morning broke gray and lowering, and the clouds rolled in heavy masses across the sky. I was sitting out on a log washing a shirt, and not distinguishing myself as a laundryman either, for one shirt will become excessively dirty in a week, and no canoeist can have more than that, as will be seen when you consider that he has to carry everything which he owns on his back. My guide had packed up our little "kit" and deposited it skilfully in the *Necoochee*—a sixteen-foot canoe of the Rice Lake pattern.

We were about to start on a cruise down a river which the lumbermen said could not be "run," as it was shallow and rocky. We could find no one who had been down it, and so, not knowing anything about it, we regarded it as a pleasant prospect. "Harrison," being a professional guide and hunter, had mostly come in contact with people—or "sports," as he called them—who had no sooner entered the woods than they were overcome with a desire to slay. No fatigue or exertion was too great when the grand purpose was to kill the deer and despoil the trout streams, but to go wandering aimlessly down a stream which by general consent was impracticable for boats, and then out into the clearings where the mountain-spring was left behind, and where logs and mill-dams and agriculturists took the place of the deer and the trout, was a scheme which never quite got straightened out in his mind. With many misgivings, and a very clear impression that I was mentally deranged, "Has" allowed that "we're all aboard."

We pushed out into the big lake and paddled. As we skirted the shores the wind howled through the giant hemlocks, and the ripples ran away into white-caps on the far shore. As I wielded my double-blade paddle and instinctively enjoyed the wildness of the day, I also indulged in a conscious calculation of how long it would take my shirt to dry on my back. It is such a pity to mix a damp shirt up with the wild storm, as it hurries over the dark woods and the black water, that I felt misgivings; but, to be perfectly accurate, they divided my attention, and, after all, man is only noble by fits and starts.

We soon reached the head of the river, and a water-storage dam and a mile of impassable rapids made a "carry" or "portage" necessary. Slinging our packs and taking the seventy-pound canoe on our shoulders, we started down the trail. The torture of this sort of thing is as exquisitely perfect in its way as any ever devised. A trunk-porter in a summer hotel simply does for a few seconds what we do by the hour, and as for reconciling this to an idea of physical enjoyment, it cannot be done. It's a subtle mental process altogether indefinable; but your enthusiast is a person who would lose all if he reasoned any, and to suffer like an anchorite is always a part of a sportsman's programme. The person who tilts back in a chair on the veranda of a summer hotel, while he smokes cigars and gazes vacantly into space, is your only true philosopher; but he is not a sportsman. The woods and the fields and the broad roll of the ocean do not beckon to him to come out among them. He detests all their sensations, and believes nothing holy except the dinner-hour, and with his bad appetite that too is flat, stale, and unprofitable. A real sportsman, of the nature-loving type, must go tramping or paddling or riding about over the waste places of the earth, with his dinner in his pocket. He is alive to the terrible strain of the "carry," and to the quiet pipe when the day is done. The campfire contemplation, the beautiful quiet of the misty morning on the still water, enrapture him, and his eye dilates, his nerves tingle, and he is in a conflagration of ecstasy. When he is going—going—faster—faster into the boil of the waters, he hears the roar and boom ahead, and the black rocks crop up in thickening masses to dispute his way. He is fighting a game battle with the elements, and they are remorseless. He may break his leg or lose his life in the tip-over which is imminent, but the fool is happy—let him die.

But we were left on the "carry," and it is with a little thrill of joy and the largest sigh of relief possible when we again settle the boat in the water. Now you should understand why it is better to have one shirt and wash it often. My "canoe kit" is the best arranged and the most perfect in the world, as no other canoeist will possibly admit, but which is nevertheless a fact. One blanket, a light shelter-tent, a cooking outfit, which folds up in a sort of Japanese way, a light axe, two canvas packs, and tea, bacon, and flour. This does not make long reading, but it makes a load for a man when it's all packed up, and a canoeist's baggage must be cut to the strength of his back. It is a great piece of confidence in which I will indulge you when I caution you not to pick out invalids for canoe companions. If a *burro* would take kindly to backwoods navigation, I should enjoy the society of one, though it would not be in the nature of a *burro* to swing an axe, as indeed there are many fine gentlemen who can not do a good job at that; and if one at least of the party cannot, the camp-fires will go out early at nights, and it is more than probable that the companions will have less than twenty toes between them at the end of the cruise.

All these arrangements being perfected, you are ready to go ahead, and in the wilderness you have only one anxiety, and that is about the "grub." If the canoe turn over, the tea, the sugar, and the flour will mix up with the surrounding elements, and only the bacon will remain to nourish you until you strike the clearings, and there are few men this side 70° north latitude who will gormandize on that alone.

The long still water is the mental side of canoeing, as the rapid is the life and movement. The dark woods tower on either side, and the clear banks, full to their fat sides, fringed with trailing vines and drooping ferns, have not the impoverished look of civilized rivers. The dark water wells along, and the branches droop to kiss it. In front the gray sky is answered back by the water reflection, and the trees lie out as though hung in the air, forming a gateway, always receding. Here and there an old monarch of the forest has succumbed to the last blow and fallen across the stream. It reaches out ever so far with its giant stems, and the first branch had started sixty feet from the ground. You may have to chop a way through, or you may force your canoe through the limbs and gather a crowd of little broken branches to escort you along the stream. The original forest tree has a character all its own, and I never see one but I think of the artist who drew second-growth timber and called it "the forest primeval." The quietness of the woods, with all their solemnity, permitting no bright or over-dressed plant to obtrude itself, is rudely shocked by the garish painted thing as the yellow polished *Necoochee* glides among them. The water-rat dives with a tremendous splash as he sees the big monster glide by his sedge home. The kingfisher springs away from his perch on the dead top with loud chatterings when we glide into his notice. The crane takes off from his grassy "set back" in a deliberate manner, as though embarking on a tour to Japan, a thing not to be hurriedly done. The mink eyes you from his sunken log, and, grinning in his most savage little manner, leaps away. These have all been disturbed in their wild homes as they were about to lunch off the handiest trout, and no doubt they hate us in their liveliest manner; but the poor trout under the boat compensate us with their thanks. The mud-turtle is making his way up-stream, as we can tell by the row of bubbles which arise in his wake; and the "skaters," as I call the little insects which go skipping about like a lawyer's point in an argument, part as we go by. The mosquitoes, those desperate little villains who dispute your happiness in the woods, are there, but they smell the tar and oil of our warpaint, and can only hum in their anger. A stick cracks in the brush, and with all the dash and confidence of a city girl as she steps from her front door, a little spotted fawn walks out on a sedge bank from among the alders. He does not notice us, but in his stupid little way looks out the freshest water-grass, and the hunter in the stern of the boat cuts his paddle through the water, and the canoe glides silently up until right under his nose. We are still and silent. The little thing raises its head and looks us full in the eye, and then continues to feed as before. I talk to him quietly, and say, "Little man, do not come near the ponds or the rivers, for you will not live to have five prongs on your antlers if any one but such good people as we see you." He looks up, and seems to say, "You are noisy, but I do not care." "Now run; and if you ever see anything in the forest which resembles us, run for your life"; and with a bound the little innocent has regained the dark aisles of the woods. You loll back on your pack, your pipe going lazily; your hat is off; you moralize, and think thoughts which have dignity. You drink in the spell of the forest, and dream of the birch barks and the red warriors who did the same thing a couple of centuries since. But as thoughts vary so much in individuals, and have but an indirect bearing on canoeing, I will proceed without them. The low swamp, with its soft timber, gives place to hills and beech ridges, and the old lord of the forest for these last

hundred years towers up majestically. The smaller trees fight for the sunlight, and thus the ceaseless war of nature goes on quietly, silently, and alone. The miserable "witch-hoppel" leads its lusty plebeian life, satisfied to spring its half-dozen leaves, and not dreaming to some day become an oak. The gentle sigh of the forest, the hum of insects, and the chatter and peal of the birds have gone into harmony with a long, deep, swelling sound, becoming louder and louder, until finally it drowns all else.

The canoe now glides more rapidly. The pipe is laid one side. The paddle is grasped firmly, and with a firm eye I regard the "grub" pack which sits up in the bow, and resolve to die if necessary in order that it may not sink if we turn over. The river turns, and the ominous growl of the rapids is at hand.

"Hold her—hold her now—to the right of the big rock; then swing to the far shore: if we go to the right, we are gone."

"All right; let her stern come round," and we drop away.

No talking now, but with every nerve and muscle tense, and your eye on the boil of the water, you rush along. You back water and paddle, the stern swings, she hangs for an instant, she falls in the current, and with a mad rush you take it like a hunting-man a six-bar gate. Now paddle, paddle, paddle. It looks bad—we cannot make it—yes—all right, and we are on the far shore, with the shallows on the other side. This little episode was successful, but, as you well know, it cannot last. The next rift, and with a bump she is hung upon a sunken rock, and —jump! jump!—we both flounder overboard in any way possible, so it is well and quickly done. One man loses his hold, the other swings the boat off, and, kicking and splashing for a foothold, the demoralized outfit shoots along. At last one is found, and then at a favorable rock we embark again.

You are now wet, but the tea and sugar are safe, so it's a small matter. A jam of logs and tops is "hung up" on a particularly nasty place, and you have a time getting the

Black Water. *Painting in private collection.*

boat around it. You walk on rotten tops while the knots stick up beneath you like sabres. "Has" floats calmly out to sea, as it were, on a detached log which he is cutting, and with a hopeless look of despair he totters, while I yell, "Save the axe, —— you— save the axe!" and over he goes, only to get wet and very disgusted, both of which will wear off in time. For a mile the water is so shallow that the boat will not run loaded, and we lead her along as we wade, now falling in over our heads, sliding on slippery stones, hurting our feet, wondering why we had come at all. The boat gets loose, and my heart stands still as the whole boat-load of blankets and grub with our pipes and tobacco started off for the settlements—or "drifting to thunder," as Bret Harte said of Chiquita. There was rather a lively and enthusiastic pursuit instituted then, the details of which are forgotten, as my mind was focussed on the grub-pack, but we got her. About this time the soles let go on my tennis shoes, and my only pair of trousers gave way. These things, however, become such mere details as to be scarcely noticed when you have travelled since sunrise up to

your waist in water, and are tired, footsore, and hungry. It is time to go ashore and camp.

You scrape away a rod square of dirt, chunks, witch-hoppel, and dead leaves, and make a fire. You dry your clothes while you wear the blanket and guide the shelter-tent, and to a casual observer it would look as though the savage had come again; but he would detect a difference, because a white man in a blanket is about as inspiring a sight as an Indian with a plug-hat.

Finally the coffee boils, the tent is up, and the bough bed laid down. You lean against the dead log and swap lies with the guide; and the greatest hunters I have ever known have all been magnificent liars. The two go together. I should suspect a man who was deficient. Since no one ever believes hunters' yarns, it has come to be a pleasurable pastime, in which a man who has not hunted considerably can't lie properly without offending the intelligence of that part of his audience who have.

The morning comes too soon, and after you are packed up and the boat loaded, if you are in a bad part of the river you do this: you put away your pipe, and with a grimace and a shudder you step out into the river up to your neck and get wet. The morning is cold, and I, for one, would not allow a man who was perfectly dry to get into my boat, for fear he might have some trepidation about getting out promptly if the boat was "hung up" on a rock; and in the woods all nature is subservient to the "grub."

Hour after hour we waded along. A few rods of still water and "Has" would cut off large chews of tobacco, and become wonderfully cynical as to the caprices of the river. The still water ends around the next point. You charge the thing nobly, but end up in the water up to your neck with the "grub" safe, and a mile or so more of wading in prospect.

Then the river narrows, and goes tumbling off down a dark cañon cut through the rocks. We go ashore and "scout the place," and then begin to let the boat down on a line. We hug the black sides like ants, while the water goes to soapsuds at our feet. The boat bobs and rocks, and is nearly upset in a place where we cannot follow it through. We must take it up a ledge about thirty feet high, and after puffing and blowing and feats of maniacal strength, we at last have it again in the water. After some days of this thing we found from a statistician we had dropped 1100 feet in about fifty-one miles, and with the well-known propensity of water to flow downhill, it can be seen that difficulties were encountered. You cannot carry a boat in the forest, and you will discover enough reasons why in a five-minute trail to make their enumeration tiresome. The zest of the whole thing lies in not knowing the difficulties beforehand, and then, if properly equipped, a man who sits at a desk the year through can find no happier days than he will in his canoe when the still waters run through the dark forests and the rapid boils below.

The Advance-Guard, or the Military Sacrifice

Where a good system of vidette-work is kept up it is seldom that the main body of the advance-guard is surprised or ambuscaded. Our American Indians when at war are much given to stalking an enemy. They charge and retreat with marvellous celerity, and by their knowledge of the country in which they operate, they always retire to the most difficult ground, of which there are vast areas in our West, of widely different sorts. The Apache takes to the high stony peaks of the Sierra, where he can look down on his pursuers. The old Comanches used to "pull out" into the great deserts of the Staked Plain, and many a command has nearly famished for water on their trail. The Northern Plains Indians thread the defiles of the Bad Lands, which are winding and devious, and of which they know every foot. This is the country that my drawing represents. It is like the bottom of the sea in contour, taking strange forms, but dry and verdureless. When troops are scouting or moving through these lands they need all their eyes, and when the vidette ranges out in front and flank he is at the mercy of his pot-hunting foe. He knows it himself, and as he moves along he's a good man if his heart doesn't thump a little. A Sioux can lay along a clay butte and "pump a Winchester" into an advancing trooper, and can only be dislodged or "developed" by the advance of a heavy body of troops. I remember to have seen two young negroes of the Ninth Cavalry go down a nasty defile

commanded by a thousand points, when they had no more chance of escape than poor shooting would afford. The Sixth Cavalry did lots of "Bad Land scouting" in the last Sioux outbreak, and from an impression I received there I got my picture, though I did not see a man killed. I have experienced myself the feeling of going up a narrow trail to a mesa which was supposed to harbor hundreds of Sioux, and I can't remember that I was enjoying myself at the time, either.

The remorselessness of war, however, makes this advance necessary, on the principle that it is better to sacrifice one or two men than a dozen, or possibly all of the command. I can recall the history of several ambuscades of United States troops in our Western Indian wars which were made possible by neglect of good advance-work; and in our earlier wars in the more eastern portions of the continent there were many such, notably that of Braddock. In reading the diary of the celebrated Major Robert Rogers, the ranger chief of 1757, I note what great stress he lays on the vidette-work in his plan of discipline, and he was the most successful Indian-fighter who ever lived in America. I cannot forbear to give some extracts:

"Whenever you are ordered out to the enemy's forts or frontiers for discoveries, if your number be small, march in a single file, keeping at such a distance from each other as to prevent one shot from killing

The Advance-Guard, or the Military Sacrifice. *Authors' photoengraving.*

two men, sending one man or more forward, and the like on each side at a distance of twenty yards from the main body."

"If you march over marshes or soft ground change your position, and march abreast of each other to prevent the enemy from tracking you, as they would do if you marched in a single file. March until it is quite dark before you encamp, which do, if possible, on a piece of ground that may afford your sentries the advantage of seeing or hearing the enemy at some considerable distance, keeping one-half of your body awake alternately through the night."

"If you oblige the enemy to retreat, be careful, in pursuit of them, to keep out your flanking parties to prevent them from gaining eminences or rising grounds, in which case they would, perhaps, be able to rally and repulse you in their turn."

"When you encamp at night fix your sentries in such a manner as not to be relieved from the main body till morning, profound secrecy and silence being often of the last importance in these cases."

"Before you leave your encampment send out small parties to scout round it, to see if there be any appearance or track of an enemy that might have been near you during the night."

"When you stop for refreshments let a small party waylay the path you came in lest the enemy should be pursuing."

"If the enemy pursue your rear, take a circle till you come to your own tracks, and there form an ambush to receive them."

All this is interesting and curious, and was well followed by that redoubtable leader. Our American Indians know everything that goes on for forty miles on every side of the movement of the main body, and our cavalrymen of the Plains have been taught the lesson. So up the cañons and over the rocks goes the individual point of the big machine, "with his life on his sleeve." There is no touch of elbow, and no comfort or glory to gain. He hears a report, feels a shock, reels in his saddle, while his stricken horse plunges under him, and then the dull brain reels and faints; but the captain in command knows that the ground in front is occupied, and take measures in accordance.

A Gallop Through the Midway

The Midway is a rather engaging place. If it were less commercial it would be great. It is not oppressively "tough." It did not shock. Mr. Henry Watterson, as he himself has assured us, and I found myself sufficiently fibrous to withstand it. One can satiate one's appetite for strange sights and sounds, and regale one's self with several hundred distinct and separate odors. He can hear a Viennese girl mix "Larboard Watch, Ahoy!" with twenty glasses of beer, or two Turks swear cheerfully at each other in perfect English. At the door of every building is a man who renders into Chicagoese the attractions within. Or, rather, he did until President Higinbotham put his vocal gymnastics under the ban; and now he earns his salary by exercising his powers of pantomime, inviting the passers-by within in an agony of dumb-show, the while violently whacking with his cane a large sign on which is printed the "patter" with which he was wont to assail the ears of the multitude. There is the muffled beating of tomtoms, the shuffling of many feet, the popcorn and lemonade, and thousands of dull, dusty, frowzy folks who stare and gape and imbibe oxlike impressions. With these are people of courage and behavior, and professional ladies from Paris with salmon-colored hair and black eyebrows. The bulk of the moving throng have "corn field" written all over them, and these children of Egypt (that is, lower Illinois) wear bonnets and costumes founded on Worth, but widely at variance. There is much merriment, especially at night, but one sees little drunkenness. The Columbian Guards do not stand in the position of a soldier; and if they did, I am not sure it would serve any good purpose beyond pleasing the eye. Strange fierce-looking negroes who have evidently not felt the elevating influence of South Carolina pass you, and Bedouins who are over-conditioned for folks who eat only barley and figs.

With the clank of a crooked sabre a man in blue clothes, turban, and red leather shoes strides down the middle of the street, and you feel with the sense of admiration creeping over you that if you were not an American you would be a savage of that type. One of Diamond Dick's Indians shuffles along in that weak-kneed, in-toed plod which speaks of the thorough horseman when he "hits the flat." And so they go —humanity in all its dissimilitude. A composite photograph might be a goat or something else dear to the Darwinian heart. After the dim wonder inspired by regarding these images of the Creator had palled, along came a polyglot whose friend I was. He was an officer in the United States navy, and this world is a very little pill to him. We did a lunch in the German *schloss,* and when the coffee, cigars, and the bill came round, I could feel the "hind *cincha"* tighten. The coffee and cigars were great, but the bill was greater, and the plunking of the buzzard dollars on the table suggested that I was paying off the mortgage on the farm. We walked up and saw the "Wild East," where the Arabs ride at top speed, and throw sticks which represent darts at each other, and catch them at times in midair. I can understand why writers and artists have dwelt so long on the Bedouin, for if he is not a dashing fellow, with his color and hightailed horse, nothing can be. The racing dromedaries, too, fill me with wonder. I can never become used to a camel; he seems so remote, does this great shuffling tortuous beast, and he is forever associating himself with old red sandstone, ichthyornes, and jokes from *Punch*.

At the place where the Bedouin women dance, wherever it is, we found a circle of honest Illinois yeomen seated about on chairs, grinning cheerfully as the dancing women whirled. They ruined the environment and consequently the dance. My polyglot friend fired Arabic at the women, close range, and they replied. The audience rewarded us with their attention, and one old lady asked me if I was a Turk—because I looked so intelligent as the conversation proceeded, I suppose—and I said: "Si, señora, me heap Turk," and she believed me, and we were both happy.

We did all the savages in turn, as every one else must do who goes there, and Buffalo Bill's besides, where I renewed my first love.

In the evening it rained, and the Midway was somewhat gloomy. The torture-dance at the Algerian Theatre was attractive to me, but the bell-boy at the Auditorium assured me that it was all a "low fake, see!" and would have explained it all if it had not been my bedtime.

Cairo Street contains the theatre where

Columbian Exposition—A Note from the Wild East in the Midway Plaisance. *Authors' photoengraving.*

the women dance in such a shockingly interesting way. It is best not to dwell on this thing. It has been sat upon by the people who best know what is proper or not, and one only goes there in order to verify their judgment. It is now a novelty to Americans, but I fear it would not stand the test of time. As I was looking at the sculptured form of a young woman in the Art Building, a rather excited rural person with a soft hat on the back of his head nudged me, and confided, "Say, the people of Kalamazoo are gettin' used to this yer," and I think that after the people of America could adjust their vision in a cold square gaze at the Cairo girls they would say, "Loie Fuller can win under a pull."

Such were my impressions at the Midway as I crawled into one of those cattle cars which bear the weary sightseer into the city. It fulfils its mission as a great educator, and the universal Yankee nation has an opportunity to observe that part of the world which does not wear Derby hats and spend its life in a top-and-bottom tussel with a mortgage bearing eight per cent.

An Outpost of Civilization

The hacienda San José de Bavicora lies northwest from Chihuahua 225 of the longest miles on the map. The miles run up long hills and dive into rocky cañons; they stretch over never-ending burnt plains, and across the beds of tortuous rivers thick with scorching sand. And there are three ways to make this travel. Some go on foot—which is best, if one has time—like the Tahuramaras; others take it ponyback, after the Mexican manner; and persons with no time and a great deal of money go in a coach. At first thought this last would seem to be the best, but the Guerrero stage has never failed to tip over, and the company make you sign away your natural rights, and almost your immortal soul, before they will allow you to embark. So it is not the best way at all, if I may judge from my own experience. We had a coach which seemed to choose the steepest hill on the route, where it then struck a stone, which heaved the coach, pulled out the king-pin, and what I remember of the occurrence is full of sprains and aches and general gloom. Guerrero, too, is only three-fourths of the way to Bavicora, and you can only go there if Don Gilberto, the *patron* of the hacienda—or, if you know him well enough, "Jack"—will take you in the ranch coach.

After bumping over the stones all day for five days, through a blinding dust, we were glad enough when we suddenly came out of the tall timber in the mountain pass and espied the great yellow plain of Bavicora stretching to the blue hills of the Sierra. In

an hour's ride more, through a chill wind, we were at the ranch. We pulled up at the entrance, which was garnished by a bunch of cow-punchers, who regarded us curiously as we pulled our aching bodies and bandaged limbs from the Concord and limped into the *patio*.

To us was assigned the room of honor, and after shaking ourselves down on a good bed, with mattress and sheeting, we recovered our cheerfulness. A hot toddy, a roaring fireplace, completed the effect. The floor was strewn with bear and wolf skin rugs; it had pictures and draperies on the walls, and in a corner a wash-basin and pitcher—so rare in these parts—was set on a stand, grandly suggestive of the refinements of luxury we had attained to. I do not wish to convey the impression that Mexicans do not wash, because there are brooks enough in Mexico if they want to use them, but wash-basins are the advance-guards of progress, and we had been on the outposts since leaving Chihuahua.

Jack's man William had been ever-present, and administered to our slightest wish; his cheerful "Good-mo'nin', gemmen," as he lit the fire, recalled us to life, and after a rub-down I went out to look at the situation.

Jack's ranch is a great straggling square of mud walls enclosing two *patios*, with adobe corrals and out-buildings, all obviously constructed for the purposes of defence. It was built in 1770 by the Jesuits, and while the English and Dutch were fighting for the possession of the Mohawk Valley, Bavicora was an outpost of civilization, as it is to-day. Locked in a strange language, on parchment stored in vaults in Spain, are the records of this enterprise. In 1840 the good fathers were murdered by the Apaches, the country devasted and deserted, and the cattle and horses hurried to the mountain lairs of the Apache devils. The place lay idle and unreclaimed for years, threatening to crumble back to the dust of which it was made. Near by are curious mounds on the banks of a dry *arroyo*. The punchers have dug down into these ruins, and found adobe walls, mud plasterings, skeletons, and bits of woven goods. They call them the "Montezumas." All this was to be changed. In 1882 an American cowboy—which was Jack—accompanied by two companions, penetrated south from Arizona, and as he looked from the mountains over the fair plain of Bavicora, he said, "I will take this." The Apaches were on every hand; the country was terrorized to the gates of Chihuahua. The stout heart of the pioneer was not disturbed, and he made his word good. By purchase he acquired the plain, and so much more that you could not ride round it in two weeks. He moved in with his hardy punchers, and fixed up Bavicora so it would be habitable. He chased the Indians off his ranch whenever he "cut their sign." After a while the Mexican *vaqueros* from below overcame their terror, when they saw the American hold his own with the Apache devils, and by twos and threes and half-dozens they came up to take service, and now there are two hundred who lean on Jack and call him *patron*. They work for him and they follow him on the Apache trail, knowing he will never run away, believing in his beneficence and trusting to his courage.

I sat on a mud-bank and worked away at a sketch of the yellow sunlit walls of the mud-ranch, with the great plain running away like the ocean into a violet streak under the blue line of the Peña Blanca. In the rear rises a curious broken formation of hills like millions of ruins of Rhine castles.

The *lobos** howl by night, and the Apache is expected to come at any instant. The old *criada* or serving-woman who makes the beds saw her husband killed at the front door, and every man who goes out of the *patio* has a large assortment of the most improved artillery on his person. Old carts with heavy wooden wheels like millstones stand about. Brown people with big straw hats and gay *serapes* lean lazily against the gray walls. Little pigs carry on the contest with nature, game-chickens strut, and clumsy puppies tumble over each other in joyful play; *burros* stand about sleepily, only indicating life by suggestive movements of their ears, while at intervals a pony, bearing its lithe rider, steps from the gate, and, breaking into an easy and graceful lope, goes away into the waste of land.

I rose to go inside, and while I gazed I grew exalted in the impression that here, in the year of 1893, I had rediscovered a Fort Laramie after Mr. Parkman's well-known description. The foreman, Tom Bailey, was dressed in store clothes, and our room had bedstead and a wash-basin; otherwise it answered very well. One room was piled high with dried meat, and the great stomachs of oxen filled with tallow; another room is a store full of goods—calicoes, buckskin, *riatas,* yellow leather shoes, guns, and other quaint plunder adapted to the needs of a people who sit on the ground and live on meat and cornmeal.

"Charlie Jim," the Chinese cook, has a big room with a stove in it, and he and the stove are a never-ending wonder to all the folks, and the fame of both has gone across the mountains to Sonora and to the south. Charlie is an autocrat in his curious Chinese way, and by the dignity of his position as Mr. Jack's private cook, and his unknown antecedents, he conjures the Mexicans and d—— the Texans, which latter refuse to take him seriously and kill him, as they would a "proper" man. Charlie Jim, in return, entertains ideas of Texans which he secretes, except when they dine with Jack, when he may be heard to mutter, "Cake

* Wolves.

"Puncher Rope Man All Same Horse." *Painting in Bradford Brinton Memorial.*

and pie no good for puncher, make him fat and lazy"; and when he crosses the *patio* and they fling a rope over his foot, he becomes livid, and breaks out, "D—— puncher; d—— rope; rope man all same horse; d—— puncher; no good that way."

The *patron* has the state apartment, and no one goes there with his hat on; but the relations with his people are those of a father and children. An old gray man approaches; they touch the left arm with the right—an abbreviated hug; say "Buenos dias, patron!" "Buenos dias, Don Sabino!" and they shake hands. A California saddle stands on a rack by the desk, and the latter is littered with photographs of men in London clothes and women in French dresses, the latter singularly out of character with their surroundings. The old *criada* squats silently by the fireplace, her head enveloped in her blue *rebozo,* and deftly rolls her ciga-rette. She alone, and one white bull-dog, can come and go without restraint.

The *administrador,* which is Mr. Tom Bailey, of Texas, moves about in the discharge of his responsibilities, and they are universal; anything and everything is his work, from the negotiation for the sale of five thousand head of cattle to the "busting" of a bronco which no one else can "crawl."

The clerk is in the store, with his pink boy's face, a pencil behind his ear, and a big sombrero, trying to look as though he had lived in these wilds longer than at San Francisco, which he finds an impossible part. He has acquired the language and the disregard of time necessary to one who would sell a real's worth of cotton cloth to a Mexican.

The forge in the blacksmith's shop is going, and one puncher is cutting another puncher's hair in the sunlight; ponies are being lugged in on the end of lariats, and thrown down, tied fast, and left in a convulsive heap, ready to be shod at the disposition of their riders.

On the roof of the house are two or three men looking and pointing to the little black specks on the plain far away, which are the cattle going into the *lagunas* to drink.

The second *patio,* or the larger one, is entered by a narrow passage, and here you find horses and saddles and punchers coming and going, saddling and unsaddling their horses, and being bucked about or dragged on a rope. In the little doorways to the rooms of the men stand women in calico dresses and blue cotton *rebozos,* while the dogs and pigs lie about, and little brown *vaqueros* are ripening in the sun. In the rooms you find pottery, stone *metates* for grinding the corn, a fireplace, a symbol of the Catholic Church, some *serapes,* some rope, and buckskin. The people sit on a mat on the floor, and make cigarettes out of native tobacco and corn-husks, or rolled *tortillas;* they laugh and chat in low tones, and altogether occupy the tiniest mental world, hardly larger than the *patio,* and not venturing beyond the little mud town of Temozachic, forty miles over the hills. Physically the men vacillate between the most intense excitement and a comatose state of idleness, where all is quiet and slothful, in contrast to the mad whirl of the roaring *rodeo.*

In the haciendas of old Mexico one will find the law and custom of the feudal days. All the laws of Mexico are in protection of the land-owner. The master is without restraint, and the man lives dependent on his caprice. The *patron* of Bavicora, for instance, leases land to a Mexican, and it is one of the arrangements that he shall drive the ranch coach to Chihuahua when it goes. All lessees of land are obliged to follow the *patron* to war, and, indeed, since the com-

A Hair-cut à la Puncher. *Authors' photoengraving.*

mon enemy, the Apache, in these parts is as like to harry the little as the great, it is exactly to his interest to wage the war. Then, too, comes the responsibility of the *patron* to his people. He must feed them in the famine, he must arbitrate their disputes, and he must lead them at all times. If through improvidence their work-cattle die or give out, he must restock them, so that they may continue the cultivation of the land, all of which is not altogether profitable in a financial way, as we of the North may think, where all business is done of the "hold you responsible, sir," basis.

The *vaqueros* make their own saddles and *reatas;* only the iron saddle-rings, the rifles, and the knives come from the *patron,* and where he gets them God alone knows, and the puncher never cares. No doctor attends the sick or disabled, old women's nursing standing between life and death. The Creator in His providence has arranged it so that simple folks are rarely sick, and a sprained ankle, a bad bruise from a steer's horn or a pitching horse, are soon remedied by rest and a good condition. At times instant and awful death overtakes the puncher —a horse in a gopher-hole, a mad steer, a chill with a knife, a blue hole where the .45 went in, a quicksand closing overhead, and a cross on a hill-side are all.

Never is a door closed. Why they were put up I failed to discover. For days I tried faithfully to keep mine shut, but every one coming or going left it open, so that I gave it up in despair. There are only two windows in the ranch of San José de Bavicora, one in our chamber and one in the blacksmith's shop, both opening into the court. In fact, I found those were the only two windows in the state, outside of the big city. The Mexicans find that their enemies are prone to shoot through these apertures, and so they have accustomed themselves to do without them, which is as it should be, since it removes the temptation.

One night the *patron* gave a *baile.* The *vaqueros* all came with their girls, and a string band rendered music with a very dancy swing. I sat in a corner and observed the man who wears the big hat and who

throws the rawhide as he cavorted about with his girl, and the way they dug up the dust out of the dirt floor soon put me to coughing. "Candles shed their soft lustre— and tallow" down the backs of our necks, and the band scraped and thrummed away in a most serious manner. One man had a harp, two had primitive fiddles, and one a guitar. One old fiddler was the leader, and as he bowed his head on his instrument I could not keep my eyes off him. He had come from Sonora, and was very old; he looked as though he had had his share of a very rough life; he was never handsome as a boy, I am sure, but the weather and starvation and time had blown him and crumbled him into a ruin which resembled the preexisting ape from which the races sprang. If he had never committed murder, it was for lack of opportunity; and Sonora is a long travel from Plymouth Rock.

Tom Bailey, the foreman, came round to me, his eyes dancing, and his shock of hair standing up like a Circassian beauty's, and pointing, he said, "Thar's a woman who's prettier than a speckled pup; put your twine on her." Then, as master of ceremonies, he straightened up and sang out over the fiddles and noise: "Dance, thar, you fellers, or you'll git the gout."

In an adjoining room there was a very heavy jug of strong-water, and thither the men repaired to pick up, so that as the night wore on their brains began to whirl after their legs, and they whooped at times in a way to put one's nerves on edge. The band scraped the harder and the dance waxed fast, the spurs clinked, and *bang, bang, bang* went the Winchester rifles in the *patio,* while the chorus "Viva el patron" rang around the room—the Old Guard was in action.

We sat in our room one evening when in filed the *vaqueros* and asked to be allowed to sing for the *patron.* They sat on my bed and on the floor, while we occupied the other; they had their hats in their hands, and their black, dreamy eyes were diverted as though overcome by the magnificence of the apartment. They hemmed and coughed, until finally one man, who was evidently the leader, pulled himself together and began, in a high falsetto, to sing; after two or three words the rest caught on, and they got through the line, when they stopped; thus was one leading and the others following to the end of the line. It was strange, wild music—a sort of general impression of a boys' choir with wild discordance, each man giving up his soul as he felt moved. The refrain always ended, for want of breath, in a low, expiring howl, leaving the audience in suspense; but quickly they get at it again, and the rise of the tenor chorus continues. The songs are largely about love and women and doves and flowers, in all of which nonsense punchers take only a perfunctory interest in real life.

These are the amusements—although the puncher is always roping for practice, and everything is fair game for his skill; hence dogs, pigs, and men have become as expert in dodging the rope as the *vaqueros* are in throwing it. A mounted man, in passing, will always throw his rope at one sitting in a doorway, and then try to get away before he can retaliate by jerking his own rope over his head. I have seen a man repair to the roof and watch a doorway through which he expected some comrade to pass shortly, and watch for an hour to be ready to drop his noose about his shoulders.

The ranch fare is very limited, and at intervals men are sent to bring back a steer from the water-holes, which is dragged to the front door and there slaughtered. A day of feasting ensues, and the doorways and the gutter-pipes and the corral fences are festooned with the beef left to dry in the sun.

There is the serious side of the life. The Apache is an evil which Mexicans have come to regard as they do the meteoric hail, the lightning, the drought, and any other horror not to be averted. They quarrel between themselves over land and stock, and there are a great many men out in the mountains who are proscribed by the government. Indeed, while we journeyed on the road and were stopping one night in a little mud town, we were startled by a fusillade of shots, and in the morning were informed

that two men had been killed the night before, and various others wounded. At another time a Mexican, with his followers, had invaded our apartment and expressed a disposition to kill Jack, but he found Jack was willing to play his game and gave up the enterprise. On the ranch the men had discovered some dead stock which had been killed with a knife. Men were detailed to roam the country in search of fresh trails of these cattle-killers. I asked the foreman what would happen in case they found a trail which could be followed, and he said, "Why, we would follow it until we came up, and then kill them." If a man is to "hold down" a big ranch in Northern Mexico he has got to be "all man," because it is "a man's job," as Mr. Bailey, of Los Ojos, said —and he knows.

Jack himself is the motive force of the enterprise, and he disturbs the quiet of this waste of sunshine by his presence for about six months in the year. With his strong spirit, the embodiment of generations of pioneers, he faces the Apache, the marauder, the financial risks. He spurs his listless people on to toil, he permeates every detail, he storms, and greater men than he have sworn like troopers under less provocation than he has at times; but he has snatched from the wolf and the Indian the fair land of Bavicora, to make it fruitful to his generation.

There lies the hacienda San José de Bavicora, gray and silent on the great plain, with the mountain standing guard against intruders, and over it the great blue dome of the sky, untroubled by clouds, except little flecks of vapor which stand, lost in immensity, burning bright like opals, as though discouraged from seeking the mountains or the sea whence they came. The marvellous color of the country beckons to the painter; its simple, natural life entrances the blond barbarian, with his fevered brain; and the gaudy *vaquero* and his trappings and his pony are the actors on this noble stage. But one must be appreciative of it all, or he will find a week of rail and a week of stage and a week of horseback all too far for one to travel to see a shadow across the moon.

"Toro, Toro!"

A distinguished newspaper man said to me the other day, in a conversation: "No, I do not like American history; it is brutal—crude—lacking in *finesse*. I prefer that of Germany, France, or Italy." His mind was a well-arranged one, and he lacked imagination. I do, however, like American history, and I think the newspaper man was probably right in his arraignment of it.

I sat on the veranda of the New York Athletic Club at Travers Island one day while and old gentleman by my side reminisced. He had gone to California as a boy, and had owned and operated a cattle ranch there before "the winter of '49," and when he had done I went home and did the picture of "Toro, Toro!" Since I have never seen an ancient California Indian do the "vaquero act," it must stand for what it is worth. And I am prepared to shift a good deal of responsibility on to the gentleman who sat talking on the veranda. The old-time vaqueros were all Indians, and their hats were imported from Chili. They dressed in cotton and leather, and were not the expensive and betinselled beings which have gone into popular fancy any more than the soldiers of Valley Forge were dressed in velvet coats and yellow silk stockings. The handkerchief over the face is worn by all cowboys in the round-up to keep the dust out of their mouths and eyes. Mexicans and Indians never take off a serape until the sun is high, for fear of pneumonia, to which they are much addicted.

I can only tell of the situation of the picture as the old gentleman narrated it, which was like this: "How the men did have to work—at daybreak in the saddle, then scattering up along the draws and cañons, far up into the mountains! Then come the wild cattle from all points, followed by the charging vaqueros, yelling, swinging their *reatas,* until the little bunches melt into the sea of horned animals around which the watchful sentinels gallop, pursuing the brutes that try to leave the herd. At times a maddened steer breaks for the hills, and away he goes, with the mettlesome little pony following, without touch of spur or rein, over gully and chaparral, while the tall graceful vaquero is slowly gathering his rope. A few times the rawhide turns slowly and gracefully in the air, and with a whiz and a jerk the noose has tightened on the horns—two quick turns about the horn of the saddle—the little pony gives a brace, and the steer goes heels up to the ground with a thud that sickens him of any further escapade."

They were glorious old days, now grown mellow to the mind of the man who had long forgotten the anxieties which must have attended his youthful days. It was a quaint baronial existence, under the blue sky, with the mountains standing about, and the whitewashed adobe lying so quiet and contented in the great valley below. The hum of insects, the cigarettes, the blue shadows and the listless waiting for the processes of nature, always slow, in contrast with the bellowing, roaring *rodeo,* the straining ropes and surging muscles, the blood in torrents—and then the profits were a neat sum for a

Toro Toro—An Old Time Californian Vaquero After a Wild Steer.
Authors' wood engraving.

young man to contemplate. But it's all past now—it's a memory. I was in California this spring for the first time, and I saw nothing of it. An old Californian out there said: "No, it's all over—these one-lunged people from New England are running this State—they are raising fruit and wheat and putting up wire fences, and they outvote us. I wish they had never come."

I agreed with him.

The Rebellion in Northern Mexico

Before now it has probably occurred to President Diaz that "kings have cares that wait upon a crown." If not, the uprising in Chihuahua will furnish an example; and yet I fear that the men who are now pressing his troops so sorely will not make a Lexington out of any town in that state, because they have already fired shots in plenty, and none of them have been "heard around the world," and, indeed, I doubt if any one but President Diaz's chief of staff has the ring of them in his ears. I travelled in Chihuahua nearly a year ago, and there was then much muttering. The killing at Tamochi had taken place, and Guerrero was full of wounded soldiers. Santa Anna Perez had not done what was expected of him as a militia chief in that fight, and was "cut off" the Mexican pay-roll, and had a skirmish with the Mexican authorities in the outlying town of Guerrero. He had withdrawn to a place of seclusion where his base of retreat could not be affected. Famine, and the natural tendency "agin the government," and the use of force as a political method, which is a Spanish political legacy to all Spanish Americans, helped him out, and he is now having a career which, while it may not be brief, owing to the terrible mountain wilderness at his back, will yet avail him nothing but the satisfaction of his natural predatory impulses. Already he has defeated, if reports are true, three forces of regular Mexican troops, and is "out still." There are rumors of the Yaqui Indians formally joining

the discontented, which is not unlikely, since they have always been at war with the federal government, and have never been formally conquered. They are a numerous and a warlike people, and with the great reach of the Sierra Madre at their back the problem of their conquest is even more difficult than was our suppression of the Apaches in Arizona and New Mexico.

Some months ago I wrote in the WEEKLY of this uprising, and, at the risk of what all prophets run, I detailed what the Mexican military authorities would be compelled to do, and by now they are doing it. I fear they have the English and American trick down there of sending out an inferior force at first, which is soundly thrashed, which emboldens the enemy, and then the regular government gets red in the face and overdoes the final *coup*.

President Diaz is open to the charge which all his enemies make against him, but he alone can handle Mexico and make life safe, industry possible, and allow civilization a chance with the bepistolled and besabred freebooters who formerly controlled the land, and when a Mexican revolution is started which has a man at its head who would not make a prison-door grin as he entered it may have American sympathies; but in this case we can afford to reserve all ours. Santa Anna helped to kill an American army officer in uniform who was in Mexico under treaty rights on an Apache trail, and every soldier north of the Rio

Grande would like to see his skin tacked up on a *corral*.

The Mexican soldiers are brave fellows. Many of them gallant officers with all the traditions of the craft. The ranks are not recruited in a praiseworthy manner outside of some of the crack regiments, and they are not very satisfactory material to turn to and say, "Come on, boys," and yet, when the conditions are right, they have put up some lovely fights in times past. In the present campaign they have a shifty and warlike race to fight under the worst possible conditions of wilderness. It is precisely like fighting Indians, only more so, since Indians did have big camps or *rancherias* and women and ponies, whereas these folks abandon such as they have and take to the mountains, with the United States on the north, in case of final overthrow.

The probabilities now are that there will be a long, tedious, and expensive campaign in northern Mexico, and just at this time, with the bad financial condition of Mexico, and the ensuing general discontent, it is not easy to concentrate too much force in one place so far from the big centres of population, which alone are vital and to be feared. At no period of his career has President Diaz had to face a situation which is as grave as this may easily become, and yet we must reserve our sympathies until an opposition appears which is not controlled by men whose motives are generated in that part of their brains which lies back of a point which in a lady is marked by her hatpin.

The Revolution in Northern Mexico—Moving Regulars to the Front. *Authors' photoengraving.*

In the Sierra Madre with the Punchers

On a chill, black morning the cabins of Los Ojos gave up their inmates at an early hour. The ponies, mules, and *burros* were herded up, and stood shivering in an angle, while about them walked the men, carefully coiling their hair lariats, and watching for an opportunity to jerk them over the heads of the selected ones. The *patron's* black pet walked up to him, but the mounts of my companion and self sneaked about with an evident desire not to participate in the present service. Old *Cokomorachie* and Jim were finally led forth, protesting after the manner of their kind. I carefully adjusted my Whitman's officer-tree over a wealth of saddle blanketing, and slung my Winchester 45-70 and my field-glasses to it. The punchers, both white and brown, and two or three women, regarded my new-fangled saddle with amused glances; indeed, Mr. Bell's Mexican wife laughed at it outright, and Tom Bailey called it "a d—— rim-fire." Another humorist thought that "it would give the chickens the pip if they got onto it"; all of which I took good-humoredly, since this was not the first time "your Uncle Samuel" had been away from home; and after some days, when a lot of men were carefully leading sore-backed horses over the mountains, I had cause to remark further on the subject. A Mexican cow-saddle is a double-barrelled affair; it will eat a hole into a horse's spine and a pair of leather breeches at the same time. If one could ask "old Jim" about that saddle of mine, I think he would give it an autograph recommend,

for he finished the trip with the hide of his back all there.

Leaving the "burro men" to haul and pull at their patient beasts as they bound on their loads, our outfit "pulled out" on what promised to be plenty of travelling. We were to do the rounds of the ranch, explore the mountains, penetrate to the old Apache strongholds, shoot game, find cliff-dwellers' villages, and I expect the dark minds of the punchers hoped for a sight at the ever-burning fire which should discover the lost mine of Tiopa. We were also promised a fight with the "Kid" if we "cut his trail"; and if he "cut ours," we may never live to regret it. Some tame Indians, just in from a hunt in the Rio Chico, had seen three fires, but they had "rolled their tails"* for Bavicora so promptly that they had not ascertained whether they were Apache or not. The same men we were in the company of had run the "Kid's" band in to the States only two months before, but on our trip that very elusive and very "bad Injun" was not encountered. Much as I should like to see him, I have no regrets, since it is extremely likely that he would have seen me first.

Our little band was composed of the *patron*, Don Gilberto; my travelling companion from New York city, who had never before been west of the Elysian Fields of New Jersey; Bailey and Bell, ranch foremen, and as dauntless spirits as ever the Texas border nurtured; the ranch bookkeeper, a young man "short" on experiences and

* Cowboy for travelling rapidly.

"long" on hope; Epitacio, an Indian hunter since outlawed; William, the colored cook; four buckskin Mexican punchers; an old man who was useless for practical purposes, but who was said to be "funny" in Spanish; and two "burro men." We were that day to go to the farthest outlying ranch, called the Casa Camadra, and then to stop for a short hunt and to give the punchers time to "gentle" some steers for work-cattle. The puncher method of doing this is beautifully simple, for any animal undergoing this is gentle or dead after it. After scouring the plain for antelope until late, we followed up a creek towards the cabin where we expected to find the punchers and the burro men with their loads of creature comforts, and as we rode in it was raining a cold sleet. The little log-cabin was low, small, and wonderfully picturesque. It was a typical "shack," such as one used to see in the Northwest when the hunters were there. Out in the rain sat two punchers, enveloped in their *serapes,* engaged in watching a half-dozen big steers eat grass. Inside of the cabin was William by a good fire in a most original fireplace, glowing with heat and pride over his corn-cakes and "marrow-gut." Between various cigarettes, the last drink of *tequela,* and the drying of our clothes, we passed the time until William had put the "grub" on a pack-saddle blanket and said, "Now, gemmen, fly in."

"Fly in" is vulgar, but it is also literal, for we did that: we did not dine—we flew in. The expression and the food were both good. Outside, the cold rain had turned into a wet snow, and we all crowded into the little place and squatted or lay about on the floor. With fingers and hunting-knives we carved and tore at the mountain of beef. The punchers consume enormous quantities of meat, and when satiated they bring forth their corn-husks and tobacco-pouches, and roll their long, thin cigarettes, which burn until they draw their *serapes* about their heads and sink back in dreamless sleep. It is all beautifully primitive, and as I rise on my elbow to look across the blanketed forms packed like mackerel in a cask, to hear their

heavy breathing, and see the fire glow, and hear the wind howl outside, I think how little it takes to make men happy. Tom Bailey and Johnnie Bell, the ranch foremen, had faces which would have been in character under a steel head-piece at Cressy, while the wildest blood of Spain, Morocco, and the American Indian ran in the veins of the punchers; and all these men were untainted by the enfeebling influences of luxury and modern life. A chunk of beef, a cigarette, an enveloping *serape,* with the Sierras for a bedroom, were the utmost of their needs.

The sunlight streamed down the big chimney, and William's "Good-mo'nin', sah," brought back my senses. Beyond his silhouette, as he crouched before the fire-place, I could hear the sputtering of the broiling steak. I repaired to the brook and smashed the ice for a rub-down. It was still drizzling, and the landscape lay under a heavy fog. Outside the cabin lay the dead body of a skinned wolf, and about a small fire crouched the punchers.

Breakfast over, the men rode off by twos into the fog, and as Tom Bailey and I jogged along together we reasoned that if we were to strike the point of the mountains and then keep well in the timber we might catch a bunch of antelope which we had "jumped" the day before on the plain below. So all day long we rode over the wet rocks, under the drip and drizzle of the mountain pines, up hill and down dale, and never "cut a sign." It was our luck; for on riding up to the "shack" we saw the bodies of deer, antelope, a big gray wolf, and the skin of a mountain-lion. We were requested to view the game, and encouraged to comment on it; but Tom and I sought a dark corner of the cabin to consume our coffee and cigarettes in silence.

At the Casa Camadra are two other log-houses, and in them live some squalid, yellow-hided humans who are to farm a little stretch of bottom-land this year. They require work-steers to do their ploughing, and Mr. Bell has brought up half a dozen vicious old "stags," which are both truculent and swift of foot. The Mexicans insist that they are not able to handle them; and Mr. Bell orders his punchers into action. I strolled out to the corrals to see the bulls "gentled." After a lot of riding and yelling they were herded and dragged into the enclosure, where they huddled while seven punchers sat on their ponies at the gate. I was standing at one corner of the corral, near the men, when out from the midst of the steers walked a big black bull, which raised its head and gazed directly at me. The bull had never before in his stupid life observed a man on foot, and I comprehended immediately what he would do next, so I "led out" for the casa at a rate of speed which the boys afterwards never grew weary of commending. No spangled *torero* of the bull-ring ever put more heart and soul into his running than did I in my great-coat and long hunting-spurs. The bull made a "fo'lorn hope" for the gate, and the gallant punchers melted away before the charge.

The diversion of the punchers made the retreat of the infantry possible, and from an intrenched position I saw the bulls tear over the hill, with the punchers "rolling their tails" behind. After an hour of swearing and hauling and bellowing, the six cattle were lugged back to the pen, and the bars put up. The punchers came around to congratulate me on my rapid recovery from a sprained ankle, when they happened to observe the cattle again scouring off for the open country. Then there was a grunting of ponies as the spurs went in, some hoarse oaths, and for a third time they tore away after the "gentle work-oxen." The steers had taken the bars in their stride. Another hour's chase, and this time the animals were thrown down, trussed up like turkeys for the baking, and tied to posts, where they lay to kick and bellow the night through in impotent rage. The punchers coiled their ropes, lit their cigarettes, and rode off in the gathering gloom. The morning following the steers were let up, and though wet and chilled, they still roared defiance. For agricultural purposes a Mexican "stag" would be as valuable as a rhinoceros or a Bengal tiger, and I await with interest the report of the death-rate at the Casa Camadra during spring ploughing.

In the handling of these savage animals the punchers are brave to recklessness, but this is partly because it seems so. In reality they have a thorough knowledge of bull nature, and can tell when and where he is going to strike as quickly as a boxer who knows by the "skim on the eye" of his opponent. But still they go boldly into the corral with the maddened brutes, seeming to pay no heed to the imminent possibilities of a trip to the moon. They toss their ropes and catch the bull's feet, they skilfully avoid his rush, and in a spirit of bravado they touch the horns, pat him on the back, or twist his tail.

After hunting for another day, with more success, we packed up and "pulled out" up the Varras Creek towards the mountains, leaving the last house behind us. Beyond was the unknown country. For many miles it had been ridden by some of the punchers, but the country is large, covered with vast mountain ranges, with wastes of stony foothills at the bases, while *barrancas* yawn at your feet, and for a great many years the policy of the Apaches has been not to encourage immigration. In 1860 a heavy band of Mexican prospectors undertook to penetrate this part in the quest of Tiopa, but they were driven out. It is now possible for strong outfits to travel its wilds with only a small chance of encountering Apache renegades, but very few have attempted it as yet. It is so remote that prospectors for silver or gold could hardly work a mine if they found one, and for other purposes it has little value. The most magnificent pine timber covers its slopes, but it would take a syndicate to deliver one log at the railroad. As we wound our way up the Varras Creek we passed beetling crags and huge pillars of porphyry rock cut into fantastic shapes by water and frost, resplendent in color, and admirably adapted for the pot-hunting of humans as affected by gentry temporarily stopping at San Carlos.

In a dell in the forest we espied some "mavericks," or unbranded stock. The punchers are ever alert for a beef without half its ears gone and a big HF burned in its flank, and immediately they perceive one they tighten their *cincha,* slip the rope from the pommel, put their hats on the back of their heads, and "light out." A cow was soon caught, after desperate riding over rocks and fallen timber, thrown down, and "hog-tied," which means all four feet together. A little fire is built; and one side of a *cincha* ring is heated red-hot, with which a rawhide artist paints HF in the sizzling flesh, while the cow kicks and bawls. She is

then unbound, and when she gets back on her feet the *vaqueros* stand about, *serape* in hand, after the bull-fighter method, and provoke her to charge. She charges, while they avoid her by agile springs and a flaunting of their rags. They laugh, and cry "Bravo toro!" until she, having overcome her indignation at their rudeness, sets off down the cañon with her tail in the air.

Thus we journeyed day by day over the hills and up the cañons, camping by night under the pines in mountain glades or deep ravines, where the sun sets at four o'clock,

On the Mountains. *Authors' photoengraving.*

while it is light above. The moon was in the full and the nights were frosty, and many times we awoke to think it morning when only our heads had become uncovered by the blankets and the big white moon shone fair upon us. Getting up in the night to poke the fire and thaw the stiffening out of one's legs is called by the boys "playing freeze-out," and we all participate in the game. A cigarette at two o'clock in the morning, with one's back to the fire, while the moon looks down on you, your comrades breathing about you, a wolf howling mournfully from a neighboring hill, the mountains towering on every side, and the tall pines painting inky shadows across the ghostly grass, is a mild sensation and rather pleasant. Some of the men are on foot, from soring their horses' backs, and their buckskin boots are wearing out, so they sit about the fire and stitch. We are all very dirty, and I no longer take comfort in watching the cook who makes the bread, for fear I may be tempted to ask him if he will not wash his hands, whereat the boys may indicate that I am a "dude," and will look down on me. The flour is nearly gone, and shortly it will not matter whether the cook's hands are rusty or not. The coffee and sugar promise to hold out. When William can no longer serve "bull gravy" with his fried meat I shall have many regrets, but they are swamped by the probabilities of a tobacco famine, which is imminent. We get deer every day, but to one not used to a strictly meat diet it begins to pall. The Indian hunter takes the stomach of a deer, fills it with meat, and deposits it under the coals. We roast it in slices and chunks, but I like it better when "jerked" brown, as it then affords somewhat more mystery to a taste already jaded with venison. In travelling with pack-animals it is the custom to make a day's march before halting, and a day's march ends about four o'clock, or when water is found. Ten hours' march will loosen one's cartridge-belt five or six holes, for venison and coffee is not a strong food. By 12 M. we acquire a wolfish yearning for the "flesh-pots," but that shortly is relieved by the contraction of the stomach, or three

or four quarts of mountain water will afford some relief. By nightfall one can "fly into" a venison steak, while cigarettes, coffee, and a desire to lie down restore one's equanimity.

We have passed some small ranges and worm our way down bottomless pits, but at last there rises ahead the main range of the Sierra Madre. From the depths of a great *barranca* we begin the climb. Never have I seen hills as sideling as these. It is terrible work for one not used to mountain-climbing and the short allowance of air one finds to subsist on. The feeling of exhaustion is almost impossible to overcome. The horses are thin, and Old Jim is developing more ribs than good condition calls for, so I walk to ease the old fellow. There are snow fields to cross, which intensifies the action. The journey is enlivened at times by shots at deer, and the rifles echo around the mountains, but being long shots they are misses. We passed the *cordon* of the mountains, and stopped on a knife-like ridge where the melting snows under one's foot ran east and west to the two great oceans. The climb from here over the main range was a bellows-bursting affair, but as we pulled on to the high *mesa* our drooping nerves were stiffened by shots, and presently deer came bounding down the ravine to our left. Jack made a bully flying shot, and the stricken deer rolled many yards, until caught by a fallen log. My companion, who was in advance, had fired into some deer, and had shot a buck which was lying down, and he was much puffed up with pride over this achievement in still-hunting. From there on we passed through the most wonderful natural deer park. The animals did not fear man, and stood to be fired at, though the open timber and absence of underbrush made the shots long-range ones. After killing all we could carry, we sat down to wait for the *burro* train.

That night we camped on a jutting crag, with the water running in the *barranca* two hundred feet below us. For a hundred miles the mountain and plain lay at our feet—a place more for an eagle's eyrie than a camp for a caravan. The night set very cold, and from out in space the moon threw its mellow light down upon us. Before the camp-fire our Indian hunter told the story of the killing of Victoria's band, where he had been among the victors, and as he threw his *serape* down, and standing forth with the firelight playing on his harsh features, he swayed his body and waved his hands, while with hoarse voice and in a strange language he gave the movement of the fight. The legend of the lost mine of Tiopa was narrated by a *vaquero* in the quiet manner of one whose memory goes far back, and to whom it is all real—about the Jesuits, the iron door over the mouth of the mine, its richness, the secrecy enjoined by the fathers on the people when they fled before the Apache devils, and how there is always a light to be kept burning at its entrance to guide them back. It was a grand theatre and an eerie scene.

On the other side of the mountain we found the trail most difficult. I would never have believed that a horse could traverse it. To say that it was steep is commonplace, and yet I cannot be believed if I say that it was perpendicular; but a man could toss his hat a mile at any moment if he pleased. Then, underfoot, it was all loose lava rock, and the little ponies had to jump and dance over the bowlders. When we had finally arrived on a grassy *mesa* I concluded that if ever again I did the like of that, it would most certainly be the result of a tremendous error in my calculations. The pack-train was here detached and sent to water, but we followed Jack to see his "discovery." After miles of travel through the dry, yellow grass we came out on a high bluff with a *barranca* at its foot, the bottom of which we could not see. On the overhanging wall opposite were Jack's cliff-dwellings, perched like dove-cots against the precipice. It was only a quarter of a mile to them, but it took two days to get there, so we did not go. There are also holes in the cliffs, and underground passages. The paths up to them are washed away, but Jack and some of his men have invaded the silent village. They climbed up with lariats, and he was let down over the cliff, but they found nothing left but dust and cobwebs.

We could not get down to water, and as our horses were thirsty and foot-sore, we "mogged along." On our ride we "cut the trail" of a big band of mustangs, or wild horses, but did not see them, and by late afternoon we found the camp, and William busy above his fire. After hunting down the valley for a few days for "burro deer" and wild turkey, we found that the tobacco was promptly giving out, according to calculations, and, being all inveterate smokers, we "made trail fast" for the Neuearachie ranch. Our ponies were jaded and sore; but having "roped" a stray pony two days before, which was now fresh, the lightest *vaquero* was put on his back, and sent hot-foot in the night to the ranch for tobacco. He made the long ride and returned at noon the next day on a fresh mount, having been thirty-six hours in the saddle. This fellow was a rather remarkable man, as it was he who, on the beginning of the trip, had brought some important mail to us one hundred and seventy miles, and after riding down two ponies he followed our trail on foot through the mountains, and overtook us as we sat resting on a log in the woods.

How we at last pulled into the ranch at Neuearachie, with its log buildings and irrigated fields, and how we "swooped down" on Mr. John Bailey, and ate up all his eggs and bread and butter at the first onset, I will not weary you with, but I believe that a man should for one month of the year live on the roots of the grass, in order to understand for the eleven following that so-called necessities are luxuries in reality. Not that I would indiscriminately recommend such a dietary abasement as ours, yet will I insist that it has killed less men than gluttony, and should you ever make the Sierra trails with the punchers, you will get rather less than more.

Julian Ralph

Being asked to write about Mr. Julian Ralph is like being asked to write about my favorite horse, or any other matter of course with myself. It's the best old horse in the world, to be sure; and Ralph, he is the most interesting man I ever met, besides being the best sort of fellow. There may be those in the world who would d—— him, but one can hardly expect me to do it, even with faint praise, and yet what I say of him is only half of the good he deserves.

He was born in New York city; and of all the conventionalities which New York has produced, he is the most New-Yorkie. It should not be imagined by this that he is a "dude," for that is not the only convention, or, indeed, the best type, produced here, but that he is very worldly, as befits a metropolitan bringing up, and is easily and quickly at home in the most unheard-of places. He was sent away to a boarding-school when so young that it did not affect his character, and then he got a college education in a printing-office. He did newspaper assignments in the back alleys, on the docks, in the hospitals, during the riots, and he has told New-Yorkers in the columns of the *Sun* how murders were done in the dark places. He has described the misery of the dirtiest slums and the brilliancy of the gayest scenes. He did the Molly Maguires, going among them into the mines and to their secret rendezvous. Eighteen years as a "special" on a New York newspaper is liable to broaden a man, and produce a fund of expanse which is beyond the ken of folks who run up and down all their lives between two points like a street car. It has enabled him to put himself in full sympathy with Indians who were most strange to him. He is about the first New-Yorker who ever wrote about the West without sneering or the South without preaching. A man can be provincial and yet be big. It is not the lot of most Americans to be able to reduce their geographical centre of gravity to a point between Park Row and Madison Square. In time it is possible for clever people to imitate the character and to play the part of a metropolitan man, but one cannot hope to deceive those to the manner born, which is what Ralph is.

After a newspaper career which has put him where he is regarded by most of his profession as the first reporter of the town, he has become known to a vastly wider circle as a contributor to HARPER'S MAGAZINE and HARPER'S WEEKLY. Out of that development has come the authorship of his books on *Canada's Frontier, Our Great West,* and *Harper's Chicago and the Fair.* In these directions he has fulfilled the promises of his old career. In Park Row he is famous as a man who can write columns of reports by the yard long about political conventions, inaugurations of Presidents, yacht-races, and whatsoever is absorbing the public attention. He has produced armfuls of good manuscript in the midst of the most terrific excitement, assisted by dozens of aids and messenger-boys, working on and on, all day and into the night, in a brain-reeling way which is miraculous. He has the "wide-open eyes of a baby" in his method of looking at things; he is original, and always fresh. He drops into a Canadian forest, a Mississippi steamboat, or the private depths of the inner office of the greatest men in America, and the Indians, the negroes, and the great men warm up instinctively and tell him the secrets of their lives. It is possible for Mr. Ralph to go right to a total stranger and become engrossed in the man's own private, personal, or business affairs in twenty minutes, and when others would be unceremoniously kicked out of the place, his strangers like it, and unburden their cares. That he ever himself developed a personal interest in any politics or business interest I could never discover. It is perhaps this disinterestedness, coupled with his reassuring appearance and personal tact, which makes this possible. The "fad" in particular which the best newspaper men cultivate is that they "never betray a confidence," but the commonest conversations in which Ralph indulges with people who "fare his way" are rendered to the public in so delicious a way that every one knows the girl on the Mississippi steamboat and her vulgar love-affair. I have seen him fishing through the ice for half an hour, with a trout tugging at his pole, while he developed the mental character of an Indian hunter, and finally lost the fish, but saved the dialect of the poor aborigine for our consumption.

Mr. Ralph's strength lies in his strong sympathies, his curious and often amusing views of things, his unconventionality, his strong color sense, and the absolute accuracy of his vision. His travels for the Harpers have made the United States and Canada Mr. Ralph's study-room. As it were, Tacoma is the mantel-piece, Colorado is an easy chair, Florida is a picture on the wall, Montreal is a bookcase, and New York city is a desk. For so large a study-room he probably knows it as no other man does in his profession. Its people are his bric-à-brac, and he loves his objects of art, and most of his curios love him—except that now and then when such a big man is moving around in great haste he may knock over some small object, but that is to be expected and excused.

If I were to strike the key-note of his character I should say "human nature"; of that he is "chock-full"; and when you can run the scale of that on a man's character you are liable to produce all the sounds.

As to his profession, he is as proud of it as any Royal Archer who ever sailed to France for glory with the mail-clad cavaliers. He has done good service in it, and his aims have always been exalted.

Personally he is a good fellow, as I have said; and that should not provoke a sneer, since the country is not overpopulated with them; and from his long experience and travel and meetings with all sorts of men he has such a vast fund of information that one almost despairs of ever broaching a subject with which he is not a little familiar.

It is better in these days to study the dollars rather than the people of this world, as Ralph does; for writers are the modern monks for economy and self-sacrifice—let us say the soldiers, for they are always in the thickest of the fray, thinking with might and main when all is gay; composed in the calamities which overtake mankind. They go when the sun shines or when the rain pours; and they are in the field when the bullets and microbes fly thickest.

A Rodeo at Los Ojos

The sun beat down on the dry grass, and the punchers were squatting about in groups in front of the straggling log and *adobe* buildings which constituted the outlying ranch of Los Ojos.

Mr. Johnnie Bell, the *capitan* in charge, was walking about in his heavy *chaparras,* a slouch hat, and a white "biled" shirt. He was chewing his long yellow mustache, and gazing across the great plain of Bavicora with set and squinting eyes. He passed us and repassed us, still gazing out, and in his long Texas drawl said, "That's them San Miguel fellers."

I looked, but I could not see any San Miguel fellows in the wide expanse of land.

"Hyar, crawl some horses, and we'll go out and meet 'em," continued Mr. Bell; and, suiting the action, we mounted our horses and followed him. After a time I made out tiny specks in the atmospheric wave which rises from the heated land, and in half an hour could plainly make out a cavalcade of horsemen. Presently breaking into a gallop, which movement was imitated by the other party, we bore down upon each other, and only stopped when near enough to shake hands, the half-wild ponies darting about and rearing under the excitement. Greetings were exchanged in Spanish, and the peculiar shoulder tap, or abbreviated embrace, was indulged in. Doubtless a part of our outfit was as strange to Governor Terraza's men—for he is the *patron* of San Miguel—as they were to us.

My imagination had never before pictured anything so wild as these leather-clad *vaqueros*. As they removed their hats to greet Jack, their unkempt locks blew over their faces, back off their foreheads, in the greatest disorder. They were clad in terra-cotta buckskin, elaborately trimmed with white leather, and around their lower legs wore heavy cowhide as a sort of legging. They were fully armed, and with their jingling spurs, their flapping ropes and buckskin strings, and with their gay *serapes* tied behind their saddles, they were as impressive a cavalcade of desert-scamperers as it has been my fortune to see. Slowly we rode back to the corrals, where they dismounted.

Shortly, and unobserved by us until at hand, we heard the clatter of hoofs, and, leaving in their wake a cloud of dust, a dozen punchers from another outfit bore down upon us as we stood under the *ramada* of the ranch-house, and pulling up with a jerk, which threw the ponies on their haunches, the men dismounted and approached, to be welcomed by the master of the *rodeo.*

A few short orders were given, and three mounted men started down to the springs, and, after charging about, we could see that they had roped a steer, which they led, bawling and resisting, to the ranch, where it was quickly thrown and slaughtered. Turning it on its back, after the manner of the old buffalo hunters, it was quickly disrobed and cut up into hundreds of small pieces, which is the method practised by the Mexican butchers, and distributed to the men.

Waving Serape to Drive Cattle. *Authors' photoengraving.*

In Mexico it is the custom for the man who gives the "round-up" to supply fresh beef to the visiting cow-men; and on this occasion it seemed that the pigs, chickens, and dogs were also embraced in the bounty of the *patron,* for I noticed one piece which hung immediately in front of my quarters had two chickens roosting on the top of it, and a pig and a dog tugging vigorously at the bottom.

The horse herds were moved in from the *llano* and rounded up in the corral, from which the punchers selected their mounts by roping, and as the sun was westering they disappeared, in obedience to orders, to all points of the compass. The men took positions back in the hills and far out on the plain; there, building a little fire, they cook their beef, and, enveloped in their *serapes,* spend the night. At early dawn they converge on the ranch, driving before them such stock as they may.

In the morning we could see from the ranch-house a great semicircle of gray on the yellow plains. It was the thousands of cattle coming to the *rodeo.* In an hour more we could plainly see the cattle, and behind them the *vaqueros* dashing about, waving their *serapes.* Gradually they converged on the *rodeo* ground, and, enveloped in a great cloud of dust and with hollow bellowings, like the low pedals of a great organ, they begin to mill, or turn about a common centre, until gradually quieted by the enveloping cloud of horsemen. The *patron* and the captains of the neighboring ranches, after an exchange of long-winded Spanish formalities, and accompanied by ourselves, rode slowly from the ranch to the herd, and, entering it, passed through and through and around in solemn procession. The cattle part before the horsemen, and the dust rises so as to obscure to unaccustomed eyes all but the silhouettes of the moving thousands. This is an important function in a cow country, since it enables the owners or their men to estimate what numbers of the stock belong to them, to observe the brands, and to inquire as to the condition of the animals and the numbers of calves and "mavericks,"

and to settle any dispute which may arise therefrom.

All controversy, if there be any, having been adjusted, a part of the punchers move slowly into the herd, while the rest patrol the outside, and hold it. Then a movement soon begins. You see a figure dash at about full speed through an apparently impenetrable mass of cattle; the stock becomes uneasy and moves about, gradually beginning the milling process, but the men select the cattle bearing their brand, and course. them through the herd; all becomes confusion, and the cattle simply seek to escape from the ever-recurring horsemen. Here one sees the matchless horsemanship of the punchers. Their little ponies, trained to the business, respond to the slightest pressure. The cattle make every attempt to escape, dodging in and out and crowding among their kind; but right on their quarter, gradually forcing them to the edge of the herd, keeps the puncher, until finally, as a last effort, the cow and the calf rush through the supporting line, when, after a terrific race, she is turned into another herd, and is called "the cut."

One who finds pleasure in action can here see the most surprising manifestations of it. A huge bull, wild with fright, breaks from the herd, with lowered head and whitened eye, and goes charging off indifferent to what or whom he may encounter, with the little pony pattering in his wake. The cattle run at times with nearly the intensity of action of a deer, and whip and spur are applied mercilessly to the little horse. The process of "tailing" is indulged in, although it is a dangerous practice for the man, and reprehensible from its brutality to the cattle. A man will pursue a bull at top speed, will reach over and grasp the tail of the animal, bring it to his saddle, throw his right leg over the tail, and swing his horse suddenly to the left, which throws the bull rolling over and over. That this method has its value I have seen in the case of pursuing "mavericks," where an unsuccessful throw was made with the rope, and the animal was about to enter the thick timber; it would be impossible to coil the rope again, and an escape would follow but for the wonderful dexterity of these men in this accomplishment. The little calves become separated from their mothers, and go bleating about; their mothers respond by bellows, until pandemonium seems to reign. The dust is blinding, and the puncher becomes grimy and soiled; the horses lather; and in the excitement the desperate men do deeds which convince you of their faith that "a man can't die till his time comes." At times a bull is found so skilled in these contests that he cannot be displaced from the herd; it is then necessary to rope him and drag him to the point desired; and I noticed punchers ride behind recalcitrant bulls and, reaching over, spur them. I also saw two men throw simultaneously for an immense creature, when, to my great astonishment, he turned tail over head and rolled on the ground. They had both sat back on their ropes together.

The whole scene was inspiring to a degree, and well merited Mr. Yorick's observation that "it is the sport of kings; the image of war, with twenty-five per cent of its danger."

Fresh horses are saddled from time to time, but before high noon the work is done, and the various "cut-offs" are herded in different directions. By this time the dust had risen until lost in the sky above, and as the various bands of cowboys rode slowly back to the ranch, I observed their demoralized condition. The economy *per force* of the Mexican people prompts them to put no more cotton into a shirt than is absolutely necessary, with the consequence that, in these cases, their shirts had pulled out from their belts and their *serapes,* and were flapping in the wind; their mustaches and their hair were perfectly solid with dust, and one could not tell a bay horse from a black.

Now come the cigarettes and the broiling of beef. The bosses were invited to sit at our table, and as the work of cutting and branding had yet to be done, no time was taken for ablutions. Opposite me sat a certain individual who, as he engulfed his food, presented a grimy waste of visage only broken by the rolling of his eyes and the snapping of his teeth.

We then proceeded to the corrals, which were made in stockaded form from gnarled and many-shaped posts set on an end. The cows and calves were bunched on one side in fearful expectancy. A fire was built just outside of the bars, and the branding-irons set on. Into the corrals went the punchers, with their ropes coiled in their hands. Selecting their victims, they threw their ropes, and, after pulling and tugging, a bull calf would come out of the bunch, whereat two men would set upon him and "rastle" him to the ground. It is a strange mixture of humor and pathos, this mutilation of calves —humorous when the calf throws the man, and pathetic when the man throws the calf. Occasionally an old cow takes an unusual interest in her offspring, and charges boldly into their midst. Those men who cannot escape soon enough throw dust in her eyes, or put their hats over her horns. And in this case there were some big steers which had been "cut out" for purposes of work at the plough and turned in. with the young stock; one old grizzled veteran manifested an interest in the proceedings, and walked boldly from the bunch, with his head in the air and bellowing; a wild scurry ensued, and hats and *serapes* were thrown to confuse him. But over all this the punchers only laugh, and go at it again. In corral roping they try to catch the calf by the front feet, and in this they become so expert that they rarely miss. As I sat on the fence, one of the foremen, in play, threw and caught my legs as they dangled.

When the work is done and the cattle are again turned into the herd, the men repair to the *casa* and indulge in games and pranks. We had shooting-matches and hundred-yard dashes; but I think no records were broken, since punchers on foot are odd fish. They walk as though they expected every moment to sit down. Their knees work outward, and they have a decided "hitch" in their gait; but once let them get a foot in a stirrup and a grasp on the horn of the saddle, and a dynamite cartridge alone could expel them from their seat. When loping over the plain the puncher is the epitome of equine grace, and if he desires to look behind him he simply shifts his whole body to one side and lets the horse go as he pleases. In the pursuit of cattle at a *rodeo* he leans forward in his saddle, and with his arms elevated to his shoulders he "plugs" in his spurs and makes his pony fairly sail. While going at this tremendous speed he turns his pony almost in his stride, and no matter how a bull may twist and swerve about, he is at his tail as true as a magnet to the pole. The Mexican punchers all use the "ring bit," and it is a fearful contrivance. Their saddle-trees are very short, and as straight and quite as shapeless as a "saw-buck pack-saddle." The horn is as big as a dinner plate, and taken altogether it is inferior to the California tree. It is very hard on horses' backs, and not at all comfortable for a rider who is not accustomed to it.

They all use hemp ropes which are imported from some of the southern states of the republic, and carry a lariat of hair which they make themselves. They work for from eight to twelve dollars a month in Mexican coin, and live on the most simple diet imaginable. They are mostly *peoned,* or in hopeless debt to their *patrons,* who go after any man who deserts the range and bring him back by force. A puncher buys nothing but his gorgeous buckskin clothes, and his big silver-mounted straw hat, his spurs, his riata, and his *cincha* rings. He makes his *teguas* or buckskin boots, his heavy leggings, his saddle, and the *patron* furnishes his arms. On the round-up, which lasts about half of the year, he is furnished beef, and also kills game. The balance of the year he is kept in an outlying camp to turn stock back on the range. These camps are often the most simple things, consisting of a pack containing his "grub," his saddle, and *serape,* all lying under a tree, which does duty as a house. He carries a flint and steel, and has a piece of sheet-iron for a stove, and a piece of pottery for boiling things in. This part of their

lives is passed in a long siesta, and a man of the North who has a local reputation as a lazy man should see a Mexican puncher loaf, in order to comprehend that he could never achieve distinction in the land where *poco tiempo* means forever. Such is the life of the *vaquero,* a brave fellow, a fatalist, with less wants than the pony he rides, a rather thoughtless man, who lacks many virtues, but when he mounts his horse or casts his riata all men must bow and call him master.

The *baile,* the song, the man with the guitar—and under all this *dolce far niente* are their little hates and bickerings, as thin as cigarette smoke and as enduring as time. They reverence their parents, they honor their *patron,* and love their *compadre.* They are grave, and grave even when gay; they eat little, they think less, they meet death calmly, and it's a terrible scoundrel who goes to hell from Mexico.

The Anglo-American foremen are another type entirely. They have all the rude virtues. The intelligence which is never lacking and the perfect courage which never fails are found in such men as Tom Bailey and Johnnie Bell—two Texans who are the superiors of any cow-men I have ever seen. I have seen them chase the "mavericks" at top speed over a country so difficult that a man could hardly pass on foot out of a walk. On one occasion Mr. Bailey, in hot pursuit of a bull, leaped a tremendous fallen log at top speed, and in the next instant "tailed" and threw the bull as it was about to enter the timber. Bell can ride a pony at a gallop while standing up on his saddle, and while Cossacks do this trick they are enabled to accomplish it easily from the superior adaptability of their saddles to the purpose. In my association with these men of the frontier I have come to greatly respect their moral fibre and their character. Modern civilization, in the process of educating men beyond their capacity, often succeeds in vulgarizing them; but these natural men possess minds which, though lacking all embellishment, are chaste and simple, and utterly devoid of a certain flippancy which passes for smartness in situations where life is not so real. The fact that a man bolts his food or uses his table-knife as though it were a deadly weapon counts very little in the game these men play in their lonely range life. They are not complicated, these children of nature, and they never think one thing and say another. Mr. Bell was wont to squat against a fireplace—*à la* Indian—and dissect the peculiarities of the audience in a most ingenuous way. It never gave offence either, because so guileless. Mr. Bailey, after listening carefully, to a theological tilt, observed that "he believed he'd be religious if he knowed how."

The jokes and pleasantries of the American puncher are so close to nature often, and so generously veneered with heart-rending profanity, as to exclude their becoming classic. The cow-men are good friends and virulent haters, and, if justified in their own minds, would shoot a man instantly, and regret the necessity, but not the shooting, afterwards.

Among the dry, saturnine faces of the cow punchers of the Sierra Madre was one which beamed with human instincts, which seemed to say, "Welcome, stranger!" He was the first impression my companion and myself had of Mexico, and as broad as are its plains and as high its mountains, yet looms up William on a higher pinnacle of remembrance.

We crawled out of a Pullman in the early morning at Chihuahua, and fell into the hands of a little black man, with telescopic pantaloons, a big sombrero with the edges rolled up, and a grin on his good-humored face like a yawning *barranca.*

"Is you frens of Mista Jack's?"

"We are."

"Gimme your checks. Come dis way," he said; and without knowing why we should hand ourselves and our property over to this uncouth personage, we did it, and from thence on over the deserts and in the mountains, while shivering in the snow by night and by day, there was Jack's man to bandage our wounds, lend us tobacco when no one else had any, to tuck in our blankets, to

amuse us, to comfort us in distress, to advise and admonish, until the last *adios* were waved from the train as it again bore us to the border-land.

On our departure from Chihuahua to meet Jack out in the mountains the stage was overloaded, but a proposition to leave William behind was beaten on the first ballot; it was well vindicated, for without William the expedition would have been a "march from Moscow." There was only one man in the party with a sort of bass-relief notion that he could handle the Spanish language, and the relief was a very slight one—almost imperceptible—the politeness of the people only keeping him from being mobbed. But William could speak German, English, and Spanish, separately, or all at once.

William was so black that he would make a dark hole in the night, and the top of his head was not over four and a half feet above the soles of his shoes. His legs were all out of drawing, but forty-five winters had not passed over him without leaving a mind which, in its sphere of life, was agile, resourceful, and eminently capable of grappling with any complication which might arise. He had personal relations of various kinds with every man, woman, and child whom we met in Mexico. He had been thirty years a cook in a cow camp, and could evolve banquets from the meat on a bull's tail, and was wont to say, "I don' know so much 'bout dese yar stoves, but gie me a camp-fire an' I can make de bes' thing yo' ever threw your lip ober."

When in camp, with his little cast-off English tourist cap on one side of his head, a short black pipe tipped at the other angle to balance the effect, and two or three stripes of white corn-meal across his visage, he would move round the camp-fire like a cub bear around a huckleberry bush, and in a low, authoritative voice have the Mexicans all in action, one hurrying after water, another after wood, some making *tortillas,* or cutting up venison, grinding coffee between two stones, dusting bedding, or anything else. The British Field-Marshal air was lost in a second when he addressed "Mister Willie" or "Mister Jack," and no fawning courtier of the Grand Monarch could purr so low.

On our coach ride to Bavicora, William would seem to go up to any ranch-house on the road, when the sun was getting low, and after ten minutes' conversation with the grave Don who owned it, he would turn to us with a wink, and say: "Come right in, gemmen. Dis ranch is yours." Sure enough, it was. Whether he played us for major-generals or governors of states I shall never know, but certainly we were treated as such.

On one occasion William had gotten out to get a hat blown off by the wind, and when he came up to view the wreck of the turn-over of the great Concord coach, and saw the mules going off down the hill with the front wheels, the ground littered with boxes and débris, and the men all lying about, groaning or fainting in agony, William scratched his wool, and with just a suspicion of humor on his face he ventured, "If I'd been hyar, I would be in two places 'fore now, shuah," which was some consolation to William, if not to us.

In Chihuahua we found William was in need of a clean shirt, and we had got one for him in a shop. He had selected one with a power of color enough to make the sun stand still, and with great glass diamonds in it. We admonished him that when he got to the ranch the punchers would take it away from him.

"No, sah; I'll take it off 'fore I get thar."

William had his commercial instincts developed in a reasonable degree, for he was always trying to trade a silver watch, of the Captain Cuttle kind, with the Mexicans. When asked what time it was, William would look at the sun and then deftly cant the watch around, the hands of which swung like compasses, and he would show you the time within fifteen minutes of right, which little discrepancy could never affect the value of a watch in the land of *mañana*.

That he possessed tact I have shown, for he was the only man at Bavicora whose relations with the *patron* and the smallest,

dirtiest Indian "kid," were easy and natural. Jack said of his popularity, "He stands 'way in with the Chinese cook; gets the warm corner behind the stove." He also had courage, for didn't he serve out the ammunition in Texas when his "outfit" was in a life-and-death tussle with the Comanches? did he not hold a starving crowd of Mexican teamsters off the grub-wagon until the boys came back?

There was only one feature of Western life with which William could not assimilate, and that was the horse. He had trusted a bronco too far on some remote occasion, which accounted partially for the kinks in his legs; but after he had recovered fully his health he had pinned his faith to *burros,* and forgotten the glories of the true cavalier.

"No, sah, Mister Jack, I don' care for to ride dat horse. He's a good horse, but I jes hit de flat for a few miles 'fore I rides him," he was wont to say when the cowboys gave themselves over to an irresponsible desire to see a horse kill a man. He would then go about his duties, uttering gulps of suppressed laughter, after the negro manner, safe in the knowledge that the *burro* he affected could "pack his freight."

One morning I was taking a bath out of our wash-basin, and William, who was watching me and the coffeepot at the same time, observed that "if one of dese people down hyar was to do dat dere, dere'd be a funeral 'fo' twelve o'clock."

William never admitted any social affinity with Mexicans, and as to his own people he was wont to say: "Never have went with people of my own color. Why, you go to Brazos to-day, and dey tell you dere was Bill, he go home come night, an' de balance of 'em be looking troo de grates in de morning." So William lives happily in the "small social puddle," and always reckons to "treat any friends of Mister Jack's right." So if you would know William, you must do it through Jack.

It was on rare occasions that William, as master of ceremonies, committed any indiscretion, but one occurred in the town of

Guerrero. We had gotten in rather late, and William was sent about the town to have some one serve supper for us. We were all very busy when William "blew in" with a great sputtering, and said, "Is yous ready for dinner, gemmen?" "Yes, William," we answered, whereat William ran off. After waiting a long time, and being very hungry, we concluded to go and "rustle" for ourselves, since William did not come back and had not told us where he had gone. After we had found and eaten a dinner, William turned up, gloomy and dispirited. We inquired as to his mood. "I do declar', gemmen, I done forget dat you didn't know where I had ordered dat dinner; but dere's de dinner an' nobody to eat it, an' I's got to leave dis town 'fore sunup, pay for it, or die." Unless some one had advanced the money, William's two other alternatives would have been painful.

The romance in William's life even could not be made mournful, but it was the "mos' trouble" he ever had, and it runs like this: Some years since William had saved up four hundred dollars, and he had a girl back in Brazos to whom he had pinned his faith. He had concluded to assume responsibilities, and to create a business in a little mud town down the big road. He had it arranged to start a travellers' eating-house; he had contracted for a stove and some furniture; and at about that time his dishonest employer had left Mexico for parts unknown, with all his money. The stove and furniture were yet to be paid for, so William entered into hopeless bankruptcy, lost his girl, and then, attaching himself to Jack, he bravely set to again in life's battle. But I was glad to know that he had again conquered, for before I left I overheard a serious conversation between William and the *patron*. William was cleaning a frying-pan by the camp-fire light, and the *patron* was sitting enveloped in his *serape* on the other side.

"Mist' Jack, I's got a girl. She's a Mexican."

"Why, William, how about that girl up in the Brazos?" inquired the *patron,* in surprise.

"Don't care about her now. Got a new girl."

"Well, I suppose you can have her, if you can win her," replied the *patron*.

"Can I, sah? Well, den, I's win her already, sah—dar!" chuckled William.

"Oh! very well, then, William, I will give you a wagon, with two yellow ponies, to go down and get her; but I don't want you to come back to Bavicora with an empty wagon."

"No, sah; I won't, sah," pleasedly responded the lover.

"Does that suit you, then?" asked the *patron*.

"Yes, sah; but, sah, wonder, sah, might I have the two old whites?"

"All right! You can have the two old white ponies;" and, after a pause, "I will give you that old *adobe* up in La Pinta, and two speckled steers; and I don't want you to come down to the ranch except on *baile* nights, and I want you to slide in then just as quiet as any other outsider," said the *patron,* who was testing William's loyalty to the girl.

"All right! I'll do that."

"William, do you know that no true Mexican girl will marry a man who don't know how to ride a charger?" continued the *patron,* after a while.

"Yes; I's been thinking of dat; but dar's dat Timborello, he's a good horse what a man can 'pend on," replied William, as he scoured at the pan in a very wearing way.

"He's yours, William; and now all you have got to do is to win the girl."

After that William was as gay as a robin in the spring; and as I write this I suppose William is riding over the pass in the mountains, sitting on a board across his wagon, with his Mexican bride by his side, singing out between the puffs of his black pipe, "Go on, dar, you muchacos; specks we ever get to Bavicora dis yar gait?"

Troop A Athletics

Troop A was first evidenced to New-Yorkers some years ago at a horse show by a lot of young men in quaint uniforms, mounted on some curious horses, and wearing a pained and uncertain expression. The other night I looked on at their tournament, and now let us—O New-Yorkers! let us blow a little; let us trumpet. It is said by the enemy to be an American trick, but it amuses us, and it can do no one any harm. Join with me when I say that Troop A is the finest troop on this crust; and if you doubt, before you howl your triumph run up to Dickel's and be convinced; and I say, where there is a better one—"standing in the shade of Brutus the Elder—I don't know."

Were not Captain Roe already immortal by reason of his courier ride of one hundred and fifty miles in twenty-two hours and a half, this his latest creation would make him so. But I fear I am not going to argue for my broad assertion very properly, since I find the condition of my mind like that of the jury which tried Tennessee's Partner—"there being no doubt in their own minds, they were willing to give the prisoner the benefit of any that might exist." So I am simply going to assume that Troop A is the best in the world, and assure all doubters of my distinguished consideration, and "be blowed to them."

Of course up at West Point they naturally receive a great many natural cavalrymen, some of whom are not ruined by being made engineer soldiers. There are those

wonderful Kuban Cossacks, but they are irregulars, as are our Indian scout corps out West, who are now being made regulars, to the utter confusion of their usefulness. If the British Military Tournament is a sample of what the British can do, they are "not in

Chasing the Ribbon. *Painting in "21" Club Collection—Peter Kriendler, President.*

it" with Troop A. And as for the big divisions of Continental Europe, it's rather an unfair comparison, since Troop A is rather an officer's cavalry school than a bunch of peasants in glittering raiment.

This annual tournament, held in their armory, is becoming year by year a New York event which in time will rank with the Horse Show and the Thanksgiving game. I only wish it could be made a full regiment instead of a troop, for it may be much needed in time by this State. Thirty days will make a fair dough-boy out of an American, but it takes three years to construct a "yellow-leg," and that, too, out of natural material. Many nations, because of their characteristics, can never have good cavalry, and Lord Wolseley has been good enough to tell us that we are one of that kind, so we must brush up. Poor old dragoons! all that is left of the romance of war

is with you, with a little glory left for the light batteries. Krag-Jörgensens have made rifle-pits and stone walls more useful than ever to the infantry, while artillery outreaches the field-glass in its zone of danger, but it's whole hog or nothing with the cavalry, just as it used to be. A fine seat, a swift sabre, and be cut into ribbons, and lie under a bush—that has always been cavalry, and it's just as bad a service for one who wants to live forever as it ever was. That's why we should be proud of Troop A, and wish it a regiment, because it's so thoroughly good.

In these games the troopers ride like fiends, and are flung around in a way which would damage a piece of rubber hose. They pound each other lustily with their broadswords, and pick up potatoes from the ground while riding sixteen-hand horses. They chase each other to get a piece of ribbon tied on the arm of one; they grab each

Mounting Double. *Authors' photoengraving.*

other and fall off their horses, and continue to maul each other in the tan bark. They mount double at a gallop, and cut heads while taking a hurdle bareback, and end up the evening by a general mêlée which is a merry slugging match, and as productive of black-and-blue spots as the "flying wedge."

Let us be proud of Troop A and nurse its squadrons, and some day it may have for us a Ziethen, a Seidlitz, a Murat, a Custer, or a Sheridan when we need one; for this easy-going fool's paradise may develop a political sore which can only be cut out with a sabre. And speaking of sabres, the one now in use by our army should be carefully laid away in an artillery museum with the other antiques, and alongside of it should go the gas-pipe with which our "dough-boys" are armed; and right next to that should be put that ridiculous little ladies' card-case called a cartridge-box, all duly labelled for posterity to wonder at, as they will at culverins, snickersnees, Tower-muskets, bone chargers, and lineal promotion.

A Model Squadron

I am not quite sure that I should not say "The Model Colonel," since every one knows men and horses are much alike when they have first passed under the eye of the recruiting officer and the remount board, and every one knows that colonels are very unlike, so that a model squadron or a model troop is certain to owe its superiority to its commander; but as we are observing the product in this instance, let the title stand as above stated.

The model squadron aforesaid is quartered across the Potomac from Washington in Fort Meyer, which is the only purely cavalry post in the country. Everywhere else the troops are mixed, and the commandant may be of any arm of the service. Here they are all cavalry, with cavalry officers and cavalry ideas, and are not hindered by dismounted theories, or pick-and-shovel work, or any of the hundreds of things which hamper equally good "yellow legs" in other posts. There are many passable misdemeanors in this post, but only one crime, and that is bad riding. There is little dismounted work, and any soldier can have his horse out on a pass, so long as he does not abuse the privilege; and when he does, it's plenty of walking falls to his lot.

There is a large brick riding-hall of approved pattern, which enables the men to do their work in all weathers. The four troops now quartered there are from the First, Seventh, Eighth, and Ninth regiments, which creates a good-natured rivalry, very conducive to thorough work. It is the opinion of General Henry that one old troop should always be left at this post as a pacesetter for the newly transferred ones, which seems reasonable.

Now to tell what the preparatory discipline is to the magnificent riding which can be seen any morning by spectators who are "game for a journey" to the fort by ten o'clock, I must say that General Guy V. Henry is a flaming fire of cavalry enthusiasm. He has one idea—a great broad expanse of principle—ever so simple in itself, but it is basic, and nothing can become so complicated that he cannot revert to his simple idea and by it regulate the whole. It is the individual training of the horse and rider. One bad rider or one unbroken horse can disarrange the whole troop movement, and "woe to him" who is not up to concert pitch! "Who is the scoundrel, the lummux, humph?" and the colonel, who is a brevet-brigadier-general, strides up and down, and fire comes from his nostrils. "Prefer charges against him, captain!" and the worst befalls. The unfortunate trooper has committed the highest crime which the commandant of Fort Meyer knows—he cannot ride.

A soldier becomes a rider by being bucketed about on a bareback horse, or he dies. The process is simple, the tanbark soft, and none have died up to date, but all have attained the other alternative. This is unimportant; but the horse—it is to his education that the oceans of patience and the mountains of intelligence are brought to bear. It is all in the books if any one cares

Throwing a Horse. *Authors' photoengraving.*

to go into it. It is the gathering of the horse; it is the legs carried to the rear of the girths; it is the perfect hand and the instant compliance of the horse with the signs as indicated by the rider; it is the backing, the passaging, the leading with either foot, and the pivoting on the front legs; it is the throwing of horses, the acquisition of gaits, and the nice bitting; it is one hundred little struggles with the brute until he comes to understand and to know that he must do his duty. It all looks beautifully simple, but in practice we know that while it is not difficult to teach a horse, it is quite another matter to unteach him, so in these horses at least no mistakes have been made. After all this, one fine sunny Friday morning the people drove out from Washington in their traps and filed into the galleries and sat down—fair women and brave men; of the former we are sure, and of the latter we trust. The colonel blew a whistle—ye gods, what a sacrilege against all the traditions of this dear old United States army!—and in rode Captain Bomus's troop of the First Plungers, which I cannot but love, since I am an honorary member of their officers' mess, and fondly remember the fellows who are now sniffing alkali dust down in Arizona. They were riding with blankets and surcingles, and did their part of a drill, the sequence of which I have forgotten, since it was divided with the three other troops—Captain Bell's, of the Seventh, Captain Hughes's, of the Ninth, and Captain Fountain's, of the Eighth. I felt a strong personal interest in some of these men, for memory took me back to a night's ride in Dakota with a patrol of the Ninth, when they were all wrapped in buffalo-skin overcoats, with white frost on their lapels; the horses' noses wore icicles, and the dry snow creaked under the tread of the hoofs as we rode over the starlit plain and through the black shadows of the *coulees*. I had pounded along also through the dust in the wake of this troop of the Eighth when it wasn't so cold, but was equally uncomfortable.

The sharp commands of the captain soon put the troop in motion, and they trotted along with a cadenced tread, every man a part of his horse; they broke into fours and wheeled to the right about, then into line and wound themselves up in the "spiral," and unwound again, and soon brought order out of a mess, and the regular canter was ever the same. Then low hurdles were strung across the hall, and by column of fours the troop went over, never breaking the formation; to the rear they turned and back again; finally they took the obstacle in line, and every horse rose as though impelled by the same mechanism. As if this was not enough, every second man was dismounted and put on double with a comrade, not with his breast to his comrade's back, but back to back, and then in line the odd cavalcade charged the hurdles, and took them every one. It was not an individual bucketing of one horse after another, but all in line and all together. After this what could there be more to test the "glue" in these troopers' seats? There was more, however, and in this wise: The saddles were put on, but without any girths, and all the movements were gone through with again, ending up with a charge down the hall, and bringing up against the wall of the spectators' stand at a sharp "halt," which would have unseated a monkey from a trick-mule.

The horses were all thrown by pulling their heads about, and one cavalryman amused himself by jumping over his prostrate mount. They rode "at will," and stood upon their knees on their horses' backs. One big animal resented carrying double, and did something which in Texas would be called "pitching," but it was scarcely a genuine sample, since the grinning soldiers made little of it.

The troop of the Ninth executed a "left backward turn" with beautiful precision, and this difficult undertaking will serve to give one an idea of the training of the mounts.

Gymnastics of all sorts were indulged in, even to the extent of turning summersaults over four horses from a spring-board. A citizen near me, whose mind had probably wandered back to Barnum and Bailey, said:

"But what's this got to do with soldiers; is it not highly flavored with circus?"

I could offer no excuse except the tradition that cavalrymen are supposed to ride well. All the men were young and in first-rate physical fix, and seemed to enjoy the thing—all except one old first sergeant, who had been time-expired these half-dozen times, whose skin was so full of bullet-holes that it wouldn't hold blood, and who had entered this new régime with many protests:

"O'me nau circus ape; I can't be leppin' around afther the likes av thim!" whereat the powers arranged it so that the old veteran got a job looking after plug tobacco, tomato-cans, tinned beef, and other "commissaries," upon which he viewed the situation more cheerfully.

The drill was tremendously entertaining to the ladies and gentlemen in the gallery, and they clapped their hands and went bustling into their traps and off down the road to the general's house, where Madam the General gave a breakfast, and the women no doubt asked the second lieutenants deliciously foolish questions about their art. The gentlemen, some of whom are Congressmen and other exalted governmental functionaries, felt proud of the cavalry, and went home with a determination to combat any one hostile to cavalry legislation, if a bold front and firm purpose could stay the desecrating hand.

But all this work is primary and elementary. The second degree is administered in field-work, comprising experimental marches, and those who know General Henry by reputation will not forget his hundred-mile march with the Ninth Cavalry at Pine Ridge, and those who know him personally will become acquainted with his theory that a cavalry command in good condition, with proper feeds, should make fifty miles a day, with a maximum on the road of ten hours a day, moving at the rate of five miles an hour in cavalry halts, the gaits being walk, trot, and leading, with a day's rest each week, to be continued indefinitely. And knowing all this, they will

be sure that the model squadron wears out a good many horseshoes in a season.

The "Cossack outposts" are another feature much insisted on, and, strange to say, this arrangement was first invented in America, despite its name (see Wagner's *Outposts*), and is an improvement on picket posts in a ratio of 240 to 324. Another movement is the "form square," which is an adaptation of the "Indian circle," it being a movement from a centre to a circle, and useful when escorting wagons or when surprised. The non-commissioned officers are sent on reconnaissance, on patrols, and are required to make maps, which are submitted to an inspector.

Another scheme which I have never seen was the linking of a troop of horses, formed in a circle, to one another, by hooking the regular cavalry links from one horse's bridle to the next one's halter ring, and then leaving them in charge of one man. I also saw the new cavalry bit for the first time. It is commended by all who use it, and I saw no horses boring on it or in the least uppish about going against it, and I never remember a horse who would not do either the one or the other to the old trap which was formerly worn.

Two other curious movements indulged in by this squadron are the firing over horses while they are lying down; and, riding double—the man faced to the rear draws his pistol, and while moving to the rear keeps shooting. It might be useful during a slow retreat, and could be done with the carbine equally well.

This whole enterprise at Fort Meyer is vastly encouraging. As one officer said, "We take no credit for it, since others could do the same if they had riding-halls and cavalry officers in command." But there are cavalry officers and there are cavalry officers, and it is not every day one is born. For thirty-five years has the old general sat in a McClellan saddle, and the tremendous enthusiasm of newly joined "sub" still remains. The very thought of a wagon arouses his indignation, and every day the mules are brought into the riding-hall, and the men initiated into the intricacies of the "diamond hitch." It takes a past-master to pack a mule in twenty-two seconds, however, and I saw that feat accomplished in General Henry's command.

It is a grand thing for the young men to have this practical training by these old veterans of the civil war and the alkali plains before they go on the retired list. It is well for a young man to know enough not to unsaddle a sweating troop of horses in a broiling sun, and to learn that it makes sore backs; and it is quite important if men can cook rations, and not go up to the sky-line of a hill when scouting, and rival the statue of "Liberty Enlightening the World," when it is clearly their business to throw what light they have behind them and not before. It takes experience to put the sole of a boot back on the upper, when it has fetched loose, with four horseshoe nails, and it is not every man that knows that the place to intrench is on the edge of a cut bank, near water, if one expects ever to get out of a round-up. No one can figure that a recruit will know how many people passed over the road before him, or which way they were going, and it takes a long head and good nerves not to pull a trigger unless the sight is dark on the object when the fight may last all day and probably all night; but all these things are not taught in school. If a horse

under him is weakening on a long march in an enemy's country, it is an ignorant fool who uses a spur instead of good sense. That's the time to unload a few dollars' worth of government property. But who can understand the value of a rubber blanket, fifty rounds of ammunition, and a pocket full of grub, with a feed of grain in the bag, but one who has tried it? There are lots of dead soldiers who would have learned these lessons if they had been older. In my opinion, the tremendous box of tricks which Uncle Sam's horses are supposed to carry has put more men afoot than will ever be admitted; but at least the old boot has gone, though there is yet room for an intelligent hand with a jack-plane to shave off that cavalry pack. I am inclined to take what every one tells me is a "cranky" view on this subject, but let it stand until the next hard campaign, and I hope to be able to be more lucid. Horses are horses, and horses are not made of wood, iron, or by rule of thumb.

To revert to Fort Meyer: it is altogether refreshing; it is worth any one's while to go there and see four troops of cavalry which cannot be beaten, and it is positively exhilarating to meet their creator, a thoroughly typical United States cavalry officer, and I'm bound to say his successor in command has had a hard pace set for him.

Troop A with the Dust On

New York's crack cavalry company has just returned from the State camp at Peekskill, and Troop A is mad away down to the heels of its boots. It's a passive rage, more correctly speaking, but it is more than disgust. Some enterprising newspaper men have written that Troop A got itself lost in Westchester County on its march up from the city. Troop A has men in it who were born and raised in Westchester County, and Troop A is full of ex-cowboys who have followed bull-trail through the Bad Lands, and Troop A, moreover, is commanded by a man who has made trails in the far West which grew to be wagon-roads and railways, and when they think of being lost in Westchester County, where a half-hour's trot to the west would make the Hudson River from any point, they are seized with one grand disgust, and they want to reason profoundly on the degeneracy of the modern press; and who can blame them, when they are buffeted below the belt in that fashion? That's the deadly insult—to say a cavalryman is lost; and laymen must understand that doctors who kill their patients, and lawyers who lose their cases, and butchers who sell bad meat, are like cavalrymen who get lost. In this contest of the pen and sword for mightiness, the pen must fight fair, or disinterested observers will have to lug out the mantle of charity, and drape the pen, and say, "Forgive it." Oh no; Troop A will eat pork, and Troop A will fight, and Troop A will get next to a com-

missary wagon before the last red gleam of sunset falls, and that's all the home a soldier knows.

That long march in the dust with the thermometer skyrocketing was intended as a lesson to the men of the troop, and they learned the lesson, as they do all others. It was a long, hot march, and any man who wasn't a good stayer would have dropped out, and they brought every man and horse in fit to work next day, and the men did their turn on guard that night. They were dusty and begrimed, and they had their coats off, and spectators who saw them arrive felt the businesslike look and bearing. All the traditions of the United States cavalry call for a man with his coat off on a hot march, and his hat should be dented and the rim knocked up, and he should look jaunty, and have a "What care I?" manner —that's the way the United States cavalrymen who have made history have all looked, and it's the unwritten regulation. The other ideas are German and parade day, and of course the spectator of United States cavalry in the field must remember that he is not looking at the Amazons in the ballet.

The troop was very popular at the camp; it was an object-lesson to the hundreds of men who had not seen cavalry. Crowds of infantry lined up around the field to watch their drill, and when they charged, and a saddle turned and threw a soldier under the pounding hoofs of the troop, and when he

A Charge in Column of Fours. *Authors' photoengraving.*

caught his horse and mounted and fell in again, they cheered him to the echo; and well they might, for it was good "sand."

It is the extras, and the extras in our militia system and the State camp in particular, which constitute its virtues rather than the parade business. For instance, when two very nice young gentlemen of the stable-guard, both covered with mud, were engaged in ploughing a furrow around the horse-shed, and doing it, too, in a manner which any agriculturist might commend, though it is almost certain that neither of them, previous to this experience, had known one end of a plough from the other, they spoke to the great coarse plough-team in a high-bred way, much as they might have spoken to trembling hunters about to do six feet three inches over the rails.

Troop A is well accoutred—or it will be when it has a new rapid-fire carbine. It has a pistol-holster adapted by Captain Roe from cowboy models, and it is possible to get it out of the case within thirty days from the first declaration of intentions, and also on the case are thimbles for twelve rounds of ammunition. The sabre is hung from the left side of the saddle forward, and the carbine, encased in a cowboy sling, hangs on the opposite side. Troop A finds difficulty in getting its boots on the morning after a rainy day, and like the rest of the National Guard is expected to rely on individual ingenuity to secure more than a dozen rounds of blank ammunition a-piece. Why, I have never been able to find out. Troop A knocks the crown of its campaign hat in with a Ninth United States cavalry twist; and if they always imitate that regiment in some other ways they will never have fault to find with themselves. They wear a yellow neckerchief, and it's as pretty as a red wagon, and carry a heavy Spanish sabre as a delicate compliment to the ordnance folks who provide a worthless weapon.

The observations of the infantry who watched the mounted drills were intelligent, as befits good Americans, for I overheard two young fellows speculating how many "yellow legs" they could spot before they were ridden down by the coming charge. They were going through the motions of loading and firing, and they were taking deadly aim every time. They were doubtless assuming that their own force was in solid array with their cartridge-boxes full; but let us hope it always would be, under the circumstances.

I followed a morning drill of the troop as it pushed itself through the lanes and woods and hills of the very broken country back of the camp. The men were dismounted and deployed, and made their way through the thick woods, the puddles, and over the stone walls, and the led-horses lay in a depression the while. It is the true American dragoon-work, and was well done in a springy and intelligent manner. These young fellows, whom I watched narrowly, were Indian-like in the selection of ground to afford them protection. They went at it with zest. One young chap could do no better than lie in the very shallowest depression on a rather flat hill, but quicksilver couldn't have gotten into the bottom of that shallow hole any deeper than he. It was very interesting work, and picturesque beyond measure to see the athletic youngsters pushing through the difficult country, and to hear the carbine fire ring, and to watch the blue smoke eddy in and out among the leaves. It's the true cavalry-work, this dismounted action; it's an American trick, and with the natural shooting quality of our people and the peculiarities of our country it has been successful. Outside of the Cossacks and the British there is no cavalry in Europe, I think, who have been able to imitate it and not impair their usefulness as true horse-soldiers. Eastern America is very rough-timbered and full of stone walls, and is altogether a most impossible cavalry country in one sense, and yet again for rapid movement and dismounted action it is the best possible place.

After this the troop went up a wooded country road, and charged in column of fours—another American cavalry trick, invented in the last war, and sneered at by Europeans, who will never understand, so we can afford not to mind. Good American cavalry should be able to charge, dismount, and deploy ahead with lightning stroke. Teach them that, and the friendly nature of the country will do the rest.

It is very remarkable how readily these young citizen soldiers take on the air of veterans, and jam their horses along through the creeks and bowlders with all the abandon of a cow-puncher or a veteran of the Indian campaigns. There is the loose easy swinging seat, the wild reining of the horse, which are peculiar to natural horse-people —by which I mean the arm extended and hand held high, to the pointing of which in any direction the horse seems to respond with an almost human intelligence.

We rode back to camp, and the horses were put up, and the men undressed and bathed themselves without anything which could be characterized as false modesty; or, for that matter—well, what is proper modesty?—who has it? "Hurry up, hurry up!" is the cry. "Why hurry up?" you ask. "Oh, we always tell every one to hurry up in Troop A." One fellow is turning back-somersaults in the company street, and

Troop A has a sense of humor. It dearly loves to guy the rest of the world, and it doesn't want to be taken seriously, as befits cavalry. Ah, youth is a delicious thing! You can see it in the company streets of A Troop—a very tornado of spirits, where the happy Hottentot would be an aged and musty ruin in comparison with these boys. After careful observation I opine that the greatest and best thing in this world is a boy twenty-one years old who is in the cavalry.

Chicago Under the Mob

I passed hundreds of burning cars, acres of old car-wheels from which the wood-work had gone up in smoke. I saw the soldiers along the track, and we were the only train in that day. Every one was asking every one else, "Do you think we will make it?" We did make it, and the following evening I went to Hammond with three companies of regular infantry, to raise the blockade of turned-over cars and spiked switches, and we let the only train out which had been over the road in twenty-four hours.

On the green of the Lake Front before the Auditorium Hotel burned the camp-fires of the troops. I went over to them and met men. There was Captain Capron, standing in front of his battery park, as natural as when I had last seen him at Pine Ridge, just after Wounded Knee. There were his troops of the gallant Seventh, and acres of infantry. The camp-fires burned, the horses stamped and struck at each other on the picket-lines, the Sibleys loomed, and the sentries paced, while the men lay about in groups. I called the attention of the officers to it, saying, "This is on the Plains, but look beyond at the gray buildings towering into the misty night, with their thousands of twinkling windows, and is this not a contrast?" We all admired; then some one broke the silence, "And this country is that for which our fathers fought!"—and a solemn pause—"I suppose we will have to fight some for it ourselves."

Well, it is a great change of air for the Seventh Cavalry. The regiment was born on the Platte River, pretty far up stream, and it has never been far enough East until the last few years to buy a fine-tooth comb or hear a hand-organ; but it is East now, and right in the middle of civilization; it is right on the scene of the great Fair, the fame of which told even Kalmuck Tartars that of all, Chicago was greatest; but it has fifty copper cylinders in its belt, and its old campaign hat on, and there are things in Chicago it doesn't like, and if you want the recreated spirit of Homer you ought to hear a Seventh Cavalry trooper tell what he thinks of Chicago's mob. Chicago's mob doesn't like the Seventh Cavalry, or at least what it has seen of it. Captain L. R. Hare, with K Troop, rode through the stock-yards over the tracks, and the mob couldn't get used to his horses, and they didn't stop to try. They called his soldiers vile names, and United States soldiers are not used to being called names, and they get mad about it. The men boil inwardly, but the order "to shoot" didn't come, so the poor soldier had to sit his horse and frown, and "cuss" inwardly. But he is bottling up a seething vat of wrath, and if it ever comes out it will scorch something. It is awful bad messing for troop-horses, charging on track; it pulls the troop in the frogs of the track, and it slips, but United States cavalry can go anywhere—that's an axiom. After the malodorous crowd of anarchistic foreign trash had run as far as its breath would hold out and the cavalry halted, a real workman

"Giving the Butt"—The Way the "Regular" Infantry Tackles a Mob.
Authors' photoengraving.

came out on a window-landing of a big factory, and shook his fist at the flying mob. "Kill 'em—kill every one of 'em, you soldiers; they are cowards; they 'ain't got no wives and children; they are cowardly whelps, and they do me harm who have a wife and children, and wants to make an honest living. Damn 'em, I wish I was a soldier." Whereat Uncle Sam's troopers felt refreshed morally.

Before the charge some men undertook to throw stones. Captain Hare raised his arm, and a man, evidently an American, came out of the crowd and harangued it: "Now go away; them's United States soldiers, and they are ordered here, and they'll shoot if they get the order—only no one's got the sand to give it to them—and if they shoot they'll kill a heap of people; they can't help it; don't curse them; curse Cleveland; he's the man that they represent;" but he was howled down by a mob too beery to comprehend even that much sense.

When I went with the three companies of infantry to Hammond, they got the order in their camp, were packed in fifteen minutes, and "right forward—fours right," they swung off down the road.

It would do any soldier's heart good, it would fairly fill his eyes, to see our United States soldiers out here—it is so refreshing to one who knows how to estimate parade-day affairs—the businesslike look, the utter "don't care" of the men, the perfect machine, the tall, bronzed young athletes with the packs and campaign hats, the water and grub and 100 rounds, the officers in flannel shirts with revolver and sword. And right here I must say that I have associated with the enlisted men of our army, and a cleaner, decenter lot of young fellows can't be found anywhere. They are pure and simple of speech, they are honest, and no man can be one who can't pass the most rigid physical examination imaginable; and to see them stand in front of the howling mobs—grim, no emotion—a perfect mental calm, generaled by the knowledge of the usefulness of the technique of their trade—to hit a man at 500 yards with a Springfield—is a simple delight. They don't think that the mob have a correct and proper appreciation of their trade, and it piques them; they have lain out on the target range at 700 yards of a long summer day, and calculated the light and the wind, and gotten up quite an enthusiasm over a painted black spot and a little record-book, and when a vicious wretch with no blood circulating above his ears calls them names their sporting blood is aroused. In spite of all their repression they have their little opportunities. An officer told me that he was escorting wagons in the early morning and went back to get one out that was stalled. A fellow on the sidewalk said, "Hello, Gen'l Miles, I'd like to kick the face off you," and this to a very little dismounted trooper.

"Hold my horse, some one," pleaded the little one.

Here the Lieutenant had business further up.

"You will, will you?" And a big tough got so awfully tangled up with 130 pounds of government clothes that he couldn't separate himself until he was in much need of a doctor. But, however, that's not much satisfaction.

The task which has fallen to the soldiers out here is something too much to ask of such men. Our statesmen fail to understand that soldiers are not police, and that police-work deteriorates troops. Soldiers only know their trade—that's fighting. They never study law or how to be diplomatically nice on occasion. They should never be made to associate with a mob, except after

their manner, which is to get strategically near enough and then shoot.

In consequence, the easy-going soldier mind out here has been strained to its utmost. When infantry must walk through a seething mass of smells, stale beer, and bad language, such as my picture indicates, they don't at all understand. The soldier idea would be to create about eleven cords of compost out of the material at hand. And, again, the soldier mind doesn't understand this Hungarian or Polack, or whatever the stuff is; he will talk to a real American striker in an undertone, and tell him it is best to go home and not get shot, but he tells me in his simple way, "Say, do you know them things ain't human?—before God I don't think they are men."

Chicago is a social island; there is nothing like it elsewhere; it has the "scourin's, the rinsin's, and the clanin's," as Mulvaney would say, and it's had some politics for twenty years which would make a moral idiot suck for his breath, and Altgeld is the crowning glory. I asked some Democratic politicians out here how he ever came to be Governor, and they said, "Do you know, we have been asking ourselves that"; and shortly they added, "but we'll see that he ain't again—if God will forgive us."

When a Governor takes the raging, savage, unthinking mob, as it stands in front of the police and the soldiers, into partnership —that's a climax.

Meanwhile this city is in a state of anarchy. With the police withdrawn to fight mobs, a man's life is not worth any more than some thief will pay for it, and every one goes about with his gun. It is much like Hayes City, Kansas, in early days. The fools are on top. I say the fools, for who will all this benefit—no one, not even the fools who are the blatant boosters of this rape of government.

Chicago Under the Law

And the troops came in by the train-load, and the Mayor and the Governor didn't want them, and neither did the mob; but the mob and the Mayor and the Governor had them, and "they had to like them, too." Slat-cars full of horses, big guns on flats, and coaches of "horse, foot, and dragoons," dusty and tough, with that delicious U.S. campaign hat knocked into a thousand fanciful ways—you can read character by that hat. Big gunners from Riley, the red of their faces running their stripes a close second—it's the kiss of the Kansas sun. They fall into the arms of the gunners from Sheridan, and pound each other on the back. "Cut the fuse to zero and turn her loose—hey, old man?"

There is infantry to throw at the birds, in full field rig, and up to the camps they come with the swing-swing, swing-swing of a thousand legs moving in unison while the dust rises. Officers with six-shooters and sword, a handkerchief around their necks, old uniforms, dust, and the hat pulled down over the right eye—the infantry "make-up" tough in their business suits. No music, no noise, no look to the right or left—just playing a professional engagement in Chicago. Cavalry go to clear the camp-grounds of the hundreds of tramps which Chicago allows to decorate her parks. It was funny to see the bums, as their beery senses returned, as they threw their eyes over this unusual molestation. One man sat up, comprehended, and shot into the air three feet, like the gentleman in *Black Crook* who comes up through the star trap, and then he struck an eleven-second gait for the crowd. One man made a talk when told to "get out." "Why?" he asked. "That's why," came the military reply, as a lieutenant and a soldier grabbed him by the scruff of the neck, spurred their horses, and he never hit the ground for a hundred yards. The poor man probably didn't understand the abrupt workings of the soldier intellect.

They are now all in camp, and the festive anarchist can come around and look over the job he has cut out for himself. The ease with which much beer is obtained in America has inflamed the imagination of this Central European peasantry here in Chicago, and they imagine they own the town. Even now there will undoubtedly be isolated acts of vandalism, which can only be of consequence if they become unbearable, in which case the people will hunt them as the stockmen used to hunt the horse-thieves out West. There are the wildest rumors afloat—there always are the most blood-curdling things which the enemy are going to do in times of war. Some fanciful chap had it that the anarchs were to hamstring the cavalry horses—how sad of him? One peculiarity of all the awful things which the enemy are going to do is that the other fellows are going to let them do it. It is very hard on the nerves of the quiet cit, but the old trooper lies back on a bale of straw and his bunky shaves him, with a horse-bucket for a lather-box. No; the trouble is all with General Miles—we have got to get him out

Major Wallace F. Randolph, 3d Artillery. *Authors' photoengraving.*

of the army before we can have any wars. He spoiled the Sioux war, and he will spoil this too—so all the soldiers think. He is too anxious to fight, and gets a lot of soldiers right up where the enemy can have fun with them, and then the enemy thinks it over carefully, and concludes to wait. It is very discouraging. And then, too, he is young, and we are likely to have him a good while yet. Major Wallace Randolph, so well known in New York, is here from Fort Riley with his war-paint on, and a new kind of shell, which he is very anxious to try. The decent people of Chicago open everything to the troops; and well they may, since their presence alone keeps the social scum from rising to the top. There is always more or less doubt about all the other forces of the law, but no one doubts the "regulars." The regulars hate the scum. The scum taunts the soldier across the street with vile language, but he, the soldier, looks deaf and dumb. One bum, in a spirit of bravado, came across the street to have fun with the soldiers, and to show his comrades what easy game soldiers were. Well, it was rather interesting. He was told to halt by a sentinel, but came on; the soldier put his gun *a porte* to bar his way, and the bum grabbed the gun. The soldier wrenched at the gun, and it was in such position that he could have run the man through with it; but in the most leisurely way up walked the other sentry and gave the tough the butt right on the temple. He dropped like a beef, and the blood came plenty. The soldiers resumed their weary round, and the friends who were to witness the fun with the soldiers came over at request and lugged off the compost. These vermin are gradually coming to understand certain phases of the military profession. Apropos of this, all the authorities on mobs—and there are books and pamphlets without number—agree that to temporize with a mob means more blood to shed in the future. Chicago should have been put under martial law immediately; a few rioters shot, and this would all have been over before now. The early fight is what a mob wants, and I do not see why the authorities should ever experiment with it. There is a big foreign population here in

Chicago, which isn't American in any particular, and it follows readily any demagogue with revolutionary tendencies; it is pitied and patted by conscienceless politicians, and I think it really believed that it would not be very difficult to turn the government over; but it now entertains some doubts on the subject. Eventually this unlicked mob will have to be shot up a little, or washed, before it will get into a mental calm.

When Debs called the strike off he showed just how great a general he was—he lost his *morale,* and his men fell over each other in getting back to work. There is a big painting establishment here in Chicago, and the men struck out of sympathy for the Pullman workers. The Pullman painters came up here and hired out in their places. Well, if you can understand that, dear reader, I cannot.

Hundreds of strikers are now cursing Debs, when they should have known what he was a week before. American workmen are having hard times to educate labor leaders. Hundreds of men are tired of the unions and their sympathy strikes. I was talking to a baker who had gone out. He had been something like two years in Chicago. He had gotten married, and was saving a little. He was ordered on strike, and had to go. In two years he had been ordered out four times, and of course his savings were dissipated. He went around to another bake-shop, but there was a crowd in front of it, and he did not dare go in for fear of his life. He had a little money left, and was going to leave the city immediately to look for a job elsewhere. Another man I talked with had been a brakeman, and had hired out to a railroad, and will go to work as soon as he feels it is safe. He said: "I have belonged to a union, and all the trouble I ever had was through that. I get along all right, and then I am ordered out, and have to go all over the country to get a new job. I am going to get a non-union job, or I'm going to work on a farm, or starve." Another man who had a family, and was on strike, said, "The trouble with the union is that the hard-working men with families are in the minority, and they can't control the unions, for a lot of young fellows get a little money ahead and want to lay off—they go on a strike, and I have to go too." Another

United States Cavalrymen Shaving. *Authors' photoengraving.*

man said, "Capital is trying to crush labor and break the unions." I asked him who brought on this trouble, the railroad managers or the unions? He said the union, and finally admitted that the riot had ruined the cause, which he attributed to the ignorant and violent foreigners at the stockyards.

From that kind of talk one can hear any extreme of opinion, such as "D—— the government!" at which point it ceases to interest me. I will leave the whole subject to the statesmen and economists, and look at the boys who are here to see that the law is upheld.

There are two strategic positions in Chicago, and General Miles has concentrated his forces there. Colonel Crofton, a sketch of whom I made, is in command on the Lake Front. Troops can be sent speedily to

Col. R. E. A. Crofton, 15th Infantry. *Painting in Montana Historical Society.*

any point in the city, and they are run out in small parties on trains to keep the roads open, and they will fire on any one who obstructs the passage. The militia, police, and marshals also do this work, but they also garrison positions of consequence. They have caught from the "regulars" the prompt and aggressive way of doing business, and are effective. One can see a caisson thunder through the streets of Chicago at full gallop, and natty hussars with cowboy hat and revolver in curious contrast with the German leg-gear as they trot along. A good type of the work is the experience of Corporal McPherson, of K Troop, Seventh Cavalry, who sat on a box-car which was uncoupled by the strikers. The train went on for a hundred yards before it stopped. The corporal was told to come down by two policemen, who then abandoned him; but with rifle and gun he stood off the threatening mob, and made his way to the rear of the train, on which sat Lieutenant Sherer and another man with levelled carbines to cover his retreat. This Sherer is a hopelessly brave chap, and he turned a switch, and stood a mob off with a gun, and arrested a rioter, and made complaint in court against him, all of which enterprise he calls "rustling for K Troop." A sentry who had been taunted and insulted for an hour as he paced his post came off guard and up to Lieutenant Brewer, his face pale with rage, and the tears streaming. "Lieutenant, can I lick that —— —? I will take off my uniform, so as not to disgrace it, and fight in my underclothes." The poor fellow had been maddened by the cowardly mob, and no soldier ought to be asked to stand such abuse. But look out, some one, for the day of reckoning. Then Father Vattmann, the post chaplain of Fort Sheridan, went into a mob with the local priest at Hammond, and quieted the crazy men, or at least he helped them to understand that the Fifteenth Infantry was there to do or die.

This is the sort of work going on, with marches of observation through the city. Then it's not all as serious as this, because you can go down to Major Randolph's tepee and hear about the old sergeant who was always whittling. A recruit came up after the mess was served, and all he could get was a blob of fat pork with bristles on it. He held out the tin plate, and in a "Johnnie-come-lately voice" said,

"Sergeant!"

No answer.

"Sergeant!" he continued.

"Hwatt!"

"Sergeant, I want to see you about my meat."

"Hwatt's the mather av tha mate?"

"Why, Sergeant, there is no lean—it's all fat."

"Now g'lang out av thet," and the sergeant gave a vicious cut at his stick; "worried to death as I am from mornin' to night wid the captain and lieutenants, de ye s'pose I've nathin' ta do but to hunt lane mate for the likes av ye? Get out."

Stubble and Slough in Dakota

Now I am conscious that all my life I have seen men who owned shot-guns and setter-dogs, and that these persons were wont at intervals to disappear from their usual haunts with this paraphernalia. Without thinking, I felt that they went to slay little birds, and for them I entertained a good-natured contempt. It came about in this wise that I acquired familiarity with "mark," and "hie-on," and "No. 6 vis No. 4's": by telegram I was invited to make one of a party in Chicago, bound West on a hunting expedition. It being one of my periods of unrest, I promptly packed up my Winchester, boots, saddle, and blankets, wired "All right—next train," and crawled into the "Limited" at Forty-second Street.

"West" is to me a generic term for that country in the United States which lies beyond the high plains, and this will account for my surprise when I walked into the private car at the St. Paul depot in Chicago and met my friends contesting the rights of occupancy with numerous setter-dogs, while all about were shot-gun cases and boxes labelled "Ammunition." After greetings I stepped to the station platform and mingled with the crowd—disgusted, and disposed to desert.

A genial young soldier who appreciated the curves in my character followed me out, and explained, in the full flush of his joyous anticipation, that we were going to North Dakota to shoot ducks and prairie chicken, and that it would be the jolliest sort of a time; besides, it was a party of good friends.

I hesitated, yielded, and enlisted for the enterprise. Feeling now that I was this far it would be good to go on and learn what there was in the form of sport which charmed so many men whose taste I respected in other matters, and once embarked I summoned my enthusiasm, and tried to "step high, wide, and handsome," as the horsemen say.

The happiness of a hunting-party is like that of a wedding, so important is it that true love shall rule. The *pièce de résistance* of our car was two old generals, who called each other by an abbreviation of their first names, and interrupted conversations by recalling to each other's memory where some acres of men were slain. "A little more of the roast beef, please—yes, that was where I was shot in this side"; and at night, when quiet reigned and we sought sleep, there would be a waving of the curtains, and a voice, "Oh, say, Blank, do you remember that time my horse was hit with the twelve-pounder?" and it banished dreams. There was a phlebotomist from Pittsburg who had shot all over the earth. He was a thorough sportsman, with a code of rules as complicated as the common-law, and he "made up tough" in his canvas shooting-clothes. There was a young and distinguished officer of the regular army who had hunted men, which excused him in the paltry undertaking before him; and, finally, three young men who were adding the accumulated knowledge of Harvard to their natural endowments. For myself, I did not see how jack-boots, spurs, and a Winchester would lend themselves to the stubble and slough of Dakota, but a collection was taken, and by the time we arrived in Valley City, Dakota, I was armed, if not accoutred, in the style affected by double-barrel men. All I now needed was an education, and between the Doctor, who explained, expostulated, and swore, and a great many "clean misses," I wore on to the high-school stage. Like the obliging person who was asked if he played on the violin, I said to myself, "I don't know, but I'll try."

In the early morning three teams drove up where our car was side-tracked, and we embarked in them. The shot-gun man affects buck-colored canvas clothes, with many pockets, and carries his cartridges in his shirt fronts, like a Circassian Cossack. He also takes the shells out of his gun before he climbs into a wagon, or he immediately becomes an object of derision and dread, or, what's worse, suddenly friendless and alone. He also refrains from pointing his gun at any fellow-sportsman, and if he inadvertently does it, he receives a fusillade such as an Irish drill-sergeant throws into a recruit when he does amiss. This day was cool and with a wind blowing, and the poor dogs leaped in delirious joy when let out from their boxes, in which they had travelled all the way from Chicago. After running the wire edge off their nerves they were gotten to range inside a township site, and we jogged along. The first thing which interested me was to hear the Doctor indicate to the driver that he did not care to participate in the driver's knowledge of hunting, and that in order to save mental wear he only had to drive the team, and stand fast when we got out, in order that from the one motionless spot on the prairie sea we could "mark down" the birds.

The immensity of the wheat-fields in Dakota is astonishing to a stranger. They begin on the edge of town, and we drive all day and are never out of them, and on either side they stretch away as far as one's eye can travel. The wheat had been cut and "shocked " which left a stubble some eight inches high. The farm-houses are far apart, and, indeed, not often in sight, but as the threshing was in progress, we saw many groups of men and horses, and the great steam-threshers blowing clouds of black smoke, and the flying straw as it was belched from the bowels of the monsters.

During the heat of the day the chickens lie in the cover of the grass at the sides of the fields, or in the rank growth of some slough-hole, but at early morning and evening they feed in the wheat stubble. As we ride along, the dogs range out in front, now leaping gracefully along, now stopping and carrying their noses in the air to detect some scent, and finally—"There's a point! Stop, driver!" and we pile out, breaking our guns and shoving in the cartridges.

"No hurry—no hurry," says the Doctor; "the dog will stay there a month." But, fired with the anticipations, we move briskly up. "You take the right and I'll take the left. Don't fire over the dog," adds the portly sportsman, with an admonishing frown. We go more slowly, and suddenly, with a "whir," up get two chickens and go sailing off. Bang! bang! The Doctor bags his and I miss mine. We load and advance, when up comes the remainder of the covey, and the bewildering plenty of the flying objects rattles me. The Doctor shoots well, and indeed prairie-chickens are not difficult, but I am discouraged. As the great sportsman Mr. Soapy Sponge used to say, "I'm a good shooter, but a bad hitter." It was in this distressful time that I remembered the words of the old hunter who had charge of my early education in .45 calibres, which ran, "Take yer time, sonny, and always see your hind sight," and by dint of doing this I soon improved to a satisfactory extent. The walking over the stubble is good exercise, and it becomes fascinating to watch the well-trained Llewellyn setters "make game," or stand pointing with their tails wagging violently in the nervous thrill of their excitement, then the shooting, and the marking down of the birds who escape the fire, that we may go to them for another "flush."

With care and patience one can bag at last the whole covey.

At noon we met the other wagons in a green swale, and had lunch, and, seated in a row under the shadow side of a straw stack, we plucked chickens, while the phlebotomist did the necessary surgery to prepare them for the cook. At three o'clock the soldier, a couple of residents, and myself started together for the evening shooting. We banged away at a thousand-yards range at some teal on a big marsh, but later gave it up, and confined ourselves to chicken. In the midst of a covey and a lot of banging I heard the Captain uttering distressful cries. His gun was leaning on a wheat "shock," and he was clawing himself wildly. "Come, help me—I am being eaten alive." Sure enough he was, for in Dakota there is a little insect which is like a winged ant, and they go in swarms, and their bite is sharp and painful. I attempted his rescue, and was attacked in turn, so that we ended by a precipitous retreat, leaving the covey of chickens and their protectors, the ants, on the field.

We next pushed a covey of grouse into some standing oats, and were tempted to go in a short way, but some farmers who were threshing on the neighboring hill blew the engine whistle and made a "sortie," whereat we bolted. At a slough which we were tramping through to kick up some birds "marked down," one suddenly got up under our feet and flew directly over the Captain, who yelled "Don't shoot!" as he dropped to the ground. It was a well-considered thing to do, since a flying bird looks bigger than a man to an excited and enthusiastic sportsman. We walked along through the stubble until the red sunset no longer gave sufficient light, and then got into our wagon to do the fourteen miles to our car and supper. Late at night we reached our car, and from it could hear "the sound of revelry." The cook did big Chicago beefsteaks by the half-dozen, for an all day's tramp is a sauce which tells.

After some days at this place we were hauled up to Devil's Lake, on the Great Northern road, which locality is without doubt the best for duck-shooting in Dakota. We were driven some sixteen miles to a spur of the lake, where we found a settler. There were hundreds of teal in the water back of his cabin, and as we took position well up the wind and fired, they got up in clouds, and we had five minutes of shooting which was gluttony. We gave the "bag" to the old settler, and the Doctor admonished him to "fry them," which I have no doubt he did.

It was six miles to a pond said to be the best evening shooting about there, and we drove over. There we met our other two teams and another party of sportsmen. The shallow water was long and deeply fringed with rank marsh grass. Having no wading-boots can make no difference to a sportsman whose soul is great, so I floundered in and got comfortably wet. After shooting two or three mud-hens, under the impression that they were ducks, the Doctor came along, and with a pained expression he carefully explained what became of people who did not know a teal from a mud-hen, and said further that he would let it pass this time. As the sun sank, the flight of ducks began, and from the far corners of the marsh I saw puffs of smoke and heard the dull slump of a report.

"Mark—left," came a voice from where the young Harvard man with the peach complexion and the cream hair had ensconced himself in the grass, and, sure enough, a flight was coming towards my lair. I waited until it was nearly over, when I rose up and missed two fine shots, while the Harvard man scored. The birds fell well out in the pond, and he waded out to retrieve them.

As I stood there the soft ooze of the marsh gradually swallowed me, and when in answer to the warning "mark" of my fellows I squatted down in the black water to my middle, and only held my gun and cartridges up, I began to realize that when a teal-duck is coming down wind you have got to aim somewhere into the space ahead of it, hoping to make a connection between your load of shot and the bird. This I did, and after a time got my first birds. The air was now full of flying birds—mallards, spoon-bills, pintails, red-heads, butter-balls, gadwalls, widgeon, and canvas-backs—and the shooting was fast and furious. It was a perfect revelry of slaughter. "Mark—mark." Bang—bang. "What's the matter of that shot?" The sun has set, and no longer bathes the landscape in its golden light, and yet I sit in the water and mud and indulge this pleasurable taste for gore, wondering why it is so ecstatic, or if my companions will not give over shooting presently. There is little probability of that, however. Only darkness can end the miseries of the poor little teal coming home to their marsh, and yet with all my sentimental emotions of

"Mark—Left." *Authors' photoengraving.*

sympathy I deplore a miss. If slough-shooting has a drawback, it is its lack of action—it is a calm, deliberate shedding of blood, and a wounding of many birds, who die in the marshes, or become easy prey for the hawks, and it's as cold-blooded as sitting in water can make it.

We give over at last, and the fortunates change their wet clothes, while those who have no change sit on the seat knee-deep in dead birds and shiver while we rattle homeward. Our driver gets himself lost, and we bring up against a wire fence. Very late at night we struck the railroad, and counted telegraph poles and travelled east until the lights of the town twinkled through the gloom. Once in the car, we find the creature comfort which reconciles one to life, and we vote the day a red-letter one. The goose-shooting came later than our visit, but the people tell marvellous tales of their numbers. They employ special guns in their pursuit, which are No. 4 gauge, single-barrelled, and very long. They throw buckshot point-blank two hundred yards, and are, indeed, curious-looking arms. The chicken-shooting is not laborious, since one rides in a wagon, and a one-lunged, wooden-legged man is as good as a four-mile athlete at it. He must know setter-dogs, who are nearly as complicated as women in their temper and ways; he must have a nose for cover, and he can be taught to shoot; he can keep statistics if he desires, but his first few experiences behind the dogs will not tempt him to do that unless his modesty is highly developed. If he becomes a shot-gun enthusiast he will discover a most surprising number of fellows—doctors, lawyers, butchers, farmers, and Indians not taxed—all willing to go with him or to be interested in his tales.

The car was to be attached to an express train bound west that night, to my intense satisfaction, and I crawled into the upper berth to dream of bad-lands elk, soldiers, cowboys, and only in the haze of fleeting consciousness could I distinguish a voice—

"Remington, I hope you are not going to fall out of that upper berth again to-night."

The Withdrawal of the U. S. Troops

When the Debs rocket came down like a stick, the order came for the withdrawal of the United States regulars from Chicago. There was much uneasiness felt by the people over this move, and I overheard sundry vicious wretches along the streets say, "Wait till the soldiers go and we will burn this town," but they haven't done so up to going to press. Possibly they could see the iron hand through the velvet, for the troops are only twenty miles out of the city, at Fort Sheridan, and in five minutes they would be trotting along the shore road, and the first thing the turbulent element would know it would have the old proposition to deal with. The troops will be kept in camp at Sheridan until there is no longer any need of their services. There are not many of them, but there are enough to uphold the law, and if Chicago wants to make a Sumter of this fort there is plenty of material left in the country to make an Appomattox of Chicago.

The order came to break camp, and the camp on the Lake Front was struck in the early morning. Then the quartermaster got into trouble with striking drivers, and it was noon before the march was begun. Poor old quartermasters! it's the fashion to "cuss them out," until I really think my sympathies are with the race. A quartermaster cannot make a striking driver work or a balking horse go. It's a sight full of sadness to see "a government six" stalled to the hubs in sand with a balky leader, and an irate quartermaster sitting on his horse blowing off steam. You must imagine several

"dough-boys" standing around in various degrees of helplessness, and covered with grime and sweat and three hours overdue for dinner. That about completes the foreground of the picture, unless you want a middle ground, which will consist of a troop of cavalry as rear-guard, who sit quietly in their saddles swearing by platoons. I suppose military trains could be marched without profanity, but I have never heard of its being done. Cromwell's troopers are the only ones who are said not to have done so, but the chances are that they had "ungodly persons" to haul the trains. Stonewall Jackson, so the story goes, had to relax his moral code in the interest of the forward movement of his mule teams on occasion.

The people of Chicago have an exaggerated idea of the destructive power of a caisson since the unfortunate accident, and, indeed, I am always interested in one myself, and confess to breathing freer when it has trundled out of sight. Any one can differentiate between three hundred rounds of shrapnel and a small bottle when it pops; so the people got behind trees and otherwise absented themselves as the Third Artillery rumbled along through the streets on its march out. The weather was frightfully hot, and the "dough-boys," in full field kit, lost flesh rapidly in the march. At the first camp out the soldiers went into Lake Michigan by the hundreds, and fine athletic fellows they were. A little swell was rolling up the beach, and the cavalry rode their horses in to drink. The Third Cavalry was mounted on

Watering the Texas Horses of the Third Cavalry in Lake Michigan.
Authors' photoengraving.

Texas horses, not one of which ever saw over a hatful of water in its life, and they had much ado to drink. A bronco would put his nose down—a swell would roll in and wet his head up to his ears, whereat he would leap ashore, and not go back again under any persuasion.

The second march was in a pouring rainstorm, and the cavalry of the rear-guards stood around and saw the "mud-splitters," as they called the infantry, file by. A Texas cavalry-horse, which could have gone at full pace over a prairie-dog town, slipped and dropped flat on a street-car track.

As the column cleared the city and got into the United States of America proper, it was saluted by the waving of flags and cheers, which was quite a relief after being in the midst of a hostile population for so long. They drew to the sides of the road, halted, and two pretty misses in a pony-trap

trotted down the centre; they blushed gorgeously as the soldiers gave them their undivided attention; and, by-the-way, how delightfully inconsistent women are, since it is an undoubted fact that they are always more interested in a petty second lieutenant than in a major of rank and discretion! The small boy is much affected by the sight of soldiers; one youngster was so much overcome that he mounted his bicycle, deserted his family entirely, and accompanied K Troop all the way to Sheridan, where he was last seen wearing a soldier's cap and helping the old first sergeant at "stables." Dogs and boys go straight to a soldier's heart, and it was with great difficulty and some heart-burning that the captain separated the boy and K Troop, and got the boy to resume his relations with the crazed mother down in Chicago. K Troop regretted the parting as much as the youngster, and not having an appreciation of the paternal ties, regarded the whole affair as unjust and tyrannical.

On the road we were joined by a full regiment made up of the Sixth, Seventh, and Third Cavalry, under Colonel Gordon. The guidon of one troop was draped for the man lost in the explosion of the caisson, and in the line of file-closers was a sergeant with his head swathed in bandages. He had lost an ear in the affair, and had never lost a minute of duty: that's good soldier stuff. The colors of the Galloping Sixth—the colonel's regiment—were decorated with flowers and escorted by the color-guard with drawn sabres. The gallant Major Lebo was there—he whom the boys of the Tenth tell of: when in the Santa Rita fight the bullets were swarming like bees, he twitched nervously at his mustache, and kept repeating, "Pretty d—— hot, pretty d—— hot," until it was suggested that he follow more conservative examples and get behind a pine-tree, where it wasn't so hot. As they prepared to go into camp they were quite impressive, so seldom is it that we see a whole cavalry regiment together in the United States. Line after line they stood in the long grass, and at the call "dismount" six hundred boots disappeared over the blanket rolls as if by machinery.

Fort Sheridan is one of the finest military posts in the country. It is nothing to Fort Riley, Kansas, if I am to believe every one. The soldiers sigh at the mention of Riley. It must be a Mohammedan paradise—an Italian garden with attar of roses and the flutter of angels' wings—this Riley. But Sheridan, begging Riley's pardon, is a fine post, with its great stone barracks, the fine quarters for its officers, its club, its forests, its winding drives, and the boom of the green surf on Lake Michigan. The great bulk of the command has "taken to the brush," as it were, and as one goes about through the timbered hills he runs over a company picket-line or a row of A tents, or the horses standing at the wheels of the guns. Cavalrymen with drawn sabres patrol the roads, and pretty women drive about in traps. The old campaign rig is put away, and the bright yellow and red and white stripes of new uniforms decorate the parade.

In the time to come Fort Sheridan should be made into a big post. The Indians are all travelling in the middle of the "white man's road," and what this government must see to now is that Chicago does not commit hari-kari.

A New Infantry Equipment

Colonel Edmund Rice, of the Fifth United States Infantry, has been through our civil war, the Franco-Prussian, and the Turco-Russian wars, and had some years of Indian work with the Fifth Infantry. He has a great many ideas about infantry, and one of them is that he has never seen United States infantry in active field-work carry what is loaded on to them by the army regulations. He knew that they ought to carry all the things prescribed, but he knew also that they never did; then he knew that it was a condition, and not a theory. And one night he had a dream, and the next day he got a seamstress to begin stitching on his idea. He thought and the seamstress stitched, until finally he made a combined military cartridge-belt and garment which could be changed from belts to garments or from garments to belts in a few moments. It was made of closely woven cotton duck, practically rain and wind proof, weighing less than the present belt plate, haversack, and canteen strap, which can now be dispensed with, and it takes the place of the cape to the overcoat, which weighs two pounds. The soldier has a cool pair of shoulder-belts for hot, and by unrolling them a short comfortable overcoat and cape for cold or stormy, weather. Worn as belts or garments, they hold the ammunition, field-glass, sword, revolver, bayonet, haversack, and canteen. The knapsack, valise-pack, and clothing-bag, or blanket and shelter-tent rolled, can be worn over the equipment. It has had the endorsement of that fearful and wonderful old Ordnance Board, and the colonel has now gone to Europe to show it there.

There is an old saying that "the calf-skin [knapsack] has killed more men than bullets or bayonets," but it cannot be said that this is true of American soldiers, because they always cut the Gordian knot by the simple process of throwing everything away. They

Rice Equipment—As Shoulder-belts.
Authors' photoengraving.

would rather do without than lug the regulation equipment. Our civil war was fought with the gun, canteen (which is too large), haversack, and a shelter-tent worn round the body. The next war will be fought with the same equipment, with the addition of a bowie-knife, bayonet, and intrenching-tool combined. I believe that every soldier ought to have three acres and a cow, but I don't believe he ought to take them to war with him. There must be a new way to carry the ammunition for the new rapid-fire gun, and obviously that must be from the shoulders. All this is to be the subject of experiment, and, indeed, the infantry which I saw at Chicago were carrying three different equipments, with varying opinions as to their merits. What man can carry in slow marches, such as a change of post or position, is one thing, and what he will carry in hard active summer campaigning is another, and five or six hundred thousand men experimented for four years once with a result as stated above.

Policing the Yellowstone

"Captain Anderson—he's the superintendent, you know—started to-day for the south of the Park; some trouble, I believe, down there. A scout thought the buffalo were being disturbed," said Lieutenant Lindsley to me at the Mammoth Hot Springs Hotel, near the entrance to the Park.

"That's unfortunate. Can I overtake him?"

"It's nearly four o'clock, but as I am going down to our camp at the Lower Geyser Basin, we can start now, and by travelling at night we can catch him before he pulls out in the morning, I think," said the yellow-leg.

So putting our belongings into a double surry, we started hot-foot through the Wonderland, leaving a band of Dakota chicken-shooters standing on the steps waving their adieux. It verified all my predictions—men who shoot chickens belong in a stage-coach —they are a "scrubby wagon outfit," as the cowboys say.

Posed on the trestled road, I looked back at the Golden Gate Pass. It is one of those marvellous vistas of mountain scenery utterly beyond the pen or brush of any man. Paint cannot touch it, and words are wasted. War, storms at sea, and mountain scenery are bigger than any expression little man has ever developed. Mr. Thomas Moran made a famous stagger at this pass in his painting; and great as is the painting, when I contemplated the pass itself I marvelled at the courage of the man who dared

the deed. But as the stages of the Park Company run over this road, every tourist sees its grandeur, and bangs away with his kodak.

As we pulled up in front of the tents of the rest camp, one of those mountain thunder-storms set in, and it was as though the New York fire department had concentrated its nozzles on the earth. The place was presided over by a classic Irishman by the name of Larry, who speedily got a roaring-hot beefsteak and some coffee on the table, and then busied himself conducting growing pools of rain-water out of the tent. Larry is justly famous on the road for his *bonhomie* and Celtic wit.

At an early hour we arose and departed —the pale moon shining through the mist of the valley, while around us rose the ghostly pines. We cowered under our greatcoats, chilled through, and saddened at remembrances of the warm blankets which we had been compelled to roll out of at this unseemly hour. At 7:30 we broke into one of those beautiful natural parks, the Lower Geyser Basin, with the sun shining on the river and the grass, and spotting the row of tents belong to D Troop, Sixth United States Cavalry. Captain Scott met us at the door, a bluff old trooper in field rig and a welcoming smile. After breakfast a soldier brought up Pat Rooney. Pat was a horse from the ground up; he came from Missouri, but he was a true Irishman nevertheless, as one could tell from his ragged hips, long drooping quarters, and a liberal show of white in his eye, which seemed to say to me, "Aisy, now, and I'm a dray-horse; but spare the brad, or I'll put ye on yer back in the bloomin' dust, I will." The saddle was put on, and I waited, until presently along came the superintendent, with his scout Burgess, three soldiers, and nine pack-mules with their creaking *aparejos,* and their general air of malicious mischief.

Pointing to a range of formidable-looking hills, the captain said, "We will pull in about there," and we mounted and trotted off down the road. What a man really needs when he does the back stretches of the Yellowstone Park is a boat and a balloon, but cavalrymen ride horses in deference to traditions. My mount, Pat, was as big as a stable door, and as light as a puff-ball on his pins. As Mr. Buckram said, "The 'eight of a 'oss 'as nothing to do with 'is size," but Patrick was a horse a man needed two legs for. Besides, he had a mouth like a bull, as does every other animal that wears that impossible bit which Uncle Sam gives his cavalry. We got along swimmingly, and, indeed, I feel considerable gratitude to Pat for the two or three thousand times he saved my life on the trip by his agility and sureness of foot.

Burgess, the scout, was a fine little piece of a man, who had served the government with credit for over thirty years. He had breasted the high divide in a dozen places, had Apache bullets whistle around and through him, and withal was modest about it. He was a quiet person, with his instinct of locality as well developed as an Indian's, and contented with life, since he only wanted one thing—a war. I think he travelled by scent, since it would have been simple enough to have gone over easier places; but Burgess despised ease, and where the fallen timber was thickest and the slopes 60°, there you would find Burgess and his tight little pony picking along.

Both Captains Anderson and Scott have a pronounced weakness for geysers, and were always stopping at every little steam-jet to examine it. I suppose they feel a personal responsibility in having them go regularly;

one can almost imagine a telegram to "turn on more steam." They rode recklessly over the geyser formation, to my discomfort, because it is very thin and hazardous, and to break through is to be boiled. One instinctively objects to that form of cooking. The most gorgeous colors are observed in this geyser formation; in fact, I have never seen nature so generous in this respect elsewhere. I wondered that the pack-mules did not walk into the sissing holes, but I suspect a mule is a bit of a geologist in his way, and as most of them have been in the government service for thirty or forty years, they have learned how to conserve their well-being. There is a tradition that one was considerably overdone once in a geyser-hole, so they may have taken warning. Who can understand a mule? The packer leads the old bell-mare off to a feeding-ground, and the whole bunch of mules go racing after her, and chains wouldn't hold them. The old bell-mare takes across a nasty chasm or a dirty slough-hole, and as the tinkle of the little cow-bell is losing itself in the timber beyond, one after another they put their ears forward and follow on.

We passed up a cleft in the hills, and were swallowed up in the pine and cedar forest. Presently the cleft ended, and nothing but good honest climbing was in front. There began my first experience in riding over the fallen timber, whiich obstructs all the northwestern Rocky Mountains. Once up in British Columbia I did it, but had trails, and I childishly imagined that there must also be trails wherever men wanted to go. Crisscross and all about lay the great peeled logs, and travel was slow, toilsome, and with anything but horses trained to it would have been impossible.

A good horse or mule, once accustomed, makes little of it, but on the steep down grades the situation is complicated by fallen logs, which it is necessary to "bucket" over, and then stop dead on an incline of 50°, with a couple of miles of tumble if he fails. The timber grew thicker, and when Burgess would get us in a hopeless sort of place, Captain A. would sing out to Captain S.,

"Burgess is on the trail now"; and when it was fairly good going, "Now he is off." But nothing could rattle Mr. Burgess, and he continued calmly on his journey, the destination of which, it seemed, could be nothing short of the moon. Finally we found ourselves seemingly so inextricably tangled up that even Burgess had to scratch his head. One mule was hung up hopelessly, while the rest crowded around us into the *chevaux-de-frise* of logs, and merrily wound through the labyrinth the old Sixth Cavalry "gag," "Here's where we trot."

To complete the effect of this passage it began to rain, and shortly to pelt us with hailstones, so we stopped under some trees to let it pass, and two people who should know better dismounted and got their saddles wet, while another, more wise in his generation, sat tight, and was rewarded later for his display of intelligence. By-and-by, wet and tired of fallen timber, we came into the Little Fire-hole Basin, and found buffalo signs in abundance. We were in great hopes of seeing some of these animals, but I may as well add that only one was seen on the trip, though there was fresh spoor, and they were undoubtedly about. We found no pony tracks either, which was more to the soldiers' liking, since they are intrusted with the protection of the Park against poachers.

In this way squads are sent over the Park, and instructed not to follow the regular

The Bell-mare Over a Bad Place. *Authors' photoengraving.*

trails, but to go to the most unfrequented places, so that they may at any time happen on a malicious person, and perhaps be able to do as one scout did—photograph the miscreant with his own camera.

After a good day's march we made camp by a little lake, and picketed our horses, while the mules ran loose around the bell-mare. Our appetites had been sharpened by a nine hours' fast, when a soldier called us to the "commissaries" which were spread out on a pack canvas. It was the usual military "grub," and no hungry man can find fault with that.

"Any man who can't eat bacon can't fight," as Captain Scott said; so if any reader wants to be a soldier he must have a mania for bacon, it seems. "This is the stuff that makes soldiers brave," he added, as the coffee-pot came around, and we fell to, and left a dreary waste of empty tins for the cook to pick up. We lighted our pipes after the banquet on the grass, and walked down to the shore of the beautiful pond, which seemed so strangely situated up there on the very crest of the continental divide. There are only three seasons in these altitudes, which the boys divide into July, August, and Winter, and the nights are always chilly. An inch or two of snow may fall even in mid-summer. In winter the snow covers the ground to a great depth, as we can tell by the trees. Nothing grows but rather stunted fir and pine and a little grass of the most hardy variety. The rounds of the Park are then made by mounting the cavalry on the *ski,* or Norwegian snow-shoe, and with its aid men travel the desolate snowclad wilderness from one "shack" to another. Small squads of three or four men are quartered in these remote recesses of the savage mountains, and remain for eight months on a stretch. The camps are provisioned for the arctic siege, and what is stranger yet is that soldiers rather like it, and freely apply for this detached service. There is little of the "pomp and vanity" in this soldiering, and it shows good spirit on the part of the enlisted men. They are dressed in fur caps, California blanket

coats, leggings, and moccasins—a strange uniform for a cavalryman, and also quite a commentary on what are commonly called the vicissitudes of the service.

In the early morning our tent was pulled down, and our bedding packed off almost before we had disentangled ourselves from its sheltering folds. The well-trained troopers went about their task of breaking camp with method and address. Burgess and a young soldier pulled a reluctant strawberry-blond mule out of the line of pack-animals, and throwing a blind over his face, proceeded to lay the blanket and adjust the *aparejo.* With a heave the *cincha* is hauled tight, and the load laid on, while the expert throws the "diamond hitch," and the mule and pack are integral parts. This packing of nine mules was accomplished with great rapidity, and laying our saddles carefully, we mounted and followed the scouts off down the trail in single file on a toilsome march which would probably not end until three or four o'clock in the afternoon. We wound around the spurs of hills, and then across a marsh, with its yielding treacherous bottom, where the horses floundered, and one mule went down and made the mud and water fly in his struggles, while my apprehensions rose to fever-pitch as I recognized my grip-sack on his load, and not likely to be benefited by the operation. At the head-waters of these rivers—and it may be said that this little purling brook is really the source of the Missouri itself, although not so described—there is an abundance of soggy marsh, which makes travel extremely difficult. In one place Captain Anderson's horse went belly-deep on a concealed quag made by a stream coming out of the side of the hill, and rolling back, fell heavily on the captain, and for a time it was rather a question whether the horse would get out or not; but by dint of exertion he regained firm ground. When a big strong horse gets into a slough the dorsal action is terrific, and it is often necessary to dismount quickly to aid him out. We crossed the great divide of the continent at a place where the slope was astonishingly steep and the fallen timber

On the Headwaters—Burgess Finding a Ford. *Painting in The Metropolitan Museum of Art, Anonymous Gift, 1962.*

thickly strewn. It was as thoroughly experimental travelling as I have ever seen, unless possibly over a lava-rock formation which I essayed last winter on the western slope of the Sierra Madre, in Chihuahua; and yet there is a fascination about being balanced on those balloonlike heights, where a misstep means the end of horse and rider. I was glad enough, though, when we struck the parklike levels of the Pitchstone plateau as the scene of our further progression. If one has never travelled horseback over the Rocky Mountains there is a new and distinct sensation before him quite as vigorous as his first six-barred gate, or his first yacht-race with the quarter-rail awash.

All through the Park were seen hundreds of wild-geese, so tame that they would hardly fly from us. It was a great temptation to shoot, but the doughty captain said he would run me off the reservation at a turkey-trot if I did shoot, and since I believed him I could restrain myself. The streams and marshes were full of beaver-dams, and

the little mud-and-stick houses rose from the pools, while here and there we saw the purl of the quiet water as they glided about. This part is exactly as primitive as when the lonely trapper Coulter made his famous journey through it, and one cannot but wonder what must have been his astonishment at the unnatural steaming and boiling of the geysers, which made the Park known from his descriptions as "Coulter's Hell."

From the breast of the mountains overlooking the great Shoshonee Lake there opened up the most tremendous sight as the waters stretched away in their blue placidity to the timbered hills. The way down to the shores was the steepest place I have ever seen horses and mules attempt. In one place, where the two steep sides of the cañon dipped together, it was cut by a nasty seam some six feet deep, which we had to "bucket over" and maintain a footing on the other side. After finding myself safely over, I watched the shower of pack-mules come sliding down and take the jump. One mule was so far overbalanced that for a moment I thought he would lose his centre of gravity, which had been in his front feet, but he sprang across to the opposite slope and was safe. Horses trained to this work do marvels, and old Pat was a "topper" at the business. I gave him his head, and he justified my trust by negotiating all the details without a miss. On a sandy "siding" he spread his feet and slid with an avalanche of detached hill-side. Old Pat's ears stuck out in front in an anxious way, as if to say, "If we hit anything solid, I'll stop"; while from behind came the cheery voice of Captain Scott, "Here's where we trot."

On the shores of the Shoshonee we camped, and walked over to the famous Union Geysers, which began to boil and sputter, apparently for our especial benefit. In a few minutes two jets of boiling water shot a hundred feet in air, and came down in rain on the other side, while a rainbow formed across it. The roar of the great geysers was awe-inspiring; it was like the exhaust of a thousand locomotives, and Mr. Burgess nudged me and remarked, "Hell's right under here."

Near the geysers, hidden away in a depression, we found a pool of water of a beautiful and curious green, while not twenty feet from it was one of a sulphur yellow. There was a big elk track in the soft mud leading into it, but no counter track coming out. There had been a woodland tragedy there.

The utility of a geyser-hole is not its least attraction to a traveller who has a day's accumulation of dust and sweat on him. I found one near the camp which ran into a little mountain stream, and made a tepid bath, of which I availed myself, and also got a cup of hot water, by the aid of which I "policed my face," as the soldiers call shaving.

The next day we encountered one of those great spongy mountain meadows, which we were forced to skirt on the rocky timber-strewn hill-sides, until finally we ventured into it. We curved and zigzagged through its treacherous mazes, fording and recrossing the stream in search of solid ground. Burgess's little gray pony put his foot forward in a gingerly way, and when satisfied, plunged in and floundered through. The pony had a positive genius for morasses. We followed him into the mud, or plunged off the steep sides into the roaring river, and, to my intense satisfaction, at last struck a good pony trail. "Now Burgess is off the trail!" we cried, whereat the modest little scout grinned cheerfully. From here on it was "fair and easy," until we came to the regular stage-road, to travel on which it seemed to us a luxury.

This expedition is typical of the manner of policing the Park, and it is generally monotonous, toilsome, and uneventful work; and the usefulness of such a *chevauchée* is that it leaves the track of the cavalry horse-shoe in the most remote parts of the preserve, where the poacher or interloper can see it, and become apprehensive in consequence of the dangers which attend his operations. That an old trapper might work quietly there for a long time I do not doubt, if he only visited his line of traps in the early morning or late evening and was careful of his trail, but such damage as he could do would be trivial. Two regiments could not entirely prevent poaching in the mountain wastes of the great reservation, but two troops are successful enough at the task. It is a great game-preserve and breeding-ground, and, if not disturbed, must always give an overflow into Montana, Wyoming, and Idaho, which will make big game shooting there for years to come. The unreasoning antipathy or malicious disregard of the American pioneer for game-laws and game-preservation is somewhat excusable, but the lines of the pioneer are now cast in new places, and his days of lawless *abandon* are done. The regulation for the punishment of Park offenders is inadequate, and should be made more severe. The Park is also full of beasts of prey, the bear being very numerous. A fine grizzly was trapped by some of the superintendent's men and shipped to the Smithsonian Institution while I was there. Near the Fountain Hotel one evening a young army surgeon and myself walked up to within one hundred and fifty yards of a big grizzly, who was not disposed to run off. Being unarmed, we concluded that our point of view was close enough, and as the bear seemed to feel the same way about it, we parted.

Americans have a national treasure in the Yellowstone Park, and they should guard it jealously. Nature has made her wildest patterns here, has brought the boiling waters from her greatest depths to the peaks which bear eternal snow, and set her masterpiece with pools like jewels. Let us respect her moods, and let the beasts she nurtures in her bosom live, and when the man from Oshkosh writes his name with a blue pencil on her sacred face, let him spend six months where the scenery is circumscribed and entirely artificial.

The Affair of the –th of July

The following is a letter from a young military aide-de-camp who was in position to see a great deal of the great riots in Chicago.

CHICAGO, July – 18–

MY DEAR FRIEND,—In your last you ask me to give you my experiences in the affair of the other day here in Chicago, and although I played but a small part, yet I do not mind adding my little quota to the volumes of matter already written on the subject. To begin with, we at headquarters had known for some time that the turbulent elements were organizing an opposition to Federal authority, and indeed after the demoralization of the police power in the affairs of Monday and Tuesday, the general issued his proclamation putting the city under martial law. The people were ordered to keep within their own doors, under penalty of shooting or drum-head court-martial, after seven o'clock in the evening, and it was also explained that any domicile harboring an active enemy was to be reduced by the sharpest means at command. The reinforcements arrived on Tuesday, and militia and police were embodied in our command. I had been out on a patrol with a troop of the Third Cavalry late in the afternoon, and I reported to the general that there was an ominous lull in the city, and that I feared the enemy were to take some active measures. We had tried, unsuccessfully, to locate the rifles looted from the gun-stores, and

also to find anything like a rendezvous of insurgents. The better class of people had nearly all left the city, and what remained were guarding their business property. Chicago streets, usually so teeming with human life, were almost deserted. No smoke came from the big chimneys, and the shops were shuttered and boarded up. A great many honest people of small means were much put to it to obtain food, and I cannot but tell you how I saw some of the troopers divide their rations with the citizens. At the time we had no intimation of the serious turn affairs would take on, but the remark of the general's, that "every soldier will die right in his tracks," had gone the rounds of the camps, and nerved the men to face the music. I was eating my dinner in the Chicago Club when I thought I heard rifle-shots. This was about nine o'clock, and the moon was shining on the Lake Front, although the side streets were dark, since the lights were out all over the city. In a minute more a squad of cavalry swept up the street at full gallop. They were heading for the general's tent, and I grabbed my cap and ran down-stairs three steps at a time. As I made my way along Michigan Avenue I could hear carbine-shots over in the city, and shortly all the bugles giving "The Assembly."

I got to headquarters, and met old Hewer of the Seventh, and it was his troops which had come in; he told me they were then standing off a mob, which was returning the fire down in the city.

I got an order from the general to deliver to the lower section of the camp, and getting on my "wheel" (which is better for this work than a horse), I pulled out. I delivered my order to Colonel Loftowne, and then waited to observe things, as I was to report back to headquarters. Rawball's battery went into "action front," two sections to a street. They were loaded, and then down on the next corner came the order through the still night to fire. A terrific flash illuminated the black square, and then with a howl down the long street went the 2¾-inch, and far down in the darkness I could see her explode; then all was silent. The signal-rockets were going from the top of the Auditorium, and I saw the answering upward sweep of the balls of fire as they were replied to farther down the street. We were on the extreme right, which was below the Art Building, and were ordered to move for an attack on the streets of the city *en échelon*. The guns limbered up, and, escorted by two companies of infantry, we passed into the dim light. At the corner of Wabash Avenue we halted.

Four or five blocks down we could both hear and see rifle-firing, evidently directed on our camp, and also a great crowd. At this juncture we heard a most awful explosion, dull and not like a rifle-canon. "Dynamite!" we all exclaimed in a breath.

"Cut the fuse to zero! Fire!" And with a terrific crash the missile sped on its way. "I think that street will be clear for a spell," drawled the captain, in his delicious old Georgia manner, as he got his guns in motion. We could hear the occasional boom of a 3-inch and the loud grinding of the Gatlings, and we knew it was enfilading our fire. The rifle-fire was silenced down the city, and the mob, as we judged by the noise, was running away. Over in the direction of the post-office we then heard rifle-shots.

"That's that outpost of the Twenty-seventh guarding the building," we said to each other. It fairly crackled now—"giving 'em hot stuff."

"Halt!" came the command, and the men stopped. "We will wait here for orders."

"What do you suppose that report was?" we asked each other as we stood on the curbing.

"It must have been dynamite. I know the sound of this ordnance too well to be mistaken," commented the captain of artillery. "What's that? Hark!" as a clatter sounded on the pavement in our rear. "It's a horse coming at full speed. Spread out, men, and stop him." And sure enough, a frightened cavalry horse came charging into the midst of the infantry, and was only stopped after he had knocked down two men.

"He only has a halter on; he's got away from the picket line; here, boys—here comes another." This one in turn was stopped, and two more which followed directly. Detailed men were sent back with the horses, while I went also to make my report. As I sped on ahead I was startled by a shot, and with a sputter I heard the bullet go to pieces at my feet. I looked around, and from the dark of a window came a flash and another sputter.

"D—— him, he is firing at me," I ejaculated, and I made the pedals fly. I had no idea of stopping, but I thought I could remember the building; and thinks I, "I am not after game, but whoever you are, I'll hunt you up, my lad."

At headquarters everything was bustle.

"Some one exploded a big dynamite bomb right in the street, in front of the Fifth Infantry camp," said Captain Moss to me, "and killed four men and wounded a dozen more. Some of the cavalry horses broke away from the picket lines and stampeded," he went on.

The hospital tents were ablaze with light, and I knew that the surgeons were at their grewsome work.

I reported for orders, and shortly was given one to deliver at my old post. Back I sped, and came near tumbling into a big hole, which I knew had been made by the dynamite bomb. I will go down another street and cross over, so as to avoid that fellow who potted at me, I reasoned; but before I turned off I saw the two infantrymen and the four old cavalry horses coming along.

"Oh, lieutenant," they called, and I went up to them. "We saw that fellow shoot at you, and McPherson held the horses and I slipped down the dark side of the street and located him. He stuck his head out of the window, and I rested across a door-post and let him have it."

"Did you hit him?"

"Well, you kin bet! He came out of that window like a turkey out of a pine-tree. A little slow at first, but kerflop at last."

So I took the street of my late enemy, and had a look at a dark object which lay on the sidewalk under the house I had located. In response to the order I bore, the infantry advanced to develop any opposition which there might be. Men were thrown out in front, and the heavy body marched in rear. We had proceeded this way for some blocks with no sound but the dropping rifle-fire some quarter of a mile to our left and behind us, when we began to find men huddled in doorways, who were promptly taken prisoners and disarmed, and sent to the rear. Some bore rifles and all had revolvers, and a hard-looking set they were. The artillery fire had demoralized them, and whatever they were to have done they had abandoned after the first shell had gone shrieking and crashing down the street.

"They'll get a drum-head in the morning, and it won't sit ten minutes," mused an officer. "I suppose they are anarchists. Well, they ought to like this; this is a sort of anarchy. It's the best we have got in our shop."

These words were scarcely spoken before a blinding flash lit up the street as lightning might. A tremendous report followed, and I was knocked down right over my bicycle, which I was trundling. I was up in an instant, and with a ringing clash an object had fallen at my feet and struck my leg a smart blow, which pained me considerably. I

reached down and picked up a Springfield rifle barrel without lock or stock. A dynamite cartridge had been exploded in our front. The infantry hesitated for a moment. Many men had been flung on their backs by the force of the concussion. "Forward!" was the command, and dropping my bicycle, I followed the dark figures of the infantry as they made their way down the sides of the streets. Half a block ahead was a great hole in the pavement, and the sidewalk was littered with cobble-stones and débris from the walls of the surrounding buildings. The bomb had been exploded over the advance-guard, and had destroyed it utterly. Which building had it come from? We stood in the doorways, and held our breath and waited. A stone dropped in the street with a crash. A tiny light appeared in one of the upper windows of a tall narrow office building. It disappeared instantly, and all was dark. Two men put their heads out of the window. "See-e!" I hissed, as a soldier drew up his rifle. All was quiet. The two heads peered down the street, and then whispered together, when shortly we caught the hollow echo of the words, "D—— 'em, they don't want any more."

"Now run for it," said the captain in command, who was a big fellow, and we all scampered off down the street to our main body. What we had discovered was reported to the battery commander. He swore a great oath.

"Bring that gun up here to this side; boost her on to the sidewalk. Come, get hold here, you fellows; lend us a hand; run her along a little; train her on that doorway. Now fire!" And then, in a high voice, "Captain, let your men cover that house with rifle-fire, and detail some men to break into a store and get inflammables."

The big gun went with a deafening crash, and the doorway was in slivers. A dropping rifle-fire rained into the windows. Crash went the big gun after a minute, but the building was dark and silent, as though holding their sputtering toys in contempt.

"I'm going to burn that building. Send a man to call out the fire department!" roared the old captain, who had now lost all his drawling, and was bellowing like a bull. After a time infantrymen came along with their arms full of bottles and cans of kerosene, and I know not what else. They had broken into a drug-store, and told the proprietor, who was found there in the darkness with his three clerks, to give them the most inflammable substances at his command.

The squad of infantry formed on the side of the street occupied by the ill-fated house, and as the big gun crashed and the rifle-fire redoubled, they dashed down the street and swarmed into the building.

"Keep up that rifle-fire!" howled the senior officer. It was bang! bang! bang! for a full minute, when a flash of light lit up the doorway, and with a rush out came the squad, and made its way to us on the run.

"We have fired the elevator shaft," said a young officer, breathing heavily with excitement. The doorway was very light now, and shortly the second-story windows over it showed yellow. Windows farther up the tall building began to redden and then to glow brightly. It was ten minutes now since the first gleam of fire, and the rifles had ceased. The building was now ablaze. A huge roaring was heard, and the black smoke poured from the hall windows, while the side windows were yet dark. A harsh yelling came from the window where I had seen the little match struck, and the thick black smoke eddied around and hid it all.

"By sections—forward—trot—march," and with a dash we moved forward past the roaring furnace and down into the darkness below.

"My orders were to move forward," muttered the old captain, as he bit at a plug of tobacco.

It was now nearly twelve o'clock, and I could hear a great deal of small-arm firing down the city on my left in front, and also the boom of cannon away on the other side of town. Shortly a note was handed me by an adjutant, and I was to go to a command on a street nearly in front of headquarters. I sped along, and shortly met men by twos and threes, wounded men going to camp, and two fellows sitting on the curbing. "Where is Captain B——'s command, my men?"

"Right on down the street—me bunkie's got it," was all I heard as I shot along.

The rifle-fire grew, and the crash of a Hotchkiss came at intervals. Then I made out a small infantry reserve, and then the guns. I found the captain, and delivered my note.

"Wait by me," said the captain, as he went into a doorway and read the order by scratching matches on his pantaloons, and the Hotchkiss nearly broke my ear-drums. "Wait a minute or so," said the captain, as he crushed the note into his trousers-pocket.

I waited, and a "kid" of the reserves, whom I knew, greeted me and explained. "They are in the depot, and we are going to carry it by storm in a minute."

Again the Hotchkiss went, and "Come on!" rang the order as the men moved forward. It was the captain, and he wanted me to "wait a minute," so, thinks I, I will wait near him; and pulling my bicycle into a dark doorway, I waited along by the captain, near the head of the procession. As we moved out from the protection of the street the report of a Hotchkiss nearly threw me from my pins, and then we ran silently under a rather hot fire from the windows and doorways. I heard the balls strike—a dull slap—and a man stumbled forward ahead of me and dropped. I sprang over him, and was soon out of fire, and with the little column passed through the big doorway under which I had so often passed with my gripsack and on the *qui vive* for a hansom-cab driver. There was a tremendous rattle of fire, the bullets struck the stonework viciously; the hollow pat sounded, and men sank reeling and lay prone under my feet. We piled in and returned the fire. It was all smoke now; nothing distinguishable. "Come on!" came a voice which interlarded itself with the reports, and we went on wildly. We were now out of the smoke, and then I saw, by the light of a fire, figures running. A man fired in our faces. He was sitting up; a bayonet went into him, and he rolled over, clutching his breast with his hands. "The house is on fire!" came the cry, and the infantry continued to discharge on the retreating figures. A great flash lighted everything, and as my senses returned, it came over me "that was a bomb." I passed my hand over my eyes. The building was on fire. I could see men lying around me breathing heavily and groaning. I got up; a voice said, "Get these men out of here!" "Get these men out of here!" I echoed, as I grabbed a big Irish sergeant, and supporting him under the arms, I strove forward. The living soldiers took hold of the dead and wounded comrades, and bore them back through the smoke and into the street. The station was now on fire, and every one was highly excited, for these bombs made strange work, and were very demoralizing.

"We Were Now Out of the Smoke." *Authors' photoengraving.*

They did no particular good to the enemy beyond that point, since they did not stop our advance, and they also demoralized the enemy quite as much as ourselves. There seemed to be no further opposition to the troops. I went back to headquarters, got my horse, and received permission to go with a detachment of cavalry. We pulled out up Michigan Avenue. We were to scout and make a junction with stock-yard troops out to the south of the city or in Washington Park. The moon was going down, and there was no sound but the clattering of the troops and the jingle of the sabres. We passed a large squad of police, with their lanterns, moving out south to protect private residences and arrest prowlers. Ahead of us we heard three revolver-shots, and galloping forward, we were hailed by a voice from a window. "They have been trying to break into my house, catch them; they are running up the street." The road here was very wide, with two rows of trees in the centre and narrow grass-plots.

"Come on!" shouted the captain, and spurring up, we moved forward.

"There they are, captain: can't you see them?" spoke the old first sergeant, as he drove his horse forward to the captain's side.

We rode over the grass-plot, and, sure enough, forms were seen to run up the steps of houses and behind shrubbery.

"Dismount!—shoot them down!" came the command, and the men sprang forward with a rush. A revolver flashed, and was followed by a dozen carbine-balls, and from the blackness of a high front stoop rolled a figure grunting and gasping. Shot after shot rang through the darkness, and the troopers routed the vermin from step and shrubbery, until shortly it ceased.

"Captain, here is Foltz—he's been shot; and McInerny—he's shot too."

I sprang up the steps of a great stone mansion and pounded on the door with the butt of my six-shooter. A window was raised and a head peered out. "What do you want?"

"We are United States cavalry, and we have two wounded men. Open your doors; we want you to put them to bed," and the window went down with a bang. Shortly the bolts were drawn, the door opened, and an old gentleman with white hair and carrying a lamp appeared.

"Certainly; bring them right in, captain," said the old gentleman, and the two men were carefully lifted and borne in by their comrades. I helped to carry one man upstairs, and to take off his great boots and to strip him.

"Is there a doctor near here, sir?" I asked.

"Right across the street; will I send my man?"

"Yes, and a-running, too," replied a comrade, who was stanching the blood on the man's chest with a bed-sheet.

We laid the man out, and I paused to note the splendor of the apartment, and to think it none too good for a brave soldier. The doctor came shortly, and I left the house. The troop was mounted and moved on. From a mansion across the street came a shot and loud shouting. We rode up and dismounted. There was a light in the front room and the door was open. The captain sprang up the steps, followed by ten or twelve men. As we entered we saw a half-dozen of the most vicious-looking wretches I have ever seen. They were evidently drunk, and did not comprehend the import of our presence. One man raised a champagne-bottle and threatened the captain. A carbine flashed—the report was almost deafening—and the drunken man dropped the bottle, threw up his hand, turned half round, and sank with a thud.

"Take these men out and shoot them, sergeant." And the now thoroughly terrorized revellers, to the number of six, were dragged, swearing and beseeching, to the pavement, and I heard shots.

The room we were in was magnificent, but in the utmost disorder. The floor was strewn with broken bottles, vases, and bric-à-brac.

A form appeared in the door. It was a woman. She was speechless with terror, and her eyes stared, and her hands were clutched. We removed our hats, and the woman closed her eyes slowly.

"Look out, captain, she's going to faint!" I cried.

The captain slapped his hat on with a crush.

"That's what she's going to do," he said, as he stood like a football-rusher before the ball is put in play.

"Grab her!" I shouted, and, with a bound, the captain made a high tackle just as the lady became limp. Out in the hall I jumped, and yelled, "Oh, you people up-stairs there, come down; come running; the lady has fainted; we are soldiers; come down; come down; come down, some-body!" And from the upper darkness a white-robed figure glided past me into the light room.

"Oh, I'm so glad!" she said, as she swept up to the rather engaging scene of the beau-tiful woman and the captain, who was "not glad," judging from his disconcerted air; and to make a story short, we left the house.

As we mounted we could see the dark-ness beginning to gray, and knew that morning would come shortly.

"It's been a nasty night's work, but if it once comes daylight I'll leave nothing of these rioters but their horrible memory," mused the old captain.

"There is a glow in the sky off there—don't you see?" I added.

"Fire! Oh, I've expected that."

As the light grayed I could see the doors of majestic residences open, windows bro-ken, and débris trailing down the steps.

"Looted."

"There are people ahead—trot!" said the captain, half turning in his saddle. The bray of the trumpet was followed by the jingle of the forward movement.

The captain pulled off to the side and shouted, "No prisoners, men—no pris-oners!" And the column swept along.

We could make out more human forms, all running by the side of the road. There were more and more fugitives as we drew nearer.

"Come on," sang out the first lieutenant, as he put his horse into a gallop and drew his six-shooter; and shortly we were among them, scattering them like chaff and firing revolver-shots into them. Up the side streets they went, scampering, terrorized.

"I guess they will keep that gait for a mile," said the lieutenant, as he turned grin-ning to me. "That is the outfit which has been looting down Michigan Avenue. I wish the light would come, and we'll give 'em hot stuff."

At Washington Park we dismounted, and shortly were joined by B Troop from Hor-don's command. They told us they had been fighting all night, and that the stock-yards and many buildings were on fire. They had encountered opposition, which seemed to be armed and to have some organization, but, laughing, he said, "They couldn't stand the 'hot stuff.'"

After this we made the ride back. It was now light, and as we rode slowly, men dis-mounted at intervals, and did some pretty work at rather long ranges with the car-bines. The enemy would see us coming, and start to run up side streets, and then, riding forward, we dismounted and potted at them. I saw a corporal "get a man" who was running upwards of six blocks away—it was luck, of course. The police were now seen posted along at intervals, and were going into houses to tell the people of the order to remain in-doors for twenty-four hours more, which was the latest from headquarters, and I suppose was intended to give the police and troops an opportunity to seek out armed insurgents.

I got back to camp, dismounted, and, being hungry, bethought me of the Audito-rium for breakfast. I didn't think, after the pounding the hotel had gotten in the early evening previous, that they would come out strong on an early breakfast, but they did fairly well. You remember Ed Kennedy, the popular clerk there—well, he was shot and badly wounded while behind the desk, after the bomb drew our fire. He will get around all right, I am told.

I saw some of the execution of those hundreds of prisoners next day, but I didn't care to see much. They piled them on flat-cars as though they had been cordwood, and buried them out in the country somewhere. Most of them were hobos, anarchists, and toughs of the worst type, and I think they "left their country for their country's good." Chicago is thoroughly worked up now, and if they keep with the present attention to detail, they will have a fine population left. The good citizens have a monster vigilance committee, and I am afraid will do many things which are not entirely just, but it is the reaction from lawlessness, and cannot be helped. They have been terribly exasperated by the rioting and license of the past. Of course, my dear friend, all this never really happened, but it all might very easily have happened if the mob had continued to monkey with the military buzz-saw.   Yours faithfully,   JACK.

Coaching in Chihuahua

That coaching is a grand sport I cannot deny, for I know almost nothing of it beyond an impression that there is a tremendous amount of mystery connected with its rites. As a sport I have never participated in it, but while travelling the waste places of the earth I have used it as a means on occasion. I never will again. There is no place to which I desire to go badly enough to go in a coach, and such points of interest as are inaccessible except by coach are off my trail. I am not in the least superstitious, and am prone to scout such tendencies; but I'm a Jonah in a stage-coach, and that is not a superstition, but a fact amply proven by many trials. I remember as a boy in Montana having been so hopelessly mixed up with a sage-bush on a dark night when the stage overturned that it left an impression on me. Later in life I was travelling in Arizona, and we were bowling along about ten miles an hour down a great "hog-back" to the plains below. A "swing mule" tripped up a "lead mule," and the stage—with myself on the box—ran over the whole six, and when the driver and I separated ourselves from the mules, shreds of harness, splinters, hair, hide, cargo, and cactus plants I began to formulate the intelligence that stage-coaching was dangerous.

While riding in an army ambulance with Major Viele, of the First Cavalry, and the late Lieutenant Clark, of the Tenth, the brake-beam broke on the descent of a hill, and we only hit the ground in the high places for about a mile. I will not insist that every man can hold his breath for five consecutive minutes, but I did it. Thereupon I formulated vows and pledges. But like the weak creature I am, I ignored all this and got into one at Chihuahua last winter, and first and last did five hundred miles of jolting, with all the incident and the regulation accident which goes to make up that sort of thing. Now I like to think that I have been through it all, and am alive and unmaimed; and I take a great deal of comfort in knowing that, however I may meet my end, a stage-coach will be in no way connected with it.

On the trip out we had mules. They were black and diminutive. To me a Mexican mule seems to be the Chinaman of the dumb animals. They are enduring beyond comprehension, and they have minds which are patient, yet alert and full of guile. The Mexican *coacheros* have their mules trained, as bankers do their depositors in our land. They back up against a wall and stand in line while one by one they are harnessed. In the early morning I liked to see the lantern-light glorify the little black creatures against the adobe wall, and hear the big *coachero* talk to his beasts in that easy, familiar way and with that mutual comprehension which is lost to those of the human race who have progressed beyond the natural state. This coachman was an enormous man—big, bony, and with Sullivanesque shoulders, gorilla hands, and a blue-black buccaneer beard; and but for a merry brown eye and a mouth set in perpet-

An Early Morning Bath. *Painting in Otto Noeding Collection, Bent Gallery, Taos, New Mexico.*

ual readiness to grin he would have belonged to the "mild-mannered" class, to which, as a matter of fact, he did not. It is written in the lease of his land that he shall drive the Bavicora ranche coach—it's fief-service, it's feudal, and it carries one back. If the little mules and ponies did not stand in the exact six feet of ground where he wanted them, he grabbed hold of them and moved them over to the place without a word, and after being located they never moved until he yanked or lifted them to their place at the pole. The guards were Mexican Indians—hair cut *à la Cosaques,* big straw hats, *serapes,* and munitions of war. William, whose ancestors had emigrated from the Congo region before the war, was to cook. He was also guide, philosopher, and friend to Mr. H. and myself in this strange land, and he made all things possible by his tact and zeal in our behalf. William knows every one in the State of Chihuahua, and he is constantly telling us of the standing and glittering position of the inhabitants of the mud huts which we pass,

until it sounds like that ghastly array of intelligence with which a society reporter quickens the social dead in a Sunday newspaper.

At night we stay at the different ranches, and, rolling ourselves up in our blankets, we lie down on the mud floors to sleep. It's not so bad after one becomes used to it, albeit the skin wears off one's femur joint. The Mexican hen is as conscientious here as elsewhere, and we eat eggs. The Mexican coffee is always excellent in quality, but the people make it up into a nerve-jerking dose, which will stand hot-water in quantities. Nearly all travellers are favorably impressed with the *frejoles* and *tortillas* of the country. The beans are good, but as old General Taylor once said, "They killed more men than did bullets in the Mexican War." Of the *tortillas* I will say, as my philosophical friend, Mr. Poultney Bigelow, says of the black bread of the Russian soldier, "It's a good strong food to march and fight on," which can in no way be a recommendation of its palatability.

The coach starts by gray dawn, and we are aroused at an early hour. The white men take sponge-baths in a wash-basin, and the native who stands about deep in the folds of his *serape* fails utterly to comprehend. He evidently thinks a lot, but he doesn't say anything. I suppose it seems like "clay-eating" or penitent mutilations to him —not exactly insanity, but a curious custom, at any rate. On the return trip we have a half-broken team of buckskin broncos, which have to be "hooked up" with great stealth. And when the coachman had climbed quietly on to the box and we were inside, the guards let go of the team, and the coachman cracked his whip, while we looked out of the window and held our breath. Then there were Horse Pyrotechniques! Ground and Lofty Tumbling! Greatest Show on Earth! for about a minute, when we made a start down the big road—or didn't, as the case might be. After the first round we often had to get out, and, two ponies having got themselves into the same collar, we would then rearrange them for better luck next time.

In Mexico they drive four mules abreast in the lead and two on the pole, which seems to be an excellent way. Mexican coachmen generally keep "belting" their stock and yelling *"Underlay-nula!"* which is both picturesque and unintelligible. Our man was, however, better educated. Forty or fifty miles is a day's journey, but the exact distance is so dependent on the roads, the load, and the desire to "get thar" that it varies greatly.

We pass the Guerrero stage as it bowls along, and hundreds of heavy, creeking ox-carts, as they draw slowly over the yellow landscape, with their freight to and from the mines. Bunches of sorrowful *burros*, with corn, wood, pottery, and hay, part as we sweep along through and by them.

We have the inspiring vista of Chihuahua before us all the time. It is massive in its proportions and opalescent in color. There are torquois hills, dazzling yellow foregrounds—the palette of the "rainbow school" is everywhere. There are little mud houses, ranches, and dirty little adobe towns to pass, which you must admire, though you may not like them. Gaunt cattle wander in their search for grass and water, and women squat by the river-bed engaged in washing or filling their *ollas*.

The people are enchanting. It is like reading the Bible to look at them, because it is so unreal; yet there they are before one, strange and mysterious, and, like other things which appeal to one's imagination, it would be a sad thing if one were to understand them. One is tempted to think that the people of our Northern races know too much for their own good. It seems remorseless, but it is so. When I heard the poor Mexican asked why he thought it had not rained in eighteen months, he said, "Because God wills it, I suppose;" we were edified by the way they shifted the responsibility which Farmer Dunn in our part of the world so cheerfully assumes.

One afternoon we were on a down-grade, going along at a fair pace, when a wheel struck a stone, placed there by some freighter to block his load. It heaved the coach, pulled out the king-pin, and let the big Concord down and over on its side. The mules went on with the front wheels, pulling Jack off the box, while we who were on top described a graceful parabolic curve and landed with three dull thuds. I was caught under the coach by one leg and held there. A guard inside made all haste to crawl out through a window, and after a bit I was released. We were all pretty badly bruised up, and Mr. H. had his foot broken. The mules were recovered, however, the coach righted, and we were again off. We made the town of Tamochica that night, and the town-folks were kind and attentive. They made crutches, heated water, and sent a man to the creek to catch leeches to put on our wounds. Two men were shot in a house near by during the night, and for a few minutes there was a lively fusillade of pistol shots. It was evident that life in Tamochica would spoil a man's taste for anything quiet, and so as soon as we could move we did it.

We passed an old church, and were

shown two Jesuits who had been dead over a hundred years. They were wonderfully preserved, and were dressed in full regalia. I wondered by what embalmer's art it had been accomplished.

A guard of punchers met us to conduct us over a mountain-pass. They were dressed in terra-cotta buckskin trimmed with white leather, and were armed for the largest game in the country. The Bavicora coach has never been robbed, and it is never going to be—or, at least that is the intention of the I-F folks. One man can rob a stage-coach as easily as he could a box of sardines, but with outriders before and behind it takes a large party, and even then they will leave a "hot trail" behind them.

One morning as I was lolling out of the window I noticed the wheel of the coach pass over a long, blue Roman candle. I thought it was curious that a long, blue Roman candle should be lying out there on the plains, when with a sudden sickening it flashed upon me—"giant powder!" The coach was stopped, and we got out. The road was full of sticks of this high explosive. A man was coming down the road leading a *burro* and picking up the things, and he explained that they had dropped out of a package from his bull-wagon as he passed the night before. We didn't run over any more pieces. If the stick had gone off there would have been a little cloud of dust on the Guerrero road, and, I hope, some regrets in various parts of the world. The incident cannot be made startling, but it put the occupants of the Bavicora coach in a quiet train of reflection that makes a man religious.

Now, as I ponder over the last stage-coach ride which I shall ever take on this earth, I am conscious that it was pleasant, instructive, and full of incident. All that might have happened did not, but enough did to satiate my taste.

Winter Shooting on the Gulf Coast of Florida

At that period in the year when the bad old lung and the inflamed bronchial tube and the festive catarrh get in their work, the fellow who likes to be amused goes off to the Mediterranean, and the fellow who likes to amuse himself hies him to Florida.

There is no reason why any one should go to Cuba, so far as I can see, and Arizona is as yet not properly appreciated by "lungers" and sportsmen as a winter resort, although it is the superior place.

This Florida sportsman goes down on the Gulf coast because there is no doubt that in remote times of the past men have caught tarpon there. He may even desire to participate in the sensations which are said to have been so dear to the tarpon fisherman when the world was young. He may even hire a boat and a darky and go up some desolate inlet and sit quietly for ten hours while the clouds roll overhead, the wind plays through the reeds, and the darky perspires quietly in the forward end of the boat: but if he has got a nerve in his body he will shortly consign tarpon to his Satanic Majesty, pull up his anchor, go back to the hotel, sell his rod and tackle to some newly arrived enthusiast, and get out his twelve-bore.

Ducks down there are confiding birds, and a boat loaded with girls and grub and Scotch whiskey and soda can be sailed right up to them while the sportsman empties his shot-gun and fills his game-bag.

Then if he has a pointer-dog he can kick up quail, or wander among the sloughs or along the beaches and bang away at the illusive jack-snipe, and if he ever hits one he can plume himself on his skill as much as he likes, but he should properly attribute it to good luck.

Winter Shooting on the Gulf Coast of Florida. *Authors' photoengraving.*

The Colonel of
the First Cycle Infantry

"You certainly are a tough outfit, colonel
—you and your night-hawks of the First
Bikes—and I am not sure you could not
have us cavalrymen going to bed with our
boots on, if we were on the other side," said
Major Ladigo, as he bit at the end of a fresh
cigar.

"Yes—bless me—Pedal's outfit might
come into camp on top of yours, Ladigo,
and where would my guns be then? I can't
have my gunners sitting on their trails all
day and all night too," sighed the big
gunner, from the other end of the tent.

"It was good work," continued the old
brigadier—"here, boy, pass those glasses—
and I have always thought well of the possibilities of that machine in a certain sort of
military operations. I don't think you can
chase Apaches with it—in fact, the only
way to chase Apaches is to agree to pay
about $500 a head for them; and also, I
don't think, Colonel Pedal—with all due respect for your enthusiasm—that you could
ever become of all-absorbing interest in
great operations between organized armies,
but I do not want to commit myself since
you seem to accomplish such feats in these
days. If we had not had a really progressive
man at the head of the army you would not
have had this opportunity; but now, Pedal,
all these fellows want to hear about your
outfit, and especially how you conducted
that affair at North Colville—they all want
to know—go ahead now—we have plenty
of time to listen," and Colonel Pedal of the

First Bikes twirled his forage cap in his two
hands and grinned pleasantly.

"Well—it was simple enough," he said.

"Oh yes—it's simple now, but how did
you get at it?" was the remark of encouragement from somewhere.

"Oh, well, you know, when I had organized and drilled this regiment, the people up
at headquarters used me in a fussy way as
orderlies, messengers, and in light outpost
work, until my outfit was scattered all over
this country, and that was not my idea at
all. I knew by long experiment that bicycles
were perfectly mobile in any country not
strictly mountainous, and my idea was that
I could fight my outfit in a new way; but
fight it, that was my idea—and march it,
too. I wanted a few holes in that flag, and
so I used to go up and labor with the general. I pleaded and begged to be turned
loose. So one afternoon the general sent for
me, and I went to headquarters.

"He said that a big band of insurgents
were gathering and organizing up at North
Colville, and that he wanted them destroyed
or dispersed, and asked me if I could do it
without asking for supports. I knew the old
man had all he could do to open the communications to the west, and that he was
going to give the bikes a try to prove what
they were good for, so I said 'Yes, sir,' right
away, though I did not know the situation
thoroughly; but I wanted a job of that sort,
and I was in for it. So he gave me orders to
that effect, and after some inquiries I left

him. Through spies he knew of this condition, and that all the communications were cut except the marine cable, which he laid in the bed of the Kaween River to Northport, and that was thirty miles from North Colville. I knew that all those upper counties were in a state of insurgency, and my orders were to destroy the rendezvous at North Colville and to then retreat; so my chief concern was to get through the country without being stopped or engaged seriously by intervening bodies of the enemy which I might encounter, and says I to myself, says I, 'Old man, show 'em what bikes are good for.' Pardon me if I become enthusiastic. I started down to my command, fell in my men, with two days' rations and one hundred and fifty rounds. I made my inspection, for, of course, you know, bike soldiers have a very complicated equipment; what with bombs, telegraphic apparatus, tools, and the extra parts of wheels, one must look well to his inspection. They have the Rice equipment—combined cartridge-belts and garment—which enables them to carry almost anything on the shouder-belt. At five o'clock we pulled out, and at dark found ourselves at our extreme outposts, as I had calculated. I did not want the enemy to see me, as I was afraid of the telegraph, but as I proceeded I tapped the wires and cut them again and again. In fact, I cut wires all night, for fear that they might not have been destroyed, or that they might have been repaired. I ran smoothly through little hamlets, and knew that I could not be overtaken. I made a slight detour around villages of any size, such as Wooddale, Rockville, and Freeport, for fear that the insurgents might be in force enough to detain me. Back of Wellsville I got awfully tangled up in a woods, and, in short, was lost; but I jumped an old cit. out of his cosey bed, put a .45 on the cabin of his intellect, a flash-lantern in his two eyes, and he looked sufficiently honest and intelligent to show us the road, which he did, and we were not detained long.

"I felt fear of Emmittstowne, as I had in-formation that the insurgents were in force there. We picked up a man on the road who seemed to be one of our sympathizers, and he informed us that there were pickets all along the road which we were travelling, and also mounted patrols. He said that there were a terrible lot of insurgents in Emmittstowne, but mostly drunk.

"Captain Bidewell, who was in command of the advance, did a rather clever piece of work here. He suspected that he would find a picket at a certain place, and sent a dismounted squad on either side of the road, which was bounded by meadow land with stone-walls, brush, and trees on either side, and he himself walked down the road with two men. They talked loudly, as though drunk, and sure enough, were shortly held up by the picket. They surrendered and expostulated in a loud voice, and offered their captors a bottle of whiskey. The advance closed in on them and even got in their rear, and, of course, held up the picket without a shot. A six-shooter argument used on these people shortly disclosed the conditions, and we advanced."

"Say, colonel, I know that Bidewell; he is organizing a bike regiment out West now—met him as I came through," interpolated a medical major.

"Yes—nice fellow—held the ten-mile record for two years before this trouble," replied Pedal; "but, as I was saying—

"Here is *How!* gentlemen!

"Well, to continue—to show you a curious phase of bicycling—my advance ran a picket farther along the road and were fired on, but, bless me, they had gone through so quickly and silently that they were not hurt, and the sergeant, who was very wise, dismounted and blew his whistle for us to advance. Bidewell dismounted and immediately advanced, and the picket, hearing his men smashing brush, retreated, and the sergeant turned a pistol loose in their faces and bellowed for them to go out in the road, throw up their hands, and surrender, which they did. You see, Colonel Ladigo, it is very hard to estimate bike forces in the night, they go so silently—they simply flit; and when you first notice them you wonder how many have gone before. A sleepy picket is waked up by a lot of bellowing and shots and smashing of brush, and he doesn't know anything, especially if the row is half in his rear. Well, the shooting must have aroused the village of Emmittstowne, and I made up my mind to run right into the town. The moon was rising, and we could see fairly well; but first I tried a little ruse with the captured picket. We advanced down the road a piece, and the men ensconced themselves in the brush, while one of the captured men stood in the middle of the road. We heard quite a party coming up the road rapidly, and the picket called out to them that it was nothing—that they had fired at some shadows, and that they might go back. Two men actually advanced to him, but he insisted that all was right, and that they might return; in fact, he protested too much, since he knew that he was lying for his life, and that the date of his demise was fixed at the instant he told the truth. We gave the town half an hour to settle down, and then started on a down grade—coasting silently. All was still. There were lights in a few saloons, and a half-dozen men, who were immediately held up and disarmed. There was evidence of a great many people in the village, since wagons and horses stood about, and tents and huts were everywhere except on the main street. I stopped in front of the hotel, and, do you know, my column got three-quarters of the way through the town before we were discovered. My column is three-quarters of a mile long, you must remember, and that was very fortunate. Some one fired a shot from a darkened window of the hotel, and I ordered my men to use their revolvers. A man can shoot a revolver with great accuracy from a wheel, as it glides so smoothly. Well, there was a deuce of a popping, and it must have fairly riddled the town. The fire was shortly returned, but in a desultory way which did not seem to do any damage, and shortly the tail of the column passed down

the street. I had set the hotel on fire before we left, and I really do not think that those fellows know what really happened there yet. I immediately cut the telegraph line, and now had nothing to interfere with my march to North Colville. I had two bikes ruined by shots, and abandoned the riders; but they made their way to our lines later. As we proceeded the country grew more flat, and we made the pedals spin; at times we overtook night prowlers—tramps, for the most part—and one rather large party of drunken insurgents, all of whom we disarmed and left tied to trees and fences along the road. Do you know, Ladigo, that one cannot hear my whole regiment on a road until it is right on top of you. I have frequently seen men ride a bicycle right up beside a man, who never heard a word until ordered to throw up his hands."

"Oh yes, Pedal, I'd like to catch your outfit at the foot of a long hill; I would fire yellow-legs into you in a way you would despise," interpolated the impetuous cavalryman, as he blew smoke at the ridge-pole and slapped his one leg over the other in a satisfied way.

"Yes, you might, Ladigo; but I'm going to spend my life trying not to let you catch me at the foot of a long hill, and if you do, you will find about one hundred bicycles piled up in the road, and it makes bad travelling for horses, especially with unshaken infantry pointing at you from behind. Well, in this case, Ladigo, I did not have any of your enterprising yellow-legs to bother me. As I was saying, we went along swimmingly until we struck Cat-tail Creek, and found the bridge burned. It was rather chilly, but I knew there was no help for it, so we got out our air-cushions and did our little swimming drill right there."

"What are your air-cushions?" inquired the medical officer with the long pipe.

"They are made of rubber, and blow up, and will sustain five equipments, and weigh fourteen pounds. Every five men have one," explained Pedal.

"Oh, I see—a quaint scheme!"

"Yes; bikes are perfectly mobile," continued Pedal, with satisfaction. "As I was saying—oh yes, we got over the river all right, but—" and here he glanced apprehensively at Ladigo—"but I forgot to mention that we lost fifteen bicycles in the passage."

"Ha—ha! oh yes—there are your dismounted men," and Colonel Ladigo beamed.

"I think horses would have stuck in the mud of Cat-tail Creek, Ladigo; fact is, horses are not perfectly mobile. I also neglected to mention that the bicycles were all fished up and joined us later. We halted on a hill off the road an hour before gray dawn, to wait for the command to close up and to eat. There are always bikes which break down, and it takes a little time to repair them; and men will fall and injure themselves more or less. But within an hour I had my command all up except five men, having marched nearly seventy miles in eleven hours, had one engagement, crossed a river. And now, Colonel Ladigo, was that not good work?"

"Oh yes, Pedal, quite good—quite good; could do it myself, though," and the soul of a cavalryman was bound to assert itself.

"Undoubtedly you could, but not next day." And Pedal lit a cigar, conscious that he had Ladigo downed, but not finally suppressed.

"My men down the road took in a cavalry patrol without a shot—actually took in a cavalry—"

"Hump—hump!" snorted Ladigo; "cavalry forsooth—a lot of d—— jays on plough-teams; cavalry, sir—"

"Here—here, Ladigo, come down," expostulated the assembled officers, and Ladigo relapsed.

"Well, after a reconnoissance and information from the patrol, I found that there were over five thousand men rendezvoused there, partly organized, and armed with all sorts of guns. Old Middle was in command —you remember Middle, formerly of the Twenty-seventh Infantry, cashiered at Fort Verde in '82."

He was known to the men present, and a few sniffs and the remark that "he was bad medicine" was all that greeted the memory of Middle.

"From the patrol I found where their camps and lines and outworks to cover the roads were, and also that it was but a quarter of a mile across a wood-lot to the road which I had intended to retire by, which ran southeast towards Spearfish and Hallam Junction, so I trundled my bikes over to it, and laid them in a column formation off the road, and left them under guard. I formed my command and turned some fellows out of some rifle-pits, which were designed to protect the road, and it was growing light. We charged into the town, which had been alarmed by our fire directed at the men in the pits. The first thing we struck was a long line of temporary camps, of what was probably a regiment, which was on the other side of a railroad embankment; but they were in a panic and offered us no resistance, while we advanced, rapidly firing, and nearly destroyed them. As we entered the town I took one battalion and directed it against the car-shops, which were full of stores and troops: these men we also nearly destroyed; and, having set fire to the shops, I entered the main part of the town, and as we advanced I had it also fired. From my right I heard heavy firing, and knew that the other command had encountered opposition; and turning to my right I struck a second railroad embankment, swarming behind with men who were standing off the advance of the other battalion. I enfiladed them, and they retired precipitously. From the net-work of railroad embankments farther up the flats north of Colville I could see masses of men forming. They began firing at me from a great distance, but we were protected by the railroad fill and did not mind it; while our sharpshooters, with their arms of longer range, annoyed the enemy quite a little, and kept up his demoralization. A great many men had gotten away from the town when I had attacked the car-shops, and I was in fear lest they might

"I Began The Retreat as I Intended." *Authors' photoengraving.*

form in my rear under the cover of the burning town, so I had my wounded removed rapidly to the hill where my bikes were left, and then retreated rapidly under the cover of the smoke. The enemy were left so completely in the air that they advanced slowly, while from the cover of the brush on the upper edge of a field I held them in play for an hour while my wounded got a good start. At last they seemed to form, and approached to my right, going around the smoke of the burning town, and as they outnumbered me four to one, they would speedily have outflanked me. I began the retreat as I had intended. I had thirty-eight badly wounded men who had to be carried in blankets, fifty-six slightly wounded who would be trundled on bicycles, and had left eighteen dead on the field."

"I say, colonel, how do you remove wounded men on bicycles?" asked some one.

"It is simple when you see it, but rather difficult to explain. If you will come down some day I will be glad to show you a wounded drill, and then you can see for yourself. By cutting sticks and tying a blanket or shelter-tent a desperately wounded man can be laid prone between two bicycles, or if slightly hurt he can be trundled or even ridden double with a comrade, while one man can move two and even three bicycles. Oh, I tell you, the bike is a great contrivance once you come to understand it," proceeded the Colonel of Cycle Infantry.

"I should like to have fought those fellows a little harder, but I was sixty miles inside of their lines, and I knew that to prolong the affair would mean that they would be heavily reinforced, and besides this was my first expedition. I had already destroyed the bigger half of the enemy and burned the town, and I did not apprehend a vigorous pursuit. What to do with my wounded was now on my mind. The country to the east of North Colville is very broken, wild, and sparsely inhabited. It had become necessary to abandon my wounded. I selected a point over twelve miles from our battle-ground, far back from the unfrequented road, in a very wild spot in the hills, and left every man not able to travel there, with all our rations and two medical officers, with ten men as a detail for the camp. My trail of course continued, and they were never suspected. Coming to the valley of the Spearfish I halted and slept my command until sundown, and then started for our lines. On the way I rode into and demoralized a half-dozen bands of armed insurgents, and struck our lines at five o'clock in the morning."

"What became of your wounded up there, colonel?" asked the medical officer with the long pipe.

"The evening following Captain Barhandle with fifty men started and made a successful march to their relief, and left two more medical officers and a lot of medical stores and rations, and came back three days after. The camp was never discovered, and was relieved when the general here made his first expedition into Wood County. They had protected themselves from prowlers by waylaying the roads, and had a dozen prisoners in camp, together with a half-dozen milch cows. My bike men are excellent foragers, since they have been so much on outpost duty."

"Suppose, Colonel Pedal, you were forced to abandon your bicycles, what would you do?"

"We had a detachment on a scout the other day who were pressed into some bad country and had to abandon their machines, which they did by sinking them in Dead Creek, and the next day we went out and recovered them. If it is desired to utterly destroy them, it can be done in an instant by stepping on the wheel and 'buckling' it, or if you remove the chain, it is useless to any one but yourself," explained the colonel.

"Now, colonel, do you consider that you can move your men successfully in a hilly or mountainous country?" inquired Ladigo.

"In all candor, no—not to a good advantage. I can march uphill as fast as infantry, and go down at limited-express speed; but I really want a rather flat country with lots of roads. I am not particular as to the quality of the roads, so there are enough of them. I can move through snow which has been tracked down by teams; I can fly on the ice; and when it is muddy there is always an inch or so beside the road which is not muddy, and that is enough for me. A favorable place for a bicycle is along a railroad track—going in the centre or at one side. When suddenly attacked, my men can get out of the road like a covey of quail, and a bicycle can be trundled across the worst possible country as fast as a man can travel, for you see all the weight of the man's gun and pack are on the wheel, which runs without an appreciable resistance, and all bike men know how to throw a bicycle over a fence with ease, and my average march is eighty miles a day. Ladigo, remember—eighty miles a day. No kind of roads, no conditions of weather, or anything but superior force can stop my command for an instant, sir;" and the colonel of cavalry rose and added, "Colonel Pedal, will you have a drink with me?"

Bear-Chasing in the Rocky Mountains

Mr. Montague Stevens is an Englishman who for the most part attends to the rounding-up of his cattle, which are scattered over the northwestern quarter of New Mexico; but he does not let that interfere with the time which all Englishmen set duly apart to be devoted to sport. His door-yard is some hundreds of miles of mountain wilderness and desolate mesa—a more gorgeous preserve than any king ever dreamed of possessing for his pleasure—with its plains dotted with antelope, and its mountains filled with cougar, deer, bear, and wild turkeys. The white race has given up the contest with nature in those parts, and it has reverted to the bear, the Navajo, and Mr. Stevens—land-grants, corrals, cabins, brands, and all else.

General Miles was conducting a military observation of the country, which is bound to be the scene of any war which the Apaches or Navajos may make; and after a very long day's march, during which we had found but one water, and that was a pool of rain-water, stirred into mud and full of alkali, where we had to let our horses into the muddy stuff at the ends of our lariats, we had at last found a little rivulet and some green grass. The coffee-pot bubbled and the frying-pan hissed, while I smoked and listened to a big escort-wagon driver, who was repairing his lash, and saying, softly, "Been drivin' a bloody lot of burros for thirty years, and don't know enough to keep a whip out of a wheel; guess I'll go to jack-punchin', 'nen I kin use a dry club."

Far down the valley a little cloud of dust gleamed up against the gray of the mountains, and presently the tireless stride of a pony shone darkly in its luminous midst. Nearer and nearer it grew—the flying tail, the regular beating of the hoofs, the swaying figure of the rider, and the left sleeve of the horseman's coat flapping purposelessly about. He crossed the brook with a splash, trotted, and, with a jerk, pulled up in our midst. Mr. Stevens is a tall, thin young man, very much bronzed, and with the set, serious face of an Englishman. He wore corduroy clothes, and let himself out of his saddle with one hand, which he also presented in greeting, the other having been sacrificed to his own shot-gun on some previous occasion. Mr. Stevens brought with him an enthusiasm for bear which speedily enveloped the senses of our party, and even crowded out from the mind of General Miles the nobler game which he had affected for thirty years.

The steady cultivation of one subject for some days is bound to develop a great deal of information, and it is with difficulty that I refrain from herein setting down facts which can doubtless be found in any good encyclopædia of natural history; but the men in the mountains never depart from the consideration of that and one other subject, which is brands, and have reached some strange conclusions—the strangest being that the true Rocky Mountain grizzly is only seen once in a man's lifetime, and that the biggest one they ever heard of leaves his tracks in this district, and costs Mr. Stevens, roughly estimating, about $416 a year to support, since that about covers the cattle he kills.

At break of day the officers, cavalrymen, escort-wagons, and pack-train toiled up the Cañon Largo to Mr. Stevens's camp, which was reached in good time, and consisted of a regular ranchman's grub-wagon, a great many more dogs of more varieties than I could possibly count, a big Texan, who was cook, and a professional bear-hunter by the name of Cooper, who had recently departed from his wonted game for a larger kind, with the result that, after the final deal, a companion had passed a .45 through Mr. Cooper's face and filled it with powder, and brought him nigh unto death, so that even now Mr. Cooper's head was swathed in bandages, and his mind piled with regrets that he had on at the time an overcoat, which prevented him from drawing his gun with his usual precision. Our introduction to the outfit was ushered in by a most magnificent free-for-all dog-fight; and when we had carefully torn the snarling, yelling, biting mass apart by the hind-legs and staked them out to surrounding trees, we had time to watch Mr. Cooper draw diagrams of bear-paws in the dust with a stick. These tracks he had just discovered up the Cañon Largo, and he averred that the bear was a grizzly, and weighed 1800 pounds, and that he had been there two years, and that all the boys had hunted him, but that he was a sad old rascal.

After lunch we pulled on up the cañon and camped. The tents were pitched and the cooks busy, when I noticed three cowboys down the stream and across the cañon, who were alternately leading their horses and stooping down in earnest consultation over some tracks on the ground. We walked over to them. There were Mr. Cooper, whose only visible eye rolled ominously, and Dan, the S. U. foreman with another puncher.

"He's usin' here," said Cooper. "That's his track, and there's his work," pointing up the hill-side, where lay the body of a five-year-old cow. We drew near her, and there was the tale of a mighty struggle, all written

out more eloquently than pen can do. There were the deep furrows of the first grapple at the top; there was the broad trail down the steep hill for fifty yards, with the stones turned over, and the dust marked with horn and hoof and claw; and there was the stump which had broken the roll down hill. The cow had her neck broken and turned under her body; her shoulder was torn from the body, her leg broken, and her side eaten into; and there were Bruin's big telltale footprints, rivalling in size a Gladstone bag, as he had made his way down to the stream to quench his thirst and continue up the cañon. The cow was yet warm—not two hours dead.

"We must pull out of here; he will come back tonight," said Cooper. And we all turned to with a will and struck the tents, while the cooks threw their tins, bags, and boxes into the wagons, whereat we moved off down wind for three miles, up a spur of the cañon, where we again camped. We stood around the fires and allowed Mr. Cooper to fill our minds with hope. "He'll shore come back; he's usin' here; an' cow outfits—why, he don't consider a cow outfit nothin'. He's been right on top of cow outfits since he's been in these parts, and thet two years gone now, when he begun to work this yer range, and do the work you see done yonder. In the mornin' we'll strike his trail, and if we can git to him you'll shore see a bar-fight."

We turned in, and during the night I was awakened twice—once by a most terrific baying of all the dogs, who would not be quieted, and later by a fine rain beating in my face. The night was dark, and we were very much afraid the rain would kill the scent. We were up long before daylight, and drank our coffee and ate our meat, and as soon as "we could see a dog a hundred yards," which is the bear-hunter's receipt, we moved off down the creek. We found that the cow had been turned over twice, but not eaten—evidently Bruin had his suspicions. The dogs cut his trail again and again. He had run within sight of our camp, had wandered across the valley hither and yon, but the faithful old hounds would not "go away." Dan sat on his pony and blew his old cow's horn, and yelled: "Hooick! hooick! get down on him. Rocks; hooick! hooick!" But Rocks could not get down on him, and then we knew that the rain had killed the scent. We circled a half-mile out, but the dogs were still; and then we followed up the Cañon Largo for miles, and into the big mountain, through juniper thickets and over malpais, up and down the most terrible places, for we knew that the bear's bed-ground is always up in the most rugged peaks, where the rimrock overhangs in serried battlements, tier on tier. But no bear.

Rocks, the forward hound, grew weary of hunting for things which were not, and retired to the rear to pay court to a lady friend; and Dan had to rope Rocks, and with some irritation he started his pony, and Rocks kept the pace by dint of legging it, and by the help of a tow from 900 pounds of horse-flesh. Poor Rocks! He understood his business; but in consequence of not being able to explain to the men what fools they were, he suffered.

The hot mid-day sun of New Mexico soon kills the scent, and we were forced to give over for the day. A cavalry sergeant shot three deer, but we, in our superior purpose, had learned to despise deer. Later I made a good two-hundred-yard centre on an antelope, and though I had not been fortunate enough in years to get an antelope, the whole sensation was flat in view of this new ambition.

On the following morning we went again to our dead cow, but nothing except the jackals had been at the bear's prey, for the wily old fellow had evidently scented our camp, and concluded that we were not a cow outfit, whereat he had discreetly "pulled his freight."

We sat on our horses in a circle, and raised our voices. In consideration of the short time at our disposal, we concluded that we could be satisfied with taking 1800 pounds of bear on the instalment plan. The first instalment was a very big piece of meat,

but was—I am going to confess—presented to us in the nature of a gift; but the whole thing was so curious I will go into it.

We hunted for two days without success, unless I include deer and antelope; but during the time I saw two things which interested me. The first was a revelation of the perfect understanding which a mountain cow-pony has of the manner in which to negotiate the difficulties of the country which is his home.

Dan, the foreman, was the huntsman. He was a shrewd-eyed, little, square-built man, always very much preoccupied with the matter in hand. He wore a sombrero modelled into much character by weather and time, a corduroy coat, and those enormous New-Mexican "chaps," and he sounded a cow-horn for his dogs, and alternately yelped in a most amusing way. So odd was this yelp that it caught the soldiers, and around their camp-fire at night you could hear the mimicking shouts of "Oh, Rocks! eh-h h! hooick! get down on him, Rocks; tohoot! tohoot!" We were sitting about on our horses in a little *sienneca,* while Dan was walking about, leading his pony and looking after his dogs.

When very near me he found it necessary to cross an *arróyo* which was about five feet deep and with perfectly perpendicular banks. Without hesitation he jumped down into it, and with a light bound his pony followed. At the opposite side Dan put up his arms on the bank and clawed his way up, and, still paying no attention to his pony, he continued on. Without faltering in the least, the little horse put his fore-feet on the bank, clawed at it once, twice, jumped, scratched, clawed, and, for all the world like a cat getting into the fork of a tree, he was on the bank and following Dan.

Later in the day, when going to our camp, we followed one of Dan's short-cuts through the mountains, and the cowboys on their mountain ponies rode over a place which made the breath come short to the officers and men behind; not that they could not cross themselves, being on foot, but that the cavalry horses could they had their solemn doubts, and no one but an evil brute desires to lead a game animal where he may lose his life. Not being a geologist, I will have to say it was a blue clay in process of rock formation, and in wet times held a mountain torrent. The slope was quite seventy degrees. The approach was loose dirt and malpais, which ran off down the gulch in small avalanches under our feet. While crossing, the horses literally stood on their toes to claw out a footing. A slip would have sent them, belly up, down the toboggan-slide, with a drop into an unknown depth at the end. I had often heard the cavalry axiom "that a horse can go anywhere a man can if the man will not use his hands," and a little recruit murmured it to reassure himself. I passed, with the loss of a quarter of the skin on my left hand, and later asked a quaint old veteran of four enlistments if he thought it was a bad place, and he said, "It's lizards, not harses, what ought to go thar."

Riding over the rough mountains all day sows poppy-seeds in a man's head, and when the big medical officer opens your tent-flaps in the morning, and fills the walls with his roars to "Get up! it's four o'clock," it is with groans that you obey. You also forego washing, because you are nearly frozen stiff, and you go out and stand around the fire with your companions, who are all cheerfully miserable as they shiver and chaff each other. It seems we do not live this life on a cold, calculating plane of existence, but on different lines, the variation of which is the chief delight of the discriminating, and I must record a distinct pleasure in elbowing fellows around a camp-fire when it is dark and cold and wet, and when you know that they are oftener in bed than out of it at such hours. You drink your quart of coffee, eat your slice of venison, and then regard your horse with some trepidation, since he is all of a tremble, has a hump on his back, and is evidently of a mind to "pitch."

The eastern sky grows pale, and the irrepressible Dan begins to "honk" on his horn, and the cavalcade moves off through the grease-wood, which sticks up thickly from the ground like millions of Omaha war-bonnets.

The advance consists of six or eight big blood-hounds, which range out in front, with Dan and Mr. Cooper to blow the horn, look out for "bear sign," and to swear gently but firmly when the younger dogs take recent deer trails under consideration. Three hundred yards behind come Scotch stag-hounds, a big yellow mastiff, fox-terriers, and one or two dogs which would not classify in a bench-show, and over these Mr. Stevens holds a guiding hand, while in a disordered band come General Miles, his son, three army officers, myself, and seven orderlies of the Second Cavalry. All this made a picture, but, like all Western canvases, too big for a frame. The sun broke in a golden flash over the hills, and streaked the plain with gold and gray greens. The spirit of the thing is not hunting but the chase of the bear, taking one's mind back to the buffalo, or the nobles of the Middle Ages, who made their "image of war" with bigger game than red foxes.

Leaving the plain we wound up a dry creek, and noted that the small oaks had been bitten and clawed down by bear to get at the acorns. The hounds gave tongue, but could not get away until we had come to a small glade in the forest, where they grew wildly excited. Mr. Cooper here showed us a very large bear track, and also a smaller one, with those of two cubs by its side. With a wild burst the dogs went away up a cañon, the blood went into our heads, and our heels into the horses, and a desperate scramble began. It is the sensation we have travelled so long to feel. Dan and Cooper sailed off through the brush and over the stones like two old crows, with their coat-tails flapping like wings. We follow at a gallop in single file up the narrow, dry watercourse. The creek ends, and we take to the steep hill-sides, while the loose stones rattle from under the flying hoofs. The rains have cut deep furrows on their way to the bed of the cañon, and your horse scratches and scrambles for a foothold. A low, gnarled branch bangs you across the face,

Crossing a Dangerous Place. *Authors' photoengraving.*

and then your breath fairly stops as you see a horse go into the air and disappear over a big log, fallen down a hill of seventy degrees' slope. The "take-off and landing" is yielding dust, but the blood in your head puts the spur in your horse, and over you go. If you miss, it is a 200-foot roll, with a 1200-pound horse on top of you. But the pace soon tells, and you see nothing but good honest climbing ahead of you. The trail of the yelling dogs goes straight up, amid scraggly cedar and juniper, with loose malpais underfoot. We arrive at the top only to see Cooper and Dan disappear over a precipice after the dogs, but here we stop. Bears always seek the very highest peaks, and it is better to be there before them if possible. A grizzly can run downhill quicker than a horse, and all hunters try to get above them, since if they are big and fat they climb slowly; besides, the mountain-tops are more or less flat and devoid of underbrush, which makes good running for a horse. We scatter out along the cordon of the range. The bad going on the rimrock of the mountain-tops, where the bear tries to throw off the dogs, makes it quite impossible to follow them at speed, so that you must separate and take your chances of heading the chase.

I selected Captain Mickler—the immaculate, the polo-player, the epitome of staff form, the trappiest trooper in the Dandy Fifth—and, together with two orderlies, we started. Mickler was mounted on a cow-pony, which measured one chain three links from muzzle to coupling. Mickler had on English riding-togs—this is not saying that the pony could not run, or that Mickler was not humorous. But it was no new experience for him, this pulling a pony and coaxing him to attempt breakneck experiments, for he told me casually that he had led bare-footed cavalrymen over these hills in pursuit of Apaches at a date in history when I was carefully conjugating Latin verbs.

We were making our way down a bad formation when we heard the dogs, and presently three shots. A strayed cavalry orderly had, much to his disturbance of mind, beheld a big silver-tip bearing down on him, jaws skinned, ears back, and red-eyed, and he had promptly removed himself to a proper distance, where he dismounted. The bear and dogs were much exhausted, but the dogs swarmed around the bear, thus preventing a shot. But Bruin stopped at intervals to fight the dogs, and the soldier fired, but without effect. If men do not come up with the dogs in order to encourage them, many will draw off, since the work of chasing and fighting a bear without water for hours is very trying. Only hounds can be depended on, as the tongues of other dogs thicken, and they soon droop when long without water. Some of the dogs may have followed the bear with cubs, but if they did we never heard of them. The one now running was an enormous silver-tip, and could not "tree." The shots of the trooper diverted the bear, which now took off down a deep cañon next to the one we were in, and presently we heard him no more. After an hour's weary travelling down the winding way we came out on the plain, and found a small cow outfit belonging to Mr. Stevens, and under a tree lay our dead silver-tip, while a half-dozen punchers squatted about it. It appeared that three of them had been working up in the foot-hills when they heard the dogs, and shortly discovered the bear. Having no guns, and being on fairly good ground, they coiled their *riatas* and prepared to do battle.

The silver-tip was badly blown, and the three dogs which had stayed with him were so tired that they sat up at a respectful distance and panted and lolled. The first rope went over Bruin's head and one paw. There lies the danger. But instantly number two flew straight to the mark, and the ponies surged, while Bruin stretched out with a roar. A third rope got his other hind-leg, and the puncher dismounted and tied it to a tree. The roaring, biting, clawing mass of hair was practically helpless, but to kill him was an undertaking.

"Why didn't you brand him and turn him loose?" I asked of the cowboy.

"Well," said the puncher, in his Texan

The Bear at Bay. *Painting in George F. Harding Museum, Chicago.*

drawl, "we could have branded him all right, but we might have needed some help in turning him loose."

They pelted him with malpais, and finally stuck a knife into a vital part, and then, loading him on a pony, they brought him in. It was a daring performance, but was regarded by the "punchers" as a great joke.

Mickler and I rode into camp, thinking on the savagery of man. One never heard of a bear which travelled all the way from New Mexico to Chicago to kill a man, and yet a man will go 3000 miles to kill a bear—not for love or fear or hate or meat; for what, then? But Mickler and I had not killed a bear, so we were easy.

One by one the tired hunters and dogs struggled into camp all disappointed, except the dogs, which could not tell us what had befallen them since morning. The day following the dogs started a big black bear, which made a good run up a bad place in

the hills, but with the hunters scrambling after in full cry. The bear treed for the dogs, but on sighting the horsemen he threw himself backward from the trunk and fell fifteen feet among the dogs, which latter piled into him *en masse,* the little fox-terriers being particularly aggressive. It was a tremendous shake-up of black hair and pups of all colors; but the pace was too fast for Bruin, and he sought a new tree. One little foxie had been rolled over, and had quite a job getting his bellows mended. This time the bear sat on a limb very high up, and General Miles put a .50-calibre ball through his brain, which brought him down with a tremendous thump, when the pups again flew into him, and "wooled him," as the cowboys put it, to their hearts' content.

While our bear-hunting is not the thing we are most proud of, yet the method is the most sportsmanlike, since nothing but the most desperate riding will bring one up with the bear in the awful country which they affect. The anticipation of having a big silver-tip assume the aggressive at any moment is inspiriting. Indeed, they often do; for only shortly before one had sprung from a thicket on to the hind-quarters of Mr. Stevens's cowboy's ponies, and it was only by the most desperate work on the part of his companion, who rode up close and shot the bear with his six-shooter, that saved his comrade's life. The horse was killed. When one thinks of the enormous strength of the silver-tip, which can overpower the mightiest steer, and bend and break its neck or tear its shoulder from its body at a stroke, one is a to say, "Do not hunt a bear unless thy skin is not dear to thee." Then the dogs must be especially trained to run bear, since the country abounds in deer, and it is difficult to train dogs to ignore their sight and scent. The cowboys account for the number of the bear in their country from the fact that it is the old Apache and Navajo range, and the incoherent mind of the savage was impressed with the rugged mass of fur and the grinning jaws of the monster which crossed his path, and he was awed by the dangers of the encounter—arrow against claw. He came to respect the apparition, and he did not know that life is only sacred when in the image of the Creator. He did not discriminate as to the value of life, but with his respect for death there grew the speculation, which to him became a truth, that the fearsome beast was of the other world, and bore the lost souls of the tribe. He was a vampire; he was sacred. O Bear!

A Cosmopolitan—
Mr. Poultney Bigelow

Personally it satisfies Mr. Bigelow to call himself an American; and that word is beginning to be used in so broad a sense that it covers every one who believes in the good destinies of this republic. He has the additional claim of a long line of New England ancestors, ending in Mr. John Bigelow, who is his father. Bigelow himself will no doubt be highly offended when I call him a cosmopolitan, or a citizen of the world, but since that will not invalidate his claims as to the detail of his Americanism, I shall so describe him; and, after all, it is much more difficult to be a cosmopolitan than an American, or any other person with one language, one set of prejudices, and curious hour for eating his breakfast.

The reason why I am asked to write about Mr. Bigelow is that I discovered him. It was in 1879, while he was the editor of the *Yale Courant*. I had such aspirations as all artists have, and I discovered that he would print one of my pictures, which he did, so I lay claim to the original discovery of Mr. Bigelow; and also, I can add to that, I made a rediscovery some years later, when he published some more of my pictures in his magazine, *Outing*. He sinned against the public, and cannot expect me to divide the responsibility.

This sketch is supposed to be a biographical shy at him, but I think biographies interest no one but the subject of them until they are about—roughly speaking—a hundred years out of print. There are exceptions to this rule, but I do not think

Bigelow would advance any claims. In order to progress I must say he was born in 1855, and he himself began to be interested in what was going on in the world when he found himself in Paris, at the age of five years, where he had been taken by his father, who was an American minister. He was there for seven years, and absorbed his French through his skin. His French to this day is not of the experimental kind, but something which any cabman can understand. The years from 1870 to 1873 were spent in Germany, and there he absorbed German and played at Cooper's Indians with the boy who is now Emperor of Germany, and was duly "rounded up" and spanked by the same pedagogue.

He had inherited the English language, and having absorbed two more, the microbe of cosmopolitanism began to generate. He lost his taste for herding sheep in Colorado, or ploughing up the gray turf of the bounding West, or some other American career which might have been open to him. The cultivation of this germ has gone on ever since, in such a way that it makes a very long story. Its first manifestation was at the end of his Freshman year at Yale, when his health gave out. He started around the world on a sailing-vessel. They doubled Cape Horn, wound around the shores of New Guinea, and the ship was totally wrecked on the Japanese coast, and the Freshman got on shore by a miracle. Some Japanese woodcutters had to be persuaded with a boat-hook not to end his promising young life right there. He staid in Japan three months, and got the language, or a big piece of it, and then to Peking. He made a highly adventurous trip to the Great Wall of China and beyond, the account of which he subsequently published in a book illustrated by himself, in consequence of which it hung fire in the second edition. He returned to California and did the Great West, without being inspired by the steer industry or the possibilities of town lots. Back in New Haven he was discovered, and graduated in '79. He studied law, but nature asserted itself, and he went to London as a foreign correspondent for the New York *Herald*. He married Miss Jaffray of this city, and it was just after my rediscovery of him when, one sunny morning in the early spring, he walked out of the office of the *Outing* magazine, of which he was editor and part owner. The mania for travel had seized him, and the magazine had to wait. This episode will indicate that he could never have been a distinguished business man in the sense that *Bradstreet* would indicate.

He had now "struck his gait," as it were. He followed literature and his own inclinations, which took him all over Europe. He was an ardent canoeist—one of the most adventurous of the cult, in fact, and has paddled his *Rob Roy* over nearly every large river in Europe and many here. He was the first man to paddle a canoe through the Iron Gates of the Danube, and to sail one around the islands of St. Thomas and St. Kitts in the Caribbean Sea. I knew of this fame of his, and desiring to catch a few beams of reflected light, I participated. We selected the Russian coast of the Baltic as a likely place, but up in St. Petersburg the Russians took the view that we had better not do the thing, and as they had all the arguments on their side, we gave up the enterprise.

Mr. Bigelow's writings are so well known to the readers in America, England, and Germany that I will not catalogue him, but rather tell what a perfect traveller he is. He does not make a "god of his belly," as I have discovered on occasions when it was dinner-time and something else was going on which we wanted to see. He would calmly postpone the dinner hour until bedtime, and then keep that date instead of trying to work in the previous one. He can, nevertheless, bring all the facts to bear on a chafing-dish when necessary, and travel third class all night, with a shake-down in a big overcoat which he carries, and which has had ten years of eventful history. He has led me into some little evasions of the Russian police which made goose-flesh, and into a bath full of ladies of the Mohammedan faith, whose friends thought well of a proposition to kill us, and nearly got me into a court ball once, which would have been worse. He does not select of necessity the shaded lanes in which to sign or imitate with his lips a Hungarian band, but does it on the boulevards or the Strassen of the big and conservative cities. He sits up all night in the café chantant in Algiers and sings songs with the chasseur d'Afrique, and it is all one to him whether it is the heartiest kind of a function in the great capitals or a break-down in a peasant's barn on the lower Danube. He knows half the distinguished soldiers and diplomats of Europe, and goes to the reviews and manœuvres on horseback behind emperors or on foot with the peasants, as the case may be, always singing or digging for facts—he has, by-the-way, a genius for facts—and yet this happy bohemian is hardened by a queer altruism, the result of a long line of old Puritans who were always unselfish enough to add the responsibilities of the rest of the world to their own. He would have liked to follow a public career in the United States, as many of his people had before him, but his generation called for scoundrels and peak-headed, pigeon brained men in public life, and to simply be honorable and intelligent was not enough. There are always men and America has its quota—who think far ahead because they have thought far behind, and because they are what is well called "level-headed," and when the dollar citizen gets up on his hind legs and thinks he is free and knows it all, he can well pause—better men do. Possibly this may not always be so, but if it continues to be so, America will need soldiers and not statesmen to control her destinies. However, he has made a career for himself in Europe, and his services may some day be utilized by his country in the diplomatic service, if we ever come to understand that the public service is better performed by such as he than by a man from our remote rural districts who has to hire a dress suit and an interpreter.

If you were to ask Mr. Bigelow what he was, he would in all probability answer, a historian. That statement could be verified by a glance at his studio, which is littered and piled with German manuscripts, books, prints, and maps, all of which he is boiling into a history. I do not care for him particularly in this rôle, for it's dull business at best. I like his little stories of his travels, his studies of current politics, his manœuvre stuff, and his knowledge of the earth. I even like his greatest eccentricity more, and that's an odd business when you have to take it for a week on a stretch. It is maps. He has thousands of maps—quarter-sectionings of Iowa, military frontiers, rivers and lakes, railroads and waterways—and he studies them whenever he sits down. He belongs to all the geographical societies, where the members wave their arms wildly at each other, and cannot even sit in their chairs from excitement, and where the stranger finds later that the whole fuss is about a nasty little creek in Central Asia; but that's better than history, because there is no excitement about history; it's all over, or will be, when this goes to press.

Cracker Cowboys of Florida

One can thresh the straw of history until he is well worn out, and also is running some risk of wearing others out who may have to listen, so I will waive the telling of who the first cowboy was, even if I knew; but the last one who has come under my observation lives down in Florida, and the way it happened was this: I was sitting in a "sto' do'," as the "Crackers" say, waiting for the clerk to load some "number eights," when my friend said, "Look at the cowboys!" This immediately caught my interest. With me cowboys are what gems and porcelains are to some others. Two very emaciated Texas ponies pattered down the street, bearing wild-looking individuals, whose hanging hair and drooping hats and generally bedraggled appearance would remind you at once of the Spanish-moss which hangs so quietly and helplessly to the limbs of the oaks out in the swamps. There was none of the bilious fierceness and rearing plunge which I had associated with my friends out West, but as a fox-terrier is to a yellow cur, so were these last. They had on about four dollars' worth of clothes between them, and rode McClellan saddles, with saddle-bags and guns tied on before. The only things they did which were conventional were to tie their ponies up by the head in brutal disregard, and then get drunk in about fifteen minutes. I could see that in this case, while some of the tail feathers were the same, they would easily classify as new birds.

"And so you have cowboys down here?" I said to the man who ran the meat-market.

He picked a tiny piece of raw liver out of the meshes of his long black beard, tilted his big black hat, shoved his arms into his white apron front, and said:

"Gawd! yes, stranger; I was one myself."

The plot thickened so fast that I was losing much, so I became more deliberate. "Do the boys come into town often?" I inquired further.

"Oh yes, 'mos' every little spell," replied the butcher, as he reached behind his weighing-scales and picked up a double-barrelled shot-gun, sawed off. "We-uns are expectin' of they-uns to-day." And he broke the barrels and took out the shells to examine them.

"Do they come shooting?" I interposed.

He shut the gun with a snap. "We split even, stranger."

Seeing that the butcher was a fragile piece of bric-à-brac, and that I might need him for future study, I bethought me of the banker down the street. Bankers are bound to be broad-gauged, intelligent, and conservative, so I would go to him and get at the ancient history of this neck of woods. I introduced myself, and was invited behind the counter. The look of things reminded me of one of those great green terraces which conceal fortifications and ugly cannon. It was boards and wire screen in front, but behind it were shot-guns and six-shooters hung in the handiest way, on a sort of disappearing gun-carriage arrangement. Shortly one of the cowboys of the street scene floundered in. He was two-thirds drunk, with brutal, shifty eyes and a flabby lower lip.

"I want twenty dollars on the old man. Ken I have it?"

I rather expected that the bank would go into "action front," but the clerk said, "Certainly," and completed this rather odd financial transaction, whereat the bull-hunter stumbled out.

"Who is the old man in this case?" I ventured.

"Oh, it's his boss, old Colonel Zuigg, of Crow City. I gave some money to some of his boys some weeks ago, and when the colonel was down here I asked him if he wanted the boys to draw against him in that way, and he said, 'Yes—for a small amount; they will steal a cow or two, and pay me that way.'"

Here was something tangible.

"What happens when a man steals another man's brand in this country?"

"He mustn't get caught; that's all. They all do it, but they never bring their troubles into court. They just shoot it out there in the bresh. The last time old Colonel Zuigg brought Zorn Zuidden in here and had him indicted for stealing cattle, said Zorn: 'Now see here, old man Zuigg, what do you want for to go and git me arrested fer? I have

A Cracker Cowboy. *Painting in "21" Club Collection—Peter Kriendler, President.*

stole thousands of cattle and put your mark and brand on 'em, and jes because I have stole a couple of hundred from you, you go and have me indicted. You jes better go and get that whole deal nol prossed;' and it was done."

The argument was perfect.

"From that I should imagine that the cow-people have no more idea of law than the 'gray apes,'" I commented.

"Yes, that's about it. Old Colonel Zuigg was a judge fer a spell, till some feller filled him with buckshot, and he had to resign; and I remember he decided a case aginst me once. I was hot about it, and the old colonel he saw I was. Says he, 'Now yer mad, ain't you?' And I allowed I was. 'Well,' says he, 'you hain't got no call to get mad. I have decided the last eight cases in yer favor, and you kain't have it go yer way all the time; it wouldn't look right;' and I had to be satisfied."

The courts in that locality were but the faint and sickly flame of a taper offered at the shrine of a justice which was traditional only, it seemed. Moral forces having ceased to operate, the large owners began to brand everything in sight, never realizing that they were sowing the wind. This action naturally demoralized the cowboys, who shortly began to brand a little on their own account —and then the deluge. The rights of property having been destroyed, the large owners put strong outfits in the field, composed of desperate men armed to the teeth, and what happens in the lonely pine woods no one knows but the desperadoes themselves, albeit some of them never come back to the little fringe of settlements. The winter visitor from the North kicks up the jacksnipe along the beach or tarponizes in the estuaries of the Gulf, and when he comes to the hotel for dinner he eats Chicago dressed beef, but out in the wilderness low-browed cow-folks shoot and stab each other for the possession of scrawny creatures not fit for a pointer-dog to mess on. One cannot but feel the force of Buckle's law of "the physical aspects of nature" in this sad country. Flat and sandy, with miles of straight pine timber, each tree an exact duplicate of its neighbor tree, and underneath the scrub palmettoes, the twisted brakes and hammocks, and the gnarled water-oaks festooned with the sad gray Spanish-moss— truly not a country for a high-spirited race or moral giants.

The land gives only a tough wiregrass, and the poor little cattle, no bigger than a donkey, wander half starved and horribly emaciated in search of it. There used to be a trade with Cuba, but now that has gone; and beyond the supplying of Key West and the small fringe of settlements they have no market. How well the cowboys serve their masters I can only guess, since the big owners do not dare go into the woods, or even to their own doors at night, and they do not keep a light burning in the houses. One, indeed, attempted to assert his rights, but some one pumped sixteen buckshot into him as he bent over a spring to drink, and he left the country. They do tell of a late encounter between two rival foremen, who rode on to each other in the woods, and drawing, fired, and both were found stretched dying under the palmettoes, one calling deliriously the name of his boss. The unknown reaches of the Everglades lie just below, and with a half-hour's start a man who knew the country would be safe from pursuit, even if it were attempted; and, as one man cheerfully confided to me, "A boat don't leave no trail, stranger."

That might makes right, and that they steal by wholesale, any cattle-hunter will admit; and why they brand at all I cannot see, since one boy tried to make it plain to me, as he shifted his body in drunken abandon and grabbed my pencil and a sheet of wrapping paper: "See yer; ye see that?" And he drew a circle **O**; and then another ring around it, thus: **◎**. "That brand ain't no good. Well, then—" And again his knotted and dirty fingers essayed the brand **I O**. He laboriously drew upon it and made **ᕮO** which of course destroyed the former brand.

"Then here," he continued, as he drew 13, "all ye've got ter do is this—313." I gasped in amazement, not at his cleverness as a brand-destroyer, but at his honest abandon. With a horrible operatic laugh, such as is painted in "The Cossack's Answer," he again laboriously drew ⊕ (the circle cross), and then added some marks which made it look like this: ⊕. And again breaking into his devil's "ha, ha!" said, "Make the damned thing whirl."

I did not protest. He would have shot me for that. But I did wish he was living in the northwest quarter of New Mexico, where Mr. Cooper and Dan could throw their eyes over the trail of his pony. Of course each man has adjusted himself to this lawless rustling, and only calculates that he can steal as much as his opponent. It is rarely that their affairs are brought to court, but when

they are, the men come *en masse* to the room, armed with knives and rifles, so that any decision is bound to be a compromise, or it will bring on a general engagement.

There is also a noticeable absence of negroes among them, as they still retain some *ante bellum* theories, and it is only very lately that they have "reconstructed." Their general ignorance is "miraculous," and quite mystifying to an outside man. Some whom I met did not even know where the Texas was which furnishes them their ponies. The railroads of Florida have had their ups and downs with them in a petty way on account of the running over of their cattle by the trains; and then some long-haired old Cracker drops into the nearest station with his gun and pistol, and wants the telegraph operator to settle immediately on the basis of the Cracker's claim for damages, which is always absurdly high. At first

Cowboys Wrestling a Bull. *Authors' photoengraving.*

the railroads demurred, but the cowboys lined up in the "bresh" on some dark night and pumped Winchesters into the train in a highly picturesque way. The trainmen at once recognized the force of the Cracker's views on cattle-killing, but it took some considerable "potting" at the more conservative superintendents before the latter could bestir themselves and invent a "cow-attorney," as the company adjuster is called, who now settles with the bushmen as best he can. Certainly no worse people ever lived since the big killing up Muscleshell way, and the romance is taken out of it by the cowardly assassination which is the practice. They are well paid for their desperate work, and always eat fresh beef or "razor-backs," and deer which they kill in the woods. The heat, the poor grass, their brutality, and the pest of the flies kill their ponies, and, as a rule, they lack dash and are indifferent riders, but they are picturesque in their unkempt, almost unearthly wildness. A strange effect is added by their use of large, fierce cur-dogs, one of which accompanies each cattle-hunter, and is taught to pursue cattle, and to even take them by the nose, which is another instance of their brutality. Still, as they only have a couple of horses apiece, it saves them much extra running. These men do not use the rope, unless to noose a pony in a corral, but work their cattle in strong log corrals, which are made at about a day's march apart all through the woods. Indeed, ropes are hardly necessary, since the cattle are so small and thin that two men can successfully "wrestle" a three-year-old. A man goes into the corral, grabs a cow by one horn, and throwing his other arm over her back, waits until some other man takes her hind leg, whereat ensues some very entertaining Græco-Roman style.

When the cow is successful, she finds her audience of Cracker cowboys sitting on the fence awaiting another opening, and gasping for breath. The best bull will not go over three hundred pounds, while I have seen a yearling at a hundred and fifty—if you, O knights of the riata, can imagine it! Still, it is desperate work. Some of the men are so reckless and active that they do not hesitate to encounter a wild bull in the open. The cattle are as wild as deer, they race off at scent; and when "rounded up" many will not drive, whereupon these are promptly shot. It frequently happens that when the herd is being driven quietly along a bull will turn on the drivers, charging at once. Then there is a scamper and great shooting. The bulls often become so maddened in these forays that they drop and die in their tracks, for which strange fact no one can account, but as a rule they are too scrawny and mean to make their handling difficult.

So this is the Cracker cowboy, whose chief interest would be found in the tales of some bushwhacking enterprise, which I very much fear would be a one-sided story, and not worth the telling. At best they must be revolting, having no note of the savage encounters which used to characterize the easy days in West Texas and New Mexico, when every man tossed his life away to the crackle of his own revolver. The moon shows pale through the leafy canopy on their evening fires, and the mists, the miasma, and the mosquitoes settle over their dreary camp talk. In place of the wild stampede, there is only the bellowing in the pens, and instead of the plains shaking under the dusty air as the bedizened vaqueros plough their fiery broncos through the milling herds, the cattle-hunter wends his lonely way through the ooze and rank grass, while the dreary pine trunks line up and shut the view.

With the Guns

Captain Dillenback, of Fort Hamilton, down New York Bay, had an idea. It was a good one, and finally the "big chiefs" who hold down the cane-bottomed chairs in the War Department put their respective names and titles and "approved and forwarded" on the application, and Secretary Lamont, who believes in letting the "man on horseback" ride, said "Yes," and the captain had the order for a summer march and camp in the famous old Berkshire Hills of Massachusetts. On the appointed day four $3\frac{2}{10}$-inch breech-loading rifles with their caissons lined up on the parade at Fort Hamilton, and each man threw out his chest, pulled in his chin, and looked as serious as the regulations require, while the captain and the battery dog inspected; then they moved off on the one-hundred-and-fifty-mile march to the point selected up in Berkshire. The battery dog in this case is worth notice because of his tremendous responsibility and the perfect way in which he does his duty. A Yorkshire terrier had been somewhere in his line of ancestors; but Battery K is a democratic lot in its feelings, and they "took on" this canine recruit, which had nothing more to offer than a good appetite and a natural aptitude for the artillery. If he had ever been in civil life he had forgotten it, and citizens who walk through Battery K's park must look sharp or the dog will nip them, and if a citizen kicks the dog he would have to lick the battery, because the men simply adore him. They feed him, pet him, stir up his fleas with a currycomb at "stables," and

scheme for the honor of being his "bunkie" at night—all of which makes a healthy life for the dog.

The march up is through a hill country, and they only attempted twenty miles a day. As they wound along the country roads and through the villages they were everywhere received with gusto by the people who viewed them. "It ain't so good as Buffalo Bill's, but it don't cost nothin', Samanthy," said one old fellow with chin whiskers. Strange to say, up in Massachusetts many good people were awed by the prospect of regular soldiers coming among them. I could not discover what basis there was for the awe, but it had possession. It might have been a legacy from the British, or possibly the reckless home-coming of the volunteers of '65; but shortly their fears began to allay, and many came to Captain Dillenback and explained that they were not only gratified to find out that his men were a decent lot of young chaps, but that they, the citizens, were very friendly with them, all of which, of course, the bronzed and rugged old soldier of thirty-five years' service could in no wise comprehend. He knows naturally that this man, so much dreaded by the smug civilian, is a happy-go-lucky fellow, better natured than his money-hunting brother; he has also seen him killed by the hundreds, and—as the captain reasons—killed for the benefit of this same smug "cit"—so why can the captain understand when the smug "cit" doesn't understand what the captain knows? The soldiers patiently opened the breech blocks, and answered millions of foolish questions about the guns and were particularly nice towards the young ladies, and the result is that the regular army is "right in it" up western Massachusetts way. Brass bands met them and kept their instruments jammed with wind; "old vets" clapped each other on their bent shoulders, and a little brine ran off their cheeks as the glorious visions of old days played through their fancies. The people gave the men "little spreads," and the officers are honorary members of more clubs than they can possibly remember, while Captain Dillenback, being a good-natured man, has to do double duty—what with fulfilling the orders to exercise his men in the conditions of actual warfare, and going to Mrs. B.'s lunch and Mr. A.'s dinner, neither of whom will take any refusal. A local paper at Great Barrington said: "This is the third time in the history of this town when artillery has been within its borders. The first time was in January, 1776, when 'a long line of sleighs, bearing cannon, mortars, cohorns, and other military stores, captured by Ethan Allen and his Green Mountain boys from Fort Ticonderoga, passed through to Dorchester to supply the sad want of artillery in Washington's army beleaguering Boston.' 'The second appearance was shortly after the surrender of Burgoyne, when a fine train of artillery, captured at Saratoga, was drawn through the village.'" Small wonder, then, that the people turned out to see.

The spot selected for the camp marks the captain as a man with an eye for the pictur-

The First Sergeant, Battery K, First Artillery, in Field Trim. *Authors' photoengraving.*

esque. Big hills on all sides, a meadow with the white tents, and the gun park with a fringe of great willow-trees shading a trout brook, which bubbles over the stones or lies lazily in deep pools. The horses stand on the picket line, sunlit, and with lowered heads and half-closed eyes, their tails drowsily beating at the flies, while the men lie under the trees after their four hours' drill with the guns. All is peace, and nature gives the lie to this noisy little detail in the sheltered valley—all is peace except the quartermaster's mind, and for quartermasters there is no peace. Under a big willow is the barber shop, which consists of a chair and a canvas bucket. The saddler sits on a fallen log, and pounds at a boot heel which has to be mended. I told him of the Tenth Cavalry soldier down in Arizona whom I had seen sitting by the side of the trail looking mournfully at a boot from which the forward part of the sole had fetched loose from the upper, and how he finally had a mental spasm, and taking out his jackknife and some horseshoe nails had repaired the boot, which was now in my collection. The soldier replied that he had been in the Fourth Cavalry, and had climbed the mountains in Arizona until his boots had worn out, when he had wrapped his feet in gunny sacking. Another man was so well set up that I felt for his history, knowing that he must have one, and sure enough he had been a first sergeant in the First Cavalry, had been discharged, tried civil life in the East, and found that old dogs don't acquire new tricks, so here he was in a battery. Another strapping fine chap was also no "ruckie." "Ten years in the Nineteenth Hussars, sir." he answered. At calisthenics the men appeared in their under-shirts, and brawny

thews and sinews are there to greet the eye of any one who loves to look on the human form.

Then it is not all dreaming under trees by purling brooks, for early each morning the horses are hooked up and moved off down the road to the drill ground on Bear Mountain, where is found one of the few available flats in this very broken country. Four hours of rapid gaits and constant going into battery, of limbering and unlimbering, makes horses and men appreciate a dinner and a nap under the willows. There is no range at Fort Hamilton, and one of the objects of the trip was to find a place to practise at the guns, but as yet this had not been determined on. Many good-natured farmers had no objection to having $3\frac{2}{10}$-inch projectiles pass over their land on their way to a distant mountain-side where the targets were, but when it was explained what shell and shrapnel were, and the strange things they did, the quiet men lost some of their enthusiasm, but no doubt a good place will shortly be found, and to the small boys of Berkshire County the noises they have been able to inject into the Fourth of July will pale into sputterings. The bang of one of these new rifles is exceedingly vicious and ought to stir up serious apprehensions in the mind of any one who is in line with their muzzles. To a spectator the drill of a battery is a most inspiring sight—quite equal to cavalry—the mad galloping of the horses, the lashing whips, the rumble of the wheels, and the sharp braying of the bugle, ending up with terrific banging of the guns as the gray smoke whirls a hundred yards in front of the long red flash, is as good as Buffalo Bill, and "it don't cost anything" to Samanthy and the good man with the chin whiskers.

Getting Hunters in Horse-Show Form

There may be a few bicycles up in the Genesee Valley, but the persons who ride them do not expect to run for Congress in that district, because the people there ride horses, and awfully good ones too, for the most part. They talk horse and think horse, and even the women are wise as serpents concerning equine matters—enough so to distress a Bull's Head dealer were one to go among them. As one goes about the country every now and then he will see in some stable a groom holding a horse by the head, while slowly walking about him is a group of men in boots or leggings, with possibly a woman or two, all silently intent on their own observations, as if it were an ancient fresco or a conqueror's tomb on which they gazed. The country-side itself is one of the most delightful pastoral landscapes in America—much the impression of England —well farmed and prosperous. Set about on the hills are the fine country-seats of the Wadsworths, the Howlands, and others, backed by big stables, all the stalls blocked with hunters, the grounds cut up with hurdles, rails, and water, stone walls and Liverpool jumps; and quite common to see are horses dancing over them as they take their exercise. One is made to wonder why there is not more of the same thing elsewhere in New York State, given up as it is to the production of gangling and nearly unsaleable trotting stock. Any good horse of the hunter type, able to clear his five feet nicely, is gold in the hands of his owner. Many of the hunters come from Canada, up Toronto

way, where years ago retired British army officers settled and raised horses from Irish hunter stock, which has made that country celebrated, and customers come in flocks to buy them. Unless a man rides at the very top weight he can be suited in his mount without importing from England or Ireland. The training of a hunter involves, first, a development of his jumping qualities in order to determine whether he will make a "hunter" or not, and on its being decided favorably a stable-boy may carry along his education until the finishing course, which must or should be given him by the master who is to hunt him. To my astonishment, a very celebrated riding man told me that occasionally an American trotting horse turns out a crack hunter, but I cannot bring myself to think that much could be hoped for from such a quarter.

Many of the farmers up Genesee way breed hunters, ride them to hounds, and if the horse performs well they sell out at a good sum to some of the gentlemen who run up there to hunt the country. When the Horse Show is on in New York great numbers of horses are shipped down to the city to participate in the contests, and many of these never return, being sold to other parts. Men who ride to hounds usually keep three horses for the purpose, and many keep more, while Mr. Howland has mounted fourteen visiting friends from his stable for one run. People are constantly changing their mounts, and naturally this buying and turning off of horses puts a man into a

Getting Hunters in Horse-show Form. *Engraving in authors' collection.*

dealer's way almost. For one who wants a horse of that character what better can he do than to go right to the stables of the big hunting men? He may not acquire their top horses, but he can find tremendous hacks which are not up to the hunting man's ideas over the timber. As I have said, one can see the hunters being schooled over the timber, which is always a good show, and he can tell the "proper" from the "flying jumper," and see all the form, never forgetting that the groom who is "up" is likely to ride amazingly well. The younger horses are first whipped along a chute and forced over rails thickly padded with straw covered with burlaps, they are then mounted by boys, until finally some few develop to horse-show form, and are entered for competition in the local show, which latter determines whether they are to command the plaudits of the multitude in the great Garden, or are simply to follow the pack over the quiet valley. I saw the gallant old Ontario brought out and put over the rails for the edification of some visitors, and he does it in his old workmanlike manner despite his lost eye and his years.

He is to be immortalized by the master, for Mr. St. Gaudens has used the grand old fellow as a model in his statue of General Sherman. Who will say that horses cannot have careers, and grand ones too? For one, I might hesitate if I had to decide to be either Ontario or some one of the millions of human beings who are not up to man-show form. Fie on this thing called contentment! Ontario may have it, though it properly only belongs to Florida negroes and housedogs. If my soul should ever transmigrate into a horse, let it be into a grand hunter's body—unbroken to harness, arched in the loin, high withers running far back, lean shoulders extended and playing like a pugilist's arms, neck supple and far from the hand, tail set high, and quarters as large as a freight-car, with my forearm like a blacksmith's; then let me have pasterns like the fencer's wrist, good long hard hoofs well open behind, and the head I must suppose to be my own. I will carry a gentleman over the country if his hands are light on my mouth and his seat is steady and well back; if we tangle up and turn over it is no more likely to hurt me than the fellow who rides me where I cannot go. If my master is a hard hunting man, I doubt not he will want me close on the dogs, in which case I must hope he will have a cool head, and will help me out of the difficulties I have to encounter in getting over the uneven ground, but by the tail of Bucephalus I hope he don't use his arms, except to steady me when I land badly or stumble on a rolling stone in some shifty going. Some men will become excited, and will not know as well as I how to negotiate the going, and if so—very well—I will leave him piled up in a ditch somewhere, waiting for whiskey-and-water and court-plaster, and go racing on after the hounds, where some better man who is riding up will see me and say it was not my fault, because he will know that my rider had no seat, because he could see that at the meet in the morning, where I kicked around a bit to loosen my sinews, and the good rider will buy me—in short, I will become possessed of a good master by my cleverness in the field; and once I have him, if he is really a good master, I will take him where he wants to go, and I will be so game that I will strain the last nerve cell to do the thing he puts me at. I may come to grief, but the good master, after he has had plaster put on his nose and liniment on his wrists, will turn over in his bed and say to himself, "I should not have put my heels into him at the last jump, because his nerves were dead, his legs heavy, and his stomach drawn into his wind." He will come out to see that the grooms rub embrocation on my knees, and repent of his ardor, while I will hope to get right in my knees as soon as he does in his wrists, whereupon we will play together some more.

Then at various times when I am a youngster I will win silver cups for him at the shows, and then in "mine age" he will not turn me off, because he will, after dinner, show his visiting friends the long row of big silver mugs on his mantel-piece, and they will all talk about me the evening through. All that will be a good business. Of course he might lose his money in Wall Street. Then, if he was a good master, he would turn me off to some friend who also liked good hunters, and the cups on the mantel-piece should go with me. If he shouldn't do this I would kick the "stuffin'" out of any unsportsmanlike character who might come to possess me. I think, too, that none of these electrical sharps will ever invent a contraption to hunt the hounds, and so long as there are cows there will be fences. However, I shall never be a horse, or anything but   FREDERIC REMINGTON.

A Practice March in Texas

There is no question in my mind as to the utility of the practice march under absolute conditions such as are bound to occur in the field of war. There seems to be a great deal of question about it by the military authorities of New York State, but I think they are wrong. One week in the field under service conditions is worth five years in a drill-hall or a month in a post camp if the basic idea is to discover how efficient troops are. Soldiers can't be made in a house. Of course it is impossible to have troops, either regulars or volunteers, in the field all the time; but that they should be in the field under service conditions for a time in every year no one can doubt, without going contrary to all ac-

A Practice March in Texas. *Authors' photoengraving.*

cepted conclusions of the greatest soldiers and to common sense of the most common kind.

It costs the government no more to keep troops in the field in small bodies than to maintain them in garrison; it induces interest in the profession, gains them experience in taking care of themselves, and fits the soldier mind to the idea that he must be able to live in a state of nature, and not in a large hotel like a man with money and the gout. These practice marches are much indulged in nowadays by the regular troops. My illustration is of two companies of the Twenty-third Infantry, under Captain Lea Febiger, which marched from Fort Clark to the East Nueces River, in Texas, last October. Their orders were for the officers and men to carry the usual field equipment—heavy-marching order, excepting knapsacks. Three days' rations were carried by the men in haversacks, while the blanket-rolls contained change of under-clothing and shelter-tent. "The command not having transportation of any kind on the march, should it become necessary to communicate with the post for any purpose whatever, may do so by bicycles, the use of which on the march by enlisted men owning them is hereby authorized," say the orders. The report of Captain Febiger says: "Each officer and man carried three days' field rations, the fresh vegetable portion being optional. which in all cases was greatly reduced, and even more so on the second day out; haversack, canteen, and blanket-roll, the last consisting of one shelter half (new pattern) and pins, one blanket, change of under-clothing, blouse, (marched in flannel shirts), one pair of socks, towel, soap, etc., and the additional rations that the haversack would not hold (about one day's), and their respective arms and belts. The total weight of the pack averaged about forty pounds, when not wet, divided as follows: Haversack, packed, 6 pounds; canteen, filled, and cup, 4 pounds; cartridge-belt and ten rounds, 1¾ pounds; rifle, 9⅓ pounds; blanket-roll 19 pounds. All officers and men did their own cooking in meat-ration can and cup.

"Four privates and one musician, with Corporal John Reeves in charge, constituted the bicycle corps, carrying their haversacks and blanket-rolls on the handle-bars, and rifles strapped to the frame. They constituted daily on the march the advance-guard, and were ready for use as messengers and couriers. Two of the machines, being secondhand, very old and worn, gave out on the march; the other four came successfully through, though not of the most expensive pattern." So much for bicycles.

"There were numerous complaints of the government shoe, and they wore much worse than those purchased outside. The new shelter-tent with the elongated rear end was very satisfactory, except that it is far from rain-proof in anything like a heavy shower." Indeed, no tent is proof, for that matter.

"The haversacks were rendered completely unfit for garrison inspection purposes, on account of the grease from the bacon carried in them;" and in conclusion the captain says that "both officers and men appreciated and have been benefited by the experience."

Squadron A's Games

A tremendous audience turned out on a very stormy night to see the final competitions of Squadron A in its new armory. The ladies swarmed the galleries, and any trooper will "ride for a fall" when they are looking on. A brass band and a pretty girl will make a soldier brave—very, very heroic —not that the squadron needs this impetus, but Squadron A is about twenty-two years of age in the aggregate, and as enthusiastic as a house on fire. The new riding-ring is of tremendous size, black with tan-bark, well lighted—altogether quite imposing. One looking on at the quiet major who is superintending events in the ring must think that the whole creation is vastly satisfactory to him after his years of hard work. Captains Bridgeman and Badgley are by this time

Tent-pegging. *Authors' photoengraving.*

3

downright veterans, while the squadron is full of material amply competent to wrestle "shave-tails."

The games were opened by a saddling-race, in which each competitor had to blanket, saddle, mount and ride to the lower end of the ring—saddle to be found properly adjusted at the finish. In this exercise "haste makes waste," so the troopers went about it like a cub bear picking huckleberries, and they did better.

The "manikin race" was funny. The blessed idea of the heroic rescue of the sorely wounded comrade lying weak and stiff is a bit hazy at best to the lay members of the audience, and it is all lost when the boys spur swiftly down the ring, throw themselves from their mounts, lay rude hands on the sausagelike image, and fling it savagely across the horse. The horse, too— he does not participate in the ethics of the drill; he only sees that a decent beast cannot be expected to be made a fool of by carrying such rubbish; so he begins to change ends with electric spirit; and what with a pivoting horse, a clumsy contrivance always observing the laws of gravitation, and a bit of nervousness about getting off on the troopers' part, the audience grins in cheerful expectancy.

Picking up the handkerchief from the ground at full career looks easy—that is to say, the average on-looker doesn't think he is seeing miracles performed right before his eyes—for which we gravely give thanks. What a refuge and a beneficence is this average person—to those who can do things which Mr. Averageman cannot! We are all average in most ways but there are fewer geniuses who can pick up handkerchiefs than one would suppose after he had seen several do it. If you don't believe me, ask a commissary sergeant; he knows what soldiers pick up quickest.

A quite formidable hedge—say five feet in the clear—was arranged by the servitors. One iron gray horse in the line of competitors said to a companion, "I'm not going to make a show of myself right before all these people; this boy will fall on my neck and

spoil my stride while he tries to hit that absurd leather head with his sword"; and the iron-gray stood on his behind legs—not once, but time after time, and the boy realized that "iron-gray" was in earnest concerning his resolve not to try the hurdle. The prejudice against the venture communicated itself to the other horses, and they carromed off at sight of the obstacle. Some were ridden so hard at it that they forgot to sidle, and a gallant sergeant did the trick and had his name shouted as victor.

The tent-pegs were set in the tan-bark while the troopers bore down on them like knights of old. They prodded viciously on their arrival, but generally succeeded only in cultivating the tan-bark around the stick. Not always so safe was it, however, for the Dacoit lying in the grass, for occasionally the offending form was tossed savagely in the air, and death lay in the track of the flying troop. The bright eyes of the women up in the galleries gleamed approval on the champions; some of them were wise enough even to know when to divide their admiration for the trooper with the horse.

The mêlée was grand. Here the idea of a fight is so insisted on that even the women know at last that these soldiers are not created to be simply beautiful. The birdcages which the combatants wear on their heads ease off feminine nerves, since they preclude any flow of claret; but the women don't know what sickly grins some of the boys drew under their masks when they got a hot wipe with a hickory stick across the back of the neck. The women also do not applaud—which is sad. There is much mystery about this cavalry business for them. The hero doesn't sing after he wipes up the villain, as he does in the opera, and the women applaud the singing and not the "wipe." But anybody can see that Squadron A's clothes fit them and that their boots glisten. The cadets on duty in the galleries dream of the day when they can draw the fire of the audience, and the Madison Avenue street-car driver told me as I lighted a cigar on his platform that "dem Troop A boys is hot stuff."

A New Idea for Soldiers

Lieutenant Charles Dodge, of the Twenty-fourth Infantry, invented a yoke some time ago which was to carry the blanket-roll of infantrymen. It was good in theory, but in practice it swayed about as the soldier marched, and the private man filed his objections. The inventor was not discouraged, knowing as he did that the knapsack would never be carried by United States soldiers, because the blanket-roll is a better method, as any infantry soldier will tell you, if you care to ask one. So he thought and contrived, until one day he filed the teeth off from the blade of a buck saw and inserted it in one edge of the dog-tent which goes about the blanket and clothing of the soldier's roll of personal plunder. This elastic spring bent under the weight of the pack and rode across the left shoulder of the man, while two little straps and buckles were attached to the strap which carries the haversack—that strap traversing the other shoulder—thus adjusting the weight of the blanket-roll to both shoulders. The roll had points of contact with the man's body at the shoulder and hip, thus preventing it from swaying, while the steel spring made it ride easily as the man walked, and also kept the weight off his breast and back, which made breathing easier and allowed the circulation of air. The cost of the improvement is a mere nothing.

He experimented with it practically by getting soldiers to carry it on marches—this being the only real test for a military equip-

ment—and the enlisted man said "it is a good thing," and that settled it. No, not quite; it ought to have, but, as a matter of fact, it didn't. There was the Quartermaster-General, but he too was favorably impressed, and I have no doubt but the Dodge blanket-roll support will be on every infantry soldier's back in course of time. The militia authorities should have a look at

The Dodge Field Equipment, or Blanket-roll Support. *Authors' photoengraving.*

this thing, and to look is to immediately adopt it. Its great merit is its absolute simplicity, since any man can immediately see what the two little straps are for. It can be taken off the person of the soldier by simply unbuckling two straps, leaving the canteen and haversack on the man. No knapsack yet invented has ever been satisfactory—first, because it heats the back of the soldier; secondly, pulls on his breastbone instead of riding on the top of the shoulders; and where it does neither of these, it is too complicated by reason of the number of buckles and straps, which are lost or get out of order, whereas simplicity should be the first essential. When this equipment is adopted, a United States infantry soldier in field equipment, as now provided will leave nothing to be desired. This is all that may be asked. If he wants to look like a street-car conductor when he gets on his good clothes, we can only deprecate his taste.

The Strange Days That Came to Jimmie Friday

The "Abwee-chemun"* Club was organized with six charter members at a heavy lunch in the Savarin restaurant—one of those lunches which make through connections to dinner without change. One member basely deserted, while two more lost all their enthusiasm on the following morning, but three of us stuck. We vaguely knew that somewhere north of the Canadian Pacific and south of Hudson Bay were big lakes and rapid rivers—lakes whose names we did not know; lakes bigger than Champlain, with unnamed rivers between them. We did not propose to be boated around in a big birch-bark by two voyagers among blankets and crackers and ham, but each provided himself a little thirteen-foot cedar canoe, twenty-nine inches in the beam, and weighing less than forty pounds. I cannot tell you precisely how our party was sorted, but one was a lawyer with eyeglasses and settled habits, loving nature, though detesting canoes; the other was nominally a merchant, but in reality an atavic Norseman of the wolf and raven kind; while I am not new. Together we started.

Presently the Abwees sat about the board of a lumbermen's hotel, filled with house-flies and slatternly waiter-girls, who talked familiarly while they served greasy food. The Abwees were yet sore in their minds at the thoughts of the smelly beds up-stairs, and discouragement sat deeply on their souls. But their time was not yet.

After breakfast they marched to the Hud-son Bay Company's store, knowing as they did that in Canada there are only two places for a traveller to go who wants anything—the great company or the parish priest; and then, having explained to the factor their dream, they were told "that beyond, beyond some days' journey"—oh! that awful beyond, which for centuries has stood across the path of the pioneer, and in these latter days confronts the sportsman and wilderness-lover—"that beyond some days' journey to the north was a country such as they had dreamed—up Temiscamingue and beyond."

The subject of a guide was considered.

Jimmie Friday always brought a big toboggan-load of furs into Fort Tiemogamie every spring, and was accounted good in his business. He and his big brother trapped together, and in turn followed the ten days' swing through the snow-laden forest which they had covered with their dead-falls and steel-jawed traps; but when the ice went out in the rivers, and the great pines dripped with the melting snows, they had nothing more to do but cut a few cords of wood for their widowed mother's cabin near the post. Then the brother and he paddled down to Bais des Pierres, where the brother engaged as a deck hand on a steamboat, and Jimmie hired himself as a guide for some bush-rangers, as the men are called who explore for pine lands for the great lumber firms. Having worked all summer and got through with that business, Jimmie bethought him to dissipate for a few days in the bustling lum-

* Algonquin for "paddle and canoe."

ber town down on the Ottawa River. He had been there before to feel the exhilaration of civilization, but beyond that clearing he had never known anything more inspiring than a Hudson Bay post, which is generally a log store, a house where the agent lives, and a few tiny Indian cabins set higgledy-piggledy in a sunburnt gash of stumps and bowlders, lost in the middle of the solemn, unresponsive forest. On this morning in question he had stepped from his friend's cabin up in the Indian village, and after lighting a perfectly round and rather yellow cigar, he had instinctively wandered down to the Hudson Bay store, there to find himself amused by a strange sight.

The Abwees had hired two French-Indian voyagers of sinister mien, and a Scotch-Canadian boy bred to the bush. They were out on the grass, engaged in taking burlaps off three highly polished canoes, while the clerk from the store ran out and asked questions about "how much bacon," and, "will fifty pounds of pork be enough, sir?"

The round yellow cigar was getting stubby, while Jimmie's modest eyes sought out the points of interest in the new-comers when he was suddenly and sharply addressed:

"Can you cook?"

Jimmie couldn't do anything in a hurry, except chop a log in two, paddle very fast, and shoot quickly, so he said, as was his wont:

"I think—I dun'no'—"

"Well, how much?" came the query.

"Two daul—ars—" said Jimmie.

The transaction was complete. The yellow butt went over the fence, and Jimmie shed his coat. He was directed to lend a hand by the bustling sportsmen, and requested to run and find things of which he had never before in his life heard the name.

After two days' travel the Abwees were put ashore—boxes, bags, rolls of blankets, canoes, Indians, and plunder of many sorts —on a pebbly beach, and the steamer backed off and steamed away. They had reached the "beyond" at last, and the odor-

iferous little bedrooms, the bustle of the preparation, the cares of their lives, were behind. Then there was a girding up of the loins, a getting out of tump-lines and canvas packs, and the long portage was begun.

The voyagers carried each two hundred pounds as they stalked away into the wilderness, while the attorney-at-law "hefted" his pack, wiped his eyeglasses with his pocket-handkerchief, and tried cheerfully to assume the responsibilities of "a dead game sport."

"I cannot lift the thing, and how I am going to carry it is more than I know; but I'm a dead game sport, and I am going to try. I do not want to be dead game, but it looks as though I couldn't help it. Will some gentleman help me to adjust this cargo?"

The night overtook the outfit in an old beaver meadow half-way through the trail. Like all first camps, it was tough. The lean-to tents went up awkwardly. No one could find anything. Late at night the Abwees lay on their backs under the blankets, while the fog settled over the meadow and blotted out the stars.

On the following day the stuff was all gotten through, and by this time the lawyer had become a voyager, willing to carry anything he could stagger under. It is strange how one can accustom himself to "pack." He may never use the tump-line, since it goes across the head, and will unseat his intellect if he does, but with shoulder-straps and a tump-line a man who thinks he is not strong will simply amaze himself inside of a week by what he can do. As for our little canoes, we could trot with them. Each Abwee carried his own belongings and his boat, which entitled him to the distinction of "a dead game sport," whatever that may mean, while the Indians portaged their larger canoes and our mass of supplies, making many trips backward and forward in the process.

At the river everything was parcelled out and arranged. The birch-barks were repitched, and every man found out what he was expected to portage and do about camp. After breaking and making camp three times, the outfit could pack up, load the canoes, and move inside of fifteen minutes. At the first camp the lawyer essayed his canoe, and was cautioned that the delicate thing might flirt with him. He stepped in and sat gracefully down in about two feet of water, while the "delicate thing" shook herself saucily at his side. After he had crawled dripping ashore and wiped his eyeglasses, he engaged to sell the "delicate thing" to an Indian for one dollar and a half on a promissory note. The trade was suppressed, and he was urged to try again. A man who has held down a canebottom chair conscientiously for fifteen years looks askance at so fickle a thing as a canoe twenty-nine inches in the beam. They are nearly as hard to sit on in the water as a cork; but once one is in the bottom they are stable enough, though they do not submit to liberties or palsied movements. The staid lawyer was filled with horror at the prospect of another go at his polished beauty; but remembering his resolve to be dead game, he abandoned his life to the chances, and got in this time safely.

So the Abwees went down the river on a golden morning, their double-blade paddles flashing the sun and sending the drip in a shower on the glassy water. The smoke from the lawyer's pipe hung behind him in the quiet air, while the note of the reveille clangored from the little buglette of the Norseman. Jimmie and the big Scotch backwoodsman swayed their bodies in one boat, while the two sinister voyagers dipped their paddles in the big canoe.

The Norseman's gorge came up, and he yelled back: "Say! this suits me. I am never going back to New York."

Jimmie grinned at the noise; it made him happy. Such a morning, such a water, such a lack of anything to disturb one's peace! Let man's better nature revel in the beauties of existence; they inflate his soul. The colors play upon the senses—the reddish-yellow of the birch-barks, the blue of the water, and the silver sheen as it parts at the bows of the canoes; the dark evergreens, the steely rocks with their lichens, the white trunks of the birches, their fluffy tops so greeny green, and over all the gold of a sunny day. It is my religion, this thing, and I do not know how to tell all I feel concerning it.

The rods were taken out, a gang of flies put on and trolled behind—but we have all seen a man fight a five-pound bass for twenty minutes. The waters fairly swarmed with them, and we could always get enough for the "pot" in a half-hour's fishing at any time during the trip. The Abwees were canoeing, not hunting or fishing; though, in truth, they did not need to hunt spruce-partridge or fish for bass in any sporting sense; they simply went out after them, and never stayed over half an hour. On a point we stopped for lunch: the Scotchman always struck the beach a-cooking. He had a "kit," which was a big camp-pail, and inside of it were more dishes than are to be found in some hotels. He broiled the bacon, instead of frying it, and thus we were saved the terrors of indigestion. He had many luxuries in his commissary, among them dried apples, with which he filled a camp-pail one day and put them on to boil. They subsequently got to be about a foot deep all over the camp, while Furguson stood around and regarded the black-magic of the thing with overpowering emotions and Homeric tongue. Furguson was a good genius, big and gentle, and a woodsman root and branch. The Abwees had intended their days in the wilderness to be happy singing flights of time, but with grease and paste in one's stomach what may not befall the mind when it is bent on nature's doings?

And thus it was that the gloomy Indian Jimmie Friday, despite his tuberculosis begotten of insufficient nourishment, was happy in these strange days—even to the extent of looking with wondrous eyes on the nooks which we loved—nooks which previously for him had only sheltered possible "dead-falls" or not, as the discerning eye of the trapper decided the prospects for pelf.

Going ashore on a sandy beach, Jimmie wandered down its length, his hunter mind seeking out the footprints of his prey. He stooped down, and then beckoned me to come, which I did.

Pointing at the sand, he said, "You know him?"

"Wolves," I answered.

"Yes—first time I see 'em up here—they be follerin' the deers—bad—bad. No can trap 'em—verrie smart."

A half-dozen wolves had chased a deer into the water; but wolves do not take to the water, so they had stopped and drank, and then gone rollicking together up the beach. There were cubs, and one great track as big as a mastiff might make.

"See that—moose track—he go by yesterday;" and Jimmie pointed to enormous footprints in the muck of a marshy place. "Verrie big moose—we make call at next camp—think it is early for call."

At the next camp Jimmie made the usual birchbark moose-call, and at evening blew it, as he also did on the following morning. This camp was a divine spot on a rise back of a long sandy beach, and we concluded to stop for a day. The Norseman and I each took a man in our canoes and started out to explore. I wanted to observe some musk-rat hotels down in a big marsh, and the Norseman was fishing. The attorney was content to sit on a log by the shores of the lake, smoke lazily, and watch the sun shimmer through the lifting fog. He saw a canoe approaching from across the lake. He gazed vacantly at it, when it grew strange and more unlike a canoe. The paddles did not move, but the phantom craft drew quickly on.

"Say, Furguson—come here—look at that canoe."

The Scotchman came down, with a pail in one hand, and looked. "Canoe—hell—it's a moose—and there ain't a pocket-pistol in this camp," and he fairly jumped up and down.

"You don't say—you really don't say!" gasped the lawyer, who now began to exhibit signs of insanity.

"Yes—he's going to be d——d sociable with us—he's coming right bang into this camp."

The Indian too came down, but he was long past talking English, and the gutturals came up in lumps, as though he was trying to keep them down.

The moose finally struck a long point of sand and rushes about two hundred yards away, and drew majestically out of the water, his hide dripping, and the sun glistening on his antlers and back.

The three men gazed in spellbound admiration at the picture until the moose was gone. When they had recovered their senses they slowly went up to the camp on the ridge—disgusted and dumfounded.

"I could almost put a cartridge in that old guncase and kill him," sighed the backwoodsman.

"I have never hunted in my life," mused the attorney, "but few men have seen such a sight," and he filled his pipe.

"Hark—listen!" said the Indian. There was a faint cracking, which presently became louder. "He's coming into camp;" and the Indian nearly died from excitement as he grabbed a hatchet. The three unfortunate men stepped to the back of the tents, and as big a bull moose as walks the lonely woods came up to within one hundred and fifty feet of the camp, and stopped, returning their gaze.

Thus they stood for what they say was a minute, but which seemed like hours. The attorney composedly admired the unusual sight. The Indian and Furguson swore softly but most viciously until the moose moved away. The Indian hurled the hatchet at the retreating figure, with a final curse, and the thing was over.

"Those fellows who are out in their canoes will be sick abed when we tell them what's been going on in the camp this morning," sighed Mr. Furguson, as he scoured a cooking-pot.

I fear we would have had that moose on our consciences if we had been there: the game law was not up at the time, but I should have asked for strength from a higher source than my respect for law.

The golden days passed and the lake grew great. The wind blew at our backs. The

Trying Moments. *Authors' photoengraving.*

waves rolled in restless surges, piling the little canoes on their crests and swallowing them in the troughs. The canoes thrashed the water as they flew along, half in, half out, but they rode like ducks. The Abwees took off their hats, gripped their double blades, made the water swirl behind them, howled in glee to each other through the rushing storm. To be five miles from shore in a seaway in kayaks like ours was a sensation. We found they stood it well, and grew contented. It was the complement to the golden lazy days when the water was glass, and the canoes rode upsidedown over its mirror surface. The Norseman grinned and shook his head in token of his pleasure, much as an epicure might after a sip of superior Burgundy.

"How do you fancy this?" we asked the attorney-at-law.

"I am not going to deliver an opinion until I get ashore. I would never have believed that I would be here at my time of life, but one never knows what a —— fool one can make of one's self. My glasses are covered with water, and I can hardly see, but I can't let go of this paddle to wipe them," shrieked the man of the office chair, in the howl of the weather.

But we made a long journey by the aid of the wind, and grew a contempt for it. How could one imagine the stability of those little boats until one had tried it?

That night we put into a natural harbor and camped on a gravel beach. The tents were up and the supper cooking, when the wind hauled and blew furiously into our haven. The fires were scattered and the rain came in blinding sheets. The tent-pegs pulled from the sand. We sprang to our feet and held on to the poles, wet to the skin. It was useless; the rain blew right under the canvas. We laid the tents on the "grub" and stepped out into the dark. We could not be any wetter, and we did not care. To stand in the dark in the wilderness, with nothing to eat, and a fire-engine playing a hose on you for a couple of hours —if you have imagination enough, you can fill in the situation. But the gods were propitious. The wind

died down. The stars came out by myriads. The fires were relighted, and the ordinary life begun. It was late in the night before our clothes, blankets, and tents were dry, but, like boys, we forgot it all.

Then came a river—blue and flat like the sky above—running through rushy banks, backed by the masses of the forest; anon the waters rushed upon us over the rocks, and we fought, plunk-plunk-plunk, with the paddles, until our strength gave out. We stepped out into the water, and getting our lines, and using our long double blades as fenders, "tracked" the canoes up through the boil. The Indians in their heavier boats used "setting-poles" with marvellous dexterity, and by furious exertion were able to draw steadily up the grade—though at times they too "tracked," and even portaged. Our largest canoe weighed two hundred pounds, but a little voyager managed to lug it, though how I couldn't comprehend, since his pipe-stem legs fairly bent and wobbled under the enormous ark. None of us by this time were able to lift the loads which we carried, but, like a Western pack-mule, we stood about and had things piled on to us, until nothing more would stick. Some of the backwoodsmen carry incredible masses of stuff, and their lore is full of tales which no one could be expected to believe. Our men did not hesitate to take two hundred and fifty pounds over short portages, which were very rough and stony, though they all said if they slipped they expected to break a leg. This is largely due to the tump-line, which is laid over the head, while persons unused to it must have shoulder-straps in addition, which are not as good, because the "breastbone," so called, is not strong enough.

We were getting day by day farther into "the beyond." There were no traces here of the hand of man. Only Jimmie knew the way—it was his trapping-ground. Only once did we encounter people. We were blown into a little board dock, on a gray day, with the waves piling up behind us, and made a difficult landing. Here were a few tiny log houses—an outpost of the Hudson Bay Company. We renewed our stock of provisions, after laborious trading with the stagnated people who live in the lonely place. There was nothing to sell us but a few of the most common necessities; however, we needed only potatoes and sugar. This was Jimmie's home. Here we saw his poor old mother, who was being tossed about in the smallest of canoes as she drew her nets. Jimmie's father had gone on a hunting expedition and had never come back. Some day Jimmie's old mother will go out on the wild lake to tend her nets, and she will not come back. Some time Jimmie too will not return—for this Indian struggle with nature is appalling in its fierceness.

There was a dance at the post, which the boys attended, going by canoe at night, and they came back early in the morning, with much giggling at their gallantries.

The loneliness of this forest life is positively discouraging to think about. What the long winters must be in the little cabins I cannot imagine, and I fear the traders must be all avarice, or have none at all; for there can certainly be absolutely no intellectual life. There is undoubtedly work, but not one single problem concerning it. The Indian hunters do fairly well in a financial way, though their lives are beset with weakening hardships and constant danger. Their meagre diet wears out their constitutions, and they are subject to disease. The simplicity of their minds makes it very difficult to see into their life as they try to narrate it to one who may be interested.

From here on was through beautiful little lakes, and the voyagers rigged blanket sails on the big canoes, while we towed behind. Then came the river and the rapids, which we ran, darting between rocks, bumping on sunken stones—shooting fairly out into the air, all but turning over hundreds of times. One day the Abwees glided out in the big lake Tesmiaquemang, and saw the steamer going to Bais des Pierres. We hailed her, and she stopped, while the little canoes danced about in the swell as we were loaded one by one. On the deck above us the passengers admired a kind of boat the like of which had not before appeared in these parts.

At Bais des Pierres we handed over the residue of the commissaries of the Abwee-Chemun to Jimmie Friday, including personally many pairs of well-worn golf-breeches, sweaters, rubber coats, knives which would be proscribed by law in New York. If Jimmie ever parades his solemn wilderness in these garbs, the owls will laugh from the trees. Our simple forest friend laid in his winter stock—traps, flour, salt, tobacco, and pork, a new axe—and accompanied us back down the lake again on the steamer. She stopped in mid-stream, while Jimmie got his bundles into his "bark" and shoved off, amid a hail of "good-byes."

The engine palpitated, the big wheel churned the water astern, and we drew away. Jimmie bent on his paddle with the quick body-swing habitual to the Indian, and after a time grew a speck on the reflection of the red sunset in Temiscamingue.

The Abwees sat sadly leaning on the after-rail, and agreed that Jimmie was "a lovely Injun." Jimmie had gone into the shade of the overhang of the cliffs, when the Norseman started violently up, put his hands in his pockets, stamped his foot, said, "By George, fellows, any D.F. would call this a sporting trip!"

Hasty-Intrenchment Drill

Hasty intrenching, so far as America is concerned, originated with the Indians, and was used by our soldiers in the Revolution; but it was only perfected in our civil war. It came to be imperative as rifle-fire increased in range and accuracy, so much so that Colonel Francis Greene tells us that

Gurko's troops carried heavy picks and shovels, by individual preference, through the Balkan campaign; this, too, when they were freezing, starving, and had their feet done up in rags. All the European armies are now provided with intrenching tools, concerning the relative value of which there is

Hasty Intrenchment Drill in the United States Army. *Authors' photoengraving.*

endless discussion. Various ones have been tried experimentally in our modern army, but none adopted. This is a bad business.

The drill now is to take the knife-bayonet and the top of the Russian meat-tin, with which every soldier is provided, and while loosening the dirt with the knife, to scoop it out with the tin. This might be difficult in frozen or hard ground, and is bad for both tin and knife. The scene of my illustration fortunately afforded loose loam, and within a few moments Captain Febiger's company of infantry were out of sight in the flat prairie. They had literally sunk into the earth, and so dry and light was the dirt that it was almost invisible at 200 yards; to a casual sight it might have been gopher diggings.

The enormous penetration of modern bolts makes soldiers throw the dirt forward for nearly four feet in order to afford any protection; and modern infantry must, in the face of an enemy, go about the country like a mole—just under the sod-line. With the command to "halt" the digging begins.

Our National Guard could not dig up armory floors, but they could do this drill at the State camp; and aside from cooking, outpost work, and shooting, it is most important to a soldier to know how to get out of sight quickly.

Uprising of the Yaqui Indians

It seems from despatches that the Yaquis are again turbulent—this time being exceptional, since they have come north through Sonora to our borders in Arizona, and have even attacked the town of Nogales by storm. Our troops are now out in Arizona, and are trying to capture such of them as cross our borders, in order to do that justice to our Mexican neighbor which international law requires of one nation toward another. But it is one of the misdeeds of Mexico that this Yaqui question was never properly settled. There are ages of politics, of frightful armed inroads and reprisals, of coveted land in question, and much misunderstanding, in consequence, between the Yaquis and the Mexican government. The Yaquis were early Christianized, in the ordinary Spanish-mission sense, and they have been handled by priests adversely to various liberal governments in Mexico—notably in the French time. They possess lands rich and fertile on the Yaqui River. They have never been able to adjust their titles to modern Mexican political law, and have in consequence to fight the covetousness of the people who are within the law. The Mexican troops have been sent against them on many occasions, have fought pitched battles, and have been soundly thrashed; they have stormed adobe forts, captured kings—notably Cajami, who was killed trying to escape, which has a sinister meaning in Mexico—but they have never subdued the Yaquis.

When the tides of battle ran against the Indians, they retreated before the troops up the Yaqui River to the desolate Sierra Madre, and from there could not be dislodged. When their lands were occupied, they sailed down and drove off the Mexicans in turn. They are a splendid people physically, industrious agriculturists, and when not at war form the best laborers in Sonora state. They work in the mines, and in Apache days were hired to convoy silver trains to the settlements, which they always did honestly, while they most successfully beat off the Apache raiders.

They were the laborers who built the Sonora Railroad, and with the money they earned they bought Winchester rifles, so that they are well armed in their encounters with the Mexican troops. They are fanatical and superstitious in their religion, and so consumed with hate toward the Mexican government that I doubt if peace can ever be made with them.

The Mexicans should be tired of trying to subdue them, it would seem, and the only solution of the problem is to conclude fair treaties with them and let Sonora enjoy peace—a thing that state has never known, what with Yaquis, Apaches, Ceris, and bandits both red and white.

Uprising of the Yaqui Indians—Yaqui Warriors in Retreat. *Authors' photoengraving.*

The Blue Quail of the Cactus

The Quartermaster and I both had trouble which the doctors could not cure—it was January, and it would not do for us to sit in a "blind"; besides, I do not fancy that. There are ever so many men who are comfortable all over when they are sitting in a blind waiting on the vagrant flying of the ducks; but it is solemn, gloomy business, and, I must say, sufficient reason why they take a drink every fifteen minutes to keep up their enthusiasm. We both knew that the finest winter resort for shot-gun folks was in the Southwest—down on the Rio Grande in Texas—so we journeyed to Eagle Pass. As we got down from the train we saw Captain Febiger in his long military cloak by a lantern-light.

"Got any quail staked out for us, Feb?" asked the Quartermaster.

"Oodles," said Febiger; "get into my trap," and we were rattled through the unlighted street out to the camp, and brought up by the Captain's quarters.

In the morning we unpacked our trunks, and had everything on the floor where we could see it, after the fashion with men. Captain Febiger's baby boy came in to help us rummage in the heaps of canvas clothes, ammunition, and what not besides, finally selecting for his amusement a loaded Colt's revolver and a freshly honed razor. We were terrorized by the possibilities of the combination. Our trying to take them away from the youngster only made him yell like a cavern of demons. We howled for his

mother to come to our aid, which she finally did, and she separated the kid from his toys.

I put on my bloomers, when the Captain came in and viewed me, saying: "Texas bikes; but it doesn't bloom yet. I don't know just what Texas will do if you parade in those togs—but you can try."

As we sauntered down the dusty main street, Texas lounged in the doorways or stood up in its buggy and stared at me. Texas grinned cheerfully, too, but I did not care, so long as Texas kept its hand out of its hip pocket. I was content to help educate Texas as to personal comfort, at no matter what cost to myself. We passed into Mexico over the Long Bridge to call on Señor Muños, who is the local czar, in hopes of getting permits to be let alone by his chaparral-rangers while we shot quail on their soil. In Mexico when the people observe an Americano they simply shrug their shoulders; so our bloomers attracted no more contempt than would an X-ray or a trolley-car. Señor Muños gave the permits, after much stately compliment and many subtle ways, which made us feel under a cloud of obligation.

The next morning an ambulance and escortwagon drove up to the Captain's quarters, and we loaded ourselves in—shotguns, ammunition, blankets, and the precious paper of Señor Muños; for, only the week before, the custom-house rangers had carefully escorted an American hunting-party a long distance back to the line for lack of the little paper and red seals. We rattled over the bridge, past the Mexican barrack, while its dark-skinned soldiery—who do not shoot quails—lounged in the sunshine against the whitewashed wall.

At the first outpost of the customs a little man, whose considerable equatorial proportions were girted with a gun, examined our paper, and waved us on our way. Under the railroad bridge of the International an engineer blew his whistle, and our mules climbed on top of each other in their terror. We wound along the little river, through irrigating ditches, past dozens of those deliciously quaint adobe houses, past the inevitable church, past a dead pony, ran over a chicken, made the little seven-year-old girls take their five-year-old brothers up in their arms for protection, and finally we climbed a long hill. At the top stretched an endless plain. The road forked; presently it branched; anon it grew into twigs of white dust on the gray levels of the background. The local physician of Eagle Pass was of our party, and he was said to know where a certain tank was to be found, some thirty miles out in the desert, but no man yet created could know which twig of the road to take. He decided on one—changed his mind—got out of the ambulance, scratched his head, pondered, and finally resolution settled on his face. He motioned the driver to a certain twig, got in, and shut his mouth firmly, thus closing debate. We smoked silently, waiting for the doctor's mind to fog. He turned uneasily in his seat, like the agitated needle of a compass, and even in time hazarded the remark that something did not look natural; but there was nothing to look at but flat land and flat sky, unless a hawk sailing here and there. At noon we lunched at the tail of the ambulance, and gently "jollied" the doctor's topography. We pushed on. Later in the afternoon the thirsty mules went slowly. The doctor had by this time admitted his doubts—some long blue hills on the sky-line ought to be farther to the west, according to his remembrance. As no one else had any ideas on the

subject, the doctor's position was not enviable. We changed our course, and travelled many weary miles through the chaparral, which was high enough to stop our vision, and stiff enough to bar our way, keeping us to narrow roads. At last the bisecting cattle trails began to converge, and we knew that they led to water—which they did; for shortly we saw a little broken adobe, a tumbled brush corral, the plastered gate of an *acéquia,* and the blue water of the tank.

To give everything its due proportion at this point, we gathered to congratulate the doctor as we passed the flask. The camp was pitched within the corral, and while the cook got supper we stood in the after-glow on the bank of the tank and saw the ducks come home, heard the mudhens squddle, while high in the air flew the long line of sand-hill cranes with a hoarse clangor. It was quite dark when we sat on the "grub" chests and ate by the firelight, while out in the desert the coyotes shrilled to the monotonous accompaniment of the mules crunching their feed and stamping wearily. To-morrow it was proposed to hunt ducks in their morning flight, which means getting up before daylight, so bed found us early. It seemed but a minute after I had sought my blankets when I was being abused by the Captain, being pushed with his foot—fairly rolled over by him—he even standing on my body as he shouted, "Get up, if you are going hunting. It will be light directly—get up!" And this, constantly recurring, is one reason why I do not care for duck-shooting.

But, in order to hunt, I had to get up, and file off in the line of ghosts, stumbling, catching on the chaparral, and splashing in the mud. I led a setter-dog, and was presently directed to sit down in some damp grass, because it was a good place—certainly not to sit down in, but for other reasons. I sat there in the dark, petting the good dog, and watching the sky grow pale in the east. This is not to mention the desire for breakfast, or the damp, or the sleepiness, but this really the larger part of duck-hunting. Of course if I later had a dozen good shots it might compensate—but I did not have a dozen shots.

The day came slowly out of the east, the mudhens out in the marsh splashed about in the rushes, a sailing hawk was visible against the gray sky overhead, and I felt rather insignificant, not to say contemptible, as I sat there in the loneliness of this big nature which worked around me. The dog dignified the situation—he was part of nature's belongings—while I somehow did not seem to grace the solitude. The grays slowly grew into browns on the sedge-grass, and the water to silver. A bright flash of fire shot out of the dusk far up in the gloom, and the dull report of a shot-gun came over the tank. Black objects fled across the sky— the ducks were flying. I missed one or two, and grew weary—none came near enough to my lair. Presently it was light, and I got a fair shot. My bird tumbled into the rushes out in front of me, and the setter bounded in to retrieve. He searched vehemently, but the wounded duck dived in front of him. He came ashore shortly, and lying down, he bit at himself and pawed and rolled. He was a mass of cockle-burs. I took him on my lap and laboriously picked cockle-burs out of his hair for a half-hour; then, shouldering my gun, I turned tragically to the water and anathematized its ducks—all ducks, my fellow-duckers, all thoughts and motives concerning ducks—and then strode into the chaparral.

"Hie on! hie on!" I tossed my arm, and the setter began to hunt beautifully—glad, no doubt, to leave all thoughts of the cockle-burs and evasive ducks behind. I worked up the shore of the tank, keeping back in the brush, and got some fun. After chasing about for some time I came out near the water. My dog pointed. I glided forward, and came near shooting the Quartermaster, who sat in a bunch of sedge-grass, with a dead duck by his side. He was smoking, and was disgusted with ducks. He joined me, and shortly, as we crossed the road, the long Texas doctor, who owned the dog, came striding down the way. He was ready for quail now, and we started.

The quail-hunting is active work. The dog points, but one nearly always finds the birds running from one prickly-pear bush to another. They do not stand, rarely flush, and when they do get up it is only to swoop ahead to the nearest cover, where they settle quickly. One must be sharp in his shooting —he cannot select his distance, for the cactus lies thick about, and the little running bird is only on view for the shortest of moments. You must overrun a dog after his first point, since he works too close behind them. The covey will keep together if not pursued with too much haste, and one gets shot after shot; still, at last you must run lively, as the frightened covey scurry along at a remarkable pace. Heavy shot are necessary, since the blue quail carry lead like Marshal Masséna, and are much harder to kill than the bob-white. Three men working together can get shooting enough out of a bunch—the chase often continuing for a mile, when the covey gradually separate, the sportsmen following individual birds.

Where the prickly-pear cactus is thickest, there are the blue quail, since that is their feed and water supply. This same cactus makes a difficulty of pursuit, for it bristles with spines, which come off on your clothing, and when they enter the skin make most uncomfortable and persistent sores. The Quartermaster had an Indian tobacco-bag dangling at his belt, and as it flopped in his progress it gathered prickers, which it shortly transferred to his luckless legs, until he at last detected the reason why he bristled so fiercely. And the poor dog—at every covey we had to stop and pick needles out of him. The haunts of the blue quail are really no place for a dog, as he soon becomes useless. One does not need him, either, since the blue quail will not flush until actually kicked into the air.

Jack and cotton-tail rabbits fled by hundreds before us. They are everywhere, and afford good shooting between coveys, it being quick work to get a cotton-tail as he flashes between the net-work of protecting cactus. Coyotes lope away in our front, but they are too wild for a shot-gun. It must

Too Big Game for Number Six. *Authors' photoengraving.*

ever be in a man's mind to keep his direction, because it is such a vastly simple thing to get lost in the chaparral, where you cannot see a hundred yards. Mexico has such a considerable territory that a man on foot may find it inconvenient to beat up a town in the desolation of thornbush.

There is an action about blue-quail shooting which is next to buffalo shooting—it's run, shoot, pick up your bird, scramble on in your endeavor to keep the skirmish-line of your two comrades; and at last, when you have concluded to stop, you can mop your forehead—the Mexican sun shines hot even in midwinter.

Later in the afternoon we get among bob-white in a grassy tract, and while they are clean work—good dog-play, and altogether

more satisfactory shooting than any other I know of—I am yet much inclined to the excitement of chasing after game which you can see at intervals. Let it not be supposed that it is less difficult to hit a running blue quail as he shoots through the brush than a flying bob-white, for the experience of our party has settled that, and one gets ten shots at the blue to one at the bob-white, because of their number. As to eating, we could not tell the difference; but I will not insist that this is final. A man who comes in from an all day's run in the brush does not care whether the cook gives him boiled beans, watermelon, or crackers and jam; so how is he to know what a bird's taste is when served to a tame appetite?

At intervals we ran into the wild cattle

which threaded their way to water, and it makes one nervous. It is of no use to say "Soo-bossy," or to give him a charge of No. 6: neither is it well to run. If the *matadores* had any of the sensations which I have experienced, the gate receipts at the bull-rings would have to go up. When a big long-horn fastens a quail-shooter with his great open brown eye in a chaparral thicket, you are not inclined to "call his hand." If he will call it a misdeal, you are with him.

We were banging away, the Quarter-master and I, when a human voice began yelling like mad from the brush ahead. We advanced, to find a Mexican—rather well gotten up—who proceeded to wave his arms like a parson who had reached "sixthly" in his sermon, and who proceeded thereat to overwhelm us with his eloquence. The Quartermaster and I *"buenos dias-ed"* and *"si, señor-ed"* him in our helpless Spanish, and asked each other, nervously, "What de'll." After a long time he seemed to be getting through with his subject, his sentences became separated, he finally emitted monosyllables only along with his scowls, and we tramped off into the brush. It was a pity he spent so much energy, since it could only arouse our curiosity without satisfying it.

In camp that night we told the Captain of our excited Mexican friend out in the brush, and our cook had seen sinister men on ponies passing near our camp. The Captain became solicitous, and stationed a night-guard over his precious government mules. It would never do to have a bandit get away with a U.S. brand. It never does matter about private property, but anything with U.S. on it has got to be looked after, like a croupy child.

We had some good days' sport, and no more formidable enterprise against the night-guard was attempted than the noisy approach of a white jackass. The tents were struck and loaded when it began to rain. We stood in the shelter of the escort-wagon, and the storm rose to a hurricane. Our corral became a tank; but shortly the black clouds passed north, and we pulled out. The twig ran into a branch, and the branch struck the trunk near the bluffs over the Rio Grande, and in town there stood the Mexican soldiers leaning against the wall as we had left them. We wondered if they had moved meanwhile.

How the Law Got into the Chaparral

"You have heard about the Texas Rangers?" said the Deacon to me one night in the San Antonio Club. "Yes? Well, come up to my rooms, and I will introduce you to one of the old originals—dates 'way back in the 'thirties'—there aren't many of them left now—and if we can get him to talk, he will tell you stories that will make your eyes hang out on your shirt front."

We entered the Deacon's cosey bachelor apartments, where I was introduced to Colonel "Rip" Ford, of the old-time Texas Rangers. I found him a very old man, with a wealth of snow-white hair and beard—bent, but not withered. As he sunk on his stiffened limbs into the arm-chair, we disposed ourselves quietly and almost reverentially, while we lighted cigars. We began the approaches by which we hoped to loosen the history of a wild past from one of the very few tongues which can still wag on the days when the Texans, the Comanches, and the Mexicans chased one another over the plains of Texas, and shot and stabbed to find who should inherit the land.

Through the veil of tobacco smoke the ancient warrior spoke his sentences slowly, at intervals, as his mind gradually separated and arranged the details of countless fights. His head bowed in thought; anon it rose sharply at recollections, and as he breathed, the shouts and lamentations of crushed men —the yells and shots—the thunder of horses' hoofs—the full fury of the desert combats came to the pricking ears of the Deacon and me.

We saw through the smoke the brave young faces of the hosts which poured into Texas to war with the enemies of their race. They were clad in loose hunting-frocks, leather leggings, and broad black hats; had powder-horns and shot-pouches hung about them; were armed with bowie-knives, Mississippi rifles, and horse-pistols; rode Spanish ponies, and were impelled by Destiny to conquer, like their remote ancestors, "the godless hosts of Pagan" who "came swimming o'er the Northern Sea."

"Rip" Ford had not yet acquired his front name in 1836, when he enlisted in the famous Captain Jack Hayes's company of Rangers, which was fighting the Mexicans in those days, and also trying incidentally to keep from being eaten up by the Comanches.

Said the old Colonel: "A merchant from our country journeyed to New York, and Colonel Colt, who was a friend of his, gave him two five-shooters—pistols they were, and little things. The merchant in turn presented them to Captain Jack Hayes. The captain liked them so well that he did not rest till every man jack of us had two apiece.

"Directly," mused the ancient one, with a smile of pleasant recollection, "we had a fight with the Comanches—up here above San Antonio. Hayes had fifteen men with him—he was doubling about the country for Indians. He found 'sign,' and after cutting their trail several times he could see that they were following him. Directly the

Indians overtook the Rangers—there were seventy-five Indians. Captain Hayes—bless his memory!—said, 'They are fixin' to charge us, boys, and we must charge them.' There were never better men in this world than Hayes had with him," went on the Colonel with pardonable pride; "and mind you, he never made a fight without winning.

"We charged, and in the fracas killed thirty-five Indians—only two of our men were wounded—so you see the five-shooters were pretty good weapons. Of course they wa'n't any account compared with these modern ones, because they were too small, but they did those things. Just after that Colonel Colt was induced to make bigger ones for us, some of which were half as long as your arm.

"Hayes? Oh, he was a surveyor, and used to go out beyond the frontiers about his work. The Indians used to jump him pretty regular; but he always whipped them, and so he was available for a Ranger captain. About then—let's see," and here the old head bobbed up from his chest, where it had sunk in thought—"there was a commerce with Mexico just sprung up, but this was later—it only shows what that man Hayes used to do. The bandits used to waylay the traders, and they got very bad in the country. Captain Hayes went after them—he struck them near Lavade, and found the Mexicans had more than twice as many men as he did; but he caught them napping, charged them afoot—killed twenty-five of them, and got all their horses."

"I suppose, Colonel, you have been charged by a Mexican lancer?" I inquired.

"Oh yes, many times," he answered.

"What did you generally do?"

"Well, you see, in those days I reckoned to be able to hit a man every time with a six-shooter at one hundred and twenty-five yards," explained the old gentleman—which no doubt meant many dead lancers.

"Then you do not think much of a lance as a weapon?" I pursued.

"No; there is but one weapon. The six-shooter when properly handled is the only weapon—mind you, sir, I say *properly,*"

and here the old eyes blinked rapidly over the great art as he knew its practice.

"Then, of course, the rifle has its use. Under Captain Jack Hayes sixty of us made a raid once after the celebrated priest-leader of the Mexicans—Padre Jarante—which same was a devil of a fellow. We were very sleepy—had been two nights without sleep. At San Juan every man stripped his horse, fed, and went to sleep. We had passed Padre Jarante in the night without knowing it. At about twelve o'clock next day there was a terrible outcry—I was awakened by shooting. The Padre was upon us. Five men outlying stood the charge, and went under. We gathered, and the Padre charged three times. The third time he was knocked from his horse and killed. Then Captain Jack Hayes awoke, and we got in a big *casa.* The men took to the roof. As the Mexicans passed we emptied a great many saddles. As I got to the top of the *casa* I found two men quarrelling." (Here the Colonel chuckled.) "I asked what the matter was, and they were both claiming to have killed a certain Mexican who was lying dead some way off. One said he had hit him in the head, and the other said he had hit him in the breast. I advised peace until after the fight. Well—after the shooting was over and the Padre's men had had enough, we went out to the particular Mexican who was dead, and, sure enough, he was shot in the head and in the breast; so they laughed and made peace. About this time one of the spies came in and reported six hundred Mexicans coming. We made an examination of our ammunition, and found that we couldn't afford to fight six hundred Mexicans with sixty men, so we pulled out. This was in the Mexican war, and only goes to show that Captain Hayes's men could shoot all the Mexicans that could get to them if the ammunition would hold out."

"What was the most desperate fight you can remember, Colonel?"

The old man hesitated; this required a particular point of view—it was quality, not quantity, wanted now; and, to be sure, he was a connoisseur. After much study by the

Colonel, during which the world lost many thrilling tales, the one which survived occurred in 1851.

"My lieutenant, Ed Burleson, was ordered to carry to San Antonio an Indian prisoner we had taken and turned over to the commanding officer at Fort McIntosh. On his return, while nearing the Nueces River, he spied a couple of Indians. Taking seven men, he ordered the balance to continue along the road. The two Indians proved to be fourteen, and they charged Burleson up to the teeth. Dismounting his men, he poured it into them from his Colt's six-shooting rifles. They killed or wounded all the Indians except two, some of them dying so near the Rangers that they could put their hands on their boots. All but one of Burleson's men were wounded—himself shot in the head with an arrow. One man had four 'dogwood switches'* in his body, one of which was in his bowels. This man told me that every time he raised his gun to fire, the Indians would stick an arrow in him, but he said he didn't care a cent. One Indian was lying right up close, and while dying tried to shoot an arrow, but his strength failed so fast that the arrow only barely left the bowstring. One of the Rangers in that fight was a curious fellow— when young he had been captured by Indians, and had lived with them so long that he had Indian habits. In that fight he kept jumping around when loading, so as to be a bad target, the same as an Indian would under the circumstances, and he told Burleson he wished he had his boots off, so he could get around good"—and here the Colonel paused quizzically. "Would you call that a good fight?"

The Deacon and I put the seal of our approval on the affair, and the Colonel rambled ahead.

"In 1858 I was commanding the frontier battalion of State troops on the whole frontier, and had my camp on the Deer Fork of the Brazos. The Comanches kept raiding the settlements. They would come down quietly, working well into the white lines,

* Arrows.

and then go back a-running—driving stolen stock and killing and burning. I thought I would give them some of their own medicine. I concluded to give them a fight. I took two wagons, one hundred Rangers, and one hundred and thirteen Tahuahuacan Indians, who were friendlies. We struck a good Indian trail on a stream which led up to the Canadian. We followed it till it got hot. I camped my outfit in such a manner as to conceal my force, and sent out my scouts, who saw the Indians hunt buffalo through spy-glasses. That night we moved. I sent Indians to locate the camp. They returned before day, and reported that the Indians were just a few miles ahead, whereat we moved forward. At daybreak, I remember, I was standing in the bull-wagon road leading to Santa Fe and could see the Canadian River in our front—with eighty lodges just beyond. Counting four men of fighting age to a lodge, that made a possible three hundred and twenty Indians. Just at sunup an Indian came across the river on a pony. Our Indians down below raised a yell —they always get excited. The Indian heard them—it was very still then. The Indian retreated slowly, and began to ride in a circle. From where I was I could hear him puff like a deer—he was blowing the bullets away from himself—he was a medicine-man. I heard five shots from the Jagers with which my Indians were armed. The painted pony of the medicine-man jumped ten feet in the air, it seemed to me, and fell over on his rider— then five more Jagers went off, and he was dead. I ordered the Tahuahuacans out in front, and kept the Rangers out of sight, because I wanted to charge home and kind of surprise them. Pretty soon I got ready, and gave the word. We charged. At the river we struck some boggy ground and floundered around considerable, but we got through. We raised the Texas yell, and away we went. I never expect again to hear such a noise—I never want to hear it—what with the whoops of the warriors—the screaming of the women and children—our boys yelling—the shooting, and the horses just a-mixin' up and a-stampedin' around," and

"We Struck Some Boggy Ground." *Authors' photoengraving.*

the Colonel bobbed his head slowly as he continued.

"One of my men didn't know a buck from a squaw. There was an Indian woman on a pony with five children. He shot the pony—it seemed like you couldn't see that pony for little Indians. We went through the camp, and the Indians pulled out—spreading fanlike, and we a-running them. After a long chase I concluded to come back. I saw lots of Indians around in the hills. When I got back, I found Captain Ross had formed my men in line. 'What time in the morning is it?' I asked. 'Morning, hell!' says he—'it's one o'clock!' And so it was. Directly I saw an Indian coming down a hill near by, and then more Indians and more Indians—till it seemed like they wa'n't ever going to get through coming. We had struck a bigger outfit than the first one. That first Indian he bantered my men to come out single-handed and fight him. One after another, he wounded five of my Indians. I ordered my

Indians to engage them, and kind of get them down in the flat, where I could charge. After some running and shooting they did this, and I turned the Rangers loose. We drove them. The last stand they made they killed one of my Indians, wounded a Ranger, but left seven of their dead in a pile. It was now nearly nightfall, and I discovered that my horses were broken down after fighting all day. I found it hard to restrain my men, they had got so heated up; but I gradually withdrew to where the fight commenced. The Indian camp was plundered. In it we found painted buffalo-robes with beads a hand deep around the edges— the finest robes I have ever seen—and heaps of goods plundered from the Santa Fe traders. On the way back I noticed a dead chief, and was for a moment astonished to find pieces of flesh cut out of him; upon looking at a Tahuahuacan warrior I saw a pair of dead hands tied behind his saddle. That night they had a cannibal feast. You see, the Tahuahuacans say that the first one of their race was brought into the world by a wolf. 'How am I to live?' said the Tahuahuacan. 'The same as we do,' said the wolf; and when they were with me, that is just about how they lived. I reckon it's necessary to tell you about the old woman who was found in our lines. She was looking at the sun and making incantations, a-cussing us out generally and elevating her voice. She said the Comanches would get even for this day's work. I directed my Indians to let her alone, but I was informed afterwards that that is just what they didn't do."

At this point the Colonel's cigar went out, and directly he followed; but this is the manner in which he told of deeds which I know would fare better at the hands of one used to phrasing and capable also of more points of view than the Colonel was used to taking. The outlines of the thing are strong, however, because the Deacon and I understood that fights were what the old Colonel had dealt in during his active life, much as other men do in stocks and bonds or wheat and corn. He had been a successful operator, and only recalled pleasantly the bull quotations. This type of Ranger is all but gone. A few may yet be found in outlying ranches. One of the most celebrated resides near San Antonio—"Big-foot Wallace" by name. He says he doesn't mind being called "Big-foot," because he is six feet two in height, and is entitled to big feet. His face is done off in a nest of white hair and beard, and is patriarchal in character. In 1836 he came out from Virginia to "take toll" of the Mexicans for killing some relatives of his in the Fannin Massacre, and he considers that he has squared his accounts; but they had him on the debit side for a while. Being captured in the Meir expedition, he walked as a prisoner to the city of Mexico, and did public work for the country with a ball-and-chain attachment for two years. The prisoners overpowered the guards and escaped on one occasion, but were overtaken by Mexican cavalry while dying of thirst in a desert. Santa Anna ordered their "decimation," which meant that every tenth man

was shot, their lot being determined by the drawing of a black bean from an earthen pot containing a certain proportion of white ones. "Big-foot" drew a white one. He was also a member of Captain Hayes's company, afterwards a captain of Rangers, and a noted Indian-fighter. Later he carried the mails from San Antonio to El Paso through a howling wilderness, but always brought it safely through—if safely can be called lying thirteen days by a water-hole in the desert, waiting for a broken leg to mend, and living meanwhile on one prairie-wolf, which he managed to shoot. Wallace was a professional hunter, who fought Indians and hated "greasers"; he belongs to the past, and has been "outspanned" under a civilization in which he has no place, and is to-day living in poverty.

The civil war left Texas under changed conditions. That and the Mexican wars had determined its boundaries, however, and it rapidly filled up with new elements of population. Broken soldiers, outlaws, poor immigrants living in bullwagons, poured in. "Gone to Texas" had a sinister significance in the late sixties. When the railroad got to Abilene, Kansas, the cow-men of Texas found a market for their stock, and began trailing their herds up through the Indian country. Bands of outlaws organized under the leadership of desperadoes like Wes Hardin and King Fisher. They rounded up cattle regardless of their owners' rights, and resisted interference with force. The poor man pointed to his brand in the stolen herd and protested. He was shot. The big owners were unable to protect themselves from loss. The property right was established by the six-shooter, and honest men were forced to the wall. In 1876 the property-holding classes went to the Legislature, got it to appropriate a hundred thousand dollars a year for two years, and the Ranger force was reorganized to carry the law into the chaparral. At this time many judges were in league with bandits; sheriffs were elected by the outlaws, and the electors were cattle-stealers.

The Rangers were sworn to uphold the

laws of Texas and the United States. They were deputy sheriffs, United States marshals —in fact, were often vested with any and every power, even to the extent of ignoring disreputable sheriffs. At times they were judge, jury, and executioner when the difficulties demanded extremes. When a band of outlaws was located, detectives or spies were sent among them, who openly joined the desperadoes, and gathered evidence to put the Rangers on their trail. Then, in the wilderness, with only the soaring buzzard or prowling coyote to look on, the Ranger and the outlaw met to fight with tigerish ferocity to the death. Shot, and lying prone, they fired until the palsied arm could no longer raise the six-shooter, and justice was satisfied as their bullets sped. The captains had the selection of their men, and the right to dishonorably discharge at will. Only men of irreproachable character, who were fine riders and dead-shots, were taken. The spirit of adventure filled the ranks with the most prominent young men in the State, and to have been a Ranger is a badge of distinction in Texas to this day. The display of anything but a perfect willingness to die under any and all circumstances was fatal to a Ranger, and in course of time they got the *moral* on the bad man. Each one furnished his own horse and arms, while the State gave him ammunition, "grub," one dollar a day, and extra expenses. The enlistment was for twelve months. A list of fugitive Texas criminals was placed in his hands, with which he was expected to familiarize himself. Then, in small parties, they packed the bedding on their mule, they hung the handcuffs and leather thongs about its neck, saddled their riding-ponies, and threaded their way into the chaparral.

On an evening I had the pleasure of meeting two more distinguished Ranger officers—more modern types—Captains Lea Hall and Joseph Shely; both of them big, forceful men, and loath to talk about themselves. It was difficult to associate the quiet gentlemen who sat smoking in the Deacon's rooms with what men say; for the tales of their prowess in Texas always ends, "and that don't count Mexicans, either." The bandit never laid down his gun but with his life; so the "la ley de huga"† was in force in the chaparral, and the good people of Texas were satisfied with a very short account of a Ranger's fight.

The most distinguished predecessor of these two men was a Captain McNally, who was so bent on carrying his raids to an issue that he paid no heed to national boundary-lines. He followed a band of Mexican bandits to the town of La Cueva, below Ringgold, once, and, surrounding it, demanded the surrender of the cattle which they had stolen. He had but ten men, and yet this redoubtable warrior surrounded a town full of bandits and Mexicans soldiers. The Mexican soldiers attacked the Rangers, and forced them back under the river-banks, but during the fight the *jefe politico* was killed. The Rangers were in a fair way to be overcome by the Mexicans, when Lieutenant Clendenin turned a Gatling loose from the American side and covered their position. A parley ensued, but McNally refused to go back without the cattle, which the Mexicans had finally to surrender.

At another time McNally received word through spies of an intended raid of Mexican cattle-thieves under the leadership of Cammelo Lerma. At Resaca de la Palma, McNally struck the depredators with but sixteen men. They had seventeen men and five hundred head of stolen cattle. In a running fight for miles McNally's men killed sixteen bandits, while only one escaped. A young Ranger by the name of Smith was shot dead by Cammelo Lerma as he dismounted to look at the dying bandit. The dead bodies were piled in ox-carts and dumped in the public square at Brownsville. McNally also captured King Fisher's band in an old log house in Dimmit County, but they were not convicted.

Showing the nature of Ranger work, an incident which occurred to my acquaintance, Captain Lea Hall, will illustrate.

† Mexican law of shooting escaped or resisting prisoners.

In De Witt County there was a feud. One dark night sixteen masked men took a sick man, one Dr. Brazel, and two of his boys, from their beds, and, despite the imploring mother and daughter, hanged the doctor and one son to a tree. The other boy escaped in the green corn. Nothing was done to punish the crime, as the lynchers were men of property and influence in the country. No man dared speak above his breath about the affair.

Captain Hall, by secret-service men, discovered the perpetrators, and also that they were to be gathered at a wedding on a certain night. He surrounded the house and demanded their surrender, at the same time saying that he did not want to kill the women and children. Word returned that they would kill him and all his Rangers. Hall told them to allow their women and children to depart, which was done; then, springing on the gallery of the house, he shouted, "Now, gentlemen, you can go to killing Rangers; but if you don't surrender, the Rangers will go to killing you." This was too frank a willingness for midnight assassins, and they gave up.

Spies had informed him that robbers intended sacking Campbell's store in Wolfe City. Hall and his men lay behind the counters to receive them on the designated night. They were allowed to enter, when Hall's men, rising, opened fire—the robbers replying. Smoke filled the room, which was fairly illuminated by the flashes of the guns —but the robbers were all killed, much to the disgust of the lawyers, no doubt, though I could never hear that honest people mourned.

The man Hall was himself a gentleman of the romantic Southern soldier type, and he entertained the highest ideals, with which it would be extremely unsafe to trifle, if I may judge. Captain Shely, our other visitor, was a herculean, black-eyed man, fairly fizzing with nervous energy. He is also exceedingly shrewd, as befits the greater concreteness of the modern Texas law, albeit he too has trailed bandits in the chaparral, and rushed in on their camp-fires at night, as two big bullet-holes in his skin will attest. He it was who arrested Polk, the defaulting treasurer of Tennessee. He rode a Spanish pony sixty-two miles in six hours, and arrested Polk, his guide, and two private detectives, whom Polk had bribed to set him over the Rio Grande.

When the land of Texas was bought up and fenced with wire, the old settlers who had used the land did not readily recognize the new régime. They raised the rallying-cry of "free grass and free water"—said they had fought the Indians off, and the land belonged to them. Taking nippers, they rode by night and cut down miles of fencing. Shely took the keys of a county jail from the frightened sheriff, made arrests by the score, and lodged them in the big new jail. The country-side rose in arms, surrounded the building, and threatened to tear it down. The big Ranger was not deterred by this outburst, but quietly went out into the mob, and with mock politeness delivered himself as follows:

"Do not tear down the jail, gentlemen— you have been taxed for years to build this fine structure—it is yours—do not tear it down. I will open the doors wide—you can all come in—do not tear down the jail; but there are twelve Rangers in there, with orders to kill as long as they can see. Come right in, gentlemen—but come fixed."

The mob was overcome by his civility.

Texas is to-day the only State in the Union where pistol-carrying is attended with great chances of arrest and fine. The law is supreme even in the lonely *jacails* out in the rolling waste of chaparral, and it was made so by the tireless riding, the deadly shooting, and the indomitable courage of the Texas Rangers.

Vagabonding with the Tenth Horse

When once an order is published in the military way it closes debate, consequently, on the day set by order for the troops to take up their outward march from Fort Assiniboine it was raining; but that did not matter. The horses in front of the officers' club stood humped up in their middles, their tails were hauled down tight and the water ran off their sides in tiny rivulets. If horses could talk they would have said, D—— the order, or at least I think they felt like their riders, and that is what they said.

It is not necessary to tell what we did in the club at that early hour of the day; but Major Wint slapped his boot-leg with his quirt and proceeded toward the door, we following. Major Kelly, who was to stay behind to guard the women and children, made some disparaging remarks about my English "riding things"—called them "the queen's breeches"—but he is not a serious man, and moreover he is Irish.

Down at the corrals the trumpets were going and the major mounted his horse. Three troops and the band of the Tenth marched out of the post and lined up on the prairie. Down the front trotted the major to inspect, while the rain pattered and drained on the oil-skin "slickers" of the cavalrymen. I rode slowly up behind the command, enjoying myself—it being such a delight for me when I see good horses and hardy men, divested of military fuss. The stately march of the Seventh New York, or Squadron A, when it is doing its prettiest, fills my eye; but it does not inflate my soul. Too deadly

prosaic, or possibly I discount it; anyhow, the Tenth Cavalry never had a "soft detail" since it was organized, and it is full of old soldiers who know what it is all about, this soldiering. They presently went slipping and sliding into column, and with the wagons following the march begins.

"Did you forget the wash-basin, Carter?" asks one of our mess.

"Yes. D—— modern invention! If this rain keeps up we won't need it," replies my host as he muffles up in his slicker, and, turning, says, "Sergeant, make the recruit sit up in his saddle—catch him lounging again make him pull mud."

"Man, sit up thar; yu ride laik yu wus in a box-car; be hittin de flat fust, yu reckon," reiterates the non-com.

And it rains, rains, rains, as mile after mile the little column goes bobity-bobity-bob up and down over the hills. But I like it. I am unable to say why, except that after I left school I did considerable of this bobity-bob over the great strange stretches of the high plains, and I have never found anything else so fascinating. The soldiers like it too, for while it is set, in its way, it is vagabonding nevertheless. I have often thought how fortunate it is that I am not secretary of war, because I should certainly burn or sell every barrack in the country and keep the soldiers under canvas and on the move.

The cavalrymen wear great oil-skin coats which cover them from hat-rim to boot-sole, in the buying of which they imitate the cow-boys, a thing which is always good for cavalry to do. There are some Montana horses in the command, fierce, vicious brutes, which do a little circus as we pass along, making every one grin smoothly except the man on the circus horse. His sentences come out in chucks: "Dog-gone, yu black son," and the horse strikes on his forefeet; "I'll break yu haid wid——" up goes the horse in front, the carbine comes out at the socket—"a rock." His hat goes off and his cup, canteen, bags and rope play a rataplan. In plugs the spur, up mounts the pony like the sweep of an angel's wing. Oh, it is good to look upon.

In the afternoon, far on ahead, we see the infantry tents with the cook-fires going. They had started the day before and were now comfortable. As the cavalry passed the "dough-boys" stood grinning cheerfully by their fires.

"Say, honey; is yu feet muddy?" sings out an ironical cavalryman to the infantry group, but the reply comes quick, "Oh, Mr. Jones, can I come up and see yu groom yu horse this evenin'?" A great guffaw goes up, while the mounted one shrugs up in his slicker and spurs along.

The picket lines go down, the wagons are unpacked, and the herds of horse go trotting off over the hill to browse and roll. Every man about camp has something to do. Here is where the first sergeant looms up, for he who can get the most jumps out of his men has the quickest and neatest camp. It takes more ability to be a good first sergeant than it does to run a staff corps. Each troop has its complement of recruits who have never been in camp before, and to them the old non-com. addresses himself as he strides about, overlooking things.

"You sergeants stand around here laik a lot come-latelies; get these men to doin' somethin'. Throw dat cigarette away. Take hold of this pin. Done yu talk back. I'll tak hold of yu in a minute, and if I do I'll spoil yu."

In the colored regiments these first sergeants are all old soldiers—thirty years and upward in the frontier service. What will be done to replace them when they expire is a question; or rather nothing will be done. Their like will never come again, because the arduous conditions which produced them can never re-occur, unless you let me be secretary of war and burn the barracks.

The tents being up we managed a very bad supper. We had suspected, but we did not know until now, that the officer who was appointed to run our mess was in love. "All the world loves a lover," but he was an exception. That night I did not sleep a wink, having drunk a quart cup of coffee—that kola-nut of the American soldier and the secret of the long marches he has made in his campaigns. I had made out to drowse a little toward morning, when a tender young Missouri mule began a shrill "haugh-ha, haugh-ha," at the approach of the hour for half rations of grain, while presently the bugles split the dawn. Shortly an orderly came in and wanted to know if he could do up my bedding. Before having fairly gotten my boots on, the tent was pulled down over my head, and there I sat in an ocean of frosty grass bounded on one side by mountains covered with snow. Across the horizon was a streak of light, before which stood my tentmates humped in their "slickers" and stamping from one foot to another as they talked.

"How are you this morning, you old citizen?" asks my host.

"If I wasn't a d—— fool I'd be miserable, thank you."

The horses are released from the picket lines and go thundering off over the hills, kicking and neighing, glad to get the frost out of their muscles. A herder tries to mount his excited horse bareback; it plunges, rears and falls backward, spilling the man, and before he recovers the horse has got away.

"Huh!" says a soldier pulling tentpegs near me; "dats de old Caesar horse; I knows him. 'Pears laik he knows a recruit when he sees one."

"What have you got for breakfast?" I ask of the lover.

"Crackers and canned tomatoes—our mess kit is not yet in order. I'll give you your breakfast bacon for dinner," he answers; but he forgets that I am solid with the infantry mess, where I betook myself.

After breakfast the march begins. A bicycle corps pulls out ahead. It is heavy wheeling and pretty bumpy on the grass, where they are compelled to ride, but they managed far better than one would anticipate. Then came the infantry in an open column of fours, heavy-marching order. The physique of the black soldiers must be admired —great chested, broad shoulder, up-standing fellows, with bull necks, as with their rifles thrown across their packs they straddle along.

United States regular infantry in full kit and campaign rig impresses one as very useful and businesslike. There is nothing to relieve the uniform or make it gay. Their whole clothing and equipment grew up in the field, and the field doesn't grow tin-pots for head-gear or white-crossbelts for the enemy to draw dead-centers on. Every means are used to keep men from falling out of ranks, for almost any reason they may allege as an excuse. Often to fall out only means that when camp is reached the unfortunate one must continue to march backward and forward before the company line, while his comrades are making themselves comfortable, until—well, until he is decided that he won't fall out again.

"I know why so many of dem battles is victorious," said one trudging darkey to another.

"Why?" he is asked.

"Dey march de men so hard to get thar, dat dey is too tired to run away."

Very naturally when with infantry and transportation, the cavalry have time to improve their mind. Later in the day the sun came out, and Major Wint made them do "some of the things which the fools write in the books," as I heard it put. We were on a perfectly flat plain where you could see for ten miles—an ideal place for paper work. The major threw an advance and flankers, and every one had a hack at the command. I forget how many troops of cavalry I represented, but I did not have enough, and notwithstanding the brilliancy of my attack I got properly "licked." At any rate, after it was all over we knew more than the fellows who write the books, and besides, it was great fun. Handling cavalry troops is an art, not a science, and it is given to few men to think and act quickly enough. As for mistakes, it is a question how many an officer ought to be allowed to make before he has to hunt up another business where he will not have to decide between right and wrong or good and bad in the fraction of a second. It is quite startling how quickly good cavalry "rides home" over eight hundred yards of ground, and when one has to do something to meet it, he has no time to whittle a stick over the matter. Moreover, I never expect to meet any really great cavalrymen who weigh over one hundred and sixty pounds.

Some of the old sergeants have been taught their battle tactics in a school where the fellows who were not quick at learning are dead. I have forgotten a great many miles of road as I talked to old Sergeant Shropshire. His experiences were grave and gay and infinitely varied.

"We used to have a fight every day down on the Washita, Mr. Remington," said he, "and them Indians used to attack accordin' to your ideas. A feller on the flanks nevah knew what minute he was goin' to have a horse-race back to the command, with anywhar from ten to five hundred Indians a close second.

"Ah, Mr. Remington, we used to have soldiers in them days. Now you take them young fellers ahead thar—lots of 'em 'll nevah make soldiers in God's world. Now you see that black feller just turnin' his head; well, he's a 'cruit, and he thinks I been abusin' him for a long time. Other day he comes to me and says he don't want no more trouble; says I can get along with him from now on. Says I to that 'cruit, 'Blame yer eyes, I don't have to get along wid you; you have to get along wid me. Understand?' " The column halted.

"What is the trouble, Shropshire?"

A "Government Six" Mired Down. *Painting, courtesy U. S. Naval Academy Museum.*

"Mule got disgusted, I reckon, sah," said he; and I rode ahead to find a "government six" stuck in the bed of a creek. I sat on the top of the bank as the dismounted men and mules and whips and sand flew, while to my ears came the lashing, the stamping, yelling and profanity. The thing was gotten out when the long lines of cavalry horses stood under the cut bank and drank at the brook, greenish-yellow with the reflection of the bank above, while the negro cavalrymen carried on conversations with their horses. Strange people, but yet not half as strange as Indians in this respect, for between these natural people and horses there is something in common which educated white men don't know anything whatever about. It is perfectly apparent that the horses understand them when they talk. This is not true

of all the men, but of the best ones. That is one reason why it ought to be legally possible, when a recruit jerks his horse's head or is otherwise impatient with him, to hit the recruit over the head with a six-shooter, whereas all an officer can now do is to take him one side and promise faithfully to murder him if he ever repeats the error.

In due time the major made a permanent camp on a flat under the Bear Paw range and everything was gotten "shipshape" and "Bristol fashion," all of which nicety is to indicate to the recruit that when he rolls over in his sleep, the operation must be attended to with geometrical reference to the center-pole of the major's tepee. All about was an inspiring sweep, high rolling plains, with rough mountains, intersecting coulées and a well-brushed creek bottom, in all, enough land to maneuver forty thousand men under cover, yet within sight of the camp, and for cavalry all one could wish. Officer's patrols were sent out to meet each other through the hills. I accompanied the major, and we sat like two buzzards on a pinnacle of rock, using our field-glasses so cleverly that no one could tell what we saw by studying our movements through their own, yet we had the contestants under sight all the time.

There was an attack on the camp led by Mr. Carter Johnson, one of the most skilful and persistent cavalrymen of the young men in the army, General Miles has said. His command was the mounted band which was to represent three troops, and with these he marched off into the hills. The camp itself was commanded on one side by a high hill on top of which the infantry rifle pitted and lay down. From here we could see everywhere, and I had previously told Mr. Johnson that I thought the camp perfectly safe, covered as it was by the intrenched infantry. It is a fact that officers have such enthusiasm each for his own arm that infantry take cavalry as they do "summer girls," whereas cavalrymen are all dying to get among "foot" and hack them up. Neither is right but both spirits are commendable.

Few cavalry orderlies stood near me while the infantry were entrenching.

"How much dirt does a dough-boy need for to protect him?" asked the saber.

"There ought to be enough on 'em to protect 'em," laughs his comrade.

But, Mr. Johnson had told me that he was going to charge the infantry just for the lark, and for this I waited. I cannot tell all that happened on that field of battle, but Mr. Johnson snapped his "wind jammers" over those hills in a most reckless manner. He met the subtle approaches of his enemy at every point, cut off a flank of the defending party, and advanced in a covered way to the final attack. He drew the fire of the infantry while replying, dismounted at long range, disappeared and reappeared, coming like mad down a cut right on top of a troop of defenders. From here on I shall not admit it was "war, but it was magnificent." On he came, with yells and straining horses, right through the camp, individual men wrestling each other off their horses, upsetting each other over the tent ropes, and then in column he took off down a cut bank at least six feet high, ploughed through the creek with the water flying, and disappeared under our hill. In an instant he came bounding up, his squad in line, the horses snorting and the darkies' eyes sticking out like saucers. It was a piece of daring riding and well delivered as a charge, but the festive dough-boys lighted cigarettes and said, "Carter, your d—— band ought to be ready for burial long before now." Heroism does not count in maneuvers and miracles are barred.

This is, in my opinion, the sort of thing our militia should undertake, and they ought to eliminate any "cut-and-dried" affairs. It should be done in September, when the weather is cool, because men not accustomed to outdoor life cannot stand immediately either extreme heat or cold and do what should be expected of them.

Permanent camps like Peekskill are but one step in advance of an armory. They were good in their day but their day is passed in our militia—we have progressed beyond it. Men will be found to like "life on the road," and officers will find that where the conditions of country are ever changing, a week's "advance and outpost" work will eclipse all the books they have ever indulged in. One of the most intelligent of military authorities, Col. Francis Green, says that our troops will never be called on to fight rural communities, but will operate in cities. This is probably true, but practice marches could be made through populous sections, with these villages, railroad tracks, fences, stone walls and other top-hamper to simulate conditions to be expected. Such a command should be constantly menaced by small detachments, under the most active and intelligent officers belonging to it, when it will be found that affairs usually made perfunctory begin to mean something to the men.

The Soledad Girls

"To-night I am going down to my ranch —the Soledad—in my private car," said the manager of the Mexican International Railroad, "and I would like the Captain and you to accompany me."

The Captain and I were only too glad; so in process of time we awoke to find our car sidetracked on the Soledad, which is in the state of Coahuila, Mexico. The chaparral spread around, rising and falling in the swell of the land, until it beat against the blue ridge of the Sierra Santa Rosa, miles to the north. Here and there the bright sun spotted on a cow as she threaded the gray stretches; a little coyote-wolf sat on his haunches on a near-by hill-side, and howled protests at his new-found companions; while dimly through the gray meshes of the leaf-denuded chaparral we could see the main ranch-house of the Soledad. We were informed at breakfast by the railroad manager that there was to be that day a "round-up," which is to say, a regular Buffalo Bill Show, with real cowboys, ponies, and cattle, all three of them wild, full of thorns, and just out of the brush.

The negro porters got out the saddles of the young women, thus disclosing their intention to ride ponies instead of in traps. We already knew that they were fearless horseback-riders, but when the string of ponies which were to be our mounts was led up by a few Mexicans, the Captain and I had our well-concealed doubts about their being proper sort of ponies for young girls to ride. We confided in an imperturbable cowboy—one of those dry Texans. He said: "Them are what we would call broke ponies, and you fellers needn't get to worryin' 'bout them little girls—you're jest a-foolin' away good time." Nevertheless, the broncos had the lurking devil in the tails of their eyes as they stood there tied to the wire fencing; they were humble and dejected as only a bronco or a mule can simulate. When that ilk look most cast down, be not deceived, gay brother; they are not like this. Their humility is only humorous, and intended to lure you on to their backs, where, unless you have a perfect understanding of the game, the joke will be on you. Instantly one is mounted, the humility departs; he plunges and starts about, or sets off like the wind, regardless of thorny bushes, tricky ground underfoot, or the seat of the rider.

The manager's wife came out of the car with her little brood of three, and then two visiting friends. These Soledad girls, as I call them, each had a sunburst of yellow hair, were well bronzed by the Mexican sun, and were sturdy little bodies. They were dressed in short skirts, with leggings, topped with Tam o' Shanters, while about their waists were cartridge-belts, with delicate knives and revolvers attached, and with spurs and *quirts* as accessories. They took up their men's saddles, for they rode astride, except the two visitors, who were older and more lately from Chicago. They swung their saddles on to the ponies, showing familiarity with the *ladigo* straps of the Texas saddles, and proudly escaping the humiliation which alights on the head of one who in the cowcamps cannot saddle his own "bronc." Being ready, we mounted, and followed a cowboy off down the road to the *rodeo*-ground. The manager and Madam Mamma rode in a buckboard, proudly following with their gaze the galloping ponies which bore their jewels. I thought they should be fearful for their safety, but after more intimate inspection, I could see how groundless was such solicitude.

I must have it understood that these little vaquero girls were not the ordinary Texas product, fed on corn-meal and bred in the chaparral, but the much looked after darlings of a fond mother. They are taken South every winter, that their bodies may be made lithe and healthy, but at the same time

two or more governesses crowd their minds with French, German, and other things with which proper young girls should be acquainted. But their infant minds did not carry back to the days when they had not felt a horse under them. To be sure, in the beginning it was only a humble donkey, but even before they knew they had graduated to ponies, and while yet ten years old, it was only by constant watch that they were kept off unbroken broncos—horses that made the toughest vaqueros throw down their hats, tighten their belts, and grin with fear.

From over the hills came the half-wild cattle, stringing along at a trot, all bearing for the open space in the waste of the chaparral where the *rodeo* occurred, while behind them followed the cowboys—gay

The Half-wild Cattle Came Down from the Hills.
The Free Library of Philadelphia.

desert figures with brown, pinched faces, long hair, and shouting wild cries. The exhilaration of the fine morning, the tramp of the thousands, got into the curls of the three little Misses Goldenhairs, and they scurried away, while I followed to feast on this fresh vision, where absolutely ideal little maids shouted Spanish at murderous-looking Mexican cow-punchers done up in bright serapes and costumed out of all reason. As the vaqueros dashed about hither and thither to keep their herds moving in the appointed direction, the infants screamed in their childish treble and spurred madly too. A bull stands at bay, but a child dashes at him, while he turns and flees. It is not their first *rodeo,* one can see, but I should wish they were with mamma and the buckboard, instead of out here in the brush, charging wild bulls, though in truth this never were written. These bulls frequently charge men, and a cow-pony turns like a ball off a bat, and a slippery seat in the saddle may put you under the feet of the outraged monarch of the range.

Driving down to the *rodeo*-ground, we all stood about on our ponies and held the herd, as it is called, the young girls doing vaquero duty, as imperturbable of mien as Mr. Flannagan, the foreman. So many women in the world are afraid of a dairy cow, even gathering up their skirts and preparing to shriek at the sight of one eating daisies. But these young women will grow up and they will be afraid of no cow. So much for a Soledad education.

The top-ropers rode slowly into the dust of the milling herd, scampered madly, cast their ropes, and came jumping to us with a blatting calf trailing at their ropes' end. Two men seized the little victim, threw him on his back, cut a piece out of his ear with a knife, and still held him in relentless grip while another pressed a red-hot branding-iron on his side, which sizzled and sent up blue smoke, together with an odor of burned flesh. The calves bawled piteously. There was no more emotion on the faces of the Soledad girls than was shown by the brown cowboys. They had often, very often,

seen this before, and their nerves were strong. Some day I can picture in my mind's eye these young girl vaqueros grown to womanhood, and being such good-looking creatures, very naturally some young man will want very badly to marry one of them for it cannot be otherwise. I only hope he will not be a thin-chested, cigarette-smoking dude, because it will be a sacrilege of nature. He must undoubtedly have played forward at Princeton or Yale, or be unworthy.

As we stood, a massive bull emerged from the body of the herd, his head thrown high, tail stiff with anger, eye rolling, and breath coming quick. He trotted quickly forward, and, lowering his head, charged through the "punchers." Instantly a small Soledad girl was after him, the vaqueros reining back to enjoy the strange ride with their eyes. Her hat flew off, and the long curls flapped in the rushing air as her pony fairly sailed over the difficult ground. The bull tore furiously, but behind him swept the pony and the child. As we watched, the chase had gone a mile away, but little Miss Yellowcurls drew gradually to the far side of the bull, quartering him on the far side, and whirling on, headed her quarry back to her audience and the herd. The rough-and-ready American range boss sat sidewise in his saddle and thought—for he never talked unnecessarily, though appreciation was chalked all over his pose. The manager and madam felt as though they were responsible for this wonderful thing. The Mexican cowboys snapped their fingers and eyes at one another, shouting quick Spanish, while the American part of the beholders agreed that it was the "limit"; "that as a picture," etc.; "that the American girl, properly environed"; "that this girl in particular," etc., was a dream. Then the bull and the girl came home; the bull to his fellows, and the girl to us. But she didn't have an idea of our admiration, because we didn't tell her; that would have been wrong, as you can imagine. Ten years will complicate little Miss Yellowcurls. Then she could be vain about such a thing; but, alas! she will not be—she will have forgotten.

A Sergeant of the Orphan Troop

While it is undisputed that Captain Dodd's troop of the Third Cavalry is not an orphan, and is, moreover, quite as far from it as any troop of cavalry in the world, all this occurred many years ago, when it was, at any rate, so called. There was nothing so very unfortunate about it, from what I can gather, since it seems to have fought well on its own hook, quite up to all expectations, if not beyond. No officer at that time seemed to care to connect his name with such a rioting, nose-breaking band of desperado cavalrymen, unless it was temporarily, and that was always in the field, and never in garrison. However, in this case it did not have even an officer in the field. But let me go on to my sergeant.

This one was a Southern gentleman, or rather a boy, when he refugeed out of Fredericksburg with his family, before the Federal advance, in a wagon belonging to a Mississippi rifle regiment; but nevertheless some years later he got to be a gentleman, and passed through the Virginia Military Institute with honor. The desire to be a soldier consumed him, but the vicissitudes of the times compelled him, if he wanted to be a soldier, to be a private one, which he became by duly enlisting in the Third Cavalry. He struck the Orphan Troop.

Physically, Nature had slobbered all over Carter Johnson; she had lavished on him her very last charm. His skin was pink, albeit the years of Arizona sun had heightened it to a dangerous red; his mustache was yellow and ideally military; while his pure Virginia accent, fired in terse and jerky form at friend and enemy alike, relieved his natural force of character by a shade of humor. He was thumped and bucked and pounded into what was in the seventies considered a proper frontier soldier, for in those days the nursery idea had not been lugged into the army. If a sergeant bade a soldier "go" or "do," he instantly "went" or "did"—otherwise the sergeant belted him over the head with his six-shooter, and had him taken off in a cart. On pay-days, too, when men who did not care to get drunk went to bed in barracks, they slept under their bunks and not in them, which was conducive to longevity and a good night's rest. When buffalo were scarce they ate the army rations in those wild days; they had a fight often enough to earn thirteen dollars, and at times a good deal more. This was the way with all men at that time, but it was rough on recruits.

So my friend Carter Johnson wore through some years, rose to be a corporal, finally a sergeant, and did many daring deeds. An atavism from "the old border riders" of Scotland shone through the boy, and he took on quickly. He could act the others off the stage and sing them out of the theatre in his chosen profession.

There was fighting all day long around Fort Robinson, Nebraska—a bushwhacking with Dull-Knife's band of the Northern Cheyennes, the Spartans of the plains. It was January; the snow lay deep on the ground, and the cold was knifelike as it thrust at the fingers and toes of the Orphan Troop. Sergeant Johnson with a squad of twenty men, after having been in the saddle all night, was in at the post drawing rations for the troop. As they were packing them up for transport, a detachment of F Troop came galloping by, led by the sergeant's friend, Corporal Thornton. They pulled up.

"Come on, Carter—go with us. I have just heard that some troops have got a bunch of Injuns corralled out in the hills. They can't get 'em down. Let's go help 'em. It's a chance for the fight of your life. Come on."

Carter hesitated for a moment. He had drawn the rations for his troop, which was in sore need of them. It might mean a court-martial and the loss of his chevrons— but a fight! Carter struck his spurred heels, saying. "Come on, boys; get your horses; we will go."

The line of cavalry was half lost in the flying snow as it cantered away over the white flats. The dry powder crunched under the thudding hoofs, the carbines banged about, the overcoat capes blew and twisted in the rushing air, the horses grunted and threw up their heads as the spurs went into their bellies, while the men's faces were serious with the interest in store. Mile after mile rushed the little column, until it came to some bluffs, where it drew reign and stood gazing across the valley to the other hills.

Down in the bottoms they espied an officer and two men sitting quietly on their horses, and on riding up found a lieutenant gazing at the opposite bluffs through a glass. Far away behind the bluffs a sharp ear could detect the reports of guns.

"We have been fighting the Indians all day here," said the officer, putting down his glass and turning to the two "non-coms." "The command has gone around the bluffs. I have just seen Indians up there on the rim-rocks. I have sent for troops, in the hope that we might get up there. Sergeant, deploy as skirmishers, and we will try."

At a gallop the men fanned out, then forward at a sharp trot across the flats, over the little hills, and into the scrub pine. The valley gradually narrowed until it forced the skirmishers into a solid body, when the lieutenant took the lead, with the command tailing out in single file. The signs of the Indians grew thicker and thicker—a skirmisher's nest here behind a scrub-pine bush, and there by the side of a rock. Kettles and robes lay about in the snow, with three "bucks" and some women and children sprawling about, frozen as they had died; but all was silent except the crunch of the snow and the low whispers of the men as they pointed to the telltales of the morning's battle.

As the column approached the precipitous rim-rock the officer halted, had the horses assembled in a side cañon, putting Corporal Thornton in charge. He ordered Sergeant Johnson to again advance his skirmish-line, in which formation the men moved forward, taking cover behind the pine scrub and rocks, until they came to an open space of about sixty paces, while above it towered the cliff for twenty feet in the sheer. There the Indians had been last seen. The soldiers lay tight in the snow, and no man's valor impelled him on. To the casual glance the rim-rock was impassable. The men were discouraged and the officer nonplussed. A hundred rifles might be covering the rock fort for all they knew. On closer examination a cutting was found in the face of the rock which was a rude attempt at steps, doubtless made long ago by the Indians. Caught on a bush above, hanging down the steps, was a lariat, which, at the bottom, was twisted around the shoulders of a dead warrior. They had evidently tried to take him up while wounded, but he had died and had been abandoned.

After cogitating, the officer concluded not to order his men forward, but he himself stepped boldly out into the open and climbed up. Sergeant Johnson immediately followed, while an old Swedish soldier by the name of Otto Bordeson fell in behind them. They walked briskly up the hill, and placing their backs against the wall of rock, stood gazing at the Indian.

With a grin the officer directed the men to advance. The sergeant, seeing that he realized their serious predicament, said:

"I think, lieutenant, you had better leave them where they are; we are holding this rock up pretty hard."

They stood there and looked at each other. "We's in a fix," said Otto.

"I want volunteers to climb this rock," finally demanded the officer.

The sergeant looked up the steps, pulled at the lariat, and commented: "Only one man can go at a time; if there are Indians up there, an old squaw can kill this command with a hatchet; and if there are no Indians, we can all go up."

The impatient officer started up, but the sergeant grabbed him by the belt. He turned, saying, "If I haven't got men to go, I will climb myself."

"Stop, lieutenant. It wouldn't look right for the officer to go. I have noticed a pine-tree, the branches of which spread over the top of the rock," and the sergeant pointed to it. "If you will make the men cover the top of the rim-rock with their rifles, Bordeson and I will go up;" and turning to the Swede, "Will you go, Otto?"

"I will go anywhere the sergeant does," came his gallant reply.

"Take your choice, then, of the steps or the pine-tree," continued the Virginian; and after a rather short but sharp calculation the Swede declared for the tree, although both were death if the Indians were on the rim-rock. He immediately began sidling along the rock to the tree, and slowly commenced the ascent. The sergeant took a few steps up the cutting, holding on by the rope. The officer stood out and smiled quizzically. Jeers came from behind the soldiers' bushes —"Go it, Otto! Go it, Johnson! Your feet are loaded! If a snow-bird flies, you will drop dead! Do you need any help? You'd make a hell of a sailor!" and other gibes.

The gray clouds stretched away monotonously over the waste of snow, and it was cold. The two men climbed slowly, anon stopping to look at each other and smile. They were monkeying with death.

At last the sergeant drew himself up, slowly raised his head, and saw snow and broken rock. Otto lifted himself likewise, and he too saw nothing. Rifle-shots came clearly to their ears from far in front— many at one time, and scattering at others. Now the soldiers came briskly forward, dragging up the cliff in single file. The dull noises of the fight came through the wilderness. The skirmish-line drew quickly forward and passed into the pine woods, but the Indian trails scattered. Dividing into sets of four, they followed on the tracks of small parties, wandering on until night threatened. At length the main trail of the fugitive band ran across their front, bringing the command together. It was too late for the officer to get his horses before dark, nor could he follow with his exhausted men, so he turned to the sergeant and asked him to pick some men and follow on the trail. The sergeant picked Otto Bordeson, who still affirmed that he would go anywhere that Johnson went, and they started. They were old hunting companions, having confidence in each other's sense and shooting. They ploughed through the snow, deeper and deeper into the pines, then on down a cañon where the light was failing. The sergeant was sweating freely; he raised his hand to press his fur cap backward from his forehead. He drew it quickly away; he stopped and started, caught Otto by the sleeve, and drew a long breath. Still holding his companion, he put his glove again to his nose, sniffed at it again, and with a mighty tug brought the startled Swede to his knees, whispering, "I smell Indians; I can sure smell 'em, Otto— can you?"

Otto sniffed, and whispered back, "Yes, plain!"

"We are ambushed! Drop!" and the two soldiers sunk in the snow. A few feet in front of them lay a dark thing; crawling to it, they found a large calico rag, covered with blood.

"Let's do something, Carter; we's in a fix."

"If we go down, Otto, we are gone; if we go back, we are gone; let's go forward," hissed the sergeant.

Slowly they crawled from tree to tree.

"Don't you see the Injuns?" said the Swede, as he pointed to the rocks in front, where lay their dark forms. The still air gave no sound. The cathedral of nature, with its dark pine trunks starting from gray snow to support gray sky, was dead. Only human hearts raged, for the forms which held them lay like black bowlders.

"Egah—lelah washatah," yelled the sergeant.

Two rifle-shots rang and reverberated down the cañon; two more replied instantly from the soldiers. One Indian sunk, and his carbine went clanging down the rocks, burying itself in the snow. Another warrior rose slightly, took aim, but Johnson's six-shooter cracked again, and the Indian settled slowly down without firing. A squaw moved slowly in the half-light to where the buck lay. Bordeson drew a bead with his carbine.

"Don't shoot the woman, Otto. Keep that hole covered; the place is alive with Indians;" and both lay still.

A buck rose quickly, looked at the sergeant and dropped back. The latter could see that he had him located, for he slowly poked his rifle up without showing his head. Johnson rolled swiftly to one side, aiming with his deadly revolver. Up popped the Indian's head, crack went the six-shooter; the head turned slowly, leaving the top exposed. Crack again went the alert gun of the soldier, the ball striking the head just below the scalp-lock and instantly jerking the body into a kneeling position.

Then all was quiet in the gloomy woods.

After a time the sergeant addressed his voice to the lonely place in Sioux, telling the women to come out and surrender—to leave the bucks, etc.

An old squaw rose sharply to her feet, slapped her breast, shouted "Lelah washatah," and gathering up a little girl and a bundle, she strode forward to the soldiers. Three other women followed, two of them in the same blanket.

"Are there any more bucks?" roared the sergeant, in Sioux.

"No more alive," said the old squaw, in the same tongue.

"Keep your rifle on the hole between the rocks; watch these people; I will go up," directed the sergeant as he slowly mounted to the ledge, and with levelled six-shooter peered slowly over. He stepped in and stood looking down on the dead warriors.

A yelling in broken English smote the startled sergeant. "Tro up your hands, you d—— Injun! I'll blow the top off you!" came through the quiet. The sergeant sprang down to see the Swede standing with carbine levelled at a young buck confronting him with a drawn knife in his hands, while his blanket lay back on the snow.

"He's a buck—he ain't no squaw; he tried to creep on me with a knife. I'm going to kill him," shouted the excited Bordeson.

"No, no, don't kill him. Otto, don't you kill him," expostulated Johnson, as the Swede's finger clutched nervously at the trigger, and turning, he roared, "Throw away that knife, you d—— Indian!"

The detachment now came charging in through the snow, and gathered around excitedly. A late arrival came up, breathing heavily, dropped his gun, and springing up and down, yelled, "Be jabbers, I have got among om at last!" A general laugh went up, and the circle of men broke into a straggling line for the return. The sergeant took the little girl up in his arms. She grabbed him fiercely by the throat like a wild-cat, screaming. While nearly choking, he yet tried to mollify her, while her mother, seeing no harm was intended, pacified her in the soft gutturals of the race. She relaxed her grip, and the brave Virginian packed her down the mountain, wrapped in his soldier cloak. The horses were reached in time, and the prisoners put on double behind the soldiers, who fed them crackers as they marched. At two o'clock in the morning the little command rode into Fort Robinson and dismounted at the guardhouse. The little girl, who was asleep and half frozen in Johnson's overcoat, would not go to her mother: poor little cat, she had found a nest. The sergeant took her into the guardhouse, where it was warm. She soon fell asleep, and slowly he undid her, delivering her to her mother.

On the following morning he came early

The Brave Cheyennes Were Running Through the Frosty Hills. *Painting in The Gund Collection of Western Art (A Traveling Exhibition of American Western Art).*

to the guard-house, loaded with trifles for his little Indian girl. He had expended all his credit at the post-trader's, but he could carry sentiment no further, for "To horse!" was sounding, and he joined the Orphan Troop to again ride on the Dull-Knife trail. The brave Cheyennes were running through the frosty hills, and the cavalry horses pressed hotly after. For ten days the troops surrounded the Indians by day, and stood guard in the snow by night, but coming day found the ghostly warriors gone and their rifle-pits empty. They were cut off and slaughtered daily, but the gallant warriors were fighting to their last nerve. Towards the end they were cooped in a gully on War-Bonnatt Creek, where they fortified; but two six-pounders had been hauled out, and were turned on their works. The four troops of cavalry stood to horse on the plains all day, waiting for the poor wretches to come out, while the guns roared, ploughing the frozen dirt and the snow over their little stronghold; but they did not come out. It was known that all the provisions they had was the dead horse of a corporal of E Troop, which had been shot within twenty paces of their rifle-pits.

So, too, the soldiers were starving, and the poor Orphans had only crackers to eat. They were freezing also, and murmuring to be led to "the charge," that they might end it there, but they were an orphan troop, and must wait for others to say. The sergeant even asked an officer to let them go, but was peremptorily told to get back in the ranks.

The guns ceased at night, while the troops drew off to build fires, warm their rigid fingers, thaw out their buffalo moccasins, and munch crackers, leaving a strong guard around the Cheyennes. In the night there was a shooting—the Indians had charged through and had gone.

The day following they were again surrounded on some bluffs, and the battle waged until night. Next day there was a weak fire from the Indian position on the impregnable bluffs, and presently it ceased entirely. The place was approached with care and trepidation, but was empty. Two Indian boys, with their feet frozen, had been left as decoys, and after standing off four troops of cavalry for hours, they too had in some mysterious way departed.

But the pursuit was relentless; on, on over the rolling hills swept the famishing troopers, and again the Spartan band turned at bay, firmly intrenched on a bluff as before. This was the last stand—nature was exhausted. The soldiers surrounded them, and Major Wessells turned the handle of the human vise. The command gathered closer about the doomed pits—they crawled on their bellies from one stack of sage-brush to the next. They were freezing. The order to charge came to the Orphan Troop, and yelling his command, Sergeant Johnson ran forward. Up from the sage-brush floundered the stiffened troopers, following on. They ran over three Indians, who lay sheltered in a little cut, and these killed three soldiers together with an old frontier sergeant who wore long hair, but they were destroyed in turn. While the Orphans swarmed under the hill, a rattling discharge poured from the rifle-pits; but the troop had gotten under the fire, and it all passed over their heads. On they pressed, their blood now quickened by excitement, crawling up the steep, while volley on volley poured over them. Within nine feet of the pits was a rim-rock ledge over which the Indian bullets swept, and here the charge was stopped. It now became a duel. Every time a head showed on either side, it drew fire like a flue-hole. Suddenly our Virginian sprang on the ledge, and like a trill on a piano poured a six-shooter into the intrenchment, and dropped back.

Major Wessells, who was commanding the whole force, crawled to the position of the Orphan Troop, saying, "Doing fine work, boys. Sergeant, I would advise you to take off that red scarf"—when a bullet cut the major across the breast, whirling him around and throwing him. A soldier, one Lannon, sprang to him and pulled him down the bluff, the major protesting that he was not wounded, which proved to be true, the bullet having passed through his heavy clothes.

The troops had drawn up on the other sides, and a perfect storm of bullets whirled over the intrenchments. The powder blackened the faces of the men, and they took off their caps or had them shot off. To raise the head for more than a fraction of a second meant death.

Johnson had exchanged five shots with a fine-looking Cheyenne, and every time he raised his eye to a level with the rock White Antelope's gun winked at him.

"You will get killed directly," yelled Lannon to Johnson; "they have you spotted."

The smoke blew and eddied over them; again Johnson rose, and again White Antelope's pistol cracked an accompaniment to his own; but with movement like lightning the sergeant sprang through the smoke, and fairly shoving his carbine to White Antelope's breast, he pulled the trigger. A 50-calibre gun boomed in Johnson's face, and a volley roared from the pits, but he fell backward into cover. His comrades set him up to see if any red stains came through the grime, but he was unhurt.

The firing grew; a blue haze hung over the hill. Johnson again looked across the glacis, but again his eye met the savage glare of White Antelope.

"I haven't got him yet, Lannon, but I will;" and Sergeant Johnson again slowly reloaded his pistol and carbine.

"Now, men give them a volley!" ordered the enraged man, and as volley answered volley, through the smoke sprang the daring soldier, and standing over White Antelope as the smoke swirled and almost hid him, he poured his six balls into his enemy, and thus died one brave man at the hands of another in fair battle. The sergeant leaped back and lay down among the men, stunned by the concussions. He said he would do no more. His mercurial temperament had undergone a change, or, to put it better, he conceived it to be outrageous to fight these poor people, five against one. He characterized it as "a d—— infantry fight," and rising, talked in Sioux to the enemy—asked them to surrender, or they must otherwise die. A young girl answered him, and said they would like to. An old woman sprang on her and cut her throat with a dull knife, yelling mean-while to the soldiers that "they would never surrender alive," and saying what she had done.

Many soldiers were being killed, and the fire from the pits grew weaker. The men were beside themselves with rage. "Charge!" rang through the now still air from some strong voice, and, with a volley, over the works poured the troops, with six-shooters going, and clubbed carbines. Yells, explosions, and amid a whirlwind of smoke the soldiers and Indians swayed about, now more slowly and quieter, until the smoke eddied away. Men stood still, peering about with wild open eyes through blackened faces. They held desperately to their weapons. An old bunch of buckskin rags rose slowly and fired a carbine aimlessly. Twenty bullets rolled and tumbled it along the ground, and again the smoke drifted off the mount. This time the air grew clear. Buffalo-robes lay all about, blood spotted everywhere. The dead bodies of thirty-two Cheyennes lay, writhed and twisted, on the packed snow, and among them many women and children, cut and furrowed with lead. In a corner was a pile of wounded squaws, half covered with dirt swept over them by the storm of bullets. One broken creature half raised herself from the bunch. A maddened trumpeter threw up his gun to shoot, but Sergeant Johnson leaped and kicked his gun out of his hands high into the air, saying, "This fight is over."

The Great Medicine-Horse

AN INDIAN MYTH OF THE THUNDER

"Itsoneorratseahoos," or Paint, as the white men called him, had the story, and had agreed to tell it to me. His tepee was not far, so "Sun-Down La Flare" said he would go down and interpret.

Sun-Down was cross-bred, red and white, so he never got mentally in sympathy with either strain of his progenitors. He knew about half as much concerning Indians as they did themselves, while his knowledge of white men was in the same proportion. I felt little confidence that I should get Paint's mysterious musings transferred to my head without an undue proportion of dregs filtered in from Sun-Down's lack of appreciation. While the latter had his special interest for me, the problem in this case was how to eliminate "Sun-Down" from "Paint." So much for interpreters.

We trudged on through the soft gray-blues of the moonlight, while drawing near to some tepees grouped in the creek bottom. The dogs came yelling; but a charge of Indian dogs always splits before an enemy which does not recoil, and recovers itself in their rear. There they may become dangerous. Sun-Down lifted the little tepee flap, and I crawled through. A little fire of five or six split sticks burned brightly in the centre, illumining old Paint as he lay back on his resting-mat. He grunted, but did not move; he was smoking. We shook hands, and Sun-Down made our peace offering to the squaw, who sat at her beading. We reclined about the tepee and rolled cigarettes. There is a solemnity about the social intercourse of old

Indian warriors which reminds me of a stroll through a winter forest. Every one knows by this how the interior of an Indian tepee looks, though every one cannot necessarily know how it feels; but most people who have wandered much have met with fleas. Talk came slow; but that is the Indian of it: they think more than they talk. Sun-Down explained something at length to Paint, and back came the heavy guttural clicking of the old warrior's words, accompanied by much subtle sign language.

"He sais he will tell you 'bout de horse. Now you got for keep still and wait; he'll talk a heap, but you'll get de story eef you don' get oneasy."

"Now, Sun-Down, remember to tell me just what Paint says. I don't care what you think Paint means," I admonished.

"I step right in hees tracks."

Paint loaded his long red sandstone pipe with the utmost deliberation, sat up on his back-rest, and puffed with an exhaust like a small stationary engine. The squaw put two more sticks on the fire, which spitted and fluttered, lighting up the broad brown face of the old Indian, while it put a dot of light in his fierce little left eye. He spoke slowly, with clicking and harsh gutturals, as though he had an ounce of quicksilver in his mouth which he did not want to swallow. After a time Sun-Down raised his hand to enjoin silence.

"He sais dat God—not God, but dat is bess word I know for white man; I have been school, and I know what he want for say ees what you say medicin', but dat ees not right. What he want for say ees de ding what direct heem un hees people what is best for do; et ees de speret what tell de ole men who can see best when dey sleep. Well —anyhow, it was long, long time ago, when hees fader was young man, and 'twas hees fader's fader what it all happened to. The Absarokees deedn't have ponies 'nough—de horses ware new in the country—dey used for get 'em out of a lac,* 'way off some- where—dey come out of de water, and dese Enjun† lay in the bulrush for rope 'em, but dey couldn't get 'nough; besides, de Enjun from up north she use steal 'em from Ab- sarokee. Well—anyhow, de medicin' tole hees fader's fader dat he would get plenty horses eef he go 'way south. So small party went 'long wid heem—dey was on foot— dey was travel for long time, keepin' in de foot-hill. Dey was use for travel nights un lay by daytime, 'cept when dey was hunt for de grub. De country was full up wid deir en- emies, but de medicin' hit was strong, and de luck was wid 'em. De medicin' hit keep tellin' 'em for go 'long—go on—on—on— keep goin' long, long time. He's been tellin' me de names of revers dey cross, but you wouldn't know dem plass by what he call 'em. Dey keep spyin' camps, but de medi- cin' he keep tellin' 'em for go on, go on, un not bodder dem camp, un so dey keep goin'."

Here Sun-Down motioned Paint, and he started his strange high-pitched voice— winking and moving his hands at Sun- Down, who was rolling a cigarette, though keeping his eyes on the old Indian. Pres- ently the talking ceased.

"He sais—dey went on—what he is tryin' for say ees dey went on so far hit was heap hot, un de Enjun dey was deeferent from what dees Enjun is. He's tryin' for to get so far off dat I don' know for tell you how far he ees."

"Never mind, Sun-Down; you stick to Paint's story," I demanded.

"Well—anyhow—he's got dees outfit hell of a long way from home, un dey met up

* Lake.   † Indian.

wid a camp un heap of pony. He was try to tell how many pony—like de buffalo used to be—more pony dan you see ober, by Gar. Den de medicin' say dey was for tac dose pony eef dey can. Well, den de outfit lay roun' camp wid de wolf-skin on—de white wolf. De Enjun he do jus' same as wolf, un fool de oder Enjun, you see; well, den come one night dey got de herds whar dey wanted 'em, un cut out all dey could drive. Et was terrible big bunch, 'cording as Paint say. Dey drive 'em all night un all nex' day, wid de horse-guides ahead, un de oders behin', floppin' de wolf-robe, un Paint say de grass will never grow where dey pass 'long; but I dink, by Gar, Paint ees talk t'ro' hees hat."

"Never mind—I don't want you to think —you just freeze to old Paint's talk, Mr. Sun-Down," I interlarded.

"Well, den—damn 'em, after dey had spoil de grass for 'bout night un day de peo- ple what dey had stole from come a-runnin'. Et was hard for drive such beeg bunch fas' —dey ought for have tac whole outfit un put 'em foot; but Paint say—un he's been horse-tief too hisself, by Gar—he say dey natu'lly couldn't; but I say—"

"Never mind what you say."

"Well, anyhow, I say—"

"Never mind, Sun-Down!"

"Well, ole Paint he say same t'ing. De oder fellers kim up wid 'em, so just natu'lly dey went fightin'; but dey had extra horses, un de oder fellers dey didn't, 'cep' what was fall out of bunch, dem bein' slow horses, un horses what was no 'count, noway. Dey went runnin' un fightin' 'way in de night; but de herd split on 'em, un hees fader's fader went wid one bunch, un de oder fellers went wid de 'split,' which no one neber heard of no more. De men what had loss de horses all went after de oder bunch. Hees fader's fader rode all dat night, all nex' day, un den stopped for res'. Dar was only 'bout ten men for look after de herd, which was more horses dan you kin see een dees valley to-day; what ees more horses dan ten men kin wrangle, 'cordin' to me."

"Never mind, Sun-Down."

"Let 'er roll, Paint," said La Flare, beginning a new cigarette.

"He sais," interrupted Sun-Down, "dey was go 'long slowly, slowly—goin' toward de villages—when one day dey was jump by Cheyenne. Dey went runnin' and fightin' till come night, un couldn't drive de herd rightly. Dey loss heap of horses, but as dey come onto divide, dey saw camp right in front of dem. It was 'mos' night, so four or five of hees fader's fader's men dey cut out a beeg bunch, un split hit off down a coulie. De Enjun foller de oder bunch, which ram right eento de village, whar de 'hole outfit went for fight lac hell. Paint's fader's fader she saw dees as she rode ober de hill. Dey was loss heap of men dat day by bein' kill un by run eento dose camp lesewise none of dem ever show up no more. Well, den, Paint say dey was keep travellin' on up dees way—hit was tac heem d—— long story for geet hees fader's fader's outfit back here, wheech ees hall right, seein' he got 'em so far 'way for begin wid."

Then Paint continued his story:

"He sais de Sioux struck 'em one day, un dey was have hell of a fight—runnin' deir pony, shootin' deir arrow. One man he was try mount fresh horse, she stan' steel un buck, buck, buck, un dees man he was not able for geet on; de Sioux dey come run, run, un dey kiell* heem. You see, when one man he catch fresh horse, he alway' stab hees played-out horse, 'cause he do not want eet for fall eento hand of de Enjun follerin'. Den White Bull's horse she run slow; he 'quirt' heem, but eet was do no good—ze horse was done; de Sioux dey was shoot de horse, un no one know whatever becom' of heem, but I dink he was kiell all right 'nough. Den 'noder man's horse she was stick hees foot in dog-hole, un de Sioux dey shoot las' man 'cept hees fader's fader. Den he was notice a beeg red horse what had alway' led de horse ban' since dey was stole. Dese Enjun had try for rope dees horse plenty times, but dey was never been able, but hees fader's fader was ride up to de head of de ban', un jus' happen for rope

*Kill.

de red horse. He jump from hees pony to dees red horse jus' as Sioux was 'bout to run heem down. De big red horse was run —run lac† hell—ah! He was run, by Gar, un de Sioux dey was—aah!—de Sioux dey couldn't run wid de big red horse nohow.

"He was gone now half-year, un he deed not know where he find hees people. He was see coyote runnin' 'head, un he was say 'good medicin'.' He foller after leetle wolf— he was find two buffalo what was kiell by lightnin', what show coyote was good medicin'. He was give coyote some meat, un nex' day he was run on some Absarokee, who was tell him whar hees people was, wheech was show how good de coyote was. When he got camp de Enjun was terrible broke up, un dey had nevar before see red horse. All of deir horses was black, gray, spotted, roan, but none of dem was red—so dees horse was tac to de big medicin' in de medicin'-lodge, un he was paint up. He got be strong wid Absarokee, un hees fader's fader was loss horse because he was keep in medicin'-tepee, un look after by big medicin'-chiefs. Dey was give out eef he was loss eet would be bad, bad for Absarokee, un dey was watch out mighty close—by Gar, dey was watch all time dees red horse. When he go out for graze, t'ree warriors was hole hees rope un t'ree was sit on deir pony 'longside. No one was ride heem."

Then, talking alternately, the story came: "He sais de horse de Absarokee was increase—plenty pony—un de mare he was all red colts; de big horse was strong. De buffalo dey was come right to de camp—by Gar, de horse was good. De Sioux sent Peace Commission for try buy de horse— dey was de beesness for Enjun down whar de summer come from, what want for geet heem back—for he was a medicin'-horse. De Absarokee dey was not sell heem. Den a big band of de Ogalalas, Brulés, Minneconjous, Sans Arcs, Cheyennes, was come for tac de red horse, dey was kiell one village, but dare was one man 'scape, what was come to red horse, un de Absarokee dey was put de red paint on deir forehead. Ah!

†Like.

"He Jumped from Hees Pony to Dees Red Horse." *Authors' photoengraving.*

de Sioux dey was not get de red horse—dey was half to go 'way. Den some time de beeg medicin'-horse was have hell of a trouble wid de bigges' medicin'-chief, right in de big medicin'-lodge. Dees word medicin' don't mean what de Enjun mean; de tent whar de sperets come for tell de people what for do, eese what dey mean; all same as Fader Lacomb he prance 'roun' when he not speak de French—dat's what dey mean. All right, he have dees trouble wid de head chief, un he keek heem een de head, un he kiell him dead. After dat he was get for be head medicin'-chief hisself, un he tole all de oder medicin'-chief what for do. He was once run 'way from de men what was hol' hees rope when he was graze—dey was scared out of deir life of heem eef dey was mak' heem mad, un he was go out een herd un kiell some horse. No one was dare go after

heem. De medicin'-men dey was go out wid de big medicin'—dey was talk come back to heem; but he wouldn't come. Den de virgin woman of de tribe—she was kind of medicin'-man herself—she was go out un make a talk; she was tell red horse to go off—dat's de way for talk to people when deir minds not lac oder people's minds—un de horse she was let heem bring heem back. After dat all de Absarokee women had for behave preety well, or de medicin'-men kiell dem, 'cause dey say de medicin'-horse she was want de woman for be better in de tribe. Be d—— good t'ing eef dat horse she 'roun' here now."

"Oh, you reptile! will you never mind this thinking—it is fatal," I sighed.

"Well, anyhow, he sais de woman dey was have many pappoose, un de colts was red, un was not curly hair, un de 'yellow eyes'* was come wid de gun for trade skin. De buffalo she was stay late; de winter was mile; de enemy no steal de pony, un de Absarokee, he tac heap scalp—all dese was medicin'-horse work. But in de moon een which de geese lay deir eggs de great horse he was rise up een de curl of de smoke of de big lodge—he was go plum' t'ro' de smoke-hole. De chief ask him for not go, but he was say he was go to fight de T'under-Bird. He say he would come back. Dey could keep his ghost. So he went 'way, un since den he has nevar come back no more. But Paint say lots of ole men use for see heem go t'ro' air wid de lightnin' comin' out of his nose, de T'under-Bird always runnin' out of hees way; he was always lick de t'under. Paint says dese Enjun have not see de medicin'-horse nowday; eef dey was see heem more, dey see no 'yellow eyes' een dees country. He sais he has seen de medicin'-horse once. He was hunt over een de mountain, but he was not have no luck; he was hungry, un was lay down by leetle fire

* White men.

een cañon. He was see de beeg medicin'-horse go 'long de ridge of de hill 'gainst de moon—he was beeg lac de new school-house. Paint got up un talked loud to de horse, askin' heem eef he was nevar come back. De horse stop un sais—muffled, lac man talk t'ro' blanket—'Yes, he was come back from speret-land, when he was bring de buffalo plenty; was roll de lan' over de white men; was fight de north wind. He sais he was come back when de Absarokee was not wear pants, was ride widout de saddle; when de women was on de square—un, by Gar, I t'ink he not come varrie soon."

"What does Paint say?"

"Ah, Paint he sais hit weel all come some day."

"Is that all?"

"Yes—dat ees all," said Sun-Down.

To be sure, there is quite as much Sun-Down in this as Paint—but if you would have more Paint, it will be necessary to acquire the Crow language, and then you might not find Paint's story just as I have told it.

Joshua Goodenough's Old Letter

The following letter has come into my possession, which I publish because it is history, and descends to the list of those humble beings who builded so well for us the institutions which we now enjoy in this country. It is yellow with age, and much frayed out at the foldings, being in those spots no longer discernible. It runs:

ALBANY June 1798.

TO MY DEAR SON JOSEPH.—It is true that there are points in the history of the country in which your father had a concern in his early life, and as you ask me to put it down I will do so briefly. Not, however, my dear Joseph, as I was used to tell it to you when you were a lad, but with more exact truth, for I am getting on in my years and this will soon be all that my posterity will have of their ancestor. I conceive that now the descendents of the noble band of heroes who fought off the indians, the Frenche and the British will prevail in this country, and my children's children may want to add what is found here in written to their own achievements.

To begin with, my father was the master of a fishing-schooner, of Marblehead. In the year 1745 he was taken at sea by a French man-of-war off Louisbourg, after making a desperate resistence. His ship was in a sinking condition and the blood was mid-leg deep on her deck. Your grandfather was an upstanding man and did not prostrate easily, but the Frencher was too big, so he was captured and later found his way as a pris-

oner to Quebec. He was exchanged by a mistake in his identity for Huron indians captivated in York, and he subsequently settled near Albany, afterwards bringing my mother, two sisters, and myself from Marblehead.

He engaged in the indian trade, and as I was a rugged lad of my years I did often accompany him on his expeditions westward into the Mohawk townes, thus living in bark camps among Indians and got thereby a knowledge of their ways. I made shift also to learn their language, and what with living in the bush for so many years I was a hand at a pack or paddle and no mean hunter besides. I was put to school for two seasons in Albany which was not to my liking, so I straight-way ran off to a hunters camp up the Hudson, and only came back when my father would say that I should not be again put with the pedegogue. For this adventure I had a good strapping from my father, and was set to work in his trade again. My mother was a pious woman and did not like me to grow up in the wilderness—for it was the silly fashion of those times to ape the manners and dress of the Indians.

My father was a shifty trader and very ventursome. He often had trouble with the people in these parts, who were Dutch and were jealous of him. He had a violent temper and was not easily bent from his purpose by opporsition. His men had a deal of fear of him and good cause enough in the bargain, for I once saw him discipline a half-negro man who was one of his boatmen for stealing his private jug of liquor from his private pack. He clinched with the negro and soon had him on the ground, where the man struggled manfully but to no purpose, for your grandfather soon had him at his mercy. "Now," said he, "give me the jug or take the consequences." The other boat paddlers wanted to rescue him, but I menaced them with my fusil and the matter ended by the return of the jug.

In 1753 he met his end at the hands of western indians in the French interest, who shot him as he was helping to carry a battoe, and he was burried in the wilderness. My mother then returned to her home in Massassuchusetts, journeying with a party of traders but I staid with the Dutch on these frontiers because I had learned the indian trade and liked the country. Not having any chances, I had little book learning concerning it. I read a few books, but fear I had a narrow knowledge of things outside the Dutch settlements. On the frontiers, for that matter, few people had much skill with the pen, nor was much needed. The axe and rifle, the paddle and pack being more to our hands in those rough days. To prosper though, men weare shrewd-headed enough. I have never seen that books helped people to trade sharper. Shortly afterwards our trade fell away, for the French had embroiled the Indians against us. Crown Point was the Place from which the Indians in their interest had been fitted out to go against our settlements, so a design was formed by His Majesty the British King to dispossess them of that place. Troops were levid in the Province and the war began. The Frenchers had the best of the fighting.

Our frontiers were beset with the Canada indians so that it was not safe to go about in the country at all. I was working for Peter Vrooman, a trader, and was living at his house on the Mohawk. One Sunday morning I found a negro boy who was shot through the body with two balls as he was hunting for stray sheep, and all this within half a mile of Vrooman's house. Then an express came up the valley who left word that the Province was levying troops at Al-

bany to fight the French, and I took my pay from Vrooman saying that I would go to Albany for a soldier. Another young man and myself paddled down to Albany, and we both enlisted in the York levies. We drawed our ammunition, tents, kettles, bowls and knives at the Albany flats, and were drilled by an officer who had been in her Majesty's Service. One man was given five hundred lashes for enlisting in some Connecticut troops, and the orders said that any man who should leave His Majesty's service without a Regular discharge should suffer Death. The restraint which was put upon me by this military life was not to my liking, and I was in a mortal dread of the whippings which men were constantly receiving for breaches of the discipline. I felt that I could not survive the shame of being trussed up and lashed before men's eyes, but I did also have a great mind to fight the French which kept me along. One day came an order to prepare a list of officers and men who were willing to go scouting and be freed from other duty, and after some time I got my name put down, for I was thought too young, but I said I knew the woods, had often been to Andiatirocte (or Lake George as it had then become the fashion to call it) and they let me go. It was dangerous work, for reports came every day of how our Rangers suffered up country at the hands of the cruel savages from Canada, but it is impossible to play at bowls without meeting some rubs. A party of us proceeded up river to join Captain Rogers at Fort Edward, and we were put to camp on an Island. This was in October of the year 1757. We found the Rangers were rough borderers like ourselvs, mostly Hampshire men well used to the woods and much accustomed to the Enemy. They dressed in the fashion of those times in skin and grey duffle hunting frocks, and were well armed. Rogers himself was a doughty man and had a reputation as a bold Ranger leader. The men declaired that following him was sore service, but that he most always met with great success. The Fort was garrissoned by His Majesty's soldiers, and I did not conceive that they were much fitted for bush-ranging, which I afterwards found to be the case, but they would always fight well enough, though often to no good purpose, which was not their fault so much as the headstrong leadership which persisted in making them come to close quarters while at a disadvantage. There were great numbers of pack horses coming and going with stores, and many officers in gold lace and red coats were riding about directing here and there. I can remember that I had a great interest in this concourse of men, for up to that time I had not seen much of the world outside of the wilderness. There was terror of the Canada indians who had come down to our borders hunting for scalps—for these were continually lurking near the cantanements to waylay the unwary. I had got acquainted with a Hampshire borderer who had passed his life on the Canada frontier, where he had fought indians and been captured by them. I had seen much of indians and knew their silent forest habits when hunting, so that I felt that when they were after human beings they would be no mean adversaries, but I had never hunted them or they me.

I talked at great length with this Shankland, or Shanks as he was called on account of his name and his long legs, in course of which he explained many useful points to me concerning Ranger ways. He said they always marched until it was quite dark before encamping—that they always returned by a different route from that on which they went out, and that they circled on their trail at intervals so that they might intercept any one coming on their rear. He told me not to gather up close to other Rangers in a fight but to keep spread out, which gave the Enemy less mark to fire upon and also deceived them as to your own numbers. Then also he cautioned me not to fire on the Enemy when we were in ambush till they have approached quite near, which will put them in greater surprise and give your own people time to rush in on them with hatchets or cutlasses. Shanks and I had finally a great fancy for each other and passed most of our time in company. He

was a slow man in his movements albeit he could move fast enough on occasion, and was a great hand to take note of things happening around. No indian was better able to discern a trail in the bush than he, nor could one be found his equal at making snow shoes, carving a powder horn or fashioning any knick-nack he was a mind to set his hand to.

The Rangers were accustomed to scout in small parties to keep the Canada indians from coming close to Fort Edward. I had been out with Shanks on minor occasions, but I must relate my first adventure.

A party . . . (here the writing is lost) . . . was desirous of taking a captive or scalp. I misdoubted our going alone by ourselves, but he said we were as safe as with more. We went northwest slowly for two days, and though we saw many old trails we found none which were fresh. We had gone on until night when we lay bye near a small brook. I was awakened by Shanks in the night and heard a great howling of wolves at some distance off together with a gun shot. We lay awake until daybreak and at intervals heard a gun fired all through the night. We decided that the firing could not come from a large party and so began to approach the sound slowly and with the greatest caution. We could not understand why the wolves should be so bold with the gun firing, but as we came neare we smelled the smoke and knew it was a camp-fire. There were a number of wolves running about in the underbrush from whose actions we located the camp. From a rise we could presently see it, and were surprised to find it contained five Indians all lying asleep in their blankets. The wolves would go right up to the camp and yet the indians did not deign to give them any notice whatsoever, or even to move in the least when one wolf pulled at the blanket of a sleeper. We each selected a man when he had come near enough, and preparing to deliver our fire, when of a sudden one figure rose up slightly. We nevertheless fired and then rushed forward, reloading. To our astonishment none of the figures moved in the least

The March of Rogers's Rangers. *Authors' photoengraving.*

but the wolves scurried off. We were advancing cautiously when Shanks caught me by the arm saying "we must run, that they had all died of the small-pox," and run we did lustilly for a good long distance. After this manner did many Indians die in the wilderness from that dreadful disease, and I have since supposed that the last living indian had kept firing his gun at the wolves until he had no longer strength to reload his piece.

After this Shanks and I had become great friends for he had liked the way I had conducted myself on this expedition. He was always arguing with me to cut off my eelskin que which I wore after the fashion of the Dutch folks, saying that the Canada indians would parade me for a Dutchman after that token was gone with my scalp. He had . . . . (writing obliterated).

Early that winter I was one of 150 Rangers who marched with Captain Rogers against the Enemy at Carrillion. The snow was not deep at starting but it continued to snow until it was heavy footing and many of the men gave out and returned to Fort Edward, but notwithstanding my exhaustion I continued on for six days until we were come to within six hundred yards of Carrillion Fort. The captain had made us a speech in which he told us the points where we were to rendevoux if we were broke in the fight, for further resistence until night came on, when we could take ourselvs off as best we might. I was with the advance guard. We lay in ambush in some fallen timber quite close to a road, from which we could see the smoke from the chimneys of the Fort and the centries walking their beats. A French soldier was seen to come from the Fort and the word was passed to let him go bye us, as he came down the road. We lay perfectly still not daring to breathe, and though he saw nothing he stopped once and seemed undecided as to going on, but suspecting nothing he continued and was captured by our people below, for prisoners were wanted at Headquarters to give information of the French forces and intentions. A man taken in this way was threatened with Death if he did not tell the whole truth, which under the circumstancs he mostly did to save his life.

The French did not come out of the Fort after us, though Rogers tried to entice them by firing guns and showing small parties of men which feigned to retreat. We were ordered to destroy what we could of the supplies, so Shanks and I killed a small cow which we found in the edge of the clearing and took off some fresh beef of which food we were sadly in need, for on these scouts the Rangers were not permitted to fire guns at game though it was found in thir path, as it often was in fact. I can remember on one occassion that I stood by a tree in a snow storm, with my gun depressed under my frock the better to keep it dry, when I was minded to glance quickly around and there saw a large wolf just ready to spring upon me. I cautiously presented my fusee but did not dare to fire against the orders. Another Ranger came shortly into view and the wolf took himself off. We burned some large wood piles, which no doubt made winter work for to keep some Frenchers at home. They only fired some cannon at us, which beyond a great deal of noise did no harm. We then marched back to Fort Edward and were glad enough to get there, since it was time for snow-shoes, which we had not with us.

The Canada indians were coming down to our Forts and even behind them to intercept our convoys or any parties out on the road, so that the Rangers were kept out, to head them when they could, or get knowledge of their whereabouts. Shanks and I went out with two Mohegon indians on a scout. It was exceedingly stormy weather and very heavy travelling except on the River. I had got a bearskin blanket from the indians which is necessary to keep out the cold at this season. We had ten days of bread, pork and rum with a little salt with us, and followed the indians in a direction

North-and-bye-East towards the lower end of Lake Champlain, always keeping to the high-ground with the falling snow to fill our tracks behind us. For four days we travelled when we were well up the west side. We had crossed numbers of trails but they were all full of old snow and not worth regarding— still we were so far from our post that in event of encountering any numbers of the Enemy we had but small hope of a safe return and had therefore to observe the greatest caution.

As we were making our way an immense painter so menaced us that we were forced to fire our guns to dispatch him. He was found to be very old, his teeth almost gone, and was in the last stages of starvation. We were much alarmed at this misadventure, fearing the Enemy might hear us or see the ravens gathering above, so we crossed the Lake that night on some new ice to blind our trail, where I broke through in one place and was only saved by Shanks, who got hold of my eel-skin que, thereby having something to pull me out with. We got into a deep gully, and striking flint made a fire to dry me and I did not suffer inconvenience.

The day following we took a long circle and came out on the lower end of the Lake, there laying two days in ambush, watching the Lake for any parties coming or going. Before dark a Mohigon came in from watch saying that men were coming down the Lake. We gathered at the point and saw seven of the Enemy come slowly on. There were three indians two Canadians and a French officer. Seeing they would shortly pass under our point of land we made ready to fire, and did deliver one fire as they came nigh, but the guns of our Mohigons failed to explode, they being old and well nigh useless, so that all the damage we did was to kill one indian and wound a Canadian, who was taken in hand by his companions who made off down the shore and went into the bush. We tried to head them unsuccessfully, and after examining the guns of our indians we feared they were so disabled that we gave up and retreated down the Lake, travelling all night. Near morning we saw a small fire which we spied out only to find a large party of the Enemy, whereat we were much disturbed, for our travelling had exhausted us and we feared the pursuit of a fresh enemy as soon as morning should come to show them our trail. We then made our way as fast as possible until late that night, when we laid down for refreshment. We built no fire but could not sleep for fear of the Enemy for it was a bright moonlight, and sure enough we had been there but a couple of hours when we saw the Enemy coming on our track. We here abandoned our bear-skins with what provissions we had left and ran back on our trail toward the advancing party. It was dark in the forest and we hoped they might not discover our back track for some time, thus giving us a longer start. This ruse was successful. After some hours travel I became so exhausted that I stopped to rest, whereat the Mohigans left us, but Shanks bided with me, though urging me to move forward. After a time I got strength to move on. Shanks said the Canadians would come up with us if we did not make fast going of it, and that they would disembowel us or tie us to a tree and burn us as was their usual way, for we could in no wise hope to make head against so large a party. Thus we walked steadily till high noon, when my wretched strength gave out so that I fell down saying I had as leave die there as elsewhere. Shanks followed back on our trail, while I fell into a drouse but was so sore I could not sleep. After a time I heard a shot, and shortly two more, when Shanks came running back to me. He had killed an advancing indian and stopped them for a moment. He kicked me vigorously, telling me to come on, as the indians would soon come on again. I got up, and though I could scarcely move I was minded diligently to persevere after Shanks. Thus we staggered on until near night time, when we again stopped and I fell into a deep sleep, but the enemy did not again come up. On the following day we got into Fort Edward, where I was taken with a distemper, was seized with very grevious pains in the head and back and a fever. They let blood and

gave me a physic, but I did not get well around for some time. For this sickness I have always been thankful, otherwise I should have been with Major Rogers in his unfortunate battle, which has become notable enough, where he was defeated by the Canadians and Indians and lost nigh all his private men, only escaping himself by a miracle. We mourned the loss of many friends who were our comrades, though it was not the fault of any one, since the Enemy had three times the number of the Rangers and hemmed them in. Some of the Rangers had surrendered under promise of Quarter, but we afterwards heard that they were tied to trees and hacked to death because the indians had found a scalp in the breast of a man's hunting frock, thus showing that we could never expect such bloody minded villiains to keep their promises of Quarter.

I was on several scouts against them that winter but encountered nothing worthy to relate excepting the hardships which fell to a Ranger's lot. In June the Army having been gathered we proceeded under Abercromby up the Lake to attack Ticonderoga. I thought at the time that so many men must be invincible, but since the last war I have been taught to know different. There were more Highlanders, Grenadiers, Provincial troops, Artillery and Rangers than the eye could compass, for the Lake was black with their battoes. This concourse proceeded to Ticondaroga where we had a great battle and lost many men, but to no avail since we were forced to return.

The British soldiers were by this time made servicible for forest warfare, since the officers and men had been forced to rid themselves of their useless incumbrances and had cut off the tails of their long coats till they scarcely reached below thir middles —they had also left the women at the Fort, browned thir gun barrels and carried thir provisions on their backs, each man enough for himself, as was our Ranger custom. The army was landed at the foot of the Lake, where the Rangers quickly drove off such small bodies of Frenchers and Indians as

Paddling the Wounded British Officer. *Painting in George F. Harding Museum, Chicago.*

opposed us, and we began our march by the rapids. Rogers men cleared the way and had a most desperate fight with some French who were minded to stop us, but we shortly killed and captured most of them. We again fell in with them that afternoon and were challenged Qui vive but answered that we were French, but they were not deceived and fired upon us, after which a hot skirmish insued during which Lord Howe was shot through the breast, for which we were all much depressed, because he was our real leader and had raised great hopes of success for us. The Rangers had liked him because he was wont to spend much time talking with them in thir camps and used also to go on scouts. The Rangers were not over fond of British officers in general.

When the time had come for battle we Rangers moved forward, accompanied by the armed boatmen and the Provincial troops. We drove in the French pickets and came into the open where the trees were felled tops toward us in a mighty abbatis, as thiough blown down by the wind. It was all we could undertake to make our way through the mass, and all the while the great breast-works of the French belched cannon and musket balls while the limbs and splinters flew around us. Then out of the woods behind us issued the heavy red masses of the British troops advancing in battle array with purpose to storm with the bayonet. The maze of fallen trees with their withered leaves hanging broke their ranks, and the French Retrenchment blazed fire and death. They advanced bravely up but all to no good purpose, and hundreds there met their death. My dear Joseph I have the will but not the way to tell you all I saw that awful afternoon. I have since been in many battles and skirmishes, but I never have witnessed such slaughter and such wild fighting as the British storm of Ticondaroga. We became mixed up—Highlanders, Grenadiers, Light Troops, Rangers and all, and we beat against that mass of logs and maze of fall-end timber and we beat in vain. I was once carried right up to the breastwork, but we were stopped by the bristling mass of sharpened branches, while the French fire swept us front and flank. The ground was covered deep with dying men, and as I think it over now I can remember nothing but the fruit bourne by the tree of war, for I looked upon so many wonderous things that July day that I could not set them downe at all. We drew off after seeing that human valor could not take that work. We Rangers then skirmished with the French colony troops and the Canada indians until dark while our people rescued the wounded, and then we fell back. The Army was utterly demoralized and made a headlong retreat, during which many wounded men were left to die in the woods. Shanks and I paddled a light bark canoe down the Lake next day, in the bottom of which lay a wounded British officer attended by his servant.

I took my discharge, and lived until the following Spring with Vrooman at German Flats, when I had a desire to go again to the more active service of the Rangers, for living in camps and scouting, notwithstanding its dangers, was agreeable to my taste in those days. So back to Albany I started, and there met Major Rogers, whom I acquainted with my desire to again join his service, whereat he seemed right glad to put me downe. I accordingly journeyed to Crown Point, where I went into camp. I had bought me a new fire-lock at Albany which was provided with a bayonet. It was short, as is best fitted for the bush, and about 45 balls to the pound. I had shot it ten times on trial and it had not failed to discharge at each pull. There was a great change in the private men of the Rangers, so many old ones had been frost bitten and gone home. I found my friend Shanks, who had staid though he had been badly frosted during the winter. He had such a hate of the Frenchers and particularly of the Canada Indians that he would never cease to fight them, they having killed all his relatives in New Hampshire which made him bitter against them, he always saying that they might as well kill him and thus make an end of the family.

In June I went north down Champlain with 250 Rangers and Light Infantry in sloop-vessels. The Rangers . . . . were . . . . (writing lost) . . . . but it made no difference. The party was landed on the west side of the Lake near Isle au Noix and lay five days in the bush, it raining hard all the time. I was out with a recoinnoitering party to watch the Isle, and very early in the morning we saw the French coming to our side in boats, whereat we acquainted Major Rogers that the French were about to attack us. We were drawn up in line to await their coming. The forest always concealed a Ranger line, so that there might not have been a man within a hundred miles for all that could be seen, and so it was that an advance party of the Enemy walked into our line and were captured, which first appraised the French of our position. They shortly attacked us on our left, but I was sent with a party to make our way through a swamp in order to attack their rear. This we accomplished so quietly that we surprized some Canada indians who were lying back of the French line listening to a prophet who was incanting. These we slew, and after our firing many French grenadiers came running past, when they broke before our line. I took a Frenchman prisoner, but he kept his bayonet pointed at me, all the time yelling in French which I did not understand, though I had my loaded gun pointed at him. He seemed to be disturbed at the sight of a scalp which I had hanging in my belt. I had lately took it from the head of an Indian, it being my first, but I was not minded to kill the poor Frenchman and was saying so in English. He put down his fire-lock finally and offered me his flask to drink liquor with him, but I did not use it. I had known that Shanks carried poisoned liquor in his pack, with the hope that it would destroy any indians who might come into possession of it, if he was taken, whether alive or dead. As I was escorting the Frenchman back to our boats he quickly ran away from me, though I snapped my fire-lock at him, which failed to explode, it having become wet from the rain. Afterwards I heard that a Ranger had shot him, seeing him running in the bush.

We went back to our boats after this victory and took all our wounded and dead with us, which last we buried on an island. Being joined by a party of Stockbridge Indians we were again landed, and after marching for some days came to a road where we recoinnoitered St. John's Fort but did not attack it, Rogers judging it not to be takeable with our force. From here we began to march so fast that only the strongest men could keep up, and at daybreak came to another Fort. We ran into the gate while a hay-waggon was passing through, and surprised and captured all the garrison, men women and children. After we had burned and destroyed everything we turned the women and children adrift, but drove the men along as prisoners, making them carry our packs. We marched so fast that the French grenadiers could not keep up, for their breeches were too tight for them to march with ease, whereat we cut off the legs of them with our knives, when they did better.

After this expedition we scouted from Crown Point in canoes, Shanks and myself going as far north as we dared toward Isle au Noix, and one day while lying on the bank we saw the army coming. It was an awsome sight to see so many boats filled with brave uniforms, as they danced over the waves. The Rangers and indians came a half a mile ahead of the Army in whale-boats all in line abreast, while behind them came the light Infantry and Grenadiers with Provincial troops on the flanks and Artillery and Store boats bringing up the Rear.

Shanks and I fell in with the Ranger boats, being yet in our small bark and much hurled about by the waves, which rolled prodigious.

The Army continued up the Lake and drove the Frenchers out of their Forts, they not stopping to resist us till we got to Chamblee, where we staid. But the French in Canada had all surrendered to the British and the war was over. This ended my service as a Ranger in those parts. I went back to Vroomans intending to go again into the indian trade, for now we hoped that the French would no longer be able to stop our enterprises.

Now my dear son—I will send you this long letter, and will go on writing of my later life in the Western country and in the War of Independence, and will send you those letters as soon as I have them written. I did not do much or occupy a commanding position, but I served faithfully in what I had to do. For the present God bless you my dear son.

JOSHUA GOODENOUGH.

Massai's Crooked Trail

It is a bold person who will dare to say that a wilder savage ever lived than an Apache Indian, and in this respect no Apache can rival Massai.

He was a *bronco* Chiricahua whose *tequa* tracks were so long and devious that all of them can never be accounted for. Three regiments of cavalry, all the scouts—both white and black—and Mexicans galore had their hack, but the ghostly presence appeared and disappeared from the Colorado to the Yaqui. No one can tell how Massai's face looks, or looked, though hundreds know the shape of his footprint.

The Seventh made some little killings, but they fear that Massai was not among the game. There surely is or was such a person as Massai. He developed himself slowly, as I will show by the Sherlock Holmes methods of the chief of scouts, though even he only got so far, after all. Massai manifested himself like the dust-storm or the morning mist—a shiver in the air, and gone. The chief walked his horse slowly back on the lost trail in disgust, while the scouts bobbed along behind perplexed. It was always so. Time has passed, and Massai, indeed, seems gone, since he appears no more. The hope in the breasts of countless men is nearly blighted; they no longer expect to see Massai's head brought into camp done up in an old shirt and dropped triumphantly on the ground in front of the chief of scouts' tent, so it is time to preserve what trail we can.

Three troops of the Tenth had gone into camp for the night, and the ghostly Montana landscape hummed with the murmur of many men. Supper was over, and I got the old Apache chief of scouts behind his own ducking, and demanded what he knew of an Apache Indian down in Arizona named Massai. He knew all or nearly all that any white man will ever know.

"All right," said the chief, as he lit a cigar and tipped his sombrero over his left eye, "but let me get it straight. Massai's trail was so crooked, I had to study nights to keep it arranged in my head. He didn't leave much more trail than a buzzard, anyhow, and it took years to unravel it. But I am anticipating.

"I was chief of scouts at Apache in the fall of '90, when word was brought in that an Indian girl named Natastale had disappeared, and that her mother was found under a walnut-tree with a bullet through her body. I immediately sent Indian scouts to take the trail. They found the tracks of a mare and colt going by the spot, and thinking it would bring them to the girl, they followed it. Shortly they found a moccasin track where a man had dismounted from the mare, and without paying more attention to the horse track, they followed it. They ran down one of my own scouts in a *tiswin** camp, where he was carousing with other drinkers. They sprang on him, got him by the hair, disarmed and bound him. Then they asked him what he had done with the girl, and why he had killed the mother

* An intoxicating beverage made of corn.

to which he replied that 'he did not know.' When he was brought to me, about dark, there was intense excitement among the Indians, who crowded around demanding Indian justice on the head of the murderer and ravisher of the women. In order to save his life I took him from the Indians and lodged him in the post guard-house. On the following morning, in order to satisfy myself positively that this man had committed the murder, I sent my first sergeant, the famous Mickey Free, with a picked party of trailers, back to the walnut-tree, with orders to go carefully over the trail and run down the mare and colt, or find the girl, dead or alive, wherever they might.

"In two hours word was sent to me that the trail was running to the north. They had found the body of the colt with its throat cut, and were following the mare. The trail showed that a man afoot was driving the mare, and scouts thought the girl was on the mare. This proved that we had the wrong man in custody. I therefore turned him loose, telling him he was all right. In return he told me that he owned the mare and colt, and that when he passed the tree the girl was up in its branches, shaking down nuts which her mother was gathering. He had ridden along, and about an hour afterwards had heard a shot. He turned his mare loose, and proceeded on foot to the *tiswin* camp, where he heard later that the old woman had been shot and the girl 'lifted.' When arrested, he knew that the other scouts had trailed him from the walnut-tree; he saw the circumstances against him, and was afraid.

"On the night of the second day Mickey Free's party returned, having run the trail to within a few hundred yards of the camp of Alcashay in the Forestdale country, between whose band and the band to which the girl belonged there was a blood-feud. They concluded that the murderer belonged to Alcashay's camp, and were afraid to engage him.

"I sent for Alcashay to come in immediately, which he did, and I demanded that he trail the man and deliver him up to me, or I would take my scout corps, go to his camp,

and arrest all suspicious characters. He stoutly denied that the man was in his camp, promised to do as I directed, and, to further allay any suspicions, he asked for my picked trailers to help run the trail. With this body of men he proceeded on the track, and they found that it ran right around his camp, then turned sharply to the east, ran within two hundred yards of a stage-ranch, thence into some rough mountain country, where it twisted and turned for forty miles. At this point they found the first camp the man had made. He had tied the girl to a tree by the feet, which permitted her to sleep on her back; the mare had been killed, some steaks taken out, and some meat 'jerked.' From thence on they could find no trail which they could follow. At long intervals they found his moccasin mark between rocks, but after circling for miles they gave it up. In this camp they found and brought to me a fire-stick—the first and only one I had ever seen—and they told me that the fire-stick had not been used by Apaches for many years. There were only a few old men in my camp who were familiar with its use, though one managed to light his cigarette with it. They reasoned from this that the man was a bronco Indian who had been so long 'out' that he could not procure matches, and also that he was a much wilder one than any of the Indians then known to be outlawed.

"In about a week there was another Indian girl stolen from one of my hay-camps, and many scouts thought it was the same Indian, who they decided was one of the well-known outlaws; but older and better men did not agree with them; so there the matter rested for some months.

"In the spring the first missing girl rode into Fort Apache on a fine horse, which was loaded down with buckskins and other Indian finery. Two cowboys followed her shortly and claimed the pony, which bore a C C C brand, and I gave it up to them. I took the girl into my office, for she was so tired that she could hardly stand up, while she was haggard and worn to the last degree. When she had sufficiently recovered

Scouts. *Authors' photoengraving.*

she told me her story. She said she was up in the walnut-tree when an Indian shot her mother, and coming up, forced her to go with him. He trailed and picked up the mare, bound her on its back, and drove it along. The colt whinnied, whereupon he cut its throat. He made straight for Alcashay's camp, which he circled, and then turned sharply to the east, where he made the big twisting through the mountains which my scouts found. After going all night and the next day, he made the first camp. After killing and cooking the mare, he gave her something to eat, tied her up by the feet, and standing over her, told her that he was getting to be an old man, was tired of making his own fires, and wanted a woman. If she was a good girl he would not kill her, but would treat her well and always have venison hanging up. He continued that he was going away for a few hours, and would come back and kill her if she tried to undo the cords; but she fell asleep while he was talking. After daylight he returned, untied her, made her climb on his back, and thus carried her for a long distance. Occasionally he made her alight where the ground was hard, telling her if she made any 'sign' he would kill her, which made her careful of her steps.

"After some miles of this blinding of the trail they came upon a white horse that was tied to a tree. They mounted double, and rode all day as fast as he could lash the pony, until, near nightfall, it fell from exhaustion, whereupon he killed it and cooked some of the carcass. The bronco Indian took himself off for a couple of hours, and when he returned, brought another horse, which they mounted, and sped onward through the moonlight all night long. On that morning they were in the high mountains, the poor pony suffering the same fate as the others.

"They stayed here two days, he tying her up whenever he went hunting, she being so exhausted after the long flight that she lay comatose in her bonds. From thence they journeyed south slowly, keeping to the high mountains, and only once did he speak, when he told her that a certain mountain pass was the home of the Chiricahuas. From the girl's account she must have gone far south into the Sierra Madre of Old Mexico, though of course she was long since lost.

"He killed game easily, she tanned the hides, and they lived as man and wife. Day by day they threaded their way through the deep cañons and over the Blue Mountain ranges. By this time he had become fond of the White Mountain girl, and told her that he was Massai, a Chiricahua warrior; that he had been arrested after the Geronimo war and sent East on the railroad over two years since, but had escaped one night from the train, and had made his way alone back to his native deserts. Since then it is known that an Indian did turn up missing, but it was a big band of prisoners, and some births had occurred, which made the checking off come straight. He was not missed at the time. From what the girl said, he must have got off east of Kansas City and travelled south and then west, till at last he came to the lands of the Mescalero Apaches, where he stayed for some time. He was over a year making this journey, and told the girl that no human eye ever saw him once in that time. This is all he ever told the girl Natastale, and she was afraid to ask him more. Beyond these mere facts, it is still a midnight prowl of a human coyote through a settled country for twelve hundred miles, the hardihood of the undertaking being equalled only by the instinct which took him home.

"Once only while the girl was with him did they see sign of other Indians, and straightway Massai turned away—his wild nature shunning even the society of his kind.

"At times 'his heart was bad,' and once he sat brooding for a whole day, finally telling her that he was going into a bad country to kill Mexicans, that women were a burden on a warrior, and that he had made up his mind to kill her. All through her narrative he seemed at times to be overcome with this blood-thirst, which took the form of a homicidal melancholia. She begged so hard for her life that he relented; so he left her in the wild tangle of mountains while he raided on the Mexican settlements. He came back with horses and powder and lead. This last was in Winchester bullets, which he melted up and recast into .50-calibre balls made in moulds of cactus sticks. He did not tell how many murders he had committed during these raids, but doubtless many.

"They lived that winter through in the Sierras, and in the spring started north, crossing the railroad twice, which meant the Guaymas and the Southern Pacific. They sat all one day on a high mountain and watched the trains of cars to by; but 'his heart got bad' at the sight of them, and again he concluded to kill the girl. Again she begged off, and they continued up the range of the Mogollons. He was unhappy in his mind during all this journey, saying men were scarce up here, that he must go back to Mexico and kill some one.

"He was tired of the woman, and did not want her to go back with him, so, after sitting all day on a rock while she besought him, the old wolf told her to go home in peace. But the girl was lost, and told him that either the Mexicans or Americans would kill her if she departed from him; so his mood softened, and telling her to come on, he began the homeward journey. They passed through a small American town in the middle of the night—he having previously taken off the Indian rawhide shoes from the ponies. They crossed the Gila near the Nau Taw Mountains. Here he stole two fresh horses, and loading one with all the buckskins, he put her on and headed her down the Eagle Trail to Black River. She now knew where she was, but was nearly dying from the exhaustion of his fly-by-night expeditions. He halted her, told her to 'tell the white officer that she was a pretty good girl, better than the San Carlos woman, and that he would come again and get another.' He struck her horse and was gone.

"Massai then became a problem to successive chiefs of scouts, a bugbear to the reservation Indians, and a terror to Arizona. If a man was killed or a woman missed, the Indians came galloping and the scouts lay on his trail. If he met a woman in the defiles, he stretched her dead if she did not please his errant fancy. He took potshots at the men ploughing in their little fields, and knocked the Mexican bulldrivers on the head as they plodded through the blinding dust of the Globe Road. He even sat like a vulture on the rim-rock and signalled the Indians to come out and talk. When two Indians thus accosted did go out, they found themselves looking down Massai's .50-calibre, and were tempted to do his bidding. He sent one in for sugar and coffee, holding the brother, for such he happened to be, as a hostage till the sugar and coffee came. Then he told them that he was going behind a rock to lie down, cautioning them not to move for an hour. That was an unnecessary bluff, for they did not wink an eye till sundown. Later than this he stole a girl in broad daylight in the face of a San Carlos camp and dragged her up the rocks. Here he was attacked by fifteen or twenty bucks, whom he stood off until darkness. When they reached his lair in the morning, there lay the dead girl, but Massai was gone.

"I never saw Massai but once, and then it was only a piece of his G string flickering in the brush. We had followed his trail half the night, and just at daylight, as we ascended a steep part of the mountains, I caught sight of a pony's head looking over a bush. We advanced rapidly, only to find the horse grunting from a stab wound in the belly, and the little camp scattered around about him. The shirt tail flickering in the brush was all of Massai. We followed on, but he had gone down a steep bluff. We went down too, thus exposing ourselves to draw his fire so that we could locate him, but he was not tempted.

"The late Lieutenant Clark had much the same view of this mountain outlaw, and since those days two young men of the Seventh Cavalry, Rice and Averill, have on separate occasions crawled on his camp at the break of day, only to see Massai go out of sight in the brush like a blue quail.

"Lieutenant Averill, after a forced march of eighty-six miles, reached a hostile camp near morning, after climbing his detachment, since midnight, up the almost inaccessible rocks, in hopes of surprising the camp. He divided his force into three parts, and tried, as well as possible, to close every avenue of escape; but as the camp was on a high rocky hill at the junction of four deep cañons, this was found impracticable. At daylight the savages came out together, running like deer, and making for the cañons. The soldiers fired, killing a buck and accidentally wounding a squaw, but Massai simply disappeared.

"That's the story of Massai. It is not as long as his trail," said the chief of scouts.

An Interesting Detail

By order of General Miles, Lieutenant Guy H. Preston, of the Ninth Cavalry, proceeds to Alaska in charge of all the pack-trains of the army.

I do not know that this distinguished duty conferred on Lieutenant Preston is a direct recognition of his heroism at the Wounded Knee fight, but certainly it recalls it.

He was with the Seventh Cavalry because he was in command of some of Taylor's Indian scouts. The fight had simmered down from a desperate hand-to-hand encounter at the outset to a desultory skirmish up the ravine, where surviving Indians had sheltered under the "cut-banks," and were doing damage to the troops.

The commanding officer desired to send a despatch to General Brooks at the Agency, acquainting him with the details of the engagement and the crippled condition of his force. After hastily preparing the missive, the Colonel looked hesitatingly about him at the officers standing near, and his gaze fell on the scout officer. He asked him "if he supposed he could get the despatch to General Brooks," and the young officer said, "I could try, sir."

The country was full of Indians, and the news of the unlooked-for engagement was travelling all over the Sioux country as fast as ponies could run. So it was exceedingly problematical as to whether he could get over the intervening eighteen miles alive.

The Colonel gave him the message, and directed him to select the fastest and best horse on the lines, and go quickly. At the picket-lines he called for the best horse there, and the soldiers gathered about to canvass the subject. There was one big bay celebrated for long-distance running. He was stripped of all surplus accoutrements. Then the Lieutenant called the soldiers who were about to come to him, and there stated his business, warning them of its danger, and asking for one volunteer. A soldier named Fellman stepped out, saying, "I will go with you, Lieutenant." He was told to strip himself and horse, which he quickly did. While this momentary wait was in progress Preston saw Captain Garlington lying there wounded, and running over, wrote a short telegram to his friends, and shaking his good arm, bade him good-by.

The Lieutenant and Fellman mounted and galloped off on the dangerous duty, while up the ravine the last scattering shots of a celebrated affair came to their ears. The soldier had a carbine and Preston a six-shooter. They skirted the half-acre of dead, wounded, and dying people where the brunt of the fight had been, hoping to get to the Fast-Horse Road, which made it only fifteen miles to the Agency. There they met Baptiste Garuier, or "Little Bat," the famous scout, with his comrades, who asked the Lieutenant where he was going. He told him; but the scout entreated him "for God's sake not to do that—that the Indians at the Agency, including Short Bull's band, just coaxed in from the Bad Lands, would hear of the fight from deserting Indian scouts before the Lieutenant's horse could get there, if they had not already heard. He assured the officer that they would all come skimming down the Fast-Horse Road to participate in the fight or to cut off any small bodies of troops, and told him he would run into them and be killed beyond the shadow of a doubt. He insisted that Preston go up the creek and take the Freight Road," which he did, thereby escaping what we now know was certain death.

The two soldiers then started on the dead run—good horses, a crisp day, and a known road. It was a ride for life. Preston put the despatch in the breast pocket of his blouse, telling Fellman, if he was potted, to take the paper and go on.

Twice at high points on the Freight Road they saw Indians in bands going to the Wounded Knee on the Fast-Horse Road, where they shortly after attacked Captain Jackson's detached force. Once the Indians saw the two straining troopers, and took "across lots" after them; but they soon discovered that the soldiers had the lead, the inside track, and the best horses; still they gave them a good race for a long distance.

Any one who has ever ridden will know that eighteen miles is a very long road at the top pace; and the Lieutenant arrived at the Agency limits in one hour, but that was some little distance from the soldier camp. The horses were "weaving" badly and staggering. The ride was made by taking the gallop up straight inclines, fast trot if steep, and the dead run (to spur) if down hill, no matter how steep or gentle, thereby making all the heavy gains in time by the down-hill work.

The hills outside of the soldier pickets were full of mounted Indians, but, with a final spurt, the two brave men went through and reached the General's tent. Here Fellman fell from his horse in a dead faint, but the first news of the Wounded Knee came in.

Such things and taking mules to the arctic regions are soldiering. Between Ringold and the Klondike, an officer hesitates between spending his money for Esquimau furs or India-silk pajamas.

The Curse of the Wolves

It was hoped, and seemed to be true, that the wolves would follow the buffalo into oblivion, but they did not do what was expected of them. When the game was cleaned out of the West, the cattle came in and the wolves developed a taste for beef just as the Indian did—perforce.

The cow-men fought them with rifle, trap, dog and poison, but the *lovo* is a smart and tenacious animal, gradually able to comprehend all these methods and to get out of their way.

They take the calves first, and then the cows; but a band of wolves can pull down the biggest steer.

The cattle made out to fight the smaller coyotes. On one big ranch I have seen a part of the cows stay with the small calves, while the other half went to water. But the range cattle never were able to cope with the big gray wolves. A rush of wolves into a band of cattle will send them off in a bawling rush, leaving one of their number a victim.

It is quite disheartening to think that such a pest cannot be gotten rid of in this advanced day; but I am afraid the cattle interest will have to put some professional wolf hunter down in the profit and loss columns before it is done.

The Essentials at Fort Adobe

The Indian suns himself before the door of his tepee, dreaming of the past. For a long time now he has eaten of the white man's lotos—the bimonthly beef-issue. I looked on him and wondered at the new things. The buffalo, the war-path, all are gone. What of the cavalrymen over at Adobe—his Nemesis in the stirring days— are they, too, lounging in barracks, since his lordship no longer leads them trooping over the burning flats by day and through the ragged hills by night? I will go and see.

The blistered faces of men, the gaunt horses dragging stiffly along to the cruel spurring, the dirty lack-lustre of campaigning—that, of course, is no more. Will it be parades, and those soul-deadening "fours right" and "column left" affairs? Oh, my dear, let us hope not.

Nothing is so necessary in the manufacture of soldiers, sure enough, but it is not hard to learn, and once a soldier knows it I can never understand why it should be drilled into him until it hurts. Besides, from another point of view, soldiers in rows and lines do not compose well in pictures. I always feel, after seeing infantry drill in an armory, like Kipling's light-house keeper, who went insane looking at the cracks between the boards—they were all so horribly alike.

Then Adobe is away out West in the blistering dust, with no towns of any importance near it. I can understand why men might become listless when they are at field-work, with the full knowledge that nothing

but their brothers are looking at them save the hawks and coyotes. It is different from Meyer, with its traps full of Congressmen and girls, both of whom are much on the minds of cavalrymen.

In due course I was bedded down at Adobe by my old friend the Captain, and then lay thinking of this cavalry business. It is a subject which thought does not simplify, but, like other great things, makes it complicate and recede from its votaries. To know essential details from unessential details is the study in all arts. Details there must be; they are the small things that make the big things. To apply this general order of things to this arm of the service kept me awake. There is first the riding—simple enough if they catch you young. There are bits, saddles, and cavalry packs. I know men who have not spoken to each other in years because they disagree about these. There are the sore backs and colics—that is a profession in itself. There are judgment of pace, the battle tactics, the use of three very different weapons; there is a world of history in this, in forty languages. Then an ever-varying *terrain* tops all. There are other things not confined to cavalry, but regarded by all soldiers. The crowning peculiarity of cavalry is the rapidity of its movement, whereby a commander can lose the carefully built up reputation of years in about the time it takes a school-boy to eat a marsh-mallow. After all, it is surely a hard profession—a very blind trail to fame. I am glad I am not a cavalryman; still, it is the

The Advance. *Authors' photoengraving.*

happiest kind of fun to look on when you are not responsible; but it needs some cultivation to understand and appreciate.

I remember a dear friend who had a taste for out-of-doors. He penetrated deeply into the interior not long since to see these same troopers do a line of heroics, with a band of Bannocks to support the rôle. The Indians could not finally be got on the centre of the stage, but made hot-foot for the agency. My friend could not see any good in all this, nor was he satisfied with the first act even. He must needs have a climax, and that not forthcoming, he loaded his disgust into a trunk line and brought it back to his club corner here in New York. He there narrated the failure of his first night; said the soldiers were not even dusty as advertised; damned the Indians keenly, and swore at the West by all his gods.

There was a time when I, too, regarded not the sketches in this art, but yearned for the finished product. That, however, is not exhibited generally over once in a generation.

At Adobe there are only eight troops— not enough to make a German nurse-girl turn her head in the street, and my friend from New York, with his Napoleonic largeness, would scoff out loud. But he and the nurse do not understand the significance; they have not the eyes to see. A starboard or a port horseshoe would be all one to them, and a crease in the saddle-blanket the smallest thing in the world, yet it might spoil a horse.

When the trumpets went in the morning I was sorry I had thought at all. It was not light yet, and I clung to my pillow. Already this cavalry has too much energy for my taste.

"If you want to see anything, you want to lead out," said the Captain, as he pounded me with a boot.

"Say, Captain, I suppose Colonel Hamilton issues this order to get up at this hour, doesn't he?"

"He does."

"Well, he has to obey his own order, then, doesn't he?"

"He does."

I took a good long stretch and yawn, and what I said about Colonel Hamilton I will not commit to print, out of respect to the Colonel. Then I got up.

This bitterness of bed-parting passes. The Captain said he would put a "cook's police" under arrest for appearing in my make-up; but all these details will be forgotten, and whatever happens at this hour should be forgiven. I had just come from the North, where I had been sauntering over the territory of Montana with some Indians and a wild man from Virginia, getting up before light—tightening up on coffee and bacon for twelve hours in the saddle to prepare for more bacon and coffee; but at Adobe I had hoped for, even if I did not expect, some repose.

In the east there was a fine green coming over the sky. No one out of the painter guild would have admitted it was green, even on the rack, but what I mean is that you could not approach it in any other way. A nice little adjutant went jangling by on a hard-trotting thoroughbred, his shoulders high and his seat low. My old disease began to take possession of me; I could fairly feel the microbes generate. Another officer comes clattering, with his orderly following after. The fever has me. We mount, and we are off, all going to stables.

Out from the corrals swarm the troopers, leading their unwilling mounts. The horses are saying, "Damn the Colonel!" One of them comes in arching bounds; he is saying worse of the Colonel, or maybe only cussing out his own recruit for pulling his *cincha* too tight. They form troop lines in column, while the Captains throw open eyes over the things which would not interest my friend from New York or the German nurse-girl.

The two forward troops are the enemy, and are distinguished by wearing brown canvas stable-frocks. These shortly move out through the post, and are seen no more.

Now comes the sun. By the shades of Knickerbocker's *History of New York* I seem now to have gotten at the beginning; but patience, the sun is no detail out in the arid country. It does more things than blister your nose. It is the despair of the painter as it colors the minarets of the Bad Lands which abound around Adobe, and it dries up the company gardens if they don't watch the *acequias* mighty sharp. To one just out of bed it excuses existence. I find I begin to soften towards the Colonel. In fact, it is possible that he is entirely right about having his old trumpets blown around garrison at this hour, though it took the Captain's boot to prove it shortly since.

The command moves out, trotting quickly through the blinding clouds of dust. The landscape seems to get right up and mingle with the excitement. The supple, well-trained horses lose the scintillation on their coats, while Uncle Sam's blue is growing mauve very rapidly. But there is a useful look about the men, and the horses show condition after their long practice march just finished. Horses much used to go under saddle have well-developed quarters and strong stifle action. Fact is, nothing looks like a horse with a harness on. That is a job for mules, and these should have a labor organization and monopolize it.

The problem of the morning was that we as an advance were to drive the two troops which had gone on ahead. These in turn were to represent a rapidly retiring rear-guard. This training is more that troops may be handled with expedition, and that the men may gather the thing, rather than that officers should do brilliant things, which they might undertake on their own responsibility in time of war, such as pushing rapidly by on one flank and cutting out a rear-guard.

Grievous and very much to be commiserated is the task of the feeling historian who writes of these paper wars. He may see possibilities or calamities which do not signify. The morning orders provide against genius, and who will be able to estimate the surgical possibilities of blank cartridges? The sergeant-major cautioned me not to indicate by my actions what I saw as we rode to the top of a commanding hill. The enemy had abandoned the stream because their retreat would have been exposed to fire. They made a stand back in the hills. The advance felt the stream quickly, and passed, fanning out to develop. The left flank caught their fire, whereat the centre and right came around at top speed. But this is getting so serious.

The scene was crowded with little pictures, all happening quickly—little dots of horsemen gliding quickly along the yellow landscape, leaving long trails of steely dust in their wake. A scout comes trotting along, his face set in an expectant way, carbine advanced. A man on a horse is a vigorous, forceful thing to look at. It embodies the liveliness of nature in its most attractive form, especially when a gun and sabre are attached. When both living equations are young, full of oats and bacon, imbued with military ideas, and trained to the hour, it always seems to me that the ghost of a tragedy stalks at their side. This is why the polo-player does not qualify sentimentally. But what is one man beside two troops which come shortly in two solid chunks, with horses snorting and sending the dry landscape in a dusty pall for a quarter of a mile in the rear? It is good—ah! it is worth any one's while; but stop and think, what if we could magnify that? Tut, tut! as I said before, that only happens once in a generation. Adobe doesn't dream; it simply does its morning's work.

The rear-guard have popped at our advance, which exchanges with them. Their fire grows slack, and from our vantage we can see them mount quickly and flee.

After two hours of this we shake hands with the hostiles and trot home to breakfast.

These active, hard-riding, straight-shooting, open-order men are doing real work, and are not being stupefied by drill-ground routine, or rendered listless by file-closer prompting or sleepy reiteration.

By the time the command dismounts in front of stables we turn longingly to the thoughts of breakfast. Every one has completely forgiven the Colonel, though I have no doubt he will be equally unpopular tomorrow morning.

But what do I see—am I faint? No; it has happened again. It looks as though I saw a soldier jump over a horse. I moved on him.

"Did I see you—" I began.

"Oh yes, sir—you see," returned a little soldier, who ran with the mincing steps of an athlete towards his horse, and landed standing up on his hind quarters, whereupon he settled down quietly into his saddle.

Others began to gyrate over and under their horses in a dizzy way. Some had taken their saddles off and now sat on their horses' bellies, while the big dog-like animals lay on their backs, with their feet in the air. It was circus business, or what they call "short and long horse" work—some not understandable phrase. Every one does it. While I am not unaccustomed to looking at cavalry, I am being perpetually surprised by the lengths to which our cavalry is carrying this Coassack drill. It is beginning to be nothing short of marvellous.

In the old days this thing was not known. Between building mud or log forts, working on the bull-train, marching or fighting, a man and a gun made a soldier; but it takes an education along with this now before he can qualify.

The regular work at Adobe went on during the day—guard mount, orders, inspection, and routine.

At the club I was asked, "Going out this afternoon with us?"

"Yes, he is going; his horse will be up at 4:30; he wants to see this cavalry," answered my friend the Captain for me.

"Yes; it's fine moonlight. The Colonel is going to an attack on Cossack posts out in the hills," said the adjutant.

So at five o'clock we again sallied out in the dust, the men in the ranks next me silhouetting one after the other more dimly until they disappeared in the enveloping cloud. They were cheerful, laughing and wondering one to another if Captain Garrard, the enemy, would get in on their pickets. He was regarded in the ranks as a sharp fellow, one to be well looked after.

At the line of hills where the Colonel stopped, the various troops were told off in their positions, while the long cool shadows of evening stole over the land, and the pale moon began to grow bolder over on the left flank.

I sat on a hill with a sergeant who knew history and horses. He remembered "Pansy," which had served sixteen years in the troop—and a first-rate old horse then; but a damned inspector with no soul came browsing around one day and condemned that old horse. Government got a measly ten dollars—or something like that. This ran along for a time; when one day they were trooping up some lonely valley, and, behold, there stood "Pansy," as thin as a snake, tied by a wickieup. He greeted the troop with joyful neighs. The soldiers asked the Captain to be allowed to shoot him, but of course he said no. I could not learn if he winked when he said it. The column wound over the hill, a carbine rang from its rear, and "Pansy" lay down in the dust without a kick. Death is better than an Indian for a horse. The thing was not noticed at the time, but made a world of fuss afterwards, though how it all came out the sergeant did not develop, nor was it necessary.

Night settled down on the quiet hills, and the dark spots of pickets showed dimly on the gray surface of the land. The Colonel inspected his line, and found everybody alert and possessed of a good working knowledge of picket duties at night—one of the most difficult duties enlisted men have to perform. It is astonishing how short is the distance at which we can see a picket even in this bright night on the open hills.

I sat on my horse by a sergeant at a point in the line where I suspected the attack would come. The sergeant thought he saw figures moving in a dry bottom before us. I could not see. A column of dust off to the left indicated troops, but we thought it a ruse of Garrard's. My sergeant, though, had really seen the enemy, and said, softly, "They are coming."

The bottom twinkled and popped with savage little yellow winks; bang! went a rifle in my ear; "whew!" snorted my big horse; and our picket went to the supports clattering.

The shots and yells followed fast. The Colonel had withdrawn the supports towards the post rapidly, leaving his picket-line in the air—a thing which happens in war; but he did not lose much of that line, I should say.

It was an interesting drill. Pestiferous little man disturbed nature, and it all seemed so absurd out there on those quiet gray hills. It made me feel, as I slowed down and gazed at the vastness of things, like a superior sort of bug. In the middle distance several hundred troops are of no more proportion than an old cow bawling through the hills after her wolf-eaten calf. If my mental vision were not distorted I should never have seen the manœuvre at all—only the moon and the land doing what they have done before for so long a time.

We reached Adobe rather late, when I found that the day's work had done wonders for my appetite. I reminded the Captain that I had broken his bread but once that day.

"It is enough for a Ninth Cavalry man," he observed. However, I out-flanked this brutal disregard for established customs, but it was "cold."

In the morning I resisted the Captain's boot, and protested that I must be let alone; which being so, I appeared groomed and breakfasted at a Christian hour, fully persuaded that as between an Indian and a Ninth Cavalry man I should elect to be an Indian.

Some one must have disciplined the Colonel. I don't know who it was. There is only one woman in a post who can, generally; but no dinners were spoiled at Adobe by night-cat affairs.

Instead, during the afternoon we were to see Captain Garrard, the hostile, try to save two troops which were pressed into the bend of a river by throwing over a bridge, while holding the enemy in check. This was as complicated as putting a baby to sleep while reading law; so clearly my point of view was with the hostiles. With them I entered the neck. The horses were grouped in the brush, leaving some men who were going underground like gophers out near the entrance. The brown-canvas-covered soldiers grabbed their axes, rolled their eyes towards the open plain, and listened expectantly.

The clear notes of a bugle rang; whackety, bang—clack—clack, went the axes. Trees fell all around. The forest seemed to drop on me. I got my horse and fled across the creek.

"That isn't fair; this stream is supposed to be impassable," sang out a lieutenant, who was doing a Blondin act on the first tree over, while beneath him yawned the chasm of four or five feet.

In less than a minute the whole forest got up again and moved towards the bridge. There were men behind it, but the leaves concealed them. Logs dropped over, brush piled on top. The rifles rang in scattered volleys, and the enemy's fire rolled out beyond the brush. No bullets whistled—that was a redeeming feature.

Aside from that it seemed as though every man was doing his ultimate act. They flew about; the shovels dug with despair; the sand covered the logs in a shower. While I am telling this the bridge was made.

The first horse came forward, led by his rider. He raised his eyes like St. Anthony; he did not approve of the bridge. He put his ears forward, felt with his toes, squatted behind, and made nervous side steps. The men moved on him in a solid crowd from behind. Stepping high and short he then bounded over, and after him in a stream came the willing brothers. Out along the bluffs strung the troopers to cover the heroes who had held the neck, while they destroyed the bridge.

Then they rode home with the enemy, chaffing each other.

It is only a workaday matter, all this; but workaday stuff does the business nowadays.

(Initial Piece) Soldier in Form of Letter T. *Drawing in George F. Harding Museum, Chicago.*

The Training of Cavalry

It was some two years since I had visited the cavalry post at Fort Myer, Virginia. At that time I had supposed that our new system of horse-training and Cossack riding had reached the limitations of man and beast. But on recently seeing the drill I was amazed to find that there are seemingly no bounds to this thing. The horses seem to use their brains almost as much as the riders use theirs, while in no circus which it has been my fortune to see has the riding equalled what all United States troopers can do at that post.

I fear almost to tell about it. I should not expect to be believed had not many thousands of delighted people witnessed the same feats by some of the same troopers at the admirable Military and Athletic Tournament held recently at the Madison Square Garden in New York.

In the first place, Colonel Sumner, commanding the Sixth Cavalry, said distinctly it was his policy not to permit anything like competition, as it would tend to the extra training of a few men at the expense of the others, and to its attendant jealousy or laxity. Consequently cooks, extra-duty men, and all other enlisted men at Fort Myer can do everything which one sees in the riding-hall. Every soldier is of necessity an athlete in training; he could not be otherwise. They are all Americans—a very high grade of young fellows—all good material for non-commissioned officers, and some for even higher honors if war should summon their energies. They are each and every one

finished horsemen as well as daring riders, not only practically, but theoretically.

Lieutenant Short of Troop A was good enough to initiate me into the opening secrets by taking two freshly arrived "remounts," not previously ridden or handled, to the riding-hall. Here he put on his "hackamore" in lieu of a bridle, and by a simple system of ropes running from broad straps around the pasterns to rings at the bottom of a broad leather surcingle he began. He slowly brought the horse to its knees, saying, "Lie—down—down—down." The horse fought, but not very hard, because Mr. Short was so patient and gentle with it. He sought not to excite or anger the animal. He would have taken all day if necessary, but after ten minutes the horse succumbed to the inevitable and lay down. It was petted and allowed to rise, when the other one was handled similarly. Thus the horses came to recognize that man was their master, and that they had nothing to fear from him.

These being particularly tractable beasts, Mr. Short said he would carry their training farther at that time, in my interest, although it was not the custom to do so, for fear of overdoing matters. He threw a horse, and upon its recovering its feet, mounted it bareback. The horse was dazed, and did not apparently mind this new indignity. It was then put through the "bending" movements by the easy leg pressure, to which it lent ready obedience. Then it was led up to a low brush hurdle at the end of a chute, and

Hurdling on Three Horses. *Painting on loan to Baltimore Museum of Art from 110th Field Artillery, Maryland National Guard, Pikesville Military Reservation.*

following a veteran troop-horse, was forced over the hurdle on a "lunge." After their first lesson these two horses were better broken than half the mounts one sees in the parks. All that remains is wrought out by patience, and never by any possibility is a horse hurt or maddened by too great a call on its energies. When the horse is issued to a soldier the man takes it to the riding-hall in his leisure moments and puts it carefully through its schooling. If a horse by over-training becomes resentful it is let out of school for the day—for all the world like a sulky boy. They do not rub an education into it.

As to the trooper, he is gone at in much the same way. It is found at long intervals that some men are too clumsy or timid for horse-soldiers, and they go elsewhere. But by proceeding gently, by a vigorous training of the muscles, the soldier gains confidence in himself. At the end of a time, which varies greatly in men, he will attempt absolutely anything with a horse, and he has so much activity, so much knowledge of how to fall, so much "horse sabé," that he is seldom hurt as he sprawls in the soft tan-bark of the ring.

Four troops were successively drilled in the hall before an admiring audience—the first two in intricate music-rides, side passages in line, lying down, and manœuvres calculated to show their perfect training.

The third troop, drilled by Lieutenant Nissen, came in bareback—and here is where I am afraid of my statements. I should not have believed it if I had not seen it. One should be or have been a bit of a

The Training of Cavalry—A Roman Race at the Riding-hall, Fort Myer, Virginia. *Painting from the Warner Collection of Gulf States Paper Corporation, Tuscaloosa, Alabama.*

horseman himself fully to appreciate such a thing. I have attempted to show in my drawings some of the most astonishing feats; and, mind you, these were performed by every horse and man on the tan-bark. The hurdle-jumping was done by men of Lieutenant Short's troop while standing up in the saddle with their coarse shoes on. This, I am told, is more difficult than when they are bareback with rubber-soled tennis-shoes.

The Roman race was indulged in by three men at a time, each controlling three horses bareback. They were in a large riding-hall, and not in a circus ring, and the horses were run at top speed—so fast, indeed, that two of them were upset on the turns.

There was much besides this—notably a soldier running beside three linked horses, vaulting while at the hurdle jump clean over two mounts to land on the nigh horse. Also, when mounted double, and at full career,

the men changed places in a most astonishing way, the front rider whirling with his back to the rear man while supported by his heel on the rear rider's toe.

It is exceedingly gratifying to know that our cavalry soldiers play their game so well. For myself, I have never seen any class of riders in any part of the world who could do as well or anything like as well—a large part of the "flash" riding of Cossacks and Comanche Indians being done by artificial aids of either saddlery or loops of various sorts which support them.

I wish those blatant patriots who are so ready to rely on our 10,000,000 able-bodied but untrained "available" men in the event of war could go and look these cavalrymen over, and ask themselves how long it will take to qualify the proper proportion of this material for troopers for the Sixth Cavalry.

How Order No. 6 Went Through

AS TOLD BY SUN-DOWN LEFLARE

We were full of venison and coffee as we gathered close around the camp fire, wiping the fitful smoke out of our eyes alternately as it came our way.

"It's blowing like the devil," said the sportsman, as he turned up his face to the pine-trees.

"Yees, sair. Maybeso dar be grass fire secon' ting we know," coincided Sun-Down Leflare.

Silver-Tip, the one who drove the wagon, stood with his back to us, gazing out across the mountain to an ominous red glare far to the south. "Ef that forest fire gets into Black Canyon, we'll be straddlin' out of yer all sorts of gaits before mornin'," he remarked.

"Cole night," observed Bear-Claw, which having exhausted his stock of English, he spoke further to Fire-Bear, but his conversation was opaque to us.

"Look at the stars!" continued the sportsman.

"Yes—pore critters—they have got to stay out all night; but I am going to turn in. It's dam cold," and Silver-Tip patted and mauled at his blankets.

"What was the coldest night you ever saw?" I asked.

He pulled off his boots, saying: "Seen heap of cold nights—dun'no' what was the coldest—reckon I put in one over on the Bull Mountains, winter of '80, that I ain't going to forget. If nex' day hadn't been a Chinook, reckon I'd be thar now."

"You have been nearly frozen, I suppose, Sun-Down?" I added.

"Yees, sair—I was cole once all right."

"Ah—the old coffee-cooler, he's been cold plenty of times. Any man what lives in a tepee has been cold, I reckon; they've been that way six months for a stretch," and having made this good-natured contribution, Silver-Tip pulled his blanket over his head.

Sun-Down's French nervousness rose. "Ah—dat mule-skinner, what she know 'bout cole?—she freeze on de green grass. I freeze seex day in de middle of de wintar over dar Buford. By gar, dat weare freeze too! Come dam near put my light out. Um-m-m!" and I knew that Sun-Down was my prey.

"How was that?"

"Over Fort Keough—I was scout for Ewers—she was chief scout for Miles," went on Leflare.

"Yas, I was scout too—over Keough—same time," put in Ramon, the club-footed Mexican.

"Yees, Ramon was scout too. Say—Miles she beeg man Eas'—hey? I see her come troo agency—well, fall of '90. Ah, she ole man; don' look like she use be sebenty-seben. Good-lookin' den."

"Wall—what you spect?" sighed his congener Ramon, in a harsh interruption. "I was good-lookin' mon myselef—sebenty-seben."

"You weare buy more squaw dan you weare eber steal—you ole frog. Dat Miles she was mak heap of trouble up dees way. I was geet sebenty dollar a month. She not trouble my people, but she was no good for Cheyenne un Sioux. Dey was nevar have one good night sleep af'er she was buil' de log house on de Tongue Rivière. Ah, ha, we was have hell of a time dem day'—don' we, Wolf-Voice?" and that worthy threw up his head quickly, and said, "Umph!"

"Well—I was wid my ole woman set in de lodge one day. Eet was cole. Lieutent Ewers she send for me. I was know I was got for tak eet or lose de sebenty. Well, I tak eet. Eet was cole.

"I was tink since, it weare dam good ting I lose dat sebenty. I was geet two pony, un was go to log house, where de officer she write all time in de book. Lieutent was say I go to Buford. I was say eet dam cole weddar for Buford. Lieutent was say I dam coffee-cooler. Well—I was not. Sitts-on-the-Point and Dick, she white man, was order go Buford wid me. Lieutent was say, when she han' me beeg lettair wid de red button, 'You keep eet clean, Leflare, un you go troo.' I told heem I was go troo, eef eet was freeze de steamboat.

"We was go out of de fort on our pony—wid de led horse. We was tak nothin' to eat, 'cause we was eat de buffalo. I was look lak de leetle buffalo—all skin. Skin hat—skin robe—skin leggin—you shoot me eef you see me. Eet was cole. We weare ride lak hell. When we was geet to Big Dry, Dick she say, 'Your pony no good; your pony not have de oat; you go back. He says he mak Buford to-morrow night. I say, 'Yees, we go back to-morrow.'

"We mak leetle sleep, un Sitts-on-the-Point he go back Keough, but I geets crazy, un say I brave man; I weel not go back; I weel go Buford, or give de dinner to de dam coyote. I weel go.

"My pony he was not able for run, un Dick she go over de heel—I was see her no more. I was watch out for de buffalo—all day was watch. I was hungry; dar was nothin' een me. All right, I was go top of de heel—I was not see a buffalo. All deese while I was head for de Mountain-Sheep Buttes, where I know Gros Ventre camp up by Buford. Eet was blow de snow, un I was

walk heap for keep warm. I was tink, eef no buffalo, no Gros Ventre camp for Leflare, by gar. I was marry Gros Ventre woman once, un eef I was geet dar I be all right. De snow she blow, un I could see not a ting. When eet geet dark, I was not know where I was go, un was lay down een de willow bush. Oh, de cole—how de hell you spect I sleep?—not sleep one wink, 'cept one. Well, my pony was try break away, but I was watch 'im, 'cept dat one wink. De dam pony what was led horse, she was geet off een de one wink. I see her track een de mornin', but I was not able for run him wid de order pony. He was geet clean away. 'Bout dat I was sorry, for een de daytime I was go keel heem eef no buffalo.

"Een de mornin' de win' she blow; de snow she blow too. Eet was long time 'fore I untie my lariat, un couldn't geet on pony 'tall—all steef—all froze. I walk long—walk long;" and Sun-Down shrugged up his shoulders and eyebrows, while he shut down his eyes and mouth in a most forlorn way. He had the quick, nervous French delivery of his father, coupled with the harsh voice of his Indian mother. There was also much of the English language employed by this waif of the plains which, I know, you will forgive me if I do not introduce.

"I deedn't know where I was—I was los' —couldn't see one ting. Was keep under cut bank for dodge win'. De snow she bank up een plass, mak me geet out on de pararie, den de win' she mak me hump. Pony he was heavy leg for punch troo de snow. All time I was watch out for buffalo, but dar was no buffalo;" and Sun-Down's voice rose in sympathy with the frightful condition which haunted his memory.

"Begin tink my medicin' was go plumb back on me. Den I tink Ewers—wish she out here wid dam old order. Eet mak me mad. Order—all time order—by gar, order soldier to change hees shirt—scout go two hundred miles. My belly she draw up like tomtom, un my head go roun', roun', lak ting Ramon was mak de hair rope wid; my han' she shake lak de leaf de plum-tree. I was fall down under cut bank, wid pony

"She Was Keep off Jus' Front of My Pony." *Painting in "21" Club Collection—Peter Kriendler, President.*

rope tie roun' me. Pony he stay, or tak me wid heem. How long I lay—well, I dun'no', but I was cole un wak up. Eet was steel—de star she shine; de win' she stop blow. Long time I was geet up slow. I was move leetle—move leetle—den I was move queek—move leetle—move queek. All right—you eat ten deer reebs while I was geet up un stan' on my feet. Pony he was white wid de snow un de fros'. Buffalo-robe she steef lak de wagon box. Long time I was move my finger—was try mak fire, un after while she blaze up. Ah, good fire—she steek in my head. Me un pony we geet thaw out one side, den oder side. I was look at pony—pony was look at me. By gar—I tink he was 'fraid I eat heem; but I was say no—I eat him by-un-by. I was melt de snow een my tin cup—was drink hot water—eet mak me strong. Den come light I was ride to

beeg butte, look all roun'—all over, but couldn't tell where I was. Den I was say, no buffalo I go Missouri Rivière.

"Long time, I was come to de buffalo. Dey was all roun'—oh, everywhere—well, hundred yard. When I was geet up close, I was aim de gun for shoot. I couldn't hole dat gun—she was wabble lak de pony tail een de fly-time. All right, I shoot un shoot at de dam buffalo, but I neber heet eem 'tall—all run off. My head she swim; my han' she shake; my belly she come up een my neck un go roun' lak she come untie. I almos' cry.

"Well—I du, 'no' jus' what den. 'Pears lak my head she go plumb off. I was wave my gun; was say I not afraid of de Sioux. Dam de Sioux!—I was fight all de Sioux in de worl'. I was go over de snow fight dem, un I was yell terrible. Eet seem lak all de

Sioux, all de Cheyenne, all de Assiniboine, all de bad Engun een de worl', she come out of de sky, all run dar pony un wave dar gun. I could hear dar pony gallop ovar my head. I was fight 'em all, but dey went 'way.

"A girl what I was use know she come drop—drop out of de sky. She had kettle of boil meat, but she was not come right up—was keep off jus' front of my pony. I was run after de girl, but she was float 'long front of me—I could not catch her. Den I don' know nothing'.

"Black George un Flyin' Medicin' was two scout come to Keough from Fort Peck. Dey saw me un follow me—dey was go to keel me, but dey see I was Leflare, so dey rope my pony, tak me een brush, mak fire, un give me leetle meat. By come night I was feel good—was geet strong.

"We was 'fraid of de Assiniboine—'cause de order fellers had seen beeg sign. I sais let us go 'way mile or so un leave fire burn here.

"Black George he sais he no dam ole woman—he brav man—fight dem—no care dam for Assiniboine.

"I say to myself, all right—Assiniboine been foller you. I go.

"Flyin' Medicin' he want for go, but George he sais Assiniboine scare woman wid hees pony track—umph! un Flyin' Medicin' she sais she no ole woman. I say, by gar, I am woman; I have got sense. You wan' stay here you be dead. Den I tak my pony un I go 'way een de dark, but I look back dar un see Medicin', she lie on de robe, Black George she set smoke de pipe, un a gray dog he set on de order side, all een de firelight. I sais dam fools.

"Well, I got for tell what happen. When I was go 'bout mile I was lay down. 'Bout one hour I hear hell of shootin'. I geet up queek, climb pony, run lak hell. I was ole woman, un I was dam glad for be ole woman. Eet was dark; pony was very thin; all same I mak heap of trail 'fore mornin' bes' I could."

I asked Sun-Down what made the shooting.

"Oh—Black George camp—course I deedn't know, but I was tink strong eet be hees camp all right 'nough. Long time after I hear how 'twas. Well—dey lay dar by de fire—Medicin' on hees back—George she set up—dog he set up order side—Assiniboine come on dar trail. I was ole woman—eef not, maybeso I was set by de fire too—humph!

"George he geet no chance fight Assiniboine. Dey fire on hees camp, shoot Flyin' Medicin' five time—all troo chest, all troo leg, all troo neck—all shoot up. Black George she was shot t'ree time troo lef' arm; un, by gar, gray dog she keel too. Black George grab hees gun un was run jump down de cut bank. Assiniboine was rush de camp un run off de pony, but George she was manage wid her lef' han' to shoot over cut bank, un dey was not dare tak Medicin's hair. Black George he was brave man. He was talk beeg, but he was as beeg as hees talk. He was scout roun', un was see no Assiniboine; he was come to Flyin' Medicin', who was go gurgle, gurgle—oh, he was all shot—all blood"—and here Sun-Down made a noise which was awfully realistic and quite unprintable, showing clearly that he had seen men who were past all surgery.

"George she raise Medicin' up, was res' hees head on hees arm, un den Medicin' was give heem hell. He was say: 'Deedn't I tole you? By gar, you dam brave man; you dam beeg fool! You do as I tole you, we be 'live, by gar. Now our time has come.' When he could speak again—when he had speet out de blood—he sais, 'Go geet my war-bag—geet out my war-bonnet—my bead shirt—my bead moccasins—put 'em on me—my time has come'; un Black George she geet out all de fine war-clothes, un she dress Medicin' up—all up een de war-clothes. 'Put my medicin'-bag on my breas'—good-by, Black George—keek de fire—good-by;' un Medicin' die all right.

"Course Black George she put out a foot un mak trail for Keough. He was haf awful time; was seex day geet to buffalo hunter camp, where she was crawl mos' of de way. De hunter was geeve heem de grub, un was pull heem to Keough een dar wagon.

Reckon he was cole, all de blood run out hees arm—nothin' to eat—seex day—reckon dat ole mule skinner she tink she was cole eef she Black George."

"What became of you meanwhile?"

"Me? Well—I was not stop until come bright day; den my pony was go deese way, was go dat way"—here Sun-Down spread out his finger-tips on the ground and imitated the staggering fore feet of a horse.

"I was res' my pony half day, un was try keel buffalo, but I was weak lak leetle baby. My belly was draw up—was go roun'—was turn upside down—was hurt me lak I had wile-cat inside my reebs. De buffalo was roun' dar. One minute I see 'em all right, nex' minute dey go roun' lak dey was all drunk. No use—I could not keel buffalo. Eet was Gros Ventre camp or bus' Leflare wid me den. All time eet very cole; fros' go pop, pop under pony feet. Guess I look lak dead man—guess I feel dam sight worse. Dat seex day she mak me very ole man.

"I was haf go slow—pony he near done —jus' walk 'long. I deedn't care dam for Assiniboine now. De gray wolf he was follow 'long behin'—two—t'ree—four wolf. I deedn't care dam for wolf. All Sioux, all Assiniboine, all wolf een de worl'—she go to hell now; I no care. I was want geet to Gros Ventre camp 'fore I die. I was walk 'long slow—was feed my pony; my feet, my han's was get cold, hard lak knife-blade. I was haf go to cut bank for fall on my pony's back—no crawl up no more. I was ride all night, slow, slow. Was sit down; wolf was come up look at me. I was tell wolf to go to hell.

"Nex' day same ting—go 'long slow. Pony he was dead; he no care for me. I can no more keek heem; I cannot use whip; I was dead.

"You ask me eef I was ever froze—hey, what you tink? Dat mule-skinner, Silver-Tip, he been dar—by gar, he nevair melt all nex' summer.

"Jus' dark I was come een big timber by creek. I was tink I die dar, for I could not mak de fire. I was stan' steel lak de steer een de coulee when de blizzair she blow.

Den what you tink? I was hear Gros Ventre woman talk 'cross de rivière. She was come geet de wattair. I was lead de pony on de hice. I was not know much, but I was wake up by fall een wattair troo crack een hice. My rein was 'roun' my shoulder; my gun she cross my two arm. I could not use my han'. When I was fall, gun she catch 'cross hice—pony was pull lak hell—was pull me out. I was wet, but I was wake up. Eef dat bridle she break, een de spring-time dey fine Leflare een wheat-fiel' down Dakotah.

"De woman was say, 'Go below—you find de ford.' Den he was run. After while I get 'cross ford—all hice. Was come dam near die standin' up. I was see leetle log house, un was go to door un pound wid my elbow. 'Let me een—let me een—I froze,' sais I, een Gros Ventre.

"Dey say, 'Who you are?'

"I sais, 'I am Leflare—I die een 'bout one minute—let me een.'

Sun-Down Leflare, Washed and Dressed Up. *Authors' photoengraving.*

"'You talk Gros Ventre; maybeso you bad Engun. How we know you Leflare?' sais de woman.

"'Eef I not Leflare, shoot when you open de door,' un dey open de door. I tink dey was come near shoot me—I was look terrible—dey was 'fraid. I grab de fire, but dey was pull me 'way. Dey was sit on me un tak off my clothes un rub me wid de snow. Well, dey was good; I dun'no' what dey do, but I was eat, eat, leetle at a time, till I was fall 'sleep. When I was wake up I was say, 'Tak dam ole order to Buford,' un I was tole de man what was tak eet I was keel heem eef he not tak eet.

"I lay een dat log house t'ree day 'fore I geet out, un den I go Buford. Dey sais de order she was all right. Den dey want me go back Keough wid order. I sais, 'Dam glad go back,' for de weddar she was fine den. 'You geeve me pony.'

"'Why geeve you pony?' sais de officer.

"'By gar, de las' order she keel my pony,' I sais."

The War Dreams

At the place far from Washington where the gray, stripped war-ships swing on the tide, and towards which the troop-trains hurry, there is no thought of peace. The shore is a dusty, smelly bit of sandy coral, and the houses in this town are built like snare-drums; they are dismal thoroughly, and the sun makes men sweat and wish to God they were somewhere else.

But the men in the blue uniforms are young, and Madame Beaulieu, who keeps the restaurant, strives to please, so it came to pass that I attended one of these happy-go-lucky banquets. The others were artillery officers, men from off the ships, with a little sprinkle of cavalry and infantry just for salt. They were brothers, and yellow-jack—hellish heat—bullets, and the possibility of getting mixed up in a mass of exploding iron had been discounted long back in their school-boy days perhaps. Yet they are not without sentiment, and are not even callous to all these, as will be seen, though men are different and do not think alike—less, even, when they dream.

"Do you know, I had a dream last night," said a naval officer.

"So did I."

"So did I," was chorussed by the others.

"Well, well!" I said. "Tell your dreams. Mr. H——, begin."

"Oh, it was nothing much. I dreamed that I was rich and old, and had a soft stomach, and I very much did not want to die. It was a curious sort of feeling, this very old and rich business, since I am neither, nor even now do I want to die, which part was true in my dream.

"I thought I was standing on the bluffs overlooking the Nile. I saw people skating, when suddenly numbers of hippopotamuses —great masses of them—broke up through the ice and began swallowing the people. This was awfully real to me. I even saw Mac there go down one big throat as easily as a cocktail. Then they came at me in a solid wall. I was crazed with fear—I fled. I could not run; but coming suddenly on a pile of old railroad iron, I quickly made a bicycle out of two car-wheels, and flew. A young hippo more agile than the rest made himself a bike also, and we scorched on over the desert. My strength failed; I despaired and screamed—then I woke up. Begad, this waiting and waiting in this fleet is surely doing things to me!"

The audience laughed, guyed, and said let's have some more dreams, and other things. This dream followed the other things, and he who told it was an artilleryman:

"My instincts got tangled up with one of those Key West shrimp salads, I reckon; but war has no terrors for a man who has been through my last midnight battle. I dreamed I was superintending two big 12-inch guns which were firing on an enemy's fleet. I do not know where this was. We got out of shot, but we seemed to have plenty of powder. The fleet kept coming on, and I

had to do something, so I put an old su-
perannuated sergeant in the gun. He
pleaded, but I said he was old, the case was
urgent, it did not matter how one died for
his country, etc.—so we put the dear old
sergeant in the gun and fired him at the
fleet. Then the battle became hot. I loaded
soldiers in the guns and fired them out to
sea until I had no more soldiers. Then I
began firing citizens. I ran out of citizens.
But there were Congressmen around somewhere there in my dreams, and though they
made speeches of protest to me under the
five-minute rule, I promptly loaded them in,
and touched them off in their turn. The fleet
was pretty hard-looking by this time, but
still in the ring. I could see the foreign
sailors picking pieces of Congressmen from
around the breech-blocks, and the officers
were brushing their clothes with their handkerchiefs. I was about to give up, when I
thought of the Key West shrimp salad. One
walked conveniently up to me, and I loaded
her in. With a last convulsive yank I pulled
the lock-string, and the fleet was gone with
my dream."

"How do cavalrymen dream, Mr.
B——?" was asked of a yellow-leg.

"Oh, our dreams are all strictly professional, too. I was out with my troop, being
drilled by a big fat officer on an enormous
horse. He was very red-faced, and crazy
with rage at us. He yelled like one of those
siren whistles out there in the fleet.

"He said we were cowards and would not
fight. So he had a stout picket-fence made,
about six feet high, and then, forming us in
line, he said no cavalry was any good which
could be stopped by any obstacle. Mind
you, he yelled it at us like the siren. He said
the Spaniards would not pay any attention to
such cowards. Then he gave the order to
charge, and we flew into the fence. We rode
at the fence pell-mell—into it dashed our
horses, while we sabred and shouted. Behind us now came the big colonel—very big
he was now, and with great red wings—saying, above all the din, 'You shall never
come back—you shall never come back!'

and I was squeezed tighter and tighter by
him up to this fence until I awoke; and now
I have changed my cocktail to a plain ver-
mouth."

When appealed to, the infantry officer
tapped the table with his knife thoughtfully:
"My dream was not so tragic; it was a
moral strain; but I suffered greatly while it
lasted. Somehow I was in command of a
company of raw recruits, and was in some
trenches which we were constructing under
fire. My recruits were not like soldiers—
they were not young men. They were past
middle age, mostly fat, and many had white
side whiskers after the fashion of the funny
papers when they draw banker types. I had
a man shot, and the recruits all got around
me; they were pleading and crying to be
allowed to go home.

"Now I never had anything in the world
but my pay, and am pretty well satisfied as
men go in the world, but I suppose the
American does not breathe who is averse to
possessing great wealth himself; so when
one man said he would give me $1,000,000
in gold if I would let him go, I stopped to
think. Here is where I suffered so keenly. I
wanted the million, but I did not want to let
him go.

"Then these men came up, one after the
other, and offered me varying sums of
money to be allowed to run away—and
specious arguments in favor of the same. I
was now in agony. D—n it! that company
was worth nearly a hundred million dollars
to me if I would let them take themselves
off. I held out, but the strain was horrible.
Then they began to offer me their daughters
—they each had photographs of the most
beautiful American girls—dozens and
dozens of American girls, each one of which
was a 'peach.' Say, fellows, I could stand
the millions. I never did 'gig' on the money,
but I took the photographs, said 'Give me
your girls, and pull your freight!' and my
company disappeared instantly. Do you
blame a man stationed in Key West for it—
do you, fellows?"

"Not by a d——d sight!" sang the company, on its feet.

"Well, you old marine, what did you dream?"

"My digestion is so good that my dreams have no red fire in them. I seldom do dream; but last night, it seems to me, I recall having a wee bit of a dream. I don't know that I can describe it, but I was looking very intently at a wet spot on the breast of a blue uniform coat. I thought they were tears—woman's tears. I don't know whether it was a dream or whether I really did see it."

"Oh, d——n your dreams!" said the Doctor. "What is that bloody old Congress doing from last reports?"

Wigwags from the Blockade

Modern war is supposed to be rapid, and we Americans think "time is money," but this war seems to be the murder of time, the slow torture of opportunity.

For seven long days and nights I have been steaming up and down on the battleship *Iowa*, ten miles off the harbor of Havana. Nothing happened. The *Mayflower* got on the land side of a British tramp and warned her off, and a poor Spanish fishing-schooner from Progreso, loaded with rotting fish, was boarded by a boat's crew from us. When the captain saw the becutlassed and bepistolled "tars" he became badly rattled, and told the truth about himself. A Spaniard has to be surprised into doing this. He had been many days out, his ice was gone, and his fish were "high." He wanted to make Havana, telling the boarding-officer that the people of Havana were very hungry. He had been boarded five times off the coast by our people; so the lieutenant—who had just gotten out of bed, by-the-way—told him to take his cargo of odors out into the open sea, and not to come back again.

The appalling sameness of this pacing up and down before Havana works on the nerves of every one, from captain to cook's police. We are neglected; no one comes to see us. All the Key West trolley-boats run to the Admiral's flag, and we know nothing of the outside. We speculate on the Flying Squadron, the *Oregon*, the army, and the Spanish. I have an impression that I was not caught young enough to develop a love of the sea, which the slow passage of each day

reinforces. I have formed a habit of damning the army for its procrastination, but in my heart of hearts I yearn for it. I want to hear a "shave-tail" bawl; I want to get some dust in my throat; I want to kick the dewy grass, to see a sentry pace in the moonlight, and to talk the language of my tribe. I resist it; I suppress myself; but my homely old first love comes to haunt me, waking and sleeping—yes, even when I look at this mountain of war material, this epitome of modern science, with its gay white officers, who talk of London, Paris, China, and Africa in one breath. Oh, I know I shall fall on the neck of the first old "dough-boy" or "yellow-leg" I see, and I don't care if he is making bread at the time!

The Morro light has been extinguished, but two powerful searches flash back and forth across the sky. "Good things to sail by," as the navigator says. "We can put them out when the time comes." Another purpose they serve is that "Jackie" has something to swear at as he lies by his loaded gun—something definite, something material, to swear at. Also, two small gunboats developed a habit of running out of the harbor—not very far, and with the utmost caution, like a boy who tantalizes a chained bear. And at places in the town arises smoke.

"What is it?" asks the captain of marines.

"Big tobacco-factories working over-time for us," replies Doctor Crandell.

I was taken down into the machinery of the ship. I thought to find in it some human

Watching the Big Search-lights in Havana. *Authors' photoengraving.*

interest. Through mile after mile of underground passages, I crawled and scrambled and climbed amid wheels going this way and rods plunging that, with little electric lights to make holes in the darkness. Men stood about in the overpowering blasts of heat, sweating and greasy and streaked with black—grave, serious persons of superhuman intelligence—men who have succumbed to modern science, which is modern life. Daisies and trees and the play of sunlight mean nothing to these—they know when all three are useful, which is enough. They pulled the levers, opened and shut cocks, showered coal into the roaring white hells under the boilers; hither and yon they wandered, bestowing mother-like attentions on rod and pipe. I talked at them, but they developed nothing except preoccupied professionalism. I believe they fairly worship this throbbing mass of mysterious iron; I believe they love this bewildering power which they control. Its problems entrance them; but it simply stuns me. At last when I stood on deck I had no other impression but that of my own feebleness, and, as I have said, felt rather stunned than stimulated. Imagine a square acre of delicate machinery plunging and whirling and spitting, with men crawling about in its demon folds! It is not for me to tell you more.

Don't waste your sympathy on these men belowdecks—they will not thank you; they will not even understand you. They are "modern"—are better off than "Jackie" and his poor wandering soul—they love their iron baby, so leave them alone with their joy. Modern science does not concern itself about death.

The *Iowa* will never be lost to the nation for want of care. By night there are dozens of trained eyes straining into the darkness, the searches are ready to flash, and the watch on deck lies close about its shotted guns. Not a light shows from the loom of the great battle-ship. Captain Evans sits most of the time on a perch upon the bridge, forty feet above the water-line. I have seen him come down to his breakfast at eight bells with his suspenders hanging down behind, indicating that he had been jumped out during the night.

The executive officer, Mr. Rogers, like the machinery down below, never sleeps. Wander where I would about the ship, I could not sit a few moments before Mr. Rogers would flit by, rapid and ghost-like—a word here, an order there, and eyes for everybody and everything. Behind, in hot pursuit, came stringing along dozens of men hunting for Mr. Rogers; and this never seemed to let up—midnight and mid-day all the same. The thought of what it must be is simply horrible. He has my sympathy—nervous prostration will be his reward—yet I greatly fear the poor man is so perverted, so dehumanized, as positively to like his life and work.

Naval officers are very span in their graceful uniforms, so one is struck when at "quarters" the officers commanding the turrets appear in their "dungaree," spotted and soiled. The *Iowa* has six turrets, each in charge of an officer responsible for its guns and hoisting-gear, delicate and complicated. In each turret is painted, in a sort of Sam Weller writing, "Remember the *Maine*." The gun-captains and turret-men acquire a strange interest and pride in their charges, hanging about them constantly.

Two gun-captains in the forward turret used to sit on the great brown barrels of the 12-inch rifles just outside the posts, guarding them with jealous care; for it is a "Jackie" trick to look sharply after his little spot on shipboard, and to promptly fly into any stranger who defiles it in any way. At times these two men popped back into their holes like prairie-dogs. It was their hope and their home, that dismal old box of tricks, and it may be their grave. I was going to die with them there, though I resolutely refused to live with them. However, the *Iowa* is unsinkable and unlickable, and the hardware on the forward turret is fifteen inches thick, which is why I put my brand on it. So good-luck to Lieutenant Van Duzer and his merry men!

"Jackie," the prevailing thing on a man-of-war, I fail to comprehend fully. He is a strong-visaged, unlicked cub, who grumbles and bawls and fights. He is simple, handy, humorous, and kind to strangers, as I can testify. The nearest he ever comes to a martial appearance is when he lines up at quarters to answer "Here!" to his name, and there is just where he doesn't martialize at all. He comes barefooted, hat on fifty ways, trousers rolled up or down, and everything blowing wide. He scratches his head or stands on one foot in a ragged line, which grins at the spectators in cheerful heedlessness, and he looks very much gratified when it is all over. His hope is for a bang-up sea-fight, or two roaring days of shore liberty, when he can "tear up the beach" with all the force of his reckless muscularity.

The marine, or sea-soldier, has succumbed to modern conditions, and now fights a gun the same as a sailor-man. He manages to retain his straight-backed discipline, but is overworked in his twofold capacity. This "soldier and sailor too" is a most interesting man to talk to, and I wish I could tell some of his stories. He marches into the interior of China or Korea to pull a minister out of the fire—thirty or forty of him against a million savages, but he gets his man. He lies in a jungle hut on the Isthmus or a "dobie" house on the West Coast while the microbes and the "dogoes" rage.

But it's all horribly alike to me, so I managed to desert. The *Winslow,* torpedero, ran under our lee one fine morning, and I sneaked on board, bound for the flag-ship —the half-way station between us and Cayo Hueso. We plunged and bucked about in the roaring waves of the Gulf, and I nearly had the breakfast shaken out of me. I assure you that I was mighty glad to find the lee of the big cruiser *New York.*

On board I found that the flag-ship had had some good sport the day previous shelling some working parties in Matanzas. Mr. Zogbaum and Richard Harding Davis had seen it all, note-book in hand. I was stiff with jealousy; but it takes more than one fight to make a war—so here is hoping!

Soldiers Who Cry

Yesterday I called at the Ninth Infantry camp, and Colonel Powell told the following in the course of conversation, and it struck me as a new note. This regiment came from Plattsburg Barracks, New York, and when the order came to go the colonel asked his captains to draw up small details out of the companies which should be left behind to guard and look after the property of the government at Plattsburg.

The colonel drew these details up in line to instruct them in their duties, which he did at some length. He said he noticed tears running down the faces of some of the men, but it did not strike him seriously at the time. He dismissed the squad and left the building; but in a string behind him came the men, crying like children. One old mustached and grizzled chap was bawling as though at his mother's funeral; he begged, he pleaded, he implored the colonel by all his gods not to leave him behind. Others did the same, standing there crying, blubbering, and beseeching Colonel Powell not to make them stay behind. The old colonel was quite taken aback. He did not know just what to do. He liked the spirit, but the discipline had never had just this sort of a shock before, and it upset him. He told the men they had been detailed by their captains to stay behind to guard property because they were steady men. It did nothing but cause more pleading and blubbering, and the colonel walked away. He did not tell me if he had a tear in his own eye when he turned his back, but the men had to be rounded sharply up and regularly made to stay. That is the kind of boys to follow the band, I say.

With the Regulars at Fort Tampa, Florida—9th U. S. Cavalry (Colored) Skirmishing Through the Pines. *Authors' photoengraving.*

The Spirit of Mahongui

It is so I have called this old document, which is an extract from the memoirs of le Chevalier Bailloquet, a Frenchman living in Canada, where he was engaged in the Indian fur trade, about the middle of the seventeenth century, and as yet they are unpublished.

It is written in English, since the author lived his latter life in England, having left Canada as the result of troubles with the authorities.

He was captured by the Iroquois, and after living with them some time, made his escape to the Dutch.

My Chevalier rambles somewhat, although I have been at pains to cut out extraneous matter. It is also true that many will not believe him in these days, for out of their puny volition they will analyze, and out of their discontent they will scoff. But to those I say, Go to your microbes, your statistics, your volts, and your bicycles, and leave me the truth of other days.

The Chevalier was on a voyage from Quebec to Montreal; let him begin:

The next day we embarqued, though not wthout confusion, because many weare not content, nor satisfied. What a pleasure ye two fathers to see them trott up and downe ye rocks to gett their manage into ye boat. The boats weare so loaded that many could not proceed if foul weather should happen. I could not persuade myself to stay wth this concourse as ye weather was faire for my journie.

Wthout adoe, I got my six wild men to paddle on ye way.

This was a fatal embarquation, butt I did not mistrust that ye Iriquoits weare abroad in ye forest, for I had been at ye Peace. Nevertheless I find that these wild men doe naught butt what they resolve out of their bloodie mindedness. We passed the Point going out of ye Lake St. Peter, when ye Barbars appeared on ye watter-side discharging their muskets at us, and embarquing for our pursuit.

"Kohe—kohe!"—came nearer ye fearsome warre cry of ye Iriquoit, making ye hearts of ye poore Hurron & ffrench alike to turn to water in their breasts. 2 of my savages weare strook downe at ye first discharge & another had his paddle cutt in twain, besides shott holes through wch the watter poured apace. Thus weare we diminished and could not draw off.

The Barbars weare daubed wth paint, wch is ye signe of warre. They coming against our boat struck downe our Hurrons wth hattchetts, such as did not jump into the watter, where also they weare in no wise saved.

But in my boat was a Hurron Captayne, who all his life-time had killed many Iriquoits & by his name for vallor had come to be a great Captayne att home and abroad. We weare resolved some execution & wth our gunns dealt a discharge & drew our cutlasses to strike ye foe. They environed us as we weare sinking, and one spake saying— "Brothers, cheere up and assure yourselfe you shall not be killed; thou art both men and

Captaynes, as I myself am, and I will die in thy defense." And ye afforesaid crew shewed such a horrid noise, of a sudden ye Iriquoit Captayne took hold about me—"Thou shalt not die by another hand than mine."

Ye savages layd bye our armes & tyed us fast in a boat, one in one boat and one in another. We proceeded up ye river, rather sleeping than awake, for I thought never to escape.

Att near sunsett we weare taken on ye shore, where ye wild men encamped bye making cottages of rind from off ye trees. They tyed ye Hurron Captayne to a trunk, he resolving most bravely but dessparred to me, and I too dessparred. Nevertheless he sang his fatal song through ye fire made him as one wth the ague. They tooke out his heart and cut off some of ye flesh of ye miserable, boyled it and eat it. This they wished not to doe att this time, but that ye Hurron had been shott wth a ball under his girdle where it was not seen, though he would have died of his desperate wound. That was the miserable end of that wretch.

Whilst they weare busy wth ye Hurron, they having stripped me naked, tyed me above ye elbows, and wrought a rope about my middle. They asked me several questions, I not being able to answer, they gave me great blows wth their fists, then pulled out one of my nails. Having lost all hopes, I resolved altogether to die, itt being folly to think otherwise.

I could not flee, butt was flung into a boat att daylight. Ye boats went all abreast, ye wild men singing some of their fatal songs, others their howls of victory, ye wild "Kohes," beating giens & parchments, blowing whistles, and all manner of tumult.

Thus did we proceed wth these ravening wolves, God having delivered a Christian into ye power of Satan.

I was nott ye only one in ye claws of these wolves, for we fell in wth 150 more of these cruels, who had Hurron captyves to ye number of 33 victimes, wth heads alsoe stuck on poles, of those who in God's mercie weare gone from their miseries. As for me, I was put in a boat wth one who had his fingers cutt

& bourned. I asked him why ye Iriquoits had broak ye Peace, and he said they had told him ye ffrench had broak ye Peace; that ye ffrench had set their pack of doggs on an olde Iriquoit woman who was eat up alive & that ye Iriquoits had told ye Hurron wild men that they had killed ye doggs, alsoe Hurrons and ffrench, saying that as to ye captyves, they would boyl doggs, Hurrons, and ffrench in ye same kettle.

A great rain arose, ye Iriquoits going to ye watter-side did cover themselvs wth their boats, holding ye captyves ye meanwhile bye ropes bound about our ancles, while we stood out in ye storm, wch was near to causing me death from my nakedness. When ye rain had abated, we pursued our way killing staggs, & I was given some entrails, wch before I had only a little parched corne to ye extent of my handfull.

At a point we mett a gang of ye head hunters all on ye shore, dancing about a tree to wch was tyed a fine ffrench mastiff dogg, wch was standing on its hinder leggs, being lashed up against a tree by its middle. Ye dogg was in a great terror, and frantic in its bonds. I knew him for a dogg from ye fort att Montroyal, kept for to give warnings of ye Enemy's approach. It was a strange sight for to see ye Heathen rage about ye noble dogg, but he itt was nevertheless wch brought ye Barbars against us. He was only gott wth great difficulty, having killed one Barbar, and near to serving others likewise.

They untyed ye dogg, I holding him one side, and ye other, wth cords they brought and tyed him in ye bow of a boat wth 6 warriors to paddle him. Ye dogg boat was ye Head, while ye rest came on up ye river singing fatal songs, triumph songs, piping, howling, & ye dogg above all wth his great noise. Ye Barbars weare more delighted att ye captyve dogg than att all of us poore Christians, for that they did say he was no dogg. Ye doggs wch ye wild men have are nott so great as wolves, they being little else & small att that. Ye mastiff was considered as a consequence to be a great interest. This one had near defeated their troupe & now was to be horridly killed after ye bloody way of ye wild men.

Att camp they weare sleep most of ye night, they being aweary wth ye torture of ye Hurron Captayne previously. Ye dogg was tyed & layd nott far off from where I was alsoe tyed, butt over him weare 2 olde men, who guarded him of a fear he would eat away his ropes. These men weare Elders or Priests, such as are esteemed for their power over spirits, & they did keep up their devil's song ye night thro.

I made a vertue of necessity & did sleep, butt was early cast into a boat to go on towards ye Enemy's countrie, tho we had raw meat given us, wth blows on ye mouth to make us ye more quickly devour itt. An Iriquoit who was the Captayne in our boat, bade me to be of a good courage, as they would not hurt me. Ye small knowledge I had of their speech made a better hope, butt one who could have understood them would have been certainly in a great terror.

Thus we journied 8 days on ye Lake Champlaine, where ye wind and waves did sore beset our endeavors att times. As for meate we wanted none, as we had a store of staggs along ye watter-side. We killed some every day, more for sport than for need. We finding them on Isles, made them go into ye watter, & after we killed above a score, we clipped ye ears of ye rest & hung bells on them, and then lett them loose. What a sport to see ye rest flye from them that had ye bells!

There came out of ye vast forest a multitude of bears, 300 at least together, making a horrid noise, breaking ye small trees. We shott att them, butt they stirred not a step. We weare much frightened that they stirred nott att our shooting. Ye great ffrench dogg would fain encounter them notwithstanding he was tyed. He made ye watter-side to ring wch his heavy voise & from his eyes came flames of fyre & clouds from out his mouth. The bears did straightway fly wch much cheered ye Iriquoits. One said to me they weare resolved nott to murder ye dogg, wch was a stone-God in ye dogg shape, or a witch, butt I could nott fully understand. Ye wild men said they had never heard their fathers speak of so many bears.

When we putt ye kettle on, ye wild man who had captured me, gave me of meate to eat, & told me a story. "Brother," says he, "itt is a thing to be admired to goe afar to travell. You must know that tho I am olde, I have always loved ye ffrench for their goodness, but they should have given us to kill ye Algonkins. We should not warre against ye ffrench, butt trade wth them for Castors, who are better for traffic then ye Dutch. I was once a Captayne of 13 men against ye Altignaonanton & ye ffrench. We stayed 3 whole winters among ye Ennemy, butt in ye daytime durst not marche nor stay out of ye deep forest. We killed many, butt there weare devils who took my son up in ye air so I could never again get him back. These devils weare as bigg as horriniacs,* & ye little blue birds wch attend upon them, said itt was time for us to go back to our people, wch being resolved to do, we came back, butt nott of a fear of ye Ennemy. Our warre song grew still on our lipps, as ye snow falling in ye forest. I have nott any more warred to the North, until I was told by ye spirits to go to ye ffrench & recover my son. My friend, I have dreamed you weare my son;" and henceforth I was not hurted nor starved for food.

We proceeded thro rivers & lakes & thro forests where I was made to support burdens. When we weare come to ye village of ye Iriquoits we lay in ye woods because that they would nott go into ye village in ye night time.

The following day we weare marched into ye brought† of ye Iriquoits. When we came in sight we heard nothing butt outcryes from one side, as from ye other. Then came a mighty host of people & payd great heed to ye ffrench dogg, wch was ledd bye 2 men while roundabout his neck was a girdle of porcelaine. They tormented ye poore Hurrons wth violence, butt about me was hung a long piece of porcelaine—ye girdle of my captor, & he stood against me. In ye meanwhile, many of ye village came about us, among wch a goode olde woman & a boy wth a hattchett came neere me. Ye olde woman covered me, & ye boy took me by my hand and led mee out of ye companie. What comforted me was that I

* Moose.   † Borough.

"This Was a Fatal Embarquation." *Authors' photoengraving.*

had escaped ye blowes. They brought me into ye village where ye olde woman showed me kindness. She took me into her cottage, & gave me to eat, butt my great terror took my stumack away from me. I had stayed an hour when a great companie came to see me, of olde men wth pipes in their mouths. For a time they sat about, when they did lead me to another cabbin, w^re they smoked & made me apprehend they should throw me into ye fyre. Butt itt proved otherwise, for ye olde woman followed me, speaking aloud, whome they answered wth a loud *ho,* then shee tooke her girdle, and about me she tyed itt, so brought me to her cottage & made me to sitt downe.

Then she gott me Indian corne toasted, & took away ye paint ye fellows had stuck to my face. A maide greased & combed my haire, & ye olde woman danced and sung, while my father bourned tobacco on a stone. They gave me a blew coverlitt, stockings, and shoes. I layed wth her son & did w^t I could to get familiarity wth them, and I suffered no wrong, yet I was in a terror, for ye fatal songs came from ye poore Hurrons. Ye olde man inquired whether I was Afferony, a ffrench. I assured him no, saying I was Panugaga, that is of their nation, for wch he was pleased.

My father feasted 200 men. My sisters made me clean for that purpose, and greased my haire. They tyed me wth 2 necklaces of porcelaine & garters of ye same. My father gave me a hattchett in my hand.

My father made a speech, showing many demonstrations of vallor, broak a kettle of cagamite wth a hattchett. So they sung, as is their usual custom. Ye banquette being over, all cryed to me "Shagon, Orimha"—that is "be hearty!" Every one withdrew to his quarters.

Here follows a long account of his daily life among the Indians, his hunting and observations, which our space forbids. He had become meanwhile more familiar with the language. He goes on:

My father came into ye cabbin from ye grand castle & he sat him downe to smoke. He said ye Elders had approved after much debate, & that ye ffrench dogg was not a witch, but ye great warrior Mahongui, gone before, whose spirit had rose up into ye ffrench dogg & had spyed ye ffrench. Att ye council even soe ye dogg had walked into ye centre of ye great cabbin, there saying loudly to ye Elders what he was & that he must be heard. His voice must be obeyed. His was not ye mocking cryes of a witch from under an olde snakeskin, butt a chief come from Paradise to comfort his own people. My father asked me if I was agreed. I said that witches did not battile as openly as ye dogg, butt doe their evil in ye dark.

These wild men are sore beset wth witches and devils—more than Christians, as they deserve to be, for they are of Satan's own belonging.

My father dreamed att night, & sang about itt, making ye fire to bourne in our cabbin. We satt to listen. He had mett ye ffrench dogg in ye forest path bye night—he standing across his way, & ye forest was light from ye dogg's eyes, who spake to my father saying, "I belong to ye dead folks—my hattchett is rust—my bow is mould—I can no longer battile wth our Ennemy, butt I hover over you in warre—I direct your arrows to their breasts —I smoothe ye little dry sticks & wett ye leaves under ye shoes—I draw ye morning mist across to shield you—I carry ye 'Kohes' back and fore to bring your terror—I fling aside ye foeman's bulletts—go back and be strong in council."

My father even in ye night drew ye Elders in ye grand cabbin. He said what he had seen and heard. Even then the great ffrench dogg gott from ye darkness of ye cabbin, & strode into ye fyre. He roared enough to blow downe castles in his might & they knew he was saying what he had told unto my father.

A great Captayne sent another night, & had ye Elders for to gather at ye grande cabbin. He had been paddling his boat upon ye river when ye dogg of Mahongui had walked out on ye watter thro ye mist. He was taller than ye forest. So he spake, saying "Mahongui says —go tell ye people of ye Panugaga, itt is time for warre—ye corne is gathered—ye deer has changed his coat—there are no more Hurrons for me to eat. What is a Panugaga village wth no captyves? Ye young men will talk as women doe, & ye Elders will grow content to watch a snow-bird hopp. Mahongui says itt is time."

Again att ye council fyre ye spirit dogg strode from ye darkness & said itt was time. Ye tobacco was bourned by ye Priests. In ye smoke ye Elders beheld ye Spirit of Mahongui. "Panugaga—Warre."

Soe my father saw ye ghost of ye departed one. He smoked long bye our cabbin fyre. He sang his battile song. I asked him to goe myself, even wth a hattchett, as I too was Panugaga. Butt he would in no wise listen. "You are nott meet," he says, "you sayest that your God is above. How will you make me believe that he is as goode as your black coats say? They doe lie & you see ye contrary; ffor first of all, ye Sun bournes us often, ye rain wetts us, ye winde makes us have shipwrake, ye thunder, ye lightening bournes & kills us, & all comes from above, & you say that itt is goode to be there. For my part, I will nott go there. Contrary they say that ye reprobates & guilty goeth downe & bourne. They are mistaken; all is goode heare. Do nott you see that itt is ye Earthe that nourishes all living creatures—ye watter, ye fishes, & ye yus, and that corne & all other fruits come up, & that all things are nott soe contrary to us as that from above. Ye devils live in ye air & they took my son. When you see that ye Earthe is our Mother, then you will see that all things on itt are goode. Ye Earthe was made for ye Panugaga, & ye souls of our warriors help us against our Ennemy. Ye ffrench dogg is Mahongui's spirit. He tells us to goe to warre against ye ffrench. Would a ffrench dogg doe that? You are nott yett Panugaga to follow your father in warre."

Sun-Down Leflare's Money

Sitting together comfortably on the front porch of the house of the man who ran the flouring-mill at the agency, Sun-Down and I felt clean, and we both had on fresh clothes. He had purchased at the trader's a cotton shirt with green stripes, which would hold the entire attention of any onlooker. We were inclined to more gayety than the smoke of the mountain camp fire superinduced, and became more important and material when the repression of the great mountains was removed.

"Well, Sun-Down, how are you feeling?" I opened.

"Feelin' pretty reech dese day," he observed, with a smile.

"Have you paid the kid's board yet?"

"Ah, by gar, I was pay dose board-money 'fore I was geet off dat pony. How you s'pose I know what weel come when I was heet de agency? Firs' fellar she wiggle de pas'eboard maybeso Sun-Down go broke. Well, I was buy de shirt un de tobac. Good shirt deese, hey? Well, den, I don' care."

"Of course you don't, my dear Mr. Leflare. Having money is a great damage to you," I continued.

"Yes, dat ees right. Money she no gran' good ting for Enjun man lak for white folk. Enjun she keep de money een hees han' 'bout long she keep de snow een hees han', but I was tell you eet was all he was geet dese day. Pony she not bring much. Enjun he can't mak de wagon 'less he 'ave de price. De dry meat, de skin, un de pony, she was what Enjun want; but he was geet leetle

now. Use for 'ave eet long time 'go; now not'ing but money! Dam!

"Back yondair, een what year you call '80—all same time de white man was hang de oddar white man so fas'—she geet be bad. De buffalo man she was come plenty wid de beeg wagon, was all shoot up de buffalo, was tak all de robe. Den de man come up wid de cow, un de soldier he was stop chasse de Enjun. De Enjun she was set roun' de log pos', un was not wan' be chasse some more—eet was do no good. Den come de railroad; aftar dat bad, all bad. Was see peop' lak you. Dey was 'ave de money, un was all time scout roun' un buy de cow. De man what was sell de cow she buy de cow some more; dey all done do not'ing but set roun' un buy de cow. I could not geet de buffalo, un could no more geet de money for be soldier scout. Well, I was not understan'—I was not know what do. We was keel de cow once—maybeso I tell you 'bout dat some time. De cowboy she say we mus' not keel de cow. We say, 'You keel our buffalo, now we mus' keel your cow.' He sais soldiers dey geet aftar us, un we don' know what do.

"I was say to Dakase un Hoopshuis: 'You mak de horse-ban' wid me. We go on de Yellowstone un sell de cowboy de pony —mak great deal of money,'" continued Sun-Down.

In hopes of development, I asked where he got all the ponies.

"Ah, nevar you min' dat. We was geet dem pony where dey was cheap." And I knew, from his cynicism, that it was an ancient form of his misbehavior. "So Dakase un me un Hoopshuis was tak de horse-ban' to Yellowstone Reever, un was hole eet by Meestar John Smeeth log house back een de foot-heel. Meestar John Smeeth he was sell de rum un deal de card een de log house. De cowboy she stop roun' Meestar John Smeeth log house, un de cowboy was raise hell. Dees rum she varrie bad medicin' for Enjun, all right; un she varrie bad for cowboy, all same. Cowboy he geet drunk, wan' all time for burn hees seex-shootair. Bad plass for Enjun when de cowboy she hise een de rum.

"Well, 'long come de cow outfeet, un Dakase un de oddar Enjun she was pull out een de foot-heel, but I was stop roun' for notice Meestar John Smeeth sell de horse-ban' to de cowboy. Meestar John Smeeth she not be varrie bes' man I evair was see. We all time look at Meestar John Smeeth varrie sharp. I was say to Meestar Smeeth, 'You sell de pony to de cowboy, un eef you geet 'nough money, you 'ave one horse when you was sell ten horse'; un I sais to heem: 'I tink you not ride varrie far on de beeg road eef you beat roun' much when you do beesness with us Enjun. I weel talk de Anglais to dose cowboy, un I weel find you out, Meestar John Smeeth.'

"'Long come de cowboy, un Meestar Smeeth she was try sell de pony; but de cowboy she weel not buy de pony, 'cause she say de bran'-iron not b'long Meestar John Smeeth. He sais, no, not b'long heem, b'long friend of hees.

"Dose cowboy dey laugh varrie loud, un dey sais, 'Guess, Meestar Smeeth, you see your frien' troo de smoke.'

"Cowboys dey go 'way. Meestar Smeeth he sais, 'I mak dat bran' b'long me,' so Dakase un Hoopshuis un me, un Meestar John Smeeth, we was work t'ree day een de corral, un we was make dat bran' b'long Meestar John Smeeth. All time dar weare a leetle white man what was hang roun' de log house un shuffle de card. He know how shuffle dose card, I tell you. He was all time fool wid de card. He wear de store clothes,

un he was not help us bran' de horse-ban', 'cause he sais, 'Dam de pony!'

"We wait roun', wait roun'. Oh, we was eat Meestar Smeeth bacon, un we was not strain ourself for de time. Meestar Smeeth he was fry de bacon un mak de bread, un he geet varrie much hope for noddar cow outfeet.

"T'ree men weare come 'long de beeg stage-road. Dey sais dar name ees Long-Horn. Well, I know what white man she call de Long-Horn now, un I 'ave know since what he call de Short-Horn. I tink eet good deal lak Enjun call de Big-Robe; I tink eet good deal lak John Smeeth. Dar ain't much Long-Horn nowday, un dar ain't so much John Smeeth as dar use be.

"All right, dey was buy de horse-ban', un was pay de money right dar. Dey was drive de pony on de beeg stage-road. Meester John Smeeth she give us de money, un sais we weel play de pokair a leetle. Dat was good beesness, so we was all set down een de log house un play de pokair. Maybeso we play one whole day. All right, dey was geet every damn cent we got; all de money what was b'long Dakase un me un Hoopshuis, un we was loss our pony un our money.

"Dakase un Hoopshuis dey geet on dar pony un go 'way, but I was stay at de log house, for I was see dat de leetle man she was deal us de skin game, but I was not see how he was do de ting. I was varrie much wan' for know how he do eet, un was tell heem I was not care eef he 'ave all my money, jus' so he show me how he deal dat skin game. I tell heem dat maybeso I keel heem eef he not show me. Well, den he was show me. He was rub my right thumb wid de powder-stone, un de skin she geet varrie sof'. Den he was show me how feel de prick een de card, un he was show me how feel de short end of de card—dose cards was 'ave de one end file' off. He was geeve me deck of dose short card, un I was set een front of dat log house, un look up at de cloud, un feel dose prick un does short card—I was feel two day steady.

"Me un de store-clothes man we was set

een front of de log house, maybeso eet t'ree day, when up de road come de t'ree Long-Horn white man what had pay for de horse-ban'. Dey was run dar horse plenty.

"I was shut my eye pretty close, un I was tink pretty queek. I was tink great deal more queek dan I was tole you 'bout dees ting. I was say, 'Sun-Down, what mak dem t'ree white man run dem horse so fas'?' I was see why. I was say to myself, Dakase un Hoopshuis she 'ave steel dem pony. I geet up un sais, 'You store-clothes man, you run aftar me or you be keel 'bout one min-ute'; un I was go roun' de corner of dat log house un geet een de cottonwoods; den we was mak de san' fly 'bout one mile. Pretty queek I was hear shootin', den I was hear not'ing. We was geet on a point of de rock, un we was see de white man: she look at our moccasin track. Dey was go back to log house, un go 'way up de stage-trail.

"I sais den: 'Store-clothes, Meestar John Smeeth ees all fix up for burn de candle ovair. Dem white mans have kill heem."

"Den we go back, scout up de log house, un fin' Meestar John Smeeth—oh, all shoot up. He was fry de bacon when dose man weare pour de lead een heem.'

"We was bury dees Smeeth, un I sais: 'Now, Meestar Store-clothes, you un I got for run lak hell. De cowboy he come pretty soon, un he come smokin'.'

"Store-clothes she sais cannot run on de horse.

"'Well,' I sais, 'you cannot run on de foot, by gar; de cowboy she 'ave your trail hot 'fore you tink.'

"I was geet down de pony from de foot-heel un was put de store-clothes man on one pony, un den I was herd dat pony all day un all night. He was groan terrible—oh, my, 'ow he was squawk, was dat leetle man! but I was leek de pony wid my rope, un de pony was run 'long pretty good wid de store-clothes man.

"He was say tak heem to railroad.

"'No,' I sais; 'go tak you wid me. We play de skin game plass I know, un eef we win, den I tak you to railroad.'

"'How far dees plass?' sais de leetle man.

"'Ah—we geet dar eef de pony hole out.' Den we was 'ave de long talk. I was say I keel heem eef he lose. He was say de oddar fellar keel heem eef he win. 'Well,' I sais, 'I sure keel you, maybeso de oddar fellar dey won't—you 'ave de bes' chance wid me.'

"He sais who de oddar fellar is?

"I tell heem dey part Enjun, part white man—dey was breeds lak me.

"I was know a breed outfeet on de breaks of de Mountain-Sheep Butte what was run de pony off un was sell heem. Dey was 'ave plenty money, un I tink we play de skin game on dem.

"When we was geet dar I was talk I fin' de store-clothes man out een de heel, un was bring heem een. He was not un'erstan' de Enjun talk. He was not know a ting 'cept deal de card, but he was know dat all right.

"Dose breed weare set roun' de camp un deal de card un drink de rum for day or so. We was not play de card much, un de store-clothes man he was lose a leetle when he was tak de chance een. Pretty soon dar was 'bout t'ree man she 'ave de money what b'long whole outfeet, un de store-clothes man he sais, 'You geet pony all fix up for run off, un tonight we play de game.' I sais: 'You geet all de money by de middle of de night-time, un don' you mees eet—I keel you. I weel turn every horse out de camp, un when I mak de sign, you follair me—queek.' Eet was 'bout ten o'clock when we was set down on de buffalo-robe un play de pokair wid de t'ree man by de fire. One man what was not play was hole de spleet steek for give de light.

"Eet was not long 'fore I was lose all de money what I was 'ave, what was what de store-clothes man 'ad geeve me. Den de lee-tle man she look at me, un she varrie much scare. He weare lak de snow; guess he nevair see much Enjun; guess he not lak what he 'ave see. I was geet up un was look at de leetle man—was look varrie smart at heem"—and here Sun-Down accompanied with a look which must have chilled the soul of the frontier gambler.

"Den I was slide 'way een de dark. I was scout up dat camp. Dey was mos' all drunk,

"He Was Laugh at Me from Between de Wheel." *Authors' photoengraving.*

'cept de t'ree man what was play de card. Dey was varrie mad, but de leetle man was not know how mad dose breeds was, 'cause de Enjun when he varrie mad she don' look defferent. Dey was lose dair money pretty fas' to de leetle man.

"I was cut de rope of de pony all roun' de camp, un dey was all go off down de creek for de watair. Dey was tie up long time. By gar, eef dar was one man see me, eet be bad for de store-clothes man, I tell you. Guess dey keel heem. No one see me. I was bring two pony up close to de camp, quiet lak, un tie dem een de bush. Den I was go to de fire. De leetle man she look at me un she *cache* all de money on de robe een hees pocket, un he tole me, 'You say I wan' queet.' De breeds dey say he mus' not queet. All right, he say, he play some more. Den dey was play, un he was deal, un dey was all 'ave de big han'ful, un bet all dair money. I was know de leetle man he sure win, un I was tak out my seex-shootair.

"Den dese breed she got varrie much excite. Oh, dey weare wile, un dey weare show down dair han' on de robe. De leetle man he was win all right. He sais he sorry—he not wan' win all dair money.

"I sais, 'You store-clothes man, you put de money een your pocket; you 'ave win all right.' One man he sais he 'ave not win all right, un he mus' geeve de money back. I was heet dees man een de head wid my gun, un he was fall down. Den dey was all jump up, un de fellar what was hole de spleet steek she drop de spleet steek. I was jump to de leetle man un say, 'Come.'

"We run queek to dose bush, geet on de pony, un we geet out. Eet was so leetle time dat dese breed dey not *sabe,* un I don' know what dey do den. I herd dat store-clothes man on de pony, un he sais, 'Now you tak me to de railroad.'

"I sais: 'Yes, now I tak you to de railroad. Guess you tink dat pretty hot pokair game?'

"He sais, eef he only geet to dat rail-road;" and Sun-Down laughed long and heartily.

"Guess dem breed fellars dey 'ave de long time for fin' dose pony. Eet was no use for me try herd dat leetle man fas' 'nough eef dose Enjun geet dose pony queek; but dey deed not, so I was geet to Glendive, what was de end of de railroad. Dat store-clothes man he was great deal more teekle dan Meestar B—— when he geet dat bull elk oddar day. He was jump up un down; he was yell; he was tank me; he was buy great deal of rum. We was have varrie good time.

"Den we was play de pokair some more —was play wid de white man. De leetle man was deal de card, un I was all time win. Was win all de white man was 'ave, un was geet a papier from one man what was what you call de mortgage for de leevery-stable. 'All right,' sais de leetle man, 'you put up your money—I put up my money un de papier—we tak de leevery-stable. Sun-Down,' he sais, 'we go eento beesness— hey?'

"So we was go eento beesness—een de beesness of de leevery-stable. I was varrie great man.

"Dat was Saturday, un Sunday I was go out to see de pries', what was tole me to come. Aftair I was see de pries' un was fix up, I come back eento de village, un was go to de leevery-stable. Dey was say I not own de leevery-stable. 'You go see your pardner,' dey sais; un I geet on my pony for fin' leetle man what was my pardner. I look all roun'. De people was say he go off on de railroad. I was run dat pony for de dam railroad.

"When I was geet dar de train, what was de freight, she weare pull out. I was see de leetle store-clothes man—my pardner—she was stan' beside de train, un he was see me.

"I ride up, but he was jump on undair de car—what you call—de car-wheel axe, un he was laugh at me from between de wheel. He was yell, 'Sun-Down, I blow een de leevery-stable las' night.'

" 'I weel blow you een,' I sais, un I fire de seex-shootair at heem, but I was unable to heet heem. De train was run fas'; my pony was not run so fas'— I could not catch heem. He was ride on de brake bettair dan on de pony;" and Sun-Down Leflare looked sad, for had not most of his real troubles come of railway trains?

"Well, Leflare," I said, as I thought of this meteoric financial tour, "nothing came of all that enterprise, did it?"

"No—no—not'ing came of dat."

Bring the Fifth Corps North

We read that the Fifth Army Corps is to be brought North, and then we read that it is not. The President should punch up those old bureaucrats of his down in Washington and have them bring that corps home—up North, and the farther North the better. It has done enough. The vitality of the men was exhausted in the terrific campaign against Santiago, and they are not fit to encounter the heat and fever. This corps is the flower of our army, and contains all the material for our future great commanders, because in it is nearly all of the regular army establishment. Other fresh troops could go in and relieve it. These new men would not be weak from hunger, fatigue, and wounds, and would bear up better.

The idea of acclimating the men which I have heard advanced is simple foolishness. It takes two years to acclimate a man to the tropics, if he doesn't die, and then he is weakened permanently. The English understand tropical campaigning, and they put strong men into a jungle, march and fight them hard until the object of the campaign is accomplished, when they are immediately withdrawn.

Bring the Fifth Corps home immediately. Justice and good policy demand it.

Colonel Roosevelt's Pride

I have been amused over Colonel Roosevelt's claims for the worth and efficitncy of his Rough Riders. It is such an old soldier trick.

Also, the curious effect it has had on the public, who, not understanding soldiers, take it seriously.

All soldiers, the world over and history through, will claim every virtue for their own regiments, privates as well as colonels, and so, too, will "Jackies" for their particular ships. Privates and Jackies will clip you on the nose if you even presume to question their claims.

Regimental affection is a grand thing, too. It means so much to the members. It involves their past and their pride.

What a poor stick a colonel would be who did not think his regiment was the best in the world, ancient or modern! And you may be sure a private who won't stand up for his regiment is wrong somehow; probably no good.

And soldiers retain this affection for their old regiments, although they may be long out of them. General Miles won't go anywhere without the Fifth Infantry if he can help it; and I firmly believe General Merritt would hang any one who said aught against the Fifth Cavalry.

By the same token soldiers and sailors will stand up for their colonel (and when they won't, it is a sure sign that the officer is sadly lacking) or their captain "to a finish" anywhere, any place, any time.

I hope the Rough Riders will never have to lick all the people that their belligerent colonel thinks they can lick. Yet it wouldn't do at all for you to go near a Rough Rider camp and say anything derogatory of Roosevelt. You would have to make good on the spot.

Sun-Down Leflare's Warm Spot

Towards mid-day the steady brilliancy of the sun had satiated my color sense, and the dust kicked up in an irritating way, while the chug-a-chug, chug-a-chug, of the ponies began to bore me. I wished for something to happen.

We had picked wild plums, which had subdued my six-hour appetite, but the unremitting walk-along of our march had gotten on my nerves. A proper man should not have such fussy things—but I have them, more is the pity. The pony was going beautifully: I could not quarrel with him. The high plains do things in such a set way, so far as weather is concerned, and it is a day's march before you change views. I began to long for a few rocks—a few rails and some ragged trees—a pool of water with some reflections—in short, anything but the horizontal monotony of our surroundings.

To add to this complaining, it could not be expected that these wild men would ever stop until they got there, wherever "there" might happen to be this day. I evidently do not have their purpose, which is "big game," close to my heart. The chickens in this creek-bottom which we are following up would suit me as well.

These people will not be diverted, though I must, so I set my self-considering eye on Sun-Down Leflare. He will answer, for he is a strange man, with his curious English and his weird past. He is a tall person of great physical power, and must in his youth have been a handsome vagabond. Born and raised with the buffalo Indians, still there was white man enough about him for a point of view which I could understand. His great head, almost Roman, was not Indian, for it was too fine; nor was it French; it answered to none of those requirements. His character was so fine a balance between the two, when one considered his environment, that I never was at a loss to place the inflections. And yet he was an exotic, and could never bore a man who had read a little history.

Sombreroed and moccasined, Sun-Down pattered along on his roan pinto, talking seven languages at the pack-ponies, and I drew alongside. I knew he never contributed to the sum of human knowledge gratuitously; it had to be irritated out of him with delicacy. I wondered if he ever had a romance. I knew if he ever had, it would be curious. We bumped along for a time doggedly, and I said,

"Where you living now, Sun-Down?"

Instantly came the reply, "Leevin' here." He yelled at a pack-horse; but, turning with a benignant smile, added, "Well, I weare leeve on dees pony, er een de blanket on de white pack-horse."

"No tepee?" I asked.

"No—no tepee," came rather solemnly for Sun-Down, who was not solemn by nature, having rather too much variety for that.

"I suppose you are a married man?"

"No—no—me not marry," came the heavy response.

"Had no woman, hey?" I said, as I gave up the subject.

"Oh, yees! woman—had seex woman," came the rather overwhelming information.

"Children too, I suppose?"

"Oh, dam, yees! whole tribe. Why, I was have boy old as you aire. He up Canada way; hees mudder he Blackfoot woman. Dat was 'way, 'way back yondair, when I was firs' come Rocky Mountain. I weare a boy."

I asked where the woman was now.

"Dead—long, long time. She got keel by buffalo. She was try for skin buffalo what was not dead 'nough for skin. Buffalo was skin her," and Sun-Down grinned quickly at his pleasantry; but it somehow did not appeal to my humor so much as to my imagination, and it revealed an undomesticated mind.

"Did you never have one woman whom you loved more than all the others?" I went on.

"Yees; twenty year 'go I had Gros Ventre woman. She was fine woman—bes' woman I evair have. I pay twenty-five pony for her. She was dress de robe un paint eet bettair, un I was mak heap of money on her. But she was keel by de Sioux while she was one day pick de wil' plum, un I lose de twenty-five pony een leetle ovair a year I have her. Sacré!

"Eef man was hab seex woman lak dat een dose day, he was not ask de odds of any reech man. He could sell de robe plenty;" and Sun-Down heaved a downright sigh.

I charged him with being an old trader, who always bought his women and his horses; and Sun-Down turned his head to me with the chin raised, while there was the wild animal in his eye.

"Buy my woman! What de 'ell you know I buy my woman?"

And then I could see my fine work. I gave him a contemptuous laugh.

Then his voice came high-pitched: "You ask me de oddar night eef I weare evair cole. Do you tink I was evair cole now? You say I buy my woman. Now I weel tell you I deed not alway buy my woman."

And I knew that he would soon vindicate

his gallantry, so I said, softly, "I will have to believe what you tell me about it."

"I don' wan' for dat agent to know 'bout all dees woman beesness. He was good frien' of mine, but he pretty good man back Eas'—maybeso he not lak me eef he know more 'bout me;" and Sun-Down regained his composure.

"Oh, don't you fret—I won't say a word," I assured him. And here I find myself violating his confidence in print; but it won't matter. Neither Sun-Down nor the agent will ever read it.

"'Way back yondair, maybeso you 'bout dees high"—and he leaned down from his pony, spreading his palm about two feet and a half above the buffalo-grass—"I was work for Meestar MacDonnail, what hab trade-pos' on Missouri Reever. I was go out to de Enjun camp, un was try for mak 'em come to Meestar MacDonnail for trade skin. Well, all right. I was play de card for dose Enjun, un was manage for geet some skin myself for trade Meestar MacDonnail. I was know dose Enjun varrie well. I was play de card, was run de buffalo, un was trap de skin.

"I was all same Enjun—fringe, bead, long hair—but I was wear de hat. I was hab de bes' pony een de country, un I was hab de firs' breech-loadair een de country. Ah, I was reech! Well, I young man, un de squaw she was good frien' for me, but Snow-Owl hab young woman, un he tink terreble lot 'bout her—was watch her all time. Out of de side of her eye she was watch me, un I was watch her out of de side of my eye—we was both watch each oddar, but we deed not speak. She was look fine, by gar! You see no woman at Billings Fair what would speet even wid her. I tink she not straight-bred Enjun woman—I tink she 'bout much Enjun as I be. All time we watch each oddar. I know eet no use for try trade Snow-Owl out of her, so I tink I win her wid de cards. Den I was deal de skin game for Snow-Owl, un was hab heem broke—was geet all hees pony, all hees robe, was geet hees gun; but eet no use. Snow-Owl she not put de woman on de blanket. I tell heem, 'You put de woman on de blanket, by gar I put twenty pony un forty robe on de blanket.'

"No, he sais he weel not put de woman on de blanket. He nevair mind de robe un de pony. He go to de Alsaroke un steal more pony, un he have de robe plenty by come snow.

"Well, he tak some young man un he go off to Alsaroke to steal horse, un I seet roun' un watch dat woman. She watch me. Pretty soon camp was hunt de buffalo, un I was hunt Snow-Owl's woman. Every one was excite, un dey don' tak no 'count of me. I see de woman go up leetle coulie for stray horse, un I follar her. I sais: 'How do? You come be my woman. We run off to Meestar MacDonnail's trade-house.'

"She sais she afraid. I tole her: 'Your buck no good; he got no robe, no pony; he go leave you to live on de camp. I am reech. Come wid me.' And den I walk up un steek my knife eento de ribs of de old camp pony what she was ride. He was go hough! hough! un was drop down. She was say she weel go wid me, un I was tie her hand un feet, all same cowboy she rope de steer down, un I was leave her dair on de grass. I was ride out een de plain for geet my horse-ban', un was tell my moccasin-boy I was wan' heem go do dees ting, go do dat ting— I was forget now.

"Well, den back I go wid de horse-ban' to de woman, un was put her on good strong pony, but I was tak off hees lariat un was tie her feet undar hees belly. I tink maybeso she skin out. Den we mak trail for Meestar MacDonnail, un eet was geet night. I was ask her eef she be my squaw. She sais she will be my squaw; but by gar she was my squaw, anyhow, eef I not tak off de raw-hide." Sun-Down here gave himself up to a little merriment, which called crocodiles and hyenas to my mind.

"I was tell you not for doubt I mak dat horse-ban' burn de air dat night. I knew eef dose Enjun peek up dat trail, dey run me to a stan'-steel. Eet was two day to Meestar MacDonnail, un I got dair 'bout dark, un Meestar MacDonnail she sais, 'When dose Enjun was come een?' I sais, 'Dey come pretty queek, I guess.'

"I was glad for geet een dat log fence. My pony she could go no more. Well, I was res' up, un maybeso eet four day when up come de 'vance-guard of dose Enjun, un dey was mad as wolf. Deedn't have nothin' on but de moccasin un de red paint. Dey was crazy. Meestar MacDonnail he not let 'em een de log fence. Den he was say, 'What een hell de mattair, Leflare?' I sais, 'Guess dey los' someting.'

"Meestar MacDonnail was geet up on de beeg gate, un was say, 'What you Enjun want?' Dey was say, 'Leflare; he stole chief's wife.' Dey was want heem for geeve me up. Den Meestar MacDonnail he got crazy, un he dam me terreble. He sais I was no beesness steal woman un come to hees house; but I was tol' heem I have no oddar plass for go but hees house. He sais, 'Why you tak woman, anyhow?' I was shrug my shouldair.

"Dose Enjun dey was set roun' on dair ham-bone un watch dat plass, un den pretty soon was come de village—dog, baby, dry meat—whole outfeet. Well, Leflare he was up in a tree, for dey was mak camp all roun' dat log fence. Meestar MacDonnail he was geet on de gate, de Enjun dey was set on de grass, un dey was talk a heap—dey was talk steady for two day. De Enjun was have me or dey was burn de pos'. Meestar MacDonnail sais he was geeve up de woman. De Enjun was say, dam de woman—was want me. I was say I was not geeve up de woman. Dat was fine woman, un I was say eef dey geet dat woman, dey must geet Leflare firs'.

"All night dar was more talk, un de Enjun dey was yell. Meestar MacDonnail was want me for mak run een de night-time, but I was not tink I geet troo. 'Well, den,' he sais, 'you geeve yourself to dose Enjun.' I was laugh at heem, un cock my breech-loadair, un say, 'You cannot mak me.'

"De Enjun dey was shoot dar gun at de log fence, un de white man he was shoot een de air. Eet was war.

"All right. Pretty soon dey was mak de

"Hees Beeg Buffalo-lance She Go Clean Troo My Shoulder." *Authors' photoengraving.*

peace sign, un was talk some more. Snow-Owl had come.

"Den I got on de gate un I yell at dem. I was call dem all de dog, all de woman een de worl'. I was say Snow-Owl he dam ole sage-hen. He lose hees robe, hees pony, hees woman, un I leek heem een de bargain eef he not run lak deer when he hear my voice. Den I was yell, bah!" which Sun-Down did, putting all the prairie-dogs into their holes for our day's march.

"Den dey was talk.

"Well, I sais, eef Snow-Owl he any good, let us fight for de woman. Let dose Enjun sen' two beeg chief eento de log fence, un I weel go out eento de plain un fight Snow-Owl for de woman. Eef I leek, dose Enjun was have go 'way; un eef dar was any one strike me but Snow-Owl, de two chief mus' die. Meestar MacDonnail he say de two chief mus' die. De Enjun was talk heap. Was say 'fraid of my gun. I was say eef I not tak my gun, den Snow-Owl mus' not tak hees bow-arrow. Den dey send de two chief

eento de log house. We was fight wid de lance un de skin-knife.

"Eet was noon, un was hot. I was sharp my knife, was tie up my bes' pony tail, un was tak off my clothes, but was wear my hat for keep de sun out of my eye. Den I was geet on my pony un go out troo de gate. I was yell, 'Come on, Snow-Owl; I teach you new game;' un I was laugh at dem.

"Does Enjun weare not to come within rifle-shot of de pos', or de chief mus' die.

"All right. Out come Snow-Owl. He was pretty man—pretty good man, I guess. Oh, eet was long time 'go. I tink he was brav' man, but he was tink too much of dat woman. He was on pinto pony, un was have not a ting on heem but de breech-clout un de bull-hide shiel'. Den we leek our pony, un we went for fight. I dun'no' jes what eet all weare;" and Sun-Down began to undo his shirt, hauling it back to show me a big livid scar through the right breast, high up by the shoulder.

"De pony go pat, pat, pat, un lak de light

in de mornin' she trabel 'cross de plain we come togaddar. Hees beeg buffalo-lance she go clean troo my shoulnar, an br'ak off de blade, un trow me off my pony. Snow-Owl she stop hees pony chuck, chunck, chinck, un was come roun' for run me down. I peeked up a stone un trow eet at heem. You bet my medicine she good; eet heet heem een de back of de head.

"Snow-Owl she go wobble, wobble, un she slide off de pony slow lak, un I was run up for heem. When I was geet dair he was geet on hees feet, un we was go at eet wid de knife. Snow-Owl was bes' man wid de lance, but I was bes' man wid de knife, un hees head was not come back to heem from de stone, for I keel heem, un I took hees hair; all de time de lance she steek out of my shoulnar. I was go to de trade-pos', un dose Enjun was yell terrebel; but Meestar MacDonnail she was geet on de gate un say dey mus' go 'way or de chief mus' die.

"Nex' morning dey was all go 'way; un Leflare he go 'way too. Meestar MacDonnail he did not tink I was buy all my squaw. Sacré!

"Oh, de squaw—well, I sol' her for one hundred dollar to white man on de Yellowstone. 'Twas t'ree year aftair dat fight;" and Sun-Down made a detour into the brushy bottom to head back the kitchen-mare, while I rode along, musing.

This rough plains wanderer is an old man now, and he may have forgotten his tender feelings of long ago. He had never examined himself for anything but wounds of the flesh, and nature had laid rough roads in his path, but still he sold the squaw for whom he had been willing to give his life. How can I reconcile this romance to its positively fatal termination?

Back came Sun-Down presently, and spurring up the cut-bank, he sang out, "You tink I always buy my squaw, hey?—what you tink 'bout eet now?"

Oh, you old land-loper, I do not know what to think about you, was what came into my head; but I said, "Sun-Down, you are a raw dog," and we both laughed.

So over the long day's ride we bobbed along together, with no more romance than hungry men are apt to feel before the evening meal. We toiled up the hills, driving the pack-horses, while the disappearing sun made the red sand-rocks glitter with light on our left, and about us the air and the grass were cold. Presently we made camp in the canyon, and what with laying our bedding, cooking our supper, and smoking, the darkness had come. Our companions had turned into their blankets, leaving Sun-Down and me gazing into the fire. The dance of the flames was all that occupied my mind until Sun-Down said, "I want for go Buford dees wintair."

"Why don't you go?" I chipped in.

"Oh—leetle baby—so long," and he showed me by spreading his hands about eighteen inches.

"Your baby, Sun-Down?"

"Yees—my little baby," he replied, meditatively.

"Why can't you go to Buford?" I hazarded.

"Leetle baby she no stan de trip. Eet varrie late een de fall—maybeso snow—leetle baby she no stand dat."

"Why don't you go by railroad?" I pressed; but, bless me, I knew that was a foolish question, since Sun-Down Leflare did not belong to the railroad period, and could not even contemplate going anywhere that way.

"I got de wagon un de pony, but de baby she too leetle. Maybeso I go nex' year eef baby she all right. I got white woman up at agency for tak care of de baby, un eet cos' me t'ree dollar a week. You s'pose I put dat baby een a dam Enjun tepee?" And his voice rose truculently.

As I had not supposed anything concerning it, I was embarrassed somewhat, and said, "Of course not—but where was the mother of the child?"

"Oh, her mudder—well, she was no Enjun. Don' know where she ees now. When de leetle baby was born, her mudder was run off on de dam railroad;" and we turned in for the night.

My romance had arrived.

Take the Army out of Politics

This grand nation is working out its immortal purposes, and I sometimes believe it contains the great hope of mankind. We have been slowly and reluctantly dragged into a war with Spain—one which we have averted for many years, but which was sure to come.

It came, and we grappled with it. After a severe struggle Spain was whipped into seeking peace terms, and now that we can mop our heads and breathe easier for a few moments, what do we find? We find we have a small modern navy which is better and more efficient than our wildest hopes could dream. Very well; it is not tinctured with politics. At least there has not appeared on the surface any of the scheming of politics. Its operations have been characterized by straightforward professional work on the part of every one connnected with the Navy Department. Every possible detail seems to have been thought out, every want anticipated. The Secretary pressed the button, and the war ships did the rest.

We found our army in different shape. We find nothing but disappointment, nothing to be proud of except the fighting ability of the line-officers and the enlisted men. The staff corps lay peacefully down on their backs at the beginning, and generals and colonels commanding troops had to detail line lieutenants to "hustle" up necessities in the open market to keep troops from starving to death. The volunteers have had a most destructive summer in the camps of instruction, and they now clamor to be mustered out. A victorious army comes home "on its back." The administration of the War Department is hopelessly discredited before the people. The deadening hand of selfish politics is laid over all.

We are enjoying an armistice at present, and with our newly acquired islands, which we desire to hold, we have almost unanimously concluded that we must have an army.

Now what will our new army be like? Will it be built along the lines dictated by military minds thinking only of effectiveness, or will ignorant and selfish politicians create it along their own lines? I am in great doubt about this matter. I only know for certain that a politico-military system will bring disaster.

However, if we are to have an army which is to do the work expected of it properly, we must at least do the following things, and doubtless many others, or we will *not* have such an army. Of which fact you can be absolutely sure.

The general of the army, or whatever major-general commands it from Washington, must be the head of the army—not in theory, but in fact. He must be the responsible head of the army—one whom we can praise if things go well, or one whom we can condemn if things go ill.

At the beginning of this Spanish war, when we should have had so much, we had nothing. The press and Congress turned hysterically on General Miles, the head of the army. It bitterly denounced him, and bade him come forward and tell them why.

He laughed at both. He could afford to do it. There was nothing else to do. Then he explained that he knew nothing more of the administration of the army than any Congressman could find out by applying to the Secretary of War. All the heads of the staff corps reported to that quaint creature, and not to him. This has been so since Grant laid down his complete control at the end of the civil war. Sherman had, as general of the army, gone to live in St. Louis because he regarded his presence in Washington as useless and humiliating. Sheridan fought various Secretaries of War with all his ardor during his incumbency; and so it has gone on to the present time despite protests and recommendations. The generals commanding our armies, after arriving at that distinction—the result of a life-long service in every grade of the establishment—after surviving fights, marchings, hunger, disease in a dozen climates, and with characters as clean as newwashed linen, come to Washington only to find themselves thrust aside by a powerful intrigue.

The high-water mark of this condition was reached when the general commanding the army had to reply to a corps commander before Santiago that he did not supersede him; he could not supersede a subordinate! So used have our soldiers become to the political head of the army that they become grotesquely mixed in their military relation; they have lost the unities. From a military standpoint the thing is funny.

The Secretaries of War have been always prominent working politicians—to a greater extent than other cabinet members. They have, with one exception since the civil war, used the department along political lines, and even this exception jealously guarded the department prerogatives. The adjutant-general has been responsible to the Secretary alone, and has come to be regarded in the army as the real working head. The fact that the adjutant-general should be the private secretary of the general in command is a long-forgotten truth.

During all these years the generals of the army have been "jollied" into making an annual report to Congress, but they were compilations of the reports of heads of staff corps, with which the generals may have had sympathy or not. In General Miles's case, he has made many recommendations to Congress which it did not act on, but which will relieve him from responsibility in cases like the present war.

The initiative of the general of the army, its natural head, is lost. For the solicitude of the tried soldier is substituted the ignorance of politicians—men who would not know a government wagon if they saw one; men who conserve their own well-being in time of peace, and who in time of war are in a state of frantic bewilderment. The adjutant-general readily succumbs to the powers he finds at his disposal in being the understudy of the Secretary, and is usually a mere tool. A tool he should be—he is nothing else, anyway—only he serves the wrong master, if you consider the well-being of the army.

So if we are to have a proper army in the future, it should have a proper head, and to him should go the heads of staff corps, utterly subservient to his orders, and the adjutant-general should be at his elbow, performing the proper functions of an adjutant. The Secretary of the War Department should be the political head and the intermediary head between the army and the President and Congress. Then the people will know who to blame if the army is not effective.

The next important thing which must come to pass before we have a good army is "an interchangeable line and staff." This should be true of every staff corps except the medical one and possibly the paymaster's.

In regard to a general staff—or more properly a war board—it is an institution which prospers best under a czar or kaiser. It needs a monarch over it who is the head of the army above all else, and who is so independent of all hampering, and so vitally solicitous of its effectiveness, that he, king-like, can demand the "best." To a czar or a kaiser the general staff is second only to God.

We Americans remark that the generals and admirals do best who have the worst signal-service staff-officers at their command. A wire to Washington is the *béte noire* of our commanders. It is an open secret that the best generals England sends out have always good communications, perfectly established, with the home government, but always, unfortunately, two days ahorseback in the rear. They consequently are two days away from interfering politicians who are at any time liable to become hysterical, and who, under such conditions, would not hesitate to sacrifice the reputations and lives of soldiers.

England has suffered from all the afflictions which we are going through, but time has taught her to let Kitchener go ahead in his own way. She only demands that he be successful, and not sacrifice troops unneccessarily. She has learned to let her tried soldiers do their duty without tricky little political pups getting under their legs when they are performing.

At present the heads of the staff are not responsible to the general of the army, and indeed things have so arranged themselves that they are responsible to no one, in a true sense. They do not and cannot be made to work together as the interests of the army dictate. So we have a lot of staff establishments going it higgledy-piggledy, and the poor line gets along as best it can. The idea that a staff is nothing but an arrangement to do the business of the army and to administer to its necessities is almost lost sight of. It is utterly independent of the fighting line, which it ignores, in fact. It is not necessary in these days to try and demonstrate that, for every day brings instances to our notice. It is inefficient; it does not do what is expected of it, and it sits up on its hind legs and tenders its excuses, and even tells us that it is doing what it should do very well, knowing that if it were under the direction of a commanding general he would break every "head" in Washington.

Generals who come from the "fighting line" do not know anything about "excuses." Such conveniences are unknown in that part of the army. If you do not do, you will not do, there.

If a general commanded the whole army, a President of the United States would not have to go to camps asking sick soldiers if they had food enough or medical attendance. He would be kept busy in Washington signing new commissions to the successors of the men whom a general would remove.

If a man came from Fort Adobe to do his three years' detail in a Washington staff corps, he would not go into a trance or a Rip Van Winkle nap. He would, in case he was in the Ordnance Bureau, take a most active interest in the introduction of smokeless powder. He would expect to have to personally use powder in the future, and he would bestir himself about the thing. Of course there could be no "close corporation"—it could not be "Ordnance Company (limited)"—because there would not be time to arrange that. He would not send Maxim, Whitehead, Lee, and the Lord only knows how many other geniuses, abroad to help fight us while trying to adopt their inventions for a close corporation to which he belonged. In short, he would be active instead of passive, and he would be in sympathy and in touch with the men who fire the powder, eat the pork when the thermometer is 100°, get lugged wounded from battlefields on improvised poles instead of proper litters. He would know what it is not to be paid promptly, and if he got a quartermaster detail, he would think out some of the problems which are in the future to confront the army. If he were in the inspector-general's department, he would inspect, and "boards of survey" would be sitting on many an incompetent officer's case who should go on the retired list for physical or mental incapacity. In short, the staff would look after the line, which it does or does not at present, as the spirit moves it. Also, favoritism would have had its day, and a big bunch of coffee-cooling cripples would find their way into private life. And he would wear his uniform in Washington as a matter of pride.

These two changes would insure us effectiveness in our army, as every good and experienced soldier with whom I have talked has told me.

There should be, either at West Point or elsewhere, an infantry and cavalry school, if we are to increase our army, where officers could be turned out for those branches. It is quite unneccessary to make engineers out of such, and for many reasons I believe it is a bad thing. I know many a fellow who is ideally fitted by instinct and physique to command infantry or cavalry who would not and could not be an engineer. I could never see even a remote connection between building an iron bridge and jockeying a troop of cavalry into form.

I might go on into a hundred details regarding a proper army organization; but let a general command an army, the staff of which is alive, and they would straighten out these things, because they would be responsible, and if let alone they would know how.

Herein lies the rub. The best foreign military experts have said that we could never have a good military administration, because of the selfish and unintelligent interruption of our legislators. Dozens of men doing dozens of things at different times cannot have a policy, nor could they maintain one if they had it.

Congress is charged by the Constitution with the duty of making rules and regulations for the government of the army and navy; and it has made such rules and regulations, especially touching the care and the distribution of government property, that red tape and inefficiency are quite inevitable. The strongest executive genius that ever lived could not administer the affairs of the army of the United States in a satisfactory way unless he disobeyed the laws which were passed by Congress. The first thing that must be done in securing such a reform in military administration as will make an efficient army will be the elimination of Congressional rule. Congress must abdicate; it must give up its power over the army, which it maintains now by making such rules and regulations that efficient administration in any staff corps is impossible. Besides that, Congressmen insist upon filling the staff corps with their favorites; so that they not only prevent proper executive action through their laws, but weaken the staff by forcing improper persons upon it.

Before this war there was an apathy on the part of the people concerning the army, which was reflected in Congress, living as it did in Washington, with nothing but an inanimate staff to remind it of the army's existence; but they have seen now that we have not 125,000 militia available for war at the drum-tap; they have seen inexperienced volunteer officers let hundreds of volunteer soldiers die uselessly or become insubordinate in camps of instruction; they have seen medical, quartermaster, ordnance, and commissary staffs standing stupidly helpless in the middle of what would have been a "licking" for us had Spain been some live power; they have seen our best two generals —Miles and Merritt—shipped off to unimportant side tracks while a "king's favorite" was allowed to puff and sweat over the only important military problem thus far presented; they have seen the politician Alger set the soldier Miles aside, while he ran the war; they have doubtless observed the cunning, the astute Secretary do his own undoing, and they will conclude that there is nothing in allowing a politician to run so important a function as a foreign war when he knows nothing about such things.

It is greatly to be hoped that when Congress takes up the new army, it will not let this discredited staff influence it. What Miles and Merritt and Wade and Henry and Lawton and Chaffee and men of that kind recommend will be right.

Another fact might as well be recognized —for it is a great truth. Militia is a broken reed. History will prove to any one who cares to go into the matter that militia has never done what was claimed for it. The extreme warlike function of which militia is capable is a "month's riot duty." This statement will doubtless come as a shock to many people, but if they go carefully over the books they will reach this conclusion, upon which all soldiers, both here and abroad, are agreed. In our case, however, they must not consider our early frontier population of Indian-fighters, because these men were born, raised, and died in forest warfare, and had nothing in common with peaceful communities.

I think probably we would best retain our militia, or State police, but I deprecate the idea that it is in any sense to be taken into account when real soldier duty is to be expected.

When Congress meets, this problem must be grappled with, and if any ignorance or peanut politics gets into the consideration of it, you can bet all your personal property that "the chickens will come home to roost." An army which has to operate in our new tropical possessions must have the decayed fingers of selfish intrigue taken from its throat, or national disaster and national disgrace will come to us, in the shape of either a foreign repulse or a killing distrust at home.

In the case of volunteer regiments having incompetent officers, which generally is bound to happen, a proper inspector-general's department reporting to the general of the army will bring forth the inevitable court martial, and all such will get their "final statements" on the spot. This is one of those matters which, I said before, will take care of itself if politics are eliminated.

I have no sympathy with idle complaining of soldier suffering which one sees so much of in the pervading newspaper. A soldier gets what God sends him. Soldiers are bound to suffer, and the most elaborate system—even the German military perfection—cannot and does not expect to remove the stones and thorns from the paths of glory. That is a part of the very hard business of war; but America will be a bad ground for the recruiting sergeant if it is not thought that good generals and good staffs are going to alleviate what God sends.

I do not intend in this paper to specifically arraign either the staff or the present administration of the army. They are both dead, and I respect the dead. All soldiers—yes, and many of them in the staff corps—have known for years that everything would break down in the event of war. They knew also that it was useless to struggle for reforms until the people had witnessed and suffered from the collapse. The poor old neglected "line" has gone on doing its duty despite every discouragement. It is more cheerful nowadays. It knows the people will not let Secretaries or mummy staff heads or Congressmen—yea, even Presidents—trifle with an institution charged with the lives of the boys which mothers lay down on the altar of the republic.

Sun-Down's Higher Self

I sat in the growing dusk of my room at the agency, before a fire, and was somewhat lonesome. My stay was about concluded, and I dreaded the long ride home on the railroad—an institution which I wish from the bottom of my heart had never been invented.

The front door opened quietly, and shut. The grating or sand-paper sound of moccasined feet came down the hall, my door opened, and Sun-Down Leflare stole in.

"Maybeso you wan' some coal on dees fire —hey?" he observed, looking in at the top of the stove.

"No, thank you—sit down," I replied, which he did, performing forthwith the instinctive act of making a cigarette.

"Sun-Down, I am going home tomorrow."

"Where you was go home?" came the guttural response.

"Back East."

"Ah, yees. I come back Eas' myself—I was born back Eas'. I was come out here long, long time 'go, when I was boy."

"And what part of the East did you come from?"

"Well—Pembina Reever—I was born een dat plass, un I was geet be good chunk of boy een dat plass—un, by gar, I wish I geet be dead man een dat plass. Maybeso I weel."

"You think you will go back some day?" I ventured.

"Oh, yees—I tink eet weel all come out dat way. Some day dat leetle baby he geet ole for mak de travel, un I go slow back dat

plass. I mak dat baby grow up where dar ees de white women un de pries'. I mak heem 'ave de farm, un not go run roun' deese heel on de dam pony." Sun-Down threw away his cigarette, and leaned forward on his hands.

"You are a Roman Catholic?" I asked.

"Yees, I am Roman Catholic. Dose pries' ees de only peop' what care de one dam 'bout de poor half-breed Enjun. You good man, but you not so good man lak de pries'. You go run roun' wid de soldier, go paint up deese Enjun, un den go back Eas'; maybeso nevair see you 'gain. Pries' he stay where we stay, un he not all de while wan' hear how I raise de hell ober de country. He keep say, 'You be good man, Sun-Down'; un, be gar, he keep tell me how for be good man.

"I be pretty good man now; maybeso eet 'cause I too ole for be bad man;" and Sun-Down's cynicism had asserted itself, whereat we laughed.

It occurred to me that time had fought for the priest and against the medicineman in these parts, and I so inquired.

"Yees, dey spleet even nowday. Pries' he bes' man for half-breed; but he be white man, un course he not know great many ting what dose Enjun know."

"Why, doesn't he know as much as the medicine-man?" came my infantlike question.

"Oh, well, pries' he good peop'; all time he varrie good for poor Sun-Down; but I keep tell you he ees white man. All time wan' take care of me when I die. Well, all right, dees Enjun medicine-man she tak care of me when I was leeve sometime. You s'pose I wan' die all time? No; I wan' leeve; un I got de medicine ober een my tepee—varrie good medicine. Eet tak me troo good many plass where I not geet troo maybeso."

"What is your medicine, Sun-Down?"

"Ah, yo nevair min' what my medicine ees. You white man; what you know 'bout medicine? I see you 'fraid dat fores' fire out dair een dose mountain. You ask de question how dose canyon run. Well, you not be so 'fraid you 'ave de medicine. De medicine she tak care dose fire.

"White man she leeve een de house; she walk een de road; she nevair go half-mile out of hees one plass; un I guess all de medicine he care 'bout he geet een hees pocket.

"I see deese soldier stan' up, geet keel, geet freeze all up; don' 'pear care much. He die pretty easy, un de pries' he all time talk 'bout die, un dey don't care much 'bout leeve. All time deese die: eet mak me seeck. Enjun she wan' leeve, un, by gar, she look out pretty sharp 'bout eet too.

"Maybeso white man she don' need medicine. White man she don' 'pear know enough see speeret. Humph! white man can't see wagon-track on de grass; don't know how he see wagon-track on de cloud. Enjun he go all ober de snow; he lie een de dark; he leeve wid dee win', de tunder—well, he leeve all time out on de grass—night-time—daytime—all de time.

"Yes, yes—certainly, Sun-Down. It is all very strange to me, but how can you prove to me that good comes to you which is due to your medicine alone?"

"Ah-h—my medicine—when weare she evair do me any good? Ah-h, firs' time I evair geet my medicine she save my life—what? She do me great deal good, I tell you. Eef dose pries' be dair, she tell, 'You geet ready for die'; but I no wan' die.

"Well, fellar name Wauchihong un me was trap de bevair ovair by de Souris Reever, un we weare not geet to dat reever one night, un weare lay down for go sleep. We weare not know where we weare. We

weare wak up een de middle of dat night, un de plain she all great beeg grass fire. De win' she weare blow hard, un de fire she come 'whew o-o-o!' We say, where we run? My medicine she tell me run off lef' han', un Wauchihong hees medicine tell heem you run off right han' way. I weare say my medicine she good: he weare say hees medicine varrie ole—have done de great ting—weare nevair fail. We follow our medicine, un so we weare part. I run varrie fas', un leetle while I fall een de Souris Reever, un den I know dose fire she not geet Leflare. My medicine was good.

"Nex' day I fin' Wauchihong dead. All burn—all black. He was burn up een dose fire what catch heem on de plain. De win' she drove de fire so fas' he could do not'-ing, un hees medicine she lie to heem.

"You s'pose de pries' he tole me wheech way for run dat night? No; she tell me behave myself, un geet ready for die right dair. Now what you tink?"

Revelations and truths of this sort were overpowering, and no desire to change a man of Sun-Down's age and rarity came to my mind; but in hopes I said, "Did it ever so happen that your medicine failed you?"

"My medicine she always good, but medicine ees not so good one time as nodder time. Do you s'pose I geet dat soldier order to Buford eef my medicine bad? But de medicine she was not ac' varrie well dat time.

"Deed you evair lie down alone een de bottom of de Black Canyon for pass de night? I s'pose you tink dair not'ing but bear een dat canyon; but I 'ave 'ear dem speerets dance troo dat canyon, un I 'ave see dem shoot troo dem pine-tree when I was set on de rim rock. Deed you evair see de top of dose reever een de moonlight? What you know 'bout what ees een dat reever? White man he don't know so much he tink he know. Guess de speeret don' come een de board house, but she howl roun' de tepie een de wintair night. Enjun see de speerets dance un talk plenty een de lodge fire; white man he see not'ing but de coffee boil.

"White man mak de wagon, un de seelver dollar, un de dam railroad, un he tink dat ees all dair ees een de country;" and Sun-Down left off with a guttural "humph," which was the midship shot of disaster for me.

"But you don't tell the priest about this medicine?"

"No—what ees de use for tell de pries'? —he ees white man."

I asked Sun-Down what was the greatest medicine he ever knew, and he did not answer until, fired by my doubts, he continued, slowly, "My medicine ees de great medicine."

A critic must be without fear, since he can never fully comprehend the intent of other minds, so I saw that fortune must favor my investigations, for I knew not how to proceed; but knowing that action is life, I walked quickly to my grip-sack and took out my silver pocket-flask, saying: "You know, Sun-Down, very well, that it is dead against the rule to give a redskin a drink on a United States agency, but I am going to give you one if you will promise me not to go out and talk about it in this collection of huts. Are you with me?"

"Long-Spur—we pretty good frien'— hey? I weel say not a ting."

Then the conventionalities were gone through with, and they are doubtless familiar to many of my readers.

"Now I tole you dees ting—what was de great medicine—but I don' wan' you for go out here een de village un talk no more dan I talk—are you me?"

"I am you," and we forgathered.

"Now le's see; I weel tole you 'bout de bigges' medicine," and he made a cigarette.

"You aire young man—I guess maybeso you not born when I was be medicine-man; but eet was bad medicine for Absaroke, un you mus' not say a ting 'bout dees to dem. I am good frien' here now, but een dose day I was good frien' of de Piegan, un dey wan' come down here to de Absaroke un steal de pony. De party was geet ready—eet was ten men, un we come on de foot. We come 'long slow troo de mountain un was hunt

for de grub. Aftair long time we was fin' de beeg Crow camp—we was see eet from de top of de Pryor Mountain. Den we go 'way back up head of de canyon, 'way een dat plass where de timber she varrie tick, un we buil' de leetle log fort, 'bout as beeg as t'ree step 'cross de meddle. We was wan' one plass for keep de dry meat; we weare not wan' any one for see our fire; un we weare put up de beeg fight dair eef de Absaroke she roun' us up.

"Een dose day de Enjun he not come een de mountain varrie much—dey was hunt de buffalo on de flat, but maybeso she come een de mountain, un we watch out varrie sharp. Every night, jus' sundown, we go out —each man by hees self, un we watch dat beeg camp un de horse ban's. Eet was 'way out on de plain great many mile. White man lak you he see not'ing, but de Enjun he mak out de tepee un de pony. I was always see much bettair dan de odder Enjun—varrie much bettair—un when we come back to de log fort for smoke de pipe, I was tole dose Enjun jus' how de country lay, un where de bes' plass for catch dem pony."

I think one who has ever looked at the Western landscape from a mountaintop will understand what Sun-Down intended by this extensive view. If one has never seen it, words will hardly tell him how it stretches away, red, yellow, blue, in a prismatic way, shaded by cloud forms and ending among them—a sort of topographical map. I can think of nothing else, except that it is an unreal thing to look at.

"Well, for begeen wid, one man she always go alone; nex' night noddair man go. Firs' man she 'ave de bes' chance, un eet geet varrie bad for las' man, 'cause dose Enjun dey catch on to de game un watch un go roun' for cut de trail. But de Enjun horse-t'ief he mak de trail lak de snake—eet varrie hard for peek up.

"I was 'ave de idea I geet be medicine-man, un I tole dem dey don' know not'ing 'cause dey cannot see, un I tole dem I see everyting; see right troo de cloud. I say each dose Enjun now you do jus' what I tole you, den you fin' de pony.

"We Come 'long Slow Troo de Mountain." *Authors' photoengraving.*

"So de firs' man he was start off een de afternoon, un we see heem no more. When de man was geet de horse, un maybeso de scalp, he skin out for de Piegan camp.

"Nex' night noddair man she go start off late œn de afternoon, un I go wid heem, un I sais, 'You stay here, pull your robe ovair your head, un I go een de brush un make de medicine for tell where ees good plass for heem to go.' When I was mak de medicine I come back, un we set dair on de mountain, un I tell heem where he go 'way out dair on de plain. I sais: 'You go down dees canyon un follow de creek down, un twenty-five mile out dair you fin' de horse ban'. You can sleep one night een de plass where I was point heem out—den you geet de pony. Eef you not fin' eet so, I am not medicine-man.'

"So dees man was go. One man she go every night, un I was set een de log fort all 'lone las' night. I was say eef deese Enjun she do what I tole heem, I be beeg great medicine-man dees time. Den I geet varrie much scarce, for I was las' man, un dose Absaroke dey sure begin see our trail, un I put out de fire een de log fort, un I go off down de mountain for geet 'way from the trail what deese Enjun she mak. I was wan' mak de fire on dees mountain, 'cause she jus' 'live wid dose grizzily-bear. I varrie much 'fraid—I sleep een de tree dat night, un jus' come day I was go down de creek een de canyon. I was walk een de water un walk on de rocks. I was geet big ban' elk to run ovair my trail. I was walk long de rim-rock, un was geet pretty well down een de plain. I was sleep dat night een de old bear cave, un I was see dees camp pretty well. Eet was good plass, 'bout ten mile out een de uppair valley of de Beeg-Horn Reever, but I was 'ave be careful, for dose Enjun dey weare run all ovair de country hunt deese horse t'ief tracks. Oh, I see dem varrie well. I see Enjun come up my canyon un pass by me so near I hear dem talk. I was scare.

"Jus' come dark I crawl up on de rim-rock, un eet was rain hard. Enjun she no lak de rain, so I sais: 'I go down now. I keep out een de heel, for I see varrie much bettair dan de Absaroke, un eef I tink dey see me I drop een de sage-bush.'" And here Sun-Down laughed, but I did not think such hide-and-seek was very funny.

"Eet geet varrie dark, un I walk up to dees camp, not more dan ten step from de tepee. I tak de dry meat off de pole un trow eet to dose dog for mak dem keep still while I was hear de Absaroke laugh un talk. De dog he bark not so much at de Enjun as eef I be de white man; jus' same de white man dog he bite de dam leg off de Enjun.

"I cut de rope two fine pony what was tie up near de lodge, un I know deese weare war-pony or de strong buffalo-horse. I lead dem out of dose camp. Eet was no use for try geet more as de two pony, for I could not run dem een de dark night. I feel dem all ovair for see dey all right. I could not see much. Den I ride off."

"You got home all right, I suppose?"

"Eef I not geet home alright by gar, I nevair geet home 'tall. Dey chasse me, I guess, but I 'ave de good long start, un I leave varrie bad trail, I tink. Man wid de led horse he can leave blind trail more def'rent dan when he drive de pony.

"When I geet to dat Piegan camp I was fin' all dose Enjun 'cept one: he was nevair come back. Un I sais my medicine she ees good; she see where no one can see. Dey all sais my medicine she varrie strong for steal de pony. I was know ting what no man she see. Dey was all fin' de camp jus' as I say so. I was geet be strong een dat camp, un dey all say I see bes' jus' at sun-down, un dey always call me de sun-down medicine."

I asked, "How did it happen that you could see so much better than the others; was it your medicine which made it possible?"

"No. I was fool dose Enjun. I was 'ave a new pair of de fiel'-glass what I was buy from a white man, un I was not let dose Enjun see dem—dat ees how."

"So, you old fraud, it was not your medicine, but the field-glasses?" and I jeered him.

"Ah, dam white man, she nevair understan' de medicine. De medicine not 'ave anyting to do wid de fiel'-glass; but how you know what happen to me een dat canyon on dat black night? How you know dat? Eef eet not for my medicine, maybeso I not be here. I see dose speeret—dey was come all roun' me—but my medicine she strong, un dey not touch me."

"Have a drink, Sun-Down," I said, and we again forgathered. The wild man smacked his lips.

"I say, Sun-Down, I have always treated you well; I want you to tell me just what that medicine is like, over there in your tepee."

"Ah, dat medicine. Well, she ees leetle bagful of de bird claw, de wolf tooth, t'ree arrow-head, un two bullet what 'ave go troo my body."

"Is that all?"

"Ah, you white man!"

With the Fifth Corps

I approach this subject of the Santiago campaign with awe, since the ablest correspondents in the country were all there, and they wore out lead-pencils most industriously. I know I cannot add to the facts, but I remember my own emotions, which were numerous, interesting, and, on the whole, not pleasant. I am as yet unable to decide whether sleeping in a mud-puddle, the confinement of a troop-ship, or being shot at is the worst. They are all irritating, and when done on an empty stomach, with the object of improving one's mind, they are extravagantly expensive. However, they satisfied a life of longing to see men do the greatest thing which men are called on to do.

The creation of things by men in time of peace is of every consequence, but it does not bring forth the tumultuous energy which accompanies the destruction of things by men in war. He who has not seen war only half comprehends the possibilities of his race. Having thought of this thing before, I got a correspondent's pass, and ensconced myself with General Shafter's army at Tampa.

When Hobson put the cork in Cervera's bottle, it became necessary to send the troops at once, and then came the first shock of the war to me. It was in the form of an order to dismount two squadrons of each regiment of cavalry and send them on foot. This misuse of cavalry was compelled by the national necessities, for there was not at that time sufficient volunteer infantry equipped and in readiness for the field. It is without doubt that our ten regiments of cavalry are the most perfect things of all Uncle Sam's public institutions. More good honest work has gone into them, more enthusiasm, more intelligence, and they have shown more results, not excepting the new navy or the postal system.

The fires of hatred burned within me. I was nearly overcome by a desire to "go off the reservation." I wanted to damn some official, or all officialism, or so much thereof as might be necessary. I knew that the cavalry officers were to a man disgusted, and thought they had been misused and abused. They recognized it as a blow at their arm, a jealous, wicked, and ignorant stab. Besides, the interest of my own art required a cavalry charge.

General Miles appeared at Tampa about that time, and I edged around towards him, and threw out my "point." It is necessary to attack General Miles with great care and understanding, if one expects any success. "General, I wonder who is responsible for this order dismounting the cavalry?" I ventured.

I think the "old man" could almost see me coming, for he looked up from the reading of a note, and in a quiet manner, which is habitual with him, said, "Why, don't they want to go?" and he had me flat on the ground.

"Oh yes, of course! They are crazy to go! They would go if they had to walk on their hands!" I said, and departed. A soldier who did not want to go to Cuba would be like a fire which would not burn—useless entirely. So no one got cursed for that business; but it is a pity that our nation finds it necessary to send cavalry to war on foot. It would be no worse if some day it should conclude to mount "bluejackets" for cavalry purposes, though doubtless the "bluejackets" would "sit tight." But where is the use of specialization? One might as well ask the nurse-girl to curry the family horse.

So the transports gathered to Port Tampa, and the troops got on board, and the correspondents sallied down to their quarters, and then came a wait. A Spanish warship had loomed across the night of some watch-on-deck down off the Cuban coast. Telegrams flew from Washington to "stop where you are." The mules and the correspondents were unloaded, and the whole enterprise waited.

Here I might mention a series of events which were amusing. The exigencies of the service left many young officers behind, and these all wanted, very naturally, to go to Cuba and get properly shot, as all good soldiers should. They used their influence with the general officers in command; they begged, they implored, and they explained deviously and ingeniously why the expedition needed their particular services to insure success. The old generals, who appreciated the proper spirit which underlay this enthusiasm, smiled grimly as they turned "the young scamps" down. I used to laugh to myself when I overheard these interviews, for one could think of nothing so much as the school-boy days, when he used to beg off going to school for all sorts of reasons but the real one, which was a ball-game or a little shooting-trip.

Presently the officials got the Spanish warship off their nerves, and the transports sailed. Now it is so arranged in the world that I hate a ship in a compound, triple-expansion, forced-draught way. Barring the disgrace, give me "ten days on the island." Do anything to me, but do not have me entered on the list of a ship. It does not matter if I am to be the lordly proprietor of the finest yacht afloat, make me a feather in a sick chicken's tail on shore, and I will thank you. So it came about that I did an unusual amount of real suffering in consequence of living on the *Segurança* during the long voyage to Cuba. I used to sit out on the afterdeck and wonder why, at my time of life, I could not so arrange that I could keep off ships. I used to consider seriously if it would not be a good thing to jump overboard and let the leopard-sharks eat me, and have done with a miserable existence which I did not seem to be able to control.

When the first landing was made, General Shafter kept all the correspondents and the foreign military attachés in his closed fist, and we all hated him mightily. We shall probably forgive him, but it will take some time. He did allow us to go ashore and see the famous interview which he and Admiral Sampson held with Garcia, and for the first time to behold the long lines of ragged Cuban patriots, and I was convinced that it was no mean or common impulse which kept up the determination of these ragged, hungry souls.

Then on the morning of the landing at Daiquiri the soldiers put on their blanket rolls, the navy boats and launches lay by the transports, and the light ships of Sampson's fleet ran slowly into the little bay and "turned everything loose" on the quiet, palm-thatched village. A few fires were burning in the town, but otherwise it was quiet. After severely pounding the coast, the launches towed in the long lines of boats deep laden with soldiery, and the correspondents and foreigners saw them go into the overhanging smoke. We held our breath. We expected a most desperate fight for the landing. After a time the smoke rolled away, and our people were on the beach, and not long after some men climbed the steep hill on which stood a block-house, and we saw presently the Stars and Stripes break from the flag-staff. "They are Chinamen!" said a distinguished foreign soldier; and he went to the other side of the boat, and sat heavily down to his reading of our artillery drill regulations.

"The Biggest Thing in Shafter's Army Was My Pack." *Authors' photoengraving.*

We watched the horses and mules being thrown overboard, we saw the last soldiers going ashore, and we bothered General Shafter's aid, the gallant Miley, until he put us all on shore in order to abate the awful nuisance of our presence.

No one had any transportation in the campaign, not even colonels of regiments, except their good strong backs. It was for every man to personally carry all his own hotel accommodations; so we correspondents laid out our possessions on the deck, and for the third time sorted out what little we could take. I weighed a silver pocket-flask for some time, undecided as to the possibility of carriage. It is now in the woods of Cuba, or in the ragged pack of some Cuban soldier. We had finally three days of crackers, coffee, and pork in our haversacks, our canteens, rubber ponchos, cameras, and six-shooter—or practically what a soldier has.

I moved out with the Sixth Cavalry a mile or so, and as it was late afternoon, we were ordered to bivouac. I sat on a hill, and down in the road below saw the long lines of troops pressing up the valley towards Siboney. When our troops got on the sand beach, each old soldier adjusted his roll, shouldered his rifle, and started for Santiago, apparently by individual intuition.

The troops started, and kept marching just as fast as they could. They ran the Spaniards out of Siboney, and the cavalry brigade regularly marched down their retreating columns at Las Guasimas, fought them up a defile, outflanked, and sent them flying into Santiago. I think our army would never have stopped until it cracked into the doomed city in column formation, if Shafter had not discovered this unlooked-for enterprise, and sent his personal aide on a fast horse with positive orders to halt until the "cracker-line" could be fixed up behind them.

In the morning I sat on the hill, and still

along the road swung the hard-marching columns. The scales dropped from my eyes. I could feel the impulse, and still the Sixth was held by orders. I put on my "little hotel equipment," bade my friends good-bye, and "hit the road." The sides of it were blue with cast-off uniforms. Coats and overcoats were strewn about, while the gray blankets lay in the camps just where the soldiers had gotten up from them after the night's rest. This I knew would happen. Men will not carry what they can get along without unless they are made to; and it is a bad thing to "make" American soldiers, because they know what is good for them better than any one who sits in a roller-chair. In the tropics mid-day marching under heavy kits kills more men than damp sleeping at night. I used to think the biggest thing in Shafter's army was my pack.

It was all so strange, this lonely tropic forest, and so hot. I fell in with a little bunch of headquarters cavalry orderlies, some with headquarters horses, and one with a mule dragging two wheels, which I cannot call a cart, on which General Young's stuff was tied. We met Cubans loitering along, their ponies loaded with abandoned soldier-clothes. Staff-officers on horseback came back and said that there had been a fight on beyond, and that Colonel Wood was killed and young Fish shot dead—that the Rough Riders were all done to pieces. There would be more fighting, and we pushed forward, sweating under the stifling heat of the jungle-choked road. We stopped and cracked cocoanuts to drink the milk. Once, in a sort of savanna, my companions halted and threw cartridges into their carbines. I saw two or three Spanish soldiers on ahead in some hills and brush. We pressed on; but as the Spanish soldiers did not seem to be concerned as to our presence, I allowed they were probably Cubans who had taken clothes from dead Spanish soldiers, and so it turned out. The Cubans seem to know each other by scent, but it bothered the Northern men to make a distinction between Spanish and Cuban, even when shown Spanish prisoners in order that

they might recognize their enemy by sight. If a simple Cuban who stole Spanish soldier clothes could only know how nervous it made the trigger fingers of our regulars, he would have died of fright. He created the same feeling that a bear would, and the impulse to "pull up and let go" was so instinctive and sudden with our men that I marvel more mistakes were not made.

At night I lay up beside the road outside of Siboney, and cooked my supper by a soldier fire, and lay down under a mango-tree on my rubber, with my haversack for a pillow. I could hear the shuffling of the marching troops, and see by the light of the fire near the road the white blanket-rolls glint past its flame—tired, sweaty men, mysterious and silent too but for the clank of tin cups and the monotonous shuffle of feet.

In the early morning the field near me was covered with the cook-fires of infantry, which had come in during the night. Presently a battery came dragging up, and was greeted with wild cheers from the infantry, who crowded up to the road. It was a great tribute to the guns; for here in the face of war the various arms realized their interdependence. It is a solace for cavalry to know that there is some good steady infantry in their rear, and it is a vast comfort for infantry to feel that their front and flanks are covered, and both of them like to have the shrapnel travelling their way when they "go in."

At Siboney I saw the first wounded Rough Riders, and heard how they had behaved. From this time people began to know who this army doctor was, this Colonel Wood. Soldiers and residents in the Southwest had known him ten years back. They knew Leonard Ward was a soldier, skin, bones, and brain, who travelled under the disguise of a doctor, and now they know more than this.

Then I met a fellow-correspondent, Mr. John Fox, and we communed deeply. We had not seen this fight of the cavalry brigade, and this was because we were not at the front. We would not let it happen again. We slung our packs and most industriously plodded up the Via del Rey until we got to within hailing distance of the picket posts, and he said: "Now, Frederic, we will stay here. They will pull off no more fights of which we are not a party of the first part." And stay we did. If General Lawton moved ahead, we went up and cultivated Lawton; but if General Chaffee got ahead, we were his friends, and gathered at his mess fire. To be popular with us it was necessary for a general to have command of the advance.

But what satisfying soldiers Lawton and Chaffee are! Both seasoned, professional military types. Lawton, big and long, forceful, and with iron determination. Chaffee, who never dismounts but for a little sleep

At the Bloody Ford of the San Juan. *Painting in "21" Club Collection—Peter Kriendler, President.*

during the darkest hours of the night, and whose head might have been presented to him by one of William's Norman barons. Such a head! We used to sit around and study that head. It does not belong to the period; it is remote, when the race was young and strong; and it has "warrior" sculptured in every line. It may seem trivial to you, but I must have people "look their part." That so many do not in this age is probably because men are so complicated; but "war is a primitive art," and that is the one objection I had to von Moltke, with his simple, student face. He might have been anything. Chaffee is a soldier.

The troops came pouring up the road, reeking under their packs, dusty, and with their eyes on the ground. Their faces were deeply lined, their beards stubby, but their minds were set on "the front"—"on Santiago." There was a suggestion of remorseless striving in their dogged stepping along, and it came to me that to turn them around would require some enterprise. I thought at the time that the Spanish commander would do well to assume the offensive, and marching down our flank, pierce the centre of the straggling column; but I have since changed my mind, because of the superior fighting ability which our men showed. It must be carefully remembered that, with the exception of three regiments of Shafter's army, and even these were "picked volunteers," the whole command was our regular army—trained men, physically superior to any in the world, as any one will know who understands the requirements of our enlistment as against that of conscript troops; and they were expecting attack, and praying devoutly for it. Besides, at Las Guasimas we got the *moral* on the Spanish.

Then came the "cracker problem." The gallant Cabanais pushed his mules day and night. I thought they would go to pieces under the strain, and I think every "packer" who worked on the Santiago line will never forget it. Too much credit cannot be given them. The command was sent into the field without its proper ratio of pack-mules, and I hope the blame of that will come home to some one some day. That was the *direct* and *only* cause of all the privation and delay which became so notable in Shafter's operations. I cannot imagine a man who would recommend wagons for a tropical country during the rainy season. Such a one should not be censured or reprimanded; he should be spanked with a slipper.

So while the engineers built bridges, and the troops made roads behind them, and until we got *"three days' crackers ahead"* for the whole command, things stopped. The men were on half-rations, were out of tobacco, and it rained, rained, rained. We were very miserable.

Mr. John Fox and I had no cover to keep the rain out, and our determination to stay up in front hindered us from making friends with any one who had. Even the private soldiers had their dog-tents, but we had nothing except our two rubber ponchos. At evening, after we had "bummed" some crackers and coffee from some good-natured officer, we repaired to our neck of woods, and stood gazing at our mushy beds. It was good, soft, soggy mud, and on it, or rather in it, we laid one poncho, and over that we spread the other.

"Say, Frederic, that means my death; I am subject to malaria."

"Exactly so, John. This cold of mine will end in congestion of the lungs, or possibly bronchial consumption. Can you suggest any remedy?"

"The fare to New York," said John, as we turned into our wallow.

At last I had the good fortune to buy a horse from an invalided officer. It seemed great fortune, but it had its drawback. I was ostracized by my fellow-correspondents.

All this time the reconnoissance of the works of Santiago and the outlying post of Caney was in progress. It was rumored that the forward movement would come, and being awakened by the bustle, I got up in the dark, and went gliding around until I managed to steal a good feed of oats for my horse. This is an important truth as showing the demoralization of war. In the pale light I saw a staff-officer who was going to

Caney, and I followed him. We overtook others, and finally came to a hill overlooking the ground which had been fought over so hard during the day. Capron's battery was laying its guns, and back of the battery were staff-officers and correspondents eagerly scanning the country with field-glasses. In the rear of these stood the hardy First Infantry, picturesquely eager and dirty, while behind the hill were the battery horses, out of harm's way.

The battery opened and knocked holes in the stone fort, but the fire did not appear to depress the rifle-pits. Infantry in the jungle below us fired, and were briskly answered from the trenches.

I had lost my canteen and wanted a drink of water, so I slowly rode back to a creek. I was thinking, when along came another correspondent. We discussed things, and thought Caney would easily fall before Lawton's advance, but we had noticed a big movement of our troops towards Santiago, and we decided that we would return to the main road and see which promised best. Sure enough, the road was jammed with horses of Grimes's battery under whip and spur. Around El Poso ranch stood Cubans, and along the road the Rough Riders— Roosevelt's now, for Wood was a brigadier.

The battery took position, and behind it gathered the foreigners, naval and military, with staff-officers and correspondents. It was a picture such as may be seen at a manœuvre. Grimes fired a few shells towards Santiago, and directly came a shrill screaming shrapnel from the Spanish lines. It burst over the Rough Riders, and the manœuvre picture on the hill underwent a lively change. It was thoroughly evident that the Spaniards had the range of everything in the country. They had studied it out. For myself, I fled, dragging my horse up the hill, out of range of Grimes's inviting guns. Some as gallant soldiers and some as daring correspondents as it is my pleasure to know did their legs proud there. The tall form of a staff-major moved in my front in jack-rabbit bounds. Prussian, English, and Japanese, correspondents, artists, all the news, and much high-class art and literature, were flushed, and went straddling up the hill before the first barrel of the Dons. Directly came the warning scream of No. 2, and we dropped and hugged the ground like starfish. Bang! right over us it exploded. I was dividing a small hollow with a distinguished colonel of the staff.

"Is this thing allowed, colonel?"

"Oh yes, indeed!" he said. "I don't think we could stop those shrapnel."

And the next shell went into the battery, killing and doing damage. Following shell were going into the helpless troops down in the road, and Grimes withdrew his battery for this cause. He had been premature. All this time no one's glass could locate the fire of the Spanish guns, and we could see Capron's smoke miles away on our right. Smoky powder belongs with arbalists and stone axes and United States ordnance officers, which things all belong in museums, with other dusty rust.

Then I got far up on the hill, walking over the prostrate bodies of my old friends the Tenth Cavalry, who were hugging the hot ground to get away from the hotter shrapnel. There I met a clubmate from New York, and sundry good foreigners, notably the Prussian (von Goetzen), and that lovely "old British salt" Paget, and the Japanese major, whose name I could never remember. We sat there. I listened to much expert artillery talk, though the talk was not quite so impressive as the practice of that art.

But the heat—let no man ever attempt that after Kipling's "and the heat would make your blooming eyebrows crawl."

This hill was the point of vantage; it overlooked the flat jungle, San Juan hills, Santiago, and Caney, the whole vast country to the mountains which walled in the whole scene. I heard the experts talk, and I love military science, but I slowly thought to myself this is not my art—neither the science of troop movement nor the whole landscape. My art requires me to go down in the road where the human beings are who do these things which science dictates,

in the landscape which to me is overshadowed by their presence. I rode slowly, on account of the awful sun. Troops were standing everywhere, lying all about, moving regularly up the jungle road towards Santiago, and I wound my way along with them, saying, "Gangway, please."

War is productive of so many results, things happen so awfully fast, men do such strange things, pictures make themselves at every turn, the emotions are so tremendously strained, that what knowledge I had fled away from my brain, and I was in a trance; and do you know, cheerful reader, I am not going to describe a battle to you.

War, storms at sea, mountains, deserts, pests, and public calamities leave me without words. I simply said, "Gangway" as I wormed my way up the fateful road to Santiago. Fellows I knew out West and up North and down South passed their word to me, and I felt that I was not alone. A shrapnel came shieking down the road, and I got a drink of water and a cracker from Colonel Garlington. The soldiers were lying alongside and the staff-officers were dismounted, also stopping quietly in the shade of the nearest bush. The column of troops was working its way into the battle line.

"I must be going," I said, and I mounted my good old mare—the colonel's horse. It was a tender, hand-raised trotting-horse, which came from Colorado, and was perfectly mannered. We were in love.

The long columns of men on the road had never seen this condition before. It was their first baby. Oh, a few of the old soldiers had, but it was so long ago that this must have come to them almost as a new sensation. Battles are like other things in nature —no two the same.

I could hear noises such as you can make if you strike quickly with a small walking-stick at a very few green leaves. Some of them were very near and others more faint. They were the Mausers, and out in front through the jungle I could hear what sounded like a Fourth of July morning, when the boys are setting off their crackers. It struck me as new, strange, almost uncanny, because I wanted the roar of battle, which same I never did find. These long-range, smokeless bolts are so far-reaching, and there is so little fuss, that a soldier is for hours under fire getting into the battle proper, and he has time to think. That is hard when you consider the seriousness of what he is thinking about. The modern soldier must have moral quality; the gorrilla is out of date. This new man may go through a war, be in a dozen battles, and survive a dozen wounds without seeing an enemy. This would be unusual, but easily might happen. All our soldiers of San Juan were for the most part of a day under fire, subject to wounds and death, before they had even a chance to know where the enemy was whom they were opposing. To all appearance they were apathetic, standing or marching through the heat of the jungle. They flattened themselves before the warning scream of the shrapnel, but that is the proper thing to do. Some good-natured fellow led the regimental mascot, which was a fice, or a fox-terrier. Really, the dog of war is a fox-terrier. Stanley took one through Africa. He is in all English regiments, and he is gradually getting into ours. His flag is short, but it sticks up straight on all occasions, and he is a vagabond. Local ties must set lightly on soldiers and fox-terriers.

Then came the light as I passed out of the jungle and forded San Juan River. The clicking in the leaves continued, and the fire-crackers rattled out in front. "Get down, old man; you'll catch one!" said an old alkali friend, and I got down, sitting there with the officers of the cavalry brigade. But promptly some surgeons came along, saying that it was the only safe place, and they began to dig the sand to level it. We, in consequence, moved out into the crackle, and I tied my horse with some others.

"Too bad, old fellow," I thought. "I should have left you behind. Modern rifle fire is rough on horses. They can't lie down. But, you dear thing, you will have to take your chances." And then I looked at the preparation for the field hospital. It was al-together too suggestive. A man came, stooping over, with his arms drawn up, and hands flapping downward at the wrists. That is the way with all people when they are shot through the body, because they want to hold the torso steady, because if they don't it hurts. Then the oncoming troops poured through the hole in the jungle which led to the San Juan River, which was our line of battle, as I supposed. I knew nothing of the plan of battle, and I have an odd conceit that no one else did, but most all the line-officers were schooled men, and they were able to put two and two together mighty fast, and in most instances faster than headquarters. When educated soldiers are thrown into a battle without understanding, they understand themselves.

As the troops came pouring across the ford they stooped as low as they anatomically could, and their faces were wild with excitement. The older officers stood up as straight as if on parade. They may have done it through pride, or they may have known that it is better to be "drilled clean" than to have a long, ranging wound. It was probably both ideas which stiffened them up so.

Then came the curious old tube drawn by a big mule, and Borrowe with his squad of the Rough Riders. It was the dynamite-gun. The mule was unhooked and turned loose. The gun was trundled up the road and laid for a shot, but the cartridge stuck, and for a moment the cheerful grin left the red face of Borrowe. Only for a moment; for back he came, and he and his men scraped and whittled away at the thing until they got it fixed. The poor old mule lay down with a grunt and slowly died. The fire was now incessant. The bullets came like the rain. The horses lay down one after another as the Mausers found their billets. I tried to take mine to a place of safety, but a sharp-shooter potted at me, and I gave it up. There was no place of safety. For a long time our people did not understand these sharp-shooters in their rear, and I heard many men murmur that their own comrades were shooting from behind. It was very demoralizing to us, and on the Spaniards' part a very desperate enterprise to lie deliberately back of our line; but of course, with bullets coming in to the front by the bucketful, no one could stop for the few tailing shots. The Spaniards were hidden in the mango-trees, and had smokeless powder.

Now men came walking or were carried into the temporary hospital in a string. One beautiful boy was brought in by two tough, stringy, hairy old soldiers, his head hanging down behind. His shirt was off, and a big red spot shone brilliantly against his marble-like skin. They laid him tenderly down, and the surgeon stooped over him. His breath came in gasps. The doctor laid his arms across his breast, and shaking his head, turned to a man who held a wounded foot up to him, dumbly imploring aid, as a dog might. It made my nerves jump, looking at that grewsome hospital, sand-covered, with bleeding men, and yet it seemed to have fascinated me; but I gathered myself and stole away. I went down the creek, keeping under the bank, and then out into the "scrub," hunting for our line; but I could not find our line. The bullets cut and clicked around, and a sharp-shooter nearly did for me. The thought came to me, what if I am hit out here in the bush while all alone? I shall never be found. I would go back to the road, where I should be discovered in such case; and I ran so quickly across a space that my sharp-shooting Spanish friend did not see me. After that I stuck to the road. As I passed along it through an open space I saw a half-dozen soldiers sitting under a tree. "Look out—sharp-shooters!" they sang out. "Wheet!" came a Mauser, and it was right next to my ear, and two more. I dropped in the tall guinea-grass, and crawled to the soldiers, and they studied the mango-trees; but we could see nothing. I think that episode cost me my sketch-book. I believe I lost it during the crawl, and our friend the Spaniard shot so well I wouldn't trust him again.

From the vantage of a little bank under a big tree I had my first glimpse of San Juan Hill, and the bullets whistled about. One would "tumble" on a tree or ricochet from the earth, and then they shrieked. Our men out in front were firing, but I could not see them. I had no idea that our people were to assault that hill—I thought at the time such an attempt would be unsuccessful. I could see with my powerful glass the white lines of the Spanish intrenchments. I did not understand how our men could stay out there under that gruelling, and got back into the safety of a low bank.

A soldier said, while his stricken companions were grunting around him, "Boys, I have got to go one way or the other, pretty damn quick." Directly I heard our line yelling, and even then did not suppose it was an assault.

Then the Mausers came in a continuous whistle. I crawled along to a new place, and finally got sight of the fort, and just then I could distinguish our blue soldiers on the hill-top, and I also noticed that the Mauser bullets rained no more. Then I started after. The country was alive with wounded men—some to die in the dreary jungle, some to get their happy-home draft, but all to be miserable. Only a handful of men got to the top, where they broke out a flag and cheered. "Cheer" is the word for that sound. You have got to hear it once where it means so much, and ever after you will grin when Americans make that noise.

San Juan was taken by infantry and dismounted cavalry of the United States regular army without the aid of artillery. It was the most glorious feat of arms I ever heard of, considering every condition. It was done without grub, without reserves of either ammunition or men, under tropical conditions. It was a storm of intrenched heights, held by veteran troops armed with modern guns, supported by artillery, and no other troops on the earth would have even thought they could take San Juan heights, let alone doing it.

I followed on and up the hill. Our men sat about in little bunches in the pea-green guinea-grass, exhausted. A young officer of the Twenty-fourth, who was very much excited, threw his arms about me, and pointing to twenty-five big negro infantrymen sitting near, said, "That's all—that is all that is left of the Twenty-fourth Infantry," and the tears ran off his mustache.

Farther on another officer sat with his arms around his knees. I knew him for one of these analytical chaps—a bit of a philosopher—too highly organized—so as to be morose. "I don't know whether I am brave or not. Now there is S——; he don't mind this sort of thing. I think—"

"Oh, blow your philosophy!" I interrupted. "If you were not brave, you would not be here."

The Spanish trenches were full of dead men in the most curious attitudes, while about on the ground lay others, mostly on their backs, and nearly all shot in the head. Their set teeth shone through their parted lips, and they were horrible. The life never runs so high in a man as it does when he is charging on the field of battle; death never seems so still and positive.

Troops were moving over to the right, where there was firing. A battery came up and went into position, but was driven back by rifle fire. Our batteries with their smoky powder could not keep guns manned in the face of the Mausers. Then, with gestures much the same as a woman makes when she is herding chickens, the officers pushed the men over the hill. They went crawling. The Spanish were trying to retake the hill. We were short of ammunition. I threw off my hat and crawled forward to have a look through my glass at the beyond. I could hardly see our troops crouching in the grass beside me, though many officers stood up. The air was absolutely crowded with Spanish bullets. There was a continuous whistle. The shrapnel came screaming over. A ball struck in front of me, and filled my hair and face with sand, some of which I did not get out for days. It jolted my glass and my nerves, and I beat a masterly retreat, crawling rapidly backwards, for a reason which I will let you guess. The small-arms rattled; now and then a wounded man came back and started for the rear, some of them shot in the face, bleeding hideously.

"How goes it?" I asked one.

"Ammunition! ammunition!" said the man, forgetful of his wound.

I helped a man to the field hospital, and got my horse. The lucky mare was untouched. She was one of three animals not hit out of a dozen tied or left at the hospital. One of these was an enormous mule, loaded down with what was probably officers' blanket rolls, which stood sidewise quietly as only a mule can all day, and the last I saw of him he was alive. Two fine officers' chargers lay at his feet, one dead and the other unable to rise, and suffering pathetically. The mule was in such an exposed position that I did not care to unpack him, and Captain Miley would not let any one shoot a horse, for fear of the demoralizing effect of fire in the rear.

A trumpeter brought in a fine officer's horse, which staggered around in a circle. I saw an English sabre on the saddle, and recognized it as Lieutenant Short's, and indeed I knew the horse too. He was the fine thoroughbred which that officer rode in Madison Square military tournament last winter, when drilling the Sixth Cavalry. The trumpeter got the saddle off, and the poor brute staggered around with a bewildered look in his eager eyes, shot in the stifle-joint, I thought; and then he sat down in the creek as a dog would on a hot day. The suffering of animals on a battle-field is most impressive to one who cares for them.

I again started out to the hill, along with a pack-train loaded with ammunition. A mule went down, and bullets and shell were coming over the hill aplenty. The wounded going to the rear cheered the ammunition, and when it was unpacked at the front, the soldiers seized it like gold. They lifted a box in the air and dropped it on one corner, which smashed it open.

"Now we can hold San Juan Hill against them garlics—hey, son!" yelled a happy cavalryman to a doughboy.

"You bet—until we starve to death."

"Starve nothing'—we'll eat them gun-teams."

Well, well, I said, I have no receipt for

licking the kind of troops these boys represent. And yet some of the generals wanted to retreat.

Having had nothing to eat this day, I thought to go back to headquarters camp and rustle something. Besides, I was sick. But beyond the hill, down the road, it was very dangerous, while on the hill we were safe. "Wait for a lull; one will come soon," advised an old soldier. It is a curious thing that battle firing comes like a big wind, and has its lulls. Now it was getting dark, and during a lull I went back. I gave a wounded man a ride to the field hospital, but I found I was too weak myself to walk far. I had been ill during the whole campaign, and latterly had fever, which, taken together with the heat, sleeping in the mud, marching, and insufficient food, had done for me.

The sight of that road as I wound my way down it was something I cannot describe. The rear of a battle. All the broken spirits, bloody bodies, hopeless, helpless suffering which drags its weary length to the rear, are so much more appalling than anything else in the world that words won't mean anything to one who has not seen it. Men half naked, men sitting down on the road-side utterly spent, men hopping on one foot with a rifle for a crutch, men out of their minds from sunstroke, men dead, and men dying. Officers came by white as this paper, carried on rude litters made by their devoted soldiers, or borne on their backs. I got some food about ten o'clock and lay down. I was in the rear at headquarters, and there were no bullets and shells cracking about my ears, but I found I had discovered no particular nervousness in myself, quite contrary to my expectations, since I am a nervous man, but there in the comparative quiet of the woods the reaction came. Other fellows felt the same, and we compared notes. Art and literature under Mauser fire is a jerky business; it cannot be properly systematized. I declared that I would in the future paint "set pieces for dining-rooms." Dining-rooms are so much more amusing than

camps. The novelist allowed that he would be forced to go home and complete "The Romance of a Quart Bottle." The explorer declared that his treatise on the "Flora of Bar Harbor" was promised to his publishers.

Soldiers always joke after a battle. They have to loosen the strings, or they will snap. There was a dropping fire in the front, and we understood our fellows were intrenching. Though I had gotten up that morning at half past three, it was nearly that time again before I went to sleep. The fever and the strong soldier-coffee banished sleep; then, again, I could not get the white bodies which lay in the moonlight, with the dark spots on them, out of my mind. Most of the dead on modern battle-fields are half naked, because of the "first-aid bandage." They take their shirts off, or their pantaloons, put on the dressing, and die that way.

It is well to bear in mind the difference in the point of view of an artist or a correspondent, and a soldier. One has his duties, his responsibilities, or his gun, and he is on the firing-line under great excitement, with his reputation at stake. The other stalks through the middle distance, seeing the fight and its immediate results, the wounded; lying down by a dead body, mayhap, when the bullets come quickly; he will share no glory; he has only the responsibility of seeing clearly what he must tell; and he must keep his nerve. I think the soldier sleeps better nights.

The next day I started again for the front, dismounted, but I only got to El Poso Hill. I lay down under a bank by the creek. I had the fever. I only got up to drink deeply of the dirty water. The heat was intense. The re-enforcing troops marched slowly up the road. The shells came railroading down through the jungle, but these troops went on, calm, steady, like true Americans. I made my way back to our camp, and lay there until nightfall, making up my mind and unmaking it as to my physical condition, until I concluded that I had "finished."

The White Forest

From the mid-winter mist and mush of New York it was a transformation to us standing there in the smoking-room of the Château Frontenac at Quebec, looking down across the grand reaches of the St. Lawrence, where the ice ran in crashing fields through the streaming water of the flood-tide. It was a cheerful view from a cheerful place, though the frost was on the pane, and the wood-work popped with the cold. Down in the street the little Canadian horses, drawing their loads, were white with rime, while their irrepressible French drivers yelled at each other until we could hear them through the double windows. There is energy in this fierce Northern air.

"Why Florida in winter? Why not Quebec?" said the old Yale stroke.

"Yes, why not?" reiterated the Essex trooper.

But the cosiness of the château did not suggest the seriousness of our purpose. We wanted to get out on the snow—to get in the snow—to tempt its moods and feel its impulses. We wanted to feel the nip of that keen outside air, to challenge a contest with our woollens, and to appropriate some of its energy. Accordingly we consulted a wise mind who sold snow-shoes, blankets, moccasins, and socks, and he did a good business.

"Shall we dress at St. Raymond or in the château?" and my companion, mindful of the severity of convention in New York, as he gazed on the litter of his new garments spread out on the floor of our room.

"We will dress here, and leave so early that Quebec will not be out of bed until we are away; but if Quebec were awake and on the streets, Quebec would not turn its head to honor our strangeness with a glance, because it would see nothing new in us;" and dress we did. We only put on three pairs of socks and one pair of flannel-lined moccasins, but we were taught later to put on all we had. As the rich man said to the reporter, when trying to explain the magnitude of his coming ball, "There will be ten thousand dollars' worth of ice-cream," so I say to you we had forty dollars' worth of yarn socks.

We had bags of blankets, hunks of fresh beef and pork, which had to be thawed for hours before cooking, and potatoes in a gunny sack, which rattled like billiard-balls, so hard were they frozen. We found great amusement on the train by rattling the bag of potatoes, for they were the hardest, the most dense things known to science.

The French drivers of the burleaus who deposited us at the train took a cheery interest in our affairs; they lashed the horses, yelled like fiends, made the snow fly around the corners, nearly ran down an early policeman, and made us happy with the animation. They are rough children, amazingly polite—a product of paternalism—and comfortable folks to have around, only you must be careful not to let them succeed in their childish endeavor to drive their horses over you. Anyway, they cheered us off through the softly falling snow of that early winter morning, and made us feel less like strangers.

At St. Raymond were the guides and little one-horse burleaus all ready for the trip to the "bush," or at least for the fifteen miles, which was as far as sleighs could go, up to old man O'Shannahan's, which is the first camp of the club. There were nearly four feet of snow on the ground, so that the regular road between the fences was drifted full, compelling the *habitants* to mark out another way with evergreen trees through their fields.

Far apart over the white landscape are set the little French cottages, with their curved roofs. They are so cosily lonely, and the rough hills go up from the valley to further isolate them. Coming along the road we met the low hauling-sleds of the natives, who ran their horses off the road into the snow halfway up their horses' sides; but the sledges were flat, and floated, as it were. Picturesque fellows, with tuques, red sashes, and fur coats, with bronzed faces, and whiskers worn under their chin, after the fashion of the early thirties. The Quebec *habitants* don't bother their heads about the new things, which is the great reason why they are the most contented people in America.

The faithful watch-dog barked at us from every cottage, and, after the manner of all honest house-dogs, charged us, with skinned lips and gleaming eye. We waited until they came near to the low-set burleau, when we menaced them with the whip, whereat they sprang from the hard road into the soft snow, going out of sight in it, where their floundering made us laugh loud and long. Dogs do not like to be laughed at, and it is so seldom one gets even with the way-side pup.

At O'Shannahan's we were put up in the little club cabin and made comfortable. I liked everything in the country except the rough look of the hills, knowing, as I do, that all the game in America has in these latter days been forced into them, and realizing that to follow it the hunter must ele-

vate himself over the highest tops, which process never became mixed in my mind with the poetry of mountain scenery.

We essayed the snow-shoes—an art neglected by us three people since our boyhood days. It is like horseback-riding—one must be at it all the time if he is to feel comfortable. Snow-shoes must be understood, or they will not get along with you.

Bebé Larette laughingly said, "Purty soon you mak de snow-shoe go more less lak dey was crazee."

Having arranged to haul the supplies into the "bush" next day, we lay down for the night in the warm cabin, tucked in and babied by our generous French guides. The good old Irishman, Mr. O'Shannahan, was the last to withdraw.

"Mr. O'Shannahan, what do the French say for 'good-night'?"

"Well, som' o' thim says 'Bung-sware,' and som' o' thim says 'Bung way';" but none of them, I imagine, say it just like Mr. O' Shannahan.

With the daylight our hut began to abound with the activities of the coming day. A guide had a fire going, and Mr. O'Shannahan stood warming himself beside it. The Essex trooper, having reduced himself to the buff, put on an old pair of moccasins and walked out into the snow. The New Jersey thermometer which we had brought along may not have as yet gotten acclimated, but it solemnly registered 5° below zero.

"Bebé, will you kindly throw a bucket of water over my back?" he asked; but Bebé might as well have been asked to kindly shoot the Essex trooper with a gun, or to hit him with an axe. Bebé would have neither ice-water, rifle, nor axe on his pious soul.

I knew the stern requirements of the morning bath, and dowsed him with the desired water, when he capered into the cabin and began with his crash towel to rub for the reaction. Seeing that Mr. O'Shannahan was perturbed, I said:

"What do you think of that act?"

"Oi think a mon is ez will aff be the soide

av this stove as to be havin' the loikes av yez poor ice-wather down his spoine."

Mr. O'Shannahan reflected and hunched nearer the box-stove, saying: "It's now gaun a year, but oi did say a mon do mooch the loikes av that wan day. He divisted himself av his last stitch, an' day*liber*ately wint out an' rowled himsilf in the snow. That before brikfast, moind ye. Oi've no doobt he's long since dead. Av the loikes av this t'ing do be goan an, an' is rayparted down en the Parliamint, they'll be havin' a law fer it—more's the nade."

After breakfast a hundred pounds of our war material was loaded on each toboggan. We girded on our snow-shoes and started out to break trail for the sledges. I know of no more arduous work. And while the weather was very cold, Mr. O'Shannahan nearly undressed us before he was satisfied at our condition for bush-ranging. We sank from eight to ten inches in the soft snow. The raising of the snow-burdened racket tells on lung and ankle and loin with killing force. Like everything else, one might become accustomed to lugging say ten pounds extra on each set of toes, but he would have to take more than a day at it. The perspiration comes in streams, which showed the good of O'Shannahan's judgment. Besides, before we had gone three miles we began to understand the mistake of not wearing our forty dollars' worth of socks. Also we had our moccasins on the outside, or next to the snow-shoes. They got damp, froze into something like sheet-iron, and had a fine ice-glaze on their bottoms which made them slip and slide backward and forward on the snow-shoes.

After three miles, Bebé readjusted and tied my moccasins, when Oliver, the cook, who was a very intelligent man, mopped his forehead with his shirt-sleeve and observed:

"Excuse me, I t'ink you bettair go back dose cabain—you are not fix hup more propair for dees beesness. Ma dear fren', dose man een Quebec what sol' you dose t'ing"—and here his quiet, patient personality was almost overcome, this human reflection of the long Northern winter could not calm himself, so he blurted, in his peaceful way—"dose man een Quebec dey weare know not'ing."

We were in the light of a great truth—the shoes would not stay on—the thongs cut our toes—we had outlived our usefulness as trailbreakers, and we succumbed. The back track was one of my greatest misfortunes in life, but it was such a measly lot of cold-finger, frozen-toe, slip-down detail that I will forbear. My companions were equally unfortunate; so when we finally fell into the arms of Mr. O'Shannahan, he said:

"Ah, a great hardship. Oi will make that matter plain to yez."

The sledges had deposited their loads halfway up the trail, the guides coming back for the night.

Next morning the remainder of our stuff was loaded, and with renewed faith we strode forth. The snow-shoes were now all right, and, with five pairs of socks apiece—one outside the moccasins—the thongs could not eat our toes. We took photographs of our moccasins—unwholesome, swollen things—and dedicated the plates to Mr. Kipling as "the feet of the young men."

The country of the Little Saguenay is as rough as any part of the Rocky Mountains. It is the custom to dress lightly for travelling, notwithstanding the 20° below zero, and even then one perspires very freely, making it impossible to stop long for a rest, on account of the chill of the open pores. Ice forms on eyebrow, hair, and mustache, while the sweat freezes in scales on the back of one's neck. The snow falls from the trees on the voyager, and melting slightly from the heat of the body, forms cakes of ice. Shades of Nansen and all the Arctic men! I do not understand why they are not all pillars of ice, unless it be that there are no trees to dump snow on them. The spruce and hemlock of these parts all point upward as straight as one could set a lance, to resist the constant fall of snow. If one leaned ever so little out of the perpendicular, it could not survive the tremendous average of fifty

Caribou Tracks. *Authors' photoengraving.*

feet of snowfall each winter. Their branches, too, do not grow long, else they would snap under the weight. Every needle on the evergreens has its little burden of white, and without intermission the snow comes sifting down from the sky through the hush of the winter. When we stopped, and the creak of the snow-shoes was still, we could almost hear our hearts beat. We could certainly hear the cracking of the tobacco burning in our pipes. It had a soothing, an almost seductive influence, that muffle of snow. So solemn is it, so little you feel yourself, that it is a consciousness which brings unconsciousness, and the calm white forest is almost deadening in its beauty. The winter forest means death.

Then came the guides dragging their toboggans, and we could hear them pant and grunt and creak and slip; how they manage the fearful work is quite beyond me. Used to it, I suppose. So are pack-mules; but think of the generations of suffering behind this which alone makes it possible. The men of the pack, the paddle, snow-shoe, toboggan, and axe do harder, more exhausting work than any other set of people; they are nearer to the primitive strain against the world of matter than are other men—they are the "wheelers," so to speak.

The last stage up the mountain was a lung-burster, but finally we got to a lake, which was our objective. It was smooth.

"Let us take off these instruments of torture and rest our feet on the smooth going," said we, in our innocence, and we undid a snow-shoe each. The released foot went into the snow up to our middles, and into water besides. We resumed our snowshoe, but the wet moccasins coming in contact with the chill air became as iron. Our frozen snow-shoe thongs were wires of steel. Our hands were cold with the work of readjustment, our bodies chilled with the waiting. It was a bad half-hour before the cabin was reached. We built a fire, but the provisions had not come up, so we sat around and gazed with glaring eyes at each other. The Essex trooper and I talked of eating the old Yale stroke, who was our companion, but we

agreed he was too tough. I was afraid for a time that a combination might be made against me on those lines, but luckily the toboggans arrived.

The log cabin was seventeen feet square, so what with the room taken by the bunks, box-stove, our provender and dunnage, the lobby of the house was somewhat crowded. There were three Americans and five Frenchmen. The stove was of the most excitable kind, never satisfied to do its mere duty, but threatening a holocaust with every fresh stick of wood. We made what we called "atmospheric cocktails" by opening the door and letting in one part of 20° below zero air to two parts of 165° above zero air, seasoned with French bitters. It had the usual effect of all cocktails; we should much have preferred the "straight goods" at, say, 70°.

In the morning we began a week's work at caribou-hunting. It is proper to state at this interval that this article can have no "third act," for success did not crown our efforts. We scoured the woods industriously behind our India-rubber, leather-lunged guides, with their expert snow-shoeing, and saw many caribou; but they saw us first, or smelled us, or heard us, and, with the exception of two "clean misses," we had no chance. It may be of interest to tell what befalls those who "miss," according to the rough law of the cabin. The returning hunter may deny it vigorously, but the grinning of the guide is ample testimony for conviction. The hunter is led to the torture tree. All the men, cook included, pour out of the cabin and line up. The "misser" is required to assume a very undignified posture, when all the men take a hack at him with a frozen moccasin. It is rude fun, but the howls of laughter ring through the still forest, and even the unfortunate sportsman feels that he has atoned for his deed.

Bebé Larette killed a young caribou, which was brought into camp for our observation. It was of a color different from what we had expected, darker on the back, blacker on the muzzle, and more the color of the tree trunks among which it lives. Indeed, we had it frozen and set up in the timber to be photographed and painted. Standing there, it was almost invisible in its sameness.

Its feet were the chief interest, for we had all seen and examined its tracks. If one puts his hand down into the track, he will find a hard pillar of snow which is compressed by their cup-like feet; and more striking still is it that the caribou does not sink in the snow as far as our big snow-shoes, not even when it runs, which it is able to do in four feet of snow with the speed of a red deer on dry ground. In these parts the caribou has no enemy but man: the wolf and the panther do not live here, though the lynx does, but I could not learn that he attacks the caribou.

From Mr. Whitney's accounts, I was led to believe the caribou was a singularly stupid beast, which he undoubtedly is in the Barren Grounds. For sportsmen who hunt in the fall of the year he is not regarded as especially difficult—he is easily shot from boats around ponds; but to kill a caribou in the Laurentian Mountains in midwinter is indeed a feat. This is due to the deathly stillness of the winter forest, and the snow-shoeing difficulties which beset even the most clever sportsman.

This brings to my mind the observation that snow-shoeing, as a hunter is required to do it when on the caribou track, has the same relationship to the "club snow-shoe run," so called, that "park riding" has to "punching cows." The men of the "bush" have short and broad oval shoes, and they must go up and down the steepest imaginable places, and pass at good speed and perfect silence through the most dense spruce and tamarack thickets, for there the caribou leads. The deep snow covers up the small evergreen bushes, but they resist it somewhat, leaving a soft spot, which the hunter is constantly falling into with fatal noise. If he runs against a tree, down comes an avalanche of snow, which sounds like thunder in the quiet.

I was brought to a perfectly fresh track of three caribou by two guides, and taking the trail, we found them not alarmed, but travelling rapidly. So "hot" was the trail that I removed the stocking from my gun-breech. We moved on with as much speed as we could manage in silence. The trees were cones of snow, making the forest dense, like soft-wood timber in summer. We were led up hills, through dense hemlock thickets, where the falling snow nearly clogged the action of my rifle and filled the sights with ice. I was forced to remove my right mitten to keep them ice-clear by warming with the bare hand. The snow-shoeing was difficult and fatiguing to the utmost, as mile after mile we wound along after those vagrant caribou. We found a small pond where they had pawed for water, and it had not yet frozen after their drink.

Now is the time when the hunter feels the thrill which is the pleasure of the sport.

Down the sides of the pond led the trail, then twisting and turning, it entered the woods and wound up a little hill. Old man Larette fumbled the snow with his bare hand; he lifted towards us some unfrozen spoor—good, cheerful old soul, his eyes were those of a panther. Now we set our shoes ever so carefully, pressing them down slowly, and shifting our weight cautiously lest the footing be false. The two hunters crouched in the snow, pointing. I cocked my rifle, one snowshoe sunk slowly under me—the snow was treacherous—and three dark objects flitted like birds past the only opening in the forest, seventy-five yards ahead.

"Take the gun, Con," I said, and my voice broke on the stillness harshly: the game was up, the disappointment keen. The reaction of disgust was equal to the suppressed elation of the second before. "Go to camp the nearest way, Larette."

The country was full of caribou. They travel constantly, not staying in one section. New tracks came every day into our little territory. We stalked and worked until our patience gave out, when we again loaded our toboggans for the back track.

At Mr. O'Shannahan's we got our burleaus, and jingled into St. Raymond by the light of the moon.

Havana Under Our Regulars

My figure of the Cuban is fairly typical of the infantry soldiers of the Cuban army. They are so diverse in their "make-ups" that, like trotting horses, they go in all shapes; but their clothes are mostly white, and their faces furnish a dark complement. The men who paraded Havana with General Gomez were almost all negroes of the most sombre hue: the light-brown variety was not conspicuous, and there was quite a following of white men. When I saw General Garcia's Oriental Army pass to the battle of Santiago, I was struck by the yellow tinge of it. To be sure, there were plenty of dark-browns and some whites, but in the main it was yellow.

When we stop to think of the thing beneath the skin, however, it must be admitted that these peasants have opposed two hundred thousand Spanish troops for three years with all their resources cut off, and they have shown stamina and fortitude. If in the future they develop "common sense" to match these qualities, they can sit at the tables in the rural *fondas* for the rest of their natural lives, drinking red wine and rum, smoking black cigars and talking of the days when they marched with Gomez. This is a thing very dear to old soldiers the world over.

The last time I was in Havana Weyler sat in the palace and dirty Spanish soldiers prowled the streets by day and by night. These much starved and abused men held up the honest wayfarer on the principal streets and got from him wherewith to buy bread. The stretches down by the wharves were little battlefields for decently dressed men after dark. The old Havana gendarme walked about or leaned against buildings, firing their cigarettes, but no one ever took them seriously—they interfered with nobody, no matter what his purpose might be.

One of Gomez's Men. *Authors' photoengraving*

The Prado at evening was a gay scene, with its swarms of Spanish officers and pretty women strolling slowly about to the music of the military bands. Much more cheerful than in these days, I must confess; but the back streets were made dangerous by starved soldiers; the insurgent bands raided the country about to the outposts on the neighboring hills, and the people in the theatres insulted Americans, thirsted for their blood, and told them so by word of mouth. Consul-General Lee employed his time in having American newspaper correspondents from the Cabanas, and the United States Government signified no more to these poor ignorant souls than a yesterday's edition—the man Lee in person was the United States of America. He was not supported by Washington, but he pounded the table in Captain-General Weyler's presence, talking loud and vigorously to good effect.

This has all changed. The city is divided into four districts, and our infantry soldiers walk along the streets with loaded Krag-Jorgensens over their shoulders, and no city in the world is policed so well. The private of infantry does not understand the Spanish language, but he comprehends a row, and at the least flicker of disorder he precipitates himself into the middle of the throng, using language fierce and loud and picturesque. No one understands the language, but every one comprehends that the vicinity of the big man with the gun should be vacant and hushed.

The liquor stores under Ludlow's administration would regard a Raines Law as unbridled license. The thirsty volunteers who come to town from the Seventh Corps are not permitted to amuse themselves after the fashion of their kind. At night the streets are quiet—almost deserted—and the criminal knows that the inarticulate Yankee will shoot him dead at the least suspicion, because how can a Yankee soldier know what else to do? At first there was some warm work, though the butt, the bayonet, and the small calibre soon brought things right.

I employed an evening with an officer going his rounds. The thing was distressingly without incident. The lights from the buildings gridironed the narrow street, the small life of the people could be seen through the open door, and slowly down the middle paced the majesty of the Great Republic in the person of Jimmie Green from Poke County, or Paddy O'Brien from "de Ate Distric'." But make no mistake about Jimmie and Pat with the "setting up," the silence of discipline, the fetich of orders and the loaded gun. There on the streets of the strange tropic city they are as impersonal as gods.

It all made me sigh for the riot and roar of Whitechapel or the lower East Side, or some of the ginger of Chicago after candlelight, and I appealed to my officer friend. I asked him to kindly hit some passing straggler over the head with his six-shooter, since I could make nothing out of all this but a pastoral.

"Well," he said, laughing, "it was more interesting at first. There was a function here, and I was told off with my company to keep the crowd back. The people pressed the marching column, and as I passed along I said to the sentry at that point, 'The crowd must be kept back.' 'Yes, sor'—and I noticed that it was Private Shaunnessy, a good old vet, and passed on. Casually turning around, I beheld the greatest commotion and rushed back.

" 'Stop, stop!' I yelled, 'I don't want you to kill them!'

"The crowd was flying from the quickly placed 'butts to the front,' and private Shaunnessy soon had room.

" 'My dear man, you must not kill them,' I said.

" 'I was not killing them, captain. I thought it best to assume a threatening attitude—sor.'

"Another soldier in dispersing a crowd pointed with his finger at them, and observed in a long southwestern drawl: 'Now —I—want—you people to get back. I know you don't understand what I am talking about but I understand my orders, and now I am going to plow into you,' with which calm statement he move forward with the light of battle in his eye. The crowd was as feathers in a wind."

But when Havana thinks over her vicissitudes in the coming years, she can say the American regular made Havana look like Sunday morning in a New England village on a summer's day, and a Spanish-American town is not like that by nature.

"Under Which King?"

HAVANA, March 10, 1899

The rural districts of Cuba are full of soldiers of the Army of Liberation. They rack along the roads on their mice-like ponies—they stroll along with their blankets and rifles. They do not seem to have any definite purpose, and doubtless have none beyond locating fruitful fields.

Our regulars have organized a patrol of certain districts, and it only happened that I noticed a haughty reserve was maintained between these two soldiery when they passed. They lack a common language, and they hardly know what their official relations are to be.

Meanwhile the poor peasant of Cuba gives both the road. He is the most ignorant being I ever saw; he has been harried by soldiers until his soul shrinks at the sight of one. These two men of my picture are friendly enough, but, like a wild animal newly caught, it will take time for him to gather the fact. The pathos of the spiritless people appeals to one's sympathies—makes him long to take them by the hand and reassure them. It would do little good; the crackers of the Relief Fund go further. He can understand that a warm heart only prompts the crackers, but man on horseback he cannot approve.

In proportion to the people the numbers who were in the Cuban army was small. The peasants, as it is the custom of the country to call them, were left helpless before the cruelty of the Spanish soldiers, and suffering also from the necessities of their own men in the field. Weyler concentrated them and intended to exterminate the race. Only the most vigorous, the most daring and enterprising, took to the *maniqua*—only those with force and cunning enough to provide themselves with arms. The men of small holdings and large families stayed on the plot of ground, and they did the suffering for both parties. Among these are many Spaniards—men who came out to labor on the land; and never having experienced the quality of mercy, they do not expect it from the victors now. But, so far as I could learn, the Cuban soldiers had not disturbed these people—quite contrary to all preconceived notions; and it is greatly to their credit. To be sure, this fellow-feeling does not extend to those who served as guerillas for Spain. These the Cubans regard as murderers, and yearn to kill. I regard their ideas on the subject as perfectly right. The guerillas were Spanish soldiers, and by the fortunes of war should leave the island which they were unable to keep.

To paraphrase: "If I were a Cuban, as I am an American, as long as there was a Spanish guerilla on the island, I would not lay down my arms—never—never—never."

When I ponder on Havana it is positively startling how little I know about it. No one can understand anything unless he lives with it. The modern facilities for going somewhere are so well adjusted that we go. Having gone to these places we come back to the quiet of our domesticity and then think about what we have seen. Our indefinite feeling is one of pity for people who are not as we are and things which are not like ours. There is no harm in this. It is typical. A Congo cannibal would not like asparagus *a la vinaigrette.*

Havana had a great call on winter-killed Americans before the war, and will have yet. It presents a change to one who wants to leave the comforts of a Northern home. It is hot, dirty, stuccoed, and picturesque. It has fine fruits, new bugs, excellent microbes, and stone floors in the bedrooms. It certainly has a sensation in store for the average American. It will give you the same nice little shock that the cold water does in the morning bath, or losing your job, or having your best girl work back in the breeching on you. Still, no one leaves his settled ways and buys steamship tickets with any idea of approving of everything he is going to see or do. The critical instinct is involved immediately. To like everything is impossible—even ordinary hoboes have tastes.

It is far from my purpose to discourage passenger traffic or the Havana habit. I have only seen Havana four times, so as a collection my experiences are incomplete. My first offence was in company with American tourists from Vera Cruz bound to New York. I dismounted at Havana from a Ward liner with a Dr. Daly of Pittsburg— since notorious for his dislike of rotten beef. We found the city full of Americans who were wintering their jaded minds, their remaining lung, or their East-wind catarrhs, but all were dressed-up, bustling and happy. Bands played in the Plaza, the Prado was thronged with carriages, mounted gendarmes sat on their horses. The shops were full of gentle-minded idiots buying those absurdly-painted bull-fight fans. The Yankee dollar twinkled on every counter. The big cafe of the Inglaterre clattered its wares. It was all very Latin, very Spanish, very agreeable.

I drove out with my friend the doctor in a rattelty-bang cab, pulled by a puppy-pony, to see an object which the serious-minded scientist said would cheer my intellect. We arrived before a rather imposing building, with its entrance closed by iron bars. Behind these were pleasing figures in white.

"This, you see, is the regular leper hospital. I am investigating leprosy—a most interesting and difficult subject. Come in." So said the doctor.

I simply smote the cabby on the head with my umbrella, not once or twice, but as fast as my arm could work, saying softly, but with great guttural force, "Go on, you yellow ——! Get up! Underlay! Vamoose! Get to hades out of here!" and I prevailed. The doctor was torn violently away from his dear scientific cripples, but he only assured me that the streets were full of them, and there was no need to run away from them. He later showed me people walking freely about the streets who were lepers. Indeed, the Chinese coolies who coaled our ship were all lepers. I parted with Havana without a pang.

But time plays strange tricks on wayward mortals. The revolution against Spain came, and Havana became the centre of the earth. Things so arranged themselves that I was expected to go to Cuba to illuminate the genius of Mr. Richard Harding Davis. We tried to run the Spanish blockade with a very narrow-waisted yacht, but the sailors did not like their job, and finally our patience gave out. The Spanish consul at Key West kept Weyler fully informed of our designs.

Mr. Davis proposed that, since we could not get in the coal-cellar window, we had best go around and knock at the front door. I should never have dreamed of such a thing, but Davis has the true newspaper impudence, so we arranged passage on the regular line steamer Olivette for Havana.

Our passports were quaint little papers, made out on some sort of custom-house blanks by a friend in Key West, but plastered with gold seals and draped with ribbons like May queens.

Upon our arrival, Consul-General Lee added us to his burden and escorted us up to the great Captain-General Weyler, who was at that time in the full glory of his "reconcentrado" and "forty-battalion" fame. To my simple democratic soul, the marble stairway of the palace which we entered looked like the Gates of Heaven. It recalled Gérôme's painting, "L'éminence Grise." There were gold-laced officers, black-robed church dignitaries, sentries and couriers coming and going, or whispering by the way. They turned lupine eyes on us, but there was no resisting Lee. To be sure, his government was affording him no support. He represented no one but himself; but his doughty presence, and, I suppose, the foresight of the Spanish, as they thought of the American millions that were behind Lee when his day should come, made courtesy possible and imperative. After being introduced, General Lee sat on a sofa, which he filled with his impassive presence; Weyler teetered in a cane rocking-chair nervously; Davis squinted at the scene for future reference, and I made the only profile of Weyler on this side of the Atlantic on my cuff.

The interview was long, and we never flattered ourselves with having impressed Weyler with our innocence. No good ever came of the beautiful papers which he said would take us everywhere. We might as well have presented a last-year's calendar to the Spanish officers. I saw ill-clad, ill-fed Spanish soldiers bring their dead and wounded into the city, dragging slowly along in ragged columns. I saw scarred Cubans with their arms bound stiffly behind them being marched to the Cabañas. They were to face the black-line in the Laurel Ditch. I saw the "reconcentrados" being hurried in by mounted guerillas, and the country was a pall of smoke from their burning homes. Sailing out past the Morro, I shook my fist at the receding town, and thought, "I shall like the town better the next time I come, because I shall never come unless in company with about one hundred thousand American soldiers."

Man only proposes, for Fate had it that the next view I got of Havana was from the deck of the battleship Iowa, Captain Robley D. Evans. We were eight miles off shore, where we sailed and sailed and sailed, up and down. Captain Evans did not like the view we got—it was too far off; but Admi-

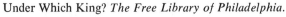

Under Which King? *The Free Library of Philadelphia.*

ral Sampson said that eight miles was the best view he could give Evans for the present. By day we gazed on the long blue shore-line, with its yellow houses, and by night we sat in the dark, behind the after turret, smoking, while we watched the big searchlights flash from the Morro. I do not know that this view of Havana put me in possession of much information concerning it, but I am bound I liked Havana better this time than before.

And, lastly, I have just been there again. This time I did not go feeling like a thief in the night or an unbidden guest, and I lived at the American Club, and sat at a mess of good old American soldiers, and ate roast beef rare. I saw the free Cubans greet their great hero with cheers as he marched in. I saw the new police being prepared to guard the interests of their own native community, and I called on General Ludlow at his office. There were no gold-laced or black-robed ones; no sentries, no fuss; nothing but a quiet engineer officer sitting at a desk before stacks of official papers, and very busy officers hurrying in and running out, all doing something useful. Soldiers patrolled the streets with loaded rifles, and nothing happened. Business men were figuring and discussing the future commercial development of the town. Every one was hopeful, and the Cubans gradually adjusting themselves to their freedom. Too much cannot be expected at once of a people who have always lived under Spanish misrule and abuse. Cuba is not a new-born country, peopled by wood-cutting, bear-fighting, agricultural folks, who must be fresh and virtuous in order to exist. It is an old country, time worn, decayed, and debauched by thieving officials and fire and sword. The people are negroes or breeds, and they were sired by Spaniards who have never had social virtues since they were overrun by the Moors.

The Cubans have known no civic rectitude; they have had no examples of honest, plain-dealing, public men; they are, in the aggregate, the most ignorant people on earth, so far as letters go. But there are in the rural districts of Cuba an honest folk, whose only aim is to till the land in safety and to be allowed to reap what they shall sow. The Nanigoes, or bands of criminal negroes which infest the cities, are a mere incident, and should be shot on sight—gotten rid of in the shortest possible way, like wild beasts, which is what will happen in the natural order of events. The people will, in my judgment, follow Gomez, who begins to develop a sanity regarding reconstruction which is good to see. And now with good American soldier governors to sit quietly by and see that no throats are cut, things will slowly come right. I very much fear this furrow to which we have set our plow will be a long one. The end is not in sight.

Physically, one is immediately impressed with the undeveloped state of Havana and Cuba generally, and of the illimitable possibilities. The Spanish officials taxed thrift right out of the island; they took industry by the neck and throttled it. The Church charged a poor man so much to get married that they, for the most part, were compelled to forego that ceremony, and when they were dead they taxed their bones. This may seem strong, but we have all seen the photographs of the piles of bones in the cemeteries which we were thrown out for arrears of taxes.

It is for no one to say how long a time it will take before Cuba is a prosperous and well-mannered country, but if we hold her up to her work, and have no nonsense in dealing with the reactionary elements, it ought not to be long. The task is delicate— this bringing of order out of chaos. The Cubans are entitled to our greatest consideration, but with "new-caught" people the grandest of all errors is indecision. No sentimentalist should go from our ports to Cuba. It is my belief that, as between the avarice of politicians and business men, the sentimentalist, with his fussy little social recipes, can do most harm in dealing with such subjects. These last are all very well in their place. We Americans understand them, but a yellow islander could never make the combination. Therefore let us continue to send honest soldiers to lead these undisciplined people.

Cuban Bandits in Santiago Province

What was said would happen has happened. The turbulent part of Garcia's old troops "has gone off the reservation." It is likely that more will go in the provinces, and then it is "up to us." That is a part of the game. We opened a jackpot and we have got to stay.

We may feel comfortable from the fact that General Wood is commanding the province of Santiago. As a youngster he followed a more sprightly people over a worse and bigger country, and he brought Geronimo's Apaches in. If he is furnished with what force he asks for he will in time quiet the country.

It is a mountainous region, covered with dense jungle, and utterly wild. The predatory bands of negro soldiery have roamed it for years. They know its trails, its fastnesses, and its commissary resources. They will be in collusion with townspeople who will renew their ammunition, and they will have perfect information of our troop movements. They will ambuscade us in bands, and then disperse as individuals. The country is hot and not healthy. So much for their part. And, oh! "lest we forget," we will in all human probabilities do what we always have done under similar circumstances—send them a Peace Commission. This will grovel and whine and make "heap good talk"; give them rations and ammunition and ask them please to be good. Never having been good, they will go out in the jungle and laugh at us. They will feel that we are afraid of them. They will murder and rob some more, and then, having gotten through with this murderous foolishness, which is traditional with us, General Wood will be asked to take up the "soldiers' burden." He will not be given a proper force. Then will ensue one of those desperate bushwhacking wars, with the bulk of the advantage on the guerillas' side. It is history that the other fellows will have to get off the earth in the long run, but it will use up plenty of good American soldiers and cost no end of money and anxiety. The only real good that ever comes of such wars is that they develop many clever young officers and make tried-out soldiers for our future use. They are the real schooling grounds for the art of war.

For our part, what we should do is to "declare them banditti." Take off the "close season" on them, as it were; offer rewards for their heads; put bands of Cuban auxiliary troops after them; stock the old Spanish block-houses with food and grain under our infantry, so that our operations could be fast and continuous, and then go in. The Spanish stayed in their block-houses or only marched a heavy column a day or so outside their own lines. The Cuban guerillas will expect us to do this—whereat they will run midship high on the shoals of error. With our infantry split up into small squads, and put out to form ambuscades all over a province, we could send mounted troops with pack-trains which could be grain-fed from the block-houses on their trail. These grain-fed horses would soon put the riders

Santiago Bandits. *The Free Library of Philadelphia.*

of the grass-fed ponies afoot. These gueril-las would not be able to stop our cavalry by fighting, and if they could be made to fight that would be all we could ask. In running away from our continuous pursuit, they would be at all times liable to run into the constantly shifting infantry ambuscades, which would greatly demoralize them.

This would be a nasty business, but I believe what we have to do could be done better in this way than in any other. It is the old tactics which Miles employed against Geronimo, and that old man was a problem in his day. Furthermore, let it be remembered that we will see many dark-moons before Cuba is rid of the bandits.

A Sketch by MacNeil

We had to laugh. I chuckled all day, it was all so quaint. But I don't see how I can tell you, because you don't know MacNeil, which is necessary.

In a labored way, MacNeil is an old frontier scout with a well-frosted poll. He is what we all call a "good fellow," with plenty of story, laugh, and shrewd comment; but his sense of humor is so ridiculously healthy, so full-bloodedly crude, that many ceremonious minds would find themselves "off side" when Mac turns on his sense of jollity. He started years ago as a scout for Sheridan down Potomac way, and since then he has been in the Northwest doing similar duty against Indians, so a life spent in the camps and foot-hills has made no "scented darling" out of old man Mac-Neil. He is a thousand-times hero, but he does not in the least understand this. If he could think any one thought he was such a thing he would opine that such a one was a fool. He has acted all his life in great and stirring events as unconscious of his own force as the heat, the wind, or the turn of tide. He is a pure old warrior, and nothing has come down the years to soften MacNeil. He is red-healthy in his sixties, and has never seen anything to make him afraid. The influence of even fear is good on men. It makes them reflective, and takes them out of the present. But even this refinement never came to Mac, and he needed it in the worst way.

So that is a bad sketch of MacNeil.

A little bunch of us sat around the hotel one day, and we were drawing Mac's covers of knowledge concerning Indians. As the conversation went on, Mac slapped his leg, and laughing, said, "The most comical thing I ever saw in my life!"

"What was that, Mac?" came a half-dozen voices, and Mac was convulsed with merriment.

"The last time the Piegans raided the Crows I was out with the First Cavalry. We were camped on the Yellowstone, and had gone to bed. I heard an Injun outside askin' about me, and pretty soon Plenty Coups comes in, sayin' the Piegans had got away with a good bunch of their ponies, but that they had found the trail crossing a little way down the river, and Big Horse and a war-band of Crows was layin' on it, and they wanted me to go 'long with them and help run it. I didn't have anything but a big government horse, and they ain't good company for Injun ponies when they are runnin' horse-thieves; besides, I didn't feel called to bust my horse helpin' Injuns out of trouble. There had got to be lots of white folks in the country, and they wa'n't at all stuck on havin' war-bands of Injuns pirootin' over the range. The Injuns wanted me to protect them from the cowboys, 'cause, you see, all Injuns look alike to a cowboy when they are runnin' over his cows. So Plenty Coups says he will give a pony, and I says, 'Mr. Injun, I will go you one.'

"I fixed up sort of warm, 'cause it was late in the fall, and threw my saddle on the pony, and joined the war-band. It was bright moon, and we ran the trail slowly until morning; and when it come day we moved along Injun fashion, which ain't slow, if you ask me about it. We kept a-pushin' until late afternoon, when we saw the Piegans, about seven miles ahead, just streakin' it over the hills. My Injuns got off their ponies, and, Injun fashion, they stripped off every rag they had on except the G-string and moccasins. This is where them Injuns is light-minded, for no man has got any call to go flirtin' with Montana weather at that time of the year in his naked hide. Old man Mac stands pat with a full set of jeans. And then we got on them ponies and we ran them Piegans as hard as we could lather till plumb dark, when we had to quit because we couldn't see. We were in an open sagebrush country. Well, it got darker and darker, and then it began to rain. I sat on my saddle and put my saddle-blanket over my head, and I was pretty comfortable. Then it began to rain for fair. Them Injuns stamped and sung and near froze to death, and I under the blanket laughing at them. 'Long 'bout midnight it began to snow, and them Injuns turned on the steam. The way they sung and stomped round in a ring tickled me near to death. The snow settled round my blanket and kept out the cold in great shape. I only had my nose out, and when it began to get gray morning I had to just yell to see them Injuns out there in five inches of snow, without a rag on, hoppin' for all they was worth. You talk about shootin' up a fellow's toes to make him dance; it wa'n't a circumstance. Them Injuns had to dance or 'cash in.' I have seen plenty of Injun dances, but that dance had a swing to it that they don't get every time.

"This Is Where Them Injuns Is Light-Minded." *Authors' photoengraving.*

"We got on the ponies and started back through the falling snow, tryin' to locate them annuity goods of theirn. 'Course we lost the Piegans. We lost ourselves, and we didn't find them clothes till afternoon, 'most eighteen miles back, and then we had to dig them up, and they was as stiff as *par-flèche*. Them was a funny bunch of warriors, I tell you.

"We found an old big-jaw* steer which some punchers had killed, and them Injuns

* A cattle disease.

eat that all right; but I wasn't hungry enough yet to eat big-jaw steer, so I pulled along down to the railroad. I got a piece of bread from a sheep-man, and when I got to Gray Cliffs, on the N. P., I was 'most frozen. My feet and knees were all swollen up.

"Whenever I gets to thinkin' 'bout them bucks jumpin' around out there in the snow all that night, and me a-settin' there under the blanket, I has to laugh. She was sure a funny old revel, boys."

And we listeners joined him, but we were laughing at MacNeil, not with him.

The Story of the Dry Leaves

If one loves the earth, he finds a liveliness in walking through the autumn woods: the color, the crackling, and the ripeness of the time appeal to his senses as he kicks his way through the dry leaves with his feet.

It is a wrong thing to dull this harmlessness, but still I must remind him that it was not always so; such leaves have been the cause of tragedy. How could bad come of such unoffending trifles? Listen.

Long ago a very old Indian—an Ottawa —recalled the sad case of Ah-we-ah from the nearly forgotten past. His case was similar to ours, only more serious, since if we could not approach a deer in the dry forest because of the noise the leaves made it meant only disappointment, but with Ah-we-ah it meant his utter undoing.

Ah-we-ah grew up or came up as all Indian boys do who manage to escape the deadfalls which nature sets in such numbers and variety for them, and was at the time of the story barely a man. His folks lived in the Northwest, in what is now known as Manitoba, and they were of the Ojibbeway people. As was a very common thing in those days, they were all murdered by the Sioux; the very last kinsman Ah-we-ah had on earth was dead when Ah-we-ah came in one day from his hunting and saw their bodies lying charred and wolf-eaten about the ashes of his father's lodge.

He found himself utterly alone in the world.

The woods Indians, who followed the moose, the bear, and trapped the small animals for the Fur Company, did not live together in great tribal bodies, as did the buffalo Indians, but scattered out, the better to follow the silent methods of their livelihood.

Ah-we-ah was thus forced to live alone in the forest that winter, and his little bark hut was cold and fireless when he came in at night, tired with the long day's hunting. This condition continued for a time, until grief and a feeling of loneliness determined Ah-we-ah to start in search of a war party, that he might accompany them against their enemies, and have an opportunity to sacrifice honorably a life which had become irksome to him.

Leaving his belongings on a "sunjegwun," or scaffold made of stout poles, he shouldered his old trade gun, his dry meat, called his wolf-dogs, and betook himself three days through the forest to the small settlement made by the hunting-camps of his tribesman, old Bent Gun,—a settlement lying about a series of ponds, of which no name is saved for this story; nor does it matter now which particular mud-holes they were—so long ago—out there in the trackless waste of poplar and tamarack.

The people are long since gone; the camps are mould; the very trees they lived among are dead and down this many a year.

So the lonely hunter came to the lodge of his friend, and sat him down on a skin, across the fire from Bent Gun; and as he dipped his hollow buffalo horn into the pot he talked of his losses, his revenge, his war-ardor, inquired where he was like to find a fellow-feeling—yes, even pleaded with the old man that he and his sons too might go forth together with him and slay some other simple savage as a spiritual relief to themselves. He chanted his war-song by the night fire in the lodge, to the discomfort and disturbance of old Bent Gun, who had large family interests and was minded to stay in his hunting-grounds, which had yielded well to his traps and stalking; besides which the snow was deep, and the Sioux were far away. It was not the proper time of the year for war.

By day Ah-we-ah hunted with old Bent Gun, and they killed moose easily in their yards, while the women cut them up and drew them to the camps. Thus they were happy in the primeval way, what with plenty of maple-sugar, bears' grease, and the kettle always steaming full of fresh meat.

But still by night Ah-we-ah continued to exalt the nobleness of the wearing of the red paint and the shrill screams of battle to his tribesmen; but old Bent Gun did not succumb to their spirit; there was meat, and his family were many. This finally was understood by Ah-we-ah, who, indeed, had come to notice the family, and one of them in particular—a young girl; and also he was conscious of the abundance of cheer in the teeming lodge.

In the contemplation of life as it passed before his eyes he found that his gaze centred more and more on the girl. He watched her cutting up the moose and hauling loads through the woods with her dogs. She was dutiful. Her smile warmed him. Her voice came softly, and her form, as it cut against the snow, was good to look at in the eyes of the young Indian hunter. He knew, since his mother and sister had gone, that no man can live happily in a lodge without a woman. And as the girl passed her dark eyes across his, it left a feeling after their gaze had gone. He was still glorious with the lust of murder, but a new impulse had seized him—it swayed him, and it finally overpowered him altogether.

When one day he had killed a moose early in the morning, he came back to the camp asking the women to come out and help him in with the meat, and Mis-kau-bun-o-kwa, or the "Red Light of the Morning," and her old mother accompanied him to his quarry.

As they stalked in procession through the sunlit winter forest, the young savage gazed with glowing eyes upon the girl ahead of him. He was a sturdy man in whom life ran high, and he had much character after his manner and his kind. He forgot the scalps of his tribal enemies; they were crowded out by a higher and more immediate purpose. He wanted the girl, and he wanted her with all the fierce resistlessness of a nature which followed its inclinations as undisturbedly as the wolf—which was his totem.

The little party came presently to the dead moose, and the women, with the heavy skinning-knives, dismembered the great mahogany mass of hair, while the craunching snow under the moccasins grew red about it. Some little distance off stood the young man, leaning on his gun, and with his blanket drawn about him to his eyes. He watched the girl while she worked, and his eyes dilated and opened wide under the impulse. The blood surged and bounded through his veins—he was hungry for her, like a famished tiger which stalks a gazelle. They packed their sleds and hung the remainder in the trees to await another coming.

The old woman, having made her load, passed backward along the trail, tugging at her head-line and ejaculating gutturals at her dogs. Then Ah-we-ah stepped quickly to the girl, who was bent over her sled, and seizing her, he threw his blanket with a deft sweep over her head; he wrapped it around them both, and they were alone under its protecting folds. They spoke together until the old woman called to them, when he released her. The girl followed on, but Ah-we-ah stood by the blood-stained place quietly, without moving for a long time.

That night he did not speak of war to old Bent Gun, but he begged his daughter of him, and the old man called the girl and set her down beside Ah-we-ah. An old squaw threw a blanket over them, and they were man and wife.

In a day or two the young man had washed the red paint from his face, and he had a longing for his own lodge, three days away through the thickets. It would not be so lonesome now, and his fire would always be burning.

He called his dogs, and with his wife they all betook themselves on the tramp to his hunting-grounds. The snow had long since filled up the tracks Ah-we-ah had made when he came to Bent Gun's camp.

He set up his lodge, hunted successfully, and forgot his past as he sat by the crackle of the fire, while the woman mended his buckskins, dried his moccasins, and lighted his long pipe. Many beaver-skins he had on his "sunjegwun," and many good buckskins were made by his wife, and when they packed up in the spring, the big canoe was full of stuff which would bring powder, lead, beads, tobacco, knives, axes, and stronding, or squaw-cloth, at the stores of the Northwest Company.

Ah-we-ah would have been destitute if he had not been away when his family were killed by the Sioux, and, as it was, he had little beyond what any hunter has with him; but he had saved his traps, his canoe, and his dogs, which in the old days were nearly everything except the lordly gun and the store of provisions which might happen.

At a camp where many of the tribe stopped and made maple-sugar, the young pair tarried and boiled sap along with the others, until they had enough sweets for the Indian year. And when the camp broke up they followed on to the post of the big company, where they traded for the year's supplies—"double-battle Sussex powder" in corked bottles, pig-lead, blue and red stronding, hard biscuit, steel traps, axes, and knives. It is not for us to know if they helped the company's dividends by the purchase of the villanous "made whiskey," as it

The Passion of Ah-we-ah. *Authors' photoengraving.*

was called in the trade parlance, but the story relates that his canoe was deep-laden when he started away into the wilderness.

The canoe was old and worn out, so Ah-we-ah purposed to make a new one. He was young, and it is not every old man even who can make a canoe, but since the mechanical member of his family had his "fire put out" by the Sioux on that memorable occasion, it was at least necessary that he try. So he worked at its building, and in due time launched his bark; but it was "quick" in the water, and one day shortly it tipped over with him while on his journey to his hunting-grounds. He lost all his provisions, his sugar, biscuits, and many things besides, but saved his gun. He was suffering from hunger when he again found the company's store, but having made a good hunt the year before, the factor made him a meagre credit of powder, lead, and the few necessary things. He found himself very poor.

In due course Ah-we-ah and his family set up their lodge. They were alone in the country, which had been hunted poor. The other people had gone far away to new grounds, but the young man trusted himself and his old locality. He was not wise like the wolves and the old Indians, who follow ceaselessly, knowing that to stop is to die of hunger. He hunted faithfully, and while he laid by no store, his kettle was kept full, and so the summer passed.

He now directed himself more to the hunting of beaver, of which he knew of the presence of about twenty gangs within working distance of his camp. But when he went to break up their houses he found nearly all of them empty. He at last discovered that some distemper had seized upon the beaver, and that they had died. He recovered one which was dying in the water, and when he cut it up it had a bloody flux about the heart, and he was afraid to eat it. And so it was with others. This was a vast misfortune to the young hunter; but still there were the elk. He had shot four up to this time, and there was "sign" of moose passing about. The leaves fell, and walking in them he made a great noise, and was forced to run down an elk—a thing which could be done by a young and powerful man, but it was very exhausting.

When an Indian hunts the elk in this manner, after he starts the herd, he follows at such a gait as he thinks he can maintain for many hours. The elk, being frightened, outstrip him at first by many miles, but the Indian, following at a steady pace along the trail, at length comes in sight of them; then they make another effort, and are no more seen for an hour or two; but the intervals in which the Indian has them in sight grow more and more frequent and longer and longer, until he ceases to lose sight of them at all. The elk are now so much fatigued that they can only move at a slow trot. At last they can but walk, by which time the strength of the Indian is nearly exhausted; but he is commonly able to get near enough to fire into the rear of the herd. This kind of hunting is what Ah-we-ah was at last compelled to do. He could no longer stalk with success, because the season was dry and the dead leaves rattled under his moccasins.

He found a band, and all day long the hungry Indian strove behind the flying elk; but he did not come up, and night found him weak and starved. He lay down by a little fire, and burned tobacco to the four corners of the world, and chanted softly his medicine-song, and devoutly hoped that his young wife might soon have meat. It might be that on his return to his lodge he would hear another voice beside that familiar one.

Ah-we-ah slept until the gray came in the east, and girding himself, he sped on through the forest; the sun came and found the buck-skinned figure gliding through the woods. Through the dry light of the day he sweated, and in the late afternoon shot a young elk. He cut away what meat he could carry in his weakness, ate the liver raw, and with lagging steps hastened backward to his far-off lodge.

The sun was again high before Ah-we-ah raised the entrance-mat of his home, and it was some moments before he could discern in the dusk that the wife was not alone. Hunger had done its work, and the young mother had suffered more than women ought.

Her strength had gone.

The man made broth, and together they rested, these two unfortunates; but on the following day nature again interposed the strain of the tightened belly.

Ah-we-ah went forth through the noisy leaves. If rain or snow would come to soften the noise; but no; the cloudless sky overspread the yellow and red of the earth's carpet. No matter with what care the wary moccasin was set to the ground, the sweesh-sweesh of the moving hunter carried terror and warning to all animal kind. He could not go back to the slaughtered elk; it was too far for that, and the wolf and wolverene had been there before. Through the long day no hairy or feathered kind passed before his eyes. At nightfall he built his fire, and sat crooning his medicine-song until nature intervened her demands for repose.

With the early light Ah-we-ah looked on the girl and her baby.

The baby was cold.

The dry breasts of Mis-kau-bun-o-kwa had been of no purpose to this last comer, but the mother resisted Ah-we-ah when he tried to take the dead child away, and he left it. This cut and maddened the hunter's mind, and he cursed aloud his medicine-bag, and flung it from him. It had not brought him even a squirrel to stay the life of his first-born. His famished dogs had gone away, hunting for themselves; they would no longer stay by the despairing master and his dreary lodge.

Again he dragged his wretched form into the forest, and before the sun was an hour high the blue smoke had ceased to curl over the woful place, and the fainting woman lay quite still on her robe. Through the dry brush and the crackling leaves ranged the starving one, though his legs bent and his head reeled. The moose could hear him for an hour.

And again at evening he returned to his bleak refuge; the hut was gray and lifeless. He dropped into his place without making a fire. He knew that the woman was going from him. From the opposite side of the wigwam she moaned weakly—he could scarcely hear her.

Ah-we-ah called once more upon his gods, to the regular thump-thump of his tomtom. It was his last effort—his last rage at fate. If the spirits did not come now, the life would soon go out of the abode of Ah-we-ah, even as the fire had gone.

He beat and sang through the doleful silence, and from the dark tamaracks the wolves made answer. They too were hungry.

The air, the leaves, the trees, were still; they listened to the low moan of the woman, to the dull thump of the tomtom, to the long piercing howl of the wolf, the low rising and falling voice of the man chanting: "He-ah neen-gui-o-ho o-ho man-i-to-we-tah-hah gah-neen-qui-o we-i-ah-nah we-he-a."

The air grew chill and cold. Ah-we-ah was aroused from his deep communion by cold spots on his face. He opened the door-mat. He peered into the gray light of the softly falling snow. The spirits had come to him, he had a new energy, and seizing his gun, the half-delirious man tottered into the forest, saying softly to himself: "A bear—I walk like a bear myself—myself I walk like a bear—a beast comes calling—I am loaded—I am ready. Oh, my spirit! Oh, my manitou!"

A black mass crossed the Indian's path—it had not heard the moccasins in the muffle of the snow. The old trade gun boomed through the forest, and the manitou had sent at last to Ah-we-ah a black bear. He tore out his knife and cut a small load of meat from the bear, and then he strode on his back track as swiftly as he could in his weakness. He came to the hole in the forest in the middle of which sat the lodge, calling: "Mis-kau-bun-o-kwa! Mis-kau-bun-o-kwa!" but there was no answer.

He quickly lighted a fire—he threw meat upon it, and bending backward from the flame, touched her, saying, "Good bear, Mis-kau-bun-o-kwa; I have a good bear for the bud-ka-da-win—for the hunger"; but Mis-kau-bun-o-kwa could not answer Ah-we-ah. The dry leaves had lasted longer than she.

The Honor of the Troop

L Troop in a volunteer regiment might be an unadulterated fighting outfit, but at first off, to volunteers, it would not be the letter L which they would fight for, so much as the mere sake of fighting, and they would never regard the letter L as of more importance than human life. Indeed, that letter would not signify to them any more than the "second set of fours," or the regimental bass drum. Later on it certainly would, but that would take a long time. In the instance of the L troop of which I speak, it had nearly one hundred years to think about, when any one in the troop cared to think about the matter at all. They were honorable years, and some of the best men living or dead have at one time or another followed that guidon. It had been through the "rifle" and "dragoon" periods of our history, and was now part of the regular cavalry establishment, and its operations had extended from Lake Erie to the city of Mexico.

Long lists of names were on its old rolls —men long since dead, but men who in the snow and on the red sands had laid down all they had for the honor of L Troop guidon. Soldiers—by which is meant the real long-service military type—take the government very much as a matter of course; but the number of the regiment, and particularly the letter of their troop, are tangible, comparative things with which they are living every day. The feeling is precisely that one has for the Alma Mater, or for the business standing of an old commercial house.

The "old man" had been captain of L for years and years, and for thirty years its first sergeant had seen its rank and file fill up and disappear. Every tenth man was a "buck" soldier, who thought it only a personal matter if he painted a frontier town up after pay-day, but who would follow L troop guidon to hell, or thump any one's nose in the garrison foolish enough to take L in vain, and I fear they would go further than this—yes, even further than men ought to go. Thus the "rookies" who came under the spell of L Troop succumbed to this veneration through either conventional decorum or the "mailed fist."

In this instance L Troop had been threading the chaparral by night and by day on what rations might chance, in hopes to capture for the honor of the troop sundry greasers, outlawed and defiant of the fulminations of the civil order of things. Other troops of the regiment also were desirous of the same thing, and were threading the desolate wastes far on either side. Naturally L did not want any other troop to round up more "game" than they did, so then horses were ridden thin, and the men's tempers were soured by the heat, dust, poor diet, and lack of success.

The captain was an ancient veteran, gray and rheumatic, near his retirement, and twenty-five years in his grade, thanks to the silly demagogues so numerous in Congress. He had been shot full of holes, bucketed about on a horse, immured in mud huts, frozen and baked and soaked until he should have long since had rank enough to get a desk and a bed or retirement. Now he was chasing human fleas through a jungle—boys' work—and it was admitted in ranks that the "old man" was about ready to "throw a curb." The men liked him, even sympathized with him, but there was that d—— G Troop in the barrack next, and they would give them the merry ha-ha when they returned to the post if L did not do something.

And at noon—mind you, high noon—the captain raised his right hand; up came the heads of the horses, and L Troop stood still in the road. Pedro, the Mexican trailer, pointed to the ground and said, "It's not an hour old," meaning the trail.

"Dismount," came the sharp order.

Toppling from their horses, the men stood about, but the individuals displayed no noticeable emotion; they did what L Troop did. One could not imagine their thoughts by looking at their red set faces.

They rested quietly for a time in the scant shade of the bare tangle, and then they sat up and listened, each man looking back up the road. They could hear a horse coming, which meant much to people such as these.

The men "thrown to the rear" would come first or "fire a shot," but with a slow pattering came a cavalry courier into view—a dusty soldier on a tired horse, which stepped stiffly along, head down, and if it were not for the dull kicking of the inert man, he would have stopped anywhere. The courier had ridden all night from the railroad, seventy-five miles away. He dismounted and unstrapped his saddle pocket, taking therefrom a bundle of letters and a bottle, which he handed to the "old man" with a salute.

The captain now had a dog-tent set up for himself, retiring into it with his letters and the bottle. If you had been there you would have seen a faint ironical smile circulate round the faces of L Troop.

A smart lieutenant, beautifully fashioned for the mounted service, and dressed in field uniform, with its touches of the "border" on the "regulations," stepped up to the dog-tent, and, stooping over, saluted, saying, "I will run this trail for a few miles if the captain will give me a few men."

"You will run nothing. Do you not see that I am reading my mail? You will retire until I direct you—"

The lieutenant straightened up with a snap of his lithe form. His eyes twinkled merrily. He was aware of the mail, he realized the bottle, and he had not been making strategic maps of the captain's vagaries for four years to no purpose at all; so he said, "Yes, sir," as he stepped out of the fire of future displeasure.

But he got himself straightway into the saddle of a horse as nearly thoroughbred as himself, and riding down the line, he spoke at length with the old first sergeant. Then he rode off into the brush. Presently six men whose horses were "fit" followed after him, and they all trotted along a trail which bore back of the captain's tent, and shortly they came back into the road. He had arranged so as to avoid another explosion from the "old man."

Then Pedro Zacatin ran the trail of three ponies—no easy matter through the maze of cattle-paths, with the wind blowing the dust into the hoof-marks. He only balked at a turn, more to see that the three did not "split out" than at fault of his own. In an opening he stopped, and pointing, said, in the harsh gutturals which were partly derived from an Indian mother, and partly from excessive cigarette-smoking: "They have stopped and made a fire. Do you see the smoke? You will get them now if they do not get away."

The lieutenant softly pulled his revolver, and raising it over his head, looked behind. The six soldiers opened their eyes wide like babies, and yanked out their guns. They raised up their horses' heads, pressed in the spurs, and as though at exercise in the riding-hall, the seven horses broke into a gallop. Pedro stayed behind; he had no further interest in L Troop than he had already displayed.

"A Beautiful Fight Ensued." *Authors' photoengraving.*

With a clattering rush the little group bore fast on the curling wreath of the campfire. Three white figures dived into the labyrinth of thicket, and three ponies tugged hard at their lariats; two shots rang, one from the officer's revolver, one from a corporal's carbine, and a bugler-boy threw a brass trumpet at the fleeting forms.

"Ride 'em down! ride 'em down!" sang out the officer, as through the swishing brush bounded the aroused horses, while the bullets swarmed on ahead.

It was over as I write, and in two minutes the three bandits were led back into the path, their dark faces blanched.

The lieutenant wiped a little stain of blood from his face with a very dirty pocket-handkerchief, a mere swish from a bush; the corporal looked wofully at a shirt-sleeve torn half off by the thorns, and the trumpeter hunted up his instrument, while a buck soldier observed, "De 'old man' ull be hotter'n chilli 'bout dis."

The noble six looked at the ignoble three half scornfully, half curiously, after the manner of men at a raffle when they are guessing the weight of the pig.

"Tie them up, corporal," said the lieutenant, as he shoved fresh shells into his gun; "and I say, tie them to those mesquit-trees, Apache fashion—sabe?—Apache fashion, corporal; and three of you men stay here and hold 'em down." With which he rode off, followed by his diminished escort.

The young man rode slowly, with his eyes on the ground, while at intervals he shoved his campaign hat to one side and rubbed his right ear, until suddenly he pulled his hat over his eyes, saying, "Ah, I have it." Then he proceeded at a trot to the camp.

Here he peeped cautiously into the "old man's" dog-tent. This he did ever so carefully; but the "old man" was in a sound sleep. The lieutenant betook himself to a bush to doze until the captain should bestir himself. L Troop was uneasy. It sat around in groups, but nothing happened until five o'clock.

At this hour the "old man" came out of his tent, saying, "I say, Mr. B——, have you got any water in your canteen?"

"Yes, indeed, captain. Will you have a drop?"

After he had held the canteen between his august nose and the sky for a considerable interval, he handed it back with a loud "Hount!" and L Troop fell in behind him as he rode away, leaving two men, who gathered up the dog-tent and the empty bottle.

"Where is that —— —— greaser? Have him get out here and run this trail. Here, you tan-colored coyote, kem up!" and the captain glared fiercely at poor Pedro, while the lieutenant winked vigorously at that perturbed being, and patted his lips with his hand to enjoin silence.

So Pedro ran the trail until it was quite dusk, being many times at fault. The lieutenant would ride out to him, and together they bent over it and talked long and earnestly. L Troop sat quietly in its saddles, grinned cheerfully, and poked each other in the ribs.

Suddenly Pedro came back, saying to the captain: "The men are in that bush—in camp, I think. Will you charge, sir?"

"How do you know that?" was the petulant query.

"Oh, I think they are there; so does the lieutenant. Don't you, Mr. B——?"

"Well, I have an idea we shall capture them if we charge," nervously replied the younger officer.

"Well— Right into line! Revolvers! Humph!" said the captain, and the brave old lion ploughed his big bay at the object of attack—it did not matter what was in front—and L Troop followed fast. They all became well tangled up in the dense chaparral, but nothing more serious than the thorns stayed their progress, until three shots were fired some little way in the rear,

and the lieutenant's voice was heard calling, "Come here; we have got them."

In the growing dusk the troop gathered around the three luckless "greasers," now quite speechless with fright and confusion. The captain looked his captives over softly, saying, "Pretty work for L Troop; sound very well in reports. Put a guard over them, lieutenant. I am going to try for a little sleep."

The reflections of L Troop were cheery as it sat on its blankets and watched the coffee in the tin cups boil. Our enterprising lieutenant sat apart on a low bank, twirling his thumbs and indulging in a mighty wonder if that would be the last of it, for he knew only too well that trifling with the "old man" was no joke.

Presently he strolled over and called the old first sergeant—their relations were very close. "I think L had best not talk much about this business. G Troop might hear about it, and that wouldn't do L any good. Sabe?"

"Divil the word kin a man say, sir, and live till morning in L Troop."

Later there was a conference of the file, and then many discussions in the ranks, with the result that L Troop shut its mouth forever.

Some months later they returned to the post. The canteen rang with praise of the "old man," for he was popular with the men because he did not bother them with fussy duties, and loud was the pæan of the mighty charge over the big insurgent camp where the three great chiefs of the enemy were captured. Other troops might be very well, but L was "it."

This hard rubbing of the feelings of others had the usual irritating effect. One night the burning torch went round and all the troopers gathered at the canteen, where the wag of G Troop threw the whole unvarnished truth in the face of L members present. This, too, with many embellishments which were not truthful. A beautiful fight ensued, and many men slept in the guard-house.

After dark, L Troop gathered back of the

stables, and they talked fiercely at each other; accusations were made, and recrimination followed. Many conferences were held in the company-room, but meanwhile G men continued to grind it in.

Two days later the following appeared in the local newspaper:

. . . . "Pedro Zacatin, a Mexican who served with troops in the late outbreak, was found hanging to a tree back of the post. There was no clew, since the rain of last night destroyed all tracks of the perpetrators of the deed. It may have been suicide, but it is thought at the post that he was murdered by sympathizers of the late revolution who knew the part he had taken against them. The local authorities will do well to take measures against lawless Mexicans from over the border who hang about this city," etc.

How the Horses Died

Having reached the firing-line, many officers left their horses tied to the brush on the sands of San Juan River. Baggage and gun mules were turned loose, and stood stupidly about. There was a constant tweet of bullets coming through the trees from the Spanish position. One horse caught three almost in a bunch; another passed through him, and he lay down on his side gasping, and another horse sat down like a dog, giving every evidence of great pain. A ball cut the skin on a mule's knee, but he only

How the Horses Died. *Painting in George F. Harding Museum, Chicago.*

stamped the leg as though to get rid of a troublesome fly.

The thing about it which was strange to me was that the horses which were untouched seemed sleepy—they gave no evidence of excitement except a slight pricking of the ears toward the hill. One almost wondered if they suspected that things were not right. Even the blood which was all about on the sands, from horses and men, did not have its general effect of scaring them.

Why do not horses die for their country? They do not have a previous intention of so doing—the act is not voluntary. Well, possibly. Neither does a conscript die voluntarily, or a man put war-stamps on checks voluntarily, but it's for the country just the same. A mule does more work for his country and more suffering than a man. It also takes more revenue stamps to keep him going. But why speak of these things? It is sufficient to know that all soldiers respect and honor all mules.

Sorrows of Don Tomas Pidal, Reconcentrado

I was driving lately with the great Cuban "war special" Sylvester Scovel along a sun-blazoned road in the Havana province, outside of Marnion; we were away beyond the patrols of the Seventh Corps. The native soldiers pattered along the road on their rat-like ponies. To them Scovel was more than a friend: he was a friend of the great chief Gomez, and that is more than enough for a Cuban.

He pointed to a ditch and to a hill, saying he had been in fights in those places—back in Maceo's time; hot little skirmishes, with no chance to put your hat on your sword. But he had always managed to get away from the Spanish; and so had Maceo—all but the one time.

Beside the road there were fine old mansions—stuccoed brick, with open windows, and with the roofs fallen in. The rank tropic vegetation was fast growing up around them, even now choking the doorways and gravel walks. And the people who lived in them? God knows!

The day grew into noon. We were hungry, and the ardent sun suggested stopping at a village which we were passing through. There was a fonda, so we got down from our carriage, and, going in, sat down at a table in a little side-room.

One is careful about the water in Cuba, and by no chance can a dirty cook get his hands on a boiled egg. We ordered coffee and eggs. A rural Cuban fonda is very close to the earth.

Through the open window could be seen the life of the village—men sitting at tables across the way, drinking, smoking, and lazing about. It was Sunday. Little children came to the window and opened their eyes at us, and we pitied their pale anæmic faces and little puffed bellies, for that terrible order of Weyler's had been particularly hard on children. There were men hanging about who looked equally hollow, but very few women.

"Reconcentrados—poor devils," observed my friend.

This harmless peasantry had suffered all that people could suffer. To look at them and to think of them was absolutely saddening. Still, the mass of suffering which they represented also deadened one's sensibilities somewhat, and for an ordinary man to put out his hand in help seemed a thing of no importance.

"I should like to know the personal experiences of one individual of this fallen people, Scovel. I can rise to one man, but two or three hundred thousand people is too big for me."

"All right," replied the alert "special." "We will take that Spanish-looking man over there by the cart. He has been starved, and he is a good type of a Cuban peasant." By the arts of the finished interviewer, Scovel soon had the man sitting at our table, with brandy-and-water before him. The man's eyes were like live coals, which is the most curious manifestation of starvation. His forehead was wrinkled, the eyebrows drawn up in the middle. He had the greenish pallor which comes when the blood is thin behind a dark, coarse skin. He did not seem afraid of us, but behind the listlessness of a low physical condition there was the quick occasional movement of a wild animal.

"Reconcentrado?"

"Si, señor. I have suffered beyond counting."

"We are Americans; we sympathize with you; tell us the story of all you have suffered. Your name? Oh! Don Tomas Pidal, will you talk to us?"

"It will be nearly three rains since the King's soldiers burned the thatch over my head and the cavalry shoved us down the road like the beasts.

"I do not know what I shall do. I may yet die—it is a small affair. Everything which I had is now gone. The Americans have come to us; but they should have come long before. At this time we are not worth coming to. Nothing is left but the land, and that the Spaniards could not kill. Señor, they of a surety would have burnt it, but that is to them impossible."

"Are you not a Spaniard by birth?"

"No; my father and mother came from over the sea, but I was born in sight of this town. I have always lived here, and I have been happy, until the war came. We did not know what the war was like. We used to hear of it years ago, but it was far to the east. The war never came to Punta Brava. We thought it never would; but it did come; and now you cannot see a thatch house or an ox, and you have to gaze hard to see any people in this country about here. That is what war does, señor, and we people here did not want war.

"Some of the valiant men who used to dwell around Punta Brava took their guns and the machete of war, and they ran away into the manigua. They used to talk in the fonda very loud, and they said they would not leave a Spaniard alive on the island. Of a truth, señor, many of those bravos have gone, they have taken many Spaniards with them to death, and between them both the people who worked in the fields died of the hunger. They ate the oxen, they burned the thatch, and the fields are grown up with bushes. There is not a dog in Punta Brava to-day.

"When the bravos ran away, the King's soldiers came into this land in numbers as great as the flies. This village sheltered many of them—many of the battalion San Quintin—and that is why the houses are not flat with the ground."

"Why did you not go out into the manigua, Don Pidal?" was asked.

"Oh, señors, I am not brave. I never talked loud in the fonda. Besides, I had a wife and five children. I lived perfectly. I had a good house of the palm. I had ten cows of fine milk and two yokes of heavy work-oxen. There were ten pigs on my land, and two hundred chickens laid eggs for me. By the sale of these and my fruit I got money. When I killed a pig to sell in Havana, it was thirty dollars. When I did not choose to sell, we had lard in the house for a month, and I had not to buy. Two of my boys, of fourteen and sixteen years, aided me in my work. We bred the beasts, planted tobacco, corn, sweet-potatoes, and plantains, and I had a field of the pineapples, besides many strong mango-trees. Could a man want for what I did not have? We ate twice a day, and even three times. We could have eaten all day if we had so desired.

"Then, señor, the tax-gatherers never suspected that I had fourteen hundred dollars in silver buried under the floor of my house. We could work as much as we pleased, or as little; but we worked, señor—all the men you see sitting about Punta Brava to-day worked before the war came; not for wages, but for the shame of not doing so. When the yokes were taken from the cattle at night and the fodder was thrown to them, we could divert ourselves. The young men put on their 'guayaberas,'* threw their saddles on their 'caballitos,'† and marched to the girls, where they danced and sang and made love. To get married it was only for the young man to have seventy dollars; the girl had to have only virtue. There was also to

* Fine shirts.   † Little horses.

go to town to buy, and then the feast-days and the Sunday nights. There was always the work—every day the same, except in the time of tobacco; then we worked into the night. In the house the women washed, they cooked, they looked after the pigs and the chickens, they had the children, and in the time of the tobacco they also went forth into the fields.

"It was easy for any man to have money, if he did not put down much on the fighting-cocks. The church cost much; there was the cura, the sacristan—many things to pay away the money for; but even if the goods from Spain did cost a great sum, because the officers of the King made many collections on them, even if the taxes on the land and the animals were heavy, yet, señor, was it not better to pay all than to have the soldiers come? Ah me, amigo, of all things the worst are the King's soldiers. It was whispered that the soldiers of your people were bad men. It was said that if they ever came to Punta Brava we should all die; but it is not so. Your soldiers do not live in other people's houses. They are all by themselves in tents up the King's road, and they leave us alone. They do nothing but bring us food in their big wagons. They lied about your soldiers. It was the talk in this country, señor, that the great people in the Free States of the North wanted to come to us and drive the King's soldiers out of the country, but it was said that your people quarrelled among themselves about coming. The great general who lived in Havana was said to be a friend to all of us, but he did not have the blue soldiers then. He is down the King's road now—I saw him the other day—and a man cannot see over the land far enough to come to the end of his tents.

'If they had been there one day the King's soldiers would not have come through my land and cut my boy to pieces in my own field. They did that, señor—cut him with the machetes until he was all over red, and they took many canastos of my fruits away. I went to the comandante to see what should be done, but he knew nothing about it.

"Then shortly a column of troops came marching by my house, and the officer said by word of mouth that we must all go to town, so that there would be none but rebels in the country. They burned my house and drove all my beasts away—all but one yoke of oxen. I gathered up some of my chickens and what little I could find about the place and put it on a cart, but I could not get my money from the burning house, because they drove us away. This was the first I felt of war.

"I thought that the King would give us food, now that he had taken us from our fields, but we got nothing from the King's officers. I could even then have lived on the outside of the town, with my chickens and what I could have raised, but it was only a short time before the soldiers of the battalion took even my chickens, and they made me move inside of a wire fence which ran from one stone fort to another. I tried to get a pass to go outside of the wire fence, and for a few weeks I was used to go and gather what potatoes I could find, but so many men were cut to pieces by the guerillas as they were coming from the fields that I no longer dared go out by day.

"We had a little thatch over our heads, but it did not keep out the rain. We became weak with the hunger. We lived in sorrow and with empty bellies. My two young children soon died, and about me many of my friends were dying like dogs. The ox-cart came in the afternoon, and they threw my two children into it like carrion. In that cart, señor, were twenty-two other dead people. It was terrible. My wife never dried her tears after that. If I had five dollars I could have gotten a box, but I did not have it. The priest would not go for less than double the price of the box, which is the custom. So my two little ones went to Guatoco on an ox-cart loaded with dead like garbage—which the Spanish comandante said we were.

"Now came the hard days, señor. Not even a dog could pick up enough in Punta Brava to keep life in his ribs. My people lay on the floor of our thatch hut, and they had not the strength to warm water in the kettle. My other child died, and again the ox-cart came. My oldest boy said he was going away and would not return. He got through the wire fence in the dark of the night, and I went with him. We got a small bunch of bananas, and in the black night out there in the manigua we embraced each other, and he went away into the country. I have not seen him since; I no longer look for him.

"Only the strongest could live, but I had hopes that by going through the fence every few nights I could keep my wife alive. This I did many times, and came back safely; but I was as careful as a cat, señor, as I crawled through the grass, for if a soldier had shot me, my wife would then have but to die. It was hard work to gather the fruit and nuts in the night, and I could not get at all times enough. My wife grew weaker, and I began to despair of saving her. One night I stole some food in a soldier's kettle from near a mess fire, and the men of the battalion fired many shots at me, but without doing me injury. Once a Spanish guerilla, whom I had known before the war came, gave me a piece of fresh beef, which I fed to my wife. I thought to save her with the beef, but she died that night in agony. There was no flesh on her bones.

"Then I ran away through the wire fence. I could not see my wife thrown on the dead-wagon, and I never came back until a few days since. I did not care if the guerillas found me. I made my way into Havana, and I got bread from the doorways at times, enough to keep me alive. There was a little work for wages along the docks, but I was not strong to do much. One night I looked between iron bars at some people of your

"This Was the First I Felt of War." *Authors' photoengraving.*

language, señor. They were sitting at a table which was covered with food, and when they saw me they gave me much bread, thrusting it out between the bars. A Spaniard would not do that.

"I was not born in a town, and when the King's soldiers sailed away I came back here to my own country. I did not like to live in Havana.

"But now I do not care to live here. I do not see, señor, why people who do not want war should have it. I would have paid my taxes. I did not care if the goods from Spain cost much. There was to get along without them if they were beyond price. It was said by the soldiers that we peasants out in the fields told the men of the manigua what the battalion San Quintin were doing. Señor, the battalion San Quintin did nothing but eat and sleep in Punta Brava. The guerillas roamed about, but I never knew whence they roamed.

"The men of the manigua took my potatoes and my plantains, but, with their guns and machetes, could I make them not to take them? Was it my fault if fifty armed men did what pleased them?

"Señor, why did not the blue soldiers of your language come to us before we died?"

This we were not able to answer.

Life in the Cattle Country

The "cattle country" of the West comprises the semi-arid belt lying between the Rocky Mountains and the arable lands of the Missouri and Mississippi Rivers, and extending from Mexico to British America. The name has been given it not because there are more cattle there than elsewhere, but because the land in its present condition is fit for little or nothing but stock raising. One who for the first time traverses the territory known abroad for its cattle, naturally expects to find the broad plains dotted with browsing herds standing knee-deep in lush pasturage; but, in fact, if he travels in the summer season, he sees the brown earth showing through a sparse covering of herbage equally brown, while he may go many miles before he comes upon a straggling bunch of gaunt, long-horned steers picking gingerly at the dry vegetation. In the humid farming regions, where corn and tame grasses can be grown for feeding, the amount of land necessary for the support of a cow is small; but upon the great plains, which lie desolate and practically dead for half the year, the conservative stockman finds it necessary to allow twenty or thirty acres for each head of his herd. No grain is raised there, and none is fed save in great emergency; the only food for the cattle is the wild grass native to the plains. This grass makes its growth in the spring; and when the rains of spring cease it is cured where it stands by the glowing sunlight. This natural hay is scant at the best, and gives little promise to the unpracticed eye;

but it is in fact very nutritious, and range cattle will thrive and fatten upon it. Every aspect of the plains suggests the necessity for avoiding the danger of overstocking; the allowance of twenty-five acres for each animal is not extravagant.

For a long time the cattle country of the Northwest was a mere stretch of wild land, wholly unbroken by fences; then the herds ranged freely under semi-occasional oversight from their owners. In that time the "cow-boy" of song and story was in his element. A gradual change has come over that old-time freedom; for where once the land was the property of the Federal government, and open to all who chose to make legitimate use of it, of late years the owners of the herds—the "cattle kings"—have acquired title to their lands, and the individual ranch has taken the place of Nature's range. Railway lines have multiplied; and with individual ownership of land has come the wire fence to mark the bounds of each man's possessions. To the wire fence more than to any other cause is due the passing of the traditional "cow-boy." Of course the fencing of the ranges is not yet universal; but every year sees a nearer approach to that end.

In former time the "round-up" was of much more importance than it is to-day; for with nothing to hinder, the cattle belonging to many owners would mix and mingle intimately, and the process of rounding up was the only method of separating them and establishing ownership. It is altogether

"The Round-up." *The Free Library of Philadelphia.*

likely the people of the next generation will see nothing of this picturesque and interesting activity.

In the cattle lands of the North, the work of rounding up begins so soon as spring is well established. During the winter the herds have been suffered to range freely, and in hard winters will often be found to have drifted far from home. The spring round-up in Nebraska and Dakota begins late in April or in May, and has for its purpose the assembling of the herds which belong to the several ranches of a neighborhood, the separation of each man's cattle from the mass, the branding of calves, etc., and the return of each herd to its own range, where the beef animals are to be put in condition for market, pending the summer and fall round-up. Cattle growers' associations have been formed in the Western States, and when the season opens each association designates the times when the several ranches within its jurisdiction shall round up their cattle, and these times are sought to be so arranged that when the first round-up is completed, say in District No. 1, District No. 2, which lies adjoining, will take up the work where No. 1 left off, and No. 3 will follow No. 2 in like manner; and in this way the round-up in the entire State consists not so much of a broken series of drives as of one long drive, with the result that practically every head of stock is discovered, identified and claimed by its owner.

Once the date is fixed for the round-up in a given district, the semi-quiescence of the winter gives instant place to hurry, bustle and strenuous activity. The "cow-ponies" which are to be ridden by the men have been upon the range through the winter, and these must be gathered up and put in condition for riding—often a task of no small difficulty, for after their winter's freedom they are not infrequently so wild as to require to be broken anew to the saddle. But, as Kipling is so fond of saying, that is another story.

The "riders" of the round-up—the men upon whom devolves the actual labor of handling the cattle—rely very greatly upon their saddle ponies. These must necessarily be trained to the work which they are to perform, and know not only the ways of men, but also the more erratic ways of the light-headed steers and cows. Ponies untrained to their duties would make endless trouble, to say nothing of greatly endangering the lives of the men. Each rider takes with him upon the round-up his own "string," consisting of ten or a dozen ponies, which are to be used in turn, so as to insure having a fresh, strong animal in instant readiness for the emergencies which are always arising, but which can never be foretold. Cow-ponies are seldom entirely trustworthy in the matter of habits and temper; but they are stout-hearted, sure-footed little beasts, who know how to keep faith in the crises of driving and "cutting out."

Besides the personal equipment of each man, the ranch sends with the party a general outfit, the principal item of which is a strong and heavy four-horse wagon, carrying bedding, food, cooking utensils, etc., and with this wagon is the man in the hollow of whose skilful hand lies the comfort and welfare of every man on the round-up— that is to say, the camp cook. Nowhere is a good cook more appreciated than in those waste places of the West. The bill of fare for the party on round-up duty is not of very great variety; the inevitable beans, salt pork, canned goods, bread and coffee make the sum total of what the men may expect to eat.

It is of great importance that this food should be well and palatably cooked; and quite independent of his abstract skill, it is always possible for the genius presiding over frying-pan and coffee-pot to make life endurable for men situated as these are. Each ranch which takes part in the round-up sends such an outfit with the men who are delegated to represent it and look after its interests, so that when the camp is pitched upon the plains it presents a very bustling and business-like appearance.

The round-up is under the direct charge of one man, known as the captain, who is sometimes selected by the association at the time of appointing the meeting, and is sometimes chosen by the ranchmen themselves when the party assembles for its work. For the time being the authority of the captain is as nearly absolute as one man's authority can be over American citizens. Violations of his orders are punishable in most cases by the assessment of arbitrary fines; but recourse is not often had to this penalty, for as a rule the men know what is expected of them, and take keen pride in doing their work well. The captain has a lieutenant chosen from the representatives of each ranch taking part in the round-up. Thus officered the force of men is ready for its work.

At the appointed time the delegates from the several ranches come straggling to the place of meeting. There is usually some delay in beginning the work, and while the captain and his aids are planning the details, the riders are wont to engage in a variety of activities, some serious, some designed for amusement—breaking unruly ponies, racing, trading, card-playing, and whatever occurs by way of passing the time. This is all put aside, however, when work actually begins; for the round-up is earnest.

With the opening of spring, when the snows have disappeared from the plains, the cattle will naturally have sought the grazing lands in the neighborhood of the watercourses; therefore, as a rule, the line travelled by the round-up lies along the valley of a small stream, extending back so far as may be necessary upon either hand.

The men are awakened in the morning long before daylight. They have probably slept on the ground, rolled in blankets and with saddles or boots for pillows. Toilets are hurriedly made, for tardiness is not tolerated. The camp breakfast is gulped down in the dark, and every man must be instantly ready to mount when the summons comes. A force of twenty or thirty men is chosen for the day's riding, and this force is divided into two parties, one of which is to cover the territory to the right and the other to the left of the line of the riders' march. For the most part, the land which borders the streams of the far Northwest is broken, rocky and ragged, and to ride a horse over it is certainly not a pleasure trip, to say nothing of the necessity for looking out sharply for straggling bunches of cattle, gathering them up and driving them forward; for range cattle are wild as deer and perverse as swine.

So soon as possible the night's camp is struck and the wagons move forward for five miles or so, where the riders are to assemble after the morning's work. The two parties of riders then strike off in opposite directions, those in each party gradually drawing further and further apart, until the dozen men form a line ten or fifteen miles in length, extending from the site of the night's camp back to the foothills bordering the stream; and then this line, with its members a mile or so apart, moves forward in the direction of the new camp, searching every nook and cranny among the rocks and hills for wandering bunches of grazing cattle. These must be assembled and driven to camp. The man on the inner end of the line keeps close to the stream, riding straight forward, while he at the other end will have to ride for perhaps thirty or forty miles, making a long circling sweep to the hills and then back to the stream. This ride is hard and often perilous, for the land is much broken and cut up by ravines and precipitous "buttes." The half-wild cattle will climb everywhere, and wherever they go the ponies must follow. It may be that in the course of the morning's drive the riders will gather many hundreds or perhaps thousands of cattle; or it is possible that no more than a score or two will be found. At any rate, the drive is carried forward with the intention of reaching camp about midday. Dinner is eaten with a ravenous appetite, but with scant ceremony, and there is no allowance of time for an after-dinner nap, for the herd gathered in the morning must be sorted over and the animals given to their several owners. This is the most trying work of the round-up. It requires clean, strong courage to ride a pony of uncertain temper

into the heart of a herd of several hundred or thousand wild cattle which are wrought up, as these are, to a pitch of high nervous excitement; but there is no other recourse.

Each ranch has its individual mark or brand, which is put upon its animals— sometimes a letter or combination of letters, and sometimes a geometrical figure.

The brands are protected by State law, somewhat after the fashion of a copyright, and each is the absolute property of the ranch which uses it. The ranches are commonly known among the cattlemen of the neighborhood by the name of the brand which they use—as "Circle-Bar Ranch," "Lazy L Ranch," etc. A lazy L is an L lying upon its side. In the work of "cutting out," a delegate from a ranch rides into the herd gathered in the morning, singles out one at a time those cattle bearing his ranch's brand, and slowly urges them to the edge of the mass, where they are taken in charge by other riders and kept together in a bunch. Great vigilance is necessary in holding out these separated bunches, for they are constantly striving to return to the main herd. The ponies used in cutting out must be the best, thoroughly broken to the work, and wise as serpents; for in case of some maddened cow or steer forming a sudden disposition to charge, the life of the rider often depends upon the willingness and cool adroitness of his pony in getting out of the way.

Once the herd is apportioned to its owners, there remains the labor of branding. Calves with their mothers are easily identified; but there will always be found some mature animals which have escaped the branding-iron in former round-ups, and which are known as mavericks. It may be imagined that the burning of a brand upon the shoulder, flank or side of a lusty two-year-old bull is fraught with considerable excitement. To do this, it is first necessary that the animal be "roped," or lariated, and thrown down. The skill of men trained to handle the rope is really admirable, and it may be remarked in passing that an expert roper is always in demand. The wildly excited steer or bull will be in full flight over the prairie, diving, dodging, plunging this way and that to escape from the inevitable noose swinging over the head of the shrill-yelling rider in pursuit. The greatest skill lies in throwing the noose so that it will settle upon the ground in such wise as to catch the fore or hind legs of the galloping beast; this is the pride of the adept roper. To throw the noose over the head or horns is a trick held in slight esteem. When the noose has settled to its place, the rider gives to his pony a well-understood signal, and the willing beast settles himself for the shock to come when the captive brings up at the end of the taut rope. The pony goes back upon his haunches, the man takes a few turns with the rope around the high horn of his saddle; then with a jerk and a jar the helpless victim throws a furious summersault, and after that there is nothing for it but to submit to fate. A second rider throws his lariat over the other pair of struggling legs, and with the brute thus pinioned the hot branding-iron is set against his side. Where the iron has touched, the hair may grow no more; or if it grows, it will be so discolored as to leave the brand easily recognizable. When the ropes are loosed the fun is fast; for the infuriated animal seeks vengeance, and will charge blindly at any moving thing within sight. The branding of calves is not child's play, but it is tame as compared with the work upon grown animals.

The work of branding concludes the most serious business of the day, save that the herd requires constant watching throughout the twenty-four hours. When night has fallen and the herd has lain down, riders are detailed to circle continually about to guard against the ever-present danger of a stampede. In the night, cattle will take fright upon very slight alarm, and often quite causelessly. One or two will rise bellowing, and in an instant the entire herd is upon its feet, crazed with fright and desiring nothing but flight. To break a stampede, it is necessary to head off the leaders and turn them back into the herd. If the onward rush can be checked and the herd induced to move around in a circle, the present danger is past; but it is impossible to foretell when another break will occur. The rider who deliberately goes in front of a stampeding herd in the pitchy darkness of a prairie night, thoughtless of everything save his duty, must be a man of fine fibre. And indeed I must say at the last that the "cow-punchers" as a class, maligned and traduced as they have been, possess a quality of sturdy, sterling manhood which would be to the credit of men in any walk of life. The honor of the average "puncher" abides with him continually. He will not lie; he will not steal. He keeps faith with his friends; toward his enemies he bears himself like a man. He has his vices—as who has not?—but I like to speak softly of them when set against his unassailable virtues. I wish that the manhood of the cow-boy might come more into fashion further East.

When a Document Is Official

William or "Billy" Burling had for these last four years worn three yellow stripes on his coat-sleeve with credit to the insignia. Leading up to this distinction were two years when he had only worn two, and back of that were yet other annums when his blue blouse had been severely plain except for five brass buttons down the front. This matter was of no consequence in all the world to any one except Burling, but the nine freezing, grilling, famishing years which he had so successfully contributed to the cavalry service of the United States were the "clean-up" of his assets. He had gained distinction in several pounding finishes with the Indians; he was liked in barracks and respected on the line; and he had wrestled so sturdily with the books that when his name came up for promotion to an officer's commission he had passed the examinations. On the very morning of which I speak, a lieutenant of his company had quietly said to him: "You need not say anything about it, but I heard this morning that your commission had been signed and is now on the way from Washington. I want to congratulate you."

"Thank you," replied William Burling, as the officer passed on. The sergeant sat down on his bunk and said, mentally, "It was a damn long time coming."

There is nothing so strong in human nature as the observance of custom, especially when all humanity practises it, and the best men in America and Europe, living or dead, have approved of this one. It has, in cases like the sergeant's, been called "wetting a new commission." I suppose in Mohammedan Asia they buy a new wife. Something outrageous must be done when a military man celebrates his "step"; but be that as it may, William Burling was oppressed by a desire to blow off steam. Here is where the four years of the three stripes stood by this hesitating mortal and overpowered the exposed human nature. Discipline had nearly throttled custom, and before this last could catch its breath again the orderly came in to tell Burling that the colonel wanted him up at headquarters.

It was early winter at Fort Adobe, and the lonely plains were white with a new snow. It certainly looked lonely enough out beyond the last buildings, but in those days one could not trust the plains to be as lonely as they looked. Mr. Sitting-Bull or Mr. Crazy-Horse might pop out of any *coulee* with a goodly following, and then life would not be worth living for a wayfarer. Some of these high-flavored romanticists had but lately removed the hair from sundry buffalo-hunters in Adobe's vicinity, and troops were out in the field trying to "kill, capture, or destroy" them, according to the ancient and honorable form. All this was well known to Sergeant Burling when he stiffened up before the colonel.

"Sergeant, all my scouts are out with the commands, and I am short of officers in post. I have an order here for Captain Morestead, whom I suppose to be at the juncture of Old Woman's Fork and Lightning Creek, and I want you to deliver it. You can easily find their trail. The order is important, and must go through. How many men do you want?"

Burling had not put in nine years on the plains without knowing a scout's answer to that question. "Colonel, I prefer to go alone." There was yet another reason than "he travels the fastest who travels alone" in Burling's mind. He knew it would be a very desirable thing if he could take that new commission into the officers' mess with the prestige of soldierly devotion upon it. Then, too, nothing short of twenty-five men could hope to stand off a band of Indians.

Burling had flipped a mental coin. It came down heads for him, for the colonel said: "All right, sergeant. Dress warm and travel nights. There is a moon. Destroy that order if you have bad luck. Understand?"

"Very well, sir," and he took the order from the colonel's hand.

The old man noticed the figure of the young cavalryman, and felt proud to command such a man. He knew Burling was an officer, and he thought he knew that Burling did not know it. He did not like to send him out in such weather through such a country, but needs must.

As a man Burling was at the ripe age of thirty, which is the middle distance of usefulness for one who rides a government horse. He was a light man, trim in his figure, quiet in manner, serious in mind. His nose, eyes, and mouth denoted strong character, and also that there had been little laughter in his life. He had a mustache, and beyond this nothing can be said, because cavalrymen are primitive men, weighing no more than one hundred and sixty pounds. The horse is responsible for this, because he cannot carry more, and that weight even then must be pretty much on the same ancient lines. You never see long, short, or odd curves on top of a cavalry horse—not with nine years of field service.

Marching down to the stables, he gave his good bay horse quite as many oats as were good for him. Then going to his quarters, he dressed himself warmly in buffalo coat, buffalo moccasins, fur cap and gloves, and

he made one saddle-pocket bulge with coffee, sugar, crackers, and bacon, intending to fill the opposite side with grain for his horse. Borrowing an extra six-shooter from Sergeant McAvoy, he returned to the stables and saddled up. He felt all over his person for a place to put the precious order, but the regulations are dead set against pockets in soldiers' clothes. He concluded that the upper side of the saddle-bags, where the extra horseshoes go, was a fit place. Strapping it down, he mounted, waved his hand at the fellow-soldiers, and trotted off up the road.

It was getting towards evening, there was a fine brisk air, and his horse was going strong and free. There was no danger until he passed the Frenchman's ranch where the buffalo-hunters lived; and he had timed to leave there after dark and be well out before the moon should discover him to any Indians who might be viewing that log house with little schemes of murder in expectance.

He got there in the failing light, and tying his horse to the rail in front of the long log house, he entered the big room where the buffalo-hunters lived; and he had timed to the results of their hard labor with each other as the pasteboards should indicate. There were about fifteen men in the room, some inviting the bar, but mostly at various tables guessing at cards. The room was hot, full of tobacco smoke and many democratic smells, while the voices of the men were as hard as the pounding of two boards together. What they said, for the most part, can never be put in your library, neither would it interest if it was. Men with the bark on do not say things in their lighter moods which go for much; but when these were behind a sage-bush handling a Sharps, or skimming among the tailing buffaloes on a strong pony, what grunts were got out of them had meaning!

Buffalo-hunters were men of iron endeavor for gain. They were adventurers; they were not nice. Three buckets of blood was four dollars to them. They had thews, strong-smelling bodies, and eager minds. Life was red on the buffalo-range in its day.

There was an intellectual life—a scientific turn—but it related to flying lead, wolfish knowledge of animals, and methods of hide-stripping.

The sergeant knew many of them, and was greeted accordingly. He was feeling well. The new commission, the dangerous errand, the fine air, and the ride had set his blood bounding through a healthy frame. A young man with an increased heart action is going to do something besides standing on one foot leaning against a wall: nature arranged that long ago.

Without saying what he meant, which was "let us wet the new commission," he sang out: "Have a drink on the army. Kem up, all you hide-jerkers," and they rallied around the young soldier and "wet." He talked with them a few minutes, and then stepped out into the air—partly to look at his horse, and partly to escape the encores which were sure to follow. The horse stood quietly. Instinctively he started to unbuckle the saddle-pocket. He wanted to see how the "official document" was riding, that being the only thing that oppressed Burling's mind. But the pocket was unbuckled, and a glance showed that the paper was gone.

His bowels were in tremolo. His heart lost three beats; and then, as though to adjust matters, it sent a gust of blood into his head. He pawed at his saddle-bags; he unbuttoned his coat and searched with nervous fingers everywhere through his clothes; and then he stood still, looking with fixed eyes at the nigh front foot of the cavalry horse. He did not stand mooning long; but he thought through those nine years, every day of them, every minute of them; he thought of the disgrace both at home and in the army; he thought of the lost commission, which would only go back the same route it came. He took off his overcoat and threw it across the saddle. He untied his horse and threw the loose rein over a post. He tugged at a big sheath-knife until it came from the back side of his belt to the front side, then he drew two big army revolvers and looked at the cylinders—they were full of gray lead. He cocked both, laid them

across his left arm, and stepped quickly to the door of the Frenchman's log house. As he backed into the room he turned the key in the lock and put it under his belt. Raising the revolvers breast-high in front of him, he shouted, "Attention!" after the loud, harsh habit of the army. An officer might talk to a battalion on parade that way.

No one had paid any attention to him as he entered. They had not noticed him, in the preoccupation of the room, but every one quickly turned at the strange word.

"Throw up your hands instantly, every man in the room!" and with added vigor, "Don't move!"

Slowly, in a surprised way, each man began to elevate his hands—some more slowly than others. In settled communities this order would make men act like a covey of quail, but at that time at Fort Adobe the six-shooter was understood both in theory and in practice.

"You there, bartender, be quick! I'm watching you." And the bartender exalted his hands like a practised saint.

"Now, gentlemen," began the soldier, "the first man that bats an eye or twitches a finger or moves a boot in this room will get shot just that second. Sabe?"

"What's the matter, Mr. Soldier? Be you *loco?*" sang out one.

"No, I am not *loco*. I'll tell you why I am not." Turning one gun slightly to the left, he went on: "You fellow with the long red hair over there, you sit still if you are not hunting for what's in this gun. I rode up to this shack, tied my horse outside the door, came in here, and bought the drinks. While I was in here some one stepped out and stole a paper—official document—from my saddle-pockets, and unless the paper is returned to me, I am going to turn both of these guns loose on this crowd. I know you will kill me, but unless I get the paper I want to be killed. So, gentlemen, you keep your hands up. You can talk it over; but remember, if that paper is not handed me in a few minutes, I shall begin to shoot." Thus having delivered himself, the sergeant stood by the door with his guns levelled. A hum of voices filled the room.

"The soldier is right," said some one.

"Don't point that gun at me; I hain't got any paper, pardner. I can't even read paper, pard. Take it off; you might git narvous."

"That sojer's out fer blood. Don't hold his paper out on him."

"Yes, give him the paper," answered others. "The man what took that paper wants to fork it over. This soldier means business. Be quick."

"Who's got the paper?" sang a dozen voices. The bartender expostulated with the determined man—argued a mistake—but from the compressed lips of desperation came the word "Remember!"

From a near table a big man with a gray beard said: "Sergeant, I am going to stand up and make a speech. Don't shoot. I am with you." And he rose quietly, keeping an inquisitive eye on the Burling guns, and began:

"This soldier is going to kill a bunch of people here; any one can see that. That paper ain't of no account. Whatever did any fool want to steal it for? I have been a soldier myself, and I know what an officer's paper means to a despatch-bearer. Now, men, I say, after we get through with this mess, what men is alive ought to take the

doggone paper-thief, stake the feller out, and build a slow fire on him, if he can be ridden down. If the man what took the paper will hand it up, we all agree not to do anything about it. Is that agreed?"

"Yes, yes, that's agreed," sang the chorus.

"Say, boss, can't I put my arms down?" asked a man who had become weary.

"If you do, it will be forever," came the simple reply.

Said one man, who had assembled his logistics: "There was some stompin' around yar after we had that drink on the sojer. Whoever went out that door is the feller what got yer document; and ef he'd a-tooken yer horse, I wouldn't think much— I'd be lookin' fer that play, stranger. But to go *cincha* a piece of paper! Well, I think you must be plumb *loco* to shoot up a lot of men like we be fer that yar."

"Say," remarked a natural observer—one of those minds which would in other places have been a head waiter or some other highly sensitive plant—"I reckon that Injun over thar went out of this room. I seen him go out."

A little French half-breed on Burling's right said, "Maybe as you keel de man what 'ave 'and you de papier—hey?"

"The Buffalo-Hunters Knew by the 'Sign' on the Trail." *Authors photoengraving.*

"No, on my word I will not," was the promise, and with that the half-breed continued: "Well, de papier ees een ma pocket. Don't shoot."

The sergeant walked over to the abomination of a man, and putting one pistol to his left ear, said, "Give it up to me with one fist only—mind, now!" But the half-breed had no need to be admonished, and he handed the paper to Burling, who gathered it into the grip of his pistol hand, crushing it against the butt.

Sidling to the door, the soldier said, "Now I am going out, and I will shoot any one who follows me." He returned one gun to its holster, and while covering the crowd, fumbled for the key-hole, which he found. He backed out into the night, keeping one gun at the crack of the door until the last, when with a quick spring he dodged to the right, slamming the door.

The room was filled with a thunderous roar, and a dozen balls crashed through the door.

He untied his horse, mounted quickly with the overcoat underneath him, and galloped away. The hoof-beats reassured the buffalo-hunters; they ran outside and blazed and popped away at the fast-receding horseman, but to no purpose. Then there was a scurrying for ponies, and a pursuit was instituted, but the grain-fed cavalry horse was soon lost in the darkness. And this was the real end of Sergeant William Burling.

The buffalo-hunters followed the trail next day. All night long galloped and trotted the trooper over the crunching snow, and there was no sound except when the moon-stricken wolves barked at his horse from the gray distance.

The sergeant thought of the recent occurrence. The reaction weakened him. His face flushed with disgrace; but he knew the commission was safe, and did not worry about the vengeance of the buffalo-hunters, which was sure to come.

At daylight he rested in a thick timbered bottom, near a cut bank, which in plains strategy was a proper place to make a fight. He fed himself and his horse, and tried to straighten and smooth the crumpled order on his knee, and wondered if the people at Adobe would hear of the unfortunate occurrence. His mind troubled him as he sat gazing at the official envelope; he was in a brown study. He could not get the little sleep he needed, even after three hours' halt. Being thus preoccupied, he did not notice that his picketed horse from time to time raised his head and pricked his ears towards his back track. But finally, with a start and a loud snort, the horse stood eagerly watching the bushes across the little opening through which he had come.

Burling got on his feet, and untying his lariat, led his horse directly under the cut bank in some thick brush. As he was in the act of crawling up the bank to have a look at the flat plains beyond, a couple of rifles cracked and a ball passed through the soldier's hips. He dropped and rolled down the bank, and then dragged himself into the brush.

From all sides apparently came Indians' "Ki-yis" and "coyote yelps." The cavalry horse trembled and stood snorting, but did not know which way to run. A great silence settled over the snow, lasting for minutes. The Sioux crawled closer, and presently saw a bright little flare of fire from the courier's position, and they poured in their bullets, and again there was quiet. This the buffalo-hunters knew later by the "sign" on the trail. To an old hunter there is no book so plain to read as footprints in the snow.

And long afterwards, in telling about it, an old Indian declared to me that when they reached the dead body they found the ashes of some paper which the soldier had burned, and which had revealed his position. "Was it his medicine which had gone back on him?"

"No," I explained, "it wasn't his medicine, but the great medicine of the white man, which bothered the soldier so."

"Hump! The great Washington medicine maybeso. It make dam fool of soldiers lots of time I know 'bout," concluded "Bear-in-the-Night," as he hitched up his blanket around his waist.

The Trouble Brothers

BILL AND THE WOLF

Sadness comes when we think of how long ago things happened. Let us not bother ourselves about time, though we cannot cease to remember that it took youth to sit up all night in the club and ride all next day, or sleep twenty-four hours on a stretch, as the situation demanded. The scene, as I recall it, demanded exactly that. The ambulances of Fort Adobé brought a party of ranking military men, sundry persons of substance, lesser mortals of much enthusiasm, and Colonel William Cody—the Great Unknown—up the long thirty miles of dusty plains from the railroad. The yellow country in the autumn is dry riding and hard work. The officers stationed at the post took a brotherly interest in the new-comers because they were also sportsmen. You could not drive an iron wedge between the plains type of officer and a sportsman without killing both. There were dinners of custom and such a gathering at the club as was unusual, where the hunting plans were keenly discussed—so keenly, in fact, that it was nearer morning than midnight when it was considered desirable to go to bed.

There were dogs which the sportsmen had brought along—fierce wolf-hounds from Russia—and Buffalo Bill had two malignant pups in which he took a fine interest. The officers at Adobé were possessed of a pack of rough Scotch hounds, besides which, if every individual soldier at the post did not have his individual doggie, I must have made a miscount. It was arranged that we consolidate the collection and run a wolf on the morrow.

When sport was in prospect, *reveille* was the usual hour, regardless of bedtime. Morning found us all mounted, and the throng of horses started up the road. The dogs were kept together; the morning was of the golden, frosty, Adobé type, and the horses could feel the run which was coming to them.

Everything was ready but the wolf. It was easy to find wolves in that country, however. We had slow dogs to trail them with. But our wolf came to us in the way money comes to a modern politician.

Bill, the chief of sports, as we called him, was riding ahead, when we saw him stop a wagon. It was driven by an old "prairie-dog,"* and on the bed of the wagon was a box made of poles and slats. Inside of this was a big gray wolf, which the man had caught in a trap without injuring it in the least. He hoped to be able to sell it at the post, but he realized his hope and his price right there. "Now, boys, we'll have a wolf-hunt; but let us go back to the post, where the ladies and the men can see it."

We could not agree whether it was the colonel's gallantry or his circus habits which prompted this move, but it was the thing which brought a blighting sorrow to Fort Adobé. We turned back, bundling Mr. Wolf down the road. He sat behind the slats, gazing far away across his native hills,

* Nondescript man of the plains.

"This Is the Way It Began." *Authors' photoengraving.*

silent and dignified as an Indian warrior in captivity.

The ladies were notified, and came out in traps. The soldiers joined us on horseback and on foot, some hundred of them, each with his pet *fice*† at his heels.

The domestic servants of the line came down back of the stables. The sentries on post even walked sidewise, that they might miss no details. Adobé was out for a race. I had never supposed there were so many dogs in the world. As pent-up canine animosities displayed themselves, they fell to taking bites at each other in the dense gathering; but their owners policed and soothed them.

Every one lined up. The dogs were arranged as best might. The wagon was driven well out in front, and Colonel William Cody

† Cur-dog.

helped the driver to turn the wolf loose, a matter which gave no trouble at all. They removed two slats, and if there had been a charge of melinite behind that wolf he could not have hit that valley any harder.

The old hounds, which had scented and had seen the wolf, straightway started on his course. With a wild yell the cavalcade sprang forward. Many cur-dogs were ridden screaming under foot. The two bronco ponies of the man who had brought the wolf turned before the rush and were borne along with the charge. Everything was going smoothly.

Of the garrison curs many were left behind. They knew nothing about wolves or field-sports, but, addled by the excitement, fell into the old garrison feuds.

At a ravine we were checked. I looked behind, and the intervening half-mile was dotted here and there with dog-fights of various proportions. Some places there were as high as ten in a bunch, and at others only couples. The infantry soldiers came running out to separate them, and, to my infinite surprise, I saw several of the dough-boys circling each other in the well-known attitudes of the prize-ring. Officers started back to pull them apart. Our dogs were highly excited. Two of them flew at each other; more sprang into the jangle. The men yelled at them and got off their horses. One man kicked another man's dog, whereat the aggrieved party promptly swatted him on the eye. This is the way it began. While you read, over a hundred and fifty men were pounding each other with virility, while around and underfoot fought each doggie with all possible vim. Greyhounds cut red slices on quarter-bred bulls; fox-terriers hung on to the hind legs of such big dogs as were fully engaged in front. Fangs glistened; they yelled and bawled and growled, while over them struggled and tripped the men as they swung for the knock-out blow. If a man went down he was covered with biting and tearing dogs. The carnage became awful—a variegated foreground was becoming rapidly red. The officers yelled at the men, trying to assert their authority, but no officer could yell as loud as the acre of dogs. By this time the men were so frenzied that they could not tell a shoulder-strap from a bale of hay. One might as well have attempted to stop the battle of Gettysburg.

Naturally this could not last forever, and gradually the men were torn apart and the dogs unhooked their fangs from their adversaries. During the war I looked towards the fort, hoping for some relief, but the half-mile was dotted here and there with individuals thumping and pounding each other, while their dogs fought at their heels. Where, where had I seen this before, thought came. Yes, yes—in Cæsar's Commentaries. They did things just this way in his time. Bare legs and short swords only were needed here.

Things gradually quieted, and the men started slowly back to the post nursing their wounds. Most of the horses had run away during the engagement. It was clear to be seen that plaster and liniment would run short at Adobé that day.

Colonel Cody sat on his horse, thinking of the destruction he had wrought.

The commanding officer gathered himself and sang out: "Say, Bill, there is your dog-goned old wolf sitting there on the hill looking at you. What do you reckon he thinks?"

"I reckon he thinks we have made trouble enough for to-day. Next time we go hunting, colonel, I think you had better leave your warriors at home," was Bill's last comment as he turned his horse's tail towards the wolf.

How Stilwell Sold Out

There always have been heroes; there always will be; and the more a nation has of them the more surely it will have roast beef for its dinner every day. We must save the records of their deeds because we are beholden to them. The kings, the cardinals, the smart fellows and the men who wrought with their hands, have to be reckoned with, as do also those chaps who owned the talents of silver in the days of yore; but they don't seem to amuse me so much as the parties of the first part.

Stilwell was one of the scouts under General Forsyth who were rounded up on the Arickere Fork of the Republican River in 1868 by the so-called "dog soldiers." These were Sioux and Cheyenne Indians, who had always been "out," as the expression went.

The affair is so well known that I won't waste time describing it, except to call to remembrance that over a thousand Indians had invested the little band on a low sand island and had shot all their horses. The white men had dug pits in the gravel, and were making a desperate fight. Three times a great band of mounted Indians charged them under cover of a heavy fire from dismounted fellows. They were repulsed, leaving dead "bucks" within ten feet of the circle. General Forsyth was shot twice. Lieutenant Beecher and the surgeon were killed. Two men were dead, four mortally wounded, four severely and ten slightly, which will indicate the desperation of the fight.

Their situation could not be worse. Relief must be had or they were doomed. No one thought of surrendering to the Indians. Such a thing had been done a few times in our history, but always by people who had very little previous knowledge of the North American aborigine. That is the potent reason why our native race has always attracted so great attention as compared with other modern savages. They were fighting for their land—they fought to the death—they never gave quarter, and they never asked it. There was a nobility of purpose about their resistance which commends itself now that it is passed.

It was my good fortune recently to meet my hero—now Judge Stilwell—at his ranch in the Big Horn Basin. Of course, I made him tell me all about the exploit which made him famous.

At the time of the episode, Jack Stilwell was a young man, and has been described by General Custer as "a mere beardless boy of perhaps 19 years, possessing a trim, lithe figure, which was well set off to great advantage by a jaunty suit of buckskin which he wore cut and fringed according to the true style of the frontiersman. In his waist-belt he carried a large-sized revolver and a hunting-knife. These with his rifle constituted his equipment. A capital shot, whether afoot or on horseback, and a perfect horseman, this beardless boy on more than one occasion proved himself a dangerous foe to the wily red man."

When I had the pleasure to observe this boy he did not answer to this description in the least. The years had their story to tell. Fat and gray hair had come, but I saw another thing which General Custer may not have had brought to his notice. Probably in his day this thing had not developed. This was a wonderfully agile mind.

Stilwell has that beautiful and homely old Missouri humorous talk, seizing the salients, like a drowning man, with sure and vigorous clutch. Jack hates many things and loves many people. He will get into his two-pony buggy instantly and pull out if he does not fancy you. Born on the frontier, and always living there, he has followed the game and the Indians into the last fastness, for the Big Horn Basin is as remote as possible now. His ranch is 150 miles from a railroad, and the old gentleman is much disturbed because a weekly paper has been started at the town of Cody, which is a day's drive from him. Says the Judge: "Next thing we know 'twill be a preacher, and then it's time for old Jack to move." He speaks Comanche, Sioux, and Spanish, in consequence of having lived among these people in his youth. He was hunting as a means of livelihood at the time of the Indian troubles in Kansas, and, when the Forsyth party was formed, enlisted in that body, which was composed of seasoned and selected men.

During the fight on the first day Stilwell and five other men on the lower end of the island were ridden over in the charge. When the Indians fell back beaten, Stilwell found he had emptied his Spencer, and only had one shot left out of the contents of two revolvers. The affair lasted but a minute, and he says he has little remembrance of it except that ponies were flying over him like a flock of pigeons, and you couldn't hear your own gun go off.

When it was quite dark the little party made their way back to the command, and there was a big conference in the pits, which had by this time been made quite protective. The idea was that some one must attempt to go through the Indian lines with the mes-

sage to Fort Wallace. It was an almost hopeless undertaking. Various ones volunteered, but Forsyth selected Jack Stilwell and an old French Rocky Mountain trapper by the name of Trudeau. He was about fifty-five years old, but had led a rough life with the American Fur Company and was much more aged than his years warranted. Also he had consumed what whiskey he could lay his hands on, and that had not improved things. He dressed in greasy buckskin, wore long hair, goatee and mustache, and would have made a proper-looking member of Napoleon's Old Guard. He had a very limited English vocabulary but made up in profanity when he lacked words. He thoroughly understood the Cheyenne language, and since Stilwell spoke Sioux they agreed to reply to any challenge in the opposite tongue to the one addressed them. They made moccasins out of their boot-tops, put on blankets, cut off a little horse meat, but they were short of tobacco. The men of the party gave them "enough," as Stilwell says, "to last till now."

The long grass was full of Indians, whose rifles flashed from time to time in the darkness across the river.

"When we were bidding the men good-by, I says, 'Boys, this year is a sellout and Jack Stilwell is going to come high.' Then the old Frenchman he says, "Yas, by —— ole man Trudeau he bring good price, too.' "

They crawled ever so slowly and silently through the pitchy darkness to the river. This they crossed half submerged, and lay a long time in the water waiting for the slow rifle-fire to indicate a place in the grass least likely to contain an Indian.

During a heavy fall of rain they got into the long grass unnoticed, and made their way back toward the hills. They were closely wrapped in their blankets and were accosted frequently by passing Indians, always replying in the other tongue. They lay still for half an hour at a time, trying to locate big bands of Indians, and when they struck some willows they crawled. The country was alive with the enemy, going or coming from the investing circle to the temporary camps.

Once the two scouts fell over a cut bank, and it nearly scared them to death for fear of detection by the sound they made.

Thinking it best not to follow up or down the river, they went out across a bald hill. It was necessary to keep a sharp lookout, because Indians always have scouts far on either side of their main body. When they could see the gray of morning coming, they crawled into the head of a dry washout, where the thick grass had grown on either side so that they could not see out of it, and there they lay all through the hot day. Stilwell thinks they had only made about three miles, and they found themselves nearer Indian camps than they had hoped for. They must have changed their direction in the darkness. The calling of the heralds in the village was faintly heard and the words of the Indian herdboys could be distinctly understood. More than once they feared detection from these youngsters through their Indian dogs.

But the day passed with nothing more serious than agitated minds, and with the darkness began their cautious journey, hoping that by morning they would be beyond the Indian scouts. Ever and again they threw themselves flat on the ground. Their constant fear was Indian dogs, which animals are quite as amiable to a white man as the latter's are towards Indians.

It was the faint first coming of the second day when they struck the south fork of the Republican and to their utter dismay found themselves in close proximity to the lower end of the Sioux village. They had wandered again in the darkness.

Quickly they hid themselves in some thick bushes on the river bank, and directly the sun came pouring over the plains. They were in for another trying day, when the minutes were hours and the hours moved with glacial slowness.

They pulled grass and covered themselves, and lay flat and famishing on the ground. They could hear the Indians burying their dead—crying and yelling. They knew their comrades were holding out, for war parties came sneaking into the village—even watering their ponies all around their hiding-place. If they had been victorious, they would have come in yelling and with great turmoil.

Several times dogs came to them, but the Indians were so preoccupied with their funerals that they did not notice. The old Frenchman hissed at these visitors like a squaw and told them to be gone, in Cheyenne, accompanying this by volleys of words such as no lady would use.

That night, when the darkness came, and the village was wailing over its dead, the two men struck out at a good round jog over a high rolling country toward Fort Wallace, leaving their blankets where they lay. It was necessary now to make time, since Wallace was many miles away, and the beleaguered scouts could not hold out forever. Having travelled all night they concluded to continue on during the daylight, and were so doing, when an Indian rode into sight. By such a lucky chance as only happens to those who take risks, there was lying near them the carcass of an old buffalo which had been killed the winter before and gutted by the wolves. Dropping, they crawled into it, or as far as they could get in. They had seen the Indian first, but by some psychic impulse peculiar to animals and Indians, the Indian turned and rode slowly along the hill toward their position.

The two frontiersmen gazed steadily at the oncoming redskin. "Does he see us?" they asked again and again. Stilwell slowly poked his rifle through a hole in the forward part of the buffalo's skin and drew a dead center on the warrior.

Meanwhile Trudeau whispered: By — — — — keel heem un we geet de horse—keel heem, Jack. We weel get on double—I weel ride behin', un we weel mak' a —— of a run for beeg timber. If those Enjun catch us I weel geet off un mak' a fight un you can geet away—keel heem, mon enfan'."

"No, he don't see us. If he does, I will soak him," replied Jack.

Thus was that Indian's life argued, and

as he rode away Stilwell felt sorry that he would never know what a good story about himself he had missed.

Trudeau's offer was rather noble, but he loved Stilwell better than anyone else in the world. All day as they lay in the dry buffalo he bemoaned Jack's failure to bag the pony. "Eef you geet dat pony you be all right. I tak' notice dat—of a fine pony. Run a heap, dat pony. He was warre-pony."

That night old Trudeau was very sick. The travelling and a bad meat diet had used him up. Stilwell had some regrets that he had not shot the warrior, but he was not then sure of catching the horse and he did not know what was on the other side of the hill.

By early morning Trudeau thought he could travel. Slowly and painfully they made their way. Their improvised moccasins were giving out—they were famished and sleepless. Late in the day the two brave men staggered into the old Denver stage road. To their delight they saw a Mexican driving toward them in a two-horse buggy. They accosted him, told their errand, and asked him to drive them back to Fort Wallace, which he refused to do. Promptly the two Spencers were held at his head and he reconsidered. By sundown they drove into Wallace, and Trudeau was lifted out of the wagon, but Stilwell delivered his message and before dark Colonel Carpenter was trotting out of the post to the relief of the scouts. He found they had fought off the Indians, but were in a pitiable condition.

Thus Trudeau and Stilwell had performed their task. In four days they had travelled one hundred and ten miles, with no food but raw horseflesh, through a country swarming with mounted Indians, but reached their destination in a state of collapse. So Jack Stilwell never "sold out" after all.

A Failure of Justice

Captain Halleran of the dragoons stepped off the way freight at Alkali Flat, which sort of place has been well described as a "roaring board and canvas city"; only in justice to certain ancient adobe huts I should mention their presence.

He was on government business connected with the Indian war then raging in the Territory, and Alkali Flat was a temporary military depot piled high with crackers, bacon, cartridges, and swarming with mules, dusty men, and all the turmoil which gathers about a place where Uncle Sam dispenses dollars to his own.

The captain was a gentleman and a scholar, but he didn't look the part. What sweat and alkali dust won't do to a uniform, sleeping on the ground in it for a month or two will do, and then he was burned like a ripe peach. This always happens to American soldiers in wars, whatever may be the case in Europe. The captain's instincts, however, had undergone no change whatever, and the dust-blown plaza did not appeal to him as he sauntered across towards the long row of one-storied shanties. There was a dismal array of signs—"The Venus," "The Medicine Queen," "The Beer Spring," "The Free and Easy"—but they did not invite the captain. There were two or three outfitting stores which relieved the business aspect, but the simple bed and board which the captain wanted was not there, unless with its tin-pan piano or gambling-chip accompaniment.

He met a man who had the local color, and asked if there was not in the town a hotel run somewhat more on the ancient lines.

"Sure there is, cap, right over to the woman's," said he, pointing. "They don't have no hell round the old woman's. That's barred in this plaza, and she can cook jes like mother. That's the old woman's over thar whar yu' see the flowers in front and the two green trees—jes nex' the Green Cloth saloon."

The captain entered the place, which was a small bar-room with a pool-table in the centre, and back of this a dining-room. Behind the bar stood a wholesome-looking woman in a white calico dress, far enough this side of middle age to make "old woman" libellous as applied to her.

"Good-evening, madam," ventured the captain, feeling that such a woman could not escape matrimony at the Flat.

"Good-evening, captain. Want some supper?"

"Yes, indeed, and I guess I will take a drink—a cocktail, if you please," as he leaned on the bar.

"Captain, the boys say I am a pretty bad bartender. I'll jes give yu' the stuff, und you can fix it up to your taste. I don't drink this, and so I don't know what men like. It's grub and beds I furnish mostly, but you can't exactly run a hotel without a bar. My customers sort of come in here and tend bar for themselves. Have a lemon-peel, captain?"

The captain comprehended, mixed and

drank his cocktail, and was ushered into the dining-room. It was half full of picturesque men in their shirt-sleeves, or in canvas and dusty boots. They were mostly red-faced, bearded, and spiked with deadly weapons. They were quiet and courteous.

Over his bottle the American is garrulous, but he handles his food with silent earnestness.

Chinamen did the waiting, and there was no noise other than the clatter of weapons, for the three-tined fork must be regarded as such. The captain fell to with the rest, and found the food an improvement on field-rations. He presently asked a neighbor about the hostess—how she managed to compete with the more pretentious resorts. Was it not a hard place for a woman to do business?

"Yes, pard, yu' might say it is rough on some of the ladies what's sportin' in this plaza, but the old woman never has no trouble." And his new acquaintance leaned over and whispered: "She's on the squar', pard; she's a plum' good woman, and this plaza sort of stands for her. She's as solid as a brick church here."

The captain's friend and he, having wrestled their ration, adjoined to the sidewalk, and the friend continued: "She was wife to an old sergeant up at the post, and he went and died. The boys here wanted a eatin'-joint, bein' tired of the local hash, which I honest can tell you was most d—— bad; so they gets her down here to ride herd on this bunch of Chinamen topside. She does pretty well for herself—gives us good grub, and all that—but she gets sort of stampeded at times over the goin's on in this plaza, and the committee has to go out and hush 'em up. Course the boys gets tangled up with their irons, and then they are packed in here, and if the old woman can't nurse 'em back to life they has to go. There is quite a little bunch of fellers here what she has set up with nights, and they got it put up that she is about the best d—— woman on the earth. They sort of stand together when any alcoholic patient gets to yellin' round the old woman's or some sportin'

lady goes after the woman's hair. About every loose feller round yer has asked the old woman to marry him, which is why she ain't popular with the ladies. She plays 'em all alike and don't seem to marry much, and this town makes a business of seein' she always lands feet first, so when any one gets to botherin', the committee comes round and runs him off the range. It sure is unhealthy fer any feller to get loaded and go jumpin' sideways round this 'dobie. Sabe?"

The captain did his military business at the quartermaster's, and then repaired to the old woman's bar-room to smoke and wait for the down freight. She was behind the bar, washing glasses.

A customer came in, and she turned to him.

"Brandy, did yu' say, John?"

"Yes, madam; that's mine."

"I don't know brandy from whiskey, John; yu' jes smell that bottle."

"The Captain Was a Gentleman and a Scholar, but He Didn't Look the Part." *Author's photo-engraving.*

John put the bottle to his olfactories and ejaculated, "Try again; that ain't brandy, for sure."

Madam produced another bottle, which stood the test, and the man poured his portion and passed out.

Alkali Flat was full of soldiers, cow-men, prospectors who had been chased out of the hills by the Apaches, government freighters who had come in for supplies, and the gamblers and whiskey-sellers who helped them to sandwich a little hilarity into their business trips.

As the evening wore on the blood of Alkali Flat began to circulate. Next door to the old woman's the big saloons were in a riot. Glasses clinked, loud-lunged laughter and demoniac yells mixed with the strained piano, over which untrained fingers banged and pirouetted. Dancers bounded to the snapping fiddle tones of "Old Black Jack." The chips on the faro-table clattered, the red-and-black man howled, while from the streets at times came drunken whoops mingled with the haw-haws of mules over in the quartermaster's corral.

Madam looked towards the captain, saying, "Did you ever hear so much noise in your life?"

"Not since Gettysburg," replied the addressed. "My tastes are quiet, but I should think Gettysburg the most enjoyable of the two. But I suppose these people think this is great fun."

"Yes, they live so quiet out in the hills that they like to get into this bedlam when they are in town. It sort of stirs them up," explained the hostess.

"Do they never trouble you, madam?"

"No—except for this noise. I have had bullets come in here, but they wasn't meant for me. They get drunk outside and shoot wild sometimes. I tell the boys plainly that I don't want none of them to come in here drunk, and I don't care to do any business after supper. They don't come around here after dark much. I couldn't stand it if they did. I would have to pull up."

A drunken man staggered to the door of the little hotel, saw the madam behind the bar, received one look of scorn, and backed out again with a muttered "Scuse me, lady; no harm done."

Presently in rolled three young men, full of the confidence which much too much liquor will give to men. They ordered drinks at the bar roughly. Their Derby hats proclaimed them Easterners—railroad tramps or some such rubbish, thought the captain. Their conversation had the glib vulgarity of the big cities, with many of their catch phrases, and they proceeded to jolly the landlady in a most offensive way. She tried to brave it out, until one of them reached over the bar and chucked her under the chin. Then she lifted her apron to her face and began to cry.

The wise mind of the captain knew that society at Alkali Flat worked like an naphtha engine—by a series of explosions. And he saw a fearful future for the small barroom.

Rising, he said, "Here, here, young men, you had better behave yourselves, or you will get killed."

Turning with a swagger, one of the hoboes said, "Ah! whose 'll kill us, youse —— ——?"

"No, he won't!" This was shouted in a resounding way into the little room, and all eyes turned to the spot from which the voice came. Against the black doorway stood Dan Dundas—the gambler who ran the faro layout next door, and in his hands were two Colts levelled at the toughs, while over them gleamed steadily two blue eyes like planetary stars against the gloom of his complexion. "No, he won't kill yu'; he don't have to kill yu'. I will do that."

With a hysterical scream the woman flew to her knight-errant. "Stop—stop that, Dan! Don't you shoot—don't you shoot, Dan! If you love me, Dan, don't, don't!"

With the quiet drawl of the Southwest the man in command of the situation replied: "Well, I reckon I'll sure have to, little woman. Please don't put your hand on my guns. Maybeso I won't shoot, but, Helen— but I ought to, all right. Hadn't I, captain?"

Many heads lighted up the doorway back

of the militant Dan, but the captain blew a whiff of smoke towards the ceiling and said nothing.

The three young men were scared rigid. They held their extremities as the quick situation had found them. If they had not been scared, they would still have failed to understand the abruptness of things; but one found tongue to blurt:

"Don't shoot! We didn't do nothin', mister."

Another resounding roar came from Dan, "Shut up!" And the quiet was opaque.

"Yes," said the captain, as he leaned on the billiard-table, "you fellows have got through your talking. Any one can see that;" and he knocked the ash off his cigar.

"What did they do, Helen?" And Dan bent his eyes on the woman for the briefest of instants.

Up went the apron to her face, and through it she sobbed, "They chucked me under the chin, Dan, and—and one of them said I was a pretty girl—and—"

"Oh, well, I ain't sayin' he's a liar, but he 'ain't got no call for to say it. I guess we had better get the committee and lariat 'em up to a telegraph pole—sort of put 'em on the Western Union line—or I'll shoot 'em. Whatever you says goes, Helen," pleaded justice amid its perplexities.

"No, no, Dan! Tell me you won't kill 'em. I won't like you any more if you do."

"Well, I sure ought to, Helen. I can't have these yer hoboes comin' round here insultin' of my girl. Now yu' allow that's so, don't yu'?"

"Well, don't kill 'em, Dan; but I'd like to tell 'em what I think of them, though."

"Turn her loose, Helen. If yu' feel like talkin', just yu' talk. You're a woman, and it does a woman a heap of good to talk; but if yu' don't want to talk, I'll turn these guns loose, or we'll call the committee without no further remarks—jes as you like, Helen. It's your play."

The captain felt that the three hoboes were so taken up with Dan's guns that Helen's eloquence would lose its force on them. He also had a weak sympathy for them, knowing that they had simply applied the low street customs of an Eastern city in a place were customs were low enough, except in the treatment of decent women.

While Dan had command of the situation, Helen had command of Dan, and she began to talk. The captain could not remember the remarks—they were long and passionate—but as she rambled along in her denunciation, the captain, who had been laughing quietly, and quizzically admiring the scene, became suddenly aware that Dan was being more highly wrought upon than the hoboes.

He removed his cigar, and said in a low voice, "Say, Dan, don't shoot; it won't pay."

"No?" asked Dan, turning his cold, wide-open blue eyes on the captain.

"No; I wouldn't do it if I were you; you are mad, and I am not, and you had better use my judgment."

Dan looked at the hoboes, then at the woman, who had ceased talking, saying, "Will I shoot, Helen?"

"No, Dan," she said, simply.

"Well, then," he drawled, as he sheathed his weapons, "I ain't goin' to trifle round yer any more. Good-night, Helen," and he turned out into the darkness.

"Oh, Dan!" called the woman.

"What?"

"Promise me that no one kills these boys when they go out of my place; promise me, Dan, you will see to it that no one kills them. I don't want 'em killed. Promise me," she pleaded out of the door.

"I'll do it, Helen. I'll kill the first man what lays a hand on the dog-gone skunks," and a few seconds later the captain heard Dan, out in the gloom, mutter, "Well, I'll be d——!"

A more subdued set of young gentlemen than followed Dan over to the railroad had never graced Alkali Flat.

Dan came back to his faro game, and, sitting down, shuffled the pack and meditatively put it in the box, saying to the case-keeper, "When a squar' woman gets in a game, I don't advise any bets."

But Alkali Flat saw more in the episode than the mere miscarriage of justice; the excitement had uncovered the fact that Dan Dundas and Helen understood each other.

Mountain Lions in Yellowstone Park

There is a strong regulation regarding the absolute letting alone of wild things in the Park. It is a proper intention to let nature take its course, but still when the superintendent clearly sees that a band of mountain lions will surely eat up all the mountain sheep in a very short time it becomes necessary for the aforesaid official to thwart the law of the mountain; also when a big grizzly gets to mixing up socially with the tourists, Captain Brown has to step in in favor of the latter, though I am not sure of the wisdom of this.

When these contingencies arise, the two scouts Whittaker and Morrison gird themselves with rifle and *ski* and proceed to equalize things, during which these two young men have some very exciting experiences. Last winter they killed five mountain lions at one time. So far this year Whittaker has bagged three, and is still hunting. As he has written, "I had a very narrow escape with these three mountain lions. I was trailing the first one when I came to a large tree. I could not see any trail, so was looking around when I heard a queer noise up in the tree. I looked up, and there he was, not fifteen feet from me, just getting ready to spring. I shot him in the shoulder while he was in the air.

"The second one I trailed to the top of a hill, walking along with my head down, when I happened to look up and there he was not five feet from me coming out from behind a rock. Just about twenty feet from him were three more. When I fired they ran away. Lieutenant Yates and myself tracked the third one to a cave in the rocks. He jumped at us, and we shot him in the air while he was springing at us. He measured seven feet nine inches."

This is the simple story of the man who did the thing. This is the way the soldiers are working to keep the Yellowstone Park for posterity. It is a pity the lions can't be allowed to live, but they are too expensive.

Now and then the death-sentence goes forth against some overconfident grizzly— always with great reluctance. When one has borne down the fortifications of the hotel meat-houses time and again, he, too, becomes aggressive and his pelt comes in. It would be better to trap these, however, and sell them alive for the benefit of the Park.

Then the coyotes kill the young antelopes and are warred against, but I very much fear the *broncho* white man of the adjacent regions is the worst of all. If it were possible to have him killed it would be a good thing for the rest of the population of the United States. The panther, the bear, and the coyote can be excused, but the white man is a selfish brute who knows he is doing wrong.

They Bore a Hand

·

When Mrs. Kessel, with the two children, saw the troops pack up and entrain their horses, she had plenty of things to do for the major besides control her feelings. It had happened so many times before that it was not a particularly distinct sensation; but the going forth of an armed man is always thrilling—yes, even after twenty years of it. She did not think, I imagine, but she knew many wives of regular army officers whom Congress had forgotten after the dead heroes had been heralded up and down the land and laid away. The "still, small voice" of the army widow doesn't make the halls of Congress yell with rage at the stern facts. But she was accustomed, since the year of their marriage, to the departure of her be-sabred husband, and that was the "worse" for which she married him. The eldest girl was as near twenty as I can tell about such things. They were excited by the fast moving of events, and the flash of steel had benumbed their reflective quality, but papa was a soldier, and Spain had to be licked. Who could do it better than papa, Oest-reicher, his orderly trumpeter, and the gallant Third, those nimble athletes who took the three bareback horses over the hurdles in the riding-hall? Who could withstand the tearing charge down the parade with the white blades flashing? Nothing but Oest-reicher with his trumpet could stop that.

Oestreicher had told them a thousand times that papa could lick any one under any conceivable circumstances. They very well knew that he had followed the flying Arapaho village far into the night, until he had captured everything; they were familiar with the niceties of the Apache round-up at San Carlos, because Oestreicher had handed the major a six-shooter at the particular in-stant, and the terrible ten days' battle with the revengeful Cheyennes, when the snow was up to the horses' bellies, had been done to death by the orderly. Papa had been shot before, but it hadn't killed him, and they had never heard of "Yellow-Jack" on the high plains. Papa did all this with Oest-reicher to help him, to be sure, for the or-derly always declared himself a full partner in the major's doings, and divided the glory as he thought best.

Oestreicher, orderly trumpeter, was white and bald. He never stated any recollections of the time before he was a soldier. He was a typical German of the soldier class; a fierce red in the face, illuminated by a long, yellowish-white mustache, but in body be-coming a trifle wobbly with age. He had been following the guidon for thirty-seven years. That is a long time for a man to have been anything, especially a trooper.

Oh yes, it cannot be denied that Oest-reicher got drunk on pay-days and state oc-casions, but he was too old to change; in his day that thing was done. Also, he had love-affairs of no very complex nature. They were never serious enough for the girls to hear of. Also, he had played the various financial allurements of the adjoining town, until his "final statement" would be the month's pay then due. But this bold humanity welled up in Oestreicher thoroughly mixed with those soft virtues which made every one come to him when he was in trouble. He was a professional soldier, who knew no life outside a Sibley or a barrack, except the major's home, which he helped the major to run. To the girls this had been always so. On the drill-ground the major undoubtedly had to be taken into account, but at the major's quarters Oestreicher had so close an alliance with madam and the girls that the "old man" made a much smaller impression. A home always should be a pure democracy.

The Kessel outfit was like this: It was "military satrap" from the front door out, but inside it was "the most lovable person commands," and Oestreicher often got this assignment.

In the barracks Oestreicher was always "Soda"—this was an old story, which may have related to his hair, or his taste, or an episode—but no man in the troop knew why. When they joined, Oestreicher was "Soda," and traditions were iron in the Third.

Oestreicher and the major got along without much friction. After pay-day the major would say all manner of harsh things about the orderly because he was away on a drunk, but in due time Oestreicher would turn up smiling. Madam and the girls made his peace, and the major subsided. He had got mad after this manner at this man until it was a mere habit, so the orderly trumpeter never came up with the court-martialling he so frequently courted, for which that worthy was duly grateful, and readily forgave the major his violent language.

For days Oestreicher and the women folks had been arranging the major's field kit. The major looked after the troops and the trumpeter looked after the major, just as he had for years and years before. When the train was about to pull out, the major kissed away his wife's tears and embraced his children, while Oestreicher stood by the back door of the Pullman, straight and solemn.

"Now look out for the major," solicited the wife, while the two pretty girls pulled the tall soldier down and printed two kisses on his red-burnt cheeks, which he received in a disciplined way.

"Feed Shorty and Bill [dogs] at four o'clock in the afternoon, and see that they don't get fed out of mess hours," said the orderly to the girls, and the women got off the cars.

And Oestreicher never knew that madam had told the major to look out well for the orderly, because he was old, and might not stand things which he had in the earlier years. That did not matter, however, because it was all a day's work to the toughened old soldier. The dogs, the horses, the errands, the girls, the major, were habits with him, and as for the present campaign —he had been on many before. It gave only a slight titillation.

Thus moved forth this atom of humanity with his thousands of armed countrymen to do what had been done before—set the Stars and Stripes over the frontier and hold them there. Indians, greasers, Spaniards—it was all the same, just so the K Troop guidon was going that way.

The "shave-tails" could kick and cuss at the criminal slowness of the troop train's progress, but Oestreicher made himself comfortable with his pipe and newspaper, wondering what kind of cousins Spaniards were to Mexicans, and speculating with another old yellow-leg on the rough forage of Cuba.

So he progressed with the well-known events to Tampa and to Daiquiri, and here he fell over a very bad hurdle. He could brown hardtack in artful ways, he did not mind the mud, he could blow a trumpet to a finish, he could ride a horse as far as the road was cut out, but the stiffened knees of the old cavalryman were badly sprung under the haversack and blanket-roll afoot.

The column was well out on the road to Siboney, when the major noted the orderly's distress: "Oestreicher, fall out—go back to the transport. You can't keep up. I will give you an order," which he did.

The poor old soldier fell to the rear of the marching men and sat down on the grass.

He was greatly depressed, both in body and mind, but was far from giving up. As he sat brooding, he noticed a ragged Cuban coming down the road on a flea-bitten pony, which was heavily loaded with the cast-off blankets of the volunteers. A quick, lawless thought energized the broken man, and he shoved a shell into his Krag carbine. Rising slowly, he walked to meet the ragged figure. He quickly drew a bead on the sable patriot, saying, "Dismount—get down—you d—— greaser!"

"No entiendo."

"Get down."

"Por Dios, hombre, que va hacer?" and at this juncture Oestreicher poked the Cuban in the belly with his carbine, and he slid off on the other side.

"Now run along—vamoose—underlay—get a gait on you," sang out the blue soldier, while the excited Cuban backed up the road, waving his hands and saying, "Bandolero, ladrone, sin verguenza—porque me roba el caballo?"

To which Oestreicher simply said, "Oh hell!"

Not for a second did Oestreicher know that he was a high agent of the law. Be it

"Get Down!" *Authors' photoengraving.*

known that any man who appropriates property of your Uncle Samuel can be brought to book. It is hard to defend his actions, when one considers his motive and the horse.

The final result was that Oestreicher appeared behind the Third Cavalry, riding nicely, with his blanket-roll before his saddle. The troops laughed, and the major looked behind; but he quickly turned away, grinning, and said to Captain Hardier: "Look at the d—— old orderly! If that isn't a regular old-soldier trick! I'm glad he has a mount; you couldn't lose him."

"Yes," replied the addressed, "you can order Oestreicher to do anything but get away from the Third. Can't have any more of this horse-stealing; it's demoralizing," and the regiment plodded along, laughing at old "Soda," who sheepishly brought up the rear, wondering what justice had in store for him.

Nothing happened, however, and presently Oestreicher sought the major, who was cursing his luck for having missed the fight at Las Guasimas. He condoled with the major in a tactful way he had, which business softened things up. While the major was watching him boil the coffee in the tin cups over a little "Indian fire," he put the order in the flames, and it went up in smoke.

"You old rascal!" was all the major said, which meant that the incident was closed.

Right glad was the major to have his orderly during the next week. The years had taught Oestreicher how to stick a dog-tent and make a bed, and how to cook and forage. Oestreicher's military conscience never vibrated over misappropriated things to eat, and Fagin could not have taught him any new arts.

Then came the fateful morning when the Third lay in the long grass under the hail of Mausers and the sickening sun. "Will the major have some water?" said Oestreicher, as he handed over one canteen.

"You go lie down there with the men and don't follow me around—you will get shot," commanded Kessel; but when he looked

around again, there was Oestreicher stalking behind. He could fool away no more energy on the man.

Then came the forward movement, the firing and the falling men, and ahead strode the officer, waving his sword and shouting fiercely. Behind followed the jaded old trumpeter, making hard going of it, but determined to keep up. His eye was not on the blazing heights, but on the small of the major's back, when the officer turned, facing him, and he ran into his arms. Down over his major's face came gushes of blood. He reeled—would have fallen but for the supporting arms of the soldier. The rush of men passed them.

They lay down in the grass. The orderly brushed the blood from the pale face, while he cut up a "first-aid" bandage and bound the wound. Then he gave him water; but the major was far gone, and the orderly trumpeter was very miserable. Oestreicher replaced the major's sword in its scabbard. Men came tottering back, holding on to their wounds.

"Say, Johnson," sung out Oestreicher to a passing soldier, "you ain't hit bad; gimme a lift with the major here." The soldier stopped, while they picked up the unconscious officer and moved heavily off towards the Red Cross flag. Suddenly they lurched badly, and all three figures sank in the pea-green grass. A volley had found them. Johnson rolled slowly from side to side and spat blood. He was dying. Oestreicher hung on to one of his arms, and the bluish-mauve of the shirt-sleeve grew slowly to a crimson lake. He sat helplessly turning his eyes from the gasping Johnson, the pale major, and the flaming hill-crest. He put his hat over the major's face. He drank from his canteen. There was nothing to do. The tropical July sun beat on them, until his head swam under the ordeal.

Presently a staff-officer came by on a horse.

"Say, captain," yelled the soldier, "come here. Major Kessel is shot in the head. Take him, won't you?"

"Oh, is that you?" said the one addressed

as he rode up, for he remembered Kessel's orderly. Dismounting, the two put the limp form on the horse. While Oestreicher led the animal, the captain held the nearly lifeless man in the saddle, bent forward and rolling from side to side. Thus they progressed to the blood-soaked sands beside the river, where the surgeons were working grimly and quickly.

It was a month before the pale old men got off the train at Burton, one an officer and the other a soldier, and many people in the station had a thrill of mingled pity and awe as they looked at them. Two very pretty girls kissed them both, and people wondered the more. But the papers next morning told something about it, and no policeman could be induced to arrest Oestreicher that day when he got drunk in Hogan's saloon, telling how he and the major took San Juan Hill.

Time wore on—wounds healed, and the troops came back from Montauk to the yelling multitudes of Burton, the home station. The winter chilled the fever out of their blood. The recruits came in and were pulled into shape, when the long-expected order of the Philippines came, and the old scenes were re-enacted, just as they had happened in the Kessel household so many times before, only with a great difference: Oestreicher was detached and ordered to stay in the guard of the post. This time the major, who was a colonel now, settled it so it would stay settled. An order is the most terrible and potent thing a soldier knows. Oestreicher shed tears, he pleaded, he got the women to help him, but the major stamped his foot and became ossified about the mouth.

Clearly there was only one thing left for Oestreicher to do in this case, and he did it with soldierly promptness. He got drunk— good and drunk—and the Third Cavalry was on its way to Manila. When the transport was well at sea from Seattle, the colonel was reading a novel on the after-deck. A soldier approached him, saluting, and saying, "I hope the colonel won't get mad—"

The colonel looked up; his eyes opened,

he said, slowly, "Well—I—will—be— d——!" and he continued to stare helplessly into the cheerful countenance of Oestreicher, orderly trumpeter, deserter, stowaway, soft food for court-martials. "How did you get here, anyway?"

Then the colonel had a military fit. He cussed Oestreicher long and loud, told him he was a deserter, said his long-service pension was in danger; and true it is that Oestreicher was long past his thirty years in the army, and could retire at any time. But through it all the colonel was so astonished that he could not think—he could only rave at the tangle of his arrangements in the old orderly's interest.

"How did you get here, anyhow?"

"Came along with the train, sir—same train you were on, sir," vouchsafed the veteran.

"Well—well—well!" soliloquized the colonel, as he sat down and took up his novel. "Get out—I don't want to see you— go away," and Oestreicher turned on his heel.

Other officers gathered around and laughed at the colonel.

"What am I to do with that old man? I can't court-martial him. He would get a million years in Leavenworth if I did. D—— these old soldiers, anyhow—they presume on their service! What can I do?"

"Don't know," said the junior major; "reckon you'll have to stay home yourself if you want to keep Oestreicher there."

It was plain to be seen that public sentiment was with the audacious and partly humorous orderly.

"Well—we—will see—we will see," testily jerked the old man, while the young ones winked at each other—long broad winks, which curled their mouths far up one side.

The colonel has been seeing ever since. I have only just found out what he "saw," by a letter from an old friend of mine out in the Philippines, which I shall quote.

"You remember Colonel Kessel's old orderly—Oestreicher? Was with us that time we were shooting down in Texas. He was ordered to stay at Jackson Barracks, but he deserted. The men hid him under their bunks on the railroad train, and then let him on the transport at Seattle. Soldiers are like boys—they will help the wicked. One day he presented himself to the old man. Oh, say—you ought to have heard the old Nan-Tan cuss him out—it was the effort of the 'old man's' life! We sat around and enjoyed it, because Oestreicher is a habit with the colonel. We knew he wouldn't do anything about it after he had blown off steam.

"Well, the night after our fight at Cabana-tuan it was dark and raining. What do you suppose I saw? Saw the 'old man' in a nipa hut with a doctor, and between them old Oestreicher, shot through the head and dying. There was the colonel sitting around doing what he could for his old dog-soldier. I tell you it was a mighty touching sight. Make a good story that—worked up with some blue-lights and things. He sat with him until he died. Many officers came in and stood with their hats off, and the colonel actually boo-hooed. As you know, boo-hooing ain't the 'old man's' long suit by a d—— sight!"

A Gallant American Officer

Colonel Hare is a long, lean, dried-out man, and he looks as though he came from Texas, which he did. He has had an interesting career since he left West Point in 1870. Nature intended him to pass his life on a horse, so she made him long in the gear and curved in the legs, as is best adapted to a saddle. His face has a high-nostriled, sharp-eyed, eager look—arranged to scent battle and to seek it.

He was Major Menill's adjutant in the Seventh Cavalry, and was one of the last men across the ford in Reno's repulse at the Little Big Horn. He it was who rode through the swarming Indians to rally Benteen and the pack-train—which he brought back to Reno's position.

He was with General Crook in his famous winter campaign against the Sioux in '76 and was with General Forsyth at the battle of Wounded Knee. He chased the "Kid" over the sands of Arizona and led his troops in the Chicago riots down the acres of railroad track where it was supposed cavalry could not go.

At the outbreak of the Spanish war he was appointed colonel of the First Texas Cavalry, which he raised, drilled and organized, and sought vainly for service in Cuba. He had Rough Riders, and, if he had been allowed to go, would undoubtedly be Governor of Texas to-day. But, no! Hare is soldier all over—he couldn't be anything but a man on a horse. He wouldn't look right in a chair any more than General Miles does. They are not built that way, either of them.

After the surrender of Cuba his regiment was disbanded and he went back to his troop, which was stationed at Vidado outside of Havana; but this didn't suit, so he raised the Thirty-third U. S. Foot and went to the Philippines as colonel with the gallant Howz and Logan for field officers.

Immediately after his arrival in the Philippines, Colonel Hare was detailed to pursue one of the scattered forces of Aguinaldo's followers, who were retreating with Lieutenant Gilmore and various naval and military prisoners held by the Filipinos. After a most arduous and never-ceasing pursuit of many days, the Filipino force was overtaken and scattered, and Lieutenant Gilmore and his fellow-prisoners were rescued.

This was not only one of the most daring, continued and persistent pursuits of this war, but has few parallels in history. For weeks the men were without regular rations, without access to supplies of any kind; they had no changes of clothing; their shoes were worn out; men dropped from the ranks daily from sickness and exhaustion, and when the final battle took place, resulting in the rescue of Lieutenant Gilmore and his fellow-prisoners, Colonel Hare had only about one hundred and twenty-six men with him, and these men were in a most deplorable condition. Nothing but the most indomi-

Colonel Luther R. Hare, Thirty-third Foot, Who Conducted the Pursuit of Aguinaldo's Forces in Northern Luzon and Rescued Lieutenant Gilmore. *The Free Library of Philadelphia.*

table will power could have kept these men up to the pursuit until the end.

For this service General Otis has recommended him for a brigadier-general. The leading trait of Colonel Hare's nature is his modesty, as well befits his calling. In his report of the affair he claims as much credit as any private soldier in the command, and no more—which will show you how absurd he can be at times with his modesty.

A Shotgun Episode

Old Captain Jack, as he is known throughout the army, and I had been working quail all the morning when we struck a stream and sat down to a small lunch, which we managed with more ease than was agreeable to us.

We began loading our pipes, and I noticed the Captain was overcome by a series of half-suppressed gurgles of amusement. He was regarding his shotgun, which leaned against a bush in front of him.

"Why this levity?" I asked. "Do you recall some hallowed memory, when you had eight dozen hard-boiled eggs instead of only two separate ones?"

When the Captain relaxed he got rid of an elegant diction, which was his at will, and to his listener became charming in something like an inverse ratio. I felt that he could be made to do a gay picture with his golden pink method, and I always cared more for the Captain's wonderful past than the inconsequential quail.

"Do you know," he replied, "I never see a shotgun but I think of my old friend Chief Winnemucca; and if he is alive I guess old Chief Winnemucca never sees one but it makes him think of his old friend Captain Jack S——."

"How now?"

"It was a little glove-call I made on old Chief Winnemucca. He was a good sort of an Injun and a heap big chief of all the Piutes up there in Nevada. He was a great friend of General Crook, and Crook admired Winnemucca, too, because he had earned his respect by lifting all Crook's horses on an occasion when the general wasn't looking. That seldom happened to Crook.

"See! this was in '77 that this shotgun business happened up at old Fort McDermitt, which was a lonely old one-company 'dobe, in the middle of a million miles of sage-brush. Right back of this post there was a high bench-land. The Indians used to sit up there and shoot into the camp in a spirit of cheerfulness, when there wasn't anything else going. I think the Eighth Infantrymen used rather to encourage the thing—for McDermitt would make a New England cemetery look like a French ball—so little episodes of this sort helped us out.

"No one else had much to do, but I was a scrub lieutenant then, and the Captain covered me with all the honors of adjutant, commissary, quartermaster, post treasurer, chaplain, and Indian agent, and I was made to scout once a month just to keep my hand in. In the post were only thirty enlisted men, and the company officers, besides a civilian doctor named Todd. This Todd was 'the original Mr. Glue from Gum Arabia' when it came to staying with a friend.

"As Indian agent I had charge of 298 solid mahogany Piutes, whom we had rounded in during the Bannock campaign. They were a touchy lot and hard to curry around the heels. I put them in a camp about a mile from the post, and old Chief Winnemucca was held personally responsible for them, but I didn't have any child-like confidence in 'Win.' He was too much of a flirt himself for a good chaperon. When you get an old Injun warmed up with corn-juice he can turn moral handsprings until you can't see anything but the buzz. However, Winnemucca had not gone 'out' and was all right in the main. He 'heap savied the white man and was many weary journeys from a fool.

"Twice each week it was my duty to run a count on these Injuns in order to get my commissary right, and to see the 'Johnny on the Spot' theory was working. But I kept missing. They worked into all kinds of numerals—sometimes going as high as 350. As rations were based on the count, and as Uncle Sam don't pay his commissary officers for Injun lawn parties, it was up to me good and hard. I was getting horribly mixed up with my books until I found that by marking down certain birds, which I could remember by their tail feathers, I discovered that they ran from one tepee to another during my tallies.

I suggested to the commanding officer, who was afterward the Colonel Corliss shot while leading the assault on El Caney, that we divide them into bands—drive a series of stakes in the parade ground—line 'em up between the stakes at attention until they could show cause why they should eat Uncle Sam's grub. This seemed to be reasonable to the K. O., but old Winnemucca and his braves made a swing-mule buck, and stopped the whole team. Still we were bound to have our way because of the books. Commissary accounts have got to be as simple as a Greek column in Washington. Postscripts about thirty men and three hundred Indians are barred.

"The order went forth, and we sat up and scratched our heads over the possibilities. No Injun came in, and we began to worry some about the lay of things. It began to look like our move. We knew that wild waves of thought came over the spirit of an Injun camp, and no man can see into the future as far as his horse's ears when the tom-toms begin to thump.

"Presently an Injun came into camp— one of the small chiefs of the Piutes, Natchez by name. His head was badly cut, he was wounded in the body, and was red all over. He said he had always been a friend of the white man; that Winnemucca's camp was full of Shoshones. His people were all drunk, and getting ready to dance—that after the dance they were coming up to wipe McDermitt off the map, and that he had only escaped with his life to tell us.

"What to do with our small force was not at all clear. Three hundred or more to thirty men, and the nearest possible relief ninety miles, was the proposition, and things due to happen on the jump. We could not take the initiative. Besides the women and children there was a lot of government property in the post.

"The Captain ordered me to go into the camp and arrest Winnemucca. He offered to spare me ten men, but I said I would go alone. I knew ten men wouldn't stand the styles down at Winnemucca's. Here is when Doctor Todd began to roll his tail—he said he would go with me. Todd would have made as good a phlebotomist with a saber as with a lancet. He was the old holiday goods.

"I went to my quarters and got a shotgun with a belt full of buck cartridges. My wife thought I was going hunting. Todd had a six-shooter, and we saddled up and started. Now this old pitcher had been to the well a good many times, but I was afraid she was going to get cracked this trip.

Winnemucca's drunken, dancing camp was a *recherché* bunch for two men to mob. I made no doubt of that. The more I thought my scheme over, however, the madder I got. I concluded to ride through the camp as hard as I could and get to Winnemucca personally. I then intended to make him protect me, or to kill him. Todd was to sit on his horse in front of the tepee and hold mine while I went in. When he heard firing he was to make a break to try and get through to the post and to leave me.

"We went through the camp, whirlwind fashion. There wasn't a buck, a squaw, or a papoose in sight, and from what I knew of

Injun domesticity, I didn't get much encouragement out of this.

"We got to the tepee—Todd held my horse, and I dove into the plant and squatted quickly down by the door. The light was bad, and I was keyed up. On the left of the tepee was old Winnemucca and Charlie Thatcher, the interpreter, lying down. Across from them were two Shoshone bucks squatting down with their blankets drawn tightly around them to their chins.

"They were all very much surprised, and somewhat drunk. I quickly shoved the double-barrel under Thatcher's ear, and told him to put his six-shooter at my feet, or I would blow his d—— head off. He did as I directed. Then I elevated the gun until it covered old Winnemucca, and he did likewise. All this time I was keeping my eyes on

the two Shoshones, and had figured to let one barrel into Winnemucca, then to let the other go at the Shoshones, while I hoped to get my hands on the six-shooters during the smoke and confusion. They were too surprised to do anything; then I jumped to my feet and told the visitors to get up and throw off their blankets. They were stark naked, and in full war paint, but unarmed.

"I made a speech which I can't remember, but I cussed them out, and held a debate with myself as to whether I ought to kill them, but anyhow they came around to my way of thinking. I told Thatcher that he would lose his hundred dollars a month from the government—that we would make an old woman out of Winnemucca, and I made the two Shoshones sit up like maids in school. But all the time I was running this

"Todd Was to Sit on His Horse in front of the Tepee, and Hold Mine While I Went In."
Authors' photoengraving.

bluff I was somewhat perturbed—would you call it—no—I was scared stiff-legged.

"Winnemucca and Thatcher promised to report at the post next day, and to run all the Shoshones out of camp during the night.

"Telling Thatcher to take the two guns out to Todd, I backed out, jumped on my horse, and we trotted out of camp. All this time there was not an Indian in sight. I don't know where they were, and I could never find out.

"They came up the next day all right, and the incident was closed. I got to be a good friend of Winnemucca's, who always hit me on the back, and said I was a 'big chief,' but if he had known how scared I was, I don't think he would have thought so.

"For shotgun work give me quail."

How a Trout Broke a Friendship

If I were an angler there would be no story, but I shall wish all my days that I had been a fisherman when I think of how my lack of experience refrigerated the nature of my old friend Joel B——.

It was early spring in Canada, and Lake Edwards was ice-water. I was camped on a point of rocks in company with three "Complete Anglers" and three French-Indians. A chilling rain had fallen incessantly for days—the fish would not be suited by any fly in our books. Everything was soggy and mildewed. An ill-tempered little box-stove smoldered, and helped Mr. Walker's creation to keep our miserable bodies alive. Our minds were becoming jaded by a draw-poker game which seemed to have had no beginning. As I view the situation from afar, I can perceive how carefully tilled was that ground to bear the seeds of trouble.

They were all friends of mine, with strong mutual sympathies in many directions; but they were fishermen, while I was not. They were men who at home have sacred dens in their houses, and in them they worship a heathen god in the form of a glass case full of dainty rods. They have hundreds of flies, suited to all kinds of moods of all kinds of fish. They have stuffed bass and wadded trout, colored artificially as falsely as a rose on Indian trade calico. There are creels, reels, silver ammunition flasks, rare prints of the forefathers of the lure, books of tall stories so dear to the craft, and things which you and I could not call by name.

In such places these men gather—through the tobacco smoke the lakes blow softly, the ponds wait idly, and the brooks bubble pleasantly in imagination.

These fellows mix fish up with their dessert and coffee, and in importance to them old Leonard is to President McKinley as a million to one.

So things to fish with to these men, things of wood and silk and steel, are invested with souls almost. They are like Japanese jugs or early English portraits to other enthusiasts.

The trout of Lake Edward floated idly beneath the boats, and if they looked at our bait they did no more, in consequence of which the anglers sat on boxes and dealt five cards round on the top of a trunk, and stub-flushes took the place of "cockie-bondhus" and "yellow sallies."

Having been ruined by the last "jackpot," I got up and trod forth into the rain, which was beating the lake into silver. I was listless—tired of the eternal "three-card draws"—tired of the rain and dreaming of elsewhere. I sauntered down towards the water and passed a shed under which were hung a great number of rods, all strung with reels, lines and flies.

"Why not fish—we came here to do that —that was our theory? Suiting the action to the thought, I took down a rod at random, called a Frenchman, and got into a boat.

We two sat there, the guide holding us a short way from the point of rocks. The rain poured in jumping drops on the flat water, while the pine forests faded softly into its obscuring sheets.

Presently one of our party, a gentleman from Pennsylvania, who must have encountered a disappointing "jack-pot," emerged from the tent, and, calling a guide, began to cast from a boat not far away.

The poker game evidently languished, since the capitalists came out in the rain and gazed about in a yawning way. They guyed Mr. Pennsylvania and me, who am no fisherman. Then they espied a bark canoe which was one of the "quickest" boats I ever saw. They remembered having recently seen an Indian stand upright in the tottlish craft—a balancing feat which was the inherited trait of ages of canoe-living ancestors. This inspired a five-dollar sporting proposition that one of them could do what the Indian had done. He pushed out in the canoe, while my friend Joel B—— stood on the rocks amusing himself with the thought of the easy five dollars.

At this point my rod doubled into something like a figure eight, then it acted like a whip-snake having a fit—it was near to parting from me at times—the reel sang and the line hissed about in the water. The Frenchman stood up in the boat and poured Lake St. John French into me in a Maxim rumble. While this was at its height, Mr. Pennsylvania hooked the mate to my whale, but he knew his business. There was a great splash in front of me, and I only glanced long enough to see that Joel B—— had won his bet.

Joel—he of the rocks—tipped backward and forward, laughing until the forests echoed with his roars. Things were all his way.

The swimmer tried to board Mr. Pennsylvania's boat, but was told to get away—not to bother his fish—that human life was nothing now—to "swim to the rocks"— "don't be a d—— fool."

The Cannuck French of my guide was beginning to tell on me. I was almost willing to let the fish go while I threw the French-

man overboard. I was so hot at him that I grew cooler toward the fish end of my troubles, and no doubt was doing better reel work for it all.

Events having slowed down a bit, Mr. Joel B—— began to observe things more closely. As he ran his eyes curiously over the activities on the water, they alighted on my rod. He gazed hard, earnestly, knowingly, at my rod. It was now in a figure eight, now bent this way, now that, being pulled half under water, and Joel B—— raised both hands high above his head while he yelled "—— —— —— ——, you have got my rod—my seventy-five-dollar Leonard rod! Cut that line, —— —— ——! What in —— do you mean by taking my best rod, —— —— ——?"

The Editor will not let me tell you all that Joel B—— vouchsafed on this galling occasion.

Now my affrighted friend walked the rocks like Mrs. Leslie Carter in the third act of "Zaza." He nearly turned handsprings; he gesticulated and roared for a boat or a deadly weapon. Steadily through it all surged his quick-chosen words of rebuke to me.

I now regretted the whole thing, but I couldn't let go, and the fish wouldn't. The seventy-five-dollar bamboo was getting action for the money, and the Frenchman knew that war had been declared.

Seeing that his present methods would never get the rod ashore without the fish, Joel B—— changed his scheme quickly, as an able tactician should. He stood still, and, beating like the leader of an orchestra, he said: "Reel him in—slowly, now—slowly—slowly. There—let him out—don't hold that rod against your belly, —— —— ——!"

There were tears streaming from the rod-owner's eye which rivaled the rain.

"Can't you check him easily—there now! Do you think you have got a bean-pole, —— —— Easy—don't get excited! Baptiste, back that boat ashore."

"If you back this boat ashore I'll murder you! By St. George, I'll burn you alive, Baptiste!" I shouted, and nothing was done.

Joel coached, more carefully now—more intelligently—and my divided interest in the trout cooled me down until, under able direction, I finally landed a five-pound trout on the rocks, and I was no fisherman. It was one of the mistakes of my life.

Joel B—— took his rod amid my apologies. He cared not for the latter. It was not the seventy-five dollars. It was that the clumsy hands of a bean-pole, worm-baiting, gill-yanking outcast had taken the soul out of Leonard's masterpiece.

No longer would that rod look out to him from the middle of the glass case, seeming to say, "Your hands and my subtle curves —what, Master—what can we not do?"

He sat around the tent and cast wolfish glances at me, and public sentiment sat stolidly by him. I carried an open jack-knife in my outside coat-pocket. I sat alone there, deep in the forest, with men whose sense of right and justice had been outraged to the breaking point. They did not even say good-by to me at the railroad station.

The moral of this unfortunate occasion is that if you are going to play marbles with Paderewski you had better take a few lessons on the piano.

Natchez's Pass

What I have in mind occurred in the days when the government expected the army to fight successfully both the wild Indians and the Department of the Interior. A military career thrives on opposition. It is the natural development of a soldier. Captain Bill Summers had buffeted through the great war, and all in all had sixteen years of formulation. He was rugged, red, fearless, and short-winded in his speech. He had found that the flag and Washington were often at odds, but he did not attempt to understand. The agency and Fort McDowell were as much at war as well could be.

There was at this time a demon in charge of the Apache agency whose name shall be Mr. Marshall East. He may have since died in a penitentiary, or have gotten through the net which justice has always set across the dark waters of opportunity: I do not know. He was a well-looking man, educated, and resourceful. Morally he liked a dirty dollar —even a bloody one, I think. He was a tool used by what was then called the "Indian Ring"—a scurvy band of political pirates, the thought of whom will always make Americans blush. Its reckless operations made a hell of the frontier. The army protested, the settlers pleaded pathetically, but the Interior Department kept its mercenaries at their posts.

The politicians grew fat, the army, the settlers, and the Indians grew thin. General Crook was in charge of the military operations against the Indians and the Interior Department. Savages constantly left the agencies on passes, when they murdered and stole. Crook's soldiers rode after them, and the government had a real war on its hands, between two of its greatest departments.

One hot day Captain Bill Summers rode into the agency at the head of his troop. After making camp he stalked into the office of Mr. Marshall East, and opened fire. "Mr. Marshall East, we have found the dead bodies of three white men over on the Rio Verde—killed by Indians, whose trail we have followed into this agency. What are you going to do about it?"

"Humph!—won't you sit down?" nodded the agent, as he fumbled some papers before him on the table.

"No, thank you. I didn't come here to sit down. I came here to arrest murderers, and I demand your aid."

"Well—arrest murderers, and don't bother me," retorted the agent.

"See here, Mr. Marshall East, you know that it is your duty to assist me by the use of your Indian police to identify these outlaws. You know, or should know, what Indians are away from the agency, or have been away, with or without passes," rejoined the Captain, now becoming alarmingly red in the face.

"I thought you came here to arrest murderers?"

"I did."

Coolly the man behind the table continued, "Well—what are you standing there for?"

The Captain was no longer standing, but

striding, heavy heeled, across the room and back to his place, where he slapped his sombrero on his head, pulling it down defiantly about his ears. "You are a scoundrel, Mr. Marshall East! You are accessory after the fact to murder!"

The agent in his turn took fire. He sprang to his feet. "You call me a scoundrel! What do you mean by coming into my office and calling me such a name? Get out of here instantly," and half turning to a long-haired, sombreroed Indian factotum, he said, "Sanchez!" Sergeant McCollough's rifle came from an "order" to a "carry" with a snap.

"Steady, sergeant," muttered the Captain. Thus the scene was arrested in its development, and all in the room stood regarding each other nervously. Presently the Captain's mustache spread, and he burst into a loud laugh. "Oh, you old dog! I know you won't bite. You would abet murder, but you would not do it with your right arm. I am going to leave this room, but not until you sit down—if I have to get my striker to pitch my dog-tent here."

Slowly the desk-man resumed his chair. Continuing, the Captain said, "Before going, I want to state carefully that you are one of the worst scoundrels I ever saw, and before I am through I will run the brand—Sroundrel—on your thick hide." Going to the door, where he stopped, with his hand on the knob, he half turned and said, "Sanchez," followed by a sneering laugh. Then he passed out, followed by the sergeant.

"I will make you pay for this!" came a muffled roar of the agent's voice through the closed door.

"Oh, I guess we will split even," mumbled the departing officer, though of a truth he did not see how.

Walking to the troop camp, the Captain took possession of an abandoned *ramada* some little distance from his men, and here he sat on his blankets, trying to soothe his disgusting thoughts with a pipe. The horses and mules and soldiers made themselves comfortable, and rested after their hard marching of the previous days. It was to

ease his command that determined the officer to stay "one smoke" at the place.

Immediately after dark, "Peaches," one of the Indian scouts of the command, slipped, ghostlike, to the opening of the *ramada,* saying, "Nan-tan!"

"What is it, Peaches?"

The ghost glided from the moonlight into the shadow, addressing his officer: "Say, Nan-tan—Injun bad—agent bad—no like you hombres. Say—me tink kill you. Tink you go make de vamoose. Sabe?"

"Oh, nonsense! Apaches won't attack me at night. Too many ghosts, Peaches."

Peaches replied, with a deprecatory turn of the hand: "No, no, Nan-tan—no *brujas* —too near agency. You vamoose—sabe?"

The Captain had an all-abiding faith in Peaches's knowledge of villany. He was just at present a friendly scout, but liable at any time to have a rush of blood to the head which would turn his hand against any man. He had been among the agency Indians all day, talking with them, and was responsive to their moods. It isn't at all necessary to beat an Indian on the head with a rock to impress his mind. He is possessed of a subtlety of understanding which is Oriental. So the Captain said, "Go, Peaches—tell Sergeant McCollough to come here."

In a few minutes the alert non-com. stood across the moonlight saluting.

"Sergeant, Peaches here has heard some alarming talk among the Indians. I don't think there is anything in it, but 'Injuns is Injuns,' you know. Tie and side-line your horses, and have your men sleep, skirmish formation, twenty-five paces out from the horses. Double your sentries. You might send a man or two up here to divide a watch over me. I want a good sleep. Understand?"

"Yes, sir. May I be one of them? It ain't far to the troop, and I can see them in the moonlight well enough."

"You had better stay with the troop. Why do you want to come up here? You can manage some sleep?" queried Summers.

"Been sleeping all afternoon, sir. Been

talking to Peaches. Don't quite make it all out. Like to come up, sir."

"Oh, well—all right, then—do as you please, but secure your horses well." Saying which, the Captain turned on his blankets to sleep.

In a half-hour's time the sergeant had arranged his troop to his satisfaction—told the old "bucks" to mind their eyes, judiciously scared the "shave-tails" into wakefulness, and with Peaches and Trooper "Long Jack" O'Brien—champion fist-mixer of the command—he stole into the Captain's *ramada*. The officer was snoring with honest, hard-going vigor.

"This do be a rale da-light," murmured Long Jack.

"Shut up—you'll wake the old man!" whispered the non-com. Silence becoming the moonlight and desert soon brooded over the plains of the agency. There was no sound save the snoring, stamping of horses on picket, and the doleful coyotes out beyond baying the mysterious light.

Through long hours Long Jack and the sergeant nodded their heads by turns. The moon was well down in the west when Peaches came over and poked the sergeant in the back with his carbine. The punched one stood up in sleepy surprise, but comprehending, shook O'Brien awake, and stepped over to where Peaches was scanning through the dead leaves which draped the *ramada*.

"Injun," whispered Peaches, almost inaudibly.

For a long time they sat gazing out at the dusky blur of the sage-brush. The sergeant, with white man's impatience, had almost concluded that the faculties of Peaches were tricking him.

"Humph!" he grunted. The hand of the Indian scout tightened like nippers of steel around his arm and opened his eyes anew. Presently he made out a sage-brush which had moved slowly several feet, when it stopped. The hand of Peaches gave another squeeze when the brush made farther progress toward the *ramada*. The sergeant stole

over to the door and put a tourniquet on Long Jack's arm which brought him in sympathy with the mysterious situation. That worthy's heart began to thump in unison with the others. A man under such circumstances can hear his own heart beat, but it is so arranged that others cannot. The sergeant pulled Long Jack's ear to his mouth, as a mother might about to kiss her infant. "Don't shoot—give them the butt." Cautiously the two Springfields were reversed. Long Jack was afraid to spit on his hands, but in lieu he ran his tongue over both before he bull-dogged them about the carbine barrel. With feet spread, the two soldiers waited, and Peaches, like a black shadow, watched the brush. The minutes passed slowly, but the suspense nerved them. After ages of time had passed they were conscious of the low rustle of a bush alongside the *ramada*—ever so faint, but they were coming. Slowly a sage-bush came around the corner, followed by the head of an Indian.

The eyes of the crawling assassin could not contract from the moonlight to meet the gloom of the interior of the house of boughs. It is doubtless true that he never had a sense of what happened, but the silence was shattered by a crash, and the soldiers sprang outside.

"Then I broake both ye un me goon."

"What in hell is the matter?" came from the awakened Captain, as he made his way out of the blankets.

A little group formed around the body, while Peaches rolled it over on its back, face upward. "Sanchez," he said, quietly. "Say, Nan-tan, maybeso you sabe Peaches. You go vamoose now?"

The captain scratched his bare head, he gave his breeches a hitch, he regarded the moon carefully, as though he had never seen it before, then he looked at the dead Indian.

"Yes, Peaches, I think I sabe. Say, sergeant, it's 'boots and saddles' on the jump. Don't say a word to the men, but bring a pack-mule up here and we'll load this carrion on it. Peaches, you blind this man's

The Captain . . . Looked at the Moon. *Authors' photoengraving.*

trail. I reckon you are Injun enough to do that. O'Brien, don't leave the stock of that rifle lying there."

The camp was soon bustling. The horses were led out, blankets smoothed, and saddles swung across. A pack-mule was led up to the Captain's *ramada* by McCollough, O'Brien, and Peaches. All four men helped to wrap up their game in a canvas. Though the mule protested vigorously, he was soon under his grewsome burden, circled tight with the diamond hitch. Having finished,

the Captain spoke: "Promise me, that you won't talk about this. I want time to think about it. I don't know the proper course to take until I consult with the military authorities. If the Indians found this out now, there would be a fight right here. If they don't, one may be averted."

" 'Twas a foine bit av woork to me credit, which will be a dead loss to me, boot I promise," replied Long Jack, and so did the others.

"Have you blinded his trail, Peaches?"

"Si, Nan-tan; Injun no see a ting," said that imp of the night.

The little command took their thudding, clanking way over the ghostly hills, trotting steadily until the sun was high, when they made an eating halt. A few days brought them into McDowell, where the Captain reported the affair. Officially his comrades did not know what to do; personally they thought he did right. They expected nothing from the Indian Ring but opposition, and they were not as strong in Washington as the politicians. But shortly time served them, as it does many who wait.

A great drought had raged in the Southwest, and many sheep-men from San Diego were driving their flocks into the Tonto Basin. One day a Mexican Indian came into Fort McDowell, stark naked and nearly exhausted. He reported that the small sheep outfit to which he belonged had been attacked by Apaches, and all murdered but himself.

Captain Summers was again ordered out with his troop to the scene of the outrage. He made forty-five miles the first day, yet with such travelling it was ten days before he came in sight of the camp. There were three tents, wind-blown and flapping. In front of the middle one lay three dead Indian bucks. The canvas walls were literally shot full of holes. As the Captain pulled back the flap of the centre tent he saw a big, blond-bearded white man sitting bolt-upright on a bed made of poles, with one arm raised in the act of ramming down a charge in a muzzle-loading rifle. He was dead, having been shot through the head. He was the owner, and a fine-looking man. His herders lay dead in the other tents, and his flocks were scattered and gone. The story of that desert combat will never be known. It was a drawn battle, because the Indians had not dared to occupy the field. The man who escaped was out in the hills, and fled at the firing.

On burying the dead the troopers found passes signed, "Marshall East, Agt.," under the belts of the dead Apaches. At last here was something tangible. Identifying each

head with its attendant pass, the Indian scouts decapitated them, stowing them in grain-bags. Back to McDowell wound the command, where a council of war was held. This resulted in the Captain's being sent to the agency, accompanied by four troops as safe-escort.

Arriving, Summers again passed the unwelcome portals of the agent's office, followed by his staff, consisting of a Lieutenant, McCollough, Long Jack, and Peaches bearing a grain-bag.

"Good-day, Mr. Marshall East. I come to reassure you that you are a great scoundrel," vouchsafed the sombreroed officer, as he lined up his picturesque company. "I see Sanchez is not here today. Away on a pass, I presume."

"I don't know how that concerns you. I have other men here, and I will not be bull-dozed by you; I want you to understand that. I intend to see if there are not influences in the world which will effectually prevent such a ruffian as you invading my office and insulting both myself and the branch of the government to which I belong."

"My dear sir," quoth the Captain, "you sign passes which permit these Indians of yours to go into white men's territory, where they every day murder women and men, and run off stock. When we run them back to your agency, you shield and protect them, because you know that if we were allowed to arrest them for their crimes, it might excite the tribe, send them on the war-path, resulting in a transfer of their responsibility to the War Department. That would interfere with your arrangements. A few dead settlers or soldiers count for little against that."

"Captain Summers, I am running this agency. I am responsible for this agency. Indians do go off this reservation at times without doubt, but seldom without a pass from me, and then with a specific object. When Indians are found outside without passes, it then becomes the duty of the army to return them to me."

In reply: "I suppose it is our duty to

bring you tarantulas and Gila monsters also; it is our duty to wear our horses' shoes off in these mountains chasing your passes with their 'specific objects.' Would you give up an Indian who we could prove had murdered, or who had tried to murder, a white man?"

"Yes—I might—under certain circumstances, with exceptional proofs," answered Mr. East.

Quickly asked the officer, "Where is Sanchez now?"

With a searching query in his eyes, the agent continued his defensive of not seeing how that concerned the Captain.

The warrior's voice rose. "Yes, sir. I will tell you how it interests me. He tried to murder me, to stab me at night—right here on this agency. Will you send your Indian police to arrest him for me?"

"Humph!—rather startling. Pray where and when did he try to murder you? What proofs have you?"

"I have three men standing here before you who saw him crawl to my *ramada* in the night with a drawn knife."

"What became of him?" drawled the agent, betraying an increasing interest.

"Will you arrest him?" insisted Summers, with his index finger elevated against the chairman.

"Not so fast, my dear Captain. He might prove an alibi. Your evidence might not be conclusive."

The Captain permitted his rather severe countenance to rest itself. McCollough and O'Brien guarded their "four aces" with a "deuce-high" lack of interest. Peaches might have been a splendid mummy from an aged tomb standing there with the sack at his feet.

Again becoming sober of mien, the Captain continued, in a voice which might have been the slow beginning of a religious service: "You are a scoundrel—you are to blame for dozens of murders in this country! Men and even women are being butchered every day because you fear to lose the opportunity to steal the property which belongs to these poor savages. I have sol-

dier comrades lying in desert graves who would be alive if you were not a coward and a thief. Only the other day Indians bearing your 'specific object' passes killed five sheep-men in the Tonto Basin."

"I have issued no passes lately."

Here the Captain pulled out all the stops in his organ. "You are a liar, and I am going to prove it."

The agent, who had been sitting lazily behind his desk, leaned forward and made the ink-bottles, pens, and erasers dance fast as he smote the table with his fist. "Leave the room—leave the room, or I will call my police!"

"Where is Sanchez?"

"I don't know," and the fist ceased to beat as he looked up sharply. "Do you?"

The Captain turned rigidly. "Peaches, show the gentleman where Sanchez is."

With a suggestion of that interest which a mender of cane-bottomed chairs might display in business, Peaches pawed in his grain-sack—peered into its dark folds—until suddenly, having assured himself, he straightened up, holding in his right hand, by its long locks, a dead head depending therefrom. Taking it gingerly, the Captain set it on the table directly before Mr. Marshall East, and arranged it squarely. With dropping jaw, the agent pushed himself back in his chair before the horrible sight.

"Yes—I know where Sanchez is. He is looking at you. Were you an accessory before the fact of his intentions? Does he seem to reproach you?" spoke the Captain.

"God!" burst from the lips of the man as he eyeballed his attendant.

"Oh—well—you recognize him, then. Here also is one of your passes. It calls for Chief Natchez, a one-eyed man, who 'specifically murdered sheep-herders with an object.' Peaches, produce Natchez!"

Again fumbling the keeper of the bag got the desired head by the hair and handed it over. It was more recent, and not so well preserved. The eyes were more human, and his grin not so sweet. This, too, was arranged to gaze on the author of passes.

"You see he has one eye—he answers the

pass. I suppose his 'specific object' was sheep."

The agent breathed heavily—not from moral shock, but at the startling exhibit. His chickens had come home to roost. His imagination had never taken him so far afield. The smooth amenities of the business world could not assert themselves before such unusual things. The perspiration rolled down his forehead. He held on to the table with both hands.

Again producing a dirty paper, the Captain read, "Pass Guacalotes" (with some description). Signed, "Marshall East. Agt., etc." Peaches dug up the deceased from the sack, handing it solemnly to the Nan-tan.

"Now, you murderer, you see your work. I wish you could see the faces of the dead sheep-herders too," and with hot impulse he rolled the head across the table. It fell into the agent's lap, and then to the floor. With a loud exclamation of "Oh—o—o!" the affrighted man bolted for the door.

Turning with the quickness of a fish, the soldier said, "Peaches, numero tres," and the third head came out of the bag like a shot.

"Murderer! Stop! Here is another 'specific object!' " but the agent was rapidly making for the door. With a savage turn the Captain hurled the dead head after him. It struck him on the back of the neck, and fell to the floor.

With a cry of fear, which cannot be interpreted on paper, the agent got through the door, followed by a chorus of "Murderer!" It was a violent scene—such as belonged to remote times, seemingly. No one knows what became of the agent. What I wonder at is why highly cultivated people in America seem to side with savages as against their own soldiers.

Billy's Tearless Woe

Mr. Bolette, ranchman, sat with me on the corral fence looking away at the yellow meadows—seeing them through our squinted eyelids, as they rolled one plain into another—growing pink and more cold, losing themselves in blue hills, until one had to squint the more to distinguish what was finally land and what was cloud form. When a mortal looks on these things he ceases to think—it does him so little good. As a mental proposition it is too exhausting. Like the ocean lying quiet at mid-day, it is only fit for brown study.

Presently our vision came back to the vicinity of the corral fence, where was passing a cow-puncher on a pony with a small basket on his arm.

"Good-by, Billy," sung out Bolette.

The individual addressed simply turned his solemn brown face to us, and broke away into a gentle lope.

"That basket is full of pie," exclaimed the ranch owner.

"Pie?"

"Yes; it's the only bait that will draw Billy off the range, 'cept medicine for a dog."

"Medicine for a dog?"

"Oh, yes; Billy's all snarled up with a Scotch stag-hound. He just is naturally in love with the beast—won't let us put out wolf poison on account of him."

The receding Billy was a handsome figure on a horse; bronzed, saturnine, silent. This might in no way distinguish him among his kind, except that it did. He was pro-nouncedly more so than others. His mission with the Coon Skin outfit was horse-wrangler and rider of the western fence. He lived in a tent miles away in a small horse pasture on the banks of the Little Big Horn, and only came up to the ranch buildings at long intervals to report matters, and petition for pie. One of Billy's few weaknesses lay strong on the fat pastries fabricated by the Coon Skin *chef*. He rarely stayed longer than was necessary to tell Mr. Bolette that "Brindle Legs" got cut up in some wire which had been carried down by the flood, that "Sloppy Weather" had a sore back, and to recommend the selling of "Magpie" before time set too strong against him, and to acquire the pie.

As Billy grew smaller on the rolling grass, Mr. Bolette observed: "That puncher don't come here often, and he don't stay long, but his dog is sick now, and he can't stay at all. It beats all how that boy hooks up to that dog. He don't appear to care for anything or anybody in the world but Keno. I don't believe that Billy has a brand on anything but that pup. Most of these punchers and line-riders tie up a little to some of the Pocahontases from the agency, but I never saw one around Billy's camp. If they ever are there, they hunt brush when they see me cleaving the air. Maybe it's a good thing for me. Most of these punchers have got a bad case of the gypsies, and that dog seems to hold Billy level. Now the dog is sick. He is getting thinner and thinner—won't eat, and I don't know what's the matter with him. Dogs don't round up much in cow-out-fits. Do you know anything about a dog? Can you feel a dog's pulse and figure out what is going on under his belt?"

I admitted my helplessness in the matter.

"Taps, chaps, and ladigo straps—if that dog don't get well my horses can look after themselves, and if he dies, Billy will make the Big Red Medicine. I lose anyway," and Mr. Bolette slid off the fence.

"I reckon we had better go over to Billy's pasture to-morrow, and shove some drugs into Keno. If it don't do any good it may help bring things to a head—so that's what we'll do."

On the morrow, late in the afternoon, we took down the bars in front of Billy's lonely tent on the banks of the Little Big Horn.

On a bright Navajo blanket in the tent lay a big, black, Scotch stag-hound—the sick Keno—Billy's idol. He raised his eyelids at us, but closed them again wearily.

"Don't touch him," sharply said Bolette. "I wouldn't touch him with a shovel in his grave when Billy wasn't around. He's a holy terror. When one of these Injuns about here wants to dine with Billy, he gets off on that hill and sings bass at Billy, till Billy comes out in front and rides the peace-sign; other-wise he wouldn't come into camp at all. An Injun would just as soon go against a ghost as this dog. Keno never did like anything about Injuns except the taste, and it's a good thing for a line-rider to have some safeguard on his mess-box. These Injuns calculate that a cow-puncher is a pretty close relation, and Injuns don't let little matters like grub stand between kinfolks. Then again there are white men who cut this range that need watching, and Keno never played favorites. He was always will-ing to hook onto anybody that showed up, and say, when that dog was in good health you wouldn't want to mix up with him much."

Over the hills from the south came a speck—a horseman—Billy himself, as the ranchman said. Slowly the figure drew on—now going out of sight in the wavy plains—moving steadily toward the tent by the river.

He dismounted at the bars with the stiff drop peculiar to his species, and, coming in, began to untackle his horse.

He never bowed to us, nor did he greet us. He never cast his eyes on us sitting there so far from any other people in that world of his. In the guild of riders politeness in any form is not an essential—indeed, it is almost a sign of weakness to their minds, because it must necessarily display emotion of a rather tender sort. Odds Fish! Zounds! Away with it. It is not of us. Suffice it to Billy that he could see us for the last three miles sitting there, and equally we were see-ing him. What more?

Untying two Arctic hares from his saddle, he straddled on his horseman's legs to Keno's bed and patted him on the head. Keno looked up and licked his hand, and then his face, as he bent toward him. For a little time they looked at each other, while Bolette and I pared softly at two sticks with our jack-knives.

Then Billy got up, came out, and began to skin his rabbits. As he slit one down, he said: "I had to work for these two jacks. When Keno was well he thinned them out round here. Whenever he got after a rabbit it was all day with him. I'm going to make some soup for him. He won't stand for no tin grub," said Billy, as he skinned away.

"Have you any idea what's the matter with the dog?" was asked.

"No, I don't savvy his misery. I'd give up good if there was a doctor within wagon-shot of this place. I'd bring him out here if I had to steal him. I'm afraid the dog has got 'to Chicago.'* He can't eat, and he's got to eat to live, I reckon. I've fixed up all kinds of hash for him—more kinds than Riley's Chinaman can make over to the station, and Keno won't even give it a smell. I lay out to shoot a little rabbit soup into him about once a day, but it's like fillin' ole ca'tridge shells. Been sort of hopin' he might take a notion to come again. Seen a man once that far gone that the boys built a box for him. And that man is a-ridin' some-where in the world to-day."

* To die.

Billy made his soup, and we put aconite and cowtownie whiskey in it. The troubled puncher poured it down Keno's resisting throat with a teaspoon until the patient fell back on the blanket exhausted. After this the poor fellow went around to the far side of the tent, and, sitting down, gazed vacantly into the woods across the Big Horn. A passing word from us met with no response. The man himself would not show his emotions, though the listless melancholy was an emotion, but the puncher did not recognize it as such. The fierce and lonely mind was being chastened, but so long as we were the other side of the canvas there could be no weakness; at least he would not have permitted that—not for an instant— had he known.

Night came on, and, with supper finished, we turned into our blankets. My eyes were

" 'Billy, I Find Him Dog . . .' "
Author's photoengraving.

opened several times during the night by the flashes of a light, and I could distinguish that it was Billy with a candle, looking over his dog.

In the morning Bolette and I rode the range in pursuit of his details of business management—fences and washouts, the new Texan two-year-olds, and the sizing up of the beef steers fit for Chicago, and then back to Billy's on the second day.

As we jogged up the river, we saw several Indians trailing about in the brush by the river—weird and highly colored figures— leading their ponies and going slowly. They were looking for a lost object, a trail possibly.

"What are they doing?" I asked.

"Don't you put in your time worrying what Injuns are doing," said Bolette. "When they are doing anything, it's worse than when they ain't doing anything. An Injun is all right when he is doing nothing. I like him laying down better than standing up."

"Oh! I say, old 'One Feather,' what you do, hey?" shouted Bolette, and "One Feather," thus addressed, came slowly forward to us.

"Ugh—Billy's dog he cow-eek—he go die —get fi' dollar mabeso we find um."

Bolette turned in his saddle to me, and with a wise, open-eyed wonderment slowly told off the words, "Billy's—kettle—is full —of mud," and I savvied.

This time we approached the camp from down the river, through a brush trail, and Bolette pulled up his horse on the fringe, pointing and saying in a whisper, "Look at Billy."

Sure enough, by the tent on a box sat the bent-over form of the puncher who despised his own emotions. His head was face downward in his hands. He was drawing on the reserve of his feelings, no doubt.

We rode up, and Bolette sang out: "Hello, Billy; hear Keno's passed it up. Sorry 'bout that, Billy. Had to go, though, I suppose. That's life, Billy. We'll all go that way, sooner or later. Don't see any use of worrying."

Billy got up quickly, saying: "Sure thing. Didn't see anything of the pup, did you?" His face was dry and drawn.

"No. Why?"

"Oh, d—n him, he pulled out on me!" and Billy started for his picketed horse.

In chorus we asked, "What do you mean —he pulled out on you?"

Turning quickly, raising his chin, and with the only arm gesture I ever saw him make, he said quickly: "He left me—he went away from me—he pulled out— savvy? Now what do you suppose he wanted to do that for? To me!"

We explained that it was a habit of animals to take themselves off on the approach of death—that they seem to want to die alone; but the idea took no grip on Billy's mind, for he still stood facing us, saying: "But he shouldn't have gone away from me —I would never have deserted him. If I was going to die for it I wouldn't have left him."

Saddling his horse, he took a pan of cooked food and started away down the river, returning after some hours with the empty tin. "I put out fresh grub every day so Keno can get something to eat if he finds it. I put little *caches* of corn-beef every few rods along the river, enough to give him strength to get back to me. He may be weak, and he may be lost. It's no use to tell me that Keno wouldn't come back to me if he could get back. I don't give a d—n what dogs do when they die. Keno wouldn't do what any ordinary dog would."

We sat about under the shadow of the great trouble, knowing better than to offer weak words to one whose rugged nature would find nothing but insult in them, when an Indian trotted up, and, leaning over his horse's neck said, "Billy, I find him dog— he in de river—drown—you follar me."

In due time we trotted in single file after the blanketed form of Know-Coose. For five miles down the Little Big Horn we wended our way, and the sun was down on the western hills when the Indian turned abruptly into some long sedge-grass and stopped his horse, pointing.

We dismounted, and, sure enough, there lay Keno—not a lovely thing to look at after two days of water and buzzards and sun.

"He must have gone to the river and fallen in from weakness," was ventured.

"No, there was water in the tent," snapped the surly cow-boy in response, for this implied a lack of attention on his part. As there was clearly no use for human comfort in Billy's case, we desisted.

The cow-puncher and the Indian went back on the dry ground, and, with their gloved hands and knives, dug a shallow grave. The puncher took a fine Navajo blanket from his saddle, and in it the carefully wrapped remains of Keno were deposited in the hole. A fifty-dollar blanket was all that Billy could render up to Keno now, excepting the interment in due form, and the rigid repression of all unseemly emotion.

"I wouldn't have pulled out on him. I don't see what he wanted to go pull out on me for," Billy said softly, as we again mounted and took up our backward march.

When we reached camp there was no Billy. After supper he did not come, and for hours there was no Billy, and in the morning there was no Billy.

"I have got it put up," soliloquized Bolette, "that Billy is making medicine over in Riley's saloon at the station, and I reckon I can get a new horse-wrangler, because if I understand the curves of that puncher's mental get-up, New Mexico or Arizona will see William Fling about ten days from now, or some country as far from Keno as he can travel on what money Riley don't get."

So it was that Keno and Billy passed without tears from the knowledge of men.

How the Worm Turned

I sat under a tropical tree, the name of which I cannot tell. Its leaves were thick, and shunted some of the rain. I was hungry, and compelled to use great forbearance toward my emaciated tobacco-bag. I derived satisfaction by glancing through the wooded glades at some hundreds of soldiers, who were just as miserable as I was—not much satisfaction, but some.

As I sat there, a horse attendant of the General's came and stood in front of me. He was a big yellow infantryman, detailed at headquarters. I knew the man—he was an acquaintance of three days' standing, and occupied at night a mudpuddle adjoining my wallow. He had rendered me several little services for which I was grateful.

"Ah do declar'," he said, as he gazed at his dripping clothes; "Ahm so dirty and wet that Ahm afraid some of these yar tropical plants will take root on me and begin to grow."

"A man of your color ought not to mind this hot country. It seems to me as though no one else could live here. For myself, I belong in the snow."

"No, sah," he protested, "Ah don't belong heah. Ma father was a Mexi-kin white man and ma mother was colored. Ah was bown in Texas and raised in New Mexico and Arizona."

My vis-a-vis sat down in the damp, and after a while spoke: "Say, Cap'en—you think thar's goin' to be a fight right soon?"

"Don't know. Why? Do you like fighting?"

"Wall—no. Can't say Ah do—can't say Ah do exactly. S'pose we've got to fight, or smother in mud, and Ah don't see much choice."

"You have been in fights, doubtless, during your long career as a soldier?" I ventured.

"Yes—'deed Ah have. Ah've fought white men and Mexikins and Injuns—and niggers, and Cubeeans—ovah to Tampa, and now we are a-goin' to get a hack at them Span-yards—on the hill yonder."

"Well, well!" I chuckled, "you seem very impartial in your selection of opponents. Uncle Sam has not been at war with niggers, as you call them. How did that happen?"

"Oh—we'uns use to fight each otha round the barracks—fight 'bout the way the pasteboards was comin'—fight 'bout the gals or any ole thing what come up. See that welt?" said my mettlesome visitor, as he rolled up the sleeve of his army shirt, displaying a long white weal on his tawny arm. "Nigger done that."

"Oh, I suppose you were one of those who helped to disgrace the negro regiments, in the riotous disturbances at Yabor City when the Fifth Corps was in camp at Tampa. You men ought to be ashamed of that."

"Tell yu honest 'bout that, Cap'en: that wasn't us that done that—that was Yabor City whiskey. When these niggers gets thar hides full of that pine-top, they don't know no mo' than some white men Ah knows

"Say, Boss, Ah Wasn't Thar—Ah Only Heared 'bout It from Men What Was."
Painting in collection of St. Lawrence University (Ray A. Jubinville).

'bout. Niggers is jus' as God made 'em, an' he didn't make 'em full of jig-juice. He left that fo' the white men to do. Cou'se Ah don't say that was right, that fightin' of the Cubeeans—at Yabor, but yu wait till these niggers put in their time on them Span-yards—ovah yondah, and yu'll say niggers is all right."

"You say you have fought white men. You are not old enough to have been in the Civil War; so how could that have been?"

"This wa'n't no civil war—this was out in Texas, whar Ah fo't white men. Say, Cap'en, be yu a Texas bown—Ah reckon not?"

Knowing that Texans were not in need of my sympathies, I protested my thoroughly judicial frame of mind concerning them.

"Well—Ah don't tell 'bout fightin' white men much. White men don't seem to want to heah 'bout it. Come to think 'bout it, Ah didn't fight that time. Ah only heared 'bout it. Yu see, Cap'en, thar's all kinds of white men. Some of them is good to people of ma

coloh, and agin, some of 'em is pizen, and the pizenest kind of white men used to live out on the plains of Texas. Them punchers and buffalo hunters and whiskey men didn't think no mo' of shootin' a po' nigger man than yu would of lightin' a cigarette. Ah have had one of them men set to shootin' at me soon as Ah come into town, and keep it up till Ah could get out of range, and my horse jus' a burnin' the grass too. He didn't hit me 'cause he was tanked up, Ah s'pose. In them days, Ah was a-servin' in the cav-alry. Say, Boss—yu needn't tell my Cap'en that—Ah don't let on Ah evah served in the cavalry."

Being reassured, he continued: "Well—Ah didn't fight, Boss—Ah only heared 'bout it. Ah reckon we'll both forget this Texas fight befo' day aftah to-morrow, when we gets tangled up with them Span-yards. Say, Boss—when all these yah cannons and bal-loons and that squirt-gun down to the Rough Riders gets to goin' and everybody is done pumpin' his Kraig—Say! that Texas fight won't cut no mo' ice than a sheep-tick in a buffalo herd."

"Go on with your Texas fight."

"Well—Ah was a-servin' in the cavalry, way back yondah at Fort Concho in Tom Green County, Texas, and them Texicans use' to shoot at us nigger soldiers on sight. They use' to run us out of town whenevah we'uns would go in to get a drink."

"Good thing," I interpolated, laughing, "keep you away from bad places."

"No, sah—Boss, yu don't think every man with a thirst ought to be shot, do yu? Reckon we'd both be shot right now. We soldiers was a-gettin' hot 'bout it, but the officers wouldn't stand fo' us goin' to town nowhow. One day Peter Jackson was orderly to the Cap'en, and he was sent into town with a note to carry. He was a-ridin' into town, 'cordin' to orders, when a bad white man come out of Bill Powell's saloon, and, drawin' his gun, he done shoot Peter off his horse. He hit him here"—pointing to his own thigh—"and Peter lay in the middle of the road, a-mo'nin'.

"His horse come back to the post a-runnin', with blood on the saddle. The guard went down and got Peter, and brung him back to camp, where he died that night. The officers tried to get the Law on some one, but the peace officers was all in cahoots with the Powell gang, and ther was nothin' doin'. We soldiers was mad 'nough tu eat railroad iron. What du yu think 'bout that —shootin' a poor soldier, what was only 'beyin' orders, jus fer fun?"

"Outrageous—perfectly outrageous."

"Well, that was what Sergeant Gadsby of F Troop said—'Perfectly outrageous,' said he. We held a meetin' in the quarters, and the Sergeant he made a speech, and the soldiers was wild. He ended up by sayin', 'If we was men, to come on.' We was all ready to 'come on,' so Gadsby took twenty-one of us —Ah didn't go—with two six-shooters apiece, and after dark we run the guard. He tole us he was a goin' down to clean out Bill Powell's saloon or die. He tole us jus what we was to do. Say, Boss, Ah wasn't thar—

Ah only heared 'bout it from men what was. Ah get to thinkin' Ah was thar sometimes, but, honest, Ah wasn't. The men walked the three miles to Powell's in the dark, and when we got there, Sergeant Gadsby opened the do', and the twenty-one soldiers walked right in—single file—and faced the bar. The room was full of men—must have been thirty-five or forty Texicans in the room. They was might'ly surprised to see us—the soldiers, Ah mean. The Sergeant was the last man to come in, and he locked the do' and put the key in his pocket. We'uns was all facin' the bar: 'What will yu have, gen'lemens?' says Gadsby. 'Whiskey,' says we. Say, boss—yu could hear your heart beat in that room, while we was a-pourin' our drinks.

"Every man bein' fixed, 'How,' says Gadsby, and we drunk.

"As we put the glasses down, Gadsby says—' 'Bout face—give 'em hell!' and every nigger turned his guns loose. Ah don't know jus' how it all was. Yu couldn't heah your own gun go off, and yu couldn't see nothin'. Pretty soon, Ah got to the do' by sliding' 'long the bar, and thar was Sergeant Gadsby, who had it open. By this time they was only a shot now and then in the room back of the smoke, but the gro'nin' and cussn' on the flo' was awful. One white man come a crawlin' tro' the smoke toward the do', and the Sergeant shot him as he lay. When we done got outside, we reloaded and waited, but only seven colored soldiers come out of Bill Powell's saloon, and some of them was bleedin'. Then we went back to the post.

"We didn't know what to do, and we lay all night a talkin'. We knew the Law would be on us. We knew the Texicans had the Law all right, so after 'stables,' we got on our horses with our arms, and we got whar ther' wa'n't no Law," concluded the narrator.

"How many white men were killed in the fight?" I asked.

"Ah don' jus' know, Boss; but Ah heared they swept up thirty-five Texicans next mornin', besides de col-lod sojers."

"Why—you didn't run away with Gadsby, did you? You say you were not in the fight."

"No, sah—Ah didn't fight, but Ah quit the cavalry so soon after that Ah didn't heah jus' how that was. Ha—yu talk 'bout Yabor City—that wasn't no red licker in that Powell fight. That was a dead squar' shake. Say, Cap'en, Ah've often wondered how many holes thar was in Powell's saloon next mornin'," laughed the horse-tender, as he got up to go over to his charges.

As he had said, "When the cannons and balloons got to goin'," I forgot all about that Texas fight for a time, but it ought not to be forgotten. When the great epic of the West is written, this is one of the wild notes that must sound in it.

A Desert Romance

A TALE OF THE SOUTHWEST

Ochoa water-hole is in no way remarkable, and not regarded as such by people in Arizona, but if the waters could speak and tell about what happened at their sides in the long ago, men would listen. Three generations of white men and Mexicans have fought Apaches since then, and one generation of Apaches has walked in the middle of the big road. There have been stories enough in the meantime. Men have struggled in crowds over similar water-holes throughout the Southwest, and Ochoa has been forgotten.

With the coming of the great war, the regular soldiers were withdrawn to participate in it. The Apaches redoubled their hostilities. This was in Cochise's day, and he managed well for them.

Volunteers entered the United States service to take the places of the departed soldiers, to hold the country, and to protect the wagon-trains then going to California. A regiment of New Mexican volunteer infantry, Colonel Simms commanding, was stationed at Fort Bowie, and was mostly engaged in escorting the caravans. There was a military order that such trains should leave the posts only on the 1st of every month, when the regular soldier escort was available; but in enterprising self-reliance the pioneers often violated this.

One lazy summer day a Texan came plodding through the dust to the sentries at Bowie. He was in a state of great exhaustion, and when taken to Colonel Simms he reported that he had escaped from a Texas emigrant caravan, which was rounded up by Apaches at Ochoa water-hole, about forty-five miles east and south of this point, and that they were making a fight against great odds. If help was not quickly forthcoming, it was death for all.

Immediately the colonel took what of his command could be spared, together with a small cavallard of little hospital mules, and began the relief march.

These America-Mexican soldiers were mountain men and strong travelers. All during the remainder of the day they shuffled along in the dust—brown, bluebearded men, shod in buckskin moccasins, of their own construction, and they made the colonel's pony trot. There are many hills and many plains in forty-five miles, and infantry is not a desert whirlwind. Night settled over the command, but still they shuffled on. Near midnight they could hear the slumping of occasional guns. The colonel well knew the Apache fear of the demons of the night, who hide under the water and earth by day, but who stalk at dark, and are more to be feared than white men, by long odds. He knew that they did not go about except under stress, and he had good hope of getting into the beleaguered wagons without much difficulty. He knew his problem would come afterward.

Guided by the guns, which the white men fired more to show their wakefulness than in hopes of scoring, the two companies trod softly in their buckskin foot-gear; but the mules struck flinty hard against the wayside rocks, and then one split the night in friendly answer to the smell of a brother mule somewhere out in the dark. But no opposition was encountered until occasional bullets came whistling over there from the wagons. "Hold on, pardners!" shouted the colonel. "This is United States infantry; let us in."

The noise located the command, and bullets and arrows began to seek them out in the darkness from all sides, but with a rush they passed into the packed wagons and dropped behind the intrenchments. The poor people of the train were greatly cheered by the advent. By morning the colonel had looked about him, and he saw a job of unusual proportions before him. They were poor emigrants from Texas, their wagons piled with common household goods and with an unusual proportion of women and children—dry, care-worn women in calico shifts, which the clinging wind blew close about their wasted and unlovely frames. In the center stood a few skeletons of horses, destined to be eaten, and which had had no grass since the train had been rounded up. What hairy, unkempt men there were lay behind their bales, long rifles in hand, bullets and powder-horns by their elbows—tough customers, who would "sell out" dearly.

Presently a very old man came to the colonel, saying he was the head person of the train, and he proposed that the officer come to his wagon, where they could talk over the situation seriously.

The colonel was at the time a young man. In his youth he had been afflicted with desk-work in the great city of New York. He could not see anything ahead but a life of absolute regularity, which he did not view complacently. He was book-taught along the lines of construction and engineering, which in those days meant anything from a smoke-house to a covered bridge. Viewed through the mist of years he must, in his day, have been a fair prospect for feminine eyes. The West was fast eating up the strong young men of the East and Simms found his way with the rest to the uttermost point of the unknown lands, and became a vagrant in Taos. Still, a man who knew as much as he did, and who could get as far West as Taos, did not have to starve to death. There were merchants there who knew the fords of the Cimarron and the dry crossings of the Mexican custom-house, but who kept their accounts by cutting notches on a stick. So Simms got more writing to do, a thing he had tried to escape by the long voyage and muling of previous days. Being young, his gaze lingered on the long-haired, buckskin men of Taos, and he made endeavor to exchange the quill for the rifle and the trap, and shortly became a protégé of Kit Carson. He succeeded so well that in the long years since he has been no nearer a pen than a sheep-corral would be.

He succumbed to his Mexican surroundings, and was popular with all. When the great war came he remembered New York and declared for the Union. Thus by hooks which I do not understand he became a colonel in the situation where I have found him.

As he approached the old man's part of the train he observed that he was richer and much better equipped than his fellows. He had a tremendous Conestoga and a spring-wagon of fine workmanship. His family consisted of a son with a wife and children, and a daughter who looked at the colonel until his mind was completely diverted from the seriousness of their present position. The raw, wind-blown, calico women had not seemed feminine to the officer, but this young person began to make his eyes pop, and his blood go charging about in his veins.

She admitted to the officer in a soft Southern voice that she was very glad he had gotten in, and the colonel said he was very glad indeed that he was there, which statement had only become a fact in the last few seconds. Still, a bullet-and-arrow-swept wagon-park was quite as compelling as the eyes of Old Man Hall's daughter, for that was her father's name. The colonel had a new interest in rescue. The people of the train were quite demoralized, and had no reasonable method to suggest as a way out, so the colonel finally said: "Mr. Hall, we must now burn all this property to prevent its falling into the hands of the enemy. I will take my hospital mules and hook them up to a couple of your lightest wagons, on which will be loaded nothing but provisions, old women, small children, and what wounded we have, and then we will fight our way back to the post."

Mr. Hall pleaded against this destruction, but the officer said that the numbers of the investing enemy made it imperative that they go out as lightly as possible, as he had no more mules and could spare no more men to guard the women. It seemed hard to burn all that these people had in the world, but he knew of no other way to save their lives.

He then had two wagons drawn out, and after a tussle got his unbroken pack-mules hooked up. Then the other stuff was piled into the remaining wagons and set on fire. The soldiers waited until the flames were beyond human control, when they sprang forward in skirmish formation, followed out of bow-shot by the wagons and women. A rear-guard covered the retreat.

As the movement began, Colonel Simms led his pony up to the daughter of Mr. Hall, and assisted her to mount. Simms was a young man, and it seemed to him more important that a beautiful young woman should be saved than some sisters who carried the curbs and collar-marks of an almost spent existence. This may not be true judgment, but Simms had little time to ponder the matter.

Now the demons of the Arizona deserts began to show themselves among the brush and rocks, and they came in boldly, firing from points of vantage at the moving troops. A few went down, but the discipline told, and the soldiers could not be checked. Scurrying in front ran the Indians, on foot and on horseback. They had few guns, and their arrows were not equal to the muzzle-loading muskets of the troops or the long rifles of the Texans. A few of the savages were hit, and this caused them to draw off.

The wounded soldiers were loaded into the wagons, which were now quite full.

What with having to stop to ram the charges home in their guns, and with the slow progress of the women on foot, the retreat dragged its toilsome way. There were bad places in the back trail—places which Simms knew the Apaches would take advantage of; but there was nothing for it but to push boldly on.

After a couple of hours the command drew near a line of bluffs up which the trail led. There was no way around. Simms halted his wagons at the foot of the coulée leading up, and sent his men in extended order on each flank to carry the line of the crest, intending to take the wagons and women up afterward. This they did after encountering some opposition, and when just in the act of reaching the level of the mesa, a score of mounted warriors dashed at the line and rode over it, down the coulée in a whirl of dust, and toward the women, who had no protection which could reach them in time to save. The men on the hill, regardless of the enemy in front, turned their muskets on the flying bunch, as did the rear-guard; but it was over with a shot, and the soldiers saw the warriors ride over the women and wagons, twanging their bows and thrusting with their lances. The mules turned, tangled in their harness, and lay kicking in a confused heap. The women ran scurrying about like quail. The cloud of dust and racing-ponies passed on, receiving the fire of the rear-guard again, and were out of range. With them went the colonel's horse and Old Man Hall's daughter, stampeded—killed by the colonel's kindness. No arm could save.

When the dust settled, several women and children lay on the sand, shot with arrows or cut by lances. The mules were rearranged, the harness was patched, and the retreat was resumed.

Old Man Hall was hysterical with tears, Simms was dumb beyond speech, as they marched along beside the clanking wagons, with their moaning loads. On all sides strode the gallant New Mexicans and

Texans, shooting and loading. The Apaches, encouraged by success, plied them with arrows and shots from every *arroyo* which afforded safe retreat. The colonel ran from one part of the line to another, directing and encouraging his men. By afternoon every one was much exhausted, Colonel Simms particularly so from his constant activity and distress of mind.

Old Man Hall had calmed down and had become taciturn, except for the working of his hollow jaws as he talked to himself. Going to the rear wagon, he took out a cotton bag, which he swung across his shoulders, and trudged along with it. "Some valuables he cherishes," thought Simms; "but to add such weight in this trying march seems strange. Demented by the loss of his daughter, probably."

Slower and slower moved the old man with his sack, falling back until he mingled with the rear-guard, and then even dropping behind that.

"Come, come, camarado, stir yourself! The Indios are just behind!" they called.

"I don't care," he replied.

"Throw away the sack. Why do you carry that? Is your sack more precious than your blood?"

"Yes, it is now," he said almost cheerfully.

"What does it contain, señor? Paper money, no doubt."

"No; it is full of pinole and pemochie and strychnine—for the wolves behind us"; and Old Man Hall trod slower and slower, and was two hundred yards in the rear before Simms noticed him.

"Halt! We will go back and get the old man, and have him put in the wagons," he said.

The soldiers turned to go back, when up from the brush sprang the Apaches, and Hall was soon dead.

"Come on; it is of no use now," signaled Simms.

"The old man is loco," said a soldier. "He had a sack of poisoned meal over his shoulder. He is after revenge."

"Poisoned meal!"

"Yes, señor; that is as he said," replied the soldier.

But under the stress Simms's little column toiled along until dusk, when they were forced to stop and intrench in a dry camp. There was no water in those parts, and the Indians had no doubt drawn off for the night—gone to the Ochoa spring, it was thought, and would be back in the morning. By early dawn the retreat started on its weary way, but no Indians appeared to oppose them. All day long they struggled on, and that night camped in the post. They had been delivered from their peril: at little cost, when the situation was considered, so men said—all except Hall's son and the young commanding officer. The caravan had violated the order of the authorities in traveling without escort, and had been punished. Old Man Hall, who had been responsible, was dead, so the matter rested.

II.

The people who had so fortunately come within the protecting lines of Bowie were quite exhausted after their almost ceaseless exertions of the last few days, and had disposed themselves as best they could to make up their lost sleep. Some of the soldiers squeezed the *tequela* pigskin pretty hard, but they had earned it.

Colonel Simms tossed uneasily on his rude bunk for some time before he gained oblivion. Something in the whole thing had been incomplete. He had had soldiers killed and soldiers wounded—that was a part of the game. Some emigrants had suffered— that could not be helped. It was the good-looking girl, gone swirling off into the unknown desert, in the dust of the Apache charge, which was the rift in the young colonel's lute, and he had begun to admit it to himself. What could be done? What was his duty in the matter? His inclination was to conduct an expedition in quest of her. He knew his Apache so well that hope died out of his mind. Even if she could get away on the colonel's swift pony, an Apache on foot could trail and run down a horse. But the tired body and mind gave over, and he

In the Desert—Don Gomez and His Lances at the Ochoa Spring.
Painting in "21" Club Collection—Peter Kriendler, President.

knew nothing until the morning light opened his eyes. Sitting opposite him on a chair was the brother of Hall's daughter, with his chin on his hands, and his long rifle across his knees.

"Good morning, Mr. Hall," he said.

"Mornin', colonel," replied Hall. "Ah 'm goin' back after my sista, colonel. Ah 'm goin' back, leastwise, to whar she was."

"So am I," spoke up Simms, like a flash, as he swung himself to his feet, "and right now." With men like Simms to think was to act.

He was refreshed by his rest, and was soon bustling about the post. The day before two companies of his regiment had come into the post on escort duty. They were pony-mounted, despite their being infantry, and were fresh. These he soon rationed, and within an hour's time had them

trailing through the dust on the back track. Hall's sad-faced son rode by his side, saying little, for both felt they could not cheer each other with words.

Late in the afternoon, when coming across the mesa which ended at the bluff where the misfortune had overtaken the girl, they made out mounted figures at the very point where they had brought up the wagons.

"If they are Apaches, we will give them a fight now; they won't have to chase us to get it, either," said the colonel, as he broke his command into a slow lope.

Steadily the two parties drew together. More of the enemy showed above the bluffs. They formed in line, which was a rather singular thing for Apaches to do, and presently a horseman drew out, bearing a white flag on a lance.

"Colonel, those are lanceros of Mexico," spoke up the orderly sergeant behind the officer.

"Yes, yes; I can see now," observed Simms. "Trot! March! Come on, bugler." Saying which, the colonel, attended by his man, rode forth rapidly, a white handkerchief flapping in his right hand.

So they proved to be, the irregular soldiers of distracted Mexico—wild riders, gorgeous in terra-cotta buckskin and red serapes, bent on visiting punishment on Apache Indians who ravaged the valleys of Chihuahua and Sonora, and having, therefore, much in common with the soldiers on this side of the line.

In those days the desert scamperers did not know just where the international boundary was. It existed on paper, no doubt, but the bleak sand stretches gave no sign. Every man or body of men owned the land as far on each side of them as their rifles would carry, and no farther. Both Mexico and the United States were in mighty struggles for their lives. Neither busied themselves about a few miles of cactus, or the rally and push of their brown-skinned irregulars.

Shortly the comandante of the lancers came up. He was a gay fellow with a brown face, set with liquid black eyes, and togged out in the rainbows of his national costume. Putting out his hand to Simms, he spoke: "Buenos dios, señor. Is it you who have killed all the Apaches?"

"Si, capitan," replied Simms. "I had the honor to command, but I do not think we killed so many."

"Madre de Dios! you call that not many! Ha, you are a terrible soldier!" And the lancer slapped him on the back. "I saw the battle-ground; I rode among the bodies as far as I could make my horse go. I saw all the burned wagons, and the Indios lying around the water-hole, as thick as flies in a kitchen. It smelled so that I did not stop to count them; they were as many as a flock of sheep. I congratulate you. Did you lose many *soldados?*"

"No capitan. I did not lose many men,

bluffs. Did you see her body there?" but I lost a woman—just down below the

In truth, the poisoned sack of meal had come only slowly into Simms's mind when he thought of the dead Indians about the waterhole, and he did not care to enlighten a foreign officer in a matter so difficult of explanation.

"No," answered the Mexican; "they were all naked Apaches—I made note of that. We looked for others, but there were none. You are a terrible soldier. I congratulate you; you will have promotion, and go to the great war in the East."

"Oh, it is nothing, I assure you," grunted Simms, as he trotted off to get away from his gruesome glories. "Come, señor; we will look at the girl's trail below the bluffs."

"Was she mounted well?" inquired the lancer, full of a horseman's instinct.

"Yes; she had a fast horse, but he had been ridden far. He was my own."

"She was of your family?"

"No, no; she was coming through with the wagon-train from Texas."

"She was a beautiful señorita?" ventured the lancer, with a sharp smile.

"Prettiest filly from Taos to New Orleans," spoke our gallant, in his enthusiasm, and then they dismounted at the wagon place, which was all beaten up with the hoof-marks of the lancers.

The best trailers among the mountain men of the command were soon on the track of the horsed Indians who had driven off the girl, and this they ran until quite dark. The enemy had gone in full flight.

Simms made his camp, and the Mexican lancer pushed on ahead, saying he would join him again in the morning.

By early light Simms had his troops in motion; but the trail was stamped up by the lancer command, and he could follow only this. He was in a broken country now, and rode far before he began to speculate on seeing nothing of his friend of yesterday. Some three hours later he did find evidence that the lancers had made a halt, but without unsaddling. Simms had run the trail carefully, and had his flankers out on the sides, to see that no one cut out from the grand track. Soon he was summoned by a flanker who waved his hat, and toward him rode the officer. Nearing, he recognized the man, who was a half-breed American, well known as a trailer of great repute.

"Colonel, here are the prints of the Apache ponies; I know by their bare feet and the rawhide shoes. Your pony is not among them; he was shod with iron. These ponies were very tired; they step short and stumble among the bushes," said the man, as he and the colonel rode along, bending over in their saddles. "See that spot on the ground. They had run the stomachs out of their horses. They stopped here and talked. They dismounted." Both the colonel and the trailer did the same. "There is no print of her shoe here," the trailer continued slowly. "See where they walked away from their horses and stood here in a bunch. They were talking. Here comes a pony-track back to them from the direction of the chase. This pony was very tired. His rider dismounted here and walked to the group. The moccasins all point toward the way they were running. They were talking. Colonel, the girl got away. I may be mistaken, but that is what the trail says. All the Indians are here. I have counted twenty ponies."

There is nothing to do in such places but believe the trail. It often lies, but in the desert it is the only thing which speaks. Taking his command again, the colonel pushed on as rapidly as he dared, while feeling that his flanking trailers could do their work. They found no more sign of the Indians, who had evidently given up the chase, thinking, probably, the wagons more important than the fast horse-girl.

All day long they progressed, the colonel wondering why he did not come up with the lancer command. Why was the Mexican in such a hurry? He did not relish the idea of this man's rescuing the girl, if that was to be fate. Long he speculated, but time brought only more doubt and suspicion. At places the Mexican had halted, and the ground was tramped up in a most meaningless way. Again the trailer came to him.

"Colonel," he said, "these people were blinding a trail. It's again' nature for humans to walk around like goats in a corral. I think they have found where the girl stopped, but I can't run my eye on her heel."

The colonel thought hard, and being young, he reached a rapid conclusion. He would follow the Mexican to the end of his road. Detailing a small body of picked trailers to follow slowly on the sides of the

The Trailer. *Authors' wood engraving.*

main trail, he mounted, and pushed on at a lope. Darkness found the Mexicans still going. While his command stopped to feed and rest, the colonel speculated. He knew the Mexicans had a long start; it was unlikely that they would stop. He thought, "I will sleep my command until midnight, and follow the trail by torch-light. I will gain the advantage they did over me last night."

After much searching on the mountainside in the gloom, some of his men found a pitch-tree, which they felled and slivered. At the appointed time the command resumed its weary way. Three hundred yards ahead, a small party followed the trail by their firelight. This would prevent, in a measure, an ambuscade. A blanket was carried ahead of the flaming stick—a poor protection from the eyes of the night, but a possible one. So, until the sky grayed in the east, the soldiers stumbled bitterly ahead on their relentless errand. It was a small gain, perhaps, but it made for success. When the torches were thrown away, they grazed for an hour, knowing that horses do not usually do that in the dark, and by day they had watered and were off. The trail led straight for Mexico.

Whatever enthusiasm the poor soldiers and horses might have, we know not, but there was a fuel added to Simms's desire, quite as great as either the pretty face of Adele Hall or his chivalric purpose kindled —it was jealousy of the lancer officer. When hate and love combine against a young man's brain, there is nothing left but the under jaw and the back of his head to guide him. The spurs chugged hard on the lathering sides, as the pursuers bore up on the flying wake of the treacherous man from Mexico.

At an eating halt which the lancers made, the trailers sought carefully until, standing up together, they yelled for the colonel. He came up, and pointing at the ground, one of the men said: "Señor, there is the heel of the white girl."

Bending over, Simms gazed down on the telltale footprint, saying, "Yes, yes; it is her shoe—I even remember that. Is it not so, Hall?" The girl's brother, upon examination, pronounced it to be his sister's shoe. Simms said: "We will follow that lancer to hell. Come on."

There were, in those days, few signs of human habitation in those parts. The hand of the Apache lay heavy on the land. The girl-stealer was making in the direction of Magdalena, the first important Mexican town en route. This was a promise of trouble for Simms. Magdalena was populous and garrisoned. International complications loomed across Simms's vision, but they grew white in the shadow of the girl, and, come what would, he spurred along, the brother always eagerly at his side.

By mid-afternoon they came across a dead horse, and soon another. The flatsoled tegua-tracks of the dismounted riders ran along in the trail of the lancer troop. The country was broken, yet at times they could see long distances ahead. Shortly the trailers found the tegua-prints turned away from the line of march, and men followed, and found their owners hidden in the mesquitbush. These, being captured, were brought to Colonel Simms, who dismounted and interrogated them, as he gently tapped their lips with the muzzle of his six-shooter to break their silence. He developed that the enemy was not far ahead; that the girl was with them, always riding beside Don Gomez, who was making for Magdalena. Further, the prisoners said they had found the white woman asleep beside her worn-out pony, which they had taken aside and killed.

This was enough. The chase must be pushed to a blistering finish. As they drew ahead they passed exhausted horses standing head down by the wayside, their riders being in hiding, doubtless. On a rise they saw the troop of lancers jogging along in their own dust, not three hundred yards ahead, while in the valley, a few miles beyond, was an adobe ranch, for which they were making. With a yell from the United States soldiers, they broke into the best run to be got out of their jaded ponies. The enemy, too, spurred up, but they were even more fatigued, and it was not many minutes before the guns began to go. A few of the enemy's horses and men fell out, wounded, and were ridden over, while the rest fled in wild panic. They had doubtless thought themselves safe from pursuit, and they would have been, had their booty been anything less than Adele Hall. Many lancers turned and surrendered when the tired horses could go no more. The commands tailed out in a long line, the better horses of the Americans mixing gradually with the weaker ones of the lancers. Still well ahead rode Don Gomez and his reluctant companion. These drew up to the blue walls of the long adobe ranch (for it was now sunset), and were given admittance, some dozen men in all, when the heavy doors were swung together and barred, just as the American advance drew rein at their portals.

Finally having all collected,—both Americans and prisoners,—and having carefully posted his men around the ranch, Simms yelled in Spanish: "Come to the wall, Capitan Gomez. I am Colonel Simms. I would speak a word with you." Again he spoke to the walls, now blackening against the failing light. From behind the adobe battlements came excited voices; the inhabitants were trying to digest the meaning of this violence, but no one answered Simms.

Turning, he gave an order. Instantly a volley of musketry started from near him, and roared about the quiet ranch.

Once more Simms raised his angry voice: "Will you come on the roof and talk to me now, Don Gomez?"

At length a voice came back, saying, "There are no windows; if I come on the roof, I will be shot."

"No, you will not be shot, but you must come on the roof."

"You promise me that?"

"Yes, I promise you that no soldier of mine will shoot at you," and in loud military language Simms so gave the order.

Slowly a dark figure rose against the greenish light of the west.

"Don Gomez, I ask you truly, has one hair of that girl's head been harmed? If you lie to me, I swear on the cross to burn you alive."

"I swear, my colonel; she is the same as when you last saw her. I did not know you were coming. I was trying to save her. I was taking her to my commander at Magdalena."

"You lie!" was the quick response from Simms, followed by a whip-like snap peculiar to the long frontier rifles. The dark form of Don Gomez turned half round, and dropped heavily out of sight on the flat roof of the adobe.

"Who fired that shot?" roared Simms.

"Ah did, sah," said Hall, stepping up to the colonel and handing him his rifle. "Ah am not one of yer soldiers, sah—I am Adele Hall's brother, and Mr. Gomez is dead. You can do what you please about it, sah."

While this conversation was making its quick way, a woman sprang up through the hole in the roof, and ran to the edge, crying, "Help Colonel Simms! Oh, help me!"

"Cover the roof with your guns, men," ordered Simms, and both he and the brother sprang forward, followed by a general closing in of the men on the building.

As they gained the side wall, Simms spoke. "Don't be scared, Miss Hall; jump. I will catch you," and he extended his arms. The girl stepped over the foot-high battlement, grasped one of the projecting roof-timbers, and dropped safely into Colonel Simms's arms. She was sobbing, and Simms carried her away from the place. She was holding tightly to the neck of her rescuer, with her face buried in a week's growth of beard.

The Strategy of the Blanket Pony

In the old days when your Uncle Samuel was trying to catch Sioux Indians with infantry, just the same as John Bull is now hunting Boers, Bill Burton was an aged captain in a regiment of foot. He was, as I have said, up in years, and it took a good bit of belting to go round his middle. He had intelligence enough, as the result of many years of soldiering, to know that General Walkaheap, who was in command, wasn't likely to catch any Indians when the Indians did not want to be caught. Almost every day, though, the Sioux used to select favorable spots from which advantage they potted at the plodding soldiers, and were gone on their rushing ponies before they could be brought to seriousness. Far out from the sides of the wagon-train plodded the dough-boys in extended order, with loaded rifles, eagerly scanning every cut-bank and sage-bush field for an Indian jack-in-the-box. Old General Walkaheap, as we will call him, was a tremendously energetic man, grown old in war, with quite too much confidence in the legs of men. Fighting flies was very exasperating to him. So day by day, including Sundays, he followed his long jaw into the heart of the Sioux buffalo range, leaving white signs many hundred miles in his rear. The angry red-men redoubled their efforts to arrest his progress—they yelled and they circled, potted and volleyed, and they burned the dry grass ahead of him, but they never rode over his thin blue line to the sugar and coffee vans, which rattled and creaked be-

tween. That was not their way, which was unfortunate for them. They knew that the dismounted soldiers could not run away, and that they would die desperately. The flour and coffee were too dear for the Sioux market.

Well, out in the van rode the General, grim and determined, quite forgetful of men's legs in his purpose to come to close quarters, or to at least occupy the heart of their hunting range. Captain Bill Burton had water blisters on his feet, his canteen was always dry, and he longed for a day's let-up, so he might wash, shave and lie quietly on his back with his pipe in his mouth "inviting his soul."

"There are those —— Indians now," he said to his trusty lieutenant, Dick Van Nick. "Steady, men! Close up your intervals. Don't fire! Let them come closer."

Down through the dry washes sped the warriors—hovering hawk-like, veering before the steady rifles and away. Again the dusty blue line stepped forward.

Captain Burton and General Walkaheap had, in times gone by but not forgotten, had their personal differences, and they were by no means admirers of each other. They seldom came nearer than they officially had to.

"If the old man would stop for a day or so once a month these Indians might give us an infantry fight. We travel so fast they can't make up their minds what to do," remarked the vinegary Burton to Van Nick.

"Yes," replied Van Nick with a deep sigh. "Say, Uncle Bill, I wonder if angels have big leather armchairs to sit in? That would pretty near fill my idea of heaven."

"Blow the angels, Dick. If I could only be a major and ride a horse, that would do."

"Well, anyhow, Uncle Bill," spoke Dick, "when we get into camp we have our little nip, while the other fellows are as dry as their belt-plates. What?"

"Yes, yes, my son—if only our fellows don't get onto us. If they do, our whiskey will last like the Irishman's—pretty d—n quick."

On the start of the expedition against the hostile Indians of the Northwest the old General had, with intent to free his loaded wagons from useless litter, ordered all the whiskey left behind. He had made the officers cache their personal belongings, only allowing each one as much as he could hold out in his right hand. But Burton and Van Nick had bought a blanket pony, which did not intrench on the government transportation, and had more bedding than would otherwise have been possible. At least that was the natural theory, when as a matter of fact in the blanket panniers were two large jugs of rare rye whiskey, carefully packed and swaddled. The column had not toiled many days before our worthies became aware that they were the only people in the camp who had any of the encouraging medicine. The blanket pony was tied behind a wagon by day, and at evening halts the captain and lieutenant personally unpacked him. They had by almost superhuman shrewdness and painstaking care managed to conceal the fact that they had a "nightcap" and an "eye-opener" at the respective times each day. There were occasional rumors among their comrades in arms to the effect that Captain Bill and his trusted Bunkie smelled of the "old thing," but they dissembled and denied. Many weary leagues lay between their cantinas of rye and a further supply, so they did not blame themselves for the selfish protection of their possession. Two jugs were enough for them personally, but among so many officers, if it were known, they would soon be drained.

Along through the buffalo grass and the gray sage tramped the soldiers—bearded and dusty and bored. Far out on the plains they could see at times their wolfish following, but they did not come near enough to give them the relaxation of a fight. At night, to be sure, they came to shoot into the camps and wagons, keeping the men awake. They made very delicate work for the pickets in the darkness, also for the officer of the guard who had to go stumbling about in the gloom. All of this exasperated the men, and particularly the old General, whose ideas of war had been gathered at such places as Chapultepec and the Death Angle. He longed to get at them; he yearned for contact with these desert hawks, and he pressed them as hard as his men could leg it or his mules be whacked along, but to no purpose. He left ambuscades for them which they never fell into. He hunted them in the darkness and the rain; but they were hunters themselves. It became utterly discouraging, so he mentally gave it up and just marched. He ceased to be interested in his own strategy.

Every one else felt the same way. Every one had ceased to expect that the regiment would get any credit out of this cheerless war, and one day Van Nick said to Uncle Billy: "It does seem kind of low-down of us to husband that rum when we could use it in the interest of the regiment—don't it, now?"

"What do you mean, Dick? You don't dream of springing it on the fellows?"

"Oh no, captain, that isn't my idea; my idea is to use it strategically."

"Use whiskey strategically?"

"Yes—give it to the Indians. It might make them fight."

"Ho, ho! I see. That's not a bad idea; but how? It's against orders to have it with us at all."

Dick thought a while, and, future general that he was to be, finally proposed that some day when they were in camp and well prepared they should drive the blanket pony out where the Indians could get him and rely on the whiskey to make the warriors brave. So their campaign was arranged, not without misgivings as to the possibilities of so sudden a conjunction of red men and red liquor. It might be a powerful combination, or a weak one, but experience of the past said yes. Shortly the train made a day's resting halt. The mules had come in from grazing and were safe within the wagon corral. Well out on each four sides of the camp lay a battalion of infantry—deployed—loaded and tired of the monotony which their shifting enemies enforced. They could put no salt on the Sioux bird's tail.

Out to the north, on some low bluffs not five hundred yards away, a considerable body of warriors were squatting beside their ponies, observing the camp. They had no desire to come nearer; keeping watch, they could both see and understand. Being all ready and the time propitious, Uncle Billy Burton and his lieutenant led the poor old blanket pony outside the line of soldiers.

"Where the —— are you going with that pony, Burton?" sang out one of a group of officers who sat playing poker on the grass.

"Oh, I am going to exercise him. He don't get work enough," responded our merry strategist with a wink.

The game stopped. Some soldier lark ahead possibly. They might be amused, they hoped.

The two officers borrowed rifles and belts as they passed through the line. Leading the loaded pony, they marched forth toward the row of grotesque figures sitting on the bluffs. When this curious trio had advanced a hundred and fifty yards the warriors out in the distance began to gird and mount. Neither did they understand. The troops had never so manœuvred before. Was it a talk which was wanted, were the soldiers sick of the long-drawn game or was it some deep-seated thoughtfulness? The Indians did not make it out. Neither did the waiting troops. They had never before seen two men leading a simple pony out into the open between two forces bent on each other's destruction. It was not in the books; it had never been told around the winter fires.

With the alert willingness to take advantage of the chances, the Sioux quirted and kicked their ponies into a proper state of anticipation of the game. The regulars sat up, spread their faces cheerfully and fingered their rifle sights up to the possible distances. Steadily the officers advanced on their curious adventure.

"Say, Uncle Bill, I think we had better stop; when they come we won't have much the best of a race back to the lines."

"All right—I think we are about right; but, Dick, I don't want this whiskey to come back on us. It won't do us a —— bit of good and may do us harm if the General gets onto it, and the boys would never let us hear the last of it. No! wait. Get your horseshoes ready. Tie them on, but hold up his tail, and for —— sake, Dick, don't get him started the wrong way or we are dirt."

Lieutenant Van Nick proceeded quickly to tie a string of mule-shoes, which he had strung on some "whang" leather, to the blanket pony's tail. He wove it in tight and strong. Meanwhile the anxious Sioux had begun to circle and hover in their bird-of-prey fashion, confident of their mobility.

"Hurry up, Dick! The d—— whelps will come soon. They will scare the pony back into the lines."

"All right, uncle—I have him fixed. Are you ready?"

"Yes—turn him loose."

This was one of those battles which had been thought out before it was begun, which seldom happens outside books. It was the soldier ideal—the real military ideal; it was what the boys at West Point had studied when they tried their simple strategy on the Academy staff, that being, in cadet theory, the way to apply talent. The captain had the thin old calico pony, loaded with his two panniers, turned toward the enemy. Dick raised the consecrated animal's tail and made a quick pass under it; he dropped the same suddenly; the string of mule-shoes clattered about its hocks; with his rifle he gave the beast a big whack and fired a cartridge over its back. The blanket pony's memories of patient treatment were all forgotten in

"The Strategy of the Blanket Pony." *University of Michigan Library.*

this sudden movement of his ganglions. He made off toward the rushing Sioux.

Turning toward their lines, the two officers ran for it—only looking back occasionally to see what the blanket pony was doing. He had run away about a hundred yards, but, upon seeing the charging Indian line, had stopped.

"Keep between the pony and our line so they won't shoot," called out the lieutenant.

This they did. The line held its fire, and the Indians rounded out the pony and bore it away.

Coming among their comrades, they were greeted with amazement. "What the —— are you doing?" "Burton, you must be crazy," etc.

"They certainly did get our pony," said Burton, grinning.

"Why didn't you lie down and let us fire over you?" was asked; but the pony strategists shed no light and walked away to speculate in quiet.

Again the soldiers lay down in groups along the line, and the poker game was resumed amid wild conjectures as to Bill Burton's sanity. They could see a possible joke in giving up the old pony, though why sacrifice all those blankets now that winter was approaching? But mostly they gave it up.

The Indians had gone out of sight beyond the bluffs. "It won't take long before we will see what our combination of reds will produce. Chemically speaking, we ought to get a wild scrap in twenty minutes or a half-hour," speculated Van Nick.

"See Bill—looking at the horizon through his glasses. Guess he's making medicine for the lost bronc," observed a poker player.

Time passed, when suddenly Captain Bill took down his glasses. "They are coming, Dick," and he ran forward. "Attention! Get ready! Now we'll have the fight of our lives, boys. Make no mistake now—they are coming home this time!" he yelled.

The line sprang to its knees; the officers drew their swords and stood to their places.

Down the bluff and over the plain came the wild, charging line of warriors—scintillating bright reds and yellows and whites—revolvers and rifles going in the air—their shrill "yips" even reaching at this distance, and the ponies beating madly. Now and then a warrior fell from his pony, and yet not a shot had been fired.

"Ready!—aim!—fire!" The gray lead sped; the blue smoke eddied out along the grass. "Load!—ready!—aim!—fire!" and again sped the deadly volley. Faintly through the smoke the soldiers saw the swift line come. In fierce nervousness they picked at their belts, threw up and down the breech-blocks and poured it in. Ponies lay kicking all along behind the Indian squadron, but on they came. Many soldiers jammed their bayonets into the sockets, many clubbed their rifles, and some lay flat on the ground.

"They are coming home!" was yelled in the captain's ear as he threw himself on the ground. The beating crowd of ponies rode over the skirmish line, but it did not fire or stop. The soldiers punched and belted with their guns. Warriors reeled and rolled like sacks of flour along the ground. There were many riderless ponies. These continued on, while the mounted ones were twisted and turned about in aimless fashion to renew the attack. Warriors were seen to roll about on the ponies' backs, some were hanging on by an eyelid, others had their arms around their ponies' necks, not seeking to control them. The soldiers ran to catch them, but found the Indians not inclined to resist.

They saw others sitting on the grass waving their arms aimlessly. They stopped to regard them wonderingly. The entire absence of offensiveness on the part of the reds was slowly understood, until men began to call, "They are drunk!" "They are all drunk!" and then they pulled what few were left from their ponies and sat on their chests.

As things began to clear, it was seen that there were no casualties among the soldiers, and the people were amazed to see Burton and Van Nick slapping their thighs and each other's backs, while they roared and screamed with laughter. The others, comprehending, began to howl, until the whole battalion, so lately grim before death, yelled in happy chorus.

"Say, Bill, why didn't you give us a drop before you got rid of that whiskey, you old villain?"

"Well, boys, you got a fight, and that's better than a drink—ain't it? You fellows would kick anyway."

The General came galloping and stood staring at his successor, but did not understand the laughter. "What was on that pony, captain?" he demanded at last.

"That was a medicine pony, General—he was loaded with The Great Spirit," returned our strategist with cheerful innocence.

The General rode away smiling. The men walked out, gathered up the drunk and wounded and the empty blanket pony, shot the downed horses and congratulated each other on the good fortunes of the S'teenth Foot, which would get ample credit, even if it was accomplished by "shrewdness and force and by deeds undone."

Western Types

THE COW-BOY

No longer strange, and become conventional, the Cow-boy is merely trying to get mountain-bred ponies to go where he wants them to go. Knowing the "Irish Pig" of their nature, he has to be fast and insistent; all of which represents a type of riding and pony "footing" easier to delineate than to perform.

The Cow-boy. *Authors' photoengraving.*

The Cossack Post (Cavalryman). *Authors' photoengraving.*

THE COSSACK POST (CAVALRYMAN)

A picket of three men is technically called a "Cossack Post," and the moonlight of the picture uncovers a United States Cavalryman on the northern plains in the almost fierce and certainly definite light of a country which has "no atmosphere," as painters phrase it. The cap and overcoat were issued for winter campaigns in that sullen cold.

The Scout. *Authors' photoengraving.*

THE SCOUT

Too well known to need particular comment. He was the white hunter who had gone to the wild countries and was employed by our troops for light-horse work in a country and among a people unknown to the Army.

The Half-breed. *Authors' photoengraving.*

THE HALF-BREED

One of the relics of the old fur company days—the descendant of white employees and Indian squaws. In great numbers of the half-breeds led a nomad existence on the plains of the Northwest, and at one time bid fair to become a separate and peculiar people. Our government through the army deported large bands from the then territory of Montana to Canada, and their expiring effort was the Louis Riel rebellion. The passing of the buffalo left them stranded, and their predatory habits made their suppression necessary, but they still exist, though robbed of their picturesque apparel and characteristic traits.

John Ermine of the Yellowstone

CONTENTS

John Ermine. *Authors' photoengraving.*

CHAPTER I

Virginia City

One fine morning in the fall of '64 Alder Gulch rolled up its shirt sleeves and fell to the upheaving, sluicing, drifting, and cradling of the gravel. It did not feel exactly like old-fashioned everyday work to the muddy, case-hardened diggers. Each man knew that by evening he would see the level of dust rise higher in his long buckskin gold-bags. All this made for the day when he could retire to the green East and marry some beautiful girl—thereafter having nothing to do but eat pie and smoke fragrant cigars in a basking sunshine of no-work. Pie up at Kustar's bake-shop was now one dollar a pie, and a pipe full of molasses and slivers was the best to be had in the market. Life was hard at Alder in those days—it was practical; and when its denizens became sentimental, it took these unlovely forms, sad to relate.

Notwithstanding the hundreds who toiled in the gulches, Virginia City itself held hurrying crowds,—Mormon freighters, pack trains, ponies, dirty men off the trails, wan pilgrims, Indians, Chinese, and almost everything else not angelic.

Into this bustle rode Rocky Dan, who, after dealing faro all night at the "Happy Days" shebang, had gone for a horseback ride through the hills to brighten his eyes and loosen his nerves. Reining up before this place, he tied his pony where a horse-boy from the livery corral could find it. Striding into that unhallowed hall of Sheol, he sang out, "Say, fellers, I've just seen a thing out in the hills which near knocked me off'en my horse. You couldn't guess what it was nohow. I don't believe half what I see and nothin' what I read, but it's out thar in the hills, and you can go throw your eyes over it yourselves."

"What? a new thing, Dan? No! No! Dan, you wouldn't come here with anything good and blurt it out," said the rude patrons of the "Happy Days" mahogany, vulturing about Rocky Dan, keen for anything new in the way of gravel.

"I gamble it wa'n't a murder—that wouldn't knock you off'en your horse, jus' to see one—hey, Dan?" ventured another.

"No, no," vouched Dan, laboring under an excitement ill becoming a faro-dealer. Recovering himself, he told the bartender to 'perform his function.' The "valley tan" having been disposed of, Dan added:—

"It was a boy!"

"Boy—boy—a boy?" sighed the crowd, setting back their 'empties.' "A boy ain't exactly new, Dan," added one.

"No, that's so," he continued, in his unprofessional perplexity, "but this was a white boy."

"Well, that don't make him any newer," vociferated the crowd.

"No, d—— it, but this was a white boy out in that Crow Injun camp, with yeller hair braided down the sides of his head, all the same Injun, and he had a bow and arrer, all the same Injun; and I said, 'Hello, little feller,' and he pulled his little bow on me, all the same Injun. D—— the little cuss, he was about to let go on me. I was too near them Injuns, anyhow, but I was on the best quarter horse in the country, as you know, and willin' to take my chance. Boys, he was white as Sandy McCalmont there, only he didn't have so many freckles." The company regarded the designated one, who promptly blushed, and they gathered the idea that the boy was a decided blonde.

"Well, what do you make of it, anyhow, Dan?"

"What do I make of it? Why, I make of it that them Injuns has lifted that kid from some outfit, and that we ought to go out and bring him in. He don't belong there, nohow, and that's sure."

"That's so," sang the crowd as it surged into the street; "let's saddle up and go and get him. Saddle up! saddle up!"

The story blew down the gulch on the seven winds. It appealed to the sympathies of all white men, and with double force to their hatred of the Indians. There was no man at Alder Gulch, even the owners of squaws,—and they were many,—who had not been given cause for this resentment. Business was suspended. Wagoners cut out and mounted team-horses; desperadoes, hardened roughs, trooped in with honest merchants and hardy miners as the strung-out cavalcade poured up the road to the plateau, where the band of Crows had pitched their tepees.

"Klat-a-way! Klat-a-way!" shouted the men as they whipped and spurred up the steeps. The road narrowed near the top, and here the surging horsemen were stopped by a few men who stood in the middle waving and howling "Halt!" The crowd had no definite scheme of procedure at any time,—it was simply impelled forward by the ancient war-shout of *A rescue! A rescue!* The blood of the mob had mounted high, but it drew restive rein before a big man who had forced his pony up on the steep hillside and was speaking in a loud, measured and authoritative voice.

The riders felt the desire for council; the ancient spirit of the witenagemote came over them. The American town meeting, bred in their bones and burned into their brains, made them listen to the big temporary chairman with the yellow lion's mane blowing about his head in the breeze. His horse did not want to stand still on the perilous hillside, but he held him there and opened.

"Gentlemen, if this yar outfit goes a-chargin' into that bunch of Injuns, them Injuns aforesaid is sure goin' to shoot at us, and we are naturally goin' to shoot back at them. Then, gentlemen, there will be a fight, they will get a bunch of us, and we will wipe them out. Now, our esteemed friend yer, Mr. Chick-chick, savvies Injuns, as you know, he bein' somewhat their way hisself —allows that they will chill that poor little boy with a knife the first rattle out of the box. So, gentlemen, what good does it all do? Now, gentlemen, I allows if you all will keep down yer under the hill and back our play, Chick-chick and me will go into that camp and get the boy alive. If these Injuns rub us out, it's your move. All what agrees to this motion will signify it by gettin' down off'en their horses."

Slowly man after man swung to the ground. Some did not so readily agree, but they were finally argued off their horses. Whereat the big chairman sang out: "The ayes have it. Come on, Mr. Chick-chick."

These two rode up the hill and over the mesa, trotting along as they talked. "Now, Chick-chick, I don't know a heap about Injuns. The most that I have seen of them was over the sights of a rifle. How are we goin' at this? Do you *habla* Crow lingo, Señor?"

"No," replied that much mixed-blooded man, "I no *cumtux* Crow, but I make the hand talk, and I can clean up a *ten-ass Chinook;* all you do is to do nothing,—you no shake hands, you say nothing, until we smoke the pipe, then you say 'How?' and shake hands all same white man. You hang on to your gun—suppose they try take it

The Chairman. *Authors' wood engraving.*

away—well, den, *icta-nica-ticki,* you shoot! Then we are dead." Having laid his plan of campaign before his brother in arms, no more was said. History does not relate what was thought about it.

They arrived in due course among the tepees of a small band of Crows. There were not probably a hundred warriors present, but they were all armed, horsed, and under considerable excitement. These Crows were at war with all the other tribes of the northern plains, but maintained a truce with the white man. They had very naturally been warned of the unusual storm of horsemen bearing in their direction, and were apprehensive concerning it. They scowled at the chairman and Mr. Chick-chick, who was an Oregon product, as they drew up. The latter began his hand-language, which was answered at great length. He did not at once calm the situation, but was finally invited to smoke in the council lodge. The squaws were pulling down the tepees; roping, bundling, screaming, hustling ponies, children, and dogs about, unsettling the statesmen's nerves mightily as they passed the pipe. The big chairman began to fancy the Indians he had seen through the sights more than these he was regarding over the pipe of peace. Chick-chick gesticulated the proposition that the white papoose be brought into the tent, where he could be seen.

The Indians demurred, saying there was no white boy—that all in the camp were Crows. A young warrior from outside broke into their presence, talking in a loud tone. An old chief looked out through the entrance-flap, across the yellow plains. Turning, he inquired what the white horsemen were doing outside.

He was told that they wanted the white boy; that the two white chiefs among them would take the boy and go in peace, or that the others would come and take him in war. Also, Chick-chick intimated that he must *klat-a-way.* The Indians made it plain that he was not going to *klat-a-way;* but looking abroad, they became more alarmed and excited by the cordon of whites about them.

"When the sun is so high," spoke Chick-chick, pointing, and using the sign language, "if we do not go forth with the boy, the white men will charge and kill all the Crows. One white boy is not worth that much."

After more excitement and talk, a youngish woman came, bearing a child in her arms, which was bawling and tear-stained,—she vociferating wildly the time. Taking the unmusical youngster by the arm, the old chief stood him before Chick-chick. The boy was near nine years of age, the men judged, white beyond question, with long, golden hair braided, Indian fashion, down the sides of his head. He was neatly clothed in dressed buckskins, fringed and beaded, and not naked or half naked, as most Indian boys are ·in warm weather. It was not possible to tell what his face looked like in repose, for it was kneaded into grotesque lumps by his cries and wailing.

"He is a Crow; his skin is white, but his heart is Absaroke. It makes us bleed to see him go; our women will mourn all this snow for him, but to save my band I give him to you. Take him. He is yours."

Chick-chick lifted the child in his arms, where the small cause of all the turmoil struggled and pulled hair until he was forced to hold him out at arm's length. Mounting, they withdrew toward their friends. The council tepee fell in the dirt—a dozen squaws tugging at its voluminous folds. The small hostage was not many yards on his way toward his own kind before the Indian camp moved off toward the mountains, urging their horses with whip and lance. This movement was accelerated by a great discharging of white men's guns, who were supposed to be sacrificing the little white Crow to some unknown passions; whereas, they were merely celebrating the advent of the white child unharmed. He was indeed unharmed as to body, but his feelings had been torn to shreds. He added his small, shrill protesting yells to the general rejoicing.

Chick-chick, or Chickens, as the miners often called him, had not entered the expedition because of his love for children, or the color of this one in particular; so, at the suggestion of the chairman, it was turned over to a benevolent saloon-keeper, who had nine notches in his gun, and a woman with whom he abided. "Gold Nugget," as he was promptly named by the diggers and freighters, was supposed to need a woman, as it was adjudged that only such a one could induce him to turn off the hot water and cease his yells.

The cavalcade reached town, to find multitudes of dirt-begrimed men thronging the streets waiting for what sensation there was left in the affair. The infant had been overcome by his exertions and was silent. They sat him on the bar of his godfather's saloon, while the men shouldered their brawny way through the crowd to have a look at him— the lost white child in the Indian dress. Many drinks and pistol shots were offered up in his honor, and he having recovered somewhat, resumed his vocal protests. These plaints having silenced the crowd, it was suggested by one man who was able to restrain his enthusiasm, that the kid ought to be turned over to some woman before he roared his head off.

Acting on this suggestion, the saloon-keeper's female friend was given charge. Taking him to her little house back of the saloon, the child found milk and bread and feminine caresses to calm him until he slept. It was publicly proclaimed by the nine-notch saloon-keeper that the first man who passed the door of the kid's domicile would be number ten to his gun. This pronunciamiento insured much needed repose to Gold Nugget during the night.

In the morning he was partially recovered from fears and tears. The women patted his face, fed him to bursting, fingered the beautiful plaits of his yellow hair, and otherwise showed that they had not surrendered all their feminine sensibilities to their tumultuous lives. They spoke to him in pleading voices, and he gurgled up his words of reply in the unknown tongue. The saloon-keeper's theory that it would be a good thing to set him up on the bar some more in order to

keep trade, was voted both inhuman and impracticable by the women. Later in the day a young man managed to get on the youngster's blind side, when by blandishments he beguiled him on to his pony in front of him. Thus he rode slowly through the streets, to the delight of the people, who responded to Gold Nugget's progress by volley and yell. This again frightened him, and he clung desperately to his new friend, who by waving his arm stilled the tempest of Virginia City's welcome, whereat the young man shouted, "Say—do you think this kid is runnin' for sheriff?"

The Gulch voted the newcomer the greatest thing that ever happened; took him into partnership, speculated on his previous career, and drank his health. Above all they drank his health. Unitedly they drank to his weird past,—his interesting present, and to his future life and happiness, far into the night. It was good for business, said the saloon-keepers one to another.

On one of the same mountain winds which had heralded his coming was borne down the Gulch next morning the tragic words, "The kid is gone!"

"Gone?" said the miners; "gone whar?"

Alder promptly dropped its pick, buckled on its artillery, and assembled before the nine-notch man. "Where has the kid gone?" it demanded.

His woman stood beside the bar, wild-eyed and dishevelled. "I don't know, gentlemen—I don't have an idea. He was playing by the door of my shack last evening. I went in the house for a minute, and when I came out he was gone. I yelled, and men came, but we could not find him hide or hair."

"If any man has got that kid away from me,—mind you this now,—he will see me through the smoke," spoke nine-notch, as he rolled his eye malevolently for a possible reply.

Long search and inquiry failed to clear matters. The tracks around the house shed no new light. The men wound their way to their cabins up and down the Gulch, only answering inquiries by, "The kid is gone."

CHAPTER II
White Weasel

For many days the Absaroke trotted and bumped along, ceaselessly beating their ponies' sides with their heels, and lashing with their elk-horn whips. With their packs and travoix they could not move fast, but they made up for this by long hours of industrious plodding. An Indian is never struck without striking back, and his counter always comes when not expected. They wanted to manœuvre their women and children, so that many hills and broad valleys would lie between them and their vengeance when it should be taken. Through the deep cañons, among the dark pine trees, out across the bold table-lands, through the rivers of the mountains, wound the long cavalcade, making its way to the chosen valley of Crowland, where their warriors mustered in numbers to secure them from all thought of fear of the white men.

The braves burned for vengeance on the white fools who dug in the Gulch they were leaving behind, but the yellow-eyed people were all brothers. To strike the slaves of the gravel-pits would be to make trouble with the river-men, who brought up the powder and guns in boats every green-grass. The tribal policy was against such a rupture. The Crows, or Sparrowhawks, as they called themselves, were already encompassed by their enemies, and only able by the most desperate endeavors to hold their own hunting-grounds against the Blackfeet, Sioux, and Cheyennes. Theirs was the pick and choosing of the northern plains. Neither too hot nor to cold, well watered and thickly grassed on the plains, swarming with buffalo, while in the winter they could retire to the upper valleys of the Big Horn River, where they were shut in by the impassable snow-clad mountains from foreign horse thieves, and where the nutritious salt-weed kept their ponies in condition. Like all good lands, they could only be held by a strong and brave people, who were made to fight constantly for what they held. The powder and guns could only be had from the white traders, so they made a virtue of necessity and held their hand.

Before many days the squaw Ba-cher-hish-a rode among the lodges with little White Weasel sitting behind her, dry-eyed and content.

Alder had lost Gold Nugget but the Indians had White Weasel—so things were mended.

His foster-mother—the one from whom the chief had taken him—had stayed behind the retreating camp, stealing about unseen. She wore the wolf-skin over her back, and in those days no one paid any attention to a wolf. In the dusk of evening she had lain near the shack where her boy was housed, and at the first opportunity she had seized him and fled. He did not cry out when her warning hiss struck native tones on his ear. Mounting her pony, she had gained the scouts, which lay back on the Indian trail. The hat-weavers (white men) should know White Weasel no more.

The old men Nah-kee and Umbas-a-hoos sat smoking over their talk in the purple shade of a tepee. Idly noting the affairs of camp, their eyes fell on groups of small urchins, which were scampering about engaging each other in mimic war. They shot blunt-headed arrows, while other tots returned the fire from the vantage of lariated ponies or friendly tepees. They further observed that little White Weasel, by his activity, fierce impulse, and mental excellence, was admittedly leading one of these diminutive war-parties. He had stripped off his small buckskin shirt, and the milk-white skin glared in the sunlight; one little braid had become undone and flowed in golden curls about his shoulders. In childish screams he urged his group to charge the other, and running forth he scattered all before his insistent assault.

"See, brother," spoke Nah-kee, "the little white Crow has been struck in the face by an arrow, but he does not stop."

"Umph—he will make a warrior," replied

the other, his features relaxing into something approaching kindliness. The two old men understood what they saw even if they had never heard of the "Gothic self-abandonment" which was the inheritance of White Weasel. "He may be a war-chief—he leads the boys even now, before he is big enough to climb up the fore leg of a pony to get on its back. The arrow in his face did not stop him. These white men cannot endure pain as we do; they bleat like a deer under the knife. Do you remember the one we built the fire on three grasses ago over by the Big Muddy when Eashdies split his head with a battle-axe to stop his noise? Brother, little White Weasel is a Crow."

"It is so," pursued the other veteran; "these yellow-eyes are only fit to play badger in a gravel-pit or harness themselves to loaded boats, which pull powder and lead up the long river. They walk all one green-grass beside their long-horned buffalo, hauling their tepee wagons over the plains. If it were not for their medicine goods, we would drive them far away."

"Yes, brother, they are good for us. If we did not have their powder and guns, the Cut-Throats [Sioux] and the Cut-Arms [Cheyennes] would soon put the Absaroke fires out. We must step carefully and keep our eyes open lest the whites again see White Weasel; and if these half-Indian men about camp talk to the traders about him, we will have the camp soldiers beat them

A Crow. *Authors' wood engraving.*

with sticks. The white traders would take our powder away from us unless we gave him to them."

"We could steal him again, brother."

"Yes, if they did not send him down the long river in a boat. Then he would go so far toward the morning that we should never pass our eyes over him again on this side of the Spiritland. We need him to fill the place of some warrior who will be struck by the enemy."

Seeing the squaw Ba-cher-hish-a passing, they called to her and said: "When there are any white men around the camps, paint the face of your little son White Weasel, and fill his hair with wood ashes. If you are careful to do this, the white men will not notice him; you will not have to part with him again."

"What you say is true," spoke the squaw, "but I cannot put black ashes in his eyes." She departed, nevertheless, glorious with the new thought.

Having fought each other with arrows until it no longer amused them, the foes of an idle hour ran away together down by the creek, where they disrobed by a process neatly described by the white men's drill regulations, which say a thing shall be done in "one time and two motions."

White Weasel was more complicated than his fellows by reason of one shirt, which he promptly skinned off. "See the white Crow," gurgled a small savage, as every eye turned to our hero. "He always has the war-paint on his body. He is always painted like the big men when they go to strike the enemy—he is red all over. The war-paint is in his skin."

"Now, let us be buffalo," spoke one, answered by others, "Yes, let us be buffalo." Accordingly, in true imitation of what to them was a familiar sight, they formed in line, White Weasel at the head as usual. Bending their bodies forward and swinging their heads, they followed down to the water, throwing themselves flat in the shallows. Now they were no longer buffalo, but merely small boys splashing about in the cool water, screaming incoherently and as nearly perfectly happy as nature ever intended human beings to be. After a few minutes of this, the humorist among them, the ultra-imaginative one, stood up pointing dramatically, and, simulating fear, yelled, "Here comes the bad water monster," whereat with shrill screams and much splashing the score of little imps ran ashore and sat down, grinning at their half-felt fear. The water monster was quite real to them. Who could say one might not appear and grab a laggard?

After this they ran skipping along the river bank, quite naked, as purposeless as birds, until they met two old squaws dipping water from the creek to carry home. With hue and cry they gathered about them, darting like quick-motioned wolves around worn-out buffalo. "They are buffalo, and we are wolves," chorussed the infant band; "bite them! blind them! We are wolves! we will eat them!" They plucked at their garments and threw dirt over them in childish glee. The old women snarled at their persecutors and caught up sticks to defend themselves. It was beginning to look rather serious for the supposed buffalo, when a young warrior came riding down, his pony going silently in the soft dirt. Comprehending the situation, and being fairly among them, he dealt out a few well-considered cuts with his pony-whip, which changed the tune of those who had felt its contact. They all ran off, some holding on to their smarts— scattering away much as the wolves themselves might have done under such conditions.

Indian boys are very much like white boys in every respect, except that they are subject to no restraint, and carry their mischievousness to all bounds. Their ideas of play being founded on the ways of things about them, they are warriors, wild animals, horses, and the hunters, and the hunted by turns. Bands of these little Crows scarcely past toddling ranged the camp, keeping dogs, ponies, and women in a constant state of unrest. Occasional justice was meted out to them with a pony-whip, but in proportions much less than their deserts.

Being hungry, White Weasel plodded home to his mother's lodge, and finding a buffalo rib roasting near the fire he appropriated it. It was nearly as large as himself, and when he had satisfied his appetite, his face and hands were most appallingly greased. Seeing this, his mother wiped him off, but not as thoroughly as his condition called for, it must be admitted. Falling back on a buffalo robe, little Weasel soon fell into a deep slumber, during which a big dog belonging to the tent made play to complete the squaw's washing, by licking all the grease from his face and hands.

In due course he arose refreshed and ready for more mischief. The first opportunity which presented itself was the big dog, which was sleeping outside. "He is a young pony; I will break him to bear a man," said Weasel to himself. Straightway he threw himself on the pup, grasping firmly with heel and hand. The dog rose suddenly with a yell, and nipped one of Weasel's legs quite hard enough to bring his horse-breaking to a finish with an answering yell. The dog made off, followed by hissing imprecations from Ba-cher-hish-a, who rubbed the little round leg and crooned away his tears. He was not long depressed by the incident.

Now all small Indian boys have a regard for prairie-dog or marmot's flesh, which is akin to the white boy's taste for candy balls and cream paste. In order to satisfy it the small Indian must lie out on the prairie for an hour under the broiling sun, and make a sure shot in the bargain. The white boy has only to acquire five cents, yet in the majority of cases that too is attended by almost overwhelming difficulties.

With three other boys White Weasel repaired to the adjoining dog-town, and having located from cover a fat old marmot whose hole was near the outskirts of the village, they each cut a tuft of grease-weed. Waiting until he had gone inside, they ran forward swiftly and threw themselves on the ground behind other dog mounds, putting up the grease-weed in front of themselves. With shrill chirping, all the marmots of this colony dived into their holes and gave the desert over to silence. After a long time marmots far away from them came out to protest against the intrusion. An old Indian warrior sitting on a near-by bluff, nursing morose thoughts, was almost charmed into good nature by the play of the infant hunters below him. He could remember when he had done this same thing—many, many grasses ago. More grasses than he could well remember.

The sun had drawn a long shadow before the fat marmot showed his head above the level of his intrenchments—his fearful little black eyes set and his ears straining. Three other pairs of black eyes and one pair of blue ones snapped at him from behind the grease-weed. There followed a long wait, after which the marmot jumped up on the dirt rim which surrounded his hole, and there waited until his patience gave out. With a sharp bark and a wiggling of his tail he rolled out along the plain, a small ball of dusty fur. To the intent gaze of the nine-year-olds he was much more important than can be explained from this view-point.

Having judged him sufficiently far from his base, the small hunters sprang to their knees, and drove their arrows with all the energy of soft young arms at the quarry. The marmot made a gallant race, but an unfortunate blunt-head caught him somewhere and bowled him over. Before he could recover, the boys were upon him, and his stage had passed.

Carrying the game and followed by his companions, Weasel took it home to his foster-mother, who set to skinning it, crooning as she did in the repeated sing-song of her race:—

> "My son is a little hunter,
> My son is a little hunter,
> Some day the buffalo will fear him,
> Some day the buffalo will fear him,
> Some day the buffalo will fear him,"

and so on throughout the Indian list until the marmot was ready for cooking.

So ran the young life of the white Crow. While the sun shone, he chased over the country with his small fellows, shooting blunt arrows at anything living of which they were not afraid. No one corrected him; no one made him go to bed early; no one washed him but the near-by brook; no one bothered him with stories about good little boys; in fact, whether he was good or bad had never been indicated to him. He was as all Crow boys are—no better and no worse. He shared the affections of his foster-parents with several natural offspring, and shared in common, though the camp took a keen interest in so unusual a Crow. Being by nature bright and engaging, he foraged on every camp kettle, and made the men laugh as they lounged in the afternoon shade, by his absurd imitations of the war and scalp dances, which he served up seriously in his infant way.

Any white man could see at a glance that White Weasel was evolved from a race which, however remote from him, got its yellow hair, fair skin, and blue eyes amid the fjords, forests, rocks, and ice-floes of the north of Europe. The fierce sun of lower latitudes had burned no ancestor of Weasel's; their skins had been protected against cold blasts by the hides of animals. Their yellow hair was the same as the Arctic bear's, and their eyes the color of new ice. Little Weasel's fortunes had taken him far afield. He was born white, but he had a Crow heart, so the tribesmen persuaded themselves. They did not understand the laws of heredity. They had never hunted those.

CHAPTER III

The Coming of The Great Spirit

With the years White Weasel spindled up into a youth whose legs quite naturally fitted around the barrel of a horse. He no longer had to climb up the fore leg of a camp-pony, but could spring on to those that ran in his father's herd and maintain his position there.

Having observed this, one night his foster-father said to him: "You are old enough, my son, to be trusted with my ponies out in the hills. You must begin to study the ponies, or you will never be able to take or hold any of your own. Not to have horses is not to hunt buffalo or go to the enemy, and not to have a wife. Go, then, when the morning comes, with your brother, and watch my herd. See that they feed safely; see that by evening they come to the lodges. You are old enough now to wear the loincloth; you must begin to be a man. You will never find your shadow-self here among the noisy lodges; it will only come to you out in the quiet of the hills. The Bad Spirits always have their arms out to clutch you when you are asleep in the night; as you ride in the shadows; when you ford the waters,—they come in the wind, the rain, the snow; they point the bullet and the battle-axe to your breast, and they will warn the Sioux when you are coming after their ponies. But out in the hills the Sak-a-war-te* will send some bird or some little wolf to you as his friend; in some way he will talk to you and give a sign that will protect you from the Bad Gods. Do not eat food or drink water; pray to him, and he will come to you; if he does not, you will be lost. You will never see the Spiritland when your body lies flat on the ground and your shadow has gone."

After saying this, his father's pipe died out, the mother put no more dry sticks on the fire, the shapes along the lodge walls died away in the gloom, and left the youth awake with a new existence playing through his brain. He was to begin to be a man. Already he had done in play, about the camp, the things which the warriors did among the thundering buffalo herds; he had imitated the fierce nervous effort to take the enemy's life in battle and the wolfish quest after ponies. He had begun to take notice of the great difference between himself and the

* Great Spirit of the Crows.

girls about the camp; he had a meaning which they did not; his lot was in the field.

Before the sun rose he was one of the many noisy boys who ran about among the horses, trailing his lariat to throw over some pony which he knew. By a fortunate jerk he curled it about one's neck, the shy creature crouching under its embracing fold, knowing full well the awful strangle which followed opposition. With ears forward, the animal watched the naked youth, as he slowly approached him along the taut rope, saying softly; "Eh-ah-h-h—um-m-m-um-m-m—eh-h-h-h-h." Tying the rope on the horse's jaw, with a soft spring he fixed himself on its back, tucking his loin-cloth under him. Now he moved to the outskirts of the thronging horses, crying softly to them as he and his brother separated their father's stock from that of the neighbor herds. He had done this before, but he had never been responsible for the outcome.

The faint rose of the morning cut the trotting herd into dull shadowy forms against the gray grass, and said as plain as any words could to White Weasel: "I, the sun, will make the grass yellow as a new brass kettle from the traders. I will make the hot air dance along the plains, and I will chase every cloud out of the sky. See me come," said the sun to White Weasel.

"Come," thought the boy in reply, "I am a man." For all Indians talk intimately with all things in nature; everything has life; everything has to do with their own lives personally; and all nature can speak as well as any Crow.

Zigzagging behind the herd, they left the smell of smoke, carrion, and other nameless evils of men behind them, until the bark of wolf-dogs dulled, and was lost to their ears.

Daylight found the two boys sitting quietly, as they sped along beside the herd of many-colored ponies. To look at the white boy, with his vermilioned skin, and long, braided hair, one would expect to hear the craunch and grind of a procession of the war-cars of ancient Gaul coming over the nearest hill. He would have been the true part of any such sight.

"Brother," spoke his companion, "we must never shut our eyes. The Cut-Arms are everywhere; they come out of the sky, they come out of the ground to take our horses. You must watch the birds floating in the air; they speak to you about the bad Indians, when you learn their talk; you must watch the wolves and the buffalo, and, above all, the antelope. These any one can understand. We must not let the ponies go near the broken land or the trees. The ponies themselves are fools, yet, if you will watch them, you will see them turn slowly away from an enemy, and often looking back, pointing with their ears. It may be only a bear which they go away from; for the ponies are fools—they are afraid of everything. The grass has been eaten off here by these buffalo, and the ponies wander. I will ride to the high hill, while you, brother, bring the herd slowly. Watch me, brother; I may give the sign of danger." Saying which, the older boy loped gracefully on ahead.

All day the herd grazed, or stood drooping, as the sun made its slow arc over the sky, while the boys sat on the ground in the shadows cast by their mounts, their eyes ceaselessly wandering. Many were the mysteries of horse-herding expounded by the one to the other. That the white Absaroke was hungry, it was explained, made no difference. Absarokes were often hungry out in the hills. The Dakotah were worse than the hunger, and to lose the ponies meant hunger in their father's lodge. This shadow-day herding was like good dreams; wait until the hail beat on the ponies' backs, and made them run before it; wait until the warriors fought about the camp, defending it; then it was hard work to hold them quietly. Even when the snow blew all ways at the same time, the Cut-Throats might come. White Weasel found a world of half-suspected things all coming to him at once, and gradually a realizing sense stole over him that the ponies and the eating and the land were very serious things, all put here for use and trouble to the Absaroke.

As the days wore on, the birds and the wild animals talked to the boy, and he un-

derstood. When they plainly hovered, or ran wildly, he helped to gather up the ponies and start them toward the lodges. If the mounted scouts came scurrying along the land, with the white dust in a long trail behind them, he headed for the cottonwoods with the herd, galloping. At times the number of the ponies in his charge changed, as his father won or lost at the game of "hand"; but after the dried-meat moon his father had brought home many new ponies from the camps of the Cut-Arms toward the Morning.

His father had often spoken praise of him beside the lodge-fire, and it made him feel good. He was beginning to be a man, and he was proud of it; he would be a warrior some day, and he would see that nothing hurtful happened to his father's horses.

It was now the month of the cold moon.[†] The skies were leaden at times; the snow-laden winds swept down from the mountains, and in the morning Weasel's skin was blue and bloodless under his buffalo-robe when he started out for the hills, where the wind had swept the snow off from the weeds and grass. Never mind, the sun of the yellow grass had not cooked the ambition out of him, and he would fight off the arrows of the cold.

His brother, being older, had at last succumbed to his thirst for glory. He had gone with some other boys to try his fortune on other people's horses. Weasel was left alone with the herd. His father often helped him to take the ponies out to good grazing, and then left him. The Absaroke had been sore pressed by the Indians out on the plains, and had retired to the Chew-cârâ-âsh-Nitishic[*] country, where the salt-weed grew. Here they could be pushed no farther. Aided by the circling wall of mountain, their own courage, and their fat horses, they could maintain themselves. Their scouts lay far out, and the camp felt as much security as a wild people can ever feel.

One day, as usual, Weasel had taken his ponies far away to fresh feed, that near the

† December.   * Big Horn Basin.

camps having been eaten off. The day was bright, but heavy, dense clouds drifted around the surrounding mountain-tops, and later they crawled slowly down their sides. Weasel noticed this as he sat shivering in his buffalo-robe; also he noticed far away other horse herds moving slowly toward the Arsha-Nitishic, along whose waters lay the camp of his people. He began to gather his ponies and rode circling about. They acted wildly—strung out and began to run. Glancing about, Weasel saw many big gray wolves loping along in unison with his charges.

It was not strange that wolves were in the vicinity of Indians. The wolves, the ravens, and the Indians were brothers in blood, and all followed the buffalo herds together. A lame or loose pony or a crippled Indian often went the way of the wolves, and many wolves' hides passed over the trader's counter. Thus they always got along together, with the raven last at the feast.

As Weasel turned his nervous eye about him, he knew that he had never seen so many wolves before. He had seen dozens and dozens, but not so many as these. They were coming in nearer to the horses—they were losing their fear. The horses were running—heads up, and blowing with loud snorts. Weasel's pony needed no whip; his dorsal action was swift and terrific.

The wolves did not seem to pay particular attention to him—they rather minded the herd. They gathered in great numbers at the head of the drove. Weasel could have veered off and out of the chase. He thought of this, but his blue eyes opened bravely and he rode along. A young colt, having lost its mother, ran out of the line of horses, uttering whinnies. Instantly a dozen gray forms covered its body, which sank with a shriek, as Weasel flashed by.

The leading ponies stopped suddenly and ran circling, turning their tails to the wolves, kicking and squealing viciously. The following ones closed up into the compact mass of horses, and Weasel rode, last of all, into the midst of them. What had been a line of rushing horses two arrow-flights long be-fore, was now a closely packed mass of animals which could have been covered by a lariat. In the middle of the bunch sat Weasel, with his legs drawn up to avoid the crushing horses. It was all very strange; it had happened so quickly that he could not comprehend. He had never been told about this. Were they really wolves, or spirits sent by the Bad Gods to destroy the boy and his horses?

All his waking hours had been spent with the ponies; he knew no other world; he had scarcely had any other thoughts. He was with them now, but instead of his protecting them they were protecting him. With their tails turned toward the circling mass of devil-animals, they struck and lashed when attacked. Nothing was heard but the snap of teeth, the stamp of hooves, the shrill squealing of horses, with an occasional thud followed by a yelp. The departing sun stole for a moment through a friendly rift in the clouds, encrimsoning the cold snow, and then departed, leaving the gray tragedy to the spirits of the night.

The smoke eddied from the top of the lodges; a bright spark showed from time to time as some one lifted an entrance flap; the ponies huddled in the dense bush; the dogs came out and barked at the wilderness of never ending plain. All was warmth and light, friendship, and safety,—even the baying wolf-dogs were only defying the shades and distances out beyond for their own amusement; it was perfunctory.

"Why does not my son come in with the ponies?" asked the foster-father of his squaw, but she could only answer, "Why?"

Wrapping his robe about him, he walked to the edge of the camp and stood long squinting across the dusky land. He saw nothing to encourage him. Possibly the ponies had come in, but why not the boy?

Oh! that was possible! That had happened! A long walk failed to locate the horses. Then he spoke to a chief, and soon all was excitement.

"The little white Crow and his horses have not come in," was repeated in every lodge.

"In the Middle of the Bunch Sat Weasel." *Authors' photoengraving.*

"The Sioux! The Sioux!" spoke the echo.

It was too dark for a search. "The Sioux" was the answer to every question, and no one hunted the Sioux by night. They might even now be on the outskirts. Swiftly the scouts made their way to the outposts. The warriors loaded their guns, and the women put out the fires. Every dog howled with all the energy of his emotional nature. There was no sleep for the Absaroke camp. It was seldom that an enemy got by the far-riding watchers of the Crow camps, but there was always a fear. It had happened.

Ba-cher-hish-a sobbed and wailed all night in her lodge, while the foster-father walked outside, speculating endlessly with his friends. Long before day he was mounted, and with a small party far on the way to the herd-grounds which he had chosen the day before.

As the plain began to unfold itself to their straining eyes, their quick ears ran ahead of them. A snarling, a horse-squealing, a curious medley of sounds, bore on them. Being old men, they knew. "It is the wolves," said they, almost in a chorus. Forward with a rush, a shrill yelling, and firing, swept the little party. The sun strove mightily to get over the mountains to help them. They now saw the solid mass of horses, with the wolves scurrying away on all sides. A faint answering human whoop came from the body of the beleaguered horse band. As the rescuers rode up, the ponies spread out from each other. Relieved from the pressure of the slimy fangs, the poor animals knew that men were better than wolves. Some of them were torn and bloody about the flanks; a few lay still on the snow with their tendons cut; but best of all which the Indians saw was little White Weasel sitting in the midst of the group. He allowed his robe to fall from his tight clutch. The men pushed their horses in among the disintegrating bunch. They saw that the boy's lips were without color, that his arms hung nerveless, but that his brave, deep eyes were open, and that they showed no emotion. He had passed the time of fear, and he had passed the time for hope, long hours ago.

They lifted him from his horse, and laid him on the ground, covered with many robes, while willing hands kneaded his marbled flesh. A fire was built beside him, and the old men marvelled and talked. It was the time when the gray wolves changed their hunting-grounds. Many had seen it before. When they sought the lower country, many grasses ago, to get away from the snow, one had known them to eat a Crow who happened in their way; this when he was a boy.

The wolves did not always act like this—not every snow. Sudden bad storms in the mountains had driven them out. The horse herds must be well looked after for a time, until the flood of wolves had passed down the valley.

The tired ponies stood about on the plain with their heads down. They, too, had become exhausted by the all-night fight. The sun came back, warm and clear, to see a more cheerful scene than it had left. Little Weasel spoke weakly to his father: "The Great Spirit came to me in the night, father, —the cold wind whispered to me that White Weasel must always carry a hoof of the white stallion in his medicine-bag. 'It is the thing that will protect you,' said the wind. The white stallion lies over there—cut down behind. Kill him, and give me one of his rear hooves, father."

Accordingly, the noble beast, the leader of the horses in battle, was relieved of what was, at best, useless suffering,—sacrificed to the gods of men, whom he dreaded less than the wolves,—and his wolf-smashing hoof did useful things for many years afterward.

CHAPTER IV

Crooked-Bear

White Weasel's tough body soon recovered from the freezing night's battle between the animals. It had never been shielded from the elements, and was meat fed. The horses ate grass, because their stomachs were so formed, but he and the wolves ate meat. They had the canines. In justice to the wolves, it must be said that all three animals represented in the fight suffered in common; for if the boy had chilled veins, and the ponies torn flanks, many wolves were stiffened out on the prairie with broken ribs, smashed joints or jaws, to die of hunger. Nature brings no soup or warmth to the creature she finds helpless.

The boy's spiritual nature had been exalted by the knowledge that the Good God had not only held him in His saving arms during the long, cold, snarling night, but He had guaranteed his continual protection and ultimate salvation. That is no small thing to any person, but to the wild man, ever in close communion with the passing of the flesh, to be on intimate terms with the something more than human is a solace that dwellers in the quiescent towns are deadened to. The boy was not taught physical fear, but he was taught to stand in abject awe of things his people did not understand, and, in consequence, he felt afraid in strange places and at inopportune times.

One evening, as the family to which White Weasel belonged sat about the blaze of the split sticks in their lodge, Fire-Bear, the medicine-man, entered, and sat down to smoke his talk with the foster-father. Between the long puffs he said: "Crooked-Bear wants us to bring the white Absaroke to him. The hot winds have come down the valley, and the snow has gone, so we can go to the mountains the next sun. Will you go with me and take the boy? The Absaroke must do as the Crooked-Bear says, brother, or who knows what may happen to us? The old man of the mountain is strong."

After blinking and smoking for a time the foster-father said: "The boy's and Crooked-Bear's skins are of the same color; they are both Sparrowhawks in their hearts. His heart may be heavy out there alone in the mountains—he may want us to leave the boy by his fire. Ba-cher-hish-a would mourn if this were done. I fear to go, brother, but must if he ask it. We will be ready when the morning comes."

When the dark teeth of the eastern mountains bit into the gray of approaching day, the two old Indians and the boy were trotting along, one behind the other. The ponies slithered in the pools and little rivulets left by the melted snow, but again taking the slow, steady, mountainous, stiff-legged, swinging lope across the dry plain, they ate the flat miles up, as only those born on the desert know how to do.

The boy had often heard of the great Crow medicine-man up in the mountains near where the tribe hovered. He seldom came to their lodges, but the Indians frequently visited him. Weasel had never seen him, for the boys of the camp were not permitted to go near the sacred places where the old man was found. He had requested this of the chiefs, and the Absaroke children drank the mystery and fear of him with their mothers' milk. He was one of the tribal institutions, a matter of course; and while his body was denied them, his advice controlled in the council-lodges. His were the words from God.

Weasel was in the most tremendous frame of mind about this venture. He was divided between apprehension and acute curiosity. He had left his mother sobbing, and the drawn face of his father served only to tighten his nerves. Why should the great man want to see White Weasel, who was only a herd-boy? Was it because his hair and his eyes were not the color of other boys'? He was conscious of this difference. He knew the traders were often red and yellow like him, and not brown and black as the other people were. He did not understand the thing, however. No one had ever said he was anything else than an Absaroke; he did not feel otherwise.

Approaching the mountains, the travellers found the snow again, and climbed more slowly along the game-trails. They had blinded their path by following up a brook which made its way down a coulée. No one left the road to Crooked-Bear's den open to the prowling enemy. That was always understood. Hours of slow winding took them high up on the mountains, the snow growing deeper and less trodden by wild animals, until they were among the pines. Making their way over fallen logs, around jagged boulders, and through dense thickets, they suddenly dropped into a small wooded valley, then up to the foot of the towering terraces of bare rock, checkered with snow, where nothing came in winter, not even the bighorns.

Soon Weasel could smell fire, then dogs barked in the woods up in front. Fire-Bear called loudly in deep, harsh Indian tones, and was answered by a man. Going forward, they came first to the dogs,—huge, bold creatures,—bigger and different than any Weasel had ever seen. Then he made out the figure of a man, low in tone and softly massed against the snow, and beside him a cabin made of logs set against the rock wall.

This was Crooked-Bear. Weasel's mind had ceased to act; only his blue eyes opened in perfect circles, seemed awake in him, and they were fixed on the man. The big dogs approached him without barking,—a bad sign with dogs. Weasel's mind did not concern itself with dogs. In response to strange words from the white medicine-man they drew away. Weasel sat on his pony while the older men dismounted and greeted Crooked-Bear. They did not shake hands— only "hat-wearers" did that. Why should an Indian warrior lose the use of his right hand for even an instant? His hand was only for his wife and children and his knife.

In response to the motion of his father's hand, the boy slid off his pony. Taking him by the shoulder, the father drew him slowly toward Crooked-Bear until they were directly in each other's presence. Weasel's eyes could open no farther. His whole training was that of an Indian. He would not have betrayed his feelings under any circumstances; he was also a boy, and the occasion was to him so momentous that he was receiving impressions, not giving them. A great and abiding picture was fast etching itself on his brain; his spongelike child-mind drank up every drop of the weird situation.

He had seen a few white men in his life. He had not forgotten Virginia City, though terror had robbed him of his powers of observation during that ordeal. He had seen the traders at the post; he had seen the few white or half-white men who lived with his people, but they were not like this one.

The old man of the mountain* was

* Old timers in Montana may remember a deformed man of wild mien and picturesque apparel who used to come into the mountain towns (there were none on the plains then) at rare intervals to do a little trading, with gold dust in payment. He would then depart for the Indian country, which was almost totally unknown to the mining people, and was often followed as far as white men dared to go. He was always a mystery. The Indians had driven the old trapping-men from the country, upon the approach of the white tide, and as yet the buffalo-hunter and cow-boy had not made their appearance.

crooked as his name implied. He also suggested a bear. He looked rude even to the Indians. It seemed that Nature had laid her hands on his shoulder and telescoped him together. He was humpbacked. His arms and legs were as other men's are, though his shortened body made his hands fall to his knees.

He was dressed in Indian buckskin, greased to a shine and bronzed by smoke. He leaned on a long breech-loading rifle, and carried a huge knife and revolver in his belt. His hat was made of wolfskin after the Indian fashion, from underneath which fell long brown hair, carefully combed, in profuse masses. Seen closely he was not old— merely past middle life. His strong features were weather-stained and care-hardened. They were sculptured with many an insistent dig by Nature, the great artist; she had gouged deep under the brows; she had been lavish in the treatment of the nose; she had cut the tiger lines fearlessly, but she had covered the mouth and lost the lower face in a bush of beard. More closely, the whole face was open, the eyes mild, and all about it was reposeful—sad resolution dominated by a dome of brain. Weasel warmed under the gaze of the kind face—the eyes said nothing but good; they did more than that: they compelled him to step forward toward the strange figure, who put his hand on Weasel's shoulder and led him tenderly in the direction of the cabin door. Weasel had lost his fear and regained the use of his mind.

As the men stooped almost on hands and knees to enter the den of Crooked-Bear, they were greeted by the acrid smell of smouldering ashes, and probably by other odors native to their noses. Crooked-Bear stirred the ashes and laid split wood on them. It was pine which spat and broke out in a bright flame, painting the wild figures against the smoked logs and rock wall. It illumined a buffalo-covered bunk, piles of *parfléche* full of dried meat, a saddle and pack panniers, cooking pots and pans on the hearth, all deeply sooted, a table and chair made with an axe, and in one corner some shelves, equally rude, piled with brown and dirty books. Many small knick-knacks intruded their useful presence as one looked with more care, but the whole was the den of a man of some remote century. The sabre-toothed tiger might snarl at the door but for the Sharp's rifle standing in the corner; that alone made time and distance.

"Your ponies must starve to-night, brother," spoke Crooked-Bear. "Go put them in my house where the horses live in summer-time. It is cold up here in the mountains—we have even no cottonwoods for them to eat. The bear and the wolves will not spring on them, though the big cats are about." All this said the white man in the language of the Absaroke, though it may be said it sounded strange in Weasel's ear. When he spoke to the dogs, the boy could not understand at all.

While the Indians looked after their ponies, the white man roasted meat and boiled coffee. On their return, seeing him cooking, Fire-Bear said: "Brother, you should have a squaw to do that. Why do you not take Be-Sha's daughter? She has the blood of the yellow-eyes in her. She would make your fire burn."

"Tut, tut," he replied, "no woman would make my fire burn. My fire has gone out." With a low laugh, Crooked-Bear added, "No woman would stay long up here, brothers; she would soon run away." Fire-Bear said nothing, for he did not understand. He himself would follow and beat the woman and make her come back, but he did not say so.

Having eaten, and passed the pipe, Fire-Bear asked the hermit how the winter was passing—how the dry meat was lasting—what fortune had he in hunting, and had any enemies beset him? He was assured his good friends, the Absaroke, had brought him enough dry meat, after the last fall hunt, to last him until he should no longer need it. The elk were below him, but plentiful, and his big dogs were able to haul enough up the hills on his sleds. He only feared for his tobacco, coffee, and ammunition; that had always to be husbanded,

being difficult to get and far to carry. Further, he asked his friend, the Indian, to take some rawhides back to the women, to be dressed and made into clothes for his use.

"Has my brother any more talking papers from the yellow-eyes? Do the white men mean to take the Sioux lands away from them? The Sioux asked the Absaroke last fall to help drive the white men out of the country, saying, 'If they take our lands to dig their badger-holes in, they will soon want yours.' The Absaroke would not help the Cut-Throats;† for they are dogs—they wag their tails before they bite," spoke Fire-Bear.

"Yes, brother," replied Crooked-Bear; "if you should, by aiding the Sioux, get rid of the white men, and even this you would not be able to do,—you would still have the Sioux, who are dogs, always ready to bite you. No, brother, have nothing to do with them, as I have counselled you. The Sak-a-war-te said this to me: 'Before the grass on the plains shoots, send a strong, fat-horse war-party to the enemy and strike hard. Sweep their ponies away—they will be full of sticks and bark, not able to carry their warriors that moon; tear their lodges down and put their fires out; make their warriors sit shivering in the plum bushes. That is the way for the Crows to have peace.' The Great Spirit has said to me: 'Tell the Absaroke that they can never run the buffalo on the plains in peace, until the Chis-chis-chash, the Dakotahs, and the Piegan dare not look them in the face. That, and that only, is the path.'"

Far into the night the men talked of the tribal policy—it was diminutive statesmanship, commercial politics with buffalo meat for money. As Crooked-Bear sat on his hewn chair, he called the boy to him, put his arm around him, and stood him against his knee. The youth's head rose above the rugged face of the master of Indian mystery; he was in his first youth, his slender bones had lengthened suddenly in the last few years, and the muscles had tried hard to catch up with them. They had no

† The Sioux.

"He Called the Boy to Him and Put His Arm Around Him." *Authors' photoengraving.*

time to do more than that, consequently Weasel was more beautiful than he would ever be again. The long lines of grace showed under the tight buckskins, and his face surveyed the old man with boyish wonder. Who can know what the elder thought of him in return? Doubtless he dreamed of the infinite possibilities of so fine a youth. He whose fire had gone out mused pleasantly as he long regarded the form in whom they were newly lighted.

Slowly he began to speak, using the Indian forms of speech, and supplementing them with the gestures which only Indians can command. "Brother, we have lived a long time. We have made the medicine strong for the Absaroke. We have taken the words of the Good Gods to the council-lodge when the tribe ran wildly and knew not which way to turn. We will follow soon the others who have gone to the Shadow-land. The Absaroke will be left behind, and

they must have wise men to guide them when we are gone. This young man will be one of those—I have seen that in my dreams. He must stay here with me in the lonely mountains, and I will teach him the great mystery of the white men, together with that of the people of his own tribe. He will visit his father's lodge whenever his heart is hungry. He owes it to himself and to his people to grow strong in the mystery, and then some day the tribe will lean on him. Shall he stay, brothers?"

White Weasel, with arms dropped to his side, made no move. The flame from the hearth lighted one of his starlike eyes as it stood open, regardful of the strange old man. The Indians passed the pipe, and for a long time there was no sound save the snapping of the fire and the pines outside popping with the cold.

At last Fire-Bear spoke: "We have had our ears open, brother. Your talk is good.

The Sak-a-war-te demands this. The boy shall stay."

Weasel's foster-father held his peace. His was the sacrifice, but the Great Spirit could not ask too much of him. In reply to another inquiry, he said that the boy should stay; then wrapping himself in his robe, he lay down before the fire to hide his weakness.

"Will you stay with me?" asked the Wonder-Worker of the boy, stroking his yellow hair and pouring the benevolence of his fire-lighted face in a steady stream on the youth.

"You have no ponies to herd, father. What shall I do?" he asked.

"I have no ponies for you to herd, but I have many mysteries here," tapping the boy's forehead with his finger, "for you to gather up and feed on, and they are greater than ponies."

"I will stay, father."

CHAPTER V

The White Medicine

That the sun rose with customary precision made little difference to the sleepers in the mountain den. Little of its light crept down the hole against the rock wall, and none of it penetrated the warm buffalo-robes. The dogs, growing uneasy, walked about and scratched at the door; they had not been disturbed by last night's vigil. Waking, one by one, the men threw off the robes and went out; all but the boy, who lay quite still, his vitality engaged in feeding the growing bones and stretching muscles.

Out by the stable Crooked-Bear said: "Take your ponies and that of the boy and ride away. They will starve here, and you must go before they weaken and are unable to carry you. A boy changes his mind very quickly, and he may not think in the sunlight what he did in the firelight. I will be kind to him. Tell Ba-cher-hish-a that her son will be a great chief in a few grasses."

Silently, as only the cats and the wolves and the Indians conduct themselves, the men with the led horses lost themselves among the trees, leaving Crooked-Bear standing by his abode with the two great cross-bred mastiffs, on their hind legs, leaning on him and trying to lick his face. As they stood together, the dogs were taller than he, and all three of them about the same color. It was a fantastic scene; a few goblins, hoarse mystery birds, Indian devils, and what not beside, might have been added to the group and without adding to its strangeness. Weasel had found a most unearthly home; but as he awoke and lay looking about the cabin, it did not seem so awfully strange. Down through the ages—borne through hundreds of wombs—in some mysterious alcove of the boy's brain had survived something which did not make the long-haired white man working about the fire, the massive dogs, the skins of wild animals, the sooty interior, look so strange.

As Weasel rose to a sitting posture on the bunk, the dogs got up also. "Down with you! Down with you, Eric! and you, Hope! You must not bother the boy," came the hermit's words of command. The dogs understood, and lay heavily down, but their eyes shone through heavy red settings as they regarded the boy with unarrested attention.

"I am afraid of your dogs, father; they are as big as ponies. Will they eat me?"

"No; do not be afraid. Before the sun goes over the mountains they will eat any one who would raise his hand against you. Come, put your hand on their heads. The Indians do not do this; but these are white dogs, and they will not bite any one who can put his hand on their heads," spoke Crooked-Bear in his labored way with the Indian tongue. He had never mastered all the clicks and clucks of it.

The meat being done, it was put on the table, and White Weasel was persuaded to undertake his first development. The hermit knew that the mind never waits on a starved belly, so he explained to the boy that only dogs ate on the ground. That was not obvious to the youngster; but he sat in the chair and mauled his piece of meat, which was in a tin plate. He drank his coffee out of a tin cup, which he could see was full better than a hollow buffalo horn, besides having the extra blandishment of sugar in it. As the hermit, occupying an up-turned pack-saddle opposite, regarded the boy, he could see that Weasel had a full forehead—that it was not pinched like an Indian's; he understood the deep, wide-open eyes which were the color of new ice, and the straight, solemn nose appealed to him also. The face was formal even to the statuesque, which is an easy way of saying he was good-looking. The bearer of these messages from his ancestors to Crooked-Bear quite satisfied him. He knew that the baby Weasel had been forcibly made to enter a life from which he himself had in mature years voluntarily fled, and for which neither was intended. They had entered from opposite doors only, and he did not wish to go out again, but the boy might. He determined to show him the way to undo the latching.

After breakfast began the slow second lesson of the white man's mystery. It was in the shape of some squaw's work, and again the boy thought unutterable protests. Crooked-Bear had killed an elk the day before, some considerable distance down the mountain, and taking his dogs with the sledges, they sallied down to get it. What with helping to push the heavy loads in aid of the dogs and his disgust of being on foot, at their noon home-coming White Weasel's interest began to flag.

Crooked-Bear noticed this, and put even more sugar into the boy's coffee. He had a way of voicing half-uttered thoughts to himself, using his native tongue, also repeating these thoughts as though to reënforce them. "I must go slow—I must go slow, or the boy will balk. I must lead him with a silken thread; the rawhide will not do—it will not do." Meanwhile the growing youth passed naturally into oblivion on the bunk.

"These Indians are an indolent people," the prophet continued. "They work only by fits and starts, but so am I indolent too. It befits our savage way of life," saying which, he put some coffee-berries into a sack and began pounding them with an axe. "I do not know—I do not remember to have been lazy; it does not matter now if I am. No one cares, and certainly I do not. I have tramped these mountains in all weathers; I have undergone all manner of hardships, yet they said I could not be a soldier in the armies down south. Of course not—of course not; a humpback could not be a soldier. He is fit only to swear at. Men would laugh at a crooked-back soldier. *She* could see nothing but my back. Ah—ah—it is past now. Men and women are not here to see my back; the trees and the clouds, the mountains and my dogs, do not look at my spine. The Indians say my back was bent by my heavy thoughts. The boy there has a straight back, and I hope he may walk among men. I will see that he does; I will give him the happiness which was denied me, and it pleases me to think that I can do this. I will create a happiness which the vicissitudes of this strange life seem to have denied him, saying, 'Weasel, you are to be a starved and naked nomad of the plains.' No! no! boy; you are not to be a starved and naked nomad of the plains. I have in my life done no intentional evil, and also I have done no intentional good; now this problem of the boy has come to me—how it reaches out its roots for the nourishing things and how its branches spread for the storms!"

Having accompanied these thoughts by the beating of the axe, the hermit arose, and stood gazing on the sleeping lad. "Oh, if I had only had your back!—oh! oh! oh! But if only you had had my opportunities and education—well, I am not a god; I am only a man; I will do what a man can."

When the boy awoke, the hermit said, "My son, did you ever make a gun speak?"

"No; my father's gun hangs with his mystery-bag on his reclining-mat, and a woman or child dare not lay their fingers on it."

"Would you like to make a gun talk?" came gently, but Weasel could only murmur. The new and great things of life were coming fast to him. He would almost have given his life to shoot a gun; to own one was like the creation, and the few similar thoughts of men; it was beyond the stars.

"Weasel," said the man, taking up a carbine, and calling him by name,—which is un-Indian,—"here is a gun; it loads in the middle; I give it to you; it is yours." With which he handed the weapon to the boy.

After some hesitation Weasel took the gun, holding it stiffly in front of him, as an altar-boy might a sacred thing. He could say nothing, and soon sat down, still holding the firearm, regarding it for a long time. When he could finally believe he was not dreaming, when he comprehended that he really did own a gun, he passed into an unutterable peace, akin to nothing but a mother and her new-born child. His white father stepped majestically from the earth that Weasel knew into the rolling clouds of the unthought places.

"To-morrow I will take my gun, and you will take your gun, and we will walk the hills together. Whatever we see, be it man or beast, your gun may speak first," proposed the prophet.

"Yes, father, we will go out with the coming of the sun. My heart is as big as the mountains; only yesterday I was a herd-boy, now I own a gun. This brought it all to me," the boy said almost to himself, as he fumbled a small bag hanging at his neck. The bag contained the dried horse's hoof.

Throwing back his long hair, the prophet fixed his face on his new intellectual garden. He saw the weeds, and he hardly dared to pull them, fearing to disturb the tender seeds which he had so lately planted. Carefully he plucked at them. "No, my son, that was not your medicine which brought the gun, but my medicine; the medicine of the white man brought it to you. The medicine of the white man brought the gun to you because the Great Spirit knew you were a white boy. The medicine of the white man is not caried in a buckskin bag; it is carried here." And the prophet laid his finger on his own rather imposing brow; he swept his hair away from it with a graceful gesture,

and smiling on the youth, he waited to see whether the seed had come up with the bad weed.

Weasel's hand left the bag, and followed down to the gun while he looked at his master. It might be so; no Indian boy whom he knew had ever had a gun. This firearm absorbed him, and the man felt it would continue to do so for some time to come; therefore he said no more.

Bright and early was the start of the hunters in the morning. They left the dogs in the cabin, and with snow-shoes slung to their backs, followed down the sledge-trail toward the bare foothills, where the game was. In and out among the shadows of the pine trees passed the figures, vigorous with the mountain ozone, and both happy in their respective ways. On reaching a proper place, they adjusted the broad, oval rackets, and skirted along the timber-line, watching the hills below them, from which the wind had blown the snow. It was not difficult to find game in those days, before the coming of the white men bearing their long-range rifles. Far our on the plain their trained eyes saw the bands of antelope, and, nearer, herds of mule-deer working about in the ravines. "But," said the boy, "my first shot must be at an elk or a bighorn, father."

"Come then, my son, we will go round this point of the hill, and on the sunny southern slope we will find the elk—great bands of them. You shall shoot one, and when you have done that, the herd-boy will be a hunter."

As had been predicted, in due course of their walk they beheld bands of elk lying about or walking slowly, their yellow backs gleaming in the morning sun. The warm winds from the valleys were coming up toward the arctic mountain-tops and away from the elk. "Take off your snow-shoes, my son; they creak on the snow—the elk will hear them; we must go down this ravine, and when we are near enough, you will shoot."

Under cover of the rocks and sparse pines they slowly made their well-considered way noiselessly, the boy's eyes blazing with the hunter's lust, and the old man watching him eagerly. From time to time the Weasel lifted his head above the rim-rock of the ravine to note the position of their approach, but the hermit's heedful eye bore only on his pupil. They had worked their way, after the hunter manner, a long distance downward, and hoped soon to be in a position for a safe shot. The cañon-like ravine which they were following narrowed suddenly; the snow lay in deep drifts against its sides, making it necessary for them to go slowly along the ledges of the rim-rock, the boy always first. As they were about to round the point where the coulée tightened, a big yellow form drifted like a wind-blown feather on to them; it suddenly appeared not twenty feet from their faces, and it was a mountain-lion. Both the men and the animal stopped, the men straightening up while the cougar crouched down. The cat bared its fangs, the boy raised his carbine; both were in search of game, but neither for what he had found. The gun reached its place; the coulée echoed with the heavy report, and through the enveloping smoke flew the great cat as though also impelled by gunpowder. The boy had not missed his mark, and the lion his only by a small margin. The steep snowdrift yielded under his frantic claws, carrying him many yards down the sides.

"Load your gun and shoot him, Weasel; I shall not shoot," came the hermit's voice. The position of his long rifle belied his words, but the youth did not look behind. He fumbled for a cartridge, was slow in working the strange mechanism of the arm, but he was ready by the time the cat, much frustrated by the unresisting snow, had nearly reached him. Again the cañon chorussed to the rifle, and as the heavy black powder-smoke drifted off on the friendly wind, the boy saw that he had killed. All had happened too quickly for his brain if not for his arm.

"Load your gun," came the voice of command in English. The tense situation made the new language strike Weasel's brain through his ear as his bullet had struck the monster. The sound of it was what conveyed the meaning, and the harsh bang of the words went home. An Indian would have had to gluck and cluck and glut for half a minute to make these three words plain. It would have sounded more like grace before meat than a command.

Weasel again broke his rifle and shoved the brass shell home, never looking elsewhere than at the yellow spot of fur on the white snow below him, as its fierce electric nerves slowly softened its expiring motions into quiet. He had never had even a dream of victory such as had taken form before him. He had known old Indian hunters who rode on a lion's skin in the ceremonial days, and he knew what warriors in the tribe wore the grizzly bear-claw necklaces—every one knew those men. Could it be that he would ride on a lion's skin? Could it be that he would carry a gun which loaded in the middle? Yes, it could be if he only had a horse, but ponies were easier than guns or lions' skins in the Indian world. What a vista of power and glory opened in the boy's mind! What vanity of his could not yet be satisfied?

The hermit glanced over the rim-rock and saw the elk in long lines trotting away; he could hear the joints cracking, but his cabin was full of meat. "Boy, this was a white man's medicine-hunt. Could any Indian do that for you?" But the boy heeded not; with a series of wolfish yells he slid down the snowy incline toward his fallen foe. The hermit followed, and drawing their knives, they raised the hide while the body was yet warm, taking head and tail and claws. Weasel was delirious with joy; he laughed and jabbered and ki-yied, while the pleased old man calculated that he had reduced the boy to a state of mind when it was safe to burden his wild young charge with something quite as serious for him as tigers' skins. He would make him begin his English.

They made their way back to the snow-shoes—back to the sledge-road—up to the cabin—received a welcome from the dogs; but the coffee had less sugar than before. Economy was a watchword with him who trailed his necessities over the long journey from the traders on pack-ponies, and so the lion skin tacked on the wall was enough for the boy.

Gradually the man brought English words into the play of conversation, and Weasel sought the key to the white medicine which had so exalted him. The nouns came first, and he soon began to piece them out with other parts of speech; his ear accustomed itself, and with it all came new and larger thoughts carefully strewn in his way by the prophet.

They hunted together; did the little healthy work found in their simple manner of life which no longer seemed fitted for women only; and the grave old man at last saw the spark which he had lighted burst into flame. It was the warmth of human kindness which is the base of everything ennobling to man.

One day when the buds of the leaves were beginning to show themselves, in response to nature's inviting smiles, the dogs barked furiously. The two dwellers of the cabin seized their rifles, ran out to places which had been selected by them for their strategic advantages in calm moments, and waited. Before long they heard challenges in the well-known Absaroke, which they answered.

"Do not talk English to your people, my son; they will not understand," said the hermit; but what he feared was their suspicion of the transformation of the lad. The Absaroke, no more than the Dakotahs, understood or loved the white man; they merely tolerated him for tribal reasons. The prophet had ingratiated himself by fortunate circumstances and an abounding tact.

The newcomers were a dozen chiefs of the tribe, the boy's Indian father among them. They drove a few led ponies belonging to Crooked-Bear, which they were returning after their wintering with the Absaroke herds. The quickly shooting mountain grasses would support them at this season.

Long and seemingly interminable talks followed the pipe about the prophet's blaz-ing hearth. He filled their minds with strong, sensible advice, reënforcing it by supposed inspired sources, until the tobacco which he had appropriated for such occasions gave out. It was a cheap and in fact the only way by which he could purchase immunity from violence—a safe wintering for his ponies and his fall supply of dried buffalo meat.

His influence was boundless, and while he hoped quite as much as the Indians that the white men would never come to these parts during his lifetime, he also knew that they would. He heard reports that the miners were invading the Sioux territory from the south; he knew gold, and he knew white men, and he realized what the combination always produced. In this strait he saw that the efforts of the Sioux would be so taxed to oppose the progress that the Absaroke would profit by their preoccupation. His revelations always favored the alliance between the Absaroke and the yellow-eyes. No one can ever know how much this forgotten hermit of the Chew-cârâ-âsh-Nitishic did for his race in the days when the Indians of the northern plains made their last stand before the white men. The Indians from King Philip's time never understood the powers, resources, and numbers of the white people. Even the Crows in those days wavered before the boastful envoys of the neighbor tribes. The Indians had hunted out of the country the Metis, the Pea-Soups, or the French half-breeds, together with the white-trappers, who had often contracted Indian marriages, and who had followed the fortunes of the early fur trade.

At that time old frontiersmen like Norris, who had for years followed up and down the plains, and across the range, admitted that a strong party of seasoned trappers was not safe east of the Big Horn Mountains.

The long palaver terminated with the Indians' promise to send out war-parties against the other tribes. The Weasel was not able to resist a very natural desire to go again to the camps, to visit his foster-mother, the boys of his childhood, and deeper yet to bear the gun and the lion's skin. The important men of the visiting party had come to regard White Weasel with some sort of veneration; he had that about him which was not quite understandable; he was supposed to be near the unknown Power.

CHAPTER VI
John Ermine

For a few days after the departure of the boy the hermit felt depressed; he had added a human interest to his life, which previously had been satisfied by communion with nature alone. The bugs, the plants, the birds, the beasts, the dogs, the hunting, had sufficed. The seat on the rock wall above the cabin, where he mused, and where his eyes went forward over interminable miles of cloud-flecked plain and tier after tier of ragged mountain ranges, had satisfied him, while his mind wandered backward among the years before he became a hermit.

But shortly the time arrived when he was compelled to make his semiannual trip with his pack-horses to the traders for his supplies of ammunition, of pots and pans, of tobacco, blankets, and foodstuffs, without which he could not exist. This journey was always tedious, hard, and dangerous; but he tried always to do it while the horses of the enemy out on the plains were thin and as yet unserviceable. With all the circumspection he was able to use, he had on several occasions nearly lost his life; but needs must, he could renounce everything on earth except his belly. However, this time he accomplished his journey, and aside from straying ponies, turning packs, with the other inevitables of desert life, he, safe and well provided, found his cabin again. The Indians had told him that White Weasel had gone with a war-party. That was nothing;— all men in the wild country were more or less at war all the time. "I hope the boy

keeps that corn-silk on his head," soliloquized the hermit; "also I think it would be a good thing for the young savage if he is forced to leave other people's alone. A fresh scalp in that boy's hand will make an extra year's work for me. It cannot be helped—it cannot be helped; it is the law of nature, only that law operates badly out here. What does it matter, however? The women can correct the loss of a man more or less in the world."

With the return of spring came the elk and bighorn. They walked into his park and blew their whistles as they smelled the odors from his hearth. The big gray bears came out of their winter caves and rumbled past his door. These were his greatest foes, constantly stampeding his ponies, even clawing at his heavy log horse-barn, where he always kept one horse to hunt the others with, and trying to circumvent his meat-arbor,—a device hung on a pole high up between two slender trees, which was operated up and down by a rawhide rope. Small black bears often put this out of action, but the dogs were usually able to chase these away. Not so with the silver-tips; for at times one of the playful brutes would come round to indulge himself in the sport of chasing Eric and Hope about the dooryard over their own preserves. They both had been slashed and hugged at intervals in their youth, and so took the big bears at their own estimate. The long, fifty-caliber rifle was called upon on such occasions, and thus far with success.

One day, at the beginning of summer, the boy returned to the hermit's nest,—was barked at, challenged, and finally greeted.

"Have you blinded your ponies' trail carefully, coming up from the valley? The enemy is abroad in the land these days," was asked and answered satisfactorily. The boy's features, which were rather grave in response to the seriousness of his life, were relaxed and beaming. There was an eagle feather in his hair, hanging down behind. He led the pony loaned by the prophet, which bore a bunch of buckskins, and was mounted on a fine animal, quite in the warrior class, with a new elkhorn saddle. His panther skin was rolled behind him. Dismounting, he carefully undid this, and from its folds drew forth a scalp—a braid of long hair, the skin stretched on a wooden ring and half covered down the plat with silver disks made of pounded silver dollars.

"It was a Dakotah, father, and I put his fire out with the medicine gun you gave me. I have danced it with the warriors; I am a warrior now."

The old man's worst fears had been realized, but after eating he had the story from White Weasel.

"When I reached the village, my father's and mother's hearts grew big at the sight of my gun and lion's skin. My mother had made the buckskins you sent down by my father into clothes both for yourself and for myself." Here he presented the hermit with his new dress, made beautiful with yellow ochre and with long fringes at back and sleeves, and open at the front, as was the white man's custom.

"Long-Horse," the boy continued, "was making up a party to go to the Dakotahs. I asked to be one of them, but he thought I was young. I said my medicine was strong and that my horse was fat. He said I was young to learn the war-path secret, but after smoking my talk he consented. I had only eight cartridges and one horse, all the other Indians having two apiece. Your old pack-pony is a warhorse now, father; he has carried a warrior," and the turquoise eyes gleamed brilliantly. "Long-Horse had a big band; we made the war-path medicine and travelled many sleeps with our backs to the sun. One morning our scouts found two men, an Absaroke and a white man, and brought them in. They belonged to the white warriors' camp, which was fighting the Dakotahs, who were all around them, and these men were going for help. Long-Horse moved toward this place guided by the men we had met. Before the sun was up, the Absaroke rode into the camp of the white soldiers, and they were glad to see us. They had the white cloth lodges and many wagons, but their horses had been taken by

the Dakotahs and they had lost some soldiers. The white men had put their dead men in the ground. I saw where they had dug in the earth and left mounds such as the prairie-dog builds. The camp was on the low ground, and back of this were bluffs. When the sun gave light, we could see the Cut-Throats swarm on their hill as the ants do when you lift a stone. There were five Cut-Throats to one white soldier, and the white men could not go out to them. While the white men had no women, they had more wagons than I could count, loaded with sugar and coffee until the wheels cut the ground. I never knew there was so much coffee and sugar; where does it come from, father? The white men are rich, and there are so few of them that each has more than he wants. In a place of that kind the Absaroke would have run away, but the white men cannot run, and they think more of the coffee and sugar than they do of their own lives. It made my head weak when I saw the enemy; they rode swiftly; they were all warriors, for they all had the war-feathers in their hair. They had guns, and as they rode they made the gestures of women and snakes and dogs at us. They rode away from a spot which they pointed at, and then they pointed at us, saying we were buffalo that always ran away like this. Long-Horse and the white chief, a big man with short hair, made a long talk. The Absaroke gave their old travelling-ponies to the white warriors, who put their own saddles on them. These white soldiers mounted the ponies on the wrong side, and tired as the horses were, they jumped like rabbits under them. Though I was afraid of the enemy, I had to laugh, father.

"When we were ready, we charged the enemy, and they fled before us; we followed them until they gained the rough hills. We fired at the Dakotahs, and they fired at us, they always working backward in the rough cañons, where we were afraid to follow on horseback because Long-Horse said they were trying to lead us into an ambuscade. All day we fought, although very few were killed. At night the white soldiers and many

Absaroke rode swiftly back to the camp. Long-Horse with half of the Absaroke stopped in the strong woods high up on one side of a ravine, and I stayed with them. I had only four cartridges left. All night we lay there and allowed their scouts to go down the cañon without firing on them. In the early morning we heard the Dakotahs coming; they rode down the cut before our faces, not knowing we were there. When Long-Horse gave his war-whoop, we all fired, and jumping on our ponies charged into them. The ground was covered with dying horses and men. My heart grew big, father; everything before my eyes swam red, and I do not remember much except that I rode behind a big Dakotah and shot him in the back. He fell from his horse to the ground and tried to gain his feet, but I rode the pack-pony over him, knocking him down so that he lay still. I turned round and shot him again before he died, and then I took his hair. He had a beautiful head-dress of feathers, which I took, but I left his gun, for it was heavy and a poor one. I chased his pony, the fine war horse which is out in the stable. The Dakotahs who were not killed had all run away, so I ran the dead man's pony back to camp, where with the help of other Indians I caught him. Long-Horse was killed, and a few Absaroke wounded, but we got many scalps, one of which is mine.

"The white soldiers took me to their lodge and gave me coffee which was heavy with sugar. They spoke your language to me, but I could not understand much of it. A half-Indian man talked the Absaroke for me in their tongue, and when I said I was a Crow,—for that is what the white men call us,—they laughed until my heart grew bad. They asked me if there were any more Crows whose hair was the color of the dry grass, and then they continued to laugh. They said I must have been born on a frosty morning. I did not know what to say, but I saw their hearts warmed to me, and I did nothing. They gave me cartridges, blankets, sugar, and coffee, until the old pack-pony could carry no more. The big chief of the

white men wanted me to stay with him, and promised to give me anything I wanted from the wagons. He talked long with the warriors, asking them to leave me with him, and the Absaroke said he could have me, but I did not want to stay. At one time I thought the white soldiers were going to make me stay, for they took me on their shoulders and carried me about the camp, laughing and yelling. I was afraid. Those men were bigger than Indians, and, father, their arms were as hard and strong as the gray bear's. They were always laughing; they roared like the buffalo bulls.

"My color is the same as theirs, father; many of them had hair like mine, though they cut it short. I am a Crow, but I do not understand these things." Whereat the boy fell into a deep meditation.

Cautiously the hermit approached. "Your heart warms to the white man, does it not, my son?"

"Yes, all white men are good to me; they give me everything I want; they are rich, and their hearts are big. They do not know how to keep their horses; they are fools about them, and they mount from the wrong side. I never heard a white man speak to a horse in that camp. When they walk up to a pony, the pony does not know whether they come as a friend or an enemy. Some day I am going to Ashar-Ra,* where the white soldiers live. They told me that when I came they would load my pony down with gifts. But I must first learn to talk as you do, father."

Here, at last, was light to brighten the hopes of the hermit. The boy's ambition had been aroused. What if he had gone to war, and what if he did have the much-treasured scalp in his possession? He had only followed the hermit's advice to his tribe concerning war. Then, too, the old man had picked up newspapers at the traders' which told of the invasion of the Black Hills by the white miners. He knew this would provoke war with the Sioux, and it occurred to him that the best possible way to introduce White Weasel to his own peo-

* Fort Ellis.

ple would be through contact with the army. He could go with them, and they might reclaim him. He could not possibly go through the industrial institutions, but he must speak English. There was plenty of time for that, since he could kill elk within a mile of his door with which to maintain himself. He would begin.

"Yes, you must work hard with me now to speak as the white men do. You will soon be a man; you are no longer a boy. You are a white man, but you were brought up by the Absaroke, and you will go back to your own people some day. The more you see them, the better you will like them."

"Why must I go to the white people, father? You do not go to them, and you are a white man."

The hunchback hermit leaned with his head on his hands for a long time; he had not foreseen this. Finally, "You will go because they are your own people; you will join them when they fight the Sioux. You think there are not many of them. Weasel, I am not a liar, and I say there are more white men on the earth than there are buffalo. You are young, you are brave, and you are straight in the back; their hearts will warm toward you. You will grow to be a white chief and own many wagons of coffee and sugar. Some day. Weasel, you will want a white woman for a wife. You have never seen a white woman; they are not like these red squaws; they are as beautiful as the morning, and some day one of them will build a fire in your heart which nothing but death can put out.

"From now on I shall no longer call you White Weasel, but will give you a white name which you must answer to. There shall be no Indian mystery about it, and you shall bear it all your life. I will call you,"— and here the hermit again relapsed into thought.

"I will call you John Ermine; that is a good strong white name, and when you are asked what it is, do not say White Weasel, —say, 'My name is John Ermine.' Now say it!" And the young man ran the thing over his tongue like a treble drag on a snare drum.

"Now again, after me: 'My—name—is— John Ermine.'" And the prophet cut the words apart with his forefinger.

John Ermine tried his name again and again, together with other simple expressions. The hermit ceased almost to address him in the Indian tongue. The broad forehead responded promptly to the strain put upon it. Before the snow came, the two had rarely to use the harsh language of the tribesmen. Gradually the pressure was increased, and besides words the hermit imposed ideas. These took root and grew in an alarming way after battling strenuously with those he had imbibed during his youth.

"And why is your name Crooked-Bear, which is Indian, while you are white?"

"My name is not Crooked-Bear, except to the Indians; my name is Richard Livingston Merril, though I have not heard the sound of it in many snows and do not care to hear it in many more. You can call me 'Comrade'; that is my name when you speak."

Sitting by their cabin door in the flecked sunlight which the pine trees distributed, the two waded carefully across the lines of some well-thumbed book, taking many perilous flying leaps over the difficult words, but going swiftly along where it was unseasoned Saxon. The prophet longed for a paper and pencil to accelerate the speed, but was forced to content himself with a sharp stick and the smoothed-out dirt before him. At times he sprinkled his sensitive plant with some simple arithmetic; again he lectured on the earth, the moon, and the stars. John Ermine did not leave a flat earth for a round one without a struggle, but the tutor ended up by carving a wooden ball which he balanced in his hand as he separated the sea from the land; he averred that he had known many men who had been entirely around it—which statement could not be disputed.

White Weasel had heard the men speak about the talking-wire and fire-wagon, but he did not believe the tales. John Ermine had more faith, although it puzzled him sorely. Raptly he listened to the long accounts of the many marvels back in the States, and his little Sioux scalp took a new significance as he tried hard to comprehend ten thousand men dying in a single battle of the Great White Man's war. Ten thousand dead men was a severe strain on his credulity when Crooked-Bear imposed it upon him. The ships which fought on the water he did not attempt at all; they were not vivid enough for his contemplation.

When were the white men coming to the Indian lands?

"Before you have a mustache, John Ermine, they will come in numbers as great as the grasshoppers, but you will not care; you are a white man."

Last but not least the prophet removed himself from his Indian pedestal in full sight of his ward. He was no prophet; he was only a man, and a poor specimen at that. Simply, and divested of much perplexity, he taught the Christian religion; told the story of Jesus, and had John Ermine repeat the Ten Commandments, which last the teacher could only marshal after many days of painful reflection, so vagrant are most men's memories as age creeps on.

CHAPTER VII

Transformation

Four years were passed by John Ermine in the cabin of the old man of the mountains, varied by visits to the Absaroke, which grew less frequent as he progressed along the white man's road, rude though the hermit's was. In the reflected light of the prophet he had a more than ordinary influence with the Indians. As his mind expanded, he began to comprehend their simplicity, and exactly why Crooked-Bear who did not violate their prejudices, could lead them by better paths.

The relationship of the two lonely men grew closer, and under the necessity of the case the hermit took Ermine to a mountain ravine some little distance from his camp. Here he operated a sluice, in connection

with a placer, in a desultory way, by which he was able to hive up enough gold dust to fill his wants from the traders. He exacted a promise from the lad that come what would he must never, by word or action, reveal the existence of this place. The hermit wanted only enough to cover his wants during his lifetime, and if no one located the place, Ermine could use it as he saw fit in after years. It would always supply his needs, and when the white men came, as they surely would, the boy might develop the property, but all would be lost without absolute secrecy. Even the Indians did not know of the placer; they always explained to the traders, when questioned concerning the hermit's gold dust, that he made it himself; his medicine was strong, etc. This they believed, and no trader could get farther. Beyond the understanding that gold dust represented the few things necessary to their simple lives, John Ermine cared no more for it than did the blue jays or the Arctic hares. The thing did not interest him beyond a rather intense dislike of the work entailed.

The hermit had often told him the story of himself and his gold. Years ago he had left the States, following the then gentle tide of adventurers who sought fortunes or found death in the unknown hills. He wanted forgetfulness, but his fellows craved gold. On one occasion he formed an alliance with a prospecting miner and an old trapper, relict of the fur-trading days, to go to a place in the Indian country, where the latter had in his wanderings discovered a placer. They outfitted in Lewiston, Idaho, and guided surely by the hunter, had reached the present scene of the hermit's domicile without accident. Finding their hopes realized, they built the log cabin against the rock wall.

As he told it: "We found the quartz-float and the miner followed it with a gold-pan. We were surprised to find we obtained colors almost from the first. We built the cabin, and put in our spare time in turning the water from the creek to one side of the gulch, so that we could get the sluice-boxes in place, and a proper flow for them, and, at the same time, work the gravel in the bottom of the creek without being inconvenienced by too great a flow of water. All this time we followed the trail to and from the cabin along the rock ledge, where no one but a goat would be apt to find it; and in every way we were careful not to attract wandering Indian hunters to ourselves.

"The miner worked slowly up the creek to where the gold became richer, until it finally petered out. He was then at a loss to account for the disappearance of the metal. This set him to thinking that he must have been working below a ledge where the gold originated. He then began to prospect for the lode itself, which, after due disappointment and effort, we found. It is the ledge which I have shown you, Ermine. The thing was buried in *débris,* and a discoloration of iron stains had confused the miner. He told me that the quartz would go a hundred dollars to the ton, and would make us all rich some day. Of course we did nothing with that, being content, for the present, with the gravel.

"We were high up on the range, away from any divides, and felt safe from wandering Indians. They could discover us only by chance, but by chance they did. One morning, when we had nearly completed the cabin, and were putting on the finishing touches, I was cooking at the fire when I heard a number of gunshots on the outside. I sprang to the half-opened door, and saw my two friends on the ground; one was dead, and the other was rolling about in agony on the pine-needles. A half-dozen Indians rushed out of the timber and soon finished their bloody work. I was so overcome, so unnerved, by the sudden and awful sight, that I could not move my hands or feet. Strangely enough, the Indians did not immediately advance on the cabin, fearing hostile shots. Since then I have found out that they knew by our tracks there were three of us. Taking positions behind trees, they waited. In the still air I could hear them talk to each other. I considered my situation hopeless, but very gradually regained my nerve. Knowing I could not defend the cabin, my mind acted quickly, as often a

man's will when he is in such desperate straits. Often I had heard the trapper, who had lived among Indians a great deal during his career, tell of their superstition, their reverence for the unusual, and their tolerance toward such things. At this time I cannot analyze the thought that came to me, but being only half dressed, I tore off my clothes, and getting on all fours, which the unusual length of my arms made possible, I ran out of the cabin, making wild noises and grotesque gestures. My faculties were so shattered at that time that I cannot quite recall all that happened. The Indians did not fire at me, nor did they appear from behind the trees. Growing weary of these antics, and feeling it was best not to prolong the situation, I worked my way toward them. If before this I had been frightened, when I came near two or three of these savages, and could look at them, it was easily seen that they were out of their minds. They were prepared for a man, but not for me. Straightening up, I walked directly to one of them and glared into his eyes. If I looked as wild as I felt, I do not wonder at his amazement. He dropped his gun, and bawled out in his native tongue, which, of course, at that time I did not understand. I answered in a soft voice, which chimed in well with his harsh howling. Presently the others came and gathered round me. I spoke in a declamatory manner for a long time, and one of them addressed some broken English to me. That man was Half-Moon, whom you know; there is French blood in him, and he had been with the traders, where he had picked up barely enough English to make himself understood.

"He asked me if I was a man, and I said, 'No, I was sent here by the Great Spirit.' I pointed to the sky, and then patted the earth, saying I lived in both places, and that when I had seen them kill white men I had come out of the ground to tell them that the Great Spirit was angry, and that they must not do it again. Oh, when I saw the weather clearing before me, I piled in my trumps; I remembered an actor named Forrest, whom you do not know, of course, but he had a way with him which I copied most accurately.

"The upshot of it all was that I gained their confidence, and felt they would not molest me so long as I could retain it. It was impossible for me to get out of their country, for there was no place in the world that suited me better. All of my worldly possessions were here, and once over the shock of the encounter, I did not especially value my life. You know the rest; no Crow comes near me, or even into this particular locality, except for reasons of Church and State. They have been good to me, and I mean to return it in so far as I can by my superior understanding of the difficulties which beset the tribe. My crooked back served me its only good turn then."

The Sioux and Cheyennes were pressed by the white tide from the south. It came curling in, roller after roller, despite the treaties with their government and in spite of the Indians who rode the country, hunting, shooting, burning, and harassing the invaders. The gold under their feet drew the huge, senseless, irresistible mass of white humanity upon them. It surged over the white soldiers who came to their aid; it flooded around the ends and crept between the crevices. Finally the reprisals of the Indians fused the white soldiers with the gold-hunters: it was war. Long columns of "pony soldiers" and "walk-a-heaps" and still longer lines of canvas-topped wagons trailed snakelike over the buffalo range. The red-men hovered and swooped and burned the dry grass ahead of them, but the fire-spitting ranks crawled hither and yon, pressing the Sioux into the country of the Crows, where great camps were formed to resist the soldiers. The poor Crows fled before them, going into the mountain valleys and inaccessible places to escape the war-ardor of the now thoroughly enraged enemy. These were lean years in the Absaroke lodges. Crooked-Bear and John Ermine dared cook their food only in the midday, fearing their smoke might be more readily seen in the quiet light of the morning and evening. They trembled after every shot at game, not

Wolf-Voice. *Painting in collection of St. Lawrence University (Ray A. Jubinville).*

knowing to whose ears the sound might carry.

Crows came sneaking into their camp, keen, scared, ghostlike creatures who brought news of the conflict. Bands of Crows had gone with the white men to ride the country in front of them. The white men could not make their own ponies run; they were as dull as buffalo; they travelled in herds, but when they moved forward, no Indians could stop them.

One day, through the shimmering heat, came Wolf-Voice, one of the messengers, with the tale how the Sioux had made a "surround" of pony soldiers on the Ease-ka-poy-tot-chee-archa-cheer* and covered a hill with their bodies. But said this one: "Still the soldiers come crawling into the country from all sides. The Sioux and the buffalo run between them. I am going down

* Little Big Horn.

the Yellowstone to help the white men. The soldiers make a scout rich."

Crooked-Bear spoke: "John Ermine, now it is time for you to play a man's part; you must go with Wolf-Voice to the soldiers. I would go myself but for my crooked back and the fact that I care nothing for either belligerents; their contentions mean nothing to me. My life is behind me, but yours is in front of you. Begin; go down the valley of the Yellowstone with Wolf-Voice; if the Sioux do not cut you off, you will find the soldiers. Enlist as a scout. I am sure they will take you."

The young man had felt that this hour would arrive, and now that it had come he experienced a particular elation. Early evening found him at the door of the cabin, mounted on one horse and leading his warpony beside him. The good-by word was all; no demonstration on the part of either man to indicate feelings, although they both were conscious of the seriousness of the parting. The horses disappeared among the trees, and the hermit sat down before his hut, intent at the blank space left by the riders. The revolt of his strong, sensitive nature against his fellows had been so complete that he had almost found happiness in the lonely mountains. While always conscious of an overwhelming loss, he held it at bay by a misanthropic philosophy. This hour brought an acute emptiness to his heart, and the falling shadows of the night brooded with him. Had he completed his work, had he fulfilled his life, was he only to sit here with his pale, dead thoughts, while each day saw the fresh bones of free and splendid animals bleach on the hillsides that he might continue? He was not unusually morbid for a man of his tastes, but his thoughts on this evening were sour. "Bah! the boy may come back; he has the habits of an Indian; he knows how to glide through the country like a coyote. The Sioux will not catch him, and I must wait and hope to see my good work consummated. Nature served that boy almost as scurvy a trick as she did me, but I thwarted her, d—— her!"

CHAPTER VIII
Playing a Man's Part

The two men rode silently, one behind the other, trailing their led ponies; the hoofs of their horses going out in sound on the pine-needles, anon cracking a dead branch as they stepped over fallen timber, or grunting under the strain of steep hillsides. Far across the wide valley the Shoshone range suddenly lost its forms and melted into blue-black against the little light left by the sun, which sank as a stone does in water. In swift pursuit of her warrior husband, came She of the night, soft and golden, painting everything with her quiet, restful colors, and softly soothing the fevers of day with her cooling lotions.

Wolf-Voice and John Ermine emerged from the woods, dog-trotting along on their ponies after the fashion of Indian kind. Well they knew the deceptions of the pale light; while it illumined the way a few steps ahead, it melted into a protecting gloom within an arrow's-flight. An unfortunate meeting with the enemy would develop a horse-race where numbers counted for no more than the swiftest horse and the rider who quirted most freely over the coulée or dog-town. The winner of such races was generally the one who had the greatest interest at stake in the outcome,—the hunted, not the hunter.

As the two riders expected, they traversed the plains without incident, forded the rivers, and two hours before sunrise were safely perched on the opposite range, high enough to look down on the eagles. These vast stretches of landscape rarely showed signs of human life. One unaccustomed to them would as soon expect to find man or horses walking the ocean's bed; their loneliness was akin to the antarctic seas. That was how it seemed, not how it was. The fierce savages who skulked through the cuts and seams made by erosion did not show themselves, but they were there and might appear at any moment; the desert brotherhood knew this, and well considered their footsteps. Seated on a rock pinnacle, amid brushwood, one man slept while the other watched. Long before nightfall they were again in motion. Around the camp, Indians are indolent, but on the war-path their exertions are ceaseless to the point of exhaustion. It was not possible to thread their way through the volcanic gashes of the mountains by night, but while light lasted they skirted along their slopes day after day, killing game with arrows which Wolf-Voice carried because of their silence and economy.

These two figures, crawling, sliding, turning, and twisting through the sunlight on the rugged mountains, were grotesque but harmonious. America will never produce their like again. Her wheels will turn and her chimneys smoke, and the things she makes will be carried round the world in ships, but she never can make two figures which will bear even a remote resemblance to Wolf-Voice and John Ermine. The wheels and chimneys and the white men have crowded them off the earth.

Buckskin and feathers may swirl in the tan-bark rings to the tune of Money Musk, but the meat-eaters who stole through the vast silences, hourly snatching their challenging war-locks from the hands of death, had a sensation about them which was independent of accessories. Their gaunt, hammer-headed, grass-bellied, cat-hammed, roach-backed ponies went with them when they took their departure; the ravens fly high above their intruding successors, and the wolves which sneaked at their friendly heels only lift their suspicious eyes above a rock on a far-off hill to follow the white man's movements. Neither of the two mentioned people realized that the purpose of the present errand was to aid in bringing about the change which meant their passing.

Wolf-Voice had no family tree. It was enough that he arrived among the traders speaking Gros Ventre; but a man on a galloping horse could see that his father was no Gros Ventre; he blew into the Crow camp on some friendly wind, prepared to make his thoughts known in his mother tongue or to embellish it with Breed-French or Chinook; he had sought the camp of the white soldiers and added to his Absaroke sundry "God-damns" and other useful expressions needed in his business. He was a slim fellow with a massive head and restless soul; a seeker after violence, with wicked little black eyes which glittered through two narrow slits and danced like drops of mercury. His dress was buckskin, cut in the red fashion; his black hat had succumbed to time and moisture, while a huge skinning-knife strapped across his stomach, together with a brass-mounted Henry rifle, indicated the danger zone one would pass before reaching his hair.

At a distance John Ermine was not so different; but, closer, his yellow braids, strongly vermilioned skin, and open blue eyes stared hard and fast at your own, as emotionless as if furnished by a taxidermist. His coat was open at the front as the white men made them; he wore blanket breeches encased at the bottom in hard elkskin leggings bound at the knee. He also carried a fire-bag, the Spencer repeating carbine given him by his comrade, together with an elk-horn whip. In times past Ermine had owned a hat, but long having outlived the natural life of any hat, it had finally refused to abide with him. In lieu of this he had bound his head with a yellow handkerchief, beside which polished brass would have been a dead and lonely brown. His fine boyish figure swayed like a tule in the wind, to the motions of his pony. His mind was reposeful though he was going to war—going to see the white men of whom he had heard so much from his tutor; going to associate with the people who lost "ten thousand men" in a single battle and who did not regard it as wonderful. He had seen a few of these after the Long-Horse fight, but he was younger and did not understand. He understood now, however, and intended to drink his eyes and feast his mind to satiety on the people of whom he was one.

As the sun westered, the two adventurers

blinded their trail in the manner most convenient at the time; a thing not so difficult to do in the well-watered northwest as in the dry deserts of the south; besides which the buffalo-hunting, horse-using Indians were not the equals of the mountain foot brethren in following trails. After doing this they doubled and twisted back on their track. While the sun was yet bright they broiled their evening meat on a tiny fire of dry sticks. Blowing the tobacco smoke to the four corners of the earth, Wolf-Voice said: "We will be rich, brother, if the Sioux do not get a chance to dry our hair; the soldiers always make their scouts rich; there is plenty to eat in their wagons, and cartridges cost nothing. The soldiers always fight; they are like the gray bears,—they do not know any better,—and then is the time when we must watch close to get away before the Sioux have an advantage of them. They are fools and cannot run. They are tied to the ground. If you get a chance to carry the talking papers from one white chief to another, they pour the money into your blanket. I have never had a paper to carry, but I think they will give you one. If they do, brother, we will take the silver and get one of the white soldiers to buy us a bottle of whiskey from the sutler." And Wolf-Voice's malignant features relaxed into a peaceful state which made Ermine laugh outright.

A bottle of whiskey and ten thousand dead men—quite a difference, thought Ermine. "That is it—that is it," continued the musing white man to himself; "he goes to war for a bottle of whiskey, and I go for ten thousand men." His unframed thoughts wrestled and twisted, lined and rounded, the idea of ten thousand men; yet the idea never took a form which satisfied him. Ten thousand buffalo—yes, he had calculated their mass; he had seen them. Ten thousand trees—that, too, he could arrange; he had blocked them out on the mountain-side. But there were many times ten thousand men who had not been killed; that he gave up altogether. Nothing had saved him but blind faith in his old comrade.

Leaving the mountains again, they stalked over the moon-lit land more like ghosts than men, and by day they lay so low that the crawling ants were their companions. By the Elk* River Wolf-Voice pointed to a long, light streak which passed through the sagebrush: "Brother, that is the sign of the white men. The buffalo, when they pass once, do not make a deeper path than that, and, brother, what is that in the road which shows so bright?"

Appropriating the gleaming thing, the Indian reached from his pony and picked it up, holding it close to his eyes for a moment before passing it to his companion. "What is that, brother?"

Ermine examined it closely, turning it in the moonlight. "I do not know; it is a paper; I will keep it until daylight."

A few steps ahead was found another glistening article, dropped by the passing soldiers. They knew what that was; it was the canteen, lost on the march, by a pony soldier. Wolf-Voice appropriated it.

"We must not stay here; the trail is old, but the Sioux will be near the soldiers. They are between us and the white men; you may be sure of that, brother," said one; and the four ponies stumbled off through the sagebrush, melting into the night.

They stopped for the day at the head of a rocky coulée, eating dried meat for fear of making a smoke. Ermine drew the paper from his pocket, laid it on the ground before him, and regarded it for a few moments; then he turned it round, seeing it was upside down by the writing on the bottom. "Bogardus," he read on the left-hand corner. The image on the card spread, opened, and flowered in Ermine's mind; it was a picture—that was plain now; it was a photograph such as he had heard Crooked-Bear tell about—an image from the sun. He had never seen one before. Wolf-Voice bent his beady eyes on the black and white thing, but it suggested nothing to him. Nature had not been black and white to his scarlet vision. The rude conventionalized lines

* Indian for Yellowstone.

painted on the buffalo-robes differentiated buffalo, ponies, and men, but this thing—"Humph!"—he lighted his pipe.

Before the persistent gaze of Ermine the face of a young woman unravelled itself from a wonderful head-gear and an unknown frock. The eyes looked into his with a long, steady, and hypnotic gaze. The gentle face of the image fascinated the lad; it stirred his imagination and added "a beautiful white woman" to his "ten-thousand-dead-men" quest. Wolf-Voice had to call him twice to take his watch, saying as he lay down, "Put the paper away, brother; it takes your eyes from the Sioux."

The travellers could not make long journeys in the short summer nights through the open country, and exercise a proper vigilance at the same time. The moon rose later every night, thus cutting their time. Neither did they see any signs of human beings or know where to find the white men; but recourse to the trail along the river, from time to time, assured them that the wagons had continued down the stream. The trail was very old, and was full of Indian pony-tracks which had followed it.

One day as they lay in a washout, Wolf-Voice pointed to columns of dust far to the south. Was it buffalo, Indians, or soldiers? The dust stayed all day in one place; it might be a buffalo-surround or big herds about camps, but this they were not able to determine.

"We will go to the dust this sleep and we will ride the war-horses; the others which we have been riding are stiff and sore; we will leave them here and come after them if we can," spoke Ermine as he braided the tail of his favorite pony. When Wolf-Voice's attention was directed elsewhere, he took his medicine, the dried hoof of the white stallion, and rubbed it gently on his pony's heels. The prophet would not approve of this, he felt, but it could do no harm, since he also prayed God to make his pony run fast and not stumble, to blind the Sioux, stop their ears, and otherwise to cherish appropriately the poor life of John Ermine

who believed in Him and now wanted His help.

Slowly they made their way south through the gloom, trusting their range-bred ponies to pick out the footing. Hour after hour they stepped along, stopping at intervals to listen.

Late at night as they made their way down a long ridge, they heard a horse whinny somewhere far down in one of the breaks of the land. Without a word they turned away from the noise. Later Wolf-Voice whispered: "Indians; the white men never let their horses loose in the night. That pony was alone, or we should have heard more sounds. He was calling his brothers. Now we must blind our trail; their scouts will find it in the morning."

Accordingly they allowed their horses to feed slowly along, not attempting to guide them, and after a mile felt that any one who should follow those tracks would think that they were loose horses grazing. By the light of the late moon they made their way more quickly, but always stopping to separate the sounds of the night—the good sounds from the bad. They could see that they were coming to the river, and as they rose on a wave of the land, they saw a few faint sparks glitter far down the valley.

"It is the white soldiers—the big fires of the white men, brother. We will go in when the sun comes up. If we should go near them now, they would fire at us. The white men shoot at anything which moves in the dark; a wolf is not safe near their camps when the sun has gone."

Before the gray of morning they were safely ensconced under a bluff, waiting for the daylight and within a mile of the long line of Sibley tents. They heard the hungry mule chorus, the clank of chains, the monotonous calls of the sentries; and the camp slowly developed before their eyes like a photographic negative in a bath of chemicals; then John Ermine began to understand ten thousand men.

Softly the metallic réveille drifted to their ears; it spread from one group of tents to

"Halt! Who Goes There." *Authors' photoengraving.*

another until the whole air danced with the delightful sound. The watchers on the sagebrush hillside were preoccupied with the movements of the soldiers. They listened to the trumpets and saw the men answer them by forming long lines. In a moment the lines broke into hurrying individuals, the fires began to send up the quiet morning smoke, while the mule chorus ceased.

As though shot out of the ground by some hidden force, Wolf-Voice bounded up. "G—— d——! Mit-wit!† Coo-ley!"* he

† Get up!　　* Run!

yelled, and as responsive as a swallow which follows the swift flight of another in play, Ermine bounded on to his horse. One look behind told the story. The Sioux were coming. He saw the lightning play of the ponies' legs, heard the whips crack on their quarters, and was away like a flash, bearing hard on the soldier camp. Before many bounds he recovered from his surprise; it was not far, and his horse was answering the medicine. He had never run like this before. The Sioux had found and followed their trail and had nearly caught them nap-

ping. After their long journey they had almost been cut off during the last mile of it.
Seeing that their prey had escaped, the
Sioux swerved like hawks, pulling up on the
hill.

Turning, Wolf-Voice and Ermine shouted
back taunts at them, fired their guns at the
group, and then leisurely loped toward the
camps. While yet quite a way out, three
white soldiers rose suddenly from a dry
wash with their rifles: "Halt! Who goes
there?"

The riders drew down to a walk, Wolf-
Voice raising his hand in the peace sign,
and saying, "We are your frens, we aire two
Crow Enjun; don' shoot!" and continued to
advance.

The soldiers stood with their guns in
readiness, while one answered: "Get off
them ponies; lay your guns on the ground.
I guess you are all right." And then, looking
at Ermine with a laugh: "Is that blonde
there a Crow? Guess them Sioux scared him
white. I've often heard tell of a man's hair
turning white in a single night."

"Ach sure, Bill, and it don't tourn a
mon's face red to be schared sthiff," observed another picket.

The faintest suggestion of a smile stole
over John Ermine as he comprehended.

"No, soldiers, we are not afraid. Why
can't you let two men go into the big camp;
are all those soldiers afraid of two men?"
And the pickets laughed at the quaint conjecture. Shortly an officer rode up on a
horse and questioned Ermine.

"Who are you?"

"We are friends of the white people. Did
you see that we are not friends of the
Sioux?"

"Yes; I saw those Indians chase you.
Were they Sioux?"

"We took that for granted." And again
the corner of John Ermine's mouth relaxed.

"Yes, of course, I admire your judgment;
come with me," replied the officer, as he
turned to ride back. The three ambled along
together. "Who are you?"

"I am a white man, and my comrade is an
Indian."

"What is your name?"

"My name is John Ermine, and I want to
be a scout. Will you take me?"

"That is not my business; but I have no
doubt the proper authority will be glad to
put you on the pay-roll. You don't seem
any more popular with the Sioux than we
are."

CHAPTER IX

In Camp

The three horsemen jogged into camp,
and it can hardly be stated who was the
more impressed by the sight—John Ermine
as he passed through the crowds of soldiers,
or the soldiers as they looked at the barebacked rider with the yellow braids and the
glaring handkerchief. They had left their
impedimenta with the worn-out ponies back
in the hills with little hope of recovering
them. The gathering men who had seen the
chase gave tokens of their approval by yelling *Ki-yis* in imitation of the Indians. "Say,
Yellow, you're no brevet"—"You wa'n't
crazy to wait for them Sioux"—"The general will feed you on mince-pie"—"You'll
be a sergeant in the rag-bag troop," and
other expressions numerous and 'uncooked'
fell on their ears. Ermine felt embarrassed
with the attention of so many people
centred on him, but his face was cut to
stand such shocks. His swift glances about
the thronging camp began to illumine the
"ten-thousand-men" proposition; he saw
lines of tents, wagons without end, but no
women; he would have to postpone that
feast.

The officer leading stopped in front of a
tent around which many officers and men
were standing or coming and going. He
spoke to one who wore a big hat and a split
blond beard, a man less pretentious in his
garb than any about him, but whose eye
arrested Ermine by the commanding keen-

ness. Dismounting, the officer, saluting, said: "General Crook, these two men were just chased into camp by Indians. They say they are Crows, or at least from the Crows, and they want to be made scouts."

"What Indians chased you?" asked the general.

"We do not know; we were waiting on the hill to come in here by daylight; they surprised us, and we did not stop to talk with them," replied John Ermine.

"Where did you come from, my boy?" he continued.

"I came from the Stinking Water country to help you fight the Sioux—myself and Wolf-Voice there," replied Ermine.

Turning to that waif, the general said, "Who are you?"

Patting his chest impressively, Wolf-Voice spoke: "Me? My mother she was Gro Ventre; I am a warrior; I spak de English; I was scout with Yellow Hair.* I am brav mans."

"Umph—no doubt," softly hazarded the Gray Fox. "You were not with him when he died? I suppose you attended to that matter with proper thoroughness. Have you seen any Sioux signs?"

"Yaas—day follar de wagon, dey aire leave dar pony-track all roun you."

Once fastening his quizzical eyes on the white lad, the general asked, "Do you talk Crow?"

"Yes."

"Can you make the hand talk?"

Ermine gave the sign for "Yes."

"Have you ever been to school?"

"No, sir."

"Who taught you to speak English?"

"My old comrade, Crooked-Bear," said Ermine.

"Crooked-Bear—Crooked-Bear," mused the general. "Oh, I give it up," as he turned away. "You are not one of the Pike County breed, it seems—Crooked-Bear—Crooked-Bear. Take them to the scout camp, Ferguson." And the general retired to his tent, somewhat perplexed by the young man's make-up.

* General Custer

The trio went on toward the scout camp, and as they passed a man on foot he inquired of Ferguson, "Where did you get that pair of aces?"

"The Sioux dealt them to me this morning; will they fill your hand?"

"Yes, sir—think they will." Then to John Ermine, "Do you savvy this country, pardner?"

"Yes, sir; I have always lived in this country," spoke he, with a wave of his arm around the horizon which had the true Indian swing to it, an accomplishment only acquired by white men after long years of association with the tribes. All the signs and gestures made by Indians are distinctive with them and are very suggestive from their constant use of the sign language. The old chief of scouts recognized the significance of the motion on the instant, and knew that one who could make it very probably possessed the other qualifications for his corps.

"What is your name?"

"John Ermine, sir," came the answer. The "sir" had been an acquisition of the last few interviews. He had heard it from the mouth of Crooked-Bear on infrequent occasions, but his quick perceptions told him that it was useful in these canvas towns.

"All right. Will you turn these men over to me for duty, Lieutenant Ferguson?" spoke the chief of scouts, who was a short infantry officer with a huge yellow mustache.

"I will," replied Ferguson, as he turned his horse. "Go with Captain Lewis there; and good luck to you, Mr. Ermine."

After answering certain questions by the chief of scouts, which were intended to prove their fitness for the job, the two late fugitives had the pleasure of knowing that Uncle Sam would open his wagons to them in return for their hair and blood when his representative should order the sacrifice. Wolf-Voice never allowed his mind to dwell on market values, and John Ermine felt that he could do what "ten thousand men" were willing to do in an emergency.

Having done with these formalities, under

the trained guidance of Wolf-Voice the two men speedily found their way to the scouts' mess, where they took a hearty toll of the government. About the cook fire squatted or sprawled the allies of the white troops. There were Crows and Indians from other tribes—together with half-breeds whose heraldic emblazonment ought to be a pretty squaw. A few white men came about from time to time, but they did not abide with the regular crew. New faces appeared as they came in from the hills to "cool coffee."

John Ermine walked aimlessly around camp, all eyes and ears. No backwoods boy at a country fair ever had his faculties so over-fed and clogged as he. In turn the soldiers attempted to engage him in conversation as he passed about among them, but the hills had put a seal of silence on his lips; he had not yet found himself amid the bustle.

Remarks which grated harshly came to his ears; the unkindness of them undermined the admiration for the white soldiers which the gentle treatment of the officers had instilled.

"Ain't that yellow handkerchief great?"—"Sure he'd do well with a hand-organ on the Bowery."—"Is he a square shake or a make-up?"—and other loose usage of idle minds.

"Say, Bill, come look at the sorrel Injun," sang one trooper to another who stood leaning on a wagon-wheel whittling a stick, to which that one replied: "You take my advice and let the sorrel Injun alone; that butcher knife on his belly is no ornament."

Captain Lewis. *Authors' wood engraving.*

By noon Ermine's mind had been so sloshed and hail-stoned with new ideas that his head was tired. They were coming so fast that he could not stow them, so he found his way back to the scout camp and lay down on a stray robe. The whole thing had not impressed him quite as he had anticipated; it had a raw quality, and he found he did not sift down into the white mass; he had a longing for the quiet of Crooked-Bear's cabin—in short, John Ermine was homesick. However, after a few hours' sleep, he became hungry, which shifted his preoccupation to a less morbid channel.

The scouts talked excitedly of the enemy with whom they had skirmished out on the hills; they discussed the location of the Sioux camp, and speculated on the intention of the Gray Fox. Sunlight or firelight never in the ages played on a wilder group than this; not on the tribes of Asiatics who swarmed in front of Alexander; not in the deserts of Northern Africa: nor on the steppes of Asia, at any period, did sun or fire cut and color cruder men than these who were taking the long, long step between what we know men are and what we think they were.

A soldier stepped briskly into the group, and touching Ermine on the shoulder, said, "The Captain wants to see you; come on." He followed to the tent designated, and was told to come in and sit down. The officer sat opposite, on a camp stool, and after regarding him kindly for a moment, said: "Your name is John Ermine and you are a white man. Where were you born?"

"I do not know, Captain, where I was born, but have lived all my life with the Crows."

"Yes; but they did not teach you to speak English."

"No; I have lived some years with my old comrade up in the mountains, and he taught me to speak English and to write it."

"Who was your old comrade, as you call him? He must have been an educated man," queried the Captain, looking insistently into Ermine's eyes.

"Captain, I cannot tell, any more than to

say that he is an educated white man, who said he is dead, that his fires have burnt out, and he asked me not to speak about him; but you will understand."

Captain Lewis did not understand, nor did he avert his perplexed gaze from Ermine. He was wondering about the boy's mind; had it become deranged? Clearly he saw that Ermine had been a captive; but this mystery of mind cultivation by one who was dead—had he struck a new scheme in psychical research? The Captain rolled a cigarette and scratched a match on the leg of his breeches.

"My old companion told me I ought to come here and help fight the Sioux."

"Have you ever been to war?"

"Yes; I took a scalp from a Sioux warrior when I was a boy, and I wear the eagle feather upright," spoke Ermine in his usual low and measured voice.

"Ho, ho! that is good. I see that you carry a Spencer carbine. I have not seen one lately; we do not use them now."

"It is the best I have, Captain." The Captain took his cigarette from his mouth and bawled: "Jones! *Oh* Jones, Jones!" Almost instantly a soldier stepped into the tent, touching his forehead in salute. "Go down and draw a carbine, fifty rounds, a saddle, blanket, and bridle." Jones disappeared. "Oh, Jones, Jones, and a shirt and hat." Then turning to Ermine, "Do you ever wear shoes?"

"Only this kind I have on, sir."

"Do you want some shoes?"

"No; I think I am better off with these. I have tried on the heavy leather shoes, but they feel as though my feet were caught in a trap."

"Ha, ha! a trap, hey—a good deal so; well any time you want anything come to me. And now, my boy, may I give you a little advice?"

"You may, sir; I shall be glad of it. I know I have much to learn," assented John Ermine.

"Well, then, you are an odd-looking person even in this camp, and that is saying much, I can assure you. I will have a hat

here in a moment which will displace that high-art headgear of yours, and may I ask if you will not take your hair out of those braids? It will be more becoming to you, will not be quite so Injuny, and I think it will not interfere with your usefulness."

"Yes, sir, I will," quietly said the young man, who forthwith undid the plats with a celerity which comes to the owners of long hair. Having finished, he gave his head a toss; the golden tresses, released from their bindings, draped his face, falling down in heavy masses over his shoulders, and the Captain said slowly, "Well, I will be good God-d—d!"

After having soothed his surprise by a repetition of this observation several times, the Captain added, "Say, you are a village beauty, Ermine, by Gad—I'd like a photograph of you." And that worthy continued to feast his eyes on the bewildering sight. It seemed almost as though he had created it.

The orderly entered at this point, loaded down with quartermaster and ordnance stuff. His hat had found its way on to the back of his head during these exertions, and he came up all standing, but the discipline told. All he did as he gazed helplessly at Ermine was to whistle like a bull elk. Quickly recovering himself, "I have the stuff, sir,—but—but I'm afraid, sir, the hat won't fit."

"All right, all right, Jones; it will do." And Jones took himself out into the darkness. To a passing comrade he 'unloaded': "Say, Steve, you savvy that blond Injun what was run in here this morning? Well, he's in the Captain's tent, and the Captain has got him to take his hair down, undo them braids, you see; and say, Steve, I am a son-of-a-gun if it ain't like a bushel of hay; say, it's a honey-cooler. You will fall dead when you see it."

Meanwhile Ermine was put in possession of the much-coveted saddle and a new gun, one with a blue barrel without a rust-spot on it anywhere, inside or out. His feelings were only held in leash by a violent repression. The officer enjoyed the proceedings hugely as the young man slipped into the new shirt and tied the yellow handkerchief round his neck. The campaign hat was a failure, as Jones had feared. It floated idly on the fluffy golden tide, and was clearly going to spoil the Captain's art work; it was nothing short of comical. Frantically the officer snatched his own hat from his camp-chest, one of the broad rolling sombreros common on the plains in those days, but now seen no more; this he clapped on Ermine's head, gave it a downward tug together with a pronounced list to the nigh side. Then, standing back from his work, he ran his eyes critically for a moment: "Good! now you'll do!"

Ermine's serious face found itself able to relax; the ripples broadened over it, his eyes closed, and his mouth opened ever so little, only escaping looking foolish by the fact that he had a reserve; he did not close or broaden too much.

"Well, my boy," said the officer, as he began to put up his papers on the chest, "go down to camp now; the outfit moves tomorrow; you'll do in a free-for-all, by Gad."

When this greeted the easy ears of our hero, he found the loud bustle, so characteristic of the white soldier, more noisy than ever. Slowly the dancing refrain passed from regiment to regiment. The thing itself is dear to the tired soldier who dreads its meaning. It was always a merry beginning, it accords with the freshness of the morning; when associated with youth it never fails to cheer the weary dragging years of him who looks behind.

The tents fluttered down; men ran about their work, munching crackers and hot bacon; they bundled and boxed and heaved things into the escort wagons. Teamsters bawled loudly—it is a concomitant with mule association; yet they were placid about their work of hooking up; their yells never interfered with their preoccupied professionalism. The soft prairie winds sighing through the dreaming teamster's horse-blankets fills his subconscious self with

cracks, whistles, howls. "You blaze!"—"Oh, Brown!"—"D—— you, Brigham!"—, ——, ——, and other phrases which cannot be printed. That mules and teamsters have never received a proper public appreciation of their importance in war is one of the disheartening injustices of the world. Orderlies and mounted officers tore about; picturesque men who had been saved from the scrap-heap of departing races ranged aimlessly or smoked placidly; they had no packing to do, their baggage was carried in their belts. One of these was John Ermine, who stood by his pony, watching Captain Lewis; this busy man with his multitudinous duties had been picked out for a guiding star. Having presently completed all the details, the Captain mounted and rode away, followed by his motley company. The camp being cleared, the officer turned, and with a wave of his hand which covered the horizon in its sweep, yelled, "Go on now; get to the hell out of here!"

In quick response the wolfish throng broke apart, loping away over the yellow landscape flaming out toward all points; the trained skirmishers trusted their instincts and their horses' heels. John Ermine rode slowly over a hill, and looking backward, saw the long, snakelike columns of horse and foot and wagons come crawling. It was the most impressive sight he had ever beheld, but he could not arrange any plan in his own mind whereby the command was going to fight the Sioux. All the Indians in his world could not and would not try to stem that advance: as well try to stop the falling of the snow or the swarms of grasshoppers. Again, there was no necessity, since the command could no more catch the Sioux than it could reach the sailing hawks or flapping ravens.

Keeping his sharp eyes circling, Ermine mused along. Yes, he remembered what Crooked-Bear had said: "The white men never go back; they do not have to hunt buffalo in order to live; they are paid by the year, and one, two, even a lifetime of years make no difference to them. They would build log towns and scare away the buffalo.

The Indians could not make a cartridge or gun," and other things which he had heard came into his mind. It was the awful stolidity of never ending time which appalled Ermine as he calculated his strategy—no single desperate endeavor would avail; to kill all those men behind him would do the Sioux no good whatever. In single battles the white men were accustomed to leave more men than that, dead, on the field. Still, think as he would, the matter was not clear to him. A mile away on his right he saw a friendly scout rise over a bluff; the horse and man made a dot on the dry yellow grass; that was the difference between the solid masses of dust-blown white men behind him and the Indian people; that sight gave him a proportion. If all these white men were dead, it would make no difference; if that Indian on the far-off hill was dead, he could never be replaced.

John Ermine felt one thing above all this abstraction: it was a deep-seated respect for the Sioux personally. Except when a fellow-scout occasionally showed himself in a distant rise, or he looked behind at the dust-pall over the soldiers, there was nothing to be seen of the Sioux; that was another difference, and one which was in no wise re-assuring to Ermine. The dry, deserted landscape was, however, an old comrade, and acted as a sedative after the flutter of the camps. The camp held dozy, full-bellied security, but these silences made his ears nervous for a rattle of shots and a pat-a, pat-a, pat-a, of rushing ponies. That is how the desert speaks.

CHAPTER X

A Brush with the Sioux

The days saw the big serpents of men crawl on and on—hither and yon over the rolling land, saw them splash through the rivers, wind round the hills, and lie comfort-

ably down at night. About them fluttered the Indian scouts like flies around a lamp,—hostiles and allies,—marking down each other's sign, dashing in and out, exchanging shots, but always keeping away from the coils of the serpents.

Many men besides Captain Lewis held out their hands to Ermine, attracted as they were, first by his picturesque appearance, fine pony, and seat, and Lewis's enthusiasm; but later by his low-voiced simplicity and acute knowledge concerning the matters about them. They in turn unravelled many tangled skeins for Ermine; regiments began to unwind into companies, details, squads; the wagons assorted themselves, and it was not long before the young scout could tell a colonel from a cook's police at a glance. Numbers of these men had seen the ten thousand men die, had been with them when they died, had even, some of them, lain down with them sapped by their own wounds, though of course they had not died. One big man slapped Ermine on the back hard enough to make him cough, and said, "I'd rather take my chance at Cold Harbor than go poking round the hills alone as you do, my boy." And Ermine had to move away quickly to avoid another exclamation point, but such little appreciation warmed him. Also the solidarity of these fellowships took the more definite form of a Colt's revolver, a copy of Upton's tactics, a pocket Bible, a comb from a bald-headed man who respected the unities, together with trifles enough to litter up his saddle-bags.

Old Major Ben Searles in particular used to centre his benevolent eyes on Ermine. He had a boy back in the States, and if he had gone to some other school than West Point might have been a superintendent of an orphan asylum as easily as the soldier which he was. Ermine's quaint questions gave him delicious little mental jolts.

"Why is it, Uncle Ben," asked Ermine, "that all these men come out here to march, get killed, freeze, and starve? They don't have any wives, and I can't see what they have to protect except their eatables."

"You see, Kid, they enlist to do what the government wants them to do, and the government wants them to make the Sioux stop killing white folks just now."

"Yes, but they won't do it. Why don't the government mount them on buffalo ponies, make them eat dried meat, and run after the Sioux instead of taking the villages to war?"

"Well, Ermine, I don't know why. I suppose that is what the Indians would like them to do, and I reckon that is the reason the soldiers don't do it. Soldiers calculate not to do what the enemy wants them to do. Don't you get discouraged; wait a year or two or three, my boy. Oh, we'll get there; we don't know how, but we always stand pat!"

"Pat? pat? What do you mean by 'standing pat'? Never heard that word. What does it mean?" questioned the young man.

Old Searles laughed. "'Pat' is a word we use in a game of cards, and it means that when you think you are licked you guess you are not. It's a great word, Ermine."

The huge column having crawled over the country as far as it was ordered, broke into divisions, some going down the river in steamboats and other parts through the hills to their far-off posts and cantonments.

The Sioux scouts regarded this as a convenient solution of the awkward situation. Neither they nor the white men could do anything with that unwieldy gathering. Two infantry regiments stayed behind as a re-

Major Ben Searles. *Authors' wood engraving.*

minder to the Sioux that the game was not played out. To one of these Captain Lewis was attached, which good fortune gave Ermine continued employment.

The soldiers began to build winter cantonments at the mouth of the Buffalo Tongue River, or, as the white men called it, "The Tongue," and to gather great quantities of stores which were hauled from Fort Benton. Here was something that the Sioux could attack; they jumped the trains savagely, burned the grass, cut in on the animals to stampede, and peppered up the men as they slept. Stores the troops must have; and though they met repulse at times, they "pounded" the trains through to the Tongue.

It was the custom for wagon trains to go into camp early in the afternoon, which gave the stock a chance to graze while it was yet daylight; it also made it possible to guard them from sudden forays by Indians. On one of these occasions Ermine was with a train which made one of the halts as usual. The Indians had not interfered, and to kill time a few officers, among whom was Searles, started a game of poker. Ermine looked on over their shoulders, trying to comprehend. He had often played the Indian game of "hand," so that poker was merely a new slide between wealth and poverty. Seeing him, Captain Lewis sent him on some trivial errand. While he was gone, an agreement was made to have him come in, and then they were to "Skin him alive" just to see how he would stand it. It worked out beautifully. First they separated what little money he had from his clothes, the officers meanwhile sitting like owls and keeping their faces sober by dint of lip-biting; then the sombrero, which was stacked up as five dollars, found its way to Captain Lewis's head in place of a very bad campaign hat. Next came off the buckskin coat, which was followed by the revolver, and slowly, so that his suspicions might not be aroused, all his personal property, including the saddle and gun, which properly did not belong to him, was laid on the grass beside the victors.

"This is going to be a cold winter, John,"

laughed one, "or else we'd let you in on that shirt."

"Want to put that pony up for a hundred, Ermine?" asked another.

"No; I'll keep the pony; he's medicine. I've often lost all I had with the plum stones. I guess I don't understand poker." And the young scout arose smiling. The officers laughed themselves into tears, jumped up, and brought comrades to see how they had trimmed John Ermine. Every one greatly enjoyed what they called Ermine's preparations for the winter. He had his government shirt, his blanket breeches, and moccasins left; he had not been so poor since he was a herd-boy, but he had known forms of poverty all his life, so it was not new. What he did not enjoy was his belittlement. The hard-working men in those dangerous, monotonous days were keen for any weakness; and when he heard their laughter he wanted a horse-bucket full of human blood to drown his thoughts. He was greatly disturbed, not so much on account of his losses, although they were everything, as he viewed them, as the ridicule in store for him at Tongue River. There is no greater stimulant to a hardy mind than poverty, and John Ermine's worked like a government-six in a mud-hole, far into the night.

The trio of gamblers, who wore their spoils on their own persons, to the huge edification of the camp, arranged to prolong the torture until they should see the young hatless, coatless, unarmed scout on his barebacked pony during the next march. At the following camp they were to play again, lose to him, and end the joke. Confidences were exchanged, and every one was as tickled as a cur with a new collar.

One of the officers of the poker engagement rode a well-bred American horse of which he was very proud. He had raced it successfully and never declined an opportunity, of which fact Ermine was aware.

It had slowly come to his mind that he had been foully dealt with, so about midnight he jumped up—he had a plan. By dint of daring, fortunate machination, and the coöperation of a quartermaster sergeant whom he took into his confidence, he watered the American horse, fed him with a heavy feed of very salt corn, and later watered him again. The horse had been on short rations and was a glutton. It was with the greatest difficulty that the noble animal managed his breakfast at all; but he was always willing at each opportunity to weaken the saline solution in his stomach.

When the train pulled out, there was Ermine, barebacked and ridiculous. He rode through the volley of jeers and approached the horse-racing officer, saying, "If you are a good gambler, come on; I will run my horse against yours, three arrow-flights and a pitch, horse against horse."

The laughing stopped; here was a new idea—the quarter-bred blood horse, with his sleek bay quarters, against the scout's pony—a good enough animal, but thin and overworked.

The officer halted and stroked his chin with his thumb and forefinger.

"Hum—hum—yes; by Gad, if my horse can't take that runt into camp, he isn't good enough for me. I'll go you."

A cheer went up from those assembled, and some hidden force carried the thrill down the train, which halted. Uncle Sam's business could wait.

The distance was paced off on the level plain; the judges were set; the scouts and officers lined up.

The American's horse's eyes fairly bulged with excitement; he broke into a dripping perspiration, but seemingly no one noticed this but Ermine. He knew that the load of water would choke him in twenty yards.

The old war-pony was thin from overwork, but responsive as a dog to his bareback rider, and dangerous-looking to one used to see ponies which show worse in condition than out, by reason of the ungraceful architectural lines.

The pistol spoke; the pony gained three jumps from the mark. The American made the best of a bad job, but Ermine was able to turn at the finish and back him over the judges' line.

The officer nearly had apoplexy, as he

pulled up. He threw himself off the horse and handed the reins to Ermine.

The action of both challenge and race had been so rapid and so badly calculated on the officer's part that he lacked time to assimilate the idea that he was a fool. He tried to maintain a composure which was lacking, as every one could see.

"If you will get all my clothes, saddle, and gun back from your comrades, I will give you your horse," said the scout.

The spectators who knew about the poker game now sat howling hopelessly on their horses' backs. Searles and the others now came to their beaten friend's aid; they shed their plunder in front of Ermine's horse, produced the saddle and gun from a near-by escort wagon, laid them carefully down with the rest, and the victor granted peace.

"Here is your horse," said Ermine, and he laughed.

The occurrence had a serious side; the three officers were quick to appreciate that. Searles stood in front of the scout and made utterance: "I want to say before all these men that the poker game was not on the square—that we robbed you purposely for a joke, and that we intended to give your property back to you to-night; and I call on all these men to witness my remarks."

"Yes, yes," came the chorus; "it was all a joke. Searles said he would give it back. Don't hold it out against him, Ermine," and other reassuring remarks. They recognized the young scout's magnanimity as a conqueror.

The laughing ceased; the thing evidently had been carried too far. It would not sound well when told at Tongue River. The unfortunate horse-race had made proper restitution impossible.

By this time John Ermine had his clothing and saddle arranged and was mounted. He spoke:—

"Well, if that is so, if it only was a joke, I suppose I ought to say that I sat up half of last night salting your horse. Look at him! He is blowing yet; he is as full of water as a drowned buffalo. I am glad it did not kill him; let us bury the axe."

Major Searles and his fellows were unlike many jokers; they slowly readjusted after the shock and laughed with the others.

The march was resumed, but the customary monotony of this slow pacing of interminable landscape was often abruptly broken by individuals ha-haing loudly, as the sequence of events took a new hold of their risibles; and Mr. John Ermine tightened in an ever increasing hold on their fancies.

Major Searles, riding beside his horse-racing *confrère,* tried to cheer him. "Brace up, compadre; that boy has you buffaloed. We are all right; we are nothing but a bunch of monkeys. The only thing we forgot was that a fellow who has lived all his life with Injuns is likely to know how to gamble and race horses. He'll be wanting to juggle the bone* for us yet, and we are bound to go him."

"You bet," came the reply; "he has got us staked out, and he can come along and do jig steps on our chest any time he feels like it. That is where we have to moisten our lips and look pleasant, too."

An old wagon boss sauntered by on his mule with its mouth *à la crocodile.*

"Ha, ha! reckon you fellers has had all the fun that's a-comin' to you. That boy had that last deck marked, bottomed, sanded, and pricked, with more up his sleeve and some in the back of his neck."

John Ermine and Wolf-Voice, meanwhile, had gone well out in front of the train, loping this way and that about the course of advance, with eyes for everything.

Presently they were seen to stop, turn, and come back, flying as fast and straight as the antelope runs.

"How now, by Gad! here's smoke for us!" said Searles. No one laughed any more.

Swift and noiseless as the birds came the scouts; nearer and nearer, until their flying horses' hair could be seen; then sounded the hoof-beats until they drew rein. Wolf-Voice's hair fairly stood up, and his fierce little eyes danced attendance; he talked all the languages he knew, and worked his free

* Indian game of "hand."

"Bullets Kicked up the Dust." *Authors' photoengraving.*

hand in most alarming sign signals to help his expression.

"What's up, Ermine?" said the Major.

"Well, Major, the ground out there is alive with fresh pony-tracks. I think you had better bunch up."

The train was strung out, having passed a bad "draw." Turning, the Major shouted: "Close up in columns of fours! Deploy that escort out!"

The order flew down the train; the whips cracked, and the straining mules trotted into position; the infantry guard ran out from the sides, shoving shells into the breech-blocks. Even while this was in motion, a torrent of Sioux poured over the bluffs, back of the flat, and came on.

The soldiers dropped on to their knees in the sagebrush. The Major spurred to the particular point for which they were headed, followed by scouts and several mounted men.

"Steady, men! hold your fire!"

The men were aiming, and each had five cartridges in his teeth. In a sonorous roll came, "Steady—steady—steady!" And the gay stream of savagery bore on.

"Fire!" Like a double drag on a drum which gradually dies, the rifles rattled down the extended line, all concentrated on the head of the flying column. The smoke played along the gray sage; there was a sharp clatter of breech-blocks, and an interval.

"Ready! Fire!" and this repeated.

The Major jogged to a wind-blown place and saw that the column had veered to its right but was not checked. Followed by his few mounted men, he rode along behind their line parallel with the head of the charge, but before the slow and steady fire the Indian line drew out. The train was caught in the circle, but the enemy had not the heart to ride over the deadly skirmish line. The close columns of wagons now turned off down toward the river, and, keeping their distances, the infantry followed it. Indian ponies lay kicking out on the dry plain, and here and there could be seen warriors who retired slowly from the racing Indians; they had been plugged.

Bullets kicked up the dust, and one or two soldiers had to be helped along by their comrades.

The heated air shimmered over the land; but for the rattle and thud of gun and pony, the clank, snort, and whip-cracks among the wagons, the great, gray plains lay silent.

No eye save that of a self-considering golden eagle looked on, and he sailed placidly far above. Ponies and mules strained and lathered, men sweated and grunted and banged to kill; nature lay naked and insensate.

The Indians made a stand under the cut banks of the river, but were flanked out. The train drove slowly into a corral form, when the mules were unhooked. The guard began to rifle-pit among the wagons, and the Indians drew off to breathe their ponies. They had stopped the train, but the "walk-a-heap" soldiers were behind the wagons, which were full of "chuck," and water was at hand. Indians always dreaded the foot-soldiers, who could not run away, and who would not surrender, but worked their long rifles to the dying gasp; they were "heap bad medicine"; they were like wounded gray bears in a den of rocks—there was no reasonable method for their capture.

Major Searles jumped from his horse, took off his hat, and mopped his forehead with his handkerchief. "So far, so good! so far, so good! but not so very d—— far either," he mused.

Towing his pony behind him, Wolf-Voice came up, legs bowed and wobbly, horseback fashion when afoot. Calling loudly, he said:—

"By Jeskris, Maje Searl, bout two-tree minit you bettar look out; dose Kul-tus-til-akum she mak de grass burn yu up, by Gar. Win' she waas come deese way."

"Yes—yes, that's right. Here you, Ermine, and you, Lieutenant Smith, take what men you want and kill a wounded mule—

drag his hide over the grass to windward; it is short and won't burn high. And, Lieutenant, give me all the men you can over here; they will try to come through the smoke." Saying which, the Major made his way to the ammunition wagons and had the mules hooked to them, intending to run these into the river in case the fire came through.

In fighting Indians, the Major, who was an old hand, knew that one must act quickly, for they are rapid tacticians and their blows come fast.

These preparations had no sooner been made than, true to Wolf-Voice's admonitions, the Indians came down, and, just out of rifle-range, started the fire down wind. Almost no air was stirring; the flames ran slowly through the short buffalo-grass, but weeds and sage made considerable smoke, which came toward the train.

The dripping carcass of the mule was dragged in a ring around the windward side of the train; the smoke eddied over the wagons; the Indians could not be seen; every man's eyes and ears were strained and fingers twitched as they lay at an "aim" or "ready," among the wagon-wheels.

The mules grew restive and sat back on their fastenings; but there, matters had been well attended to, for the side-lines and hobbles were leathered and laced.

To the silent soldiers this was one of the times when a man lives four years in twenty minutes; nothing can be compared to it but the prolonged agony between your "Will you have me?" and her "yes" or "NO."

As the fire came nearer, they heard its gentle crackle, crackle; their nerves all crackled in unison. It reached the bloody ring left by the poor mule—"would the d—— Injuns never come?" At the guard line the flames died and crackled no more. The smoke grew thinner, and at last they saw out through it; the Indians held themselves safely out of rifle-shot.

"Hum," said Searles, as he stepped down from a wagon-wheel, "they didn't want any of this chicken pie." And then he did what he was never known to do under ordinary circumstances; and when he was through, the men cheered, and every mule-skinner who had heard him envied a man who could talk it off just like that.

"Ah, Maje Searl," chimed in Wolf-Voice, "don' you been scare; dose Injuns no say goo'by yet, mabeso."

And they did not say good-by. They dismounted and went behind the washes in the shallow river. They peppered and banged the men as they watered the stock, the perilous trip only being made behind a strong skirmish line with three men hit and a half-dozen mules. The soldiers ate a quiet supper and put out the fires before the sun went down. The Indians, with the declining light, crawled in on the train and pecked at the monster.

"Pe-e-e-eing" went a bullet on a wagon-tire; "slap" went another on a wagon-box; "thud," as one buried in a grain-bag; "phud," and the ball made a mule grunt; but the echoing Springfields spit their 45's at the flashes.

Searles sent for Ermine and Wolf-Voice, and sitting on the grass behind a barricade of grain-sacks, he began: "We are corralled, and I haven't escort enough to move. I can hold out till snow, but can't graze my stock. Some one has to go back for reënforcements. Will you go? It can be made on a good horse by morning."

"Well, Major, I'll try it. I can go if I can get through with a fair start. The moon will come up later, and I must go now while there is a chance," said Ermine.

"Will you go also, Mr. Wolf-Voice?"

"Well, hit be good chance for geet keel. Yaes, I go, mebeso, feefty doaller," vouchsafed that worthy, after nicely balancing the chances.

"What do you want for going, John Ermine?" asked the Major.

"I don't want anything. I came to fight the Sioux. I do not go to war for fifty dollars." But it was too dark for the half-breed to see the contempt in Ermine's face, so he only shrugged his shoulders and contented himself with, "Oh, weel, mabeso dose sol-dier-man go for not so much. I do not."

"All right, all right! I'll give you an order

for fifty dollars. Here are the papers." And the Major handed one to each. "Now, don't lose them, whatever else you do."

"Ma pony, she steef, no good. I was go on de foot." And Wolf-Voice proceeded to skin off his motley garments. In these desperate situations he believed in the exemplar of his name; its methods were less heroic but more sure.

Ermine half stripped himself, and his horse wholly; bound up the tail, and in the gloom rubbed the old dried horse's hoof on his heels. It had, at least, never done any harm, and at times favored him. Sak-a-war-te and the God of the white men—he did not know whether they were one or two. Trusting his valuables to the care of the Major, he was let out of the corral after a good rattle of firing, into the darkness, away from the river.

Only a few rifles ripped the night air in response to this, which he took to indicate that the better part of the Indians were along the river. He glided away, leading his pony, and the last the soldiers saw was the flash of a gun turned in an opposite direction from the wagon train. Neither Wolf-Voice or Ermine again appeared.

The slow fight continued during the night and all the next day, but by evening the Indians disappeared. They had observed the approach of reënforcements, which came in during the following morning, led by Ermine. Wolf-Voice, who had been on foot, did not make the rapid time of his mounted partner, but had gone through and acquired the fifty dollars, which was the main object.

CHAPTER XI

The Truth of the Eyes

The soldiers who had been in the wagon-train fight carried John Ermine's fame into cantonments, and Major Searles never grew tired of the pæan:—

"I do not go to war for fifty dollars,
You can bet your boots that isn't not me
    lay.
When I fight, it's only glory which I
    collars,
Also to get me little beans and hay."

But his more ardent admirers frowned on this doggerel, and reminded the songsters that no one of them would have made that courier's ride for a thousand acres of Monongahela rye in bottles. As for Wolf-Voice, they appreciated his attitude. "Business is business, and it takes money to buy marbles," said one to another.

But on the completion of the rude huts at the mouth of the Tongue, and when the last wagon train had come through, there was an ominous preparation for more serious things. It was in the air. Every white soldier went loping about, doing everything from greasing a wagon to making his will.

"Ah, sacre, John," quoth Wolf-Voice, "am much disturb; dese Masta-Shella* waas say dis big chief—what you call de Miles? —she medicin fighter; she very bad mans; she keep de soldiers' toes sore all de taime. She no give de dam de cole-moon, de yellow-grass moon; she hump de Sioux. Why for we mak to trouble our head? We have dose box, dose bag, dose barrel to heat, en de commissaire—wael 'nough grub las' our lifetaime; but de soldier say sure be a fight soon; dat Miles she begin for paw de groun' —it be sure sign. Wael, we mak' a skin dat las fight, hey, John?"

Ermine in his turn conceived a new respect for the white soldiers. If their heels were heavy, so were their arms when it came to the final hug. While it was not apparent to him just how they were going to whip the Sioux and Cheyenne, it was very evident that the Indians could not whip the soldiers; and this was demonstrated directly when Colonel Miles, with his hardy infantry, charged over Sitting Bull's camp, and while outnumbered three to his one, scattered and drove the proud tribesmen and looted their tepees. Not satisfied with this,

* White men.

the grim soldier crawled over the snow all winter with his buffalo-coated men, defying the blizzards, kicking the sleeping warriors out of their blankets, killing and chasing them into the cold starvation of the hills. So persistent and relentless were the soldiers that they fought through the captured camps when the cold was so great that the men had to stop in the midst of battle to light fires, to warm their fingers, which were no longer able to work the breech-locks. Young soldiers cried in the ranks as they perished in the frigid atmosphere; but notwithstanding, they never stopped. The enemy could find no deep defile in the lonely mountains where they were safe; and entrench where they would among the rocks, the steady line charged over them, pouring bullets and shell. Ermine followed their fortunes and came to understand the dying of "the ten thousand men." These people went into battle with the intention of dying if not victorious. They never consulted their heels, no matter what the extremity. By the time of the green grass the warriors of the northern plains had either sought their agencies or fled to Canada. Through it all Ermine had marched and shot and frozen with the rest. He formed attachments for his comrades—that enthusiastic affection which men bring from the camp and battle-field, signed by suffering and sealed with blood.

CHAPTER XII

Katherine

The snow had gone. The plains and boxlike bluff around the cantonments had turned to a rich velvet of green. The troops rested after the tremendous campaigns in the snow-laden, wind-swept hills, with the consciousness of work well done. The Indians who had been brought in during the winter were taking their first heart-breaking steps along the white man's road. The army teams broke the prairie, and they were planting the seed. The disappearance of the buffalo and the terrible white chief Bear-Coat,* who followed and fought them in the fiercest weather, had broken their spirits. The prophecies of the old beaver-men, which had always lain heavily on the Indian mind, had come true at last—the whites had come; they had tried to stop them and had failed.

The soldiers' nerves tingled as they gathered round the landing. They cheered and laughed and joked, slapped and patted hysterically, and forgot the bilious officialism entirely.

Far down the river could be seen the black funnel of smoke from the steamboat—their only connection with the world of the white men. It bore letters from home, luxuries for the mess-chest, and best of all, news of the wives and children who had been left behind when they went to war.

Every one was in a tremor of expectancy except the Indians, who stood solemnly apart in their buffalo-robes, and John Ermine. The steamboat did not come from their part of the world, and brought nothing to them; still Ermine reflected the joyousness of those around him, and both he and the Indians knew a feast for their eyes awaited them.

In due course the floating house—for she looked more like one than a boat—pushed her way to the landing, safe from her thousand miles of snags and sandbars. A cannon thudded and boomed. The soldiers cheered, and the people on the boat waved handkerchiefs when they did not use them to wipe happy tears away; officers who saw their beloved ones walked to and fro in caged impatience. When the gang-planks were run out, they swarmed aboard like Malay pirates. Such hugging and kissing as followed would have been scandalous on an ordinary occasion; lily-white faces were quite buried in sun-burnt mustaches on mahogany-brown skins. The unmarried men all registered a vow to let no possible occasion to

* General Miles.

get married escape them, and little boys and girls were held aloft in brawny arms paternal. A riot of good spirits reigned.

"For Heaven's sake, Mary, did you bring me my summer underwear?"

"Oh, don't say you forgot a box of cigars, Mattie."

"If you have any papers or novels, they will save me from becoming an idiot," and a shower of childish requests from their big boys greeted the women.

In truth, it must be stated that at this period the fashion insisted upon a disfigurement of ladies which must leave a whole generation of noble dames forgotten by artists of all time. They loosened and tightened their forms at most inappropriate places; yet underneath this fierce distortion of that bane of woman, Dame Fashion, the men were yet able to remember there dwelt bodies as beautiful as any Greek ever saw or any attenuated Empire dandy fancied.

"Three cheers for the first white women on the northern buffalo range!"

"See that tent over there?" asked an officer of his 'Missis,' as he pointed toward camp; "well, that's our happy home; how does it strike you?"

A bunch of "shave-tails" were marched ashore amid a storm of good-natured raillery from the "vets" and mighty glad to feel once again the grit under their brogans. Roustabouts hustled bags and boxes into the six-mule wagons. The engine blew off its exhaust in a frail attempt to drown the awful profanity of the second mate, while humanity boiled and bubbled round the great river-box.

The Indians stood motionless, but their keen eyes missed no details of the strange medley. Ermine leaned on a wagon-tail, carefully paring a thin stick with a jack-knife. He was arrayed for a gala day in new soldier trousers, a yellow buckskin shirt beautifully beaded by the Indian method, a spotted white handkerchief around his neck, buckskin leggings on the lower leg above gay moccasins, a huge skinning-knife and revolver in his belt, and a silver watch chain. His golden hair was freshly combed, and his big rakish sombrero had an eagle feather fastened to the crown, dropping idly to one side, where the soft wind eddied it about.

The John Ermine of the mountain den was a June-bug beside this butterfly, but no assortment of color can compete with a scarlet blanket when the clear western sun strikes on it; so in consequence Ermine was subdued by Wolf-Voice, who stood beside him thus arrayed.

As the people gathered their bags and parcels, they came ashore in small groups, the women and children giving the wild Indians the heed which their picturesque appearance called for, much of this being in the form of little shivers up and down the spine. A true old wolf-headed buffalo Indian would make a Japanese dragon look like a plate of ice-cream, and the Old Boy himself would have to wave his tail, prick up his sharp ears, and display the best of his Satanic learning to stand the comparison.

Major Searles passed on with the rest, beaming like a June morning, his arms full of woman's equipment—Mrs. Searles on one side and his daughter on the other.

"Hello, Ermine."

"How do, Major?" spoke the scout as he cast his whittling from him.

"This is John Ermine, who saved my life last winter, my dear. This is Mrs. Searles, John."

She bowed, but the scout shook hands with her. Miss Searles, upon presentation, gave Ermine a most chilling bow, if raising the chin and dropping the upper eyelids can be so described; and the man who pushed his pony fearlessly among the whirling savages recoiled before her batteries and stood irresolute.

Wolf-Voice, who had not been indicated by the Major, now approached, his weird features lighted up with what was intended as pleasantry, but which instead was rather alarming.

"How! how me heap glad to see you." And to Miss Searles, "How! how you heap look good." After which they passed on.

"My, my, papa, did you ever see such beautiful hair as that man Ermine has?" said Katherine Searles. "It was a perfect dream."

"Yes, good crop that—'nough to stuff a mattress with; looks better to-day than when it's full of alkali dust," replied the Major.

"If the young man lost his hat, it would not be a calamity," observed the wife.

"And, papa, who was that dreadful Indian in the red blanket?"

"Oh, an old scoundrel named Wolf-Voice, but useful in his place. You must never feed him, Sarah, or he will descend on us like the plague of locusts. If he ever gets his teeth into one of our biscuits, I'll have to call out the squad to separate him from our mess-chest."

A strange thought flashed through John Ermine's head—something more like the stroke of an axe than a thought, and it had deprived him of the power of speech. Standing motionless and inert, he watched the girl until she was out of sight. Then he walked away from the turmoil, up along the riverbank.

Having gained a sufficient distance, he undid the front of his shirt and took out a buckskin bag, which hung depended from his neck. It contained his dried horse's hoof and the photograph of a girl, the one he had picked up in the moonlight on the trail used by the soldiers from Fort Ellis.

He gazed at it for a time, and said softly, "They are the same, that girl and this shadow." And he stood scrutinizing it, the

Katherine. *Authors' wood engraving.*

The Englishman. *Authors' wood engraving.*

eyes looking straight into his as they had done so often before, until he was intimate with the image by a thousand vain imaginings. He put it back in his bag, buttoned his shirt, and stood in a brown study, with his hands behind his back, idly stirring the dust with the point of one moccasin.

"It must have been—it must have been Sak-a-war-te who guided me in the moonlight to that little shadow paper there in the road—to that little spot in all this big country; in the night-time and just where we cut that long road; it means something—it must be." And he could get no farther with his thoughts as he walked to his quarters.

Along the front of the officers' row he saw the bustle, and handshaking, laughter, and quick conversation. Captain Lewis came by with a tall young man in citizen's clothes, about whom there was a blacked, brushed, shaved appearance quite new on the Tongue.

"I say, and who is that stunning chap?" said this one to Lewis, in Ermine's hearing.

"One of my men. Oh, come here, Ermine. This is Mr. Sterling Harding, an Englishman come out to see this country and hunt. You may be able to tell him some things he wants to know."

The two young men shook hands and stood irresolutely regarding each other. Which had the stranger thoughts concerning the other or the more curiosity cannot be stated, but they both felt the desire for better acquaintance. Two strangers on meeting always feel this—or indifference, and sometimes repulsion. The relations are established in a glance.

"Oh, I suppose, Mr. Ermine, you have shot in this country."

"Yes, sir,"—Ermine had extended the "sir" beyond shoulder-straps to include clean shirts,—"I have shot most every kind of thing we have in this country except a woman."

"Oh! ha! ha ha!" And Harding produced a cigar-case.

"A woman? I suppose there hasn't been any to shoot until this boat came. Do you intend to try your hand on one? Will you have a cigar?"

"No, sir; I only meant to say I had shot things. I suppose you mean have I hunted."

"Yes, yes—exactly; hunted is what I mean."

"Well then, Mr. Sterling Harding, I have never done anything else."

"Mr. Harding, I will leave you with Ermine; I have some details to look after. You will come to our mess for luncheon at noon?" interjected Captain Lewis.

"Yes, with pleasure, Captain." Whereat the chief of scouts took himself off.

"I suppose, Mr. Ermine, that the war is quite over, and that one may feel free to go about here without being potted by the aborigines," said Harding.

"The what? Never heard of them. I can go where I like without being killed, but I have to keep my eyes skinned."

"Would you be willing to take me out? I should expect to incur the incidental risks of the enterprise," asked the Englishman, who had taken the incidental risks of tigers in India and sought "big heads" in many countries irrespective of dangers.

"Why, yes; I guess Wolf-Voice and I could take you hunting easily enough if the Captain will let us go. We never know here what Bear-Coat is going to do next; it may be 'boots and saddles' any minute," replied the scout.

"Oh, I imagine, since Madam has appeared, he may remain quiet and I really understand the Indians have quite fled the country," responded Harding.

"Mabeso; you don't know about Indians, Mr. Harding. Indians are uncertain; they may come back again when their ponies fill up on the green grass."

"Where would you propose to go, may I ask?"

Ermine thought for a time, and asked, "Would you mind staying out all one moon, Mr. Harding?"

"One moon? You mean thirty days. Yes, three moons, if necessary. My time is not precious. Where would you go?"

"Back in the mountains—back on the Stinking Water; a long way from here, but a good place for the animals. It is where I come from, and I haven't been home in nearly a year. I should like to see my people," continued Ermine.

"Anywhere will do; we will go to the Stinking Water, which I hope belies its name. You have relatives living there, I take it."

"Not relatives; I have no relations anywhere on the earth, but I have friends," he replied.

"When shall we start?"

Ermine waved his hand a few times at the sky and said "So many," but it failed to record on the Englishman's mind. He was using the sign language. The scout noted this, and added, "Ten suns from now I will go if I can."

"Very well; we will purchase ponies and other necessaries meanwhile, and will you aid me in the preparations, Mr. Ermine? How many ponies shall we require?"

"Two apiece—one to ride and the other to pack," came the answer to the question.

A great light dawned upon Harding's mind. To live a month with what one Indian pony could carry for bedding, clothes, cartridges, and food. His new friend failed, in his mind, to understand the requirements of an English gentleman on such quests.

"But, Mr. Ermine, how should I transport my heads back to this point with only one pack-animal?"

"Heads? heads? back here?" stumbled the light-horseman. "What heads?"

"Why, the heads of such game as I might be so fortunate as to kill."

"What do you want of their heads? We never take the heads. We give them to our little friends, the coyotes," queried Ermine.

"Yes, yes, but I must have the heads to take back to England with me. I am afraid, Mr. Ermine, we shall have to be more liberal with our pack-train. However, we will go into the matter at greater length later."

Sterling Harding wanted to refer to the Captain for further understanding of his new guide. He felt that Lewis could make the matter plain to Ermine by more direct methods than he knew how to employ. As the result of world-wide wanderings, he knew that the Captain would have to explain to Ermine that he was a crazy Englishman who was all right, but who must be humored. To Harding this idea was not new; he had played his blood-letting ardor against all the forms of outlandish ignorance. The savages of many lands had eaten the bodies of which the erratic Englishman wanted only the heads.

So to Lewis went Harding. "I say, Captain, your Ermine there is an artless fellow. He is proposing to Indianize me, to take me out for a whole moon, as he calls it, with only one pack-pony to carry my belongings. Also he fails, I think, to comprehend that I want to bring back the heads of my game."

"Ha! I will make that plain to him. You see, Mr. Harding, you are the first Englishman he ever encountered; fact is he is range bred, unbranded and wild. I have ridden him, but I use considerable discretion when I do it, or he would go up in the air on me," explained Lewis. "He is simple, but he is honest, faithful, and one of the very few white men who know this Indian country. Long ago there were a great many hunters and trappers in these parts; men who worked for the fur companies, but they have all been driven out of the country of late years by the Indians, and you will be lucky to get Ermine. There are plenty of the half-breeds left, but you cannot trust them. They might steal from you, they might abandon you, or they might kill you. Ermine will probably take you into the Crow country, for he is solid with those people. Why, half the time when I order Crow scouts to do something they must first go and make a talk with Ermine. He has some sort of a pull with them—God knows what. You may find it convenient to agree with him at times when you naturally would not; these fellows are independent and follow their fancies pretty much. They don't talk, and when they get an idea that they want to do anything, they proceed immediately to do it. Ermine has been with me nearly a year now, but I never know what minute I am to hear he has pulled out."

Seeing Ermine some little distance away, the Captain sent an orderly after him. He came and leant with one hand on the tent-pole of the fly.

"Ermine, I think you had better take one or two white packers and at least eight or ten animals with you when you go with Mr. Harding."

"All right, sir, we can take as many packers as he likes, but no wagons."

Having relieved the scout of his apprehensions concerning wagons, the bond was sealed with a cigar, and he departed, thinking of old Crooked-Bear's prediction that the white men would take him to their hearts. Underneath the happy stir of his faculties on this stimulating day there played a new emotion, indefinite, undefinable, a drifting, fluttering butterfly of a thought which never alighted anywhere. All day long it flitted, hovered, and made errant flights across his golden fancies—a glittering, variegated little puff of color.

CHAPTER XIII

Playing with Fire

On the following morning Harding hunted up John Ermine, and the two walked about together, the Englishman trying to fire the scout with his own passion for strange lands and new heads.

To the wild plainsman the land was not new; hunting had its old everyday look, and the stuffed heads of game had no significance. His attention was constantly interrupted by the little flutter of color made more distinct by a vesper before the photograph.

"Let us go and find your friend, Wolf-Voice," said Harding, which they did, and the newcomer was introduced. The Englishman threw kindly, wondering eyes over the fiercely suspicious face of the half-breed, whose evil orbs spitted back at him.

"Ah, yees—you was go hunt. All-right; I weel mak' you run de buffalo, shoot dose elk, trap de castor, an you shall shake de han' wid de grizzly bear. How much money I geet—hey?"

"Ah, you will get the customary wages, my friend, and if you give me an opportunity to shake hands with a grizzly, your reward will be forthcoming," replied the sportsman.

"Very weel; keep yur heye skin on me, when you see me run lak hell—weel, place where I was run way from, dare ees mousier's grizzly bear, den you was go up shake han', hey?"

Harding laughed and offered the man a cigar, which he handled with four fingers much as he might a tomahawk, having none of the delicate art native to the man of cigars or cigarettes. A match was proffered, and Wolf-Voice tried diligently to light the wrong end. The Englishman violently pulled Ermine away, while he nearly strangled with suppressed laughter. It was distinctly clear that Wolf-Voice must go with them.

"Your friend Wolf-Voice seems to be quite an individual person."

"Yes, the soldiers are always joshing him, but he doesn't mind. Sometimes they go too far. I have seen him draw that skinning-knife, and away they go like a flock of birds. Except when he gets loaded with soldier whiskey, he is all right. He is a good man away from camp," said Ermine.

"He does not appear to be a thoroughbred Indian," observed Harding.

"No, he's mixed; he's like that soup the

company cooks make. He is not the best man in the world, but he is a better man in more places than I ever saw," said Ermine, in vindication.

"Shall we go down to the Indian camp and try to buy some ponies, Ermine?"

"No, I don't go near the Sioux; I am a kind of Crow. I have fought with them. They forgive the soldiers, but their hearts are bad when they look at me. I'll get Ramon to go with you when you buy the horses. Ramon was a small trader before the war, used to going about with a half-dozen pack-horses, but the Sioux ran him off the range. He has pack saddles and rawhide bags, which you can hire if you want to," was explained.

"All right; take me to Ramon if you will."

"I smoke," said Ermine as he led the way.

Having seen that worthy depart on his trading mission with Harding in tow, Ermine felt relieved. Impulse drew him to the officers' row, where he strolled about with his hands in his cartridge-belt. Many passing by nodded to him or spoke pleasantly. Some of the newly arrived ladies even attempted conversation; but if the soldiers of a year ago were difficult for Ermine, the ladies were impossible. He liked them; their gentle faces, their graceful carriage, their evident interest in him, and their frank address called out all his appreciation. They were a revelation after the squaws, who had never suggested any of these possibilities. But they refused to come mentally near him, and he did not know the trail which led to them. He answered their questions, agreed with whatever they said, and battled with his diffidence until he made out to borrow a small boy from one mother, proposing to take him down to the scout camp and quartermaster's corral to view the Indians and mules.

He had thought out the proposition that the Indians were just as strange to the white people as the white people were to them, consequently he saw a social opening. He would mix these people up so that they could stare at each other in mutual perplex-ity and bore one another with irrelevant remarks and questions.

"Did Mr. Butcher-Knife miss Madam Butcher-Knife?" asked a somewhat elderly lady on one occasion, whereat the Indian squeezed out an abdominal grunt and sedately observed to "Hairy-Arm," in his own language, that "the fat lady could sit down comfortably," or words that would carry this thought.

The scout who was acting as their leader upon this occasion emitted one loud "A-ha!" before he could check himself. The lady asked what had been said. Ermine did not violate a rule clearly laid down by Crooked-Bear, to the effect that lying was the sure sign of a man's worthlessness. He answered that they were merely speaking of something which he had not seen, thus satisfying his *protégé*.

After a round or two of these visits this novelty was noised about the quarters, and Ermine found himself suddenly accosted. By his side was the original of his cherished photograph, accompanied by Lieutenant Butler of the cavalry, a tall young man whose body and movements had been made to conform to the West Point standards.

"Miss Searles has been presented, I believe. She is desirous of visiting the scout camp. Would you kindly take us down?"

John Ermine's soul drifted out through the top of his head in unseen vapors, but he managed to say that he would. He fell in beside the young woman, and they walked on together. To be so near the reality, the literal flesh and blood of what had been a long series of efflorescent dreams, quite stirred him. He gathered slowly, after each quick glance into the eyes which were not like those in the photograph; there they were set and did not resent his fancies; here they sparkled and talked and looked unutterable things at the helpless errant.

Miss Searles had been to a finishing school in the East, and either the school was a very good one or the little miss exceedingly apt, but both more probably true. She had the delicate pearls and peach-bloom on her cheeks to which the Western sun and winds are such persistent enemies, and a dear little nose tipped heavenward, as careless as a cat hunting its grandmother.

The rustle of her clothes mingled with little songs which the wind sang to the grass, a faint freshness of body with delicate spring-flower odors drifted to Ermine's active nostrils. But the eyes, the eyes, why did they not brood with him as in the picture? Why did they arch and laugh and tantalize?

His earthly senses had fled; gone somewhere else and left a riot in his blood. He tripped and stumbled, fell down, and crawled over answers to her questions, and he wished Lieutenant Butler was farther away than a pony could run in a week.

She stopped to raise her dress above the dusty road, and the scout overrode the alignment.

"Mr. Ermine, will you please carry my parasol for me?"

The object in question was newer to him than a man-of-war would have been. The prophet had explained about the great ships, but he had forgotten parasols. He did not exactly make out whether the thing was to keep the sun off, or to hide her face from his when she wanted to. He retraced his steps, wrapped his knuckles around the handle with a drowning clutch, and it burned his hand. If previously it had taken all his force to manœuvre himself, he felt now that he would bog down under this new weight. Atlas holding the world had a flying start of Ermine.

He raised it above her head, and she looked up at him so pleasantly, that he felt she realized his predicament; so he said, "Miss Searles, if I lug this baby tent into that scout camp, they will either shoot at us, or crawl the ponies and scatter out for miles. I think they would stand if you or the Lieutenant pack it; but if I do this, there won't be anything to see but ponies' tails wavering over the prairie."

"Oh, thank you; I will come to your rescue, Mr. Ermine." And she did.

"It is rather ridiculous, a parasol, but I do not intend to let the sun have its way with me." And glancing up, "Think if you had

always carried a parasol, what a complexion you would have."

"But men don't carry them, do they?"

"Only when it rains; they do then, back in the States," she explained.

Ermine replied, "They do—hum!" and forthwith refused to consider men who did it.

"I think, Mr. Ermine, if I were an Indian, I should very much like to scalp you. I cannot cease to admire your hair."

"Oh, you don't have to be an Indian, to do that. Here is my knife; you can go ahead any time you wish," came the cheerful response.

"Mr. Butler, our friend succumbs easily to any fate at my hands, it seems. I wonder if he would let me eat him," said the girl.

" 'Will You Please Carry My Parasol for Me?' " *Authors' photoengraving.*

"I will build the fire and put the kettle on for you." And Ermine was not joking in the least, though no one knew this.

They were getting into the dangerous open fields, and Miss Searles urged the scout in a different direction.

"Have you ever been East?"

"Yes," he replied, "I have been to Fort Buford."

The parasol came between them, and presently, "Would you like to go east of Buford—I mean away east of Buford," she explained.

"No; I don't want to go east or west, north or south of here," came the astonishing answer all in good faith, and Miss Searles mentally took to her heels. She feared seriousness.

"Oh, here are the Indians," she gasped, as they strode into the grotesque grouping. "I am afraid, Mr. Ermine—I know it is silly."

"What are you afraid of, Miss Searles?"

"I do not know; they look at me so!" And she gave a most delicious little shiver.

"You can't blame them for that; they're not made of wood." But this lost its force amid her peripatetic reflections.

"That's Broken-Shoe; that's White-Robe; that's Batailleur—oh, well, you don't care what their names are; you probably will not see them again."

"They are more imposing when mounted and dashing over the plains, I assure you. At a distance, one misses the details which rather obtrude here," ventured Butler.

"Very well; I prefer them where I am quite sure they will not dash. I very much prefer them sitting down quietly—such fearful-looking faces. Oh my, they should be kept in cages like the animals in the Zoo. And do you have to fight such people, Mr. Butler?"

"We do," replied the officer, lighting a cigarette. This point of view was new and amusing.

One of the Indians approached the party. Ermine spoke to him in a loud, guttural, carrying voice, so different from his quiet use of English, that Miss Searles fairly jumped. The change of voice was like an explosion.

"Go back to your robe, brother; the white squaw is afraid of you—go back, I say!"

The intruder hesitated, stopped, and fastened Ermine with the vacant stare which in such times precede sudden, uncontrollable fury among Indians.

Again Ermine spoke: "Go back, you brown son of mules; this squaw is my friend; I tell you she is afraid of you. I am not. Go back, and before the sun is so high I will come to you. Make this boy go back, Broken-Shoe; he is a fool."

The old chieftain emitted a few hollow grunts, with a click between, and the young Indian turned away.

"My! Mr. Ermine, what are you saying? Have I offended the Indian? He looks daggers; let us retire—oh my, let us go—quick—quick!" And Ermine, by the flutter of wings, knew that his bird had flown. He followed, and in the safety of distance she lightly put her hand on his arm.

"What was it all about, Mr. Ermine? Do tell me."

Ermine's brain was not working on schedule time, but he fully realized what the affront to the Indian meant in the near future. He knew he would have to make his words good; but when the creature of his dreams was involved, he would have measured arms with a grizzly bear.

"He would not go back," said the scout, simply.

"But for what was he coming?" she asked.

"For you," was the reply.

"Goodness gracious! I had done nothing; did he want to kill me?"

"No, he wanted to shake hands with you; he is a fool."

"Oh, only to shake hands with me? And why did you not let him? I could have borne that."

"Because he is a fool," the scout ventured, and then in tones which carried the meaning, "Shake hands with you!"

"I see; I understand; you were protecting me; but he must hate you. I believe he will harm you; those dreadful Indians are so relentless, I have heard. Why did we ever go near the creatures? What will he do, Mr. Ermine?"

The scout cast his eye carefully up at the sky and satisfied the curiosity of both by drawling, "A—hu!"

"Well—well, Mr. Ermine, do not ever go near them again; I certainly would not if I were you. I shall see papa and have you removed from those ghastly beings. It is too dreadful. I have seen all I care to of them; let us go home, Mr. Butler."

The two—the young lady and the young man—bowed to Ermine, who touched the brim of his sombrero, after the fashion of the soldiers. They departed up the road, leaving Ermine to go, he knew not where, because he wanted to go only up the road. The abruptness of white civilities hashed the scout's contempt for time into fine bits; but he was left with something definite, at least, and that was a deep, venomous hatred for Lieutenant Butler; that was something he could hang his hat on. Then he thought of the "fool," and his footsteps boded ill for that one.

"That Ermine is such a tremendous man; do you not think so, Mr. Butler?"

"He seems a rather forceful person in his simple way," coincided the officer. "You apparently appeal to him strongly. He is downright romantic in his address, but I cannot find fault with the poor man. I am equally unfortunate."

"Oh, don't, Mr. Butler; I cannot stand it; you are, at least, sophisticated."

"Yes, I am sorry to say I am."

"Oh, please, Mr. Butler," with a deprecating wave of her parasol, "but tell me, aren't you afraid of them?"

"I suppose you mean the Indians. Well, they certainly earned my respect during the last campaign. They are the finest light-horse in the world, and if they were not encumbered with the women, herds, and villages; if they had plenty of ammunition and the buffalo would stay, I think there would be a great many army widows, Miss Searles."

"It is dreadful; I can scarcely remember my father; he has been made to live in this beast of a country since I was a child." Such was the lofty view the young woman took of her mundane progress.

"Shades of the vine-clad hills and citron groves of the Hudson River! I fear we brass buttoners are cut off. I should have been a lawyer or a priest—no, not a priest; for when I look at a pretty girl I cannot feel any priesthood in my veins."

Miss Searles whistled the bars of "Halt" from under the fortification of the parasol.

"Oh, well, what did the Lord make pretty women for?"

"I do not know, unless to demonstrate the foolishness of the line of Uncle Sam's cavalry," speculated the arch one. "Mr. Butler, if you do not stop, I shall run."

"All right; I am under arrest, so do not run; we are nearly home. I reserve my right to resume hostilities, however. I insist on fair play with your sage-brush admirer. Since we met in St. Louis, I have often wondered if we should ever see each other again. I always ardently wished we could."

"Mr. Butler, you are a poor imitation of our friend Ermine; he, at least, makes one feel that he means what he says," she rejoined.

"And you were good enough to remind me that I was sophisticated."

"I may have been mistaken," she observed. She played the batteries of her eyes on the unfortunate soldier, and all of his formations went down before them. He was in love, and she knew it, and he knew she knew it.

He felt like a fool, but tried not to act one, with the usual success of lovers. He was an easy victim of one of those greatest of natural weaknesses men have. She had him staked out and could bring him into her camp at any time the spirit moved her. Being a young person just from school, she found affairs easier than she had been led to suspect. In the usual girl way she had studied her casts, lures, and baits, but in reality they all seemed unnecessary, and she began to think some lethal weapon which would keep her admirers at a proper distance more to the purpose.

The handsome trooper was in no great danger, she felt, only she must have time; she did not want everything to happen in a minute, and the greatest dream of life vanish forever. Besides, she intended never, under any circumstances, to haul down her flag and surrender until after a good, hard siege.

They entered the cabin of the Searles, and there told the story of the morning's adventures. Mrs. Searles had the Indians classified with rattlesnakes, green devils, and hyenas, and expected scenes of this character to happen.

The Major wanted more details concerning Ermine. "Just what did he say, Butler?"

"I do not know; he spoke in some Indian language."

"Was he angry, and was the Indian who approached you mad?"

"They were like two dogs who stand ready to fight,—teeth bared, muscles rigid, eyes set and just waiting for their nerves to snap," explained Butler.

"Oh, some d—— Indian row, no one knows what, and Ermine won't tell; yet as a rule these people are peaceful among themselves. I will ask him about it," observed the Major.

"Why can't you have Mr. Ermine removed from that awful scout camp, papa? Why can't he be brought up to some place near here? I do not see why such a beautiful white person as he is should have to associate with those savages," pleaded the graceful Katherine.

"Don't worry about Ermine, daughter; you wouldn't have him rank the Colonel out of quarters, would you? I will look into this matter a little."

Meanwhile the young scout walked rapidly toward his camp. He wanted to do something with his hands, something which would let the gathering electricity out at his finger-ends and relieve the strain, for the trend of events had irritated him.

Going straight to his tent, he picked up his rifle, loaded it, and buckled on the belt containing ammunition for it. He twisted his six-shooter round in front of him, and worked his knife up and down in its sheath. Then he strode out, going slowly down to the scout fire.

The day was warm; the white-hot sun cut traceries of the cottonwood trees on the ground. A little curl of blue smoke rose straight upward from the fire, and in a wide ring of little groups sat or lounged the scouts. They seemingly paid no attention to the approach of Ermine, but one could not determine this; the fierce Western sun closes the eyelids in a perpetual squint, and leaves the beady eyes a chance to rove unobserved at a short distance.

Ermine came over and walked into the circle, stopping in front of the fire, thus facing the young Indian to whom he had used the harsh words. There was no sound except the rumble of a far-off government mule team and the lazy buzz of flies. He deliberately rolled a cigarette. Having done this to his satisfaction, he stooped down holding it against the coals, and it was ages before it caught fire. Then he put it to his lips, blew a cloud of smoke in the direction of his foe, and spoke in Absaroke.

"Well, I am here."

The silence continued; the Indian looked at him with a dull steady stare, but did nothing; finally Ermine withdrew. He understood; the Indian did not consider the time or opportunity propitious, but the scout did not flatter himself that such a time or place would never come. That was the one characteristic of an Indian of which a man could be certain.

CHAPTER XIV

In Love

John Ermine lay on his back in his tent, with one leg crossed over the other. His eyes were idly attracted by the play of shadows on the ducking, but his mind was visiting other places. He was profoundly discontented. During his life he had been at all times an easy-going person—taught in a rude school to endure embarrassing calamities and long-continued personal inconveniences by flood and hunger, bullets and snow. He had no conception of the civilized trait of acquisitiveness whereby he had escaped that tantalization. He desired military distinction, but he had gotten that. No man strode the camp whose deeds were better recognized than his, not even the Colonel commanding.

His attitude toward mankind had always been patient and kindly except when urged into other channels by war. He even had schooled himself to the irksome labor at the prophet's mine, low delving which seemed useless; and had acquiesced while Crooked-Bear stuffed his head with the thousand details of white mentality; but now vaguely he began to feel a lack of something, an effort which he had not made—a something he had left undone; a difference and a distinction between himself and the officers who were so free to associate with the creature who had borrowed his mind and given nothing in return. No one in the rude campaigning which had been the lot of all since he joined had made any noticeable social distinction toward him—rather otherwise; they had sought and trusted him, and more than that, he had been singled out for special good will. He was free to call at any officer's quarters on the line, sure of a favorable reception; then why did he not go to Major Searles's? At the thought he lay heavier on the blanket, and dared not trust his legs to carry out his inclinations.

The camp was full of fine young officers who would trust their legs and risk their hearts—he felt sure of that. True, he was subject to the orders of certain officials, but so were they. Young officers had asked him to do favors on many occasions, and he did them, because it was clear that they ought to be done, and he also had explained devious plains-craft to them of which they had instantly availed themselves. The arrangement was natural and not oppressive.

Captain Lewis could command him to ford a rushing torrent: could tell him to stand on his head and be d—— quick about it, and of course he would do anything for him and Major Searles; they could ask nothing which the thinker would not do in a lope. As for Colonel Miles, the fine-looking man who led "ten thousand" in the great white battles, it was a distinction to do exactly what he ordered—every one did that; then why did he not go to Major Searles's quarters, he kept asking himself. He was not afraid of Colonel Miles or Captain Lewis or Major Searles or any officer, but—and the thought flashed, he was wary of the living eyes of the beloved photograph. Before these he could not use his mind, hands, or feet; his nerves shivered like aspen leaves in a wind, and the blood surged into his head until he could see nothing with his eyes; cold chills played up and down his spine; his hair crawled round under his sombrero, and he was most thoroughly miserable, but some way he no longer felt contentment except while undergoing this misery.

He lay on the blanket while his thoughts alternately fevered and chilled his brain. So intense were his emotions that they did more than disorder his mind: they took smart hold of his very body, gnawing and constricting his vitals until he groaned aloud.

No wild beast which roamed the hills was less conscious, ordinarily, of its bodily functions than Ermine. The machinery of a perfect physique had always responded to the vital principle and unwound to the steady pull of the spring of life, yet he found himself now stricken. It was not a thing for the surgeon, and he gradually gave way before its steady progress. His nature was a rich soil for the seeds of idealism which warm imagination constantly sprinkled, and the fruits became a consuming passion.

His thoughts were burning him. Getting up from his bed, he took a kettle and small axe, saddled his pony, and took himself off toward the river. As he rode along he heard the Englishman call out to him, but he did not answer. The pony trotted away, leaving the camp far behind, until he suddenly came to a little prairie surrounded by cotton-woods, in the middle of which were numbers of small wick-e-ups made by the Indians for sweat-baths. He placed his blankets and ponchos over one, made a fire and heated a number of rocks, divested himself of his clothing, and taking his pail of water got inside, crouching while he dashed handfuls of water over the hot rocks. This simple remedy would do more than cleanse the skin and was always resorted to for common ills by the Indians. After Ermine came out he plunged into the cold waters of the Yellowstone and dressed himself, but he did not feel any better. He mounted and rode off, forgetting his axe, blankets, and pail; such furnishings were unconsidered now. In response to a tremendous desire to do something, he ran his pony for a mile, but that did not calm the yearning.

"I feel like a piece of fly-blown meat," he said to himself. "I think I will go to Saw-Bones and let him have a hack at me; I never was so sick before." And to the cabin of the surgeon he betook himself.

That gentleman was fussing about with affairs of his own, when Ermine entered.

"Say, doctor, give me some medicine."

"What's the matter with you?" asked the addressed, shoving his sombrero to one side and looking up incredulously.

"Oh, I'm sick."

"Well, where are you sick?"

Ermine brushed his hair from off his forehead, slapped his leggings with his quirt, and answered, "Sick all over—kind of low fever, like a man with a bullet in him."

"Bilious, probably." And the doctor felt his pulse and looked into his bright, clear eyes.

"Oh, nonsense, boy—you are not sick. I guess loafing around is bad for you. The Colonel ought to give you a hundred miles with his compliments to some one; but here is a pill which will cure you." Saying which, the physician brought out his box containing wheat bread rolled into small balls, that

he always administered to cases which he did not understand or to patients whom he suspected of shirking on "sick report."

Ermine swallowed it and departed.

The doctor tipped his sombrero forward and laughed aloud in long, cadenced peals as he sorted his vials.

"Sick!" he muttered; "funny—funny—funny sick! One could not kill him with an axe. I guess he is sick of sitting round—sick to be loping over the wild plains. Humph—sick!"

Ermine rode down the officers' row, but no one was to be seen. He pulled his horse's head up before Major Searles's door, but instantly slapped him with his whip and trotted on to his tent.

"If that fool Indian boy would only show himself," he thought; but the Indian was not a fool, and did not. Again Ermine found himself lying on his back, more discontented than ever. The day waned and the shadows on the tent walls died, but still he lay. Ramon stuck his head in at the flaps.

"Well—ah got your British man hees pony, Ermine—trade twenty-five dollar in goods for five pony."

"Oh, d—— the Englishman," was the response to this, whereat Ramon took a good long stare at his friend and withdrew. He failed to understand the abruptness, and went away wondering how Ermine could know that he had gouged Mr. Harding a little on the trade. Still this did not explain; for he had confidence in his own method of blinding his trail. He was a business man and a moral cripple.

The sun left the world and Ermine with his gloomy thoughts.

* * *

Late at night Captain Lewis sat at his desk writing letters, the lamp spotting on the white disk of his hat, which shaded his face, while the pale moonlight crept in through the open door. A sword clanked outside, and with a knock the officer of the guard hurriedly entered.

"Say, Bill, I have your scout Ermine down by the guard-house, and he's drunk. I didn't lock him up. Wanted to see you first. If I lock him up, I am afraid he'll pull out on you when he comes to. What shall I do?"

"The devil you say—Ermine drunk? Why, I never knew him to drink; it was a matter of principle with him; often told me that his mentor, whoever he was, told him not to."

"Well, he's drunk now, so there you are," said the officer.

"How drunk?"

"Oh, good and drunk."

"Can he walk?" Lewis queried.

"No; all he can do is lay on his back and shoot pretty thick Injun at the moon."

"Does every one know of this?"

"No; Corporal Riley and Private Bass of Company K brought him up from Wilmore's whiskey-shack, and they are sitting on his chest out back of the guard-house. Come on," spoke the responsible one.

Lewis jumped up and followed. They quickly made their way to the spot, and there Lewis beheld Ermine lying on his back. The moonlight cut his fine face softly and made the aureole of his light hair stand away from the ground. He moaned feebly, but his eyes were closed. Corporal Riley and Private Bass squatted at his head and feet with their eyes fastened on the insensible figure. Off to one side a small pile of Ermine's lethal weapons shimmered. The post was asleep; a dog barked, and an occasional cow-bell tinkled faintly down in the quartermaster's corral.

"Gad!" gasped Lewis, as he too stooped down. "How did this happen, Corporal?"

"Well, I suppose we might as well tell it as it is," Bass replied, indirectly conscious of the loyalty he owed his brother sinner. "We ran the guard, sir, and went down to Wilmore's, and when we got there, we found this feller pretty far gone with drink. He had his guns out, and was talking Injun, and he had Wilmore hiding out in the sagebrush. I beefed him under the ear, and we took his guns away, sir. I didn't hurt him much; he was easy money with his load, and then we packed him up here, and I told the officer of the guard, sir."

"Well," said Lewis, finally, "make a chair of your hands and bring him down to my quarters."

The soldiers gathered up the limp form, while Lewis took the belt and pistols.

"No use of reporting this?"

"No," answered the officer of the guard.

The men laid him out on the Captain's bed after partially disrobing him, and started to withdraw.

"Go to your quarters, men, and keep your mouths shut; you will understand it is best for you."

The two saluted and passed out, leaving the Captain pacing the floor, and groping wildly for an explanation.

"Why, I have offered that boy a drink out of my own flask on campaign, when we were cold enough and tired enough to make my old Aunt Jane weaken on her blue ribbon; but he never did. That was good of the men to bring him in, and smart of Welbote not to chuck him in the guard-house. Sailor's sins! he'd never stand that; it would kill his pride, and he has pride, this long-haired wild boy. He may tell me in the morning, but I am not so sure of that. Laying down on his luck is not the way he plays it. I don't doubt it was an accident, and maybe it will teach him a d—— good lesson; he'll have a head like a hornets' nest to-morrow morning."

The Captain, after a struggle with the strange incident, sought his couch, and when he arose next morning betook himself to Ermine's room. He found him asleep amid the tangle of his wonderful hair, and he smiled as he pictured the scout's surprise when he awoke; in fact, he pulled himself together for a little amusement. A few remarks to reënforce the headache would do more good than a long brief without a big 'exhibit A,' such as would accompany the awakening.

The steady gaze of the Captain awoke the scout, and he opened his eyes, which wandered about the room, but displayed no interest; they set themselves on the Captain's form, but refused to believe these dreams, and closed again. The Captain grinned and addressed the empty room:—

"How would you like to be a millionaire and have that headache? Oh, gee—'twould bust a mule's skull."

The eyes opened again and took more account of things; they began to credit their surroundings. When the scene had assembled itself, Ermine sat up on the bed, saying, "Where am I? what hit me?" and then he lay down again. His dream had come true; he was sick.

"You are in my bed, so stay there, and you will come out all right. You have been making the Big Red Medicine; the devil is pulling your hair, and every time he yanks, he will say, 'John Ermine, don't do that again.' Keep quiet, and you will get well." After saying which Lewis left the room.

All day long the young man lay on the bed; he was burning at the stake; he was being torn apart by wild horses; the regimental band played its bangiest music in his head; the big brass drum would nearly blow it apart; and his poor stomach kept trying to crawl out of his body in its desperate strife to escape Wilmore's decoction of high-wine. This lasted all day, but by evening the volcano had blown itself out, when a natural sleep overcame him.

Captain Lewis had the knowledge of certain magic, well enough known in the army, to alleviate Ermine's condition somewhat, but he chose not to use it; he wanted 'exhibit A' to wind up in a storm of fireworks.

As Ermine started out the next morning Lewis called, "Hey, boy, how did you come to do it?"

Ermine turned a half-defiant and half-questioning front to Lewis and tossed his matted hair. "I don't know, Captain; it all seems as though I must have fallen off the earth; but I'm back now and think I can stay here."

"Well, no one knows about it except myself, so don't say a word to any one, and don't do it again—sabe?"

"You bet I won't. If the soldiers call that drowning their sorrows, I would rather get along with mine."

CHAPTER XV

Bringing in the Wolf

"Going to follow the dogs to-day, Lewis?" said Lieutenant Shockley, poking his head in the half-open door.

"Yes, reckon I'll give this chair a vacation; wait a minute," and he mauled the contents of his ditty-box after the manner of men and bears when in search of trifles. A vigorous stirring is bound to upheave what is searched for, so in due course the Captain dug up a snaffle-bit.

"I find my horse goes against this better than the government thing—when the idea is to get there and d—— formations."

"Well, shake yourself, Lewis; the people are pulling out."

"What, ahead of the scouts?" laughed the chief of them.

"Yes; and you know the line never retires on the scouts; so smoke up."

The orderly having changed the bits, the two mounted and walked away. "'Spose this is for the Englishman. Great people these Englishmen—go trotting all over the earth to chase something; anything will do from rabbits to tigers, and niggers preferred," said Lewis.

"Must be a great deprivation to most Englishmen to have to live in England where there is nothing to chase. I suppose they all have this desire to kill something; a great hardship it must be," suggested Shockley.

"Oh, I think they manage," continued Lewis; "from what I understand the rich and the great go batting about the globe after heads; the so-so fellows go into the army and navy to take their chance of a killing, and the lower orders have to find contentment in staying at home, where there is no amusement but pounding each other."

"There goes your friend Ermine on that war-pony of his; well, he can show his tail to any horse in cantonments. By the way, some one was telling me that he carries a

Shockley. *Authors' wood engraving.*

medicine-bag with him; isn't he a Christian?"

"Oh, I don't know. He reminds me of old Major Doyle of ours, who was promoted out of us during the war, but who rejoined in Kansas and was retired. You don't remember him? He was an Irishman and a Catholic; he had been in the old army since the memory of man runneth not to the contrary, and ploughed his way up and down all over the continent. And there was Major Dunham—you know him. He and Doyle had been comrades since youth; they had fought and marched together, spilled many a noggin in each other's honor, and who drew the other's monthly pay depended on the paste-boards. Old Doyle came into post, one day, and had a lot of drinks with the fellows as he picked up the social threads. Finally he asked: 'Un' phware is me ole friend, Dunham? Why doesn't he come down and greet me with a glass?'

"Some one explained that old Dunham had since married, had joined the church, and didn't greet any one over glasses any more.

"'Un' phwat church did he join?'

"Some one answered, the Universalist Church.

"'Ah, I see,' said Doyle, tossing off his drink, 'he's huntin' an aisy ford.' So I guess that's what Ermine is doing."

They soon joined the group of mounted officers and ladies, orderlies, and nondescripts of the camp, all alive with anticipations, and their horses stepping high.

"Good morning, Mr. Harding; how do you find yourself?" called out Captain Lewis.

"Fine—fine, thank you."

"How are you mounted?"

Harding patted his horse's neck, saying: "Quite well—a good beast; seems to manage my weight, but I find this saddle odd. Bless me, I know there is no habit in the world so strong as the saddle. I have the flat saddle habit."

"What we call a rim-fire saddle," laughed Searles, who joined the conversation.

"Ah—a rim-fire, do you call them? Well, do you know, Major, I should say this saddle was better adapted to carrying a sack of corn than a man," rejoined Harding.

"Oh, you'll get along; there isn't a fence nearer than St. Paul except the quartermaster's corral."

"I say, Searles," spoke Lewis, "there's the Colonel out in front—happy as a boy out of school; glad there's something to keep him quiet; we must do this for him every day, or he'll have us out pounding sage-brush."

"And there's the quartermaster with a new popper on his whip," sang some voice.

"There is no champagne like the air of the high plains before the sun burns the bubble out of it," proclaimed Shockley, who was young and without any of the saddle or collar marks of life; "and to see these beautiful women riding along—say, Harding, if I get off this horse I'll set this prairie on fire," and he burst into an old song:—

"Now, ladies, good-by to each kind, gentle
    soul,
Though me coat it is ragged, me heart it is
    whole;
There's one sitting yonder I think wants a
    beau,
Let her come to the arms of young Billy
    Barlow."

And Shockley urged his horse to the side of Miss Katherine Searles.

Observing the manœuvre, Captain Lewis poked her father in the ribs. "I don't think your daughter wants a beau very much,

Major; the youngsters are four files deep around her now."

" 'Tis youth, Bill Lewis; we've all had it once, and from what I observe, they handle it pretty much as we used to."

"The very same. I don't see how men write novels or plays about that old story; all they can do is to invent new fortifications for Mr. Hero to carry before she names the day."

Lieutenant Shockley found himself unable to get nearer than two horses to Miss Searles, so he bawled: "And I thought you fellows were hunting wolves. I say, Miss Searles, if you ride one way and the wolf runs the other, it is easy to see which will have the larger field. My money is on you—two to one. Who will take the wolf?"

"Oh, Mr. Shockley, between you and this Western sun, I shall soon need a new powder puff."

"Shall I challenge him?" called Bowles to the young woman.

"Please not, Mr. Bowles; I do not want to lose him." And every one greeted Shockley derisively.

"Guide right!" shouted the last, putting his horse into a lope. Miss Searles playfully slashed about with her riding-whip, saying, "Deploy, gentlemen," and followed him. The others broke apart; they had been beaten by the strategy of the loud mouth. Lieutenant Butler, however, permitted himself the pleasure of accompanying Miss Searles; his determination could not be shaken by these diversions; he pressed resolutely on.

"I think Butler has been hit over the heart," said one of the dispersed cavaliers.

"You bet, and it is a disabling wound too. I wonder if Miss Searles intends to cure him. When I see her handle her eyes, methinks, compadre, she's a cruel little puss. I wouldn't care to be her mouse."

"But, fellows, she's pretty, a d—— pretty girl, hey!" ventured a serious youngster. "You can bet any chap here would hang out the white flag and come a-running, if she hailed him."

And so, one with another, they kept the sacred fire alight. As for that matter, the aforesaid Miss Puss knew how her men valued the difficulties of approach, which was why she scattered them. She proposed to take them in detail. Men do not weaken readily before each other, but alone they are helpless creatures, when the woman understands herself. She can then sew them up, tag them, and put them away on various shelves, and rely on them to stay there; but it requires management, of course.

"I say, Miss Searles, those fellows will set spring guns and bear traps for me to-night; they will never forgive me."

"Oh, well, Mr. Shockley, to be serious, I don't care. Do you suppose a wolf will be found? I am so bored." Which remark caused the eminent Lieutenant to open his mouth very wide in imitation of a laugh, divested of all mirth.

"Miss Katherine Searles," he said, in mock majesty, "I shall do myself the honor to crawl into the first badger-hole we come to and stay there until you dig me out."

"Don't be absurd; you know I always bury my dead. Mr. Butler, do you expect we shall find a wolf? Ah, there is that King Charles cavalier, Mr. Ermine—for all the world as though he had stepped from an old frame. I do think he is lovely."

"Oh, bother that yellow Indian; he is such a nuisance," jerked Butler.

"Why do you say that? I find him perfectly new; he never bores me, and he stood between me and that enraged savage."

"A regular play. I do not doubt he arranged it beforehand. However, it was well thought out—downright dramatic, except that the Indian ought to have killed him."

"Oh, would you have arranged it that way if you had been playwright?"

"Yes," replied the bilious lover.

Shaking her bridle rein, she cried, "Come, Mr. Shockley, let us ride to Ermine; at least you will admire him." Shockley enjoyed the death stroke which she had administered to Butler, but saying to himself as he thought of Ermine, "D—— the curly boy," and followed his charming and difficult quarry. He alone had ridden true.

The independent and close-lipped scout was riding outside the group. He never grew accustomed to the heavy columns, and did not talk on the march—a common habit of desert wanderers. But his eye covered everything. Not a buckle or a horse-hair or the turn of a leg escaped him, and you may be sure Miss Katherine Searles was detailed in his picture.

He had beheld her surrounded by the young officers until he began to hate the whole United States army. Then he saw her dismiss the escort saving only two, and presently she reduced her force to one. As she came toward him, his blood took a pop into his head, which helped mightily to illumine his natural richness of color. She was really coming to him. He wished it, he wanted it, as badly as a man dying of thirst wants water, and yet a whole volley of bullets would not disturb him as her coming did.

"Good morning, Mr. Ermine; you, too, are out after wolves, I see," sang Katherine, cheerily.

"No, ma'm, I don't care anything about wolves; and why should I care for them?"

"What are you out for then, pray?"

"Oh, I don't know; thought I would like to see you after wolves. I guess that's why I am out," came the simple answer.

"Well, to judge by the past few miles I don't think you will see me after them to-day."

"I think so myself, Miss Searles. These people ought to go back in the breaks of the land to find wolves; they don't give a wolf credit for having eyes."

"Why don't you tell them so, Mr. Ermine?"

"The officers think they know where to find them; they would not thank me, and there might not be anywhere I would go to find them. It does not matter whether we get one or none, anyhow," came Ermine's sageness.

"Indeed, it does matter. I must have a wolf."

"Want him alive or dead?" was the low question.

"What! am I to have one?"

"You are," replied the scout, simply.

"When?"

"Well, Miss Searles, I can't order one from the quartermaster exactly, but if you are in a great hurry, I might go now."

"Mr. Ermine, you will surely kill me with your generosity. You have offered me your scalp, your body, and now a wolf. Oh, by the way, what did that awful Indian say to you? I suppose you have seen him since."

"Didn't say anything."

"Well, I hope he has forgiven you; but as I understand them, that is not the usual way among Indians."

"No, Miss Searles, he won't forgive me. I'm a-keeping him to remember you by."

"How foolish; I might give you something for a keepsake which would leave better memories, do you not think so?"

"You might, if you wish to."

The girl was visibly agitated at this, coming as it did from her crude admirer. She fumbled about her dress, her hair, and finally drew off her glove and gave it to the scout, with a smile so sweet and a glance of the eye which penetrated Ermine like a charge of buckshot. He took the glove and put it inside of the breast of his shirt, and said, "I'll get the wolf."

Shockley was so impressed with the conversation that he was surprised into silence, and to accomplish that phenomenon took a most powerful jolt, as every one in the regiment knew. He could talk the bottom out of a nose-bag, or put a clock to sleep. Ordinary verbal jollity did not seem at all adequate, so he carolled a passing line:—

"One little, two little, three little Injuns,
  Four little, five little, six little Injuns,
Seven little, eight little, nine little Injuns,
      Ten little Injun boys."

This came as an expiring burst which unsettled his horse though it relieved him. Shockley needed this much yeast before he could rise again.

"Oh, Mr. Shockley, you must know Mr. Ermine."

"I have the pleasure, Miss Searles; haven't I, Ermine?"

The scout nodded assent.

"We were side by side when we rushed the point of that hill in the Sitting Bull fight last fall; remember that, Ermine?"

"Yes, sir," said the scout; but the remembrance evidently did not cause Ermine's E string to vibrate. Fighting was easier, freer; but altogether it was like washing the dishes at home compared with the dangers which now beset him.

Suddenly every one was whipping and spurring forward; the pack of greyhounds were streaking it for the hills. "Come on," yelled Shockley, "here's a run." And that mercurial young man's scales tipped right readily from his heart to his spurs.

"It's only a coyote, Miss Searles," said Ermine; but the young woman spatted her horse with her whip and rode bravely after the flying Shockley. Ermine's fast pony kept steadily along with her under a pull; the plainsman's long, easy sway in the saddle was unconscious, and he never took his eyes from the girl, now quite another person under the excitement.

Every one in the hunting-party was pumping away to the last ounce. A pack of greyhounds make a coyote save all the time he can; they stimulate his interest in life, and those who have seen a good healthy specimen burn up the ground fully realize the value of passing moments.

"Oh, dear; my hat is falling off!" shrieked the girl.

"Shall I save it, Miss Searles?"

"'Yes! yes! Catch it!" she screamed.

Ermine brought his flying pony nearer hers on the off side and reached his hand toward the flapping hat, struggling at a frail anchorage of one hat-pin, but his arm grew nerveless at the near approach to divinity.

"Save it! save it!" she called.

"Shall I?" and he pulled himself together.

Dropping his bridle-rein over the pommel of his saddle, standing in his stirrups as steadily as a man in church, he undid the hat with both hands. When he had released

it and handed it to its owner, she heard him mutter hoarsely, "My God!"

"Oh, Mr. Ermine, I hope the pin did not prick you."

"No, it wasn't the pin."

"Ah," she ejaculated barely loud enough for him to hear amid the rushing hoof-beats.

The poor man was in earnest, and the idea drove the horses, the hounds, and the coyote out of her mind, and she ran her mount harder than ever. She detested earnest men, having so far in her career with the exception of Mr. Butler found them great bores; but drive as she would, the scout pattered at her side, and she dared not look at him.

These two were by no means near the head of the drive, as the girl's horse was a stager, which had been selected because he was highly educated concerning badger-holes and rocky hillsides.

Orderlies clattered behind them, and Private Patrick O'Dowd and Private Thompson drew long winks at each other.

"Oi do be thinkin' the long bie's harse cud roon fasther eff the divil was afther him. Faith, who'd roon away from a fairy?"

"The horse is running as fast as is wanted," said Thompson, sticking his hooks into the Indian pony which he rode.

"Did yez obsarve the bie ramove the hat from the lady, and his pony shootin' gravel into our eyes fit to smother?" shouted O'Dowd, using the flat of his hand as a sounding-board to Thompson.

"You bet, Pat; and keeping the gait he could take a shoe off her horse, if she wanted it done."

"They say seein's believin', but Oi'll not be afther tellin' the story in quarters. Oi'm eaight year in the ahrmy, and Oi can lie whin it's convanient."

The dogs overhauled the unfortunate little wolf despite its gallant efforts, and it came out of the snarling mass, as some wag had expressed it, "like a hog going to war —in small pieces." The field closed up and dismounted, soldier fashion, at the halt.

"What's the matter with the pony to-day,

Ermine? Expected you'd be ahead of the wolf at least," sang out Lewis.

"I stopped to pick up a hat," he explained; but Captain Lewis fixed his calculating eye on his man and bit his mustache. Events had begun to arrange themselves; that drunken night and Ermine's apathy toward the Englishman's hunting-party—and he had stopped to pick up her hat—oho!

Without a word the scout regained his seat and loped away toward the post, and Lewis watched him for some time, in a brown study; but a man of his years often fails to give the ardor of youth its proper value, so his mind soon followed more natural thoughts.

"Your horse is not a very rapid animal, I observe, Miss Searles," spoke Butler.

"Did you observe that? I did not notice that you were watching me, Mr. Butler."

"Oh, I must explain that in an affair of this kind I am expected to sustain the reputation of the cavalry. I forced myself to the front."

"Quite right. I kept the only man in the rear, who was capable of spoiling your reputation; you are under obligations to me."

"That wild man, you mean. He certainly has a wonderful pony, but you need not trouble about him if it is to please me only."

"I find this sun becoming too insistent; I think I will go back," said Katherine Searles. Many of the women also turned their horses homeward, leaving only the more pronounced types of sportsmen to search for another wolf.

"Having sustained the cavalry, I'll accompany you, Katherine."

"Miss Searles, please!" she said, turning to him, and the little gem of a nose asserted itself.

"Oh, dear me! What have I done? You permitted me to call you Katherine only last night."

"Yes, but I do not propose to divide my friendship with a nasty little gray wolf which has been eaten up alive."

The officer ran his gauntlet over his eyes.

"I am such a booby. I see my mistake, Miss Searles, but the idea you advance seems so ridiculous—to compare yourself with a wolf."

"Oh, I say, Miss Searles," said Shockley, riding up, "may I offer you one of my gauntlets? The sun, I fear, will blister your bare hand."

"No, indeed." And Butler tore off a glove, forcing it into her hand. She could not deny him, and pulled it on. "Thank you; I lost one of mine this morning."

Then she turned her eyes on Mr. Shockley with a hard little expression, which sealed him up. He was prompt to feel that the challenge meant war, and war with this girl was the far-away swing of that gallant strategic pendulum.

"Yes," Shockley added, "one is apt to drop things without noting them, in a fast rush. I dropped something myself this morning."

"Pray what was it, Mr. Shockley?"

"It was an idea," he replied with a shrug of the shoulders.

"An idea?" laughed she, appreciating Shockley's discretion. "I hope you have more of them than I have gloves."

"I have only one," he sighed.

"Are all soldiers as stupid as you are, my dear sir?"

"All under thirty, I am sorry to say," and this from Shockley too. Miss Searles applied the whip; but go as she would, the two officers did not lose again the idea, but kept their places beside her.

"You are not very steady under fire," laughed Shockley.

"You are such an absurd person."

"I may be a blessing in disguise."

"You may be; I am unable to identify you."

"The chaperon is waving her whip at us, Miss Searles," cautioned Butler.

"Private O'Dowd is my chaperon, and he can stand the pace," she replied.

The young woman drove on, leaving a pall of dust behind, until the little party made the cantonment and drew rein in front of the Searleses' quarters. Giving her hand to the orderly, she dismissed her escort and disappeared.

"Well, Katherine," said Mrs. Searles, "did you enjoy your ride?"

"Yes, mother, but my horse is such an old poke I was nowhere in the race."

"The Major says he is a safe horse; one which can be relied on, and that is more important than speed. I do not want your neck broken, my dear."

"Neither do I want my neck broken, but I should like to be somewhere in sight during a run. The young officers desert me once a wolf is sighted; they forget their manners at the first flash of a greyhound."

"I know, daughter, but what can you expect? They go out for that purpose."

"Mr. Ermine doesn't, or at least he is polite enough to say that he goes out to see me run, and not the wolf. If he is not sophisticated, he seems to have the primitive instincts of a gentleman."

"Mr. Ermine, forsooth!" And Madam Searles betrayed some asperity. "Is he presumptuous enough to present you with compliments? You had better maintain your distance."

"He is a perfectly delightful man, mother; so thoughtful and so handsome."

"Tut tut, Katherine; he is only an ordinary scout—a wild man."

"I don't care; I like him."

"Katherine, what are you thinking of?"

"Oh, I don't know, mother; I am thinking what an absurd lot men are. They insist on talking nonsense at me. They do not seem to preserve their reserve; they are not a bit like the men back in the States."

"Well, my daughter, you must be careful not to provoke familiarity. Young women are rather scarce out here, and you are not without your charms. I believe you use your eyes more than you should. Have a care; do not forget that quiet modesty is the most becoming thing in the world for a woman."

"I am sure I do nothing; in fact, I have to be constantly menacing these military youths to keep them from coming too near, especially Mr. Shockley and Mr. Butler. I am in distress every minute for fear Mr. Butler will say more than I am ready to hear."

Mrs. Searles was by no means averse to Butler's attentions to her daughter. "A very fine young man," was her comment when she thought of him. Both women knew that the Lieutenant was ready to draw his sabre in Katherine's behalf.

Katherine had met Butler while visiting St. Louis the year before, had come to know him well, and didn't pretend to dislike him. His father and mother were dead, but his people were of consequence.

Mrs. Searles determined to ask the Major to make some inquiries about her daughter's suitor, and meanwhile dismissed Katherine with the caution not to tempt this midday sun overmuch; "It will soon turn your peach-blow into russet apples," she told her, "and men, you know, like the peach-blow. Without it you might be less troubled by the young officers."

* * *

The sun was about to depart. The families of the officers were sitting under their *ramadas* enjoying the cool. Butler and Shockley with two or three other men were seated with the Searleses when their attention was attracted by a commotion down by the quarters.

"What's the circus?"

"Don't make out; seems to be coming this way. It is—why, it is the scout Ermine!"

The group sat expectantly and witnessed the approach of John Ermine on his horse. At some distance to one side rode Wolf-Voice, and gradually through the dusk they made out some small animal between them —a dog-like thing.

The riders drew up before the Searleses' hut, and every one rose. The object was a scared and demoralized wolf with his tail between his legs. His neck was encircled by two rawhide lariats which ran to the pommels of the riders.

Touching his hat, Ermine said, "Miss Searles, I have brought you the wolf."

"Goodness gracious, Mr. Ermine! I only said that in fun. What can I possibly do with a wolf?"

"I don't know. You said you wanted one, so here he is."

"Yaes," said Wolf-Voice, with an oath, "she was bite my harm hoff; you no want heem; I skin her alive." He had previously warned Ermine that no one but a d—— fool would want a live wolf.

"Well, daughter, what you going to do with it? Start a Zoo? I don't know where we can put him," spoke Major Searles, in perplexity.

"He will have to roost high if the dogs find out about this visitation," observed Shockley.

"How did you get him, Ermine?"

"Dug him out of his den, and before we got him roped he pinched Wolf-Voice, and I had a hard time to keep him from killing the beast."

"Yaes; no want him, an' we dig a hole mile deep mabeso—dig ever since sun she so high, ten-as tol-a-pas." And in his disgust Wolf-Voice was about to slacken his rope.

"Hold up there; don't turn that animal loose near here! Take him down to the corral and lock him up. We'll see to-morrow what can be done with him," spoke Searles.

Ermine and Wolf-Voice turned and drifted out into the gathering darkness with their forlorn tow, while a few soldiers with clubs fought the dogs off as they gradually began to gather around their natural enemy.

"Why, I only asked for a wolf in the most casual way—in a joking way; you heard me, Mr. Shockley."

"Yes, I did hear you, but I also heard him say you should have one, and I thought at the time he looked serious about it."

"I was so astonished that I did not properly thank him," she added; "and the Indian was in a lovely humor over the whole episode; his disgust was most apparent. I must be more careful what I say to Mr. Ermine."

"I have it," cried the Major; "we'll make up a purse, buy the wolf, and run him so soon as he gets over the effects of his capture."

"No, no, papa, you must not offend Ermine with money. He would be awfully offended; that would be the very last thing to do to him."

CHAPTER XVI

A Hunt

A troop of cavalry trotted along through the early morning dust, and Lieutenant Butler drew out at the Searleses' quarters, tying his horse for a moment in front, while he went inside. It was early for casual people. He did not stay long, but the sergeant in the rear thought he saw a girl come to the door and kiss him good-by. As the officer dashed to the head of the troop, the old sergeant dipped a smiling countenance deep into a plug of tobacco.

"Hello! there goes Butler with his troop," said Mr. Harding to Captain Lewis, as they basked in the morning sun before that officer's quarters.

"Yes, he goes to escort some wagons; but the fact is, internecine war has broken out in the post, and he goes for the good of the service. It's all about a damn little yellow dog."

"A dog make a war! How, pray?"

"Oh gee! yes! Dogs and rum and women make all the trouble there is in the army, and particularly dogs. That sounds odd, doesn't it? Nevertheless, it's a hard, dry fact. Soldiers take to dogs, and it's always 'kick my dog kick me' with these bucks. That troop had a miserable runt of a *fice,* and he's smart the same as such pups often are. The cavalrymen have taught him to nip at infantrymen, which they think is great fun. Some of the infantrymen got tired of sewing up three-cornered tears in their galligaskins and allowed they would assassinate said *fice.* Here is where these baby cavalrymen lose their temper and threaten to fire on the company-quarters of any outfit which bags Fido—and that's war. It has been fixed up. Some officer has arranged an armistice, and meanwhile the troop gets a few miles in the sage-brush, which, it is hoped, will be credited to the pup, whereat he won't be so popular."

"Ah, a very sad case for the doggie,"

added Harding; "he was taught to take wrong views of the service."

"Let us go down and take a look at Ermine's wolf," said Lewis, and the two proceeded to the quartermaster's corral, where they found a group standing about the wolf.

It was held by a stout chain and lay flat on the ground, displaying an entire apathy concerning the surroundings, except that it looked "Injuny," as a passing mule-skinner observed.

"When I see one of those boys, it makes my back come up like a cat's," said Lewis. "A bunch of them nearly pulled me down two years ago on the Canadian. I fired all my ammunition at them and got into camp just about the right time; a half a mile more and I would have got my 'final statement.'"

"Yes, I have hunted them in Poland, on moonlight nights. A wolf in the deep forests on a moonlight night harmonizes better than one tied by a chain, with twenty men staring at him in broad daylight."

An irrepressible private shoved his nose into the circle, looked at the captive, and departed saying:—

> "He enlisted in the army,
>   The bullets took their toll,
> The wolves got his body,
>   And the divil got his soul.
>   Om-a yah-ha-ha."

Poor wolf! He possessed too many attributes of man to ingratiate himself. He did not admit their superiority, and lay stoically under the heel of the conqueror; all thumbs were down for him.

He was aposthrophized by a soldier: "Ah, me innocent-lukin' child of the divil—wait till ye git thim hoop-shnake dawgs afther yez."

Major Searles rode in through the gate and sang out: "The Colonel has a few papers to sign, after which he says we will chase the wolf; so you can get ready, gentlemen, those who care to run." And then to Ermine, who stood near: "Miss Searles thinks that will be a proper disposition of your valuable present. Can you manage to turn him loose?"

"Why, yes, I suppose we can. Putting the ropes on him is easier than taking them off. I won't take him out until you are all ready; every dog in the camp will fly at him. Can I have four or five soldiers to drive them off? Wolf-Voice and myself will be on horseback, and can't protect him."

"Certainly, certainly!" And under the Major's directions various soldiers armed themselves with whips, and undertook to make a rear-guard fight with the garrison pups.

Horses were saddled, and went clattering to all points of the post. The certainty of a run drew every one out. Shockley aided Miss Searles to mount, saying, "I am on duty to-day; my thoughts will fly where my pony should. You cannot doubt where he would go."

"Poor man, do not look so woebegone; it does not become you. I like you better when you sing than when you cry."

"If you didn't make me cry, I should sing all the time."

"Oh, that would be bad for your voice, my dear Mr. Shockley, as we say on a letter head." And she mocked him beyond her rapier point, as she rode along, followed by the rapidly receding words:—

> "Don't forget me, Molly darling;
>   Put your little hand in mine.
> Tell me truly that you love me,
>   And—"

The rest died behind her.

"He is such a nice fellow," she mused, "but there's more music in his soul than in his throat. I shall miss him to-day, but not so much as I shall Mr. Butler; and there is my knight of the yellow hair. Oh! I must be careful of him. He is such a direct person, there is no parrying his assault. His presence has a strange effect on me; I do not understand it; he is queer. What a pity he is not an officer, with short hair; but pshaw! I might not like him then; how absurd, I do not like him now." And thus the girlish emotions swayed her pretty head, not stopping to clarify, man fashion. They flitted about on every little wind, and alighted nowhere for more than a few seconds.

Other women joined her, and a few men, all making for the quartermaster's.

"Your mother finds herself past riding, Miss Katherine," spoke one merry matron, to whom age had been generous, and who was past it herself, did she but know it.

"Yes, mother takes that view. I am afraid I cannot sustain the reputation of the Searles outfit, as the phrase goes here. My horse is a Dobbin—papa is so absurdly careful. There is no fun in being careful."

"Oh, the Major is right. He knows the value of that little nose of yours, and doesn't want it ploughed in the dirt. Noses which point upward, just ever so little, lack the severity of those that point down, in women; that is what the men tell me, Katherine."

The girl glanced at her companion, and doubted not that the men had said that to her.

"I don't care to go through life thinking of my nose," she added.

"No, indeed; never think of your nose; think of what men think of it."

"I can go home and do that, Mrs. Gooding; out here my horse seems more to the point than my nose." At this juncture some men opened the corral gate, and the women passed in.

Seeing the wolf flattened out like an un-oratorical man at a banquet, who knows he is next on the toast-list, Miss Searles exclaimed, "Poor creature! it seems such a shame."

And the others added, "Now that I see him I feel like a butcher."

"Let him go, Major; we will not have his murder on our conscience," continued a third.

"I should as soon think of killing a canary in a cage." And thus did the gentler sex fail at this stage; but when the Colonel rode out of the enclosure, they all followed.

The wolf rose to its feet with a snap as the half-breed and Ermine approached, curling their lariats. A few deft turns, and the ropes drew around the captive's throat. A man undid the chain, the horse started,

and the wild beast drew after, a whizzing blur of gray hair.

There was some difficulty in passing the gate, but that was managed. The remembrance of yesterday's experience in the rawhide coils came back to the wolf. It slunk along, tail down, and with head turning in scared anxious glances. Behind followed the rear-guard, waving their whips at various feeble-minded ki-yis which were emboldened by their own yelling.

"Colonel, give me a good start; this is a female wolf. I will raise my hat and drop it on the ground when it is time to let the dogs go! We may have trouble clearing away these ropes," talked Ermine, loudly.

"Sacre—mi-ka-tic-eh muck-a-muck—dees dam wolf he have already bite de hole in my rope ver near," and Wolf-Voice gave a severe jerk. To be sure, the animal was already playing havoc with his lariat by savage side-snaps which bade fair shortly to shred it.

"Watch my hat, Colonel; she may get away from us before we are ready."

Well outside of the post the Colonel halted his field and waited; all eyes bent on the two wild men, with their dangerous bait, going up the road. The nimble ponies darted about in response to the riders' swayings, while at intervals the wolf gave an imitation of a pin-wheel.

When well out, Wolf-Voice yelled, "Ah, dare go my rope!"

The wolf had cut it, and turning, fixed its eyes on Ermine, who stopped and shook his lariat carefully, rolling it in friendly circles toward the wolf. Wolf-Voice drew his gun, and for an appreciable time the situation had limitless possibilities. By the exercise of an intelligence not at all rare in wild creatures, the wolf lay down and clawed at the rope. In an instant it was free and galloping off, turning its head to study the strategy of the field.

"Wait for the people; she's going for the timber, and will get away," shouted Ermine, casting his big sombrero into the air.

The dogs held in leash never lost sight of

the gray fellow, and when let go were soon whippeting along. The horses sank on their quarters and heaved themselves forward until the dusty plain groaned under their feet.

"Ki-yi-yi-yi," called the soldiers, imitating the Indians who had so often swept in front of their guns.

The wolf fled, a gray shadow borne on the wind, making for the timber in the river-bottom. It had a long start and a fair hope. If it had understood how vain the noses of greyhounds are, it might have cut its angle to cover a little; for once out of sight it might soon take itself safely off; but no wild animal can afford to angle much before the spider dogs.

The field was bunched at the start and kicked up a vast choking dust, causing many slow riders to deploy out on the sides, where they could at least see the chase and the going in front of them. Wolf-Voice and Ermine had gone to opposite sides and were lost in the rush.

Ermine's interest in the wolf departed with it. He now swung his active pony through the dirt clouds, seeking the girl, and at last found her, well in the rear as usual, and unescorted, after the usual luck she encountered when she played her charms against a wolf. She was trying to escape from the pall by edging off toward the river-bank. Well behind strode the swift war-pony, and Ermine devoured her with his eyes. The impulse to seize and bear her away to the inaccessible fastnesses of which he knew was overcome by a fear of her—a fear so great that his blood turned to water when his passion was greatest.

Time did not improve Ermine's logistics concerning this girl; he wanted her, and he did not know in the least how to get her. The tigers of his imagination bit and clawed each other in ferocious combat when he looked at her back as she rode or at her pensive photograph in the quiet of his tent. When, however, she turned the battery of her eyes on him, the fever left him in a dull, chilly lethargy—a realization of the hope-lessness of his yearning; and plot and plan and assuage his fears as he might, he was always left in a mustache-biting perplexity. He could not at will make the easy reconnaissance of her fortresses which the young officers did, and this thought maddened him. It poisoned his mind and left his soul like a dead fish cast up on a river-bank.

Ermine had known the easy familiarity of the Indian squaws, but none of them had ever stirred him. The vast silence of his mountain life had rarely been broken by the presence of men, and never by women. The prophet had utterly neglected the boy's emotions in the interest of his intellect. The intense poverty of his experience left him without any understanding of the most ordinary conventions or casual affairs of white men's lives. All he knew was gathered from his observation of the rude relations of frontier soldiers on campaign. The visions of angels never exalted a fasting mediæval monk in his cell as did the advent of this white woman to Ermine, and they were quite as nebulous.

The powerful appeal which Katherine Searles made to his imagination was beyond the power of his analysis; the word Love was unknown to his vocabulary. He wanted her body, he wanted her mind, and he wanted her soul merged with his, but as he looked at her now, his mouth grew dry, like a man in mortal fear or mortal agony.

And thinking thus, he saw her horse stop dead—sink—and go heels up and over in a complete somersault. The girl fluttered through the air and struck, raising a dust which almost concealed her. A savage slap of his quirt made his pony tear the ground in his frantic rush to her aid. No one noticed the accident, and the chase swept around the bluffs and left him kneeling beside her. She showed no sign of life; the peach-blow left her cheeks an ivory white, set with pearls when the high lights showed, but there was no blood or wound which he could see.

Her mount struggled to extract his poor broken foreleg from a gopher-hole, where it

"He Bore the Limp Form to the Sands."
Authors' photoengraving.

was sunk to the elbow. He raised his head, with its eyes rolling, and groaned in agony.

If this had been a man, or even any other woman, Ermine would have known what to do. In his life a wounded or broken man had been a frequent experience. As he took her wrist to feel her pulse, his own hands trembled so that he gave over; he could feel nothing but the mad torrent of his own blood.

Turning his face in the direction where the hunt had gone, he yelled, "Help! help!" but the sound never reached the thudding hunt. Putting his arm under her shoulder, he raised her up, and supporting her, he looked hopelessly around until his eye fell on the Yellowstone only a short distance away. Water had always been what the wounded wanted. He slowly gathered her in his arms, gained his feet, and made his way toward the river. A gopher-hole had planned what Ermine never could; it had brought her body to him, but it might be a useless gift unless the water gave him back her life.

He bore the limp form to the sands beside the flowing river and laid it down while he ran to fill his hat with water. He made fast work of his restoration, rubbing her wrists and sprinkling her forehead with water; but it was long before a reward came in the way of a breath and a sigh. Again he raised her in a sitting position against his knee.

"Breathe, Katherine—try again—now breathe." And he pressed her chest with his hand, aiding nature as best he knew, until she sighed again and again.

The girl was half damp in death, while like a burning mine the pent-up fire-damp exploded and reverberated through the veins of the young man. Oh, if he could but impart his vitality to her. Possibly he did, for presently her weakness permitted her to note that the sky was blue, that the tree-tops waved in familiar forms, that the air flooded her lungs, and that a cooling rain was falling. Again she drifted somewhere away from the earth in pleasant passage through kaleidoscopic dreams of all a girl's subconsciousness ever offers.

Her eyes spread, but soon closed in complete rest against the easy cradle. She sensed kindly caresses and warm kisses which delighted her. The long yellow hair hung about her face and kept it shadowed from the hot sun.

"Oh my! Oh my! Where am I? Is that you —How do I—" but the effort exhausted her.

"God—God—Sak-a-war-te come quick! It will be too late." He put more water on her face.

* * *

The hunt missed the wolf in the cover of the river-bottom. It doubled on the dogs, and out of sight was out of mind with the fast-running hounds.

"She gave us a run, anyhow," sang out Major Searles to Wolf-Voice.

"Yaes, d—— him; she give me a bite and two run. What good was come of eet, hey—why ain't you keel him first plass, by Gar?"

"Oh! you are a poor sport, Wolf-Voice."

"Am poor sport, hey? All right; nex' wolf she not tink dat, mabeso."

Laughing and talking, they trotted home, picking up belated ones who had strung behind the fastest horses.

"Where is Miss Searles, Major?" spoke one.

"That's so! don't know; had a slow horse; by Gad, we must look this up." And the now anxious father galloped his mount. The others followed sympathetically. Rounding the bluffs, they saw Ermine's pony quietly feeding.

"Where is Ermine?" came a hail of questions, and presently they almost ran over the girl's horse, now lying on its side, breathing heavily, and no longer trying to disengage his leg from the gopher-hole.

"The horse is in a gopher-hole," said some one; "and see here—look at the dirt; he has thrown Miss Searles; here is where she struck."

"Yes, but where is she? where is she?" ejaculated the Major, in a nervous tremor of excitement. "Where is my girl?"

Wolf-Voice had dismounted and found Ermine's trail, which he followed toward the river.

"Come!" he called. "Am show you dose girl!"

While an orderly stayed behind to shoot the horse and get the empty saddle, the group followed hard on the half-breed.

"Done you ride on de trail, you was keep behine. Dey girl was broke his neck, an' Ermine am pack him."

Stepping briskly forward, the plainsman made quick work of empty moccasin tracks and burst through the brush. A pistol-shot rang in the rear; an orderly had shot the horse. A cry of "Help, help!" responded from the river beyond the cottonwoods, and the horses ploughed their way to the sands. The people all dismounted around the limp figure and kneeling scout. Her pale face, the

hat with the water in it, and the horse in the gopher-hole made everything clear.

"Here, Swan, ride to the post for an ambulance," spoke the Major, as he too knelt and took his daughter in his arms. "Ride the horse to death and tell the ambulance to come running." Some of the women brought their ministering hands to bear and with more effect.

"What happened, Katherine?" whispered her father amid the eager silence of the gathered people.

"What did I do?" she pleaded weakly.

"How was it, Ermine?"

"Her horse put his foot in a hole; he is out there now. I saw her go down. Then I tried to save her. Will she live?"

Ermine's eager interest had not departed because of the advent of so many people. He still continued to kneel and to gaze in rapture at the creature of his hopes and fears. No one saw anything in it but the natural interest of one who had been left with so much responsibility.

"If you men will retire, we will endeavor to find her injuries," spoke one of the older ladies; so the men withdrew.

Every one asked eager questions of the scout, who walked hat in hand, and had never before shown perturbation under the trying situations in which he and the soldiers had been placed.

"I knew that wolf would get away in the timber, and I wasn't going to ride my pony for the fun of seeing it, so I was behind. Miss Searles's horse was slow, and I noticed she was being left; then she went down and I didn't know what to do,"—which latter statement was true.

He had done as well under the circumstances as any man could, they all admitted. A magpie on an adjoining limb jeered at the soldiers, though he made no mention of anything further than the scout had admitted.

In due course the ambulance came bounding behind the straining mules. Mrs. Searles was on the seat with the driver, hatless, and white with fear. The young woman was placed in and taken slowly to quarters.

Being the only witness, Ermine repeated his story until he grew tired of speech and wanted only silence which would enable him to think. The greatest event of his life had happened to him that morning; it had come in a curious way; it had lasted but a few moments, but it had added new fuel to his burning mind, which bade fair to consume it altogether.

Miss Searles's injuries consisted of a few bruises and a general shock from which she would soon recover, said the doctor, and the cantonment slowly regathered its composure, all except Shockley, who sat, head down, in most disordered thought, slowly punctuating events as they came to him, by beating on the floor with his scabbard.

"And she gave him her glove and she never gave me any glove—and she never gave Butler her glove that I know of; and he gave her a wolf and he was with her when this thing happened. Say, Shockley, me boy, you are too slow, you are rusty; if you saw an ancient widow woman chopping wood, you would think she was in love with the wood-pile." And thus did that worthy arrive at wrong conclusions. He would not give himself the credit of being only a man, whom God in the wisdom of His creation did not intend to understand women and thus deaden a world.

The camp was in ignorance of the points of contact between Katherine Searles and the scout; it felt none of the concern which distressed Shockley.

Miss Searles had known Butler back in the States; they were much together here on the Yellowstone, and it was pretty generally admitted that in so far as she was concerned Lieutenant Butler had the biggest pair of antlers in the garrison. That young officer was a fine soldier—one of the best products of West Point, and was well connected back East, which was no small thing in an affair of this nature. Also his fellows easily calculated that he must have more than his pay. Shockley, however, continued to study the strategy of the scout Ermine, and he saw much to fear.

CHAPTER XVII

A Proposal

"Oh! I say, Captain Lewis, I am all ready to start. I have Ramon, a cook, and Wolf-Voice, together with pack-animals, but I can't get your man Ermine to say when he will go."

"That's odd, Harding; I don't know of anything to detain him. But go slow; he's like all these wild men up here; when they will they will, and when they won't, they'll lay down on you. I'll go round and scout him up. What is the matter so far as you can determine?"

"I can't determine. He says he will go, but will not name any exact time; tells me to push on and that he will catch up. That is a curious proposition. He is willing to take my money—"

"Oh! whoa up, Mr. Harding! That fellow doesn't care anything about your money—make no mistake about that. Money means no more to him than to a blue jay. He wanted to go back to his own country and was willing, incidentally, to take you. I'll see; you wait here awhile;" saying which, Captain Lewis went in search of his man, whom he found whittling a stick pensively.

"Hello, my boy, you don't seem to be very busy. Suppose your heart is out in the hills chasing the elk and bear."

"No, Captain; I don't care much about the hills."

"Or the Crow squaws?"

"D—— the Crow squaws!" And Ermine emphasized this by cutting his stick through the middle.

"Want to stay here?"

"Yes, I am getting so I like this camp; like the soldiers—like the wagons—kind of like the whole outfit."

"Like to chase wolves?" interrupted the officer.

Ermine slowly turned up his head and settled his fathomless blue eyes on Lewis, but he said nothing.

"Well, Mr. Harding is all set. You said you would go with him; a soldier must keep his word."

"I will go with him."

"When?"

Again Ermine shaved some delicate slivers off the stick; suddenly he threw it away, shut up his knife, and arose. "If Mr. Harding will pull out now, Wolf-Voice will show him the way. I shall know where the Indian takes him, and in four days I will walk into his camp. The pack-ponies travel slowly, I do not care to punch pack-horses; that will do for Ramon and the cook."

"Does that go?"

"I have said it. Did I ever lie, Captain Lewis?"

"All right. Mr. Harding will go now. I will attend to that." With this Lewis left him, and in two hours the little cavalcade trotted westward, out into the hot, sunlit plains, carrying faith in Ermine's word. The scout, leaning on a log stable, saw them go.

Three days took their slow departure, and on the morrow Ermine would have to make good his word to follow the Englishmen. He would have liked to stay even if his body suffered slow fire, but excuses would not avail for his honor. A soldier's honor was something made much of in these parts; it pegged higher than the affairs of the flesh.

He had not been able to see Miss Searles, and he wondered what she would feel, or think, or say. He was a thief when he remembered the stolen kisses, and he dared not go to the Searleses' home to inquire after her. All this diffidence the public put down to apathy; he had done his duty, so why further concern himself?

After supper he strolled along the officers' row, desperately forlorn, but hoping and yearning, barely nodding his head to passers-by.

Major Searles approached him with the nervous stride habitual to a soldier, and held out his hand, saying bluffly: "Of course, I can't thank you enough for your attention to my daughter, Ermine. But for your fortunate presence there at the time of the accident, things might have been bad; how bad I fear to contemplate. Come to my quarters, my boy, and allow my daughter to thank you. She is quite recovered. She is sitting out-of-doors. She hasn't been abroad much. Such a fall would have killed an older woman."

Together they made their way to the house, and Ermine passed under the *ramada* with his hat off. Mrs. Searles shook his hand and said many motherly things due on such occasions.

"Please forgive me if I do not rise; it is the doctor's orders, you know." And Miss Searles extended her hand, which the scout reverently took. To have seen him one would have fancied that, after all, manners must have been made before men; which idea is, of course, absurd.

In response to their inquiries, he retold the story of the accident and of his ministrations and perplexities. He did not embellish, but left out very important details, wondering the while if they were dead to all but his memory.

"She should not ride so poor a horse," ventured Ermine.

"She should not have been left unattended." And this severity was directed at Major Searles by his wife, to which he feebly pleaded vain extenuations, without hope of their acceptance.

"No, no my dear; you were always a careless person; one is never safe to place dependence on you in minor matters. I declare, all men are alike—leastwise soldiers are. A blanket and a haversack, and the world may wag at will, so far as they concern themselves." Rising, she adjusted her hat, saying: "I must run down to Mrs. Taylor's for a minute. Her baby is very ill, and she has sent for me. You will stay here, Major," and she swept out.

"When do you depart for your hunting with Mr. Harding, Ermine?" asked Searles.

"I must go soon. He left camp three days ago, and I have promised to follow."

"I should think you would be delighted to hunt. I know I should if I were a man," cheerfully remarked the young woman.

"I have always hunted, Miss Searles. I think I should like to do something else."

"What, pray?"

"Oh, I don't know, something with a white shirt in it."

"Isn't that foolish? There is no more fun in a white shirt than there is in a buckskin one, and there is no fun in either when it rains, I am told."

A passing officer appealed to the Major to come out; he was needed, together with other requests to follow, with reasons why haste was important.

"All right, I will be back in a moment, daughter." And the officer took himself off in complete disobedience of his wife's orders.

"Don't be gone long, father; there is no one here but Mary and the striker. You know I cannot depend on them."

"You keep the wolves off, Ermine; I won't be gone a minute." And Ermine found himself alone again with Katherine.

This time she was not pale unto death, but warm and tingling. Her lover's hands and feet took better care of themselves on a horse than in a chair, but the gloom under the porch at least stayed some of the embarrassment which her eyes occasioned him. Indeed, it is well known that lovers prefer night attacks, and despite the law and the prophets, they manage better without an audience.

She gained a particularly entrancing attitude in her chair by a pussy-cat wiggle which let the point of her very small foot out of concealing draperies. One hand hung limply toward Ermine over the arm of the chair, and it seemed to scream out to him to take hold of it.

"And when do you go, Mr. Ermine?"

This seemed safe, and along the lines of his self-interest.

"I go to-morrow; I have given my word."

"Very naturally there can be nothing to delay you here," she continued; "the fighting is over, I hear."

"There is something in the world beside fighting."

"Yes?" she evaded.

"Yes, you detain me."

"I!" and the little foot went back to its nest; the extended hand rose in protest. "I detain you! My dear Mr. Ermine, I do not understand how I detain you; really, I am quite recovered from my fall."

"You may have got well, Miss Searles, but I am not. Do you remember?"

"Remember—remember—do I remember? What should I remember? I am told you were very good to me, but I was laboring under such a shock at the time that you cannot expect much of my memory."

"I was but little better off."

"And were you injured also?"

"Yes, so bad that I shall never get well unless you come to my rescue."

"I come to your rescue! What can I do?" Her sword waved in tierce and seconde.

"Be my wife; come, girl, be my wife."

He had beaten down her guard; the whole mass was in the fire. The dam had broken; he led his forlorn hope into the breach. "Come, Katherine, say you will marry me; say it and save me."

"Oh," she almost screamed, "I can't do that; why, my mother would never consent to it," she appealed in bewilderment.

He had risen and taken a step forward. "What has your mother to say? Say you will be my wife, Katherine."

"Careful, careful, Mr. Ermine; restrain yourself, or I shall call a servant. No, no, I cannot marry you. Why, what should we do if I did? We should have to live in the mule corral."

"No, come to the mountains with me. I will make you a good camp."

She almost laughed aloud at this. "But I should make a poor squaw. I fear you would have many quarrels with your dinner. Besides, my father would not let me marry you. I like you, and you have been very good to me, but I had no idea we had gotten so far as this. Don't you think you Western men cover the ground a little too fast?"

Ermine drew back. "Why did you kiss me?"

"I didn't," she snapped. Her manner grew cold and strange to him. He had never seen this mood before. It chilled him not a little, and he sat down again in the chair. His assault had been repulsed. They were now looking straight into each other's eyes. Fear had departed from Ermine's and all graciousness from hers. Divested of their seductive flashes, he saw the eyes of his photograph, and slowly reaching into the bosom of his shirt, drew out the buckskin bag and undid it. Turning to the straining light, he gazed a moment, and then said, "It is you!"

"I!—what is I?"

"Yes! it is you!" and he handed the much-soiled photograph labelled "Bogardus" to her.

She regarded it. "Why, how on earth did you come by this, Mr. John Ermine?"

"Sak-a-war-te sent it to me in the night, and he made it talk to me and he made me swear that I would seek the woman until I found her. Then she would be my wife. I have found you—I do not know—my head is burning—"

She scanned the photograph, and said in an under-tone: "Taken last year in New York, and for him; yet you have it away out here in the middle of this enormous desert. He surely would not give it away to you. I do not understand." And she questioned him sharply as she returned the card.

"Who is this Sak-a-war-te?"

"He is God," said the scout.

"Oh!" she started up. The little miss had never heard God connected with affairs of this sort. An active fear of the fire which burned this extraordinary man's head began to oppress her.

"It is very strange. What has your god got to do with me,—with my—oh, you are joking, Mr. Ermine," she again appealed, a shadow of her old smile appearing.

"No, no; I am not joking. I have found you. I must believe what the spirits say to me when they take my mind from me and give it to you," returned the excited man.

"But really—I did not mean to take your mind. I haven't it anywhere about me. You have dreamed all this."

"Yes; it may be only a dream, Miss Searles, but make it come true; please make it all come true. I should like to live such a dream."

"Oh, my good man, I cannot make the dreams of casual people come true, not such serious dreams as yours."

"You say you would have to live in the corral with mules. Is that because I have so little money?"

"No, it is not money. I do not know how much you have."

"I have often taken enough gold out of the ground in a few days to last me a year."

"Yes, yes, but that is not the only thing necessary."

"What is necessary, then? Tell me what you want."

"There would have to be a great deal of love, you know. That is why any one marries. I have been flattered by the attentions of many cavaliers like yourself, Mr. Ermine, but I could not marry any one of them unless I loved him."

"And then you do not love me," this in a low, far-away voice, lopping each word off as though with an axe.

"No, I do not. I have given you no reason to think I did. I like you, and I am sorry for you, now that I know in what way you regard me. Sit down again and let me tell you." She crouched herself on the edge of her chair, and he sat in his, revolving his big hat in both hands between his knees. He was composed, and she vaguely felt that she owed him a return for his generous acts of the past. She had the light touch of mature civilization and did not desire her darts to be deadly. Now that one had laid this simple nature low, she felt a womanly impulse to nurse the wound.

"Some terrible mistake has been made. Believe me, I am truly sorry that our relationship has not been rightly understood." Here she paused a moment to take a long breath and observe the effect of her words on the one who had so easily lost his head. "No, I simply admired you, Mr. Ermine, as I do many of the brave men about here. I was not thinking of marrying any one. As for living in the mule corral, I was only joking about that. There might be worse places. I should dearly love a gold mine, but don't you understand there would have to be something else—I should have to give you something before we thought of marrying."

"I see it; it all comes to me now," he labored. "You would have to give me something, and you won't give me yourself. Then give me back my mind—give me the peace which I always had until I saw you. Can you do that, Miss Searles? Can you make John Ermine what he was before the steamboat came here, and let him mount his pony and go away?"

It was all so strange, this quiet appeal, that she passed her hand across her forehead in despair.

"If you will not make my dreams come true; if you will not say the things which the photograph does; if you will not do what God intends,—then I must take my body away from here and leave my shadow, my mind, and my heart to be kicked about among the wagons and the dogs. And I know now that you will soon forget me. Then I will be John Ermine, riding among the hills, empty as an old buffalo carcass, moving without life, giving no thought to the sunshine, not feeling the wind nor caring how the birds fly or the animals run. If you will not marry me—"

"Stop, please stop. I cannot stand this sort of thing, my dear Mr. Ermine. There are other young women besides myself. Go about the world, back in the States; you will find whole oceans of them, and without flattery, I feel you will soon find your mind again."

"You have my mind. You have all the mind I ever had." And his voice dropped until she could distinguish only wild gutturals. He was talking to himself in the Indian language.

Springing up quickly, she flew into the house, out through it to the rear steps, where she fell upon the neck of Mary, the cook, to the utter consternation of a soldier, who, to all appearances, was there with a similar ambition so to do. This latter worthy

flung himself out into the darkness. The cook held Katherine, expecting the entire Sioux tribe to come pouring through the front door on the instant, and at this belated interval Mrs. Searles entered her own porch.

"Why, Mr. Ermine, where is Katherine, and where is the Major? Why, you are all alone!" And she came up standing.

"Yes, I am all alone," said the scout, quietly, rising from the chair and putting on his sombrero. Before she could comprehend, he was gone.

CHAPTER XVIII

Man to Man

The Major sauntered in shortly and found Mrs. Searles standing over Katherine's chair, trying to dry her tears and gather the reasons for her grief. Mary's Indians not having appeared, she stood in the doorway, with her apron raised to a sort of feminine "charge bayonets."

"What in the devil is the circus?" demanded the father.

"It's nothing, father; I am nervous, that is all."

"Now, Major Searles, I want you to sit down and keep quiet. You will drive me frantic. Why did you run away when I clearly told you to stay here?" Her tones were dry with formality.

Against all manner of people and happenings the Major joyfully pitted his force and cunning. His only thought in a great crisis was his six-shooter; but he always hesitated before anything which concerned Mrs. Searles and a military order. These impelled obedience from the very nature of things. "But what has happened? What must I do?"

"You must sit down," said his wife; and he sat down. Affairs of this kind could be cleared only by women; he was conscious that he could not hurry matters.

"Now what has happened, Katherine? Will you tell me? Who did it?" pleaded the mother.

"Why, it is nothing, only that horrible scout wanted to marry me. Did you ever hear anything so ridiculous?" said the girl, sitting up and made defiant by the idea.

"Did he do anything?" and the Major again forgot his orders and rose truculently.

"Benjamin!" said Mrs. Searles, with asperity; and he again subsided. Like most soldiers and sailors, he was imperfectly domesticated.

"He wanted to marry you?" she continued with questioning insistence.

"Yes, he said I must marry him; that God wanted me to, and he also said he had lost his mind—"

"Well, I think he has," observed the mother, catching this idea, which was at least tangible to her. "Is that all, Katherine?"

"Is that all, mother? Why, isn't that enough?"

"I mean, he simply asked you to marry him—properly—he wasn't insulting—insistent beyond—"

"No, he did nothing else, though he went about it in a most alarming way."

"You said, No!"

"I most emphatically did, mother."

"What then?"

"Then he began mumbling Indian and scared me nearly to death. I ran to Mary."

"Dade an' she did, mum; an' I'm afther loosin' my sinses thinkin' thim rid-divils what do be ploughin' the land down be the river was devastating the cantonmint for to pass the time. An' ets only some bye afther wantin' to marry her—the swate thing."

Mrs. Searles interposed, "Mary!" and the domestic retired to the sable silences of the rear steps, to split a joke with one Private O'Shane, should he venture to return.

"The social savagery of this place is depressing. To think of my daughter living in a log-cabin, cooking bear meat for a long-haired wild man. In the future, Benjamin Searles, I trust you will not feel called upon to introduce your fantastic acquaintances to this house. You can sit on the corral fence to entertain them. That is where they belong. I suppose next, an out-and-out Indian will want to be my son-in-law."

"I certainly will see that the man does not again obtrude himself. I do not understand his nerve in this matter. Lewis thinks the boy's ridgepole is crooked; but he is harmless and has done many good and gallant deeds. As for his proposing, I simply think he doesn't know any better. For my part, I think it is about time that the engagement to Mr. Butler is announced; it will put an end to this foolishness all round," added the father. "I am going out to see Lewis about this fellow now."

"Ben Searles, I hope you are not going to do anything rash," pleaded the mother.

"Of course not, my dear; the situation doesn't call for any temperature beyond blood-heat. I only want to put a cooling lotion on the base of that scout's brain. He must stop this dreaming habit."

Having found Lewis at his quarters and seated himself, the Major began, "Now, Captain, what do you think of this Ermine of yours—is he crazy?"

"Is he crazy? Why, what has he done now?"

"Well, by Gad, he came to my house this evening, and when I stepped out for a minute he proposed marriage to my daughter—wanted her to marry him! Now, how's that strike you? Is it just gall, or does he need a physician?"

"Well, I will be d——d; proposed marriage, hey! Looks like he ought to have an opiate," concluded Lewis. "You know, now that I think of it, I have a little mistrusted him before. He has shown signs of liking your daughter, but I never regarded the matter seriously—didn't ever credit him with being an entire fool. The boy's queer, Searles—mighty queer, but he never did anything wrong; in fact, he is a pretty good boy—a heap different from most of these double-belted, sage-bush terrors. Then, of course, he was born and raised in the wilderness, and there is a whole lot of things he don't savvy. Probably he has lost his head over your daughter and he can't see why he hasn't a chance. I will send for him, and we will make a big talk, and I'll send him away to Harding." Turning, the Captain yelled, "Orderly! Jones! Oh, Jones!"

"Yes, sir," responded Jones, as he appeared in the doorway.

"Go find the scout Ermine, if you can, and tell him to report to me immediately. If you don't find him in half an hour, let it go until to-morrow—understand?

"As I was saying, you see, Major, if this thing wasn't vinegar, it would be sugar. When I think of him proposing—say, I have to laugh. There is one thing about him which kept me guessing: it is the Indian reserve of the fellow. He goes round here like a blue-moon, and if you should hit him over the head with an axe, I don't think he would bat an eye. He never complains, he never questions, and when you are right up against it, as we were a half-dozen times last winter, he is Johnny-on-the-spot. So you see, if he fell in love, no one would hear the splash. Now that he is in love, we want to tighten the curb chain; he might—well, he might take it into his head to do something, and that something might be just what we would never think of."

Thus the two speculated until the sandpaper grating of Ermine's moccasins on the porch warned them, and looking up they beheld the scout, standing with his rifle in the hollow of his left arm. This was unusual and produced several seconds of very bad silence. Captain Lewis held up his hand in mockery of the "peace sign," and said: "I see you're fixed for war, Ermine. Sit down over there. I want to talk to you."

The scout removed his hat and sat down, but with the ominous rifle in place. He had been told by the orderly whom he was to encounter; and it had come over him that wanting to marry Katherine Searles might be some crime against the white man's law. He had seen very natural actions of men punished under those laws during his sojourn in camp.

"Ermine, I understand that during the temporary absence of her father this evening, you asked Miss Searles to marry you."

"I did, sir."

"Very well. Don't you think you took an unfair advantage of her father's absence?"

"I don't know, sir. A man doesn't speak to a woman before other men," replied Ermine, dubiously.

The Captain emitted a slight cough, for the blow had staggered him a little. He knew the law of convention, and he knew the customs of men; but they did not separate readily in his mind.

"In any event, Ermine, the young lady had given you no encouragement which would warrant you in going to the length of proposing marriage to her."

This was an assertion which Ermine did not care to discuss. His views would not coincide, and so he fumbled his hat and made no reply.

"I may state that you are not warranted in aspiring to the hand of Miss Searles for many reasons; further, that she distinctly doesn't want attention of any kind from you. To this I will add, her father and mother forbid you all association in the future—do you understand?"

This, also, failed to break the scout's silence.

"And," interpolated the father, "I may add that my daughter is already engaged to be married to Lieutenant Butler, which will end the matter."

If the evening's occurrences had set the nerves of the Searles family on edge, it had torn the scout's into shreds; but he managed his stoicism.

"Now, my boy," continued Captain Lewis, with a sense of benevolence, "we do not mean to be hard on you. We all, including Miss Searles, feel a great pity for you in this matter."

"Pity—pity—what is pity?" saying which the boy's eyes took on an unnatural glow and he rose to his feet. Lewis quickly added, "I mean that we feel for you."

"I know what you feel for me, Captain Lewis, and Major Searles," and it was evident that Ermine was aroused. "You feel that I am an uneducated man, without money, and that I do not wear a white shirt; that I tuck my pants in my leggings and that I sleep among the Indians. I know you think I am a dog. I know Miss Searles thinks I belong in the corral with the mules; but, by G——, you did not think I was a dog when the Sioux had your wagon-train surrounded and your soldiers buffaloed; you did not think I was a dog when I stood beside the Colonel, and neither did Sitting Bull. You did not think I was a dog when I kept you all from freezing to death last winter; but here among the huts and the women I am a dog. I tell you now that I do not understand such men as you are. You have two hearts: one is red and the other is blue; and you feel with the one that best suits you at the time. Your blue heart pities me. Me, a warrior and a soldier! Do you give pity with your coffee and sow-belly? Is that what you feed a soldier on? Hum-m— G——!" And the scout slapped his hat on his head.

"Steady, steady, my boy; don't you go up in the air on us," said Lewis, persuasively. "I did not mean to offend you, and we want to be friends; but you keep your feet on the ground and don't go raring and pitching, or we may forget you."

"Yes; that is it,—forget me; you may forget me. What's more, you can do it now. I am going far away, so that your eyes will not remind you."

"You are going to make your word good to Mr. Harding, are you not?" asked the chief of scouts.

"What good is a dog's word?" came the bitter reply.

The Major said little, but remained steadily studying the face of the scout; rising, he approached him with extended hand. "If you are going away, let us part friends, at least. Here is my hand, and I shall not forget you; I shall not forget your services to me or mine, and I do not think you are a dog. When you calm down you may find that you have been unjust to Captain Lewis and myself."

The scout took the Major's hand mechanically, and also that of Lewis, which the latter offered in turn, saying:—

"In the morning I will see that you get your pay, and if you conclude to return, I will find you employment."

"Thank you, sir; I care nothing for the pay. I did not come here for money; I came here to help you fight the Sioux, and to be a man among white men." And once more the young man relapsed into the quiet of his ordinary discourse.

"You certainly have shown yourself a man among men; no one has ever questioned that," said the Major.

"Then why is it wrong for a man among men to want your daughter to be his wife?"

"It is not wrong, but you have gone about the matter wrong. I have tried to make it plain that her hand is promised to Mr. Butler."

As this was said, two horses trotted up to Captain Lewis's quarters. A man dismounted, gave his horse to the other, and Butler himself strode heavily into the room. He was quite gray with dust, with a soiled handkerchief about his neck, unshaven, booted, and armed.

"Hello, Major! Hello, Lewis! I'm just in with my troop, and if you will pardon me, I will have a word with Mr. Ermine here." His manner was strained, and knowing the situation as they all did, the two older officers were alarmed.

"Hold up there, Butler; never mind your word to-night; wait until morning."

Butler paid no attention, but addressed the scout with icy directness. "May I ask, Mr. Ermine, if you have in your possession a photograph of Miss Searles?"

"I have."

"Have you it about your person at present?"

"I have, sir."

"Then, Mr. Ermine, I have the word of Miss Searles for it, that the photograph in question was one she had taken, of which there is only one copy in the world, and which was given to me, and lost by myself, somewhere on the road between here and

"A Tremendous Bang Roared Around the Room." *Authors' photoengraving.*

Fort Ellis. It must be my property. If you will let me see it, I can soon identify it. In which case I demand that you hand it over to me."

"Mr. Butler, you will only get that photograph from off my dead body. You have Miss Searles; is not that enough?"

"I will then take it by force from you!" A tremendous bang roared around the room, and the little group was lost in smoke.

Butler turned half round, his six-shooter going against the far wall with a crash. He continued to revolve until caught in the Major's arms. Lewis sprang to his desk, where his pistol lay, and as he turned, the smoke lifted, revealing Butler lying against the Major's chest, wildly waving his left arm and muttering savagely between short breaths. Ermine was gone.

"Fire on that man!" yelled Lewis to the orderly outside, taking one shot himself at the fleeing figure of the scout.

The soldier jerked his carbine and thrashed about the breech-block with a cartridge. "I can't see him, Captain!" he shouted.

"Fire at him, anyway! Fire, I tell you!" And the man discharged his rifle in the direction in which Ermine's figure had disappeared.

Simultaneously with the shots, the garrison bugles were drawling "Taps," but they left off with an expiring pop. The light did not go out in quarters, and the guard turned out with much noise of shoe leather and rattle of guns. This body soon arrived, and Lewis spoke from the porch of his quarters.

"The scout, Ermine, has just shot Lieutenant Butler in the arm! He ran that way! Chase him! Go quickly, or he will get away. Shoot instantly if he resists; and he will, I think."

The guard shuffled off in the darkness and beat up the camp to no purpose. The soldiers stood about, speculating in low voices and gradually quieting as the word passed about on the uneasy wings of gossip that Ermine had shot Butler in the arm, wounding him badly, and that the scout had gone into the earth or up in the air, for divil the hide nor hair of him could the guard find.

When the orderly had come for Ermine and told him who wanted to see him, the scout scented trouble ahead. According to the immemorial practices of the desert at such times, he had saddled his pony, tying him in the darkest and most unlikely place he could find, which was between two six-mule wagons outside the corral. He armed himself and obeyed the summons, but he intended never to let a hand be placed on his shoulder; and he chose death rather than the military court which sat so gravely around the long table at headquarters. He fully expected to depart for the mountains on the morrow, but his hand was forced. The quick episode of Butler, ending in the shot and his flight, had precipitated matters. Shortly he found himself seated on his horse between the wagons, while the denizens of the cantonments swarmed around. A group searched the corral with lanterns, and he heard one soldier tell another what had happened, with the additional information that Butler was not seriously injured. Armed men passed close to him, and he knew that discovery meant probable death, because he would not hold up his hands. Despite the deadly danger which encompassed him, he found time for disappointment in the news that Butler was only wounded. Even now he would go to his enemy and make more sure, but that enemy was in the hospital surrounded by many friends. She, too, was probably there, weeping and hating the responsible one,—a fugitive criminal driven into the night. The silken robes of self-respect had been torn from Ermine, and he stood naked, without the law, unloved by women, and with the hand of all men turned against him. The brotherhood of the white kind, which had promised him so much, had ended by stealing the heart and mind of the poor mountain boy, and now it wanted his body to

work its cold will on; but it could have that only dead. This he knew as he loosed five cartridges, putting them between his teeth and clutching his loaded rifle. Would the search never cease? The lanterns glided hither and yon; every garrison cur ran yelping; the dull shuffling of feet was coming directly to the wagons which stood apart from other objects, and a dog ran under the wagon. With their eyes on the ground, an officer and two men towered above the light of a lantern. They were coming directly to the wagons. He kicked the pony and galloped softly out. Instantly the men began calling, "Halt! halt! G—— d—— you, halt!" but the ghostly pony only answered feebly the lantern light. "Bang! bang! bang!" came the shots, which "zee-weeped" about his ears. He doubled quickly in the dark and trotted to the edge of the camp, which buzzed loudly behind him. He knew he must pass the sentries, but he took the chance. His apprehensions were quickly answered. "Halt!"—the man was very near, but it was very dark. "Bang!"—it missed, and he was away. He stopped shortly, dismounted, and ran his hand completely over the body of the pony; it was dry. "Good!" For a half-hour he walked over the herd-grounds, crossing, circling, and stopping; then back as near to the post as he dared. At last he turned and rode away. He was thoroughly familiar with the vicinity of the camp, and had no trouble so long as the post lights guided him.

The mountain boy had brought little to the soldier camp but the qualities of mind which distinguished his remote ancestors of the north of Europe, who came out of the dark forests clad in skins, and bearing the first and final law of man, a naked sword on a knotted arm. An interval of many centuries intervened between him and his fellows; all the race had evolved, all the laws which they had made for the government of society, all the subtle customs which experience had decreed should circumscribe associates, were to him but the hermit's gossip in idle hours at the cabin. The bar sinister was on his shield; his credentials were the advice of an unreal person to fight in common with the whites. He came clad in skins on a naked horse, and could barely understand English when it was in the last adulteration; and still he had made his way without stumbling until the fatal evening. Now he was fleeing for life because he had done two of the most natural things which a man can do.

"Good-by, good-by, white men, and good-by, white woman; the frost is in your hearts, and your blood runs like the melting snow from the hills. When you smile, you only skin your fangs; and when you laugh, your eyes do not laugh with you. You say good words which mean nothing. You stroke a man's back as a boy does a dog's, and kick him later as a boy does. You, woman, you who pick men's hearts and eat them as a squaw does wild plums, I want no more of you. You, Butler, I wish were out here in the dark with me; one of us would never see the sun rise. You would force me!" and the scout vented himself in a hollow laugh which was chill with murder.

The lights were lost behind the rise of the land, and the pony trotted along. No horse or man not raised on the buffalo range could travel in that darkness; but both of them made steady progress.

"Those Indians will have to crawl on their knees a whole day to pick up my pony tracks on the herd ground. The Crows will never try to follow me; the Shoshone may when the white men offer a reward. That fool of a boy may see his chance to even up the insult which I gave before the woman. He can shake her hand now for all I would do. I will ride for two hours before the sun comes, and then let the pony feed."

Patting his horse's neck, he added: "And then, my boy, we will blind our trail in some creek. I will rub the medicine on your heels, you shall gallop until dark, and no horse in that camp will get near enough to spoil my sleep."

Keeping along the river flats, floundering occasionally and dismounting to lead through the dry washes, he kept steadily on, impelled by the fear that the Indian scouts and cavalry might not stop for his trail, but deploy out at daybreak, and ride fast to the west, in the hopes that he had not yet made a long start in the darkness. There was only the danger that his horse might lame himself in the night; but then he could go back in the hills and make a skulk on foot. Even to be brought to bay had no great terror; Ermine held his life lightly in the hollow of his hand.

He mused as he rode: "They took my hair out of the braids and let it flow in the wind; then they said I was a white man. I may be one; but I wish now I had forgotten my color and I would not be so empty-handed this night. If I had followed my Indian heart, I could have stolen that girl out from under the noses of those soldiers, and I may do it yet. When she was riding, I could have taken her away from the hunting-party, rawhided her on to her horse, and left no more sign than a bird behind us; but when she looked at me, my blood turned to water. O Sak-a-war-te, why did you not take the snake's gaze out of her eyes, and not let poor Ermine sit like a gopher to be swallowed? God, God, have you deserted me?"

CHAPTER XIX

Flight

Ermine understood the "talking wire,"—the telegraph had been made plain to him,—and he knew the soldiers were stretching one into the west. He sheered away from the white man's medicine, going up a creek where only the silent waters swirling about his horse's legs could know the story of his ride, which secret they would carry to the eternal sea.

The gallant pony's blood was rich from the grain-sacks; he had carried a rider in the strain of many war-trails, and his heart had not yet failed. In the prime of life, he was now asked to do the long, quick distance that should lose the white man; those mighty people who bought the help of mercenary men; whose inexhaustible food came in the everlasting wagons; and who spoke to each other twenty sleeps apart. His rider had violated their laws, and they would have him. Only the pony could save.

Having walked the bed of the creek as far as he deemed necessary, Ermine backed his pony out of the stream into some low bushes, where he turned him about and rode away. All day over the yellow plains and through the defiles of the hills loped the fugitive. Once having seen buffalo coming in his direction, he travelled for miles along a buffalo path which he judged they would follow. If by fortune they did, he knew it would make the scouts who came after rub their eyes and smoke many pipes in embarrassment. Not entirely satisfied with his precautions,—for he thought the Indians would cast ahead when checked,—he continued to urge the pony steadily forward. The long miles which lay before his pursuers would make their hearts weak and their ponies' forelegs wobble.

He reflected that since he was indeed going to join Mr. Harding's party at the secret place in Gap-full-of-arrow-holes,* why would not Lewis's scouts follow the easy trail made by their ponies and trust to finding him with them; and again, would the Englishman want his company under his altered status? This he answered by saying that no horse in the cantonment could eat up the ground with his war-pony; and as for the Englishman, he could not know of the late tragedy unless the accused chose to tell him. What of his word? Why was he keeping it? With a quick bullet from his rifle had gone his honor, along with other things more material. Still, the Gap lay in his way, so he could stop without inconvenience, at least long enough for a cup of coffee and some tobacco. The suddenness of his departure had left him no time to gather the most simple necessities, and he was living

by his gun. Only once did he see Indians far away in the shimmer of the plains. He had dropped into the dry washes and sneaked away. They might be Crows, but the arrows of doubt made sad surgery in his poor brain; the spell of the white man's vengeance was over him. Their arms were long, their purses heavy; they could turn the world against him. From their strong log-towns they would conjure his undoing by the devious methods which his experience with them had taught him to dread. The strain of his thoughts made his head ache as he cast up the events which had forced him to this wolfing through the lonely desert. He had wanted to marry a pretty girl whose eyes had challenged him to come on, and when he had ventured them, like a mountain storm the whole cantonment rattled about his head and shot its bolts to kill. As the girl had fled his presence at the mere extension of his hand, in swift response to her emotions the whole combination of white humanity was hard on the heels of his flying pony.

* * *

From the summit of the red cliffs Ermine looked down into the secret valley of his quest, and sitting there beside a huge boulder he studied the rendezvous. There were Ramon's pack-ponies—he remembered them all. There curled the smoke from the tangle of brushwood in the bottom, and finally Wolf-Voice and Ramon came out to gather in the horses for the night. He rode down toward them. Their quick ears caught the sound of the rattle of the stones loosened by his mount, and they stopped. He waved his hat, and they recognized him. He came up and dismounted from his drooping horse, stiff-hided with lather and dust, hollow-flanked, and with his belly drawn up as tight as the head of a tom-tom.

"Are you alone in the camp? Has no one been here?"

"No; what for waas any one been here?" asked and answered the half-breed. "De King George Man† she waas set by dose

---

* Pryor Gap.

† Any person who belonged to the Queen.

fire an' waas ask me 'bout once a minit when waas Ermine come."

The men drove the horses in while Ermine made his way through the brush to the camp-fire.

"Aha! Glad to see you, Mr. Ermine. Gad! but you must have put your horse through. He is barely holding together in the middle. Picket him out, and we will soon have some coffee going."

Ermine did as directed and was soon squatting before the fire with his cup and plate. To the hail of questions he made brief response, which Harding attributed to fatigue and the inclination of these half-wild men not to mix discourse with the more serious matter of eating.

"How did you leave every one at the camp?"

Ermine borrowed a pipe and interspersed his answers with puffs.

"Left them in the night—and they were all sitting up to see me off. My pony is weak, Mr. Harding. Will you give me a fresh one in the morning? We ought to start before daylight and make a long day of it."

"My dear man, before daylight? Are we in such haste? It seems that we have time enough before us."

"This is a bad country here. Indians of all tribes are coming and going. We are better off back in the range. In two or three sleeps we will be where we can lie on the robe, but not here;" saying which, Ermine rolled up in his saddle blanket, and perforce the others did likewise, in view of the short hours in store.

The last rasping, straining pack-rope had been laid while yet the ghostly light played softly with the obscurity of the morning. The ponies were forced forward, crashing through the bushes, floundering in the creek, cheered on by hoarse oaths, all strange to the ear of Harding. The sedate progression of other days was changed to a fox-trot—riding-whips and trail-ropes slapping about the close-hugged tails of the horses.

Harding congratulated himself on the unexpected energy of his guide; it would pro-

duce results later when wanted in the hunting. The ponies strung out ahead to escape the persecution of the lash, but Wolf-Voice saw something new in it all, and as he rode, his fierce little eyes gleamed steadily on Ermine. The half-breed knew the value of time when he was pushing the horses of the enemy away from their lodges, but these horses had no other masters. He turned his pony alongside of Ermine's.

"Say, John, what for you waas keep look behin'? Who you 'fraid follar dese pony? Ain't dose Canada-man pay for dese pony —sacre, what you was do back de camp dare? De Sioux, she broke hout?" And the half-breed's mischievous eye settled well on his confrère.

"Well, I did that back there which will make the high hills safer for me than any other place. Don't say anything to Mr. Harding until I feel safe. I want to think."

"You waas shoot some one, mabeso?"

"Yes—that —— —— Butler. He said he would force me to give up the paper we found in the moonlight on the soldier trail down the Yellowstone a year ago. He pulled his pistol, and I shot him."

"You kiell heem—hey?"

"No, caught him in the arm, but it will not kill him. I may go back and do that— when the soldiers forget a little."

"Den you waas run away—hey?"

"Yes; I made the grass smoke from Tongue River to here. I don't think they can follow me, but they may follow this party. That's why I look behind, Wolf-Voice, and that's why I want you to look behind."

"What for you waas come to de King George Man, anyhow?"

"I wanted coffee and tobacco and a fresh pony and more cartridges, and it will be many moons before John Ermine will dare look in a trader's store. If the white men come, I will soon leave you; and if I do, you must stay and guide Mr. Harding. He is a good man and does what is right by us."

"Ah!" hissed the half-breed, "old Broken-Shoe and White-Robe, she ain' let dose Engun follar you. You spose dey let dose

Crow tak de ack-kisr-attah* to Crooked-Bear's boy? Humph, dey 'fraid of hees medecin'."

"Well, they will pile the blankets as high as a horse's back, and say to the Shoshone, 'Go get the yellow-hair, and these are your blankets.' What then?"

"Ugh! ugh!—a-nah," grunted the half-breed; "de —— —— Shoshone, we will leek de pony—come—come!"

The energy of the march, the whacking ropes, and scampering horses passed from satisfaction to downright distress in Mr. Harding's mind. He pleaded for more deliberation, but it went unheeded. The sun had gone behind the hard blue of the main range before they camped, and the good nature of the Englishman departed with it.

"Why is it necessary to break our cattle down by this tremendous scampering? It does not appeal to my sense of the situation."

"Wael, meester, wan more sun we waas en de hiell—den we have long smoke; all you waas do waas sit down smoke your pipe—get up—kiell dose grizzly bear—den sit down some more."

But this observation of the half-breed's was offset by Ramon, who was cleaning a frying-pan with a piece of bread, and screwing his eyes into those of Wolf-Voice. The matter was not clear to him. "What good can come of running the legs off the ponies? Why can't we sit down here and smoke?"

"You waas trader—you waas spend all de morning pack de pony—spend all the afternoon unpack heem—a man see your night fire from stan where you waas cook your breakfast—bah!" returned Wolf-Voice.

This exasperated Ramon, who vociferated, "When I see men run the pony dat way, I was wander why dey run dem." Wolf-Voice betook himself to that ominous silence which, with Indians, follows the knife.

Ermine was lame in the big white camp, but out here in the desert he walked ahead; so, without looking up, he removed his

* Soldiers.

pipe, and said in his usual unemotional manner, "Shut up!" The command registered like a gong.

Wolf-Voice sat down and smoked. When men smoke they are doing nothing worse than thinking. The cook ceased doing the work he was paid for, and also smoked. Every one else smoked, and all watched the greatest thinker that the world has ever known—the Fire.

The first man to break the silence was the Englishman. Whether in a frock coat, or a more simple garment, the Englishman has for the last few centuries been able to think quicker, larger, and more to the purpose in hours of bewilderment, than any other kind of man. He understood that his big purpose was lost in this "battle of the kites and crows." The oak should not wither because one bird robbed another's nest. As a world-wide sportsman he had seen many yellow fellows shine their lethal weapons to the discomfiture of his plans; and he knew that in Ermine he had an unterrified adversary to deal with. He talked kindly from behind his pipe. "Of course, Ermine, I am willing to do what is proper under any and all circumstances, and we will continue this vigorous travel if you can make the necessity of it plain to me. Frankly, I do not understand why we are doing it, and I ask you to tell me."

Ermine continued to smoke for a time, and having made his mind up he removed his pipe and said slowly: "Mr. Harding, I shot Butler, and the soldiers are after me. I have to go fast—you don't—that's all."

The gentleman addressed opened wide eyes on his guide and asked in low amaze-

Ramon. *Authors' wood engraving.*

ment, "D—— me—did you? Did you kill him?"

"No," replied Ermine.

Rising from his seat, Mr. Harding took the scout to one side, out of reach of other ears, and made him tell the story of the affair, with most of the girl left out.

"Why did you not give him the photograph?"

"Because he said he would make me give it and drew his pistol, and what is more, I am going back to kill the man Butler—after a while. We must go fast to-morrow, then I will be where I am safe, for a time at least."

All this gave Harding a sleepless night. He had neither the power nor the inclination to arrest the scout. He did not see how the continuance of his hunt would interfere with final justice; and he hoped to calm the mood and stay the murderous hand of the enraged man. So in half-bewilderment, on the morrow, that staid traveller found himself galloping away from the arms of the law, in a company of long-haired vagabonds; and at intervals it made him smile. This was one of those times when he wished his friends at home could have a look at him.

"Say, Wolf-Voice," said he, "Ermine says he is going back to kill Lieutenant Butler sometime later."

"He says dat—hey?"

"Yes, he says that."

"Wiell den—she wiell do eet—var much, 'fraid—what for she wan kiell dose man Butler? She already waas shoot heem en the harm."

"I think Ermine is jealous," ventured Harding.

"What you call jealous?" queried the half-breed.

"Ermine wants Butler's girl and cannot get her; that is the trouble."

"Anah-a! a bag of a squaw, ees eet?" and Wolf-Voice ran out to head a pack-horse into the line of flight. Coming back he continued: "Say, Meester Harding, dese woman he ver often mak' man wan' kiell some ozer man. I have done dose ting."

"Whew!" said Harding, in amazement, but he caught himself. "But, Wolf-Voice, we do not want our friend Ermine to do it, and I want you to promise me you will help me to keep him from doing it."

"'Spose I say, 'Ermine, you no kiell Meester Butler'—he teel me to go to hell, mabeso—what den?"

"Oh, he may calm down later."

"Na—Engun she no forget," cautioned the half-breed.

"But Ermine is not an Indian."

"Na, but she all de same Engun," which was true so far as that worthy could see.

"If we do not stop him from killing Butler, he will hang or be shot for it, sooner or later, and that is certain," said Harding.

"Yees—yees; deese white man have funny way when one man kiell 'nozer. Ermine ees brave man—he eese see red, an' he wiell try eet eef he do hang. No one eese able for stop heem but deese Crooked-Bear," observed the half-breed.

"Is Crooked-Bear an Indian chief?"

"Na; she ain' Enjun, she ain' white man; she come out of the groun'. Hees head eet waas so big an' strong eet were break hees back for to carry eet."

"Where does this person live?" ventured Harding.

"Where she eese lieve, ah?—where Ermine an' his pony can find heem," was the vague reply. "You no wan' Ermine for kiell deese Butler; weel den, you say, 'Ermine, you go see Crooked-Bear—you talk wid heem.' I weel take you where you wan' go een de montaign for get de grizzly bear."

"I suppose that is the only solution, and I suppose it is my duty to do it, though the thing plays havoc with my arrangements."

Later the trail steepened and wound its tortuous way round the pine and boulders, the ponies grunting under their burdens as they slowly pushed their toilsome way upwards. When Ermine turned here to look back he could see a long day's march on the trail, and he no longer worried concerning any pursuit which might have been in progress. They found their beds early, all being exhausted by the long day's march, particularly the fugitive scout.

On the following morning, Harding suggested that he and Ermine begin the hunting, since fresh meat was needed in camp; so they started. In two hours they had an elk down and were butchering him. The antlers were in the velvet and not to the head-hunter's purpose. Making up their package of meat and hanging the rest out of the way of prowling animals, to wait a pack-horse, they sat down to smoke.

"Are you still intending to kill Mr. Butler?" ventured Harding.

"Yes, when you are through hunting, I shall begin—begin to hunt Butler."

"You will find your hunting very dangerous, Ermine," ventured Harding.

"It does not matter; he has got the girl, and he may have my life or I shall have his."

"But you cannot have the girl. Certainly after killing Butler the young lady will not come to you. Do you think she would marry you? Do you dream you are her choice?"

"No, the girl would not marry me; I have forgotten her," mused Ermine, as he patiently lied to himself.

"Does this maiden wish to marry Butler?" asked Harding, who now recalled garrison gossip to the effect that all things pointed that way.

"She does."

"Then why do you kill the man she loves?"

"Because I do not want to think he is alive."

The wide vacancy of the scout's blue eyes, together with the low deliberation in his peaceful voice, was somewhat appalling to Harding. He never had thought of a murderer in this guise, and he labored with himself to believe it was only a love-sickness of rather alarming intenseness; but there was something about the young man which gave this idea pause. His desperation in battle, his Indian bringing-up, made it all extremely possible, and he searched in vain for any restraining forces. So for a long time they sat by the dead elk, and Harding sorted and picked out all the possible reasons he could conjure as to why Ermine

should not kill Butler, until it began to dawn upon him that he was not replying to his arguments at all, but simply reiterating his own intentions despite them. He then recalled cases in England where fists had been the arguments under a rude lover's code; only out here the argument was more vital, more insistent, and the final effect left the lady but one choice should she care to interest herself in the affair.

Resuming his talk, Harding suggested that his guide go to his own friends, who might advise him more potently than he was able, and ended by asking pointedly, "You have friends, I presume?"

"I have one friend," answered the youth, sullenly.

"Who is he?"

"Crooked-Bear," came the reply.

"Crooked-Bear is your friend; then you must listen to him; what he advises will probably be the thing to do."

"Of course I will listen to him. He is the only person in the world I care for now. I have often heard him talking to himself, and I think he has known a woman whom he cannot forget," spoke Ermine. "He will not want me to seek my enemy's life. I have talked too much, Mr. Harding. Talk weakens a man's heart. I will make no more talk."

"Well, then, my man, go to your friend; I can do nothing more," and Harding arose. They tied their meat on the saddles, mounted, and sought their camp. On the following morning Ermine had gone.

CHAPTER XX

The End of All Things

The heart of the rider hung like a leaden weight in his body, as he cast accustomed glances at the old trail up the mountain to Crooked-Bear's cabin. He heard the dogs bark, and gave the wolf's call which was the hermit's countersign. The dogs grew menacing at his unfamiliar scent, but a word satisfied them. A dog forgets many things about a person in a year, but never his voice. From out of a dark corner came the goblin of the desolate mountain, ready with his gun for the unwelcome, but to greet Ermine with what enthusiasm his silent forest ways had left him. For a long time they held each other's hands, while their faces lighted with pleasure; even the warmth of kindliness kindling in the scout's as he stood in the presence of one who did not seek him with the corner of his eyes.

As they built the fire and boiled the water, the old man noted the improved appearance of his protégé—the new clothes and the perfect equipment were a starched reminder of the glories of the old world, which he had left in the years long gone. He plied his questions, and was more confused to uncover Ermine's lack of enthusiasm concerning the events which must have been tremendous, and with difficulty drew the belated news of war and men and things from him. Then like the raising of a curtain, which reveals the play, the hermit saw suddenly that it was heavy and solemn—he was to see a tragedy, and this was not a play; it was real, it was his boy, and he did not want to see a tragedy.

He feared to have it go on; he shut his eyes for a long time, and then rose to his feet and put his hands on the young man's shoulders. He sought the weak gleam of the eyes in the dusk of the cabin. "Tell me, boy, tell me all; you cannot hide it any more than a deer can hide his trail in the snow. I can read your thoughts."

Ermine did not immediately reply, but the leaden heart turned slowly into a burning coal.

"Crooked-Bear, I wanted a white girl for my wife, and I shot a soldier, who drew a revolver and said he would force me to give him her picture which I had in my pocket, and then I ran away, everybody shooting at me. They may even come here for me. They want to stand me up beside the long table with all the officers sitting around it, and

they want to take me out and hang me on a tree for the ravens and magpies to pick at. That is what your white people want to do to me, Crooked-Bear, and by God they are going to have a chance to do it, for I am going back to kill the man and get the girl or die. Do you hear that, Crooked-Bear, do you hear that?"

The hermit's arms dropped to his side, and he could make no sound or sign. "Sit down, be quiet, boy; let us talk more of this thing. Be calm, and I can find a reason why you will not want to stain your hands with this man's blood. When I sent you to the white men to do a man's work in a white man's way, I did not think you would lock horns with any buck you met on the trail, like the dumb things that carry their reason for being on the point of their antlers—sit down." And the long arms of the hermit waved with a dropping motion.

Ermine sat down, but by no means found his composure. Even in the darkness his eyes gave an unnatural light, his muscles twitched, and his feet were not still. "I knew, Crooked-Bear, I knew you would talk that way. It is the soft talk of the white men. She made a fool of me, and he was going to put his foot on me as though John Ermine was a grasshopper, and every white man would say to me after, 'Be quiet, Ermine, sit down.' Bah! I will be quiet and I will sit down until they forget a little, and then—" Ermine emitted the savage snarl of a lynx in a steel trap. Slapping his knee, he continued: "The white men in the camp are two-sided; they pat you with a hand that is always ready to strike. When the girl looked at me, it lighted a fire in my heart, and then she blew the flame until I was burning up. She told me as well as any words can say, 'Come on,' and when I offered her my hand she blatted like a fawn and ran away. As if that were not enough, this Butler walked into the room and talked to me as though I were a dog and drew his gun; everything swam before my eyes, and they swim yet, Crooked-Bear. I tell you I will kill him as surely as day follows night. These soldiers talk as white and soft as milk when it suits their plan, but old Major Searles says that they stand pat in war, that they never give up the fight, that they must win if it takes years to do it. Very well, I shall not forget that."

"But, my boy, you must not see red in a private feud; that is only allowed against the enemies of the whole people. Your heart has gone to your head; you can never win a white woman by spilling the blood of the other man who happens to love her also. That is not the way with them."

"No, it is not the way with them; it is the way with their women to set a man on fire and then laugh at him, and it is the way with their men to draw a gun. What do they expect, Crooked-Bear? I ask you that!"

"Who was the girl, Ermine?"

The scout unwrapped the package from his bosom, and handed the photograph to the old man, saying, "She is like that."

The hermit regarded the picture and ventured, "An officer's daughter?"

"Yes; daughter of Major Searles."

"Who was the man you shot?"

"A young pony soldier,—an officer; his name is Butler." And gradually Ermine was led to reveal events to the wise man, who was able to piece out the plot with much knowledge not natural to the wilds of the Rocky Mountains. And it was a tragedy. He knew that the girl's unfortunate shot had penetrated deeper than Ermine's, and that the Law and the Lawless were in a death grapple.

They sought their bunks, and in the following days the prophet poured much cold water on Ermine's determination, which only turned to steam and lost itself in the air. The love of the woman and the hate of the man had taken root in the bedrock of his human nature, and the pallid "should nots" and "must nots" of the prophet only rustled the leaves of Ermine's philosophy.

"He has taken her from me; he has made me lose everything I worked for with the white men; he has made me a human wolf, and I mean to go back and kill him. You say I may lose my life; ho! what is a dead man? A dead man and a buffalo chip look

just alike to these mountains, to this sky, and to me, Crooked-Bear," came the lover's reply.

And at other times: "I know, Crooked-Bear, that you wanted a girl to marry you once, and because she would not, you have lived all your life like a gray bear up here in these rocks, and you will die here. I am not going to do that; I am going to make others drink with me this bitter drink, which will sweeten it for me."

Sadly the hermit saw this last interest on earth pass from him; saw Fate wave her victorious banners over him; saw the forces of nature work their will; and he sank under the burden of his thoughts. "I had hoped," he said to himself, "to be able to restore this boy to his proper place among the white people, but I have failed. I do not understand why men should be so afflicted in this world as Ermine and I have been, but doubtless it is the working of a great law, and possibly of a good one. My long years as a hunter have taught me that the stopping of the heart-beat is no great thing—it is soon over; but the years of living that some men are made to undergo is a very trying matter. Brave and sane is he who keeps his faith. I fear for the boy."

After a few weeks Ermine could no longer bear with the sullen savagery of his emotions, and he took his departure. Crooked-Bear sat by his cabin door and saw him tie his blanket on his saddle; saw him mount and extend his hand, which he shook, and they parted without a word. They had grown accustomed to this ending; there was nothing in words that mattered now. The prophet's boy disappeared in the gloom of the woods, snapping bushes, and rolling stones, until there was no sound save the crackling of the fire on the lonely hearth.

As Ermine ambled over the yellow wastes, he thought of the difference between now and his going to the white man one year ago. Then he was full of hopes; but now no Crow Indian would dare be seen in his company—not even Wolf-Voice could offer him the comfort of his reckless presence. He was compelled to sneak into the Absaroke camp in the night, to trade for an extra pony with his relatives, and to be gone before the morning. The ghostly tepees, in the quiet of the night, seemed to dance around him, coming up, and then retiring, while their smoke-flaps waved their giant fingers, beckoning him to be gone. The dogs slunk from him, and the ponies walked away. The curse of the white man was here in the shadows, and he could feel the Indians draw their robes more closely over their heads as they dreamed. The winds from the mountains blew on his back to help him along, and whispered ugly thoughts. All the good of the world had drawn away from Ermine, and it seemed that the sun did not care to look at him, so long was he left to stumble through the dark. But Nature did not paint this part of her day any blacker than she had Ermine's heart; each footfall of his pony took him nearer to death, and he whipped on impatiently to meet it. Hope had long since departed—he could not steal the girl; he realized the impossibility of eluding pursuit; he only wanted to carry Butler with him away from her. All the patient training of Crooked-Bear, all the humanizing influence of white association, all softening moods of the pensive face in the photograph, were blown from the fugitive as though carried on a wind; he was a shellfish-eating cave-dweller, with a Springfield, a knife, and a revolver. He had ceased to think in English, and muttered to himself in Absaroke. As his pony stumbled at a ford in the river, he cut it savagely with his whip,—the pony which was the last of his friends,—and it grunted piteously as it scrambled for its foothold.

Day after day he crawled through the rugged hills far from the places where men might be; for every one was his enemy, and any chance rifle would take away from him his vengeance. The tale of his undoing had travelled wide—he found that out in the Crow camp; Ba-cher-hish-a had told him that through her tears. He could trust no one; the scouts at Tongue River might be apathetic in an attempt to capture him, but they could not fail to report his presence if seen in the vicinity. Butler was probably in the middle of the log-town, which swarmed with soldiers, but it was there he must go, and he had one friend left, just one; it is always the last friend such a one has,—the Night.

Having arrived in the vicinity of the post, he prowled out on foot with his only friend. It was early, for he must do his deed while yet the lights were lit. Any one moving about after "taps" would surely be investigated by the guard. The country was not yet tranquil enough to permit of laxity in the matter of sentry duty, and the soldiers counted "ten" very fast after they challenged. He had laid aside his big hat, and was wrapped in his blanket. Many Indians were about, and he was less apt to be spoken to or noticed. He moved forward to the scout fire, which was outside of the guard-line, and stood for a time in some brushwood, beyond the play of the flames. He was closely enveloped in his blanket, and although Indians passed quite near him, he was not noticed. Suddenly he heard a detail of wagons clanking up the road, and conjectured rightly that they would go into the post. He ran silently toward them, and stooping low, saw against the skyline that the cavalry guard had worked up in front, impatient to shave the time when they should reach their quarters.

It was a wood train, and it clanked and ground and jingled to the quartermaster's corral, bearing one log on the last wagon which was John Ermine and his fortunes. This log slid to the ground and walked swiftly away.

* * *

The time for "taps" was drawing near, and the post buzzed in the usual expectation of that approaching time of quiet. A rifle-shot rang loud and clear up on the officers' row; it was near Major Searles's house, every one said as they ran. Women screamed, and Tongue River cantonment laid its legs to the ground as it gathered to the place. Officers came with revolvers, and the guard with lanterns. Mrs. Searles and her daughter were clasped in each other's arms, while Mary, the cook, put her apron over her head. Searles ran out with his gun; the shot had been right under the window of his sitting-room. An Indian voice greeted him, "Don' shoot; me killi him."

"Who in h—— are you?" swore Searles, at a present.

"Don' shoot, me Ahhæta—all same Sharp-Nose—don' shoot—me killi him."

"Killi who? Who have you killed? Talk up quick!"

"Me killi him. You come—you see."

By this time the crowd drew in with questions and eager to help. A sergeant arrived with a lantern, and the guard laid rude hands on the Crow scout, Sharp-Nose, who was well known. He was standing over the prostrate figure, and continued to reiterate, "Me killi him."

The lantern quickly disclosed the man on the ground to be John Ermine, late scout and fugitive from justice, shot through the heart and dead, with his blanket and rifle on the ground beside him. As he looked through the window, he had been stalked and killed by the fool whom he would not allow to shake hands with Katherine Searles, and a few moments later, when Sharp-Nose was brought into her presence, between two soldiers, she recognized him when he said, "Mabeso, now you shake hands."

"Yes, I will shake hands with you, Sharp-Nose," and half to herself, as she eyed her malevolent friend, she muttered, "and he kept you to remember me by."

A Few Words from Mr. Remington

From behind the breastworks of his big desk the editor is banging at me to write about myself. I find the thought very chilly out here in the garish light, but his last shot says, "If you don't, I will send a person to interview you, and he will probably misquote you." Quite so—one doesn't need that character of help when about to play the fool; so if you find the going heavy, gentle reader, camp here.

I had brought more than ordinary schoolboy enthusiasm to Catlin, Irving, Gregg, Lewis and Clark, and others on their shelf, and youth found me sweating along their

The Map in the Sand. *University of Michigan Library.*

tracks. I was in the grand silent country following my own inclinations, but there was a heavy feel in the atmosphere. I did not immediately see what it portended, but it gradually obtruded itself. The times had changed.

Evening overtook me one night in Montana, and I by good luck made the campfire of an old wagon freighter who shared his bacon and coffee with me. I was nineteen years of age and he was a very old man. Over the pipes he developed that he was born in Western New York and had gone West at an early age. His West was Iowa. Thence during his long life he had followed the receding frontiers, always further and further West. "And now," said he, "there is no more West. In a few years the railroad will come along the Yellowstone and a poor man can not make a living at all."

There he was, my friend of the open, sleeping in a blanket on the ground (it snowed that night), eating his own villanies out of his frying-pan, wearing a cotton shirt open at the throat, and hunting his horses through the bleak hills before daylight; and all for enough money to mend harness and buy wagon grease. He had his point of view and he made a new one for me.

The old man had closed my very entrancing book almost at the first chapter. I knew the railroad was coming—I saw men already swarming into the land. I knew the derby hat, the smoking chimneys, the cordbinder, and the thirty-day note were upon us in a resistless surge. I knew the wild riders and the vacant land were about to vanish forever, and the more I considered the subject the bigger the Forever loomed.

Without knowing exactly how to do it, I began to try to record some facts around me, and the more I looked the more the panorama unfolded. Youth is never appalled by the insistent demands of a great profession, because it is mostly unconscious of their existence. Time unfolds these abruptly enough. Art is a she-devil of a mistress, and, if at times in earlier days she would not even stoop to my way of thinking, I have persevered and will so continue. Some day, who knows, she may let me tell you some of my secrets. Meanwhile be patient, and if the recording of a day which is past infringes on the increasing interest of the present, be assured there are those who will set this down in turn and everything will be right in the end. Besides, artists must follow their own inclinations unreservedly. It's more a matter of heart than head, with nothing perfunctory about it. I saw the living, breathing end of three American centuries of smoke and dust and sweat, and I now see quite another thing where it all took place, but it does not appeal to me.

Frederic Remington.

Jefferson as a Painter

I found Joseph Jefferson, a few years ago, in a secluded spot on the west coast of Florida, and he invited me into his den. I had known before that he painted, but I did not know that he gave so much time to it. The studio was an honest workshop, with paint and brushes in hopeless crisscross all over the place, like a tamarack swamp after the fire has swept it, canvases piled against the walls, and Mr. Jefferson in a new character. His tea-gown or blouse was long and voluminous, and gracefully daubed with stray paint. His long hair had fallen in a shock over his eyes, pulled there in the nervous moments when the thrill of color had robbed him of his consciousness, and from under it shone the quaint face which three generations of Americans can recall to their fancy.

"Are you going to paint to-day, Mr. Jefferson?" I asked.

"Of course!"

"What?" I ventured.

"Oh, bless you, I don't know! I never know what I am going to paint."

This was quite a shock to my ideas, but I gradually recovered as my brain titillated with the new idea. My own pictures, if at all successful, are finished before they are begun, but, on a little reflection, "there is no one way in art." Only teachers have methods; artists play with color and line unconsciously.

The medium he was using was a body water-color which is treated with varnish and has the effect of oil. It is laid on many shades lighter, and gathers intensity after the varnish is applied. After squeezing tube after tube on his palette and throwing them on the floor, he jerked things about, and I smiled at the hopeless confusion he had got things into as he said,

"I have the best girl in the world to look after this room, but she puts things away where I cannot find them." And he then mixed every article in the room up in a despairing manner.

Continuing, he said, "In this medium you have the compensation that if the results are not just what you intended, they are often much better."

Here was the key—he had the color sense developed beyond all else. "I have no method beyond this fussing with color, except to stop short when the thing suits me," he added; and picking up a sponge, he applied great sweeps of sky tone in his enthusiastic way.

"I account this"—holding up the dripping sponge—"the best weapon, after my fingers and thumb." And he gave the sky a few vicious wipes with the superior weapon.

"Clouds," he went on, "are not intellectual, you see; they do not know where they are going. A premeditated cloud—can you imagine it?" And the sponge worked vigorously, and the clouds blew over and under each other on the canvas just as they would in nature, until he sprang up and said, "There!"

At this stage I was in hopes that the earth under them would be made to do something specific. But no; a great tree trunk grew out of nothing instantly, as the blood follows in the track of a saber-stroke. The smaller trees were massed in battalions, and limbs were made with the feather of a buzzard's wing used as a brush.

"Neither are the branches of trees intellectual; they all happen," he said.

Pressed by me to betray his thoughts, he did so reluctantly: "Oh, I suppose I am thinking of Canada—those moss-covered rocks, big trees, and purling brooks." But I could see that he did not want to realize anything.

"I want to paint the woods as you see them when you are not looking at them," he exclaimed. It was his protest against realism. He wanted his pictures to be those of his strange mind, and not those which the negro sees who rows his boat when he goes fishing. It is the grotesque fancy which created Rip after the twenty years' working in a new field.

The trees he painted are mysterious—they do strange things, and end and begin nowhere.

I have travelled five thousand miles to be able to differentiate as to some drawing of horses, but I would not have mentioned that to Mr. Jefferson for worlds, so far were our instincts apart; and so I sat behind his chair, and my mind grew blank to see this highly organized, nervous mind, half drunk with the play of the color in paint as he swept his canvas and prodded his palette, while his hands fairly shook with excitement. He sat back with a sigh as the result caught his errant fancy. All these strange doings had to overcome themselves in my mind before I could lend it in sympathy to his works, but presently I felt their quaint charm, simplicity of purpose, and odd little accidents, which were beautiful. But again I found myself in rebellion; I entered into a conspiracy with Mrs. Jefferson, who constantly tried to inveigle her husband from his studio in the interest of his health.

He espied a little pieced-up board shanty on the sands of the Gulf. I suggested that we paint that since it pleased him.

"No—not now."

"When?"

"Oh, I shall paint that next year some time, or possibly not in two years," he soliloquized.

"But," said I, in my rebellion, "you may not be here; besides, I think the house will rot down in less time than that."

"As we see it when we are not looking at it, my boy;" and I knew he was right.

Then, as our boat glided in the quiet creeks where the sedgegrass shot downward its reflections, where the palms waved gracefully and the limbs of the water-oaks did crazy angles, he noted things, and said, "I will remember that." He walked the woods, with bowed head, and hands clasped behind him, and he held his fishing-rod listlessly as his eyes sought the clouds. His mind was gathering the treasures of nature to his storebox, to be seen later when he was not looking.

The Way of an Indian

White Otter's Own Shadow

White Otter's heart was bad. He sat alone on the rimrocks of the bluffs overlooking the sunlit valley. To an unaccustomed eye from below he might have been a part of nature's freaks among the sand rocks. The yellow grass sloped away from his feet mile after mile to the timber, and beyond that to the prismatic mountains. The variegated lodges of the Chis-chis-chash village dotted the plain near the sparse woods of the creek-bottom; pony herds stood quietly waving their tails against the flies or were driven hither and yon by the herdboys—giving variety to the tremendous sweep of the Western landscape.

This was a day of peace—such as only comes to the Indians in contrast to the fierce troubles which nature stores up for the other intervals. The enemy, the pinch of the shivering famine, and the Bad Gods were absent, for none of these things care to show themselves in the white light of a mid-summer's day. There was peace with all the world except with him. He was in a fierce dejection over the things which had come to him, or those which had passed him by. He was a boy—a fine-looking, skillfully modeled youth—as beautiful a thing, doubtless, as God ever created in His sense of form; better than his sisters, better than the four-foots, or the fishes, or the birds, and he meant so much more than the inanimate things, in so far as we can see. He had the body given to him and he wanted to keep it, but there were the mysterious demons of the darkness, the wind and the flames; there were the monsters from the shadows, and from under the waters; there were the machinations of his enemies, which he was not proof against alone, and there was yet the strong hand of the Good God, which had not been offered as yet to help him on with the simple things of life; the women, the beasts of the fields, the ponies and the war-bands. He could not even protect his own shadow, which was his other and higher self.

His eyes dropped on the grass in front of his moccasins—tiny dried blades of yellow grass, and underneath them he saw the dark traceries of their shadows. Each had its own little shadow—its soul—its changeable thing—its other life—just as he himself was cut blue-black beside himself on the sand-stone. There were millions of these grass-blades, and each one shivered in the wind, maundering to itself in the chorus, which made the prairie sigh, and all for fear of a big brown buffalo wandering by, which would bite them from the earth and destroy them.

White Otter's people had been strong warriors in the Chis-chis-chash; his father's shirt and leggins were black at the seams with the hair of other tribes. He, too, had stolen ponies, but had done no better than

He Looked on the Land of His People and He Hated All Vehemently. *Painting in the Gund Collection of Western Art* (*A Traveling Exhibition of American Western Art*).

that thus far, while he burned to keep the wolf-totem red with honor. Only last night, a few of his boy companions, some even younger than himself, had gone away to the Absaroke for glory and scalps, and ponies and women—a war-party—the one thing to which an Indian pulsed with his last drop.

He had thought to go also, but his father had discouraged him, and yesterday presented him with charcoal-ashes in his right hand, and two juicy buffalo-ribs with his left. He had taken the charcoal. His father said it was good—that it was not well for a young man to go to the enemy with his shadow uncovered before the Bad Gods.

Now his spirits raged within his tightened belly, and the fierce Indian brooding had driven him to the rim-rock, where his soul rocked and pounced within him. He looked at the land of his people, and he hated all vehemently, with a rage that nothing stayed but his physical strength.

Old Big Hair, his father, sitting in the shade of his tepee, looked out across at his son on the far-off sky-line, and he hid his head in his blanket as he gazed into his medicine-pouch. "Keep the enemy and the

Bad Gods from my boy; he has no one to protect him but you, my medicine."

Thus hour after hour there sat the motionless tyro, alone with his own shadow on the hill. The shades of all living nature grew great and greater with the declining sun. The young man saw it with satisfaction. His heart swelled with brave thoughts, as his own extended itself down the hillside—now twenty feet long—now sixty—until the western sun was cut by the bluffs, when it went out altogether. The shadow of White Otter had been eaten up by the shadow of the hill. He knew now that he must go to the westward—to the western mountains, to the Inyan-kara, where in the deep recesses lay the shadows which had eaten his. They were calling him, and as the sun sank to rest, White Otter rose slowly, drew his robe around him, and walked away from the Chis-chis-chash camp.

The split sticks in Big Hair's lodge snapped and spit gleams of light on the old warrior as he lay back on his resting-mat. He was talking to his sacred symbols. "Though he sleeps very far off, though he sleeps even on the other side, a spirit is what I use to keep him. Make the bellies of animals full which would seek my son; make the wolf and the bear and the panther go out of their way. Make the buffalo herds to split around my son, Good God! Be strong to keep the Bad God back, and all his demons—lull them to sleep while he passes; lull them with soft sounds."

And the Indian began a dolorous chanting, which he continued throughout the night. The lodge-fires died down in the camp, but the muffled intone came in a hollow sound from the interior of the tepee until the spirit of silence was made more sure, and sleep came over the bad and good together.

Across the gray-greens of the moonlit plains bobbed and flitted the dim form of the seeker of God's help.

Now among the dark shadows of the pines, now in the gray sage-brush, lost in the coulees, but ceaselessly on and on, wound this figure of the night. The wolves sniffed along on the trail, but came no nearer.

All night long he pursued his way, his muscles playing tirelessly to the demands of a mind as taut as bowstring.

Before the morning he had reached the Inyan-kara, a sacred place, and begun to ascend its pine-clad slopes. It had repulsion for White Otter, it was sacred—full of strange beings not to be approached except in the spiritual way, which was his on this occasion, and thus he approached it. To this place the shadows had retired, and he was pursuing them. He was in mortal terror— every tree spoke out loud to him; the dark places gave back groans, the night-winds swooped upon him, whispering their terrible fears. The great underground wildcat meowed from the slopes, the red-winged moon-birds shrilled across the sky, and the stone giants from the cliffs rocked and sounded back to White Otter, until he cried aloud:

"O Good God, come help me. I am White Otter. All the bad are thick around me; they have stolen my shadow; now they will take me, and I shall never go across to live in the shadow-land. Come to White Otter, O Good God!"

A little brown bat whirled round and round the head of the terror-stricken Indian, saying: "I am from God, White Otter. I am come to you direct from God. I will take care of you. I have your shadow under my wings. I can fly so fast and crooked that no one can catch up with me. No arrow can catch me, no bullet can find me, in my tricky flight. I have your shadow and I will fly about so fast that the spirit-wildcats and the spirit-birds and the stone giants cannot come up with me or your shadow, which I carry under my wings. Sit down here in the dark place under the cliffs and rest. Have no fear."

White Otter sat him down as directed, muffled in his robe. "Keep me safe, do not go away from me, ye little brown bat. I vow to keep you all my life, and to take you in the shadow-land hereafter, if ye will keep me from the demons now, O little brown bat!" And so praying, he saw the sky pale in the east as he lay down to sleep. Then he looked all around for his little brown bat, which was no more to be seen.

The daylight brought quiescence to the fasting man, and he sank back, blinking his hollow eyes at his shadow beside him. Its possession lulled him, and he paid the debt of nature, lying quietly for a long time.

Consciousness returned slowly. The hot sun beat on the fevered man, and he moved uneasily. To his ears came the far-away beat of a tom-tom, growing nearer and nearer until it mixed with the sound of bells and the hail-like rattle of gourds. Soon he heard the breaking of sticks under the feet of approaching men, and from under the pines a long procession of men appeared—but they were shadows, like water, and he could see the landscape beyond them. They were spirit-men. He did not stir. The moving retinue came up, breaking now into the slow side-step of the ghost-dance, and around the form of White Otter gathered these people of the other world. They danced "the Crazy

Dance" and sang, but the dull orbs of the faster gave no signs of interest.

"He-eye, he-eye! we have come for you—come to take you to the shadow-land. You will live on a rocky island, where there are no ponies, no women, no food, White Otter. You have no medicine, and the Good God will not protect you. We have come for you—hi-ya, hi-ya, hi-yah!"

"I have a medicine," replied White Otter. "I have the little brown bat which came from God."

"He-eye, he-eye! Where is your little brown bat? You do not speak the truth—you have no little brown bat from God. Come with us, White Otter." With this one of the spirit-men strode forward and seized White Otter, who sprang to his feet to grapple with him. They clinched and strained for the mastery, White Otter and the camp-soldier of the spirit-people.

"Come to me, little brown bat," shouted the resisting savage, but the ghostly crowd yelled, "Your little brown bat will not come to you, White Otter."

Still he fought successfully with the spirit-soldier. He strained and twisted, now felling the ghost, now being felled in turn, but they staggered again to their feet. Neither was able to conquer. Hour after hour he resisted the taking of his body from off the earth to be deposited on the inglorious desert island in the shadow-land. At times he grew exhausted and seemed to lie still under the spirit's clutches, but reviving, continued the struggle with what energy he could summon. The westering sun began lengthening the shadows on the Inyan-kara, and with the cool of evening his strength began to revive. Now he fought the ghost with renewed spirit, calling from time to time on his medicine-bat, till at last when all the shadows had merged and gone together, with a whir came the little brown bat, crying "Na-hoin [I come]."

Suddenly all the ghost-people flew away, scattering over the Inyan-kara, screaming, "Hoho, hoho, hoho!" and White Otter sat up on his robe.

The stone giants echoed in clattering chorus, the spirit-birds swished through the air with the whis-s-s-tling noise, and the whole of the bad demons came back to prowl, since the light had left the world, and they were no longer afraid. They all sought to circumvent the poor Indian, but the little brown bat circled around and around his head, and he kept saying: "Come to me, little brown bat. Let White Otter put his hand on you; come to my hand."

But the bat said nothing, though it continued to fly around his head. He waved his arms widely at it, trying to reach it. With a fortunate sweep it struck his hand, his fingers clutched around it, and as he drew back his arm he found his little brown bat dead in the vise-like grip. White Otter's medicine had come to him.

Folding himself in his robe, and still grasping the symbol of the Good God's protection, he lay down to sleep. The stone giants ceased their clamors, and all the world grew still. White Otter was sleeping.

In his dreams came the voice of God, saying: "I have given it, given you the little brown bat. Wear it always on your scalp-lock, and never let it away from you for a moment. Talk to it, ask of it all manner of questions, tell it the secrets of your shadow-self, and it will take you through battle so fast that no arrow or bullet can hit you. It will steal you away from the spirits which haunt the night. It will whisper to you concerning the intentions of the women, and your enemies, and it will make you wise in the council when you are older. If you adhere to it and follow its dictation, it will give you the white hair of old age on this earth, and bring you to the shadow-land when your turn comes."

The next day when the sun had come again, White Otter walked down the mountain, and at the foot met his father with ponies and buffalo-meat. The old man had followed on his trail, but had gone no farther.

"I am strong now, father. I can protect my body and my shadow—the Good God has come to Wo-pe-ni-in."

II

The Brown Bat Proves Itself

Big Hair and his son, White Otter, rode home slowly, back through the coulees and the pines and the sage-brush to the camp of the Chis-chis-chash. The squaws took their ponies when they came to their lodge.

Days of listless longing followed the journey to the Inyan-kara in search of the offices of the Good God, and the worn body and fevered mind of White Otter recovered their normal placidity. The red warrior on his resting-mat sinks in a torpor which a sunning mud-turtle on a log only hopes to attain to, but he stores up energy; which must sooner or later find expression in the most extended physical effort.

Thus during the days did White Otter eat and sleep, or lie under the cottonwoods by the creek with his chum, the boy Red Arrow—lying together on the same robe and dreaming as boys will, and talking also, as is the wont of youth, about the things which make a man. They both had their medicine —they were good hunters, whom the camp soldiers allowed to accompany the parties in the buffalo-surround. They both had a few ponies, which they had stolen from the Absaroke hunters the preceding autumn, and which had given them a certain boyish distinction in the camp. But their eager minds yearned for the time to come when they should do the deed which would allow them to pass from the boy to the warrior stage, before which the Indian is in embryo.

Betaking themselves oft to deserted places, they each consulted his own medicine. White Otter had skinned and dried and tanned the skin of the little brown bat, and covered it with gaudy porcupine decorations. This he had tied to his carefully cultivated scalplock, where it switched in the passing breeze. People in the camp were beginning to say "the little brown bat boy" as he passed them by.

But their medicine conformed to their wishes, as an Indian's medicine mostly has to do, so that they were promised success in their undertaking.

Old Big Hair, who sat blinking, knew that the inevitable was going to happen, but he said no word. He did not advise or admonish. He doted on his son, and did not want him killed, but that was better than no eagle-plume.

Still the boys did not consult their relatives in the matter, but on the appointed evening neither turned up at the ancestral tepee, and Big Hair knew that his son had gone out into the world to win his feather. Again he consulted the medicine-pouch and sang dolorously to lull the spirits of the night as his boy passed him on his war-trail.

Having traveled over the table-land and through the pines for a few miles, White Otter stopped, saying: "Let us rest here. My medicine says not to go farther, as there is danger ahead. The demons of the night are waiting for us beyond, but my medicine says that if we build a fire the demons will not come near, and in the morning they will be gone."

They made a small fire of dead pine sticks and sat around it wrapped in the skins of the gray wolf, with the head and ears of that fearful animal capping theirs— unearthly enough to frighten even the monsters of the night.

Old Big Hair had often told his son that he would send him out with some war-party under a chief who well knew how to make war, and with a medicine-man whose war-medicine was strong; but no war-party was going then and youth has no time to waste in waiting. Still, he did not fear pursuit.

Thus the two human wolves sat around the snapping sticks, eating their dried buffalo-meat.

"To-morrow, Red Arrow, we will make the war-medicine. I must find a gray spider, which I am to kill, and then if my medicine says go on, I am not afraid, for it came direct from the Good God, who told me I should live to wear white hair."

"Yes," replied Red Arrow, "we will make

the medicine. We do not know the mysteries of the great war-medicine, but I feel sure that my own is strong to protect me. I shall talk to a wolf. We shall find a big gray wolf, and if as we stand still on the plain he circles us completely around, we can go on, and the Gray Horned Thunder-Being and the Great Pipe-Bearing Wolf will march on our either side. But if the wolf does not circle us, I do not know what to do. Old Bear-Walks-at-Right, who is the strongest war-medicine-maker in the Chis-chis-chash, says that when the Gray Horned Thunder-Being goes with a war party, they are sure of counting their enemies' scalps, but when the Pipe-Bearing Wolf also goes, the enemy cannot strike back, and the Wolf goes only with the people of our clan."

Thus the young men talked to each other, and the demons of the night joined in their conversation from among the tree-tops, but got no nearer because the fire shot words of warning up to them, and the hearts of the boys were strong to watch the contest and bear it bravely.

With the first coming of light they started on—seeking the gray spider and the gray wolf. After much searching through the rotting branches of the fallen trees, White Otter was heard calling to Red Arrow: "Come! Here is the gray spider, and as I kill him, if he contains blood I shall go on, but if he does not contain blood my medicine says there is great danger, and we must not go on."

Over the spider stooped the two seekers of truth, while White Otter got the spider on the body of the log, where he crushed it with his bow. The globular insect burst into a splash of blood and the young savage threw back his shoulders with a haughty grunt, saying, "My medicine is strong—we shall go to the middle of the Absaroke village," and Red Arrow gave his muttered assent.

"Now we must find a wolf," continued Red Arrow, and they betook themselves through the pines to the open plains, White Otter following him but a step in rear.

In that day wolves were not hard to find in the buffalo country, as they swarmed around the herds and they had no enemies. Red Arrow arrogated to himself the privilege of selecting the wolf. Scanning the expanse, it was not long before their sharp eyes detected ravens hovering over a depression in the plain, but the birds did not swoop down. They knew that there was a carcass there and wolves, otherwise the birds would not hover, but drop down. Quickly they made their way to the place, and as they came in range they saw the body of a half-eaten buffalo surrounded by a dozen wolves. The wolves betook themselves slowly off, with many wistful looks behind, but one in particular, more lately arrived at the feast, lingered in the rear.

Selecting this one, Red Arrow called: "O gray wolf of my clan, answer me this question. White Otter and I are going to the Absaroke for scalps—shall we have fortune, or is the Absaroke medicine too strong?"

The wolf began to circle as Red Arrow approached it and the buffalo carcass. Slowly it trotted off to his left hand, whereat the anxious warrior followed slowly.

"Tell me, pretty wolf, shall White Otter's and my scalps be danced by the Absaroke? Do the enemy see us coming now—do they feel our presence?" And the wolf trotted around still to the left.

"Come, brother. Red Arrow is of your clan. Warn me, if I must go back." And as the Indian turned, yet striding after the beast, it continued to go away from him, but kept an anxious eye on the dead buffalo meanwhile.

"Do not be afraid, gray wolf; I would not rise my arm to strike. See, I have laid my bow on the ground. Tell me not to fear the Absaroke, gray wolf, and I promise to kill a fat buffalo-cow for you when we meet again."

The wolf had nearly completed his circle by this time, and once again his follower spoke.

"Do you fear me because of the skin of the dead wolf you see by my bow on the ground? No, Red Arrow did not kill thy brother. He was murdered by a man of the dog clan, and I did not do it. Speak to me— help me against my fears." And the wolf barked as he trotted around until he had made a complete circle of the buffalo, whereat Red Arrow took up his bow and bundle, saying to White Otter, "Now we will go."

The two then commenced their long quest in search of the victims which were to satisfy their ambitions. They followed up the depression in the plains where they had found the buffalo, gained the timber, and walked all day under its protecting folds. They were a long way from their enemies' country, but instinctively began the cautious advance which is the wild-animal nature of an Indian.

The old buffalo-bulls, elk and deer fled from before them as they marched. A magpie mocked at them. They stopped while White Otter spoke harshly to it: "You laugh at us, fool-bird, because we are boys, but you shall see when we come back that we are warriors. We will have a scalp to taunt you with. Begone now, before I pierce you with an arrow, you chattering woman-bird." And the magpie fluttered away before the unwonted address.

In the late afternoon they saw a band of wolves pull down and kill a fawn, and ran to it, saying, "See, the Pipe-Bearing Wolf is with us; he makes the wolves to hunt for us of his clan," and they despoiled the prey.

Coming to a shallow creek, they took off their moccasins and waded down it for a mile, when they turned into a dry watercourse, which they followed up for a long distance, and then stopped in some thick brush which lined its sides. They sat long together on the edge of the bushes, scanning with their piercing eyes the sweep of the plains, but nothing was there to rouse their anxiety. The wild animals were feeding peacefully, the sun sank to rest, and no sound came to them but the cry of the nightbirds.

When it was quite dark, they made a small fire in the depths of the cut, threw a small quantity of tobacco into it as a sacrifice, cooked the venison and went to sleep.

It was more than mere extension of interest with them; it was more than ambition's haughtiest fight; it was the sun-dried, wind-shriveled, tried-out atavistic blood-thirst made holy by the approval of the Good God they knew.

The miniature war-party got at last into the Absaroke country. Before them lay a big camp—the tepees scattering down the creek-bottom for miles, until lost at a turn of the timber. Eagerly they studied the cut and sweep of the land, the way the tepees dotted it, the moving of the pony herds and the coming and going of the hunters, but most of all the mischievous wanderings of the restless Indian boys. Their telescopic eyes penetrated everything. They understood the movements of their foes, for they were of kindred nature with their own.

Their buffalo-meat was almost gone, and it was dangerous to kill game now for fear of attracting the ravens, which would circle overhead and be seen from the camp. These might attract an investigation from idle and adventurous boys and betray them.

"Go now; your time has come," said the little brown bat on White Otter's scalplock.

"Go now," echoed Red Arrow's charm.

When nothing was to be seen of the land but the twinkle of the fires in the camp, they were lying in a deep washout under a bluff, which overlooked the hostile camp. Long and silently they sat watching the fires and the people moving about, hearing their hum and chanting as it came to them on the still air, together with the barking of dogs, the nickering of ponies, and the hollow pounding on a log made by old squaws hacking with their hatchets.

Slowly before the drowse of darkness, the noises quieted and the fires died down. Red Arrow felt his potent symbols whispering to him.

"My medicine is telling me what to do, White Otter."

"What does it say?"

"It says that there is a dangerous mystery in the blue-and-yellow tepee at the head of the village. It tells me to have great care," replied Red Arrow.

"Hough, my medicine says go on; I am to be a great warrior," replied White Otter.

After a moment Red Arrow exclaimed: "My medicine says go with White Otter, and do what he says. It is good."

"Come then; we will take the war-ponies from beside the blue-and-yellow tepee. They belong to a chief and are good. We will strike an Absaroke if we can. Come with me." White Otter then glided forward in the darkness toward the camp. When quite near, they waited for a time to allow the dogs to be still, and when they ceased to tongue, they again approached with greater caution.

Slowly, so as not to disturb the animals of the Indians, they neared the blue-and-yellow tepee, squatting low to measure its gloom against the sky-line. They were among the picketed ponies, and felt them all over carefully with their hands. They found

the clip-maned war-ponies and cut the ropes. The Indian dogs made no trouble, as they walked their booty very slowly and very quietly away, as though they wandered in search of food. When well out of hearing, they sprang on their backs and circled back to the creek-bottom.

Nearing this, they heard the occasional inharmonious notes of an Indian flute-horn among the trees. Instantly they recognized it as an Indian lover calling for his sweetheart to come out from the lodges to him.

"Hold the ponies, Red Arrow. My medicine tells me to strike," and White Otter slid from his horse. He passed among the tepees at the end of the village, then quickly approached the direction of the noise of the flute.

The lover heard his approaching footsteps, for White Otter walked upright until the notes stopped, when he halted to await

"O Gray Wolf of My Clan—Shall We Have Fortune?" *Painting in the Gund Collection of Western Art (A Traveling Exhibition of American Western Art).*

their renewal. Again the impatient gallant called from the darkness to his hesitating one, and our warrior advanced with bared knife in one hand, and bow in the other with an arrow notched.

When quite near, the Absaroke spoke in his own language, but White Otter, not understanding, made no reply, though advancing rapidly. Alas for the surging blood which burns a lover's head, for his quick advance to White Otter discovered for him nothing until, with a series of lightning-like stabs, the knife tore its way into his vitals—once, twice, three times, when, with a wild yell, he sank under his deluded infatuation.

He doubtless never knew, but his yell had found its response from the camp. Feeling quickly, White Otter wound his hand among the thick black hair of his victim's head, and though it was his first, he made no bad work of the severance of the prize, whereat he ran fast to his chum. Attracted by the noise, Red Arrow rode up, and they were mounted. Cries and yells and barking came from the tepees, but silently they loped away from the confusion—turning into the creek, blinding the trail in the water for a few yards and regaining the hills from a much-tracked-up pony and buffalo crossing. Over the bluffs and across the hills they made their way, until they no longer heard the sounds of the camp behind them.

Filled with a great exultation, they trotted and loped along until the moon came up, when White Otter spoke for the first time, addressing it: "Pretty Mother of the Night—time of the little brown bat's flight—see what I have done. White Otter is no longer a boy." Then to his pony: "Go on quickly now, pretty little war-pony. You are strong to carry me. Do not lame yourself in the dog-holes. Carry me back to the Chis-chis-chash, and I promise the Mother of the Night, now and here, where you can hear me speak, that you shall never carry any man but White Otter, and that only in war."

For three days and nights they rode as rapidly as the ponies could travel, resting an hour here and there to refresh themselves. Gradually relaxing after this, they assumed the fox-trot of the plains pony; but they looked many times behind and doubled often in their trail.

Seeing a band of wolves around a buffalo-bull which was fighting them off, they rode up and shot arrows into it—the sacrifice to the brother of the clan who had augured for them. Red Arrow affected to recognize his old acquaintance in the group.

As they rode on, White Otter spoke: "I shall wear the eagle-feather standing up in my scalplock, for I struck him with a hand-weapon standing up. It shall wave above the bat and make him strong. The little brown bat will be very brave in the time to come. We took the clipped and painted war-ponies from under the chief's nose, Red Arrow."

"Yes, I did that—but my medicine grew weak when it looked at the great camp of the Absaroke. Your medicine was very strong, White Otter; there is no old warrior in the Chis-chis-chash whose is stronger. I shall take the charcoal again, and see if the Good God won't strengthen my medicine."

Time brought the victors in sight of their village, which had moved meanwhile, and it was late in the evening.

"Stay here with the ponies, Red Arrow, and I will go into my father's lodge and get red paint for us. We will not enter until to-morrow."

So White Otter stole into his own tepee by night—told his father of his triumph—got a quantity of vermilion and returned to the hills. When he and Red Arrow had bedaubed themselves and their ponies most liberally, they wrapped the scalp to a lance which he had brought out, then moved slowly forward in the morning light on their jaded ponies to the village, yelling the long, high notes of the war-whoop. The people ran out to see them come, many young men riding to meet them. The yelling procession came to the masses of the people, who shrilled in answer, the dogs ki-yied, and old trade-guns boomed. White Otter's chin was high, his eyes burned with a devilish light through the red paint, as he waved the lance slowly, emitting from time to time above the din his battle-cry.

It was thus that White Otter became a man.

III

The Bat Devises Mischief Among the Yellow-Eyes

White Otter, the boy, had been super-seded by the man with the upright eagle-feather, whom people now spoke of as Ho-to-kee-mat-sin, the Bat. The young women of the Chis-chis-chash threw approving glances after the Bat as he strode proudly about the camp. He was possessed of all de-sirable things conceivable to the red mind. Nothing that ever bestrode a horse was more exquisitely supple than the well-laid form of this young Indian man; his fame as a hunter was great, but the taking of the Absaroke scalp was transcendent. Still, it was not possible to realize any matrimonial hopes which he was led to entertain, for his four ponies would buy no girl fit for him. The captured war-pony, too, was one of these, and not to be transferred for any woman.

The Bat had conjured with himself and conceived the plan of a trip to the far south —to the land of many horses—but the time was not yet.

As the year drew on, the Chis-chis-chash moved to the west—to the great fall buffalo-hunt—to the mountains where they could gather fresh tepee-poles, and with the hope of trade with the wandering trap-per bands. To be sure, the Bat had no skins or ponies to barter with them, but good for-tune is believed to stand in the path of every young man, somewhere, some time, as he wanders on to meet it. Delayed ambition did not sour the days for the Indian. He knew that the ponies and the women and the chieftainship would come in the natural way; besides which, was he not already a warrior worth pointing at?

He accompanied the hunters when they made the buffalo-surround, where the bel-lowing herds shook the dusty air and made the land to thunder while the Bat flew in swift spirals like his prototype. Many a car-cass lay with his arrows, driven deep, while the squaws of Big Hair's lodge sought the private mark of the Bat on them.

The big moving camp of the Chis-chis-chash was strung over the plains—squaws, dogs, fat little boys toddling after possible prairie dogs, tepee ponies, pack-animals with gaudy squaw trappings, old chiefs stalking along in their dignified buffalo-robes—and a swarm of young warriors rid-ing far on either side.

The Bat's and Red Arrow's lusty fire had carried them far in the front, and as they slowly raised the brow of a hill they saw in the shimmer of the distance a cavalcade with many two-wheeled carts—all dragging wearily over the country.

"The Yellow-Eyes!" said the Bat.

"Yes," replied Red Arrow. "They always march in the way the wild ducks fly—going hither and yon to see what is happening in the land. But their medicine is very strong; I have heard the old men say it."

"Hough! it may be, but is not the medi-cine of the Chis-chis-chash also strong? Why do we not strike them, Red Arrow? That I could never understand. They have many guns, blankets, paints, many strong ponies and the strong water, which we might take," added the Bat, in perplexity.

"Yes, true, we might take all, but the old men say that the Yellow-Eyes would not come again next green grass—we would make them afraid. They would no more bring us the powder and guns or the knives. What could we do without iron arrow-heads? Do you remember how hard it was to make bone arrow-heads, when we were boys and could not get the iron? Then, the Yellow-Eyes are not so many as the Chis-chis-chash, and they are afraid of us. No, we must not make them more timid," re-plied the wise Red Arrow.

"But we may steal a gun or a strong pony when they do not look," continued the in-domitable Bat.

"Yes—we will try."

"I will go down the hill, and make my pony go around in a circle so that the camp may send the warriors out to us," saying which, the Bat rode the danger-signal, and the Chis-chis-chash riders came scurrying over the dry grass, leaving lines of white dust in long marks behind them. Having assembled to the number of a hundred or so, the chiefs held a long consultation, each talking loudly from his horse, with many gestures. After some minutes, the head war-chief declared in a high, rough voice that the man must go to the Yellow-Eyes with the peace-sign, and that they must not do anything to make the Yellow-Eyes afraid. The white men had many guns, and if they feared the Indians they would fire on them, when it would be impossible to get near the powder and paints and knives which were in the carts.

The warriors took each from a little bag his paints and plumes. Sitting in the grass, they decorated themselves until they assumed all hues—some red, and others half white or red across the face, while the ponies came in for streaks and daubs, grotesque as tropic birds.

So over the hill rode the line of naked men, their ponies dancing with excitement, while ahead of them a half-breed man skimmed along bearing a small bush over his head. The cavalcade of the Yellow-Eyes had halted in a compact mass, awaiting the oncoming Indians. They had dismounted and gone out on the sides away from the carts, where they squatted quietly in the grass. This was what the Yellow-Eyes always did in war.

A warrior of the Yellow-Eyes came to meet them, waving a white cloth from his gun-barrel after the manner of his people, and the two peace-bearers shook hands. Breaking into a run, the red line swept on, their ponies' legs beating the ground in a vibratory whirl, their plumes swishing back in a rush of air, and with yelps which made the white men draw their guns into a menacing position.

At a motion of the chief's arm, the line stopped. The Yellow-Eyed men rose slowly from the grass and rested on their long rifles, while their chief came forward.

For a long time the two head men sat on their ponies in front of the horsemen, speaking together with their hands. Not a sound was to be heard but the occasional stamp of a pony's hoof on the hard ground. The beady eyes of the Chis-chis-chash beamed malevolently on the white chief— the blood-thirst, the warrior's itch, was upon them.

After an understanding had been arrived at, the Indian war-chief turned to his people and spoke. "We will go back to our village. The Yellow-Eyes do not want us among their carts—they are afraid. We will camp near by them to-night, and to-morrow we will exchange gifts. Go back, Chis-chis-chash, or the white chief says it is war. We do not want war."

The two camps were pitched that night two miles apart; the Yellow-Eyes intrenched behind their packs and carts, while the Indians, being in overwhelming strength, did much as usual, except that the camp-soldiers drove the irrepressible boys back, not minding to beat their ponies with their whips when they were slow to go. There was nothing that a boy could do except obey when the camp-soldier spoke to him. He was the one restraint they had, the only one.

But as a mark of honor, the Bat and Red Arrow were given the distinguished honor of observing the Yellow-Eye camp all night, to note its movements if any occurred, and with high hearts they sat under a hill-top all through the cold darkness, and their souls were much chastened by resisting the impulses to run off the white man's ponies, which they conceived to be a very possible undertaking.

Nothing having occurred, they returned before daylight to their own camp to so inform the war-chief.

That day the Chis-chis-chash crowded around the barricade of the Yellow-Eyes, but were admitted only a few at a time. They received many small presents of coffee and sugar, and traded what ponies and robes they could. At last it became the time for the Bat to go into the trappers' circle. He noted the piles of bales and boxes as he passed in, a veritable mountain of wealth; he saw the tall white men in their buckskin and white blanket suits, befringed and beribboned; their long, light hair, their bushy beards, and each carrying a well-oiled rifle. Ah, a rifle! That was what the Bat wanted; it displaced for the time all other thoughts of the young warrior. He had no robes and came naked among the traders—they noted him—only an Indian boy, and when all his group had bartered what they had, the half-breed who had ridden with the peace-branch spoke to him, interpreting: "The white chief wants to know if you want to buy anything."

"Yes. Tell the white chief that I must have a gun, and some powder and ball."

"What has the boy to give for a gun?" asked a long-bearded leader.

"A pony—a fast buffalo pony," replied our hero through the half-breed.

"One pony is not enough for a gun; he must give three ponies. He is too young to have three ponies," replied the trader.

"Say to the Yellow-Eye that I will give him two ponies," risked the Bat.

"No, no; he says three ponies, and you will not get them for less."

"Let me see the gun," demanded the boy. A gun was necessary for the Bat's future progression.

A subordinate was directed to show a gun to him, which he did by taking him one side and pulling one from a cart. It was a long, yellow-stocked smoothbore, with a flintlock. It had many brass tacks driven into the stock, and was bright in its cheap newness. As the Bat took it in his hand, he felt a nervous thrill, such as he had not experienced since the night he had pulled the dripping hair from the Absaroke. He felt it all over, smoothing it with his hand; he cocked and snapped it; and the little brown bat on his scalplock fairly yelled, "Get your ponies, get your ponies—you must have the gun."

Returning the gun, the Bat ran out, and after a time came back with his three ponies, which he drove up to the white man's pen, saying in Chis-chis-chash: "Here are my ponies. Give me the gun."

The white chief glanced at the boy as he sat there on a sturdy little clip-maned war-pony—the one he had stolen from the Absaroke. He spoke, and the interpreter continued: "The trader says he will take the pony you are riding as one of the three."

"Tell him that I say I would not give this pony for all the goods I see. Here are my three ponies; now let him give me the gun before he makes himself a liar," and the boy warrior wore himself into a frenzy of excitement as he yelled: "Tell him if he does not give me the gun he will feel this war-pony in the dark, when he travels; tell him he will not see this war-pony, but he will feel him when he counts his ponies at daylight. He is a liar."

"The white chief says he will take the war-pony in place of three ponies, and give you a gun, with much powder and many balls."

"Tell the Yellow-Eye he is a liar, with the lie hot on his lips," and the Bat grew quiet to all outward appearance.

After speaking to the trader, the interpreter waved at the naked youth, sitting there on his war-pony: "Go away—you are a boy, and you keep the warriors from trading."

With a few motions of the arms, so quickly done that the interpreter had not yet turned away his eye, the Bat had an arrow drawn to its head on his leveled bow and covering the white chief.

Indians sprang between; white men cocked their rifles; two camp-soldiers rushed to the enraged Bat, and led his pony quietly away, driving the three ponies after him.

The trading progressed throughout the day, and at night the Indians all came home, but no one saw the Bat in his father's lodge, and also Red Arrow was missing. All the Indians had heard of how the white trader had lied to the boy, and they knew the retribution must come. The trading was over; the white men had packed up their goods; had shaken hands with the chiefs and head men, promising to come again when the grass was green.

The Chis-chis-chash were busy during the ensuing days following the buffalo, and their dogs grew fat on the leavings of the

The Interpreter Waved at the Youth, Sitting There on His War-pony.
Painting in George F. Harding Museum, Chicago.

carcasses. The white traders drew their weary line over the rolling hills, traveling as rapidly as possible to get westward of the mountains before the snows encompassed them. But by night and by day, on their little flank, in rear or far in front, rode two vermilion warrior-boys, on painted ponies, and one with an eagle-plume upright in his scalplock.

Old Delaware hunters in the caravan told the white chief that they had seen swift pony-tracks as they hunted through the hills; and that, too, many times. The tracks showed that the ponies were strong and went quickly—faster than they could follow on their jaded mounts. The white chief must not trust the solitude.

But the trailing buffalo soon blotted out the pony-marks; the white men saw only the sailing hawks, and heard only bellowing and howling at night. Their natures responded to the lull, until two horse-herders grew eager in a discussion, and did not notice that the ponies and mules were traveling rapidly away to the bluffs. Two ponies ran hither and thither behind the horses. There was method in their movements—were they wild stallions? As the white men moved out toward the herd, still gazing ardently, they saw one of these ponies turn quickly, and as he did so a naked figure shifted from one side to the other of his back.

"Indians! Indians!" A pistol was fired— the herders galloped after.

The horse-thieves sat upon their ponies, and the long, tremulous notes of the war-whoop were faintly borne on the wind to the camp of the Yellow-Eyes. Looking out across the plains, they saw the herd break into a wild stampede, while behind them sped the Bat and Red Arrow, waving long-lashed whips to the ends of which were suspended blown-up buffalo-bladders, which struck the hard ground with sharp, explosive thumps, rebounding and striking again. The horses were terrorized, but, being worn down, could not draw away from the swift and supple war-steeds. There were more than two hundred beasts, and the white men were practically afoot.

Many riders joined the pursuit; a few lame horses fell out of the herd and out of the race—but it could have only one ending with the long start. Mile by mile the darkness was coming on, so that when they could no longer see, the white pursuers could hear the beat of hoofs, until that, too, passed—and their horses were gone.

That night there was gloom and dejection around the camp-fires inside the ring of carts. Some recalled the boy on the war-pony with the leveled bow; some even whispered that Mr. McIntish had lied to the boy, but no one dared say that out loud. The factor stormed and damned, but finally gathered what men he could mount and prepared to follow next day.

Follow he did, but the buffalo had stamped out the trail, and at last, baffled and made to go slow by the blinded sign, he gave up the trail to hunt for the Chis-chis-chash village.

After seven days' journey he struck the carcasses left in the line of the Indians' march, and soon came up with their camp, which he entered with appropriate ceremony, followed by his seven retinues—half-breed interpreter, Delaware trailers, French horse-herders, and two real Yellow-Eyed men—white Rocky Mountain trappers, rifle-bearing and born in Kentucky.

He sought the head chief, and they all gathered in the council tepee. There they smoked and passed the pipe. The squaws brought kettles of buffalo-meat, and the eager youngsters crowded the door until a camp-soldier stood in the way to bar them back. The subchiefs sat in bronze calm, with their robes drawn in all dignity about them.

When all was ready, Mr. McIntish stood in the middle of the lodge and spoke with great warmth and feeling, telling them that

Chis-chis-chash warriors had stolen his horse-herd—that he had traced it to their camp and demanded its return. He accused them of perfidy, and warned them that from thence on no more traders would ever come into their country, but would give their guns to the Absaroke, who would thus be able to overwhelm them in war.

When he had finished and sat down, the head chief arose slowly, and stepping from the folds of his robe, he began slowly to talk, making many gestures. "If the white chief had tracked the stolen ponies to his camp, let him come out to the Indian pony-herds and point them out. He could take his horses."

The face of the trader grew hard as he faced the snare into which the chief had led him, and the lodge was filled with silence.

The camp-soldier at the entrance was brushed aside, and with a rapid stride a young Indian gained the center of the lodge, and stood up very straight in his nakedness. He began slowly, with senatorial force made fierce by resolve. "The white chief is a liar. He lied to me about the gun; he has come into the council tepee of the Chis-chis-chash and lied to all the chiefs. He did not trail the stolen horses to this camp. He will not find them in our pony-herds. I—the boy—I stole all the white chief's ponies, in the broad daylight, with his whole camp looking at me. I did not come in the dark. He is not worthy of that. He is a liar, and there is a shadow across his eyes. The ponies are not here. They are far away—where the poor blind Yellow-Eyes cannot see them even in dreams. There is no man of the Chis-chis-chash here who knows where the horses are. Before the liar gets his horses again, he will have his mouth set on straight," and the Bat turned slowly around, sweeping the circle with his eyes to note the effect of his first speech, but there was no sound.

Again the trader ventured on his wrongs—charged the responsibility of the Bat's actions on the Chis-chis-chash, and pleaded for justice.

The aged head chief again rose to reply,

"I Will Tell the White Man How He Can Have His Ponies Back."
Painting in George F. Harding Museum, Chicago.

saying he was sorry for what had occurred, but he reminded McIntish that the young warrior had convicted him of forged words. What would the white chief do to recompense the wrong if his horses were returned? He also stated that it was not in his power to find the horses, and that only the young man could do that.

Springing again to his feet, with all the animation of resolution, the Bat's voice clicked in savage gutturals. "Yes, it is only with myself that the white liar can talk. If the chiefs and warriors of my tribe were to take off my hide with their knives—if they were to give me to the Yellow-Eyes to be burnt with fire—I would not tell where the ponies lie hidden. My medicine will blind your eyes as does the north wind when he comes laden with snow.

"I will tell the white man how he can have his ponies back. He can hand over to me now the bright new gun which lies by his side. It is a pretty gun, better than any Indian has. With it, his powder-horn and his bullet-bag must go. If he does this, he can have back all his horses, except those I

choose to keep. Is it good? I will not say it again. I have spoken."

The boy warrior stood with arms dropped at his sides, very straight in the middle of the tent, the light from the smokehole illumining the top of his body while his eye searched the traders.

McIntish gazed through his bushy eyebrows at the victor. His burnt skin turned an ashen-green; his right hand worked nervously along his gun-barrel. Thus he sat for a long time, the boy standing quietly, and no one moved in the lodge.

With many arrested motions, McIntish raised the rifle until it rested on its butt; then he threw it from himself, and it fell with a crash across the dead ashes of the fire, in front of the Bat. Stripping his powder-horn and pouch off his body, violently he flung them after, and the Bat quickly rescued them from among the ashes.

Gathering the tokens and girding them about his body, the Bat continued: "If the white liar will march up this river one day and stop on the big meadows by the log house, which has no fire in it; if he will keep his men quietly by the log house, where they can be seen at all times; if he will stay there one day, he will see his ponies coming to him. I am not a boy; I am not a man with two tongues; I am a warrior. Go, now— before the camp-soldiers beat you with sticks."

IV

The New Lodge

The Yellow-Eyes had departed, and at the end of four days the Bat and Red Arrow drove a band of thirty ponies and mules onto the herd-grounds, where they proceeded to cut them into two bunches— fifteen horses for each young man. This was not a bad beginning in life, where ponies and robes were the things reckoned. The Bat got down from his horse and tossed a little brother onto it, telling him to look after them. The copper-colored midget swelled perceptibly as he loped away after the Bat's nineteen horses, for the twentieth, which was the war-pony, was taken to be picketed by Big Hair's Lodge.

As the Bat stalked among the Chis-chis-chash, he was greeted often—all eyes turned to him. No mere boys dared longer to be familiar; they only stood modestly, and paid the tribute to greatness which much staring denotes. The white man's new rifle lay across his left arm, his painted robe dragged on the ground, his eagle-feather waved perpendicularly above the dried bat's skin, the sacred red paint of war bloodied his whole face, and a rope and a whip— symbols of his success with horses— dangled in his right hand, while behind him followed the smart war-pony, covered with vermilion hand-prints as thickly as the spots on a brook-trout. The squaws ran from their fleshing, their chopping or their other work to look at the warrior who made all the camp talk. Wisdom mellowed by age, in

the forms of certain old men, sat back and thought disturbedly of the future, as is the wont of those who have little time to live. They feared for the trade with the Yellow-Eyes, for no Chis-chis-chash could forge iron into guns and knives, which were the arbiter between the tribes. This the Bat had brought upon them. But still they thought more than they said; warriors as promising as this young one did not often appear.

There was a feast at the lodge. The Bat told his exploits to the warriors, as he strode about the night-fire in the tepee, waving his arms, giving his war-yell until he split the air and made his listeners' ears ring.

On the morrow, men from the military order of the "red lodges," the "miayuma," came to the Bat with charcoal, and he fasted many days before undergoing his initiation. The sacred symbols of the body, their signs and ceremonies, were given him, and he had become a pillar in the Chis-chis-chash social structure.

The nights were growing cold, and occasional bleak winds blew down from the great mountains, warning the tribe to be about its mission. The loads of dry meat made the horses weary, when the camp was broken; the tepee-poles were bright and new, and the hair began to grow on the ponies.

One day, as they moved, they could see far ahead on the plains the colorless walls of Fort Laramie, and the wise-men feared for their reception, but the pillage of the traders' horses sat lightly on the people. The Yellow-Eyes should have a care how they treated the Chis-chis-chash. It was in their power to put out the white man's fires. The Bat's people were an arrogant band, and held their heads high in the presence of aliens. Their hands were laid heavily and at once on anyone who stood in their path. All the plains tribes, the French Indians at the posts and the Yellow-Eyed trapper-bands stood in awe of them. With the exception of the chief, the people had never been inside of the second gate at Laramie. They traded through a hole in the wall, and even then the bourgeois Papin thought he played with fire. Their haughty souls did not brook refusal when the trader denied them the arrangement of the barter.

The tribe encamped, and got rid of what ponies, robes and meats it could dispose of for guns and steel weapons, and "made whisky." The squaws concealed the arms while the warriors raged, but the Chis-chis-chash in that day were able to withstand the new vices of the white men better than most people of the plains.

On one occasion, the Bat was standing with a few chiefs before the gateway of the fort. Papin opened the passage and invited them to enter. Proudly the tall tribesmen walked among the *engagés*—seeming to pay no heed, but the eye of an Indian misses nothing. The surroundings were new and strange to the young man. The thick walls seemed to his vagabond mind to be built to shield cowards. The white men were created only to bring goods to the Indians. They

were weak, but their medicine was wonderful. It could make the knives and guns, which God had denied to the Bat's people. They were to be tolerated; they were few in number—he had not seen over a hundred of them in all his life. Scattered here and there about the post were women, who consorted with the *engagés*—half-breeds from the Mandans and Delawares, Sioux and many other kinds of squaws; but the Chis-chis-chash had never sold a woman to the traders. That was a pride with them.

The sisterhood of all the world will look at a handsome man and smile pleasantly; so nothing but cheerful looks followed the Bat as he passed the women who sat working by the doorways. They were not ill-favored, these comforters of the workmen, and were dressed in bright calicoes and red strouding, plentifully adorned with bright beads. The boy was beginning to feel a subtle weakening in their presence. His fierce barbarism softened, and he began

Nothing But Cheerful Looks Followed the Bat. *Painting in George F. Harding Museum, Chicago.*

to think of taking one. But he put it aside as a weakness—this giving of ponies for these white men's cast-offs. That thought was unworthy of him—a trade was not his wild way of possessing things.

He stood quietly leaning against a door on Papin's balcony, observing the men laboring about the enclosure, his lip curling upward with fine contempt. The "dogs" were hewing with axes about some newly made carts, or rushing around on errands as slaves are made to do. Everyone was busy and did not notice him in his brown study.

From within the room near by he heard a woman sing a few notes in an unknown tongue. Without moving a facial muscle, he stepped inside the room, and when his eye became accustomed to the light, saw a young squaw, who sat beading, and wore a dress superior to that of the others. She stared a moment and then smiled. The Bat stood motionless for a long time regarding her, and she dropped her gaze to her needlework.

"I' nisto' niwon [You were humming]," spoke the statued brave, but she did not understand.

Again came the clicking gutturals of the harsh Chis-chis-chash tongue: "Whose squaw are you?"—which was followed by the sign-talk familiar to all Indians in those days.

The woman rose, opening her hand toward him and hissing for silence. Going to the door, she looked into the sunlighted court, and, pointing to the factor who was directing workmen, replied, "Papin." He understood.

She talked by signs as she drew back, pointing to the Bat, and then ran her hand across her own throat as though she held a knife, and then laughed while her eyes sparkled.

Again he understood, and for the first time that day he smiled. There are no preliminaries when a savage warrior concludes to act. The abruptness of the Bat's love-making left room for few words, and his attentions were not repulsed except that the fear of her liege lord out by the carts made her flutter to escape that she might reassure herself. She was once again covered by the sweep of the warrior's robe, and what they whispered there, standing in its folds, no man can tell. The abrupt entrance of Papin drowned all other thoughts, and filled the quiet fort with a whirl of struggles and yells, in which all joined, even to the dogs.

The outcome was that the Bat found himself thrown ignominiously into the dust outside the walls, and the gate slammed after him. He gathered himself together and looked around. His humiliation was terrible —complete. Nothing like this had occurred before. Cowardly French half-breeds had laid their hands on the warrior's body, even on his sacred bat and eagle plume; and they had been content to throw him away as though he were a bone—merely to be rid of him. His rage was so great that he was in a torpor; he did not even speak, but walked away hearing the shrieks of the squaw being beaten by Papin.

Going to the camp, he got a pony and rode to the hills, where he dismounted and sat down. The day passed, the night came, and morning found the Bat still sitting there.

He seemed not to have moved. His eye burned with the steady glare of the great cats until, allowing his robe to fall away, he brought out his firebag and lighted his pipe. Standing up, he blew a mouthful of smoke to each of the four corners of the world; then lowered his head in silence for a long while. He had recovered himself now.

Presently he mounted and rode toward camp; his eyes danced the devil's dance as they wandered over the battlements of Fort Laramie. He wanted a river of blood—he wanted to break the bones of the whites with stone hatchets—he wanted to torture with fire. He would have the girl now at any cost.

After eating at Big Hair's lodge, he wandered over to the Fort. He said not a word to anyone as he passed. An old chief came out of the gate, turned the corner, saw the Bat, and said: "The white chief says you

The Ceremony of the Fastest Horse. *Painting in George F. Harding Museum, Chicago.*

tried to steal his squaw. His heart is cold to-ward our people. He will no longer trade with us. What have you done?"

The Bat's set eyes gazed at the old man, and he made no reply, but stood leaning against the walls while the chief passed on.

No one noticed him, and he did not move for hours. He was under that part of the wall behind which was the room of the woman, and not unexpectedly he heard a voice from above in the strange language which he did not understand. Looking up, he saw that she was on the roof. He motioned her to come down to him, at the same time taking his rifle from under his robe.

The distance was four times her height, but she quickly produced a rawhide lariat, which she began to adjust to a timber that had been exposed in the roof, dirt having been washed away. Many times she looked back anxiously, fearful of pursuit, until, testing the knot and seeming satisfied, she threw her body over the edge and slid down.

The Bat patted her on the back, and instinctively they fled as fast as the woman could run until out of rifle-shot, when her new brave stayed her flight and made her go slowly that they might not attract attention. They got at last to the pony-herds, where the Bat found his little brother with his bunch of ponies. Taking the cherished war-pony and two others, he mounted his new woman on one, while he led the other beside his own. They galloped to the hills. Looking back over the intervening miles of plain, their sharp eyes could see people running about like ants, in great perplexity and excitement. Papin had discovered his woes, and the two lovers laughed loud and long. He had made his slaves lay violent hands on the Bat, and he had lashed the girl Seet-se-be-a (Mid-day Sun) with a pony-whip, but he had lost his woman.

Much as the Bat yearned to steep his hands in the gore of Papin, yet the exigencies of the girl's escape made it impossible now, as he feared pursuit. On the mountain-ridge they stopped, watching for the pursuing party from the Fort, but the Cheyennes swarmed around and evidently Papin was perturbed.

So they watched and talked, and fondled each other, the fierce Cheyenne boy and Minataroe girl—for she proved to be of that tribe—and they were married by the ancient rites of the ceremony of the Fastest Horse.

Shortly the tribe moved away to its wintering-grounds, the young couple following after. The Bat lacked the inclination to stop long enough to murder Papin; he deferred that to the gray future, when the "Mid-day Sun" did not warm him so.

As they entered the lodges, they were greeted with answering yells, and the sickening gossip of his misadventure at Laramie was forgotten when they saw his willing captive. The fierce old women swarmed around, yelling at Seet-se-be-a in no complimentary way, but the fury of possible mothers-in-law stopped without the sweep of the Bat's elkhorn pony-whip.

Before many days there was a new tepee among the "red lodges," and every morning Seet-se-be-a set a lance and shield up beside the door, so that all people should know by the devices that the Bat lived there.

V

"The Kites and the Crows"

The Bat had passed the boy stage. He was a Chis-chis-chash warrior now, of agile body and eager mind. No man's medicine looked more sharply after his physical form and shadow-self than did the Bat's; no young man was quicker in the surround; no war-pony could scrabble to the lariat ahead of his in the races. He had borne more bravely in the Sun-dance than all others, and those who had done the ceremony of "smoking his shield" had heard the thick

bull's-hide promise that no arrow or bullet should ever reach the Bat. He lost the contents of his lodge at the game of the plum-stones—all the robes that Seet-se-be-a had fleshed and softened, but more often his squaw had to bring a packpony down to the gamble and pile it high with his winnings. He was much looked up to in the warrior class of the Red Lodges, which contained the tried-out braves of the Cheyenne tribe; moreover old men—wise ones—men who stood for all there was in the Chis-chis-chash talked to him occasionally out of their pipes, throwing measuring glances from under lowering brows in his direction to feel if he had the secret Power of the Eyes.

The year passed until the snow fell no longer and Big Hair said the medicine chiefs had called it "The Falling Stars Winter" and had painted the sign on the sacred robes. The new grass changed from yellow to a green velvet, while the long hair blew off the horses' hides in bunches and their shrunken flanks filled up with fat. As nature awoke from the chill and began to circulate, the Indians responded to its feel. They stalked among the pony herds, saying to each other, "By the middle of the moon of the new Elk Horns, these big dogs will carry us to war."

The boys of the camp herded the ponies where the grass was strongest, and the warriors watched them grow. It was the policy of the tribe to hang together in a mass against the coming of the enemy, for the better protection of the women and the little ones, but no chiefs or councils were strong enough to stop the yearning of the young Cheyennes for military glory. All self-esteem, all applause, all power and greatness, came only down that fearful road—the war-trail. Despite the pleadings of tribal policy Iron Horn, a noted war- and mystery-man, secretly organized his twenty men for glorious death or splendid triumph. Their orders went forth in whispers. "By the full of the moon at the place where the Drowned Buffalo water tumbles over the rocks one day's pony-travel to the west."

Not even Seet-se-be-a knew why the Bat was not sitting back against his willow-mat in the gray morning when she got up to make the kettle boil, but she had a woman's instinct which made her raise the flap to look out. The two war-ponies were gone. Glancing again behind the robes of his bed she saw, too, that the oiled rifle was missing. Quickly she ran to the lodge of Red Arrow's father, wailing, "My man has gone, my man has gone—his fast ponies are gone—his gun has gone," and all the dogs barked and ran about in the shadows while Red Arrow's mother appeared in the hole in the tepee, also wailing, "My boy has gone, my boy has gone," and the village woke up in a tumult. Every one understood. The dogs barked, the women wailed, the children cried, the magpies fluttered overhead while the wolves answered back in piercing yells from the plains beyond.

Big Hair sat up and filled his pipe. He placed his medicine-bag on a pole before him and blew smoke to the four sides of the earth and to the top of the lodge saying: "Make my boy strong. Make his heart brave, oh Good Gods—take his pony over the dog-holes—make him see the enemy first!" Again he blew the smoke to the deities and continued to pray thus for an hour until the sunlit camp was quiet and the chiefs sat under a giant cotton-wood, devising new plans to keep the young men at home.

Meanwhile from many points the destined warriors loped over the rolling landscape to the rendezvous. Tirelessly all day long they rose and fell as the ponies ate up the distance to the Drowned Buffalo, stopping only at the creeks to water the horses. By twos and threes they met, galloping together—speaking not. The moon rose big and red over their backs, the wolves stopped howling and scurried one side—the ceaseless thud of the falling hoofs continued monotonously, broken only by the crack of a lash across a horse's flank.

At midnight the faithful twenty men were still seated in a row around Iron Horn while the horses, too tired to eat, hung their heads. The old chief dismissed his war party saying, "To-morrow we will make the mystery—we will find out whether the Good Gods will go with us to war or let us go alone."

Sunrise found the ponies feeding quietly, having recovered themselves, while the robed aspirants sat in a circle. The grass had been removed from the enclosed space and leveled down.

A young man filled the long medicine-pipe and Iron Horn blew sacrificial puffs about him, passing it in, saying: "Let no man touch the pipe who has eaten meat since the beginning of the last sun. If there are any such he must be gone—the Good Gods do not speak to full men." But the pipe made its way about the ring without stopping.

Iron Horn then walked behind the circle sticking up medicine-arrows in the earth—arrows made sacred by contact with the great medicine of the Chis-chis-chash and which would hold the Bad Gods in check while the Good Gods counseled.

Resuming his seat, he spoke in a harsh, guttural clicking: "What is said in this circle must never be known to any man who does not sit here now. The Bad Gods will hear what the Good Gods say in such an event and the man who tells against them will be deserted by the Good Gods forever. Every man must tell all his secrets—all the things he has thought about his brothers since the last war-medicine; all that the gods have whispered in his dreams. He must tell all and forever say no more," and Iron Horn rested on his words for a moment before continuing his confession:

"Brothers, I am a great medicine-man—no arrow can touch me—I do not fear men. I am too old for the women to look upon. I did not say it at the time, but when the sun was low on the land last winter, I made it turn blue for a time. I made it cold in the land. Our horses were poor, and when I made the sun blue we crusted the buffalo and killed many with our lances. Brothers, it was I who made the sun blue in the winter.

"Brothers, I love you all—I shall say no

more," and Iron Horn threw tobacco on the earth in front of him.

A young man next to him dropped his robe from about his body and with fierce visage spoke excitedly, for it was his first confession and his Indian secretiveness was straining badly under the ordeal. It was mostly about gallantries and dreams—all made like the confessions which followed. They were the deeds and thoughts common to young Indian men.

The men now began to paint themselves and to take their paraphernalia from their war-bags and put it on. Iron Horn said: "Brothers—when it is dark I will put a medicine-arrow into the ground where my feet are now, and if in the morning it has not moved, we will go back to the lodges, but if it has moved, we will go in the direction in which it points.

"When we start toward the enemy no man must eat, drink or sit down by day, no matter how long or fatiguing the march; if he halts for a moment he must turn his face toward his own country so that the gods may see that it is his wish to return there. We must sleep with our own faces toward our village. No two men must lie covered by the same robe. We must not ride or walk in a beaten path lest the spirit of the path go running on ahead of us to warn the enemy, and if by chance we do, we must come to the big medicine and rub it on the horses' legs to ward off the danger."

This said, Iron Horn said much more to his young braves—all the demon fears which the savage mind conjures in its contact with the supernatural, together with stated forms of decorations to be painted on the ponies, and then he dismissed them, saying, "Come to the circle before the moon rises while it is yet dark, but meanwhile sit each man alone and in silence and we will see what the Good Gods do with the arrows."

The warriors led their ponies off to various points in the savage gorge and sat motionless the livelong day while the river rushed ceaselessly over the wild rocks and the ravens soared in the blue heavens.

By night they came gliding back, picking their way among the rocks, and stood by the bared earth of the mystery place. The chief struck a light and, bending over, saw the arrow lying out in the middle of the space many feet away from where he had placed it. The smooth earth was dotted by the tracks of coyotes, but the arrow pointed nearly southwest and it was the way they must take. Rising, he pointed, saying: "The Good Gods say we must go this way— where they point. The medicine is strong— the gods sent their little medicine-wolves to show us."

They struck a pole in the center of the circle, and when the moon rose each warrior approached it and either hung some piece of rag or buckskin on it or put various implements at its foot, muttering meanwhile prayers for protection and success and rubbing the pole with his weapons to vitalize them spiritually.

By the full light of the moon the mounted men, each leading a horse, rode slowly off, one after the other, into the hills, and they did not halt until nearly morning when they again sat in a magic circle and took heed of the medicine-arrows before lying down to sleep in a long row, facing toward the village.

The day following found the small war-party advancing cautiously, preceded far in advance on its flanks by watchful scouts. They were all eyes for any hunting bands of Utes or Shoshones and might see the Yellow-Eyes trooping along in a line as the ducks fly.

For days marched the band, winding through the lands or splashing through the flat rivers until early one morning they observed one of the scouts far in advance, flashing a looking-glass from a hilltop. Lashing their horses they bore on toward him, dashing down the cut banks at reckless speed or clambering up them helter-skelter. No inequalities of ground opposed their desperate speed.

Arriving at the place, they rode boldly up to the mounted scout and far down on the plains saw three Yellow-Eyes driving twelve pack animals heavily loaded. They paused to repaint their faces and put the sacred war-marks on the ponies, not forgetting to tie up their tails before continuing the mad charge. The poor beaver-hunters saw the on-coming, knew their danger, and instantly huddled their horses and began dropping their packs. They had selected a slight knoll of the prairie and before many minutes had a rude barricade constructed with their packages. Dropping behind this they awaited the Indians with freshly primed rifles and pistols.

The Chis-chis-chash rode in a perfect line and when within a hundred yards gave shrill "ki-yi's," lashed their whips and the ponies clattered through the dust. It would be all over with the three luckless trappers in an instant. When nearly half the distance had been consumed three rifles cracked. Iron Horn and another warrior reeled on their mounts but clung desperately, stopping in no way the rush. In an instant, when it seemed as if the Indians were about to trample the Yellow-Eyes, a thin trail of fire ran along the grass from the barricade and with a blinding flash a keg of powder exploded with terrific force right under the front feet of the rushing ponies. Pistols cracked from behind the pile of roped goods. Four ponies lay kicking on the grass together with six writhing men, all blackened, bleeding and scorched. The other ponies reeled away from the shock—running hopelessly from the scene. All but one, for the Bat pulled desperately at his hair lariat

The Fire Eater Raised His Arms.
Authors' photoengraving.

which was tied to the under jaw of the horse. Striking his pony across the head with his elk-horn whip and, lashing fiercely, he rushed the pony right to the barricade. Firing his rifle into it swerving, he struck the bunch of trapper-horses which had already begun to trot away from the turbulent scene, and drove them off in triumph. He alone had risen superior to the shock of the white man's fire trap.

Four of the wounded Indians got slowly to their feet, one after the other, and walked painfully away. The whites had reloaded meanwhile and fatally shot the last man as he was nearly out of range.

When the defeated party came together, it made a mystic circle in the turf of open prairie, not over three arrow flights from the Yellow-Eyes, and there sat down. In the center lay the Indian dead and three more sightless with their hair singed off and their bodies horribly scorched, while Iron Horn was stretched on a blanket, shot through the body and singing weakly his death-song.

"Let the Bat take the medicine—he is a strong warrior—the bursting fire did not stop him. He ate the fire. I am a great warrior—I am a great medicine-man, but I could not eat the fire. Brothers, the scalps of the beaver-hunters must dry in the Red Lodges." Then the dying warrior became incoherent and scarcely mumbled. The Bat took black paint from his fire bag and rubbed it on the face of the dying man while the decreased circle of warriors yelped the death-cry dolorously. For an hour this continued, rising and rising in scales until the sadness had changed to fury. The Bat held the medicine toward the sun saying: "Mia-yu-ma—nis heva—la ma—nih. Nis tako navero nao' hiko' no hi. (Red Lodges—he has taken pity on us. He will make you strong—I am strong.)"

They took the dead and wounded and deposited them near where the led-horses were kept. The injured men were attended to, and the dead buried carefully in robes.

"One warrior lies dead near the feet of Yellow-Eyes; if they get his scalp he will go to the hungry islands in the middle of the Big Water and we shall never see him in the spirit-land. We must not let them touch his hair, brothers. If the Yellow-Eyes come from behind their packs we must charge—we must eat the flying fire or all be rubbed out. If they do not come out the ravens will not have to wait long for the feast." Thus said the Bat. He had kept his word about going farther toward the enemy than any other and was now moved to resort to strategy. He did not martial his warriors in a line but deployed them about the citadel of the plains. That place, robbed of its horrors, gave no sign of life except a burned and injured pony which raised itself and slowly moved its head from side to side in its agony. But behind it there was promise of deadly rifles and the bursting fire.

The warriors stood like vultures on the plains, by twos and threes, smoking and feeding their ponies from their lariats. They spoke of the chief no longer as the Bat but called him "Fire Eater" or "The Man who eats the Flying Fire." The ravens hovered about the place and wise, gray wolves sat haunched in a still larger ring without. Slowly the sun moved across the heavens. The scene was quiet and pitiful.

Night came on but nothing happened. Before the moon rose out of the darkness a rifle flashed behind the bales, when again the quiet became intensified by the explosion. The wolves sung their lullaby of death, but on the prairie that was as the ceaseless, peaceful surging of the waves on the ocean sand.

When the warriors returned in small parties to their camp for refreshment they saw the dead body of Owl Bear—he who had fallen outside the barricade of the Yellow-Eyes. The Fire Eater had brought it in during the night—having approached and carried it away—drawing the fire of the rifle but saving the hair and shadow-self of his brother.

For seven days the Chis-chis-chash stood about the doomed place. Twice they had approached it and had lost another warrior, shot by the fatal rifle of the beaver-men. Then they had drawn off and given up in the face of the deadly shooting—concluding to let nature work for the victory.

At last, becoming eager and restless, the Fire Eater's war-party galloped out toward the fort. His brothers, seeing this rashness, closed in with him, but no sign of life came from the stronghold.

Boldly he rode up to the edge of the bales of goods, and glancing over saw the swelled and blackened bodies of the three beaver-men and knew by the skinned lips and staring eyes that thirst had done its work. The braves gathered, but no man dismounted and one by one they turned and rode away. "The bad spirits of the dead may get into our bodies—come away—come away—the sun shines now, but we must be far away when the night sets in. Our medicine-arrows will keep them off after that," said the Fire Eater.

Much cast down the Red Lodge warriors gathered up their dead and rode slowly back toward the village.

On the morning of the second day the Cheyennes awoke to find the Fire Eater gone, but he had left his horses on their hands. "The young chief's heart is sad. He has gone away by himself. He will not want us to follow him. He cannot go into the village with our dead and wear the mourning paint," whispered they, one to another.

This was true—for the fierce spirit of the young man could not brook defeat. The Chis-chis-chash should never see blackened ashes on a cheek which was only fitted for the red paint. The shield of the Fire Eater should never face to the lance—the little brown bat flapped fiercely in the wind and screamed for blood and scalp braids. The warrier traveled lazily on his journey—light-hearted and fiercely resolved.

After many days of wolfish travel he saw signs of the vicinage of the Shoshone Indians. They were a hungry band who had come out of the mountains and were hunting the buffalo. He followed the pony tracks where they were not lost in the buffalo trails, finding picked bones, bits of castaway clothing and other signs, until he saw the scouts of the enemy riding about the hills.

Approaching carefully in the early night and morning he found the camp and lay watching for depressions in the fall of some bluffs. But the young men were ceaselessly active, and he did not see an opportunity to approach. During the night he withdrew to a pine-clad rocky fortress which promised better concealment, and his surprise was great in the morning to see the Shoshones preparing to make buffalo-surround in the valley immediately in front of him. From all directions they came and encompassed the buffalo below.

The Fire Eater carefully pressed down the tuft of loose hair which sat upright on the crown of his head after the manner of his people, and leaving his rifles he walked down toward the seething dust-blown jumble where the hunters were shearing their bewildered game. No one noticed him and the dust blew over him from the herd. Presently a riderless pony came by and seizing its lariat he sprang on its back. He rode through the whirling dust into the surround, and approaching an excited and preoccupied Shoshone, stabbed him repeatedly in the back. The Indian yelled, but no one paid any attention in the turmoil. The Fire Eater slung his victim across his pony, taking his scalp. He seized his lance and pony and rode slowly away toward the bluffs. After securing his rifle he gained the timber and galloped away.

On his road he met a belated scout of the enemy coming slowly on a jaded horse. This man suspected nothing until the Fire Eater raised his rifle when he turned away to flee. It was too late and a second scalp soon dangled at the victor's belt. He did not take the tired horse for it was useless.

Swiftly he rode now for he knew that pursuit was sure, but if one was instituted it never came up, and before many days the Cheyennes rode along his own tepee, waving the emblem of his daring, and the camp grew noisy with exultation. The mourning paint was washed from each face and the old pipe-men said, "The Bat will be a great leader in war—his medicine is very strong and he eats fire." The chiefs and council

The Fire Eater Slung His Victim Across His Pony, Taking His Scalp.
Painting in George F. Harding Museum, Chicago.

withheld their discipline, and the Fire Eater grew to be a great man in the little world of the Chis-chis-chash, though his affairs proportionately were as the "Battles of the Kites and Crows."

VI

The Fire Eater's Bad Medicine

The Chis-chis-chash had remembered through many "green grasses" that the Fire Eater had proven himself superior to the wrath of the Bad Gods who haunt the way of the men who go out for what the Good Gods offer—the ponies, the women and the scalps. He had become a sub-chief in the Red Lodge military clan. He had brought many painted war-bands into the big camp with the scalps of their tribal enemies dangling from their lance heads. The village had danced often over the results of his victories. Four wives now dressed and decorated his buffalo robes. The seams of his clothes were black with the hair of his enemies, as he often boasted, and it required four boys to herd his ponies. His gun was reddened, and there were twenty-four painted pipes on his shield indicative of the numbers who had gone down before him in war. In the time of the ceremonies, his chief's war-bonnet dragged on the ground and was bright with the painted feathers which belonged to a victor. He hated the Yellow-Eyes—not going often to their posts for trade, and like a true Indian warrior he despised a beaver trap. It was conceded by old men that time would take the Fire Eater near to the head chieftainship, while at all times the young men were ready to follow him to the camp of the foe.

One day in the time of the yellow-grass the Fire Eater had sat for hours, without moving, beside his tepee, looking vacantly out across the hills and speaking to no human being. His good squaws and even his much cherished children went about the camping space quietly, not caring to disturb the master. He was tired of the lazy sunshine of home; the small cackle of his women, one to another, annoyed him; he was strong with the gluttony of the kettle which was ever boiling; the longing for fierce action and the blood-thirst had taken possession of him. Many times he reached up with his hand to the crown of his head and patted the skin of the little brown bat, which was his medicine. This constantly talked to him in his brown study, saying: "Look—look at the war-ponies—the big dogs are fat and kick at each other as they stand by the wooden pins. They are saying you are too old for them. They think that the red hands will no more be painted on their flanks."

But the warrior, still with his sleepy dog-stare fixed on the vacant distance, answered the bat-skin: "We will seek the help of the Good Gods to-night; we will see if the path is clear before us. My shadow is very black beside me here—I am strong." Thus the Indian and his medicine easily agreed with each other in these spiritual conversations —which thing gave the Fire Eater added respect for the keeper of his body and his shadow-self.

Far into the night the preoccupied Indian leaned against his resting-mat watching the little flames leaping from the split sticks as his youngest squaw laid them on the fire.

After a time he sprang to his feet and drove the woman out of the lodge. Untying his war-bags he produced a white buffalo-robe and arranged it to sit on. This was next to the bat-skin his strongest protector. When seated on it he lost contact with the earth—he was elevated above all its influences. Having arranged his gun, shield and war-bonnet over certain medicine-arrows, the sacred bat-skin was placed on top. This last had, in the lapse of years, been worn to a mere shred and was now contained in a neat buckskin bag highly ornamented with work done by squaws. Lighting his medicine-pipe, after having filled it in the formal manner due on such occasions, he blew the sacrificial whiffs to the four corners of the world, to the upper realms and to the lower places, and then addressed the Good Gods. All the mundane influences had departed—even his body had been left behind. He was in communion with the spirit-world—lost in the expectancy of revelation. He sang in monotonous lines, repeating his extemporizations after the Indian manner and was addressing the Thunder Bird—the great bird so much sought by warriors. He sat long before his prayers were heeded, but at last could hear the rain patter on the dry sides of the tepee, and he knew that the Thunder Bird had broken through the air to let the rain fall. A great wind moaned through the encampment and in crashing reverberations the Thunder Bird spoke to the Fire Eater: "Go —go to the Absaroke—take up your pony-whip—your gun wants to talk to them— your ponies squeal on the ropes—your bat says no arrow or bullet can find him—you will find me over your head in time of danger. When you hear me roar across the sky and see my eyes flash fire, sit down and be still; I am driving your enemies back. When you come again back to the village you must sacrifice many robes and ponies to me." Lower and lower spoke the great bird as he passed onward—the rain ceased to beat—the split sticks no longer burned—the Fire Eater put up the sacred things and was alone in the darkness.

In the early morning the devotee stalked over to the great war-prophet—a mystery-man of the tribe who could see especially far on a contemplated war-path. The sun was bright when they were done with their conversation, but the signs were favorable to the spirit of war. The Thunder Bird had on the preceding night also told the war-prophet that the Chis-chis-chash had sat too long in their lodges, which was the reason why he had come to urge activity.

Accordingly—without having gone near the boiled meat—the Fire Eater took the war-pipe around the Red Lodges and twenty young men gladly smoked it. In council of the secret clan the war-prophet and the sub-chief voiced for war. The old chiefs and the wise men, grown stiff from riding and conservative toward a useless waste of young warriors, blinked their beady eyes in protest, but they did not imperil their popularity by advice to the contrary. The young men's blood-thirst and desire for distinction could not be curbed.

So the war-prophet repaired to his secret lodge to make the mystery, while the warriors fasted until it was done. Everything about the expedition had been faithfully attended to; all the divinities had been duly consulted; the council had legitimatized it; the Fire Eater had been appointed leader; the war-prophet had the secret protection forthcoming, and no band had lately gone forth from the village with so many assurances of success.

For many days the little streak of ponies wound over the rolling brown land toward the north. Each man rode a swift horse and led another alongside. Far ahead ranged the cautious spies; no sailing hawk, no wailing coyote, no blade of grass did anything which was not reasoned out by mind or noted by their watchful eyes.

The Absaroke were the friends of the Yellow-Eyes who had a little fort at the mouth of the Muscleshell, where they gave their guns and gauds in great quantities. The Chis-chis-chash despised the men who wore hats. They barely tolerated and half protected their own traders. Nothing seemed so desirable as to despoil the Absaroke traders. They had often spied on the fort but always found the protecting Absaroke too numerous. The scouts of the Fire Eater, however, found immense trace of their enemy's main camp as it had moved up the valley of the Yellowstone. They knew that the Absaroke had finished their yellow-grass trading and had gone to hunt the buffalo. They hoped to find the little fort unprotected. Accordingly they sped on toward that point, which upon arrival they found sitting innocently alone in the grand landscape. Not a tepee was to be seen.

Having carefully reconnoitered and considered the place, they left their horses in a dry washout and crawled toward it through the sagebrush. As the sky grew pale toward the early sun there was no sign of discovery from its silent pickets. When within a hundred yards, in response to the commanding war-cry of the Fire Eater, they rose like ghosts from the sage and charged fast on the stockade. The gray logs stood stiffly unresponsive and gave no answering shots or yells as the Indians swept toward it. The gate was high, but the attacking force crept up on one another's bent backs as they strove for the interior. A tremendous commotion arose; rifles blazed inside and out. Two or three Indians sprang over but were shot down. Hatchets hacked at the timbers; gun-muzzles and drawn arrows sought the crevices in the logs; piercing yells rose above the hoarse shouts of the besieged, for the stockade was full of white men.

The savages had not noticed a great number of Mackinaw boats drawn up on the river bank and concealed by low bushes. These belonged to a brigade of freighters who were temporarily housed in the post. As the surprised whites and creoles swarmed to the defense, the Indians found themselves outnumbered three to one. The Fire Eater, seeing several braves fall before the ever-increasing fire from the palisades and knowing he could not scale the barrier, ordered a withdrawal. The beaten band drew slowly away carrying the stricken brothers.

The medicine was bad—the war-prophet had not had free communication with the mystery of the Good Gods. Some one had allowed himself to walk in a beaten path or had violated the sacred rights of the war-path. The skin of the little brown bat did not comfort the Fire Eater in his fallen state. He cast many burning glances back at the logs now becoming mellowed by the morning light. The sun had apparently thrown its protection over them, and the omen struck home to the wondering, savage mind. He remembered that the old men had always said that the medicine of the Yellow-Eyes was very strong and that they always

fought insensibly, like the gray bears. The flashing rifles which had blown their bodies back from the fort had astonished these Indians less by their execution, than the indication they gave that the powers of darkness were not with them. They looked askance at the Fire Eater for their ill-success. He was enraged—a sudden madness had overpowered and destroyed his sense of the situation. One of those moods had come upon the savage child-mind when the surging blood made his eyes gleam vacantly like the great cat's.

Slowly the dismayed band withdrew to the washout—casting backward glances at the walls which had beaten down their ambitions and would paint the tribes with ashes and blood-sacrifices for the lost. When there, they sat about dejectedly, finding no impulse to do more. From out of the west, in response to their blue despondency, the clouds blew over the plains—the thunder rumbled—the rain came splashing and beating and then came in blinding sheets. The Fire Eater arose and standing on the edge of the bank raised his arms in thanks to the Thunder Bird for his interposition in their behalf saying: "Brothers, the Thunder Bird has come to his poor warriors to drive our enemies back as was promised to the prophet. He will put out the fires of the Yellow-Eyes, behind their medicine-logs. We are not afraid—our medicine is strong."

The rain poured for a time but abated gradually as the crashing Thunder Bird hurried away to the rising sun, and with a final dash it separated into drops, letting the sunlight through the departing drizzle. The warriors began drying their robes and their weapons—preoccupied with the worries so much dampness had wrought to their powder and bowstrings. Suddenly one of them raised his head, deerlike, to listen. As wild things they all responded, and the group of men was statuesque as it listened to the beat of horses' hoofs. As a flock of blackbirds leave a bush—with one motion—the statuary dissolved into a kaleidoscopic twinkle of movement as the warriors grabbled and ran and gathered. They sought their ponies' lariats, but before they could mount a hundred mounted Yellow-Eyes swept down upon them, circling away as the Indians sowed their shots among them. But they were surrounded. The Thunder Bird had lied to the Chis-chis-chash—he had chosen to sacrifice the Fire Eater and the twenty Red Lodge braves. There was now no thought of arresting the blow—there was but to die as their people always did in war. The keepers of the Red Lodge counting robes might cross the red pipes out with black, but they should not wash them out entirely.

The beaver-men—the traders—the creoles and the half-breeds slid from their horses and showered their bullets over the washout, throwing clouds of wet dirt over the braves crowding under its banks. The frightened Indian ponies swarmed out of one end of the cut, but were soon brought back and herded together in the sagebrush by the moccasin-boys of the Yellow-Eyes.

In maddened bewilderment the Fire Eater leaped upon the flat plain, made insulting gestures and shouted defiant words in his own language at the flashing guns. Above the turmoil could be heard the harsh, jerky voice which came from the bowels of the warrior rather than from his lips. No bullet found him as he stepped back into cover, more composed than when he had gone out. The nervous thrill had expended itself in the speech. To his own mind the Fire Eater was a dead man, his medicine had departed; his spiritual protection was gone. He recognized that to live his few remaining hours was all—he had only to do the mere act of dying and that he would do as his demon nature willed it. His last sun was looking down upon him.

The Yellow-Eyes knew their quarry well. They recognized of old the difference between an Indian cooped up in a hole in a flat plain and one mounted on a swift war-pony, with a free start and the whole plain for a race track. They advanced with all caution—crawling, sneaking through sage and tufted grass. Occasionally as an Indian

exposed himself for fire, a swift bullet from a beaver-man's long rifle crashed into his head, rolling him back with oozing brains. The slugs and ounce-balls slapped into the dirt from the muskets of the creole *engagés* and they were losing warrior after warrior. By cutting the dirt with their knives the Indians dug into the banks and, avoiding a fire which raked the washout and by throwing the dirt up on either side, they protected their heads as they raised to fire.

A man walking over the flats by midday would have seen nothing but feeding ponies and occasional flashes of fire close to the grass, but a flying raven would have gloated over a scene of many future gorges. It would have seen many lying on their backs in the ditch—lying quite still and gazing up at his wheeling flight with stony gaze. Still there were others, rolling over on their backs to load their guns and again turning on their bellies to fire them.

The white men had no means of knowing how successful had been their rifle-fire and they hesitated to crawl closer. Each party in turn taunted the other in unknown tongue, but they well knew that the strange voices carried fearful insult from the loud defiance of the intonation. The gray bears or the mountain cats were as merciful as any there. As the sun started on its downward course the nature of the Gothic blood asserted itself. The white men had sat still until they could sit still no longer. They had fasted too long. They talked to each other through the sagebrush and this is what happened when they cast the dice between death and dinner.

A tall, long-haired man, clad in the fringed buckskin of a Rocky Mountain trapper of the period, passed slowly around the circle of the siege, shouting loudly to those concealed among the brush and grasses. What he said the Chis-chis-chash did not know, but they could see him pointing at them continually.

The Fire Eater raised his voice: "Brothers, keep your guns full of fire; lay all your arrows beside you. The Yellow-Eyes are going to kill us as we do the buffalo in a surround. Brothers, if the Thunder Bird does not come, our fires will go out now. We will take many to the spirit-land."

Having completed the circle the tall white man waved a red blanket and started on a run toward the place where the Indians lay. From all sides sprang the besiegers, converging with flying feet. When nearly in contact the Indians fired their guns, killing and wounding. The whites, in turn, excitedly emptied theirs and through the smoke with lowered heads charged like the buffalo. The bowstrings twanged and the ravens could only see the lightning sweep of axes and furious gun-butts going over the pall of mingled dust and powder smoke. If the ravens were watching they would have seen nothing more except a single naked Indian run out of the turmoil, and, after a quick glance backward, speed away through the sagebrush. He could not fight for victory now; he sought only to escape; he was deserted by his gods; he ran on the tightened muscles of a desperate hope.

A bunch of horses had been left huddled by a squad of the enemy who had gone in with the charge on post, and for these the Fire Eater made. No one seemed to notice the lone runner until a small herds-boy spied him, whereat he raised his childish treble, but it made no impression. The Fire Eater picked up a dropped pony-whip and leading two ponies out of the bunch, mounted and lashed away. He passed the screaming boy within killing distance, but it was an evil day.

Before the small herder's voice asserted itself he was long out of rifle-shot but not out of pony-reach. A dozen men dashed after him. The warrior plied his whip mercilessly in alternate slaps on each pony-quarter and the bareback savage drew steadily away to the hills. For many miles the white men lathered their horses after, but one by one gave up the chase. The dice doubtless said dinner as against an Indian was a double mount, and many will think they gave a wise choice.

On flew the Fire Eater. Confusion had come to him. The bat on his scalp-lock said never a word. His heart was upside down

within him. His shadow flew away before him. The great mystery of his tribe had betrayed and bewitched him. The Yellow-Eyed medicine would find him yet.

From a high divide the fugitive stopped beside a great rock to blow his horses, and he turned his eyes on the scene of ill-fate. He saw the Yellow-Eyes ride slowly back to their medicine-logs. For a long time he stood—not thinking, only gazing heavy-headed and vacant.

After a time he pulled his ponies' heads up from the grass and trotted them away. Growing composed with his blood stilled, thoughts came slowly. He thanked the little brown bat when it reminded him of his savior. A furious flood of disappointment overcame him when he thought of his lifelong ambitions as a warrior—now only dry ashes. Could he go back to the village and tell all? The council of the Red Lodges would not listen to his voice as they had before. When he spoke they would cast their eyes on the ground in sorrow. The Thunder Bird had demanded a sacrifice from him when he returned. He could not bear the thoughts of the wailing women and the screaming children and the old men smoking in silence as he passed through the camp. He would not go back. He had died with his warriors.

When the lodges lay covered with snow the Chis-chis-chash sang songs to the absent ones of the Fire Eater band. Through the long, cold nights the women sat rocking and begging the gods to bring them back their warriors. The green-grass came and the prophet of the Red Lodges admitted that the medicine spoke no more of the absent band. By yellow-grass hope grew cold in the village and socially they had readjusted themselves. It had happened in times past that even after two snows had come and gone warriors had found the path back to the camp, but now men saw the ghost of the Fire Eater in dreams, together with his lost warriors.

Another snow passed and still another. The Past had grown white in the shadows of an all-enduring Present when the Chis-chis-chash began to hear vague tales from their traders of a mighty war-chief who had come down to the Shoshones from the clouds. He was a great "wakan" and he spoke the same language as the Chis-chis-chash. This chief said he had been a Cheyenne in his former life on earth, but had been sent back to be a Shoshone for another life. The Indians were overcome by an insatiate curiosity to see this being and urged the traders to bring him from the Shoshones—promising to protect and honor him.

The traders, dominated by avarice, hoping to better their business, humored the stories and enlarged upon them. They half understood that the mystery of life and death is inextricably mixed in savage minds —that they come and go, passing in every form from bears to inanimate things or living in ghosts which grow out of a lodge fire. So for heavy considerations in beaver skins they sent representatives to the Shoshones, and there, for an armful of baubles, they prevailed upon those people to allow their supernatural war-chief to visit his other race out on the great meadows.

"If, in the time of the next green-grass," said the trader, "the Chis-chis-chash have enough beaver—we will bring their brother who died back to their camps. We will lead him into the tribal council. If, on the other hand, they do not have enough skins, our medicine will be weak."

In the following spring the tribe gathered at the appointed time and place, camping near the post. The big council-lodge was erected, the great ceremonial-pipe filled and the council-fire kept smoldering.

When the pipe had passed slowly and in form, the head-chief asked the trader if he saw beaver enough outside his window. This one replied that he did and sent for the man who had been dead.

The council sat in silence with its eyes upon the ground. From the commotion outside they felt an awe of the strange approach. Never before had the Chis-chis-chash been so near the great mystery. The door-flap was lifted and a fully painted, gorgeously arrayed warrior stepped into the center of the circle and stood silently with raised chin.

There was a loud murmur on the outside that the lodge was like a grave. A loud grunt came from one man—followed by another until the hollow walls gave back like a hundred tom-toms. They recognized the Fire Eater, but no Indian calls another by his name.

Raising his hand with the dignity which Indians have in excess of all other men, he said: "Brothers, it makes my heart big to look at you again. I have been dead, but I came to life again. I was sent back by the gods to complete another life on earth. The Thunder Bird made the Yellow-Eyes kill all my band when we went against the Absaroke. My medicine grew weak before the white man's medicine. Brothers, they are very strong. Always beware of the medicine of the traders and the beaver-men. They are fools and women themselves, but the gods give them guns and other medicine things. He can make them see what is to happen long before he tells the Indians. They have brought me back to my people, and my medicine says I must be a Chis-chis-chash until I die again. Brothers, I have made my talk."

VII

Among the Pony-Soldiers

The burial scaffold of the Fire Eater's father had rotted and fallen down with years. Time had even bent his own shoulders, filled his belly and shrunk his flanks. He now had two sons who were of sufficient age to have forgotten their first sun-dance medicine, so long had they been warriors of distinction. He also had boys and girls of less years, but a child of five snows was the only thing which could relax the old man's features, set hard with thought and time and toil.

Evil days had come to the Buffalo Indians. The Yellow-Eyes swarmed in the Indian country, and although the red warriors rode their ponies thin in war, they could not drive the invaders away. The little bands of traders and beaver-men who came to the camps of the Fire Eater's boyhood with open hands were succeeded by immense trains of wagons, drawn by the white man's buffalo. The trains wound endlessly toward the setting sun—paying no heed to the Indians. Yellow-Eyes came to the mountains where they dug and washed for the white man's great medicine, the yellow iron. The fire boats came up the great river with a noise like the Thunder Bird—firing big medicine-guns which shot twice at one discharge.

The Fire Eater, with his brothers of the Chis-chis-chash, had run off with the horses and buffalo of these helpless Yellow-Eyes until they wanted no more. They had knocked them on the head with battle-axes in order to save powder. They had burned the grass in front of the slow-moving trains and sat on the hills laughing at the discomfiture caused by the playful fires. Notwithstanding, all their efforts did not check the ceaseless influx and a vague feeling of alarm began to pervade them.

Talking-men came to them and spoke of their Great Father in Washington. It made them laugh. These talking-men gave them enough blankets and medicine-goods to make the travvis poles squeak under the burden. When these men also told them that they must live like white men, the secret council lost its dignity entirely and roared long and loud at the quaint suggestion.

Steadily flowed the stream of wagons over the plains though the Indians plied them with ax and rifle and fire. Sober-minded old chiefs began to recall many prophecies of the poor trappers who told how their people swarmed behind them and would soon come on.

Then began to appear great lines of the Great Father's warriors—all dressed alike and marching steadily with their wagons drawn along by half-brothers to the horse. These men built log forts on the Indian lands and they had come to stay.

The time for action had come. Runners went through the tribes calling great councils which made a universal peace between the red brothers. Many and fierce were the fights with these blue soldiers of the Great Father. The Indians slew them by hundreds at times and were slain in turn. In a grand assault on some of these which lay behind medicine-wagons and shot medicine-guns, the Indian dead blackened the grass and the white soldiers gave them bad dreams for many days.

The talking-wives and the fire wagon found their way, and the white hunters slew the buffalo of the Indians by millions, for their hides.

Every year brought more soldiers who made more log forts from which they emerged with their wagons, dragging after the trace of the Chis-chis-chash camp, and disturbing the buffalo and the elk. To be sure, the soldiers never came up because the squaws could move the travvis more rapidly than the others could their wagons, but it took many young men to watch their movements and keep the grass burning before them. Since the Indians had made the wagon fight, they no longer tried to charge the soldiers, thinking it easier to avoid them. The young men were made to run their ponies around the Yellow-Eyes before it was light enough in the morning for them to shoot, and they always found the Yellow-Eyes heavy with sleep; but they did not grapple with the white soldiers because they found them too slow to run away and enemies who always fought wildly, like bears. Occasionally the Indians caught one of them alive, staked him out on a hill, and burned him in sight of his camp. These Yellow-Eyes were poor warriors, for they always whined and yelled under the torture. Half-breeds who came from the camp of the Yellow-Eyes said that this sight always made the white soldiers' blood turn to water. Still the invaders continued to crawl slowly along the dusty valleys. The buffalo did not come up from the south—from the caves of the Good Gods where they were made—in such numbers as they once did and the marching soldiers frightened those which did and kept them away. The young warriors never wearied of the excitement of these times, with its perpetual war-party, but old men remembered the prophecies of the beaver-men and that the times had changed.

The Fire Eater as he talked to old Weasel Bear over their pipes and kettles said:

"Brother—we used to think Yellow Horse had lost the Power of his Eyes when he came from his journey with the talking white man. We thought it had been made to dream by the Yellow-Eyes. We have seen the talking-wives and we have seen fire wagons. We have seen the white men come until there are as many as all the warriors in this camp. All the foolish half-breeds say it is as the talking-men say. Brother, I have seen in my dreams that there are more of them than the buffalo. They have their caves to the east as the buffalo do to the south, and they come out of them in the time of the green-grass just as the buffalo do. The Bad Gods send the Yellow-Eyes and the Good Gods send the buffalo. The gods are fighting each other in the air."

Weasel Bear smoked in silence until he had digested the thoughts of his friend when he replied:

"Your talk is good. Two grasses ago I was with a war-party and we caught a white man between the bends of the Tois-ta-to-e-o. He had four eyes and also a medicine-box which we did not touch. All the hair on his head and face was white as the snow. While we were making the fire to burn him with he talked much strong talk. Before we could burn him he sank down at our feet and died a medicine-death. We all ran away. Bad Arm, the half-breed who was with us, said the man had prophesied that before ten snows all our fires would be put out by his people. Brother, that man hath the Power of the Eyes. I looked at him strong while he talked. I have seen him in my dreams—I am afraid."

The Fire Eater continued:

"You hear our young scouts who come in tell us how the white soldiers are coming in droves this grass. There are walking-sol-diers, pony-soldiers, big guns on wheels and more wagons than they can count. Many of their scalps shall dry in our lodges, but, brother, we cannot kill them all."

In accordance with the tribal agreements, the Chis-chis-chash joined their camp with the Dakota, and together both tribes moved about the buffalo range. Every day the scouts came on reeking ponies to the chiefs. The soldiers were everywhere marching toward the camps. The council fire was always smoldering. The Dakota and Chis-chis-chash chiefs sat in a dense ring while Sitting Bull, Gall, Crazy Horse and all the strong men talked. They regarded the menace with awe; they feared for the camp with its women and children, but each voice was for war. It was no longer poor beaver-men or toiling bull-wagons; it was crowds of soldiers coming up every valley toward the villages which before had been remote and unmolested. If any soothsayer could penetrate the veil of the future he held his peace in the councils. The Indians tied up their ponies' tails for the struggle and painted for war. Three cartridges were all a fine buffalo robe would bring from a trader and even then it was hard to get them, but, if the lodges had few robes, many brass-bound bullets reposed in the war-bags.

The old thrill came over the Fire Eater in these agitated times. He could no longer leap upon his pony at full gallop but rode a saddle. The lodge chafed him until he gathered up a few young men who had been acting as spies and trotted forth on a coyote prowl. For many days they made their way toward the south. One day as he sat smoking by a small fire on a mountain-top, somewhat wearied with travel—the restless young men came trotting softly back over the pine needles, saying,

"Come out and you will see the white soldiers." He mounted and followed and, sitting there amid the mountain tangle, he saw his dreams come true. The traders and the talking-men had not lied about the numbers of their people, for his eye did not come to the rear of the procession which wound up the valley like a great snake. There were pony-soldiers, walking-soldiers, guns on wagons, herds of the white men's buffalo, and teams without end. The Fire Eater passed his hands across his eyes before another gaze reassured him, and having satisfied himself he asked a young man, "Brother, you say there are as many more soldiers up north by the Yellowstone?"

"There are as many more—I saw them with my own eyes and Blow Cloud over there has seen as many to the east. He could not count them."

For an hour the spies watched the white columns before the Fire Eater turned his pony and, followed by his young men, disappeared in the timber.

Upon his arrival at the big camp the Fire Eater addressed the council:

"I have just come five smokes from the south, and I saw the white soldiers coming. I could not count them. They crawl slowly along the valley and they take their wagons to war. They cannot travel as fast as our squaws, but they will drive the buffalo out of the land. We must go out and fight them while our villages lie here close to the mountains. The wagon-soldiers cannot follow the women's pack-horses into the mountains."

The council approved this with much grunting, and the warriors swarmed from the villages—covering the country until the coyotes ran about continually to get out of their way. No scout of the enemy could penetrate to the Indian camps. The Indians burned the grass in front of the oncoming herds; they fired into the enemy's tents at night, and as the pony-soldiers bathed naked in the Yellowstone, ran their horses over them. They would have put out many white soldiers' fires if the wagon-guns had not fired bullets which burst among them.

But it was all to no purpose. Slowly the great snakes crawled through the valleys and the red warriors went riding back to the village to prepare for flight.

One morning the Fire Eater sat beside his lodge fire playing with his young son—a thing which usually made his eyes gleam. Now he looked sadly into the little face of the boy who stood holding his two great scalp-braids in his chubby hands. He knew that in a day or two the camp must move and that the warriors must try to stop the Yellow-Eyes. Taking from his scalp a buckskin bag which contained his bat-skin medicine he rubbed it slowly over the boy's body and it made the boy laugh. The sun was barely stronger than the lodge fire when from far away on the hills beyond the river came a faint sound borne on the morning wind, yet it electrified the camp, and from in front of the Fire Eater's tent, a passing man split the air with the wolfish war-yell of the Chis-chis-chash. As though he had been a spiral spring released from pressure, the Fire Eater regained his height. The little boy sat briskly down in the ashes, adding his voice to the confusion which now reigned in the great camp in a most disproportionate way. The old chief sprang to his doorway in time to see a mounted rider cut by who shrieked, "The pony-soldiers are coming over the hills," and disappeared among the tepees.

With intense fingers the nerved warrior readjusted his life treasure, the bat-skin, to his scalp-lock, then opening his war-bags, which no other person ever touched on pain of death, he quickly daubed the war-paint on his face. These two important things having been done, he filled his ammunition bag with a double handful of cartridges, tied his chief's war-bonnet under his chin, and grasping his rifle, war-ax and whip, he slid out of the tepee. An excited squaw hastily brought his best war-pony with its tail tied up, as it always was in these troublesome times. The Fire Eater slapped his hand violently on its quarters and, when he raised it, there was the red imprint of the hand of war. The frightened animal threw back its head and backed away, but, with a bound like a panther, the savage was across its back, a thing which, in tranquil times, the old man was not able to do.

This was the first time in years that the warrior had a chance to wear his war-bonnet in battle. Rapidly adjusting his equipment as he sat his plunging horse, he brought his quirt down with a full-arm swing and was away. By his side many sturdy war-ponies spanked along. At the ford of the river they made the water foam, and the far side muddy, with their drip. They were grotesque demons, streaked and daubed, on their many-colored ponies. Rifles clashed, pony-whips cracked, horses snorted and blew, while the riders emitted the wild yelps which they had learned from the wolves. Back from the hills came their scouts sailing like hawks, scarcely seeming to touch the earth as they flew along. "The pony-soldiers are coming—they are over the hill," they cried. The crowded warriors circled out and rode more slowly as their chiefs marshaled them. Many young Red Lodge braves found the Fire Eater place, boys who had never seen the old man in war, but who had listened in many winter lodges where his deeds were "smoked." As they looked at him now they felt the insistency of his presence—felt the nervous ferocity of the wild man; it made them eager and reckless, and they knew that such plumes as the Fire Eater wore were carried in times like these.

The view of the hill in front was half cut by the right bank of the coulee up which they were going, when they felt their hearts quicken. One, two, a half dozen, and then the soldiers of the Great Father broke in a flood across the ridge, galloping steadily in column, their yellow flags snapping. The Fire Eater turned and gave the long yell and was answered by the demon chorus—all whipping along. The whole valley answered in kind. The rifles began to pop. A bugle rang on the hill, once, twice, and the pony-soldiers were on their knees, their front a blinding flash, with the blue smoke rolling down upon the Indians or hurried hither and thither by the vagrant winds. Several followers of the Fire Eater reeled on their ponies or waved from side to side or clung desperately to their ponies' necks, sliding slowly to the ground as life left them. Relentless whips drove the maddened charge into the pall of smoke, and the fighting men saw everything dimly or not at all.

The rushing Red Lodges passed through the line of the blue soldiers, stumbling over them and striking downward with their axes. Dozens of riderless troop-horses mingled with them, rushing aimlessly and tripping on dangling ropes and reins. Soon they were going down the other side of the hill and out of the smoke; not all, for some had been left behind. Galloping slowly, the red warriors crowded their cartridges into their guns while over their heads poured the bullets of the soldiers who, in the smoke, could no longer be seen. On all sides swarmed the rushing warriors mixed inextricably with riderless troop-horses mad with terror. As the clouds of Indians circled the hill, the smoke blew slowly away from a portion of it, revealing the kneeling soldiers. Seeing this the Fire Eater swerved his pony and, followed by his band, charged into and over the line. The whole whirling mass of horsemen followed. The scene was now a mass of confusion which continued for some time, but the frantic Fire Eater, as ne dashed about, could no longer find any soldiers. As the tumult quieted and the smoke gave back, they all seemed to be dead. Dismounting, he seized a soldier's hair and drew his knife, but was not able to wind his fingers into it. He desisted and put back his knife muttering, "A dog—he had not the hair of a warrior—I will not dance such a scalp."

The Fire Eater looked around him and saw the warriors hacking and using their knives, but the enemy had been wiped out. Horses lay kicking and struggling, or sat on their haunches like dogs with the blood pouring from their nostrils. He smiled at the triumph of his race, mounted his pony and with his reeking war-ax moved through the terrible scene. The hacking and scalping was woman's work—anyone could count a *coup* here. As for the Fire Eater, his lodge was full of trophies, won in single combat. Slowly he made his way down the line of horror until he came to the end—to the place where the last soldier lay dead, and he passed on to a neighboring hill to view the scene. As he stood looking, he happened to cast his eyes on the ground and there saw a footprint. It was the track of a white man's moccasins with the iron nails showing, and it was going away from the scene of action. Turning his pony, he trotted along beside the trail. Over the little hills it ran through the sagebrush. Looking ahead, the Fire Eater saw a figure in a red blanket moving rapidly away. Putting his pony to speed, he bore down with his rifle cocked upon the man. The figure increased its gait, and the red blanket fell from the shoulders revealing a blue soldier. It was but an instant before the pony drew up alongside and the white man stood still, breathing heavily. The Fire Eater saw that his enemy had no gun, the thought of which made him laugh—"A naked warrior; a man without even a knife; does the man with the iron moccasins hope to outrun my war-pony?"

The breathless and terrified white man held out his hand and spoke excitedly, but the Fire Eater could not understand. With menacing rifle he advanced upon his prey, whereat the white man, suspecting his purpose, quickly picked up a loose stone and threw it at him but only hit the pony. The Fire Eater straightway shot the soldier in the thigh and the latter sat down in the dirt. The old chief got off his horse, chuckling while he advanced, and sat down a few yards from the stricken man. He talked to him saying: "Brother I have you now. You are about to die. Look upon the land for the last time. You came into my country to kill me, but it is you who are to be killed."

The white soldier could not make out the intention of the Indian for the language was mild and the face not particularly satanic. He pleaded for his life, but it had no effect upon the Fire Eater, who shortly arose and approached him with his battle-ax. The man

The Rushing Red Lodges Passed Through the Line of the Blue Soldiers.
Painting in George F. Harding Museum, Chicago.

saw clearly now what was to happen and buried his face in his hands. Too often had the hunter-warrior stood over his fallen quarry to feel pity; he knew no more of this than a bird of prey, and he sank his three-pronged battle-ax into the soldier's skull and wiped it on his pony's shoulder saying: "Another dog's head; I will leave him for the women and the boys. If he had thrown away his iron moccasins his fire would not be out. I give the meat to the little gray wolves and to the crowd which bring us messages from the spirit-world," and he resumed his mount.

Riding back, he saw the squaws swarming over the battlefield, but the warriors had gone. Men that he met in the valley told him that they had more soldiers surrounded in the bluffs up the valley, but that the white-faces could not get away and that the Indians were coming back for fresh ponies. Enough men had been left to hold the besieged.

Coming to his lodge he got a new pony, and, as he mounted, said to his youngest wife: "Wan-ha-ya, give me my little boy; put him up behind me on my pony. I will show him war."

The squaw held the chubling and put him on the desired place where he caught on like a burr. The Fire Eater made his way to the battle ground. There the squaws were stripping and mutilating. Finding a dead soldier who was naked, he dismounted, setting the boy on the ground. Pulling his great knife from its buckskin sheath, he curled the fat little hand around its shaft and led him to the white body. "Strike the enemy, little son, strike like a warrior," and the Fire Eater, simulating a blow, directed the small arm downward on the corpse. Comprehending the idea, the infant drew up and drove down, doing his best to obey the instructions, but his arm was far too weak to make the knife penetrate. The fun of the thing made him scream with pleasure, and the old Fire Eater chuckled at the idea of his little warrior's first *coup*. Then he rode back to the lodge.

VIII

The Medicine-Fight of the Chis-chis-chash

Hither and yon through the valleys dragged the wagon-soldiers, while the Indians laughed at them from the hills. In the time of the yellow-grass the tribe had made a successful hunt and the sides of their lodges were piled high with dry meat. Their kettles would boil through this snow.

As the tops of the mountains grew white, the camp was moved into a deep gorge of the Big Horn Mountains out of the way of the trailing Yellow-Eyes. For a thousand feet the rock walls rose on either side. A narrow brook wound down between their narrow ways. Numerous lateral cañons crossed the main one, giving grass and protection to their ponies. As it suited the individual tastes of the people, the lodges were placed in cozy places.

They felt secure in their eerie home, though the camp-crier frequently passed shouting, "Do not let your ponies wander down the cañon and make trails for the Yellow-Eyes to see." The women worked the colored beads and porcupine quills, chatted with one another, or built discreet romances, as fancy dictated. The men gambled, or made smoke-talks by the night fires. It was the Indian time of social enjoyment.

Restless young men beat up the country in search of adventure; and only this day a party had arrived with Absaroke scalps which they were dancing after the sun had gone. The hollow beat of the tom-toms multiplied against the sides of the cañon, together with wild shrieking and yelling of the rejoicers; but the old Fire Eater had grown weary of dancing scalps. He had danced his youthful enthusiasm away. Thus he sat on this wild, whooping night with old Big Hand by his side to smoke his talk, and with his son asleep across his lap.

"Where did the war-party leave its trail as it came to the lodges?" he asked.

Big Hand in reply said: "The man who strikes said they came over the mountains— that the snow lay deep. They did not lead up from the plains. They obeyed the chiefs. If it was not so, the camp-soldiers would have beaten them with sticks. You have not heard the women or the dogs cry."

"It is good," continued the Fire Eater. "The wagon-soldiers will not find a trail on the high hills. The snow would stop their wheels. They will dream that the Chis-chis-chash were made into birds and have flown away."

Then Big Hand: "I have heard, brother, that ponies passed the herders at the mouth of the cañon last smoke. It was cold, and they had their robes tight over their heads. It is bad."

"Yes, you talk straight. It is bad for the pony trails to show below where the land breaks. Some dog of an Absaroke who follows the gray fox may see them. Ponies do not go to live in the hills in the time of snow. The ponies will not travel straight, as the herders drive them back. They will understand. With another sun, I shall call the council. It will talk the herders' eyes open. The young men have closed ears in these days. The cold makes their bones stiff. Brother, when we were young we could see a horse pass in the night. We could smell him. We could tell if he had a man on his back."

Big Hand gave wise consideration to his companion's statement, saying it was as he spoke. "Brother, those big horses which we took from the pony-soldiers run badly in the herd. They gather in a bunch and run fast. They go over the herders when they see the valley. They will do nothing unless you strike them over the head. They are fools like their white riders were."

So the old men gravely passed the pipe over the little things of life, which to them bore all their interest in the world. The squaw combed her hair and put fresh sticks on the fire from time to time. After a time the boy woke up and stretched himself cubbishly across his father's knees. The ancient one gave him a piece of fresh meat, which he held in both hands as he gnawed it, smearing his chubby face with grease. Having devoured his morsel he blinked sleepily, and the old Indian tucked him away in the warm recesses of his old buffalo-robe couch, quite naked, as was their custom to sleep during the winter nights. Long sat the smokers, turning their tongues over youthful remembrances, until Big Hand arose and drawing his robe about him, left the lodge.

The Fire Eater removed the small buckskin bag which contained his little brown bat's skin from his scalp-lock and smoked to it saying, "Keep the big horses from running down the cañon—keep the eyes of the herders open while I sleep—keep the little boy warm—keep the bad spirits outside the lodge after the fire can no longer see them." With these devotions concluded, he put the relic of the protection of the Good Gods in his war-bag which hung on his resting-mat over his head. Undressing, he buried himself in his buffalo robes. The fire died down, the tom-toms and singing in the adjoining lodges quieted gradually, and the camp slept.

In the ceaseless round of time the night was departing to the westward when, as though it were in a dream, the old warrior was conscious of noise. His waking sense was stirred. Rapid, frosty cracking of snow ground by horse-hoofs came through the crevices of his covering. All unusual, he sat up with a savage bang, as it were, and bent a stiff ear to the darkness. His senses were electric, but the convolutions of his brain were dead. A rifle shot, far away but unmistakable. Others followed; they came fast, but not until the clear notes of a bugle blazed their echoing way up the rock walls did he, the Fire Eater, think the truth. He made the lodge shake with the long yell of war. He did the things of a lifetime now and he did them in a trained, quick way. He shoveled his feet into his moccasins and did no more because of the urgency of the case; then he reached for his rifle and belt and stood in the dark lodge aroused. His sleep was gone but he did not comprehend. Listening for the briefest of moments, he heard amid the yelping of his own people the dull, resonant roar which he knew was the white man's answer.

Fired into a maddened excitement, he snatched up his precious boy and seizing a robe, ran out of the lodge followed by his squaw. Overhead the sky was warming but the cañon was blue dark. Every moment brought the shots and roar nearer. Plunging through the snow with his burden, the Fire Eater ran up a rocky draw which made into the main cañon. He had not gone many ar-row-flights of distance before the rushing storm of the pony-soldiers swept past his deserted lodge. Bullets began to whistle about him, and, glancing back, he saw the black form of his squaw stagger and lie slowly down in the snow. He had, by this time, quite recovered the calm which comes to the tired-out man when tumult overtakes him. Putting the boy down on a robe behind a rock, and, standing naked in the frosty air, he made his magazine gun blaze until empty. Resuming his burden, he ran on higher up the rocks until he was on the ta-ble-land of the top of the cañon. Here he resumed his shooting, but the darkness and distance made it difficult to see. Other Indians joined him and they poured their bullets into the pony-soldiers.

The Bad God had whispered to the Yel-low-Eyes; they had made them see under the snow. The Chis-chis-chash were dead men, but they would take many with them to the spirit-land. The Fire Eater felt but a few cartridges in his belt and knew that he must use them sparingly. The little boy sat crying on the buffalo robe. Holding his smoking rifle in one hand, he passed the other over his scalp-lock. The bat-skin medicine was not there. For the first time since the Good Gods had given it to him, back in his youth, did he find himself without it. A nameless terror overcame him. He was a truly naked man in the snow, divested of the protection of body and soul.

Shoving cartridges into his magazine, he made his way down, the light snow flying before him. Rounding the rocks he could see down into the main cañon; see the pony-soldiers and their Indian allies tearing down and burning the lodges. The yellow glare of many fires burned brightly in contrast with the cold blue of the snow. He scanned narrowly the place where his own lodge had been and saw it fall before many hands to be taken to their fires. The bat-skin—the hand of the Good Gods—was removed from him; his shadow was as naked as his back.

In the snow a hundred yards below him lay his young squaw, the mother of his boy, and she had not moved since she lay down.

As the pony-soldiers finally saw the stark figure of the Indian among the rocks they sent a shower of bullets around him. He had no medicine; the Bad Gods would direct the bullets to his breast. He turned and ran frantically away.

The last green-grass had seen the be-plumed chief with reddened battle-ax leading a hundred swift warriors over the dying pony-soldiers, but now the cold, blue snow looked on a naked man running before bullets, with his medicine somewhere in the black smoke which began to hang like a pall over the happy winter-camp of the bravest Indians. The ebb and flow of time had fat-tened and thinned the circumstances of the Fire Eater's life many times, but it had never taken his all before. It had left him nothing but his boy and a nearly empty gun. It had placed him between the fire of the soldiers' rifles and the cruel mountain winds which would pinch his heart out.

With his boy at his breast he flew along the rim-rock like a crow, hunting for shelter from bullets and wind. He longed to expend his remaining cartridges where each would put out a white man's fire. Recovering from their surprise, the Indians gathered thickly on inaccessible heights and fought stiffly back. Being unable to follow them, the pony-soldiers drew back; but, as they retreated, they left the village blazing, which the Chis-chis-chash could not prevent. Their rifles had only handed them over to the hungry winter.

The Fire Eater sat muffled on a ledge,

firing from time to time, and anxiously scanning his shots. The cold made him shake and he could not hold his rifle true. His old, thin blood crept slowly through his veins, and the child cried piteously. His fires were burning low; even the stimulus of hate no longer stirred him as he looked down on the white men who had burned his all and shot his wife and were even then spattering his den in the rocks with lead. He gave up, overpowered by the situation. With infinite difficulty he gathered himself erect on his stiffened joints and took again his burden in his trembling arms. Standing thus on the wind-swept height, with the bullets spotting the rocks around him, he extended his right hand and besought the black, eddying smoke to give him back his bat-skin; he begged the spirits of the air to bring it to him. He shouted his harsh pathos at a wild and lonely wind, but there was no response.

Then off through the withering cold and powdery snow moved the black figure of despair tottering slowly away from the sound of rifles which grew fainter at each step. He chattered and mumbled, half to himself,

He Shouted His Pathos at a Wild and Lonely Wind, But There Was No Response. *Authors' photoengraving.*

half to the unseen influences of nature, while the child moaned weakly under his clutched robe. When he could but barely hear the noises of the fight, he made his way down into the cañon where he shortly came upon a group of his tribesmen who had killed a pony and were roasting pieces over a log fire. They were mostly women and children or old, old men like himself. More to note than their drawn and leathery faces was the speechless terror brooding over all. Their minds had not digested their sudden fate. If the young warriors broke before the guns of the pony-soldiers, worse yet might overtake them, though the wind-swept table-lands dismayed them equally with the bullets. Munching their horse meat, clutching their meager garments, they elbowed about the fires, saying little. In their homeless helplessness their souls deadened. They could not divine the immediate future. Unlike the young warriors whose fires flashed brighter as the talons of death reached most fiercely for them, they shuddered and crouched.

Warriors came limping back from the battle, their robes dyed with a costly vermilion. They sat about doing up their wounds in filthy rags, or sang their death-songs amid the melancholy wailing of the squaws.

Having warmed himself and quieted the boy, the Fire Eater stalked down the cañon, past the smoking poles, stopping here and there to pick up fragments of skins which he used to swaddle the boy. Returning warriors said the soldiers were going away, while they themselves were coming back to get warm. Hearing this, the old man stalked down the creek toward the place where his lodge had been. He found nothing but a smoldering heap of charred robes and burnt dried meat. With a piece of lodge pole he poked away the ashes, searching for his precious medicine and never ceasing to implore the Good Gods to restore it to him. At last, dropping the pole, he walked up the side cañon to the place where his wife had fallen. He found her lying there. Drawing aside the robe he noticed a greenish pallor and fled from Death.

Finding the ponies tethered together by their necks, he caught them and improvising packs out of old robes and rawhide, he filled them with half-burnt dried meat. With these he returned to the fires where he constructed a rude shelter for the coming night. The boy moaned and cried through the shivering darkness as the old Fire Eater rocked him in his arms to a gibberish of despairing prayer.

Late in the night, the scouts came in, saying that the walking-soldiers were coming, whereat the Indians gathered their ponies and fled over the snow. The young men stayed where from the cliffs they fought back the soldiers. Many weak persons in the retreating band sat down and passed under the spell of the icy wind. The Fire Eater pressed along, carrying his rifle and boy, driving his ponies in a herd with others. It was too cold for him to dare to ride a horse. The crying boy shivered under the robe. The burden-bearer mumbled the troubled thoughts of his mind: "My mystery from the Good Gods is gone; they have taken it; they gave it to the fire. I am afraid."

Hour after hour he plodded along in the snow. His body was warmed by his exertions and the boy felt cold against his flesh. He noted this, but with the passing moments the little frame grew more rigid and more cold until to the Fire Eater it felt like a stone image. Stopping with his back to the wind, he undid the robe and fingered his burden. He knew that the shadow had gone; knew that the bad spirits had taken it away. "Oh, Bad Gods! Oh, Evil Spirits of the night, come take my shadow! You have stolen my boy, you have put out my lodge-fire; put out the fire of my body! Take vengeance on me! I am deserted by the Good Gods! I am ready to go! I am waiting!"

Thus stood in the bleak night this victim of his lost medicine; the fierce and cruel mysteries of the wind tugged at his robe and flapped his long hair about his head. Indians coming by pushed and pulled him along. Two young men made it a duty to aid the despairing chief. They dragged him until they reached a cañon where fires had been lighted around which were gathered the fugitives. The people who had led him had supposed that his mind was wandering under suffering or wounds. As he sank by the side of the blaze he dropped the robe and laid the stiffened body of his frozen boy across his knees. The others peered for a time with frightened glances at the dead body, when with cries of "Dead, dead!" they ran away, going deeper down the cañon. The Fire Eater sat alone, waiting for the evil spirits which lurked out among the pine trees, to come and take him. He wanted to go to the spirit-land where the Cheyennes of his home and youth were at peace in warm valleys, talking and eating.

EX LIBRIS

NOTES

When Remington arrived in the White-water River bottoms of south-central Kansas in early March 1883, his immediate reaction was that he could profitably engage in the raising of sheep. He used his inheritance to purchase a 320-acre ranch and set about the necessary structural improvements.

At first the privations, the treeless plain, and the wearing labor produced a severe depression. Then Remington recovered his customary ebullience. He engaged help to do the heavy work and spent his days with cronies. By July, he was off on a junket into the Southwest.

In mid-October 1883, Remington lived the rollicking twenty-four hours he narrated in "Coursing Rabbits on the Plains" (*Outing,* May 1887). This is a relatively long tale for Remington, told in the same straightforward language he employed in his letters.

The cast of characters is complex. The narrator is Fred Remington. His mare was Terra-Cotta. The host was Robert or Bob, surname Camp, astride old Jane. Phip was Bob's cook and rode Bob's mule. James or Jim was Chapman (or Chapin) who mounted Push-Bob and petted Peg-Leg. John S was Jack Smith, who owned the greyhound. Charlie B on the blue mare was Charles Birch, "the best fellow in the world." Bill Carr, really Kehr (or Kerr), was Fred Remington's ranch hand, racing Prince. It was old John Mitchner who led the pack with the "cow-skin" racer, and old John's boy cooked. Remington referred to

Kehr as Carr without being aware of the correct spelling, although they ate and bunked together for almost a year. His misspelling of friends' names was a lifelong failing.

The actual coursing of the rabbits is treated as a casual affair, personal to these participants. It was, however, an organized sport. The meet of the American Coursing Club was initiated as an annual event in Kansas in 1886. There, the greyhounds killed the rabbits.

The day that Remington described is underlaid with the resentment of the community against these young squires. Old John grouses, "My hoss stock ain't nothin' to brag on now, because I hain't got the money that you fellers down in the creek has got fer to buy 'em with." Later, John gloats, "Thar now, I've been a layin' fer you fellers ever since I came inter these yar parts."

That was the start of Remington's disenchantment with sheep ranching. When he was arrested for a Christmas Eve prank that aroused the enmity of the townspeople, it was the end. He had never taken hold of the routine drudgery of the business. With local unpopularity added on, he offered the ranch for sale and left the area about the end of January 1884.

After Remington became famous years later, his old sheep-raising neighbors did not associate the great artist with the Fred Remington they had known. When they found out, they commemorated him by naming a school after him, but the art he had strewn generously around the countryside was all gone.

Bibliographic sources for this period are Allen, Myra Brown, Dary, Hassrick, Mechem, Peabody Centennial, and Robert Taft (see Bibliography).

Remington moved to a rooming house in Kansas City. He was listed in the 1884 city directory as a hardware dealer and had a silent partnership in the saloon where the literati gathered. Remington was labeled a bon vivant, a frequenter of the theater, the billiard hall, the restaurant, the bar, and the roadhouse. He married Eva Caten in Gloversville, New York, on October 1, 1884, and brought her West to live.

When Remington's investments failed and his painting sales were few, Eva Remington returned East before the beginning of the summer of 1885. Remington bought a work horse for fifty dollars and spent the remainder of his funds again sketching in the Southwest. While there is no definite record of where he went, he did in this period sketch Oklahoma scenes that were sold to New York editors in later years. After borrowing the train fare, he joined his wife in Brooklyn in September 1885.

Success came as a Christmas present, when at twenty-four, he sold his first signed illustration.

The head of the publishing house of Harper, J. Henry Harper, looked on Remington as his personal discovery that fall. "Tell me about the West," he demanded of the commission-seeking Remington, who had appeared in cowboy garb. Remington told the tales that Harper was expecting. To ensure he held Harper's attention, Remington fabricated a scenario about how he won the train fare East that he had actually borrowed: He had whipped out his Colt to fend off cardsharpers plucking an eastern drummer and then sat guard all night, gun at ready, to save the sleeping tenderfoot. Remington—as good a self-salesman as any drummer—claimed to be just in from the train trip the grateful drummer bought. (The source is Harper.)

Remington became a most important

Harper artist and, later on, writer. His illustrations appeared in ten *Harper's Weekly* issues in 1886. He was sent by Harper on a southwestern and Mexican trip in June of 1886 to gather sketches for illustrations of articles written by other *Harper's* writers.

"A Peccary Hunt in Northern Mexico" (*Harper's Weekly,* December 1, 1888) starts from Hermosillo. A slender literary accomplishment, the article draws succinctly on an unusual outdoors episode. It continues in the first person to describe confidently an event where the writer participates with confessedly less success than the gracious and humble locals.

For the 1886 assignment by Harper and for the 1888 trip for Century, Remington maintained daily journals. The 1886 journal puts Remington in the right place for "Peccary Hunt" but it does not record the event.

This trip was the start of Remington's continuing romance with Mexico despite confrontations with the residents. "I was amused on the train," he said in his journal, "to see one very good looking Mexican girl spit—she had the art." The hackmen in his journal and the hangers on in the article both "no doubt had knives under their tunics" to Remington's suspicious eye. Cannot help seeing the "villian" in the face of every Mexican, he noted.

Bibliographic sources for this period are (Denver) *Republican,* Dippie, Exman, Harper, Hassrick, McCracken, Taft papers, and Vail.

The year 1887 was the consolidation of Remington's position as an illustrator. His work appeared in *Harper's Bazaar, Harper's Weekly, Harper's Young People, London Graphic, Outing,* and *St. Nicholas.* From *Century* he received the major assignment of illustrating Theodore Roosevelt's "Ranch Life and the Far West." He probably also visited the Pacific Northwest the summer of 1887. He mentioned meeting a sketch-shy Blackfoot at the Bow River that year.

It was R. W. Gilder, editor of *The Century Magazine,* who took credit for launching Remington as a writer. When the two were discussing a trip for the summer of

1888 so that Remington could illustrate articles on Indian tribes, Gilder asked whether Remington had had experience in writing, in order to eliminate sending another man. Remington replied in jest that all he had ever written was his name on the reverse of a railroad pass. "Coursing Rabbits" had been printed in *Outing,* however, so Gilder commissioned the Indian articles along with their illustrations.

The first of Remington's *Century* pieces was "Horses of the Plains" (*Century,* January 1889). The manuscript was submitted as "Descendents of the Barbs" before the 1888 trip but was rewritten and resubmitted September 6, 1888. Continued melding of parts of the original with the amendments resulted in an article where every paragraph sounds fine but the over-all concept is muddy. By October 30, 1888, Remington was still making corrections and additions and had accepted the suggestion of the final title. Nevertheless, a letter from Eva Remington to Horace Sackrider the month of publication boasts that the Century people tell Fred he is quite a literary man. (Source is Taft papers.)

Years later, in November of 1894, when Owen Wister was mining Remington for nuggets of Western lore, Remington garbled his reply to a Wister inquiry about the genealogy of the bronco: "I wrote an article in 'The Century'—The horse of the Plains '87—I went into that—I cant find the article.—Cortez had horses but they must have been all killed—subsequent importations—stolen and lost—the Sioux have a legend of the first horses—they were stolen from Mexico. 'Cayuse'—a north Western indian tribe who raised good horses—the term grew and is localized in the north west.—'mustang'—a California word for a steed.—much used by '49 but never established in use (out of story books) East of Mountains.—'broncho'—'wild' Spanish—means anything north of where the people don't understand Spanish.—"

It did not appear that the five-year interval since the publication of "Horses of the Plains" improved Remington's clarity in this essay. The sources are Vail and Wister papers.

What did improve was Remington's standard of living. In 1885 he had squeezed into shared quarters on South Ninth Street in Brooklyn. Before November 2, 1886, the Remingtons were in a rooming house at 165 Ross Street in Brooklyn. Until 1888 they were in an apartment at 360 West Fifty-eighth Street in Manhattan. In 1889 they lived in a small house in the upper city at 561 Mott Avenue, and by 1890 they were established in their New Rochelle mansion. What paid the bills was Remington's organized devotion to writing and illustrating. It was the first task he had ever had where work was fun.

"A Scout with the Buffalo-Soldiers" (*Century,* April 1889) is a prime example of the blending of word and picture so that they enhance each other. The article resulted from the 1888 trip as indicated by Remington's journal. His letters to his wife in 1888 run along the high spots of the text, occasionally adding a fillip of emotion to reveal the Remington who would so test himself physically in the exercise of his trade.

Remington in his journal observed that he was greatly gratified to be able to say that he liked the Negro as a soldier in almost every particular. "The best d—— soldiers in the world," prudishly recorded a man known for his cursing.

He had written his wife June 7, 1888: "To night I sleep in an infantry camp and go on the trail with them until to morrow noon. The day following I start on a scout with Clarke up through the San Carlos way to Apache (Fort). I will be gone two or three weeks and you will not hear from me very often. Am well. Take good care of yourself. Yours Respt. Frederic Remington. Excuse the Yours Respt. It was a slip.—love."

June 22 he reported back in, a little early: "My dear girl. We just returned this afternoon from a two weeks scout up as far as the Pinal Mountains. it was tough—the toughest thing I ever went through. The climb was like going continually up stairs only often steeper. I puffed like a tug boat. we camped—saw a wild bull fight—the next day I was very sore. I leave here Tuesday for Fort Sill Indian Territory. I will certainly be home before the 1st August and will probably come before. love & kisses from Your Fred."

(Sources are Hassrick, Taft papers, and Helen Card papers.)

The 1888 journal places Remington "On the Indian Reservations" (*Century,* July 1889). It has been said that Remington here headed a routine account of Apache Indian observations with a three-year-old Geronimo adventure just as an attention-getting device. This then can be construed as a matter of mechanical technique in writing, as an illustration might be made evocative by the exaggerated stance of the figures, a typical Remington mannerism in his art.

The real reason for Remington's dragging in the old Geronimo encounter is probably not technique at all. His 1885 sketches of the warlike Geronimo gave him his start. His first signed illustration was *The Apache War* with the skinny little *Indian Scouts on Geronimo's Trail*. He naturally thought back to his Geronimo days when he confided to his 1888 journal: "The Apaches are most uninteresting tribes aside from their war like characteristic. No tradition."

Another criticism of Remington is that he here admits: "I believe that no white man can ever penetrate the mystery of the Indian mind or explain the reason of their acts." This 1889 statement is used to discredit Remington writing as an Indian in *The Way of an Indian* in 1906, as if a 1909 painting of full-color impressions could be denied because 1889 paintings were grisaille and literal. Remington's friend Theodore Roosevelt picked this up in his February 20, 1906, letter quoted in the Introduction, by saying that despite the old disclaimer, to another white man Remington certainly sounded like he understood Indians.

Remington's use of his field journal is manifold. He reuses in his articles whole paragraphs that have been only slightly fleshed out from the journal. He keys bits of lingo to remind himself of a joke. He lists pictures to be painted and records painterly colors. He finds his intended articles in the parade of events. And, in the personal sense, he records his wins as an Indian trader accumulating painting props for the studio. Some were losses: "Camped in a beautiful post oak and black jack grove . . . along came a Witchita Indian—little boy on horse—nicely dressed—I wanted to trade for boy's clothes—we agreed on 10 dollars —I proffed 10 bill—he said 'no wayno me ketch em white money—heap no good maybe so'—no trade."

By July 1, 1888, Remington was writing home from Henrietta, Texas: "Here I am at last—had a devil of a time—the mosquitoes like to have eaten me up—and oh oh oh how hot it is here—I am dirty and look like the devil and feel worse and there is not help for me. I am nearly starved to death— this Texas grub is something frightful. and my room—I wish you could see it. you would smile. well all this is very discouraging but its an artists life. Your old boy, Fred."

"Artist Wanderings Among the Cheyennes" (*Century,* August 1889) is the final portion of the 1888 "vacation with pay," to use Helen Card's expression. How much pay is the matter Remington took up with Gilder at *Century,* April 6, 1889: "At your convenience I trust you will have the goodness to conclude the business transaction regarding the two Indian articles which I wrote for your magazine. I was paid $100 on account for the two articles as you had not had time then, in the office to look the matter up thoroughly. If there is any more coming to me I should like to know it and if not the determination of that fact will have a soothing effect on my mind. I have not inquired into this matter in so long a time that I thought I would remind your people of it."

Assuming that the illustrations for the two articles were separately compensated, the $100 on account for the writing was not too far short of what was due, even though the articles totaled about 13,600 words.

Remington's rate at that time in his career would have been about $10 per thousand words, and not more than $12.50 per thousand. His first illustrations for *Outing* were paid for at $10 each. It is obvious that it took a multiplicity of appearances to produce an income. It is also true that Remington did not write again for *Century* until 1902.

(Sources are Dippie, Taft papers, and White.)

"Two Gallant Young Cavalrymen" (*Harper's Weekly,* March 22, 1890) is Remington at the beginning of the decade that solidly established him at the top level of the golden age of illustration. Here he puffs General Miles and Lieutenant Clarke. This is a redo of his "A Scout with the Buffalo-Soldiers" given immediacy and retold in connection with the capture of a few renegade Apaches who had ambushed an Arizona freighter.

Clarke's heroic episode was originally reported in the *Harper's Weekly* of June 19, 1886. It appeared next as a full-page Remington illustration, August 21, 1886, "Soldiering in the Southwest—The Rescue of Corporal Scott," where one of Clarke's troopers is quoted, "He'd 've fairly dusted 'way fum dar to save he own hide whole if he wa'n't a—fightin' man—fightin' man, I tell you and it jes do 'im good to see a—Injun. An' he don't forgit a man in his 'stress."

Remington felt that singling his friend Clarke out for praise would help Clarke in his military career, even though some old commanders regarded Clarke as a "broncho in barracks." Clarke in his September 13, 1890, letter to Remington had more knowledge than he was aware of in his joke, "Well you will ruin me yet and I wont be able to descend into the valleys only 'on high places will I touch.'" Clarke did endanger his prospects by forcing confrontations with the hidebound military staff.

"Chasing a Major-General" (*Harper's Weekly,* December 6, 1890, *Pony Tracks*) is the earliest of the pieces reprinted in book form during Remington's life. After appear-

ing in the 1895 anthology *Pony Tracks,* it was repeated in the 1899 anthology *Stories of Peace and War.* "Chasing" follows Remington's penchant for titles employing the *-ing* suffix, as in Coursing, Wanderings, Training, Coaling, Galloping, and the choice Vagabonding.

Remington had met General Miles during the 1886 trip for *Harper's:* "Sunday. Left Tucson on the morning train—My hotel chap made a grievous error and only charged me $5.00 for what ought to have been $10.00. more luck than I generally have. I was introduced to Genl Miles by Capt Thompson. I felt his presence before conscious of his identity. A good style of man. His personal looks I shall never forget —He gave me the usual 'great man' reception which is one I ask and expect—that being a recognition of the fact that you are not a lower animal."

General Miles's buttering of the young Remington made a connection important to Miles for twenty years. "Chasing" is a prime example, a moody nocturnal feature story set above the realities of the coming Indian war. The background to the story is Remington as *Harper's Weekly* correspondent attached to the Cheyenne Indian Commission headed by General Miles. Lieutenant Sydenham on the spot saw Remington as "a fat citizen dismounting from a troop horse, with closely shaven head, an easy graceful waddle, fair complexion, blue eyes, light hair, smooth face—a big good-natured overgrown boy."

Miles's commission decided to force the Cheyenne from their reservation, although ultimately the influence of the regular army in the neighboring post protected the Cheyenne and they were allowed to stay. Meanwhile, Remington followed the general on his wild charges through the dark.

(Sources are the Taft papers, Sydenham, and *Montana the magazine.*)

"The Art of War and Newspaper Men" (*Harper's Weekly,* December 6, 1890) is Remington as the spokesman for the army, to explain why the disposition of the troops against the Indians suddenly required secrecy. The answer is that the Interior Department had educated enough Indians so that troop movements disclosed in the newspapers were known to all.

It is implicit that before this date, the Indian-fighting army had issued its news releases under the assumption that Indians could not read.

While Remington had been "Chasing a Major-General," the escort for the general had been the Northern Cheyenne Scouts under Lieutenant Ned Casey. Earlier in 1890, Casey had proposed to his superiors that a troop of Indian scouts be established with full military status but not attached to a regular army unit. Remington reported on Casey's immediate success both in "Chasing a Major-General" and in "Indians as Irregular Cavalry" (*Harper's Weekly,* December 27, 1890). Remington pleaded the army's case in what he called a scheme of regeneration for the native American race.

Hamilton Wright Mabie, the historian, had previously stated the opposite position: "Although Mr. Remington's descriptions are undoubtedly faithful as impressions, what is known as the Indian Question has made great progress through the Interior Department." In the same issue of *Harper's Weekly* as Remington's article, President Harrison apparently expressed himself as favoring Remington's approach, while the January 10, 1891, issue also enlisted General Miles and Red Cloud. The March 26, 1892, issue reported an enabling measure pending in Congress to legislate the military view. *Harper's Weekly* took a negative editorial position, partially because "Indians drink unspeakable mixtures at frontier saloons."

The Indian-fighting army was appreciative of Remington's attention. Remington's article also referred to Lieutenant S. C. Robertson's Crow Scout Corps at Fort Custer. Robertson wrote Remington December 31: "When fifty or sixty years hence you depart from mundane affairs and join, in the happy hunting grounds, the spirits of the Indians your clever pencil has created,

I'll see that the U. S. Army—scouts included—keep your grave green."

Robertson did not live to keep his promise. He resigned from the cavalry June 30, 1893, and died two months later. His epitaph was in a letter Remington had written to Powhatan Clarke June 27, 1893: "As for Robertson—he's a d—— sight better soldier drunk than any fellow who will come at me, is sober." The source is Hassrick.

Meanwhile, back at the office, we have Remington's December 10 letter to Schell, art director of *Harper's:* "Here are the illustrations for my article which will come down Saturday on 'Indians as Irregular Cavalry'—you can use them as you see fit. Please do not make pencil marks on the front side of the water colors." Under the terms of his illustrating arrangement with *Harper's,* Remington was entitled to the return of the originals. He wanted the originals clean for resale.

"Indians as Irregular Cavalry" was never included in the Remington anthologies. The article represented a military point of view that fell before civilian insistence on a pastoral program of assimilating the Indian into white society, a program that did not work.

(Sources are *Harper's Weekly,* Hassrick, and *Montana the magazine.*)

The world of arts and letters was smaller in the 1890s. Members of cliques like those affiliated with *Harper's* engaged in public strokings of each other. In the January 17, 1891, *Harper's Weekly,* Julian Ralph, who was an author whose work Remington illustrated, wrote a glowing profile on Remington. The tone of the piece was "Born a country boy, his ancestors have responded to every call to arms upon this soil." Ralph also claimed that "at the first public notice of the strange aberration of the Indians concerning their 'Messiah,' " Remington's unique judgment took him to the scene of the fighting just as it began. Later biographers extended this to say Remington was the only correspondent on the scene for the Sitting Bull uprising. This is mainly predicated on the postcard Remington sent Harper from Chicago after December 10, 1890: "I leave here to-night for Rapid City—near Deadwood. There is going to be a row—that's settled—it was good judgment to come I think—excuse postal."

Remington's article was "The Sioux Outbreak in South Dakota" (*Harper's Weekly,* January 24, 1891, *Pony Tracks*). J. Frank Dobie labeled it superb reporting. What it is is not reporting of the main event, the Wounded Knee fight, but a feature article on the aftermath in terms of the soldiers' reactions.

The Wounded Knee battle occurred December 29, 1890, about twelve miles east and north of the Pine Ridge Agency. Remington's accounts of his participation, "Lieutenant Casey" and "The Sioux Outbreak," are quite clear and have been verified in detail by Robert Taft. The night of December 25, Remington was camped at Hermoso south of Rapid City. By December 26 he had marched to the Cheyenne River, north of the Agency. December 27 and 28, he moved down the river and onto the bluffs. The day of the battle, Remington started for the Pine Ridge Agency twenty-five miles away but was turned back by the Sioux.

Remington did not arrive at the Agency until two days after. The artist correspondents who drew the first published illustrations of the fight itself were Dan Smith and Rufus Zogbaum, neither of whom appears to have been present. The press corps on the scene included at least twenty-two correspondents, one a woman who was the first female "special." Only three correspondents were present at the battle. (The source is Knight.)

None of the participants knew at the time that this was the end of the Indian Wars.

In "Lieutenant Casey's Last Scout" (*Harper's Weekly,* January 31, 1891, *Pony Tracks*), Remington recounts his adventures with Casey up to December 25, 1890. His conclusion is based on his reading the news report of Casey's having been shot.

After Remington left for home, Casey and his Indian scouts were part of the troops surrounding a large Sioux camp following Wounded Knee. While General Miles was attempting to negotiate the end of the hostilities, Casey took it on himself January 7, 1891, to approach the Sioux to seek an audience with Red Cloud. The meeting was denied. Casey was returning to his scouts when he was assassinated by Plenty Horses, a Sioux who had attended Carlisle for five years. At Plenty Horses' trial for murder, he testified he had shot Casey so he could make a place for himself among his people rather than continuing in a lonely role as an educated man in the wild tribe.

Remington never did report the trial and its outcome. Plenty Horses was acquitted, on the ground that he could have considered Casey a spy, in a time of war. And Casey's efforts with the "Indians as Irregular Cavalry" were eroded as the scouts were first absorbed into the regular army and then in 1895 terminated.

In Remington's account, when he fended off the "little buck" who tried to slip behind him, by holding out his hand and saying, "How, colah?" Remington not only countered the threatened movement with "Peace, friend" but also contributed to the career of his fellow artist Charles Schreyvogel. "How Kola" was painted by Schreyvogel in 1901, as he had used "My Bunkie" in 1899 after Remington's "The Wounded Bunkie" of 1896.

(Sources are the Card papers, Dobie, McCracken, and *Montana the magazine.*)

"General Miles's Review of the Mexican Army" (*Harper's Weekly,* July 4, 1891) is another example of Remington's continued infatuation with American military brass and with Mexico. Although he was on an assignment for *Harper's,* he would have gone wherever Miles requested. He was undoubtedly pleased that the destination was his "magnificent" Mexico, where Miles was on vacation with his family. (The source is Miles.)

"A Day with the Seventh Regiment"

(*Harper's Weekly,* July 18, 1891) is the expression of Remington's preoccupation both with the glorified killing he foresaw resulting from the next war and with the practice for war that the military would get through putting down the mobs that sprang from labor unrest.

The senior *Harper's* illustrator W. A. Rogers wrote in his autobiography that a stranger meeting Remington would come away with the impression that he had met a man of blood and iron. Rogers felt it was the picturesqueness of battles that misled Remington into an imaginary love for kill and be killed, blood and more blood, whereas Remington was really a big overgrown boy, full of the charm of make-believe. Rogers' apologia might have been correct, but until 1899 Remington's writings, his letters, and his speech are full of variations on the idea that the business of a soldier is to be ready to die.

And, as Remington said in this article, in the absence of war and Indians the next best target for fighting was the mob. As early as 1877, federal troops had been required to restore order to the railroad system after unprecedented violence and arson in reaction to a wage cut during a depression. Labor unrest spread. Twice as many strikes occurred in 1886 as in any previous year. That May, the Haymarket bombing of the police took place during an anarchist meeting protesting the killing of a striker. Men of Remington's class seriously considered the danger of revolution brought on by "communist" labor leaders.

To maintain his contact with the West, Remington had been corresponding with Powhatan Clarke in order to induce Clarke to use a camera. The early days of the venture produced Clarke letters like the one of September 13, 1890, concerning a camera lent to Clarke by Remington: "Sent outfit to Dragoon Pass while I spent the day in a dark room. Took train to Dragoon with two Indians & joined outfit they were tickled to death over the ride in the 'Soon Wagon' train started [   ] said to Brakeman put my camera and lantern off in Tucson All

right said he I'll put her off at Benson. To cut story short the camera has been traced to Oakland Cal and traces lost."

At this point, Clarke's successes with the new camera brought Remington's own attention to the West. In August 1891, Remington wrote Schell at Harper's: "I have just received a nice lot of instantaneous photos from an officer in the 10th cavalry and suggest that I be allowed to do a page on 'Training Cavalry Horses to Jump Obstacles' [*Harper's Weekly,* September 19, 1891]. It would be something on the order of my 'Breaking cav horses to stand fire' published some time since. They jump logs —dead cattle—rocks &c.—you can catch the idea."

In early 1890 "Breaking Horses" had been Remington illustrations with copy by a staff writer. Here text and pictures were both Remington.

"Coolies Coaling a Ward Liner—Havana" (*Harper's Weekly,* November 7, 1891) shows another facet of the personality of Remington's class. That is the overwhelming fear of the dilution of the Saxon race because of the approximately six million foreigners who entered the United States during Remington's lifetime.

The "Coolies" incident occurred during Remington's return from Vera Cruz to New York after the illustration assignment with General Miles in Mexico. As described again eight years later in "Under Which King?" a second fear was implicit—the violent aversion to human deformity.

The article originated with Remington's August 22, 1891, letter to Schell: "I ship today a drawing for a 'double' in the Weekly entitled 'Genus horribile—or Chinese coolies coaling a Ward Line Steamer in Havana.' I can write about it—if you desire —they were the hardest looking outfit of humanity I ever saw and while having no claims to interest in a 'sassiety' way yet socially they were engaging to the last degree especially since they are coming up here by the hundreds and are all lepers."

The drawing was used as a single-page illustration (rather than the "double") and it was as true as it could have been, in contrast to the rant of the article. The man more rabid than Remington was the author, Poultney Bigelow, to whom Remington wrote in May 1893: "Jews, Injuns, Chinamen, Italians, Huns—the rubbish of the Earth—I hate."

Actually, Bigelow had slightly different spots. He loved the Huns. When Bigelow published Remington's private letters in 1929, he commented: "As we read Remington's diatribes against nations and races, we must bear in mind that he knew of them only the poorest." (The source is Bigelow.)

There is also a February 7, 1909, letter on the subject that is from Theodore Roosevelt to Remington: "I entirely agree that the Asiatic must be kept out. I am keeping him out."

In that sense, "Coolies Coaling" could be considered to have been national policy.

"A Merry Christmas in a Sibley Tepee" (*Harper's Weekly,* December 5, 1891) was the fourth of the *Harper's* pieces to have been reprinted in *Pony Tracks*. This is a flashback in time to the previous year's holiday at the end of the Indian wars. It is all mood and generality without mention of specific events or personalities.

"The Galloping Sixth" (*Harper's Weekly,* January 16, 1892) was not reprinted in *Pony Tracks*. It had produced an explosion from the protagonist, General Carr, who failed to provide Remington with what Remington expected, the usual "great man" reception.

The same day the article was published in *Harper's Weekly,* it also appeared in the *Army and Navy Journal,* along with an editorial praising Remington. This could not have pleased Carr. He was a brevet major general, standing at that moment for promotion to fill an existing vacancy in a permanent grade. Carr's second lieutenant, Alonzo Gray, wrote the editor of the *Journal* for publication, February 6, 1892: "I suppose Mr. Remington is like all newspaper correspondents who, when they visit military camps expecting to find news and find none, make it themselves because their

very existence depends upon their supplying their papers with news. It was doubtless this which led Mr. Remington to hold Brevet Major General Eugene A. Carr up to ridicule."

The first reply published in the *Journal* came February 20 from W. C. Brown, first lieutenant, 1st Cavalry: "The readers must have read with no little regret Lieut. Gray's uncalled for attack on that distinguished artist and friend of the Army. It would be in far better taste for us to 'chip in' and present him with a handsome testimonial in recognition of his services in presenting to the public a faithful picture of the work."

The same issue carried a letter from Richard Harding Davis as managing editor of *Harper's Weekly:* "The only reason I can see for this epistle in which the writer represented Mr. Remington as ridiculing General Carr was his desire to curry favor with his superior officer. Mr. Remington does not 'make his living' gathering news, but on the contrary supports five or six large magazines and keeps them living well. He is also the mainstay of different Secretaries of War, and Generals know it, and get up Indian Wars for him to illustrate with themselves in the foreground."

Another word on correspondents was from Lieutenant Alvin Sydenham which appeared in *Harper's Weekly* August 13, 1892. He wrote about the little regular army: "The only attention we ever get that is truly valuable is when Mr. Remington or Mr. Zogbaum makes a tour of our camps. They are the best friends we have."

His description as a bacon and forage colonel never ceased rankling Carr. Seven years later Remington was required to answer Mr. Harper: "As for Gen'l Carr's letter I dont see why he lugs in that old subject. He took offense where I intended none —I apologized & explained in Army & Navy Journal at the time and supposed the incident was closed. I do not understand from the letter why he brings it up. I have met him since and he was pleasant to me. But I cant bother about that now." A search of the *Journal* files at the West Point Cadet Library turned up no such Remington apology.

"An Appeal for Justice" (*Harper's Weekly*, July 9, 1892) was Remington's attempt on behalf of the army to renew the pleas of the article "Indians as Irregular Cavalry." The goal was the same, to have the control of the Indians shifted from the civilian bureau to the military.

"Buffalo Bill in London" (*Harper's Weekly*, September 3, 1892) and "Military Athletics at Aldershot" (*Harper's Weekly*, September 10, 1892) were the consequences of Remington's aborted trip to Russia with Poultney Bigelow. Remington had sailed for England May 23, 1892, to join Bigelow. They were *Harper's* correspondents commissioned to report on a canoe trip down the Volga. The Russians suspected Bigelow of serving as a German spy and Remington as his recording accomplice so the Volga trip was not sanctioned.

By June 11, 1892, Remington was back in Germany, writing to his friend Julian Ralph: "Here I am on German soil—thank God. Bigelow and I have been fired bodily out of Russia. We dodged the police telegrams and got off with our notes and sketches—you talk about Ingins—they aint in it."

Passing through England, Remington gathered the material for the two articles and wrote to Bigelow, who had remained in Europe: "I have got some London clothes and am a very nice young man but have great difficulty with the cab drivers whose pronunciation of English is so different from mine."

In a July 25, 1893, letter marked confidential, General Miles wrote Remington: "I am much interested in the article in which you illustrated the Prussian Army." Suspected by the Russians to have been a German spy, Remington was now called upon to report on the German military. Thirty years later, Remington's sister-in-law wrote that Bigelow and Remington might have been classified in Russia as "travellers who knew too much." The source is Caten.

Before the receipt of Miles's letter, though, Remington was off to Mexico for another *Harper's* assignment: "My dear Bigelow," he wrote January 29, 1893. "To-morrow—to-morrow I start for 'my people' —d—— Europe—the Czar—The Arts the Conventionalities—the cooks and the dudes and the women—I go to the simple men. — men with the bark on—the big mountains— the great deserts the scrawney ponies—I'm happy."

In "Buffalo Bill" the misspelling "guacho" is Remington's.

"The Uprising in Chihuahua" (*Harper's Weekly*, May 6, 1893) reported on the Mexican portion of the trip. It placed Remington in Mexico in April 1893. It was requested by *Harper's Weekly* as background to their news coverage of the abortive revolution. It also had a sequel, "The Rebellion in Northern Mexico" (*Harper's Weekly*, December 30, 1893). Remington's serious writing on Mexico began in *Harper's Monthly* the end of the year.

The shift in outlets from *Harper's Weekly* to *Harper's Monthly* becomes confusing chronologically. As is reflected in the names, the *Weekly* would carry a piece two weeks or more after submission, while the *Monthly* was two months or more. The *Weekly* was a newspaper, the *Monthly* a magazine.

"Black Water and Shallows" (*Harper's Monthly*, August 1893) was probably written following Remington's vacation at Cranberry Lake in the summer of 1892, and, of course, preceded the Mexican trip.

Of the previous twenty-two published pieces, all but the "Coolies Coaling" were Western- or military-oriented. "Black Water . . ." was Remington's first article on the Adirondacks. Remington retained the strongest emotional ties with the North Country of New York State, where he was born and buried. Married there in 1884, he returned in 1885 and at least 1887, 1889, 1891, and 1892 when he canoed down the Oswegatchie River with his favorite Adirondack guide, Has Rasbeck.

Remington had met Owen Wister the first time by chance in Yellowstone in the fall of

1893. As soon after as February 8, 1894, Remington wrote Wister: "Well compadre, what do you think of 'Black water and shallows'—Fly into me and jump on me and make it so that when I convalesce I will know more."

"The Advance-Guard, or the Military Sacrifice" (*Harper's Weekly,* September 16, 1893) implicitly recognized that the Indian wars were over. Remington is henceforth a historian of the West and not a correspondent. In reusing here the setting of the 1890 "Sioux Outbreak," Remington bridged history back to 1757 for Major Robert Rogers and to 1755 for Braddock.

Travel west by rail along the northern route in the fall of 1893 involved a pause in Chicago. There the World's Columbian Exposition was the center of national interest. It was the stopping point for many writers and illustrators, including Remington in "A Gallop Through the Midway" (*Harper's Weekly,* October 7, 1893). Remington discusses the racing dromedaries he had seen there, associating them with the prehistoric Ichthyornes and the Exposition's notorious Loie Fuller's serpentine dance. He failed to mention that in the drawings section of the fine arts exhibition there were shown no fewer than fifteen of his works.

Remington's spring 1893 trip to Mexico not only produced the previously mentioned "The Uprising in Chihuahua" but also led to three leisurely articles published in *Harper's Monthly.* Remington's February 7 letter from Chihuahua to J. Henry Harper reports on the reception Bill Harper, who had accompanied Remington, is receiving and adds that they leave the next morning for the four days' stage ride that is described in the beginning of "An Outpost of Civilization" (*Harper's Monthly,* December 1893, *Pony Tracks*). They are on their way to Bavicora in the northwest part of the state of Chihuahua, forty miles above Temósachic (shown in an atlas). The owner of the ranch is El Patron, otherwise Don Gilberto in Mexico and Jack Gilbert in the United States.

Many years later, Remington's St. Lawrence County friend John Howard thought he had been along on this trip. Remington's letter in the authors' collection calls his companion "Bill," however, and the text (p. 113) in *Pony Tracks* mentions "my travelling companion from New York city" from which Howard was not.

Remington is then treated to an excursion "In the Sierra Madre with the Punchers" (*Harper's Monthly,* February 1894, *Pony Tracks*). The party returns to an outlying ranch of Bavicora for "A Rodeo at Los Ojos" (*Harper's Monthly,* March 1894, *Pony Tracks*). Thereafter, Jack Gilbert's man William takes Remington and Bill Harper by wagon back to Chihuahua for the connection with the Pullman to El Paso and on to California.

"Toro, Toro!" (*Harper's Weekly,* December 9, 1893) was an incongruous bow toward the historical California cowboy, in the tracks of the California painters James Walker, William Hahn, and Charles Nahl. While Remington never had a pupil, he did touch and influence young artists like Maynard Dixon, Charles Chapman, and Sally Farnham. When the Western sculptor Arthur Putnam applied for his first art schooling, he offered rough sketches of horses reminiscent of Remington, explaining that Remington had been on the Putnam ranch near San Diego in 1893 and Putnam's task had been to get the horses to "cut up" for Remington's sketches. (The source is Heyneman.)

Remington was now thirty-two and a firm member of the eastern publishing establishment. He had all of the illustrating and writing assignments he wished to undertake. His immediate associates were Wister, Ralph, Bigelow, Kemble, and Roosevelt. When a laudatory article needed writing for a member of the group, another member was called upon, such as Remington handling the February 24, 1894, puffing of "Julian Ralph" (*Harper's Weekly,* February 24, 1894).

This service even involved notifying Ralph about the article in advance and accepting Ralph's editing, as Remington indicated in his letter of February 1894: "Go to Harpers and read my article on you— have re written it."

A coy acknowledgment was also called for, as in Remington's January 3, 1891, letter to Ralph concerning an article by Ralph on Remington: "I like to think of myself as you wrote but 'I dasnt.' "

Although the extensive trek to remote Bavicora had enabled Remington to discover frontier cowboys who were still left in the reaches, it was apparent by 1894 that the Indian-fighting army had become a peacetime army. Many of Remington's military friends were either out of the West, like General Miles stationed in Chicago, or dead, like Powhatan Clarke and Robertson. In order to continue to report on the cavalry, for his own sustenance and to comfort his friends in the service, Remington wrote about "Troop A Athletics" (*Harper's Weekly*, March 3, 1894), "A Model Squadron" (*Harper's Weekly,* June 9, 1894, *Pony Tracks*), and "Troop A with the Dust On" (*Harper's Weekly,* July 7, 1894). He had earlier suggested Troop A as a publishable subject in a December 16, 1891, letter to Arthur B. Turner, an editor at *Harper's,* but then he was still fresh from "Sioux Outbreak" and "Lieutenant Casey" so he requested a *Harper's* writer to supplement his Troop A illustrations. In 1894 Remington did his own writing, even though the justification for the articles was mainly social, with these genteel military types performing acrobatics on horseback as the prelude to a reception by the officers' wives.

After the Indian-fighting army and the circus-performing army came the mob-controlling army. The most critical example of labor unrest in Remington's time was the Pullman strike in Chicago in 1894. Employees of the Pullman Palace Car factory had walked off the job in response to a series of wage cuts. The result was the ending of railroad service to the West. President Cleveland directed General Miles to ensure the maintenance of law and order. This involved operating trains with troops and dispersing protesting civilians.

Miles in his memoirs says that "some unimportant question arose" to cause the strike that forced two billion dollars of transportation property to remain idle. After the mob stoned an engineer to death, Miles wrote, he persuaded Cleveland to provide three thousand troops to deal with the mob whose leaders were preaching rebellion in a city where all the gun stores had been sold out. The presence of the troops enabled Miles, he said, to compel the city to use police to prevent civilian assembly. The troops were on stand-by for two weeks, then moved by Miles to a neighboring encampment for autumn maneuvers which he called "very beneficial and much enjoyed."

Remington reflected the military viewpoint in "Chicago Under the Mob" (*Harper's Weekly,* July 21, 1894), "Chicago Under the Law" (*Harper's Weekly,* July 28, 1894), and "The Withdrawal of the U. S. Troops" (*Harper's Weekly,* August 11, 1894). To Remington, these are his old Saxon associates of the 7th Cavalry facing down Europe's "rinsins and lavins," the rinsings and leavings. "The Withdrawal" involved the assembly of the regulars in Fort Sheridan, a roundup of the scrappy fighters of the plains.

"The Affair of the –th of July" (*Harper's Weekly*, February 2, 1895, *Pony Tracks*) is Remington six months later rewriting the resolution of the Pullman strike in the manner that he on behalf of the military would have preferred. Remington's view was entirely compatible with General Miles's and President Cleveland's expressions in Miles's memoirs. "The Affair," as fiction, was printed in the same issue of *Harper's Weekly* as the news coverage of "The Strike in Brooklyn," where the lead illustration depicted an actual happening, "Firing at the Mob." The editorial position of *Harper's Weekly* was: "From the first the managers of the [Brooklyn] strike have acted as the enemies of the nation and of mankind."

As opposed to the free use of imagination in stories like "The Affair," when Remington was reporting he was quite factual. He was not, however, above shading the truth or deleting a complication to strike a mood.

The Beginning of "Stubble and Slough in Dakota" (*Harper's Monthly,* August 1894, *Pony Tracks*) presupposes the impromptu response of a free spirit to an unexpected invitation. In fact, Remington's October 30, 1893, letter to Harper indicates that his just completed trip to Dakota and Yellowstone, via Chicago, was an assignment. It was one where his rate of pay for writings was appropriate for a beginner rather than an author-illustrator with Remington's enormous following: "I do not at all understand what the basis of my pay is for work for your house. Stubble & Slough in Dakota was one article—gotten on a trip which I had talked with you about and said that three articles might be gotten out of—to which you consented—they to pass muster at your discretion. I only got two—that being one. For some 4000 words I get $50 and numerous drawings are made only two pages and not paid for at $125 a page. This I do not understand and did not expect."

For his Harper writings, Remington was still receiving a tyro's $12 a thousand words. According to Owen Wister's diary for 1893, *Harper's* started him at $12, then immediately raised him to $20, then $30, then $35, all before anything of importance had been written. Wister had the technique of bluffing *Harper's* into increasing its rates.

In the same diary, Wister related lunching on September 8, 1893, at Norris Basin in Yellowstone, and unexpectedly coming upon his idol, Remington, whom he had not previously met. Remington had just completed the expedition he reported on in "Policing the Yellowstone" (*Harper's Weekly,* January 12, 1895, *Pony Tracks*). Wister saw Remington was a 240-pound huge rollicking animal with quick and forcible artistic insight, politically compatible. Remington kept no diary then, but it would appear that he saw Wister as a gold mine of Western stories needing illustration. At that point he skipped the third story for *Harper's* and returned eastward by train with Wister. This began a long illustrator-writer relationship.

Remington also carried on elaborate correspondence with military officials, often providing requested advice on ordnance items, caps, canteens, and organization. For Secretary of War Daniel Lamont, for example, Remington was a bridge to junior officers. When "A New Infantry Equipment" (*Harper's Weekly,* September 22, 1894) was introduced, Remington was the acknowledged expert.

It is difficult to keep the chronology straight on the pieces being written and published at this time. In October 1893 *Harper's Weekly* bought "Policing the Yellowstone" but only printed the piece in January 1895. Similarly, "Coaching in Chihuahua" (*Harper's Weekly,* April 13, 1895), the sixth article produced by Remington from his February 1893 visit to Mexico, was written about January 1894.

The writing of "Winter Shooting on the Gulf Coast of Florida" (*Harper's Weekly,* May 11, 1895) is dated by letters Remington wrote to Wister. One letter from Jacksonville, Florida, at the end of January 1895 stated: "Old lady has 'grip' and we have been detained here until Thursday morning when we go to Punta Gorda—where the festive tarpon monkeys and the quail and jack snipe range."

The second letter, dated February 1, 1895, was from Punta Gorda, where he observed the scenes he reported in "Cracker Cowboys of Florida" (*Harper's Monthly,* August 1895, *Crooked Trails*): "Come down—deer—bear—tarpon—red snapper —ducks birds of paradise—curious cowboys who shot up the rail road trains."

In a third letter, about February 10, Remington continued on their mutual subject the cowboy: "There is a man down on this neck of land who owns 90 000 head of cattle—but that's another story."

For his model of "Cracker Cowboy," Remington is believed to have used Bone Mizell, an illiterate drinker who lisped. When asked by a judge how long it had been since his last drunk, Mizell lisped, "A momph." Pressed, he added, "Hang hit, jedge, I fought ever'body knowed what a momph is—hit's firty days." A top cow hunter, Mizell paid off his hands by withdrawing funds from an Arcadia bank against a blank check signed by his boss. His death certificate in 1921 read: "Moonshine—went to sleep and did not wake up." (The source is Smiley.)

In the spring of 1895, Remington was cajoling Wister into writing the essay "The Evolution of the Cow-puncher." Remington wanted the essay for *Harper's Monthly,* a more remunerative medium, but Wister appears to have seen conflict with "Cracker Cowboys." Remington as an evasion told Wister about June 1895 that "Cracker Cowboys" would be in the *Weekly,* confirmed this two weeks later, and then in July mentioned in passing: "My 'Cracker Cow Boys' went into the Magazine," the *Monthly.* Wister's essay appeared September 1895, one month after "Cracker Cowboys."

Remington had mentioned to Wister in the fall of the previous year that he was writing "Bicycle Infantry." This was "The Colonel of the First Cycle Infantry" (*Harper's Weekly,* May 18, 1895, *Pony Tracks*). It has been speculated that this originated from the Wister article on "The National Guard of Pennsylvania," but the same subject was being explored by the military on three continents. There was, for example, an article "Cyclist Infantry" in *Harper's Weekly,* February 11, 1893. The same issue as Wister's "Pennsylvania Guard" piece carried a Thulstrup illustration of the Japanese "Bicycle Corps." And Poultney Bigelow in an October 19, 1895, review of the German Grand Manœuvres concluded: "It is very doubtful if the U. S. army could use a 'Bike Brigade' to advantage." (The source on Wister is Vorpahl.)

In October 1894 Remington had been part of General Miles's entourage for "Bear-Chasing in the Rocky Mountains" (*Harper's Monthly,* July 1895, *Pony Tracks*). Other accounts of this incident can be found in General Miles's *Personal Recollections* and in Montague Stevens', the host, *Meet Mr. Grizzly.* There is also an undated letter of Remington's to Grandpa Sackrider: "Have been thinking of you—have just

come from a bear hunt in New Mexico— chased them with hounds, we on horseback. Great sport—got a silver-tip 700 lbs one black 300 lbs. Cow-boy caught the silver tip with the ropes—three of them & killed him with rocks and a knife. They had no guns.— I shot an antelope at 200 yards through the heart. Haven't had much fun this year—had to hustle for a living but you see Harpers and know about how I do it."

In his mid-November 1894 letter to Wister, Remington mentioned: "Stevens had a hell of a time killing off & running out thieves—Had 5000 in bank—to go to the man who killed the man who killed him."

Remington's respect for Stevens produced confusion over who would write "Bear-Chasing." Stevens' November 29, 1894, letter to Remington indicated he thought Remington wanted Wister to do the article. In early December 1894, Remington wrote Wister to invite him to a meeting with Stevens that never came off. About July 1895, Remington blithely wrote Wister: "Stevens thought (he misunderstood me) that you were to do the bear hunt—which I have written and which I can do much better than you because it was a lot of little things which happened and very little bear and you were not there anyway." Remington signed his letter "Frederic (O Bear)" in response to a coy note from Wister: "Why in h—— Oh Bear Don't you write to me." Remington then put a postscript to his letter: "Never use that 'O Bear' again—I have ended my bear article 'Oh Bear.'"

The last "Bear-Chasing" note was Miles's June 25, 1895, letter to Remington: "Your descriptive powers are certainly very good. I think you will in time develope as much skill with the pen as you have genius with the brush. There is a bright future for you if you will adhere to my council."

"A Cosmopolitan—Mr. Poultney Bigelow" (*Harper's Weekly,* July 20, 1895) is a model of an intimate biographical sketch. The same page of that issue continued with a sketch on Remington by Julian Ralph. In only eight years, Ralph pointed out, Remington had become "the most vigorous and busiest artist in America." He is an "uncommonly able writer, with "his Thackeray-like knack at portraying a character or a scene with a rollicking pencil." As "a war artist in peace," Remington "loves the American soldier." His "life-work" is "to leave a pictured record of the conquest of the country west of the Alleghanies."

The reference to Thackeray came from an undated letter, Remington to Ralph: "Am reading Thackery—that's the way to become great—read Thackery—Davis got great by doing it and so can you and I sonny." The books Remington inherited from his father included Thackeray's *Vanity Fair* (New York: Harper & Brothers, 1868), signed S. P. Remington inside the front cover (Hough collection).

Ralph did not mention the publication by *Harper's* that same week of Remington's first book, the anthology *Pony Tracks*. In January 1895 Remington had entered into the publishing agreement calling for the generous royalty of 10 per cent of retail price with escalations to 15 per cent for sales over three thousand copies. The dedication of the book is "to the fellows who rode the ponies that made the tracks." *Pony Tracks* reprints fifteen of the forty-two pieces described above, taking most but not all of the effective writing. The order of the articles' appearance in the book is not the same as the order in which they were published. Many illustrations are omitted or moved away from the relevant text.

Reviews quoted in *Harper's* advertisements were: "A series of vigorous graphic sketches of life on the great plains and upon the mountains" (Chicago *Inter-Ocean*). "This is a spicy account of real experiences among Indians and cowboys. No better illustrated book of frontier adventure has been published" (Boston *Journal*). "The pictures are better than the articles, and the articles are very good indeed, which is equivalent to saying that the pictures are remarkably fine" (Brooklyn *Times*).

Pony Tracks was published at $3.00. It was still in print for Christmas 1898, then priced at $1.75.

In Ralph's article on Remington, he as an intimate described Remington's studio without mentioning that in the summer of 1895, Remington was deeply involved in the modeling of his first and most famous bronze sculpture, the "Bronco Buster."

"With the Guns" (*Harper's Weekly,* August 17, 1895) is the beginning of a transitional period in which Remington's writing left the hard realist idiom. "Getting Hunters in Horse-Show Form" (*Harper's Weekly,* November 16, 1895) presents a Remington confident enough to portray himself as a horse, the animal he felt he knew the best. As a horse, he strains "the last nerve-cell."

And "Dear Nerve Cell" it is he addresses Wister in his early November 1895 letter that begins with a reference to Remington's second painting exhibition: " 'I open' as the theatrical folks say on Nov 14 and sell everything but 'the old lady' on the night of Nov 19. That *sale*—the bronze—magazines Horse Show pictures—a patent I am trying to engineer—a story (good one) which I *can't* write about canoeing (by the way I'm going to do that all over again with you to make copy) and several other things make life perfectly *Chineese coolie* to me."

This is typical of Remington's promises to Wister about relinquishing subjects. Remington exhorted Wister to write about American cowboys in genre situations which Remington illustrated. In return, Remington seldom wrote about the cowboys. On some military and outdoors subjects that Remington had originated, he promised to let Wister do the writing. In most instances, however, Remington had already written these pieces.

In comparison with painting or sculpting, writing was a chore for Remington, as it is for most writers. Remington said he wrote primarily because he felt he had to explain the milieu of his paintings. Inducing Wister to write about cowboys freed Remington from that task. It may even be that if Remington had considered Wister adequate to write competently about the army and the Indian as well as the cowboy, Remington would not have had to write at all.

The day after the November 19 auction sale, Theodore Roosevelt addressed Remington: "In your last Harpers article you used the adjective 'gangling'; where did you get it? It was a word of my childhood that I once used in a book myself, and everybody assured me it did not have any real existence beyond my imagination." Roosevelt did not keep Remington's response, but Roosevelt was correct that "gangling" would have been a colloquialism in 1895.

"A Practice March in Texas" (*Harper's Weekly*, January 4, 1896), "Squadron A's Games" (*Harper's Weekly*, March 28, 1896), and "A New Idea for Soldiers" (*Harper's Weekly*, May 2, 1896) represent Remington concentrating on the peacetime army at a low ebb in his life. As Remington wrote to Ralph April 6, 1896: "I am plugging away at my game—nothing is happening—we rather hope for a war with Spain. Bigelow is in Egypt, Davis in Moscow."

The canoe story, "The Strange Days That Came to Jimmie Friday" (*Harper's Monthly*, August 1896), was one that Remington had held out as a possible collaboration ostensibly to be rewritten by Wister. This was reprinted in both *Crooked Trails* and *Stories of Peace and War*.

One of Remington's Abwees was Edward H. Wales, a millowner and customer. Typical Remington promotional letters to Wales ran: "The expedition starts on Friday morning—no deadly weapons but 1 flask and your water color kit . . . a camera will be found useful in our business. —We are about to discover whether light blue fluid runs in your veins or lots of good red corpsiclues—and by God I have my doubts."

Careful reading of Remington's writings reveals many bits of autobiography, such as where he was in a prior year or who his companion was on an earlier trip. There also may be found the orgins of or inspiration for the titles for future paintings, as in "Jimmie Friday" there is the reference to "the howl of the weather" that became a famous *Collier's* print in 1907.

"Hasty-Intrenchment Drill" (*Harper's Weekly*, August 8, 1896) is Remington in the capacity of the military expert he had become, just as "Uprising of the Yaqui Indians" (*Harper's Weekly*, August 29, 1896) relies on Remington's experiences in and studies of northern Mexico.

In "The Blue Quail of the Cactus" (*Harper's Monthly*, October 1896, *Crooked Trails*), the "quartermaster" is Captain Jack Summerhayes. Mrs. Summerhayes wrote one of the very few reminiscences of Eva Remington who was "little Eva" who stood by Remington "through all the reverses of his early life" as "his guiding star." To Mrs. Summerhayes, Remington was a deep thinker who liked to solve all questions for himself. "And so we sat" during the delightful evenings after dinner in Remington's studio, "Frederic and Jack stretched out in their big leather chairs puffing away at their pipes and Eva with her needlework."

"How the Law Got into the Chaparral" (*Harper's Monthly*, December 1896) is the lead story in Remington's second anthology, *Crooked Trails*.

Remington's late February 1896 letter to Wister was along the usual light lines: "Just back from Texas & Mexico—got an article —good illustrations but I tumble down on the text—its a narrative of the Texas Rangers—I call it 'How the law got into the chaparral.' May have to ask you to bisect, cross-cut—spay alter, eliminate, quarter & have dreams over it and sign it with the immortal sig of he who wrote 'Where Francy was bred'—had a good time—painted— shot—loafed—quit drinking on Feb 1 for ever and got some ideas."

Remington no more turned "How the Law" over to Wister than he quit drinking. (The sources are White, Card papers, and Summerhayes.)

"Vagabonding with the Tenth Horse" (*Cosmopolitan*, February 1897) is Remington in a new publication for his writings. This precluded the piece from having been republished in one of his anthologies because all were brought out by Harper and drawn only from Harper periodicals.

"Vagabonding" also proffers morsels of collateral value. It gives, for example, still another slant at Remington's 1881 fortune-hunting trip to Montana by referring to his fascination then with riding over the high plains. It also repeats the 1888 statement of Remington's unexpected admiration for the black soldier, a change from his 1886 expressions when blacks were one of the many groups Remington ran down. And "Vagabonding" notes the unusual usage of a bicycle corps on the high plains.

"The Soledad Girls" (*Harper's Round Table,* May 4, 1897, *Crooked Trails*) was from the "Blue Quail" trip with Captain Summerhayes. It earned the unique credit line of "Fred" Remington. Fred is what Remington was called, but his writing credits were as Frederic.

The girls described in the article were young. Their age did not qualify them as women, so that Remington was free to portray them as attractive and feminine. Part of the masculine mystique Remington affected was that he simply could not draw a woman, that even his wife considered leaving him after she had posed for him. Remington felt threatened by relationships with women other than his wife, but not apparently by young girls. He called his wife "Kid."

"A Sergeant of the Orphan Troop" (*Harper's Monthly,* August 1897, *Crooked Trails*) introduces the compassionate soldier. The story involves the Northern Cheyenne Indians, who were defeated in 1876 and sent by the Indian Bureau to live with the Southern Cheyenne. Dying and unwanted there, they began an open and generally peaceful trek north. When they refused to return to the Southern Cheyenne, they were starved and then in 1879 slaughtered by United States troops in a manner finally considered "outrageous" by the heroic protagonist, Carter Johnson.

Remington refers to the Northern Cheyenne as brave in action and bushwhacked in consequence. Previous heroes like Lieutenant Casey had been understanding of particular Indian groups, but in "Orphan Troop" Carter Johnson verges on disobedience in reaction to "these poor people" and their wounded squaws. Remington still speaks from the soldier's position, not the Indian's, in describing this twenty-year-old episode.

Johnson wrote Remington July 27, 1897: "I have just read your Orphan Troop and you have certainly given a wonderfully accurate description of that affair. Your illustrations are very true to life. I must admit that I am delighted with your description, and my vanity is more than satisfied. In reading the story and looking at the illustrations I was carried back many years, and the whole affair appeared before my eyes in the most vivid manner. I have actually read the story three times in the last 24 hours. Alas for human vanity—Poor mortal man —even the best can be greatly spoiled by the pen and pictures of you cunning fellows."

Remington sent the letter along to *Harper's:* "Please return this letter—its from my hero in last story."

It has been claimed that Remington received letters from and had photographs of Sun-Down Leflare, the interpreter in "The Great Medicine-Horse: An Indian Myth of the Thunder" (*Harper's Monthly,* September 1897, *Sundown Leflare*). The point of the claim is that Remington's fiction sprang from some sort of reality.

Leflare was the subject of five Remington stories assembled into the unhyphenated Harper book *Sundown Leflare*. We have here retained the original hyphen used in *Harper's Monthly,* for a variety of reasons: First, Sun-Down is visually in keeping with the character. Sundown is eastern and modern. A sundowner was a British drink. Second, we have throughout retained the stylings in the first publication of a piece. Third, the thought that changes made in republication would have been improvements does not generally apply to Remington. He customarily accepted revisions where made by persons he considered authorities in a field not his. Fourth, these re-edited changes are sometimes obvious typographical errors. In "Orphan Troop," for example, "the little column . . . drew rein" became "reign."

And finally, if Sun-Down had been a real person, it would have been as the original hyphenate. That was how Remington identified him, although letters to Harper and to Wales provide a third choice, "Sun Down"—two words, no hyphen.

Sun-Down is an instance of a character taking hold of his author. Launched as just an interpreter for the chief Remington names "old Paint," Sun-Down becomes central to four more 1898 stories. As Remington wrote Bigelow August 9, 1897: "Europe is all right for most everybody but me—I am going to do America—its new—its to my taste. I am writing short stories—got a hummer in the next Harper magazine—dialect, by G-D, and that will give Alden a hemorage unless its a top roper." Alden was an editor of *Harper's Monthly*.

"Joshua Goodenough's Old Letter" (*Harper's Monthly,* November 1897) appears to have been one of Remington's favorite pieces in that it was reprinted in paper wraps in 1897 as *A Rogers Ranger in the French and Indian War, 1757–1759* (Remington's second book), again in 1898 in *Crooked Trails,* and again in 1899 in *Stories of Peace and War.* The research for "Joshua Goodenough" would have been considerable, and there was no expert criticism of Remington's historical detail such as arose eight years later concerning the "Great Explorers" series in *Collier's.*

For "Massai's Crooked Trail" (*Harper's Monthly,* January 1898, *Crooked Trails*), the then Assistant Secretary of the Navy, Theodore Roosevelt, wrote his December 28, 1897, letter of praise: "Are you aware, O sea-going plainsman, that aside from what you do with the pencil, you come closer to the real thing with the pen than any other man in the western business? And I include Hough, Grinnell and Wister. Your articles have been a growing surprise. I don't know how you do it, any more than I know how Kipling does it; but somehow you get close not only to the plainsman and soldier, but to the half-breed and Indian, in the same way Kipling does to the British

Tommy and the Gloucester codfisher. Without stopping your work with the pencil, I do hope you will devote more and more time to the pen."

Roosevelt said that Remington's stories and sketches will "live and will make the cantos in the last Epic of the Western Wildernesses before it ceased being a wilderness." Roosevelt's reference to "sea-going" related to the steady pressure to involve Remington in painting and writing about the navy in addition to the army.

Massai's biography up to the point of the story is as Remington gave it. A real Chiricahua Apache, his name was also given as Masai, Ma-si, Matse, and Masse. After escaping from the Geronimo train near Springfield, Missouri, in 1886, he reappeared in Arizona a year later without having been seen in the intervening twelve hundred miles. It is said that Massai was killed in Mexico, although General Miles claimed that credit for United States troops. (The sources are Monahan and Miles.)

"An Interesting Detail" (*Harper's Weekly,* January 8, 1898) is Remington's memory of the events of the Indian Wars triggered by current news. Fort Ringgold was on the river at Rio Grande City, Texas. The climate was so hot that cotton uniforms were worn all year. The reference to India-silk pajamas would be to the fabric then called pongee, used in semitropical areas. The duty assigned to Lieutenant Preston "to Alaska in charge of all the pack-trains of the army" would more likely have been the personal charge of one command of pack trains in the Klondike. (The source is a letter from Henry B. Davis, jr.)

"Interesting Detail," written from the standpoint of the cavalry, was followed by "The Curse of the Wolves" (*Collier's,* January 27, 1898), written from the standpoint of the stockmen. "The Curse of the Wolves" is the first of the *Collier's* pieces through which Remington later became one of the highest paid American illustrators.

"The Essentials at Fort Adobe" (*Harper's Monthly,* April 1898, *Crooked Trails*) is the Western cavalry in its peacetime training simulations, its activity more civilized but not necessarily more sensible than the Indian who at the opening of the article is sunning himself while dreaming of the past.

"The Training of Cavalry" (*Harper's Weekly,* April 2, 1898) is "A Model Squadron," revisited at Fort Myer after four years. This time the troopers are performing their equestrian circus to demonstrate their readiness for the coming war, absolutely unaware of the extent to which they had become bright vestiges.

The second of the Sun-Down Leflare stories is "How Order No. 6 Went Through" (*Harper's Monthly,* May 1898, *Sundown Leflare*). The format is the favorite Remington device of a character reminiscing about the old days. This is the point of Remington's need to write, to record in words as well as pictures and bronzes the West that was his stock in trade, even though he had personally experienced it as such a brief flash. In early 1898 the frontier West was already passed over.

At no time, though, did Remington forget that literature and art were his vocation, his means of earning the expanding sums required by his standard of living. Even his friends and fellow Abwees fed the Remington pot, as he wrote in the undated letter: "My dear Wales. I have the picture back of the 'starving' of Sun Down Leflare which you said you wanted. Do you want it at $100."

"The War Dreams" (*Harper's Weekly,* May 7, 1898) is Remington on a totally new tack, the Spanish-American War. Augustus Thomas recollected that Remington had from childhood adored the memory of his father in a cavalry uniform. When Remington wrote to his uncle from Highland Military Academy in 1878, he promised: "There is just one obstruction between me and prosperity, that is, if Uncle Sam ever gets into any delicate controversy I will leave my bones where thousands of patriotic Americans have deposited theirs within the past fifteen years."

Remington's letters to his friends in the mid-1890s are obsessed with the coming war. He wrote Wister the beginning of November 1895: "I think I smell *war* in the air." Again to Wister in April 1896: "I expect you will see a big war with Spain over here and will want to come back—and see some more friends die. *Cuba libre* It does seem tough that so many Americans had had to be and have still got to be killed to free a lot of d—— niggers who are better off under the yoke. There is something Fatefull in our destiny that way. This time however we will kill a few Spaniards instead of Anglo Saxons which will be proper and nice."

In December 1896 Remington had been sent with Richard Harding Davis as an artist correspondent on William Randolph Hearst's yacht *Vamoose* to report on the Cuban insurgents for Hearst's newspaper the New York *Journal*. Remington wrote to his wife from Key West: "Xmas. Dear Kid. Vamoose is now being painted grey—it is blowing hard and we may not go before tomorrow night. See Chicago banks are unsafe—watch out and if you think New York gets weak check out most of our money."

When the weather blocked *Vamoose* from delivering the correspondents to the insurgents, Davis and Remington on January 9, 1897, embarked for Havana on a commercial passenger ship. By January 24 Remington wired Hearst: "There will be no war. I wish to return." The reply Hearst may have made was: "You furnish the pictures and I'll furnish the war." (The source is Lundberg.)

Remington returned anyhow, and wrote to Ralph January 26, 1897: "I am a yellow Kid Journalist as you may see. I have been in Cuba for them. I have fallen—I now compete for preferment with Anna Held and other ladies. Oh God Julian why did this cup come to us. How does the artist boy progress."

Then, after the incident of the sinking of the *Maine* in February 1898, the Spanish-American War was declared.

In the period of inactivity for the invading army in Tampa, "The War Dreams" provided a prophetic note. Two of the dreams are nightmares, two are jokes, and the fifth is a variation of "men must fight and women must weep."

The next week Remington was on the battleship *Iowa* for a (to him) boring patrol of Havana harbor. His report was "Wigwags from the Blockade" (*Harper's Weekly*, May 14, 1898, *Men with the Bark On*), reprinted in book form as "The Bowels of a Battle-ship." A week at sea made Remington yearn for the army, "to talk the language of my tribe." And it should be parenthetically noted here that the Victorian reference "in a sort of Sam Weller writing" is to Thomas Onwhyn, called Peter Palette or Samuel Weller, the English illustrator, caricaturist, and engraver who died in London in 1886.

"Soldiers Who Cry" (*Harper's Weekly*, May 21, 1898) is an anecdote.

The "simulated spellings" in "The Spirit of Mahongui" (*Harper's Monthly*, June 1898, *Crooked Trails*) is Remington taking "Joshua Goodenough" back another hundred years. This is an extract, so called, that appears incomplete, in an experimental form not repeated.

"Mahongui" is the last of the pieces reprinted in Remington's third book, the anthology *Crooked Trails* published by *Harper's* in 1898 at $2.00 with the comment: "There are one or two departures in the present volume from Mr. Remington's accustomed haunts—departures which led him into the storied past; but in them he remains as virile and as convincing as we have been accustomed to find him in more familiar scenes."

The Chicago *Dial* review was: "All in all, Mr. Remington's book is a delightful one. . . . The volume is a comely one, and it will make a tempting gift-book when the Holiday season comes."

All of *Crooked Trails* was written after the demise of the Indian-fighting army. There are ten pieces, five historical, two outdoors, two travel, and "Fort Adobe" about the peacetime cavalry.

The fourth Remington book was published in January 1890 as *Sundown Leflare*.

It included "Medicine Horse" and "Order No. 6," then continued with "Sun-Down Leflare's Money" (*Harper's Monthly*, July 1898), which is Sun-Down in 1897 reminiscing about 1880. "Sun-Down Leflare's Warm Spot" (*Harper's Monthly*, September 1898) has the fifty-five-to-sixty-year-old Sun-Down telling a story of 1877. The mature Remington confesses here that the "chug-a-chug, chug-a-chug of the ponies began to bore," although such riding on the high plains was "fascinating" only a year earlier in "Vagabonding." "Sun-Down's Higher Self" (*Harper's Monthly*, November 1898) is a story of 1880. The book editor transposed "Money" and "Warm Spot" to correct the chronology.

The stories had been written by March 1898, the date Remington entered into his usual royalty agreement with Harper & Brothers. When the book was published, it was not widely reviewed or noticed or sold. A reason given is that it purported to be a novel, whereas it is an anthology of loosely related Sun-Down stories.

The real cause of the lack of success of this warm bit of local color puzzled Remington, as is implicit in his convolute February 3, 1899, letter to J. Henry Harper: "In reply to your answer to suggestion that 'Sun Down Leflare' be put on book-stands—the thing occurred to me that it should be found there when I suggested the form of its publication and its price $1.25—and now friends ask me why they do not find it there etc not having time to go to the big book stores etc. Of course, I know nothing of trade conditions and may overestimate my own book etc though I should like to understand why my book is not available for the popular exposure in order that I may not in the future try to do something in a line which does not seem successful."

By 1907, when Remington listed his books in an interview with Perriton Maxwell, *Sundown Leflare* was one he omitted.

Another reason for the failure of *Sundown Leflare* may have been that it was issued so soon after the Spanish-American War. In the time between the writing of the Sun-Down stories and their reprinting,

Remington had been primarily involved in covering the war. He landed in Cuba June 22, bivouacked on the invasion with the Sixth Cavalry, and wrote his wife June 29, 1898: "We are about five miles from Santiago and except the fight which the cavalry brigade had the other day the Spanish have not opposed us—everything is quiet. The first night ashore it rained and I slept all night wet.—I stayed with the 6th but found they did not move forward so I started. I have an awful cold—& cant get over it.— The country is healthy and few men are sick. If I could get my hammock some cigars and a quart of whiskey I would be it. But I am seeing all the actualities of campaigning."

Immediately thereafter, Remington was with the correspondents on the spot July 1 for the El Caney attack, to see true "campaigning." He became exposed to Spanish sharpshooters, and then was emotionally stunned by "men dead, and men dying," by what was later described in the editorial "The Horrors of Our War" (*Harper's Weekly,* September 10, 1898): "Without proper clothing or proper food for the tropics, the troops were rushed into Cuba, under a commander incompetent to do what might have been done to remedy the evils, and, after a free fight against a weak enemy, Santiago was taken, and disease and famine entered."

Following San Juan Hill, Remington was invalided home, the victim of the same fever that precipitated "Bring the Fifth Corps North" (*Harper's Weekly,* August 13, 1898). In this article Remington was emphasizing Colonel Roosevelt's letter as it was reported August 3: "If we are kept here [in Cuba] it will, in all human probability, mean an appalling disaster, for the surgeons here estimate that over half the army, if kept here during the sickly season, will die."

"Colonel Roosevelt's Pride" (*Harper's Weekly,* August 27, 1898) also played the Roosevelt tune, as "Take the Army out of Politics" (*Harper's Weekly,* October 15, 1898) echoed General Miles.

Soon after his return from Cuba, Remington wrote the undated letter: "My dear Mr. Harper—I will undertake an article on my personal observations on the war, and will do it as soon as I can." The result was "With the Fifth Corps" (*Harper's Monthly,* November 1898, *Men with the Bark On*). The worst this article was called was "a small masterpiece."

Even Emerson Hough, who had little good to say about Remington, declared: "At the time of our opera-bouffe war with Spain, when all the country was palpitating with high-geared war stories, the best war story written was by Frederic Remington." C. C. Buel of *Century* wrote October 28, 1898: "I have just finished your experience With the Fifth Corps and I want to thank you for leaving your fellows of the quill so far behind. A well-conducted artist in the field should subordinate himself to the professional word-painters, while travelling in their company. But here you are making the best pictures of the Santiago Campaign, and on top of that outdoing everybody with a description of the scenes and the emotions of that memorable advance to San Juan."

Geo. E. Morris of The Players club wrote November 3, 1898: "I dont want to swell your head but really it is exactly what every body has always wanted and never gotten until now. & if you had never done anything else it ought to make you famous." H. C. DuVal of the Grand Central Depot wrote the same day: "It has received more attention, gone deeper than all the stuff written by all the bunch of other writers put together. The Brooklyn Barnard Club is composed of ladies and gentlemen residing on Brooklyn Heights interested in art and literature. Perhaps you would not mind giving a little talk."

The year 1898 thus ended for Remington with a torrent of books, articles, illustrations, paintings, sculptures, and campaigns having been realized. Hamlin Garland, the novelist, recalled Christmas 1898 at The Players: "Frederic Remington was at the club in one of his most cantankerous moods. 'You mustn't criticize the army in its relation to the Indians—military men best friends of Indian.' He is never fluent at his best, and on this occasion he was trucu-

lent and hesitant. I don't like him or his illustrations. His red men and trappers are all
drawn from one model. I admire certain aspects of his work. He is a man of power but
has very little poetry in his writing or illustrations. I don't see how he does so much
work."

When Wister and Remington had by
1902 diverged in their views of the Indian,
Garland was as far to the "Indian is
Beauty" side of Remington as Wister's
"Good Indian is Dead Indian" was to the
other.

The impact of the Santiago campaign on
Remington was apparent. The volume of his
work decreased. As a painter, he reflected
Impressionism and favored nocturnes. As a
writer, he spiritually joined with the Indians
in the equivalent of feeling his medicine and
he sensed their aura. As a man, he became
moody again, in spells, and foresaw his end.
And withal, his popular success was enormous.

"The White Forest" (*Harper's Monthly*,
December 1898, *Men with the Bark On*)
presages the change. (The piece was written the previous winter.) This is a happy
Remington testing himself against "the winter forest" that "means death," realizing that
a wayside pup would hate being laughed at,
and failing to kill a caribou in his sights.

After having been a tourist in Havana in
1891, an artist in Havana unable to reach
the Insurgents in 1897, and a war correspondent for the Santiago campaign in
1898, Remington's fourth Cuban trip was in
1899 to report on the military occupation
for *Collier's Weekly.* "Havana Under Our
Regulars" (*Collier's*, April 1, 1899) is a
mellow Remington who describes dark-
brown and white and yellow Cuban soldiers
in terms of, "When we stop to think of the
thing beneath the skin." "Under Which
King?" (*Collier's*, April 8, 1899) is a
relaxed view that saves its message for the
end—occupation should be controlled by
the military not the "sentimentalist" civilian.

"Cuban Bandits in Santiago Province"
(*Collier's*, April 22, 1899) is a Remington
primer on how to fight against a guerrilla

force in a hostile territory. The statement of
the problem is contemporary; the solution is
based on General Miles's pursuit of Geronimo.

Set in the Yellowstone in the 1880s, "A
Sketch by MacNeil" (*Harper's Monthly*,
May 1899, *Men with the Bark On*) is again
an odd note. When the old scout is evalu-
ated, it is his unthinking bravery that now
makes him less a person: "The influence of
even fear is good on men. It makes them
reflective, and takes them out of the present." The younger listeners elicit Mac's leg-
slapper that has him starved and frostbitten
in a venture with what he considers a
"funny bunch" of Crows, but the men are
not admiring the "pure old warrior."
Rather, they "were laughing at MacNeil,
not with him."

Remington before Santiago had a weakness as a storyteller. When the Indians
swooped down on the army wagon, no matter how desperate the circumstance, the
young soldier was bound to survive. When
he returned from Cuba, he began to change
in mood and spirit. "The White Forest" had
hinted of death. "The Story of the Dry
Leaves" (*Harper's Monthly*, June 1899,
Men with the Bark On) kills, not in war,
but through starvation, not men flaunting
danger, but a newborn infant and then its
mother.

Even stranger, this tragic ending follows
Remington's first romantic love scene, where
"The blood surged and bounded through
his veins—he was hungry for her, like a
famished tiger which stalks a gazelle." Remington's lovers are not two gazelles who rub
noses.

Death continues in "The Honor of the
Troop" (*Harper's Monthly*, July 1899, *Men
with the Bark On*). The traducer of "The
Honor" of L Troop is hung. This simplistic
story could have been written ten years before: The murdered man is a "greaser."

"How the Horses Died" (*Harper's
Weekly*, July 15, 1899) is the reprise of a
little section of "With the Fifth Corps."
"Sorrows of Don Tomas Pidal, Reconcentrado" (*Harper's Monthly*, August 1899,

Men with the Bark On) is the death of a Cuban family in a Spanish concentration camp.

As Remington told Julian Ralph in a letter the middle of June 1900: "I am sorry for your generally ruined condition but I believe that mostly befals warriors—I didn't get over Santiago for a year and I dont want any more." Howard Pyle in his March 29, 1899, letter to Remington was sensitive to Remington's unease: "I received your letter the other day and read it with no small amusement. At the same time there was an under current of something else than jocularity that caused me a feeling of real discomfort—a feeling that somehow you were not happy."

By September 1, 1899, though, Remington had come to his resolve, as he wrote to Wister: "Just back from two months in Montana and Wyoming—had a good time—as Miss Columbia said to Uncle Sam *'That was my war'*—that old cleaning up of the West—that is the war I am going to put in the rest of my time at."

Remington's primary involvement was with the cavalry and the Indian. For that reason, the writer Emerson Hough deprecated Remington as the eastern progenitor of the Wild West school. Remington, though, was not only a railroad-transported visitor to the West. He was a serious student. In his 1909 response to Mrs. Glentworth Butler, he wrote: "Andy Adams is the historian of the cattle trail." In the course of this long letter on ranching, he began: "It is a good deal as though you suddenly asked the Dr. 'now tell me all about medicine.'" "Life in the Cattle Country" (*Collier's,* August 26, 1899) is the serious essay on ranching that Remington could have referred Mrs. Butler to. Oddly enough, the interior illustrations were photographs.

"When a Document Is Official" (*Harper's Monthly,* September 1899, *Men with the Bark On*) describes a cavalryman's death where Remington offers a message that is new. After Remington's experiences in Santiago, his reader cannot assume that an official assignment in the hands of a brave and experienced man will be completed. When the cavalryman is distracted by a forthcoming promotion so that he incurs the hostility of buffalo hunters who side with the Indians, he lets down his guard. The heroic act that discloses his position to the Indians causes his death. To the Indian observer, he is a "dam fool." In 1891, though, Remington had eulogized the careless Casey: "Where one like Casey goes down there are many places where Sorrow will spread her dusky pinions and the light grow dim."

In October 1899 Harper & Brothers published Remington's fifth book, the odd little anthology *Stories of Peace and War.* It contained "Chasing a Major-General," published originally in December 1890, "The Strange Days that Came to Jimmie Friday, from August 1896, and "Joshua Goodenough's Old Letter," from November 1897. The book is distinguished by Remington's given name having been printed on the cover as Frederick. This was a misspelling that accompanied Remington all his life, and amazingly, he never let on that it bothered him. To Remington, though, his Frederic was Saxon and desirable, while Frederick was German.

"The Trouble Brothers: Bill and the Wolf" (*Harper's Monthly,* November 1899, *Men with the Bark On*) has no such complexity as "When a Document."

When Remington wrote about events he had not witnessed, he either relied on observers or did his homework. In "How Stilwell Sold Out" (*Collier's,* December 16, 1899), Remington did both. He had begun researching Forsyth's 1868 fight on the Republican River for the painting in his 1897 book *Drawings.* He had an elaborate exchange of correspondence with Forsyth, who provided maps, personal photos, and complete data: "By the way give Roman Nose a war bonnet—one that trailed from his head floating well to the rear and almost sweeping the ground. It must have been nearly or quite seven feet in length."

Forsyth also referred Remington to the

article "A Frontier Fight" in *Harper's Monthly,* June 1895, where Forsyth described "Pierre Truedeau, an old and experienced trapper, and a young fellow named Jack Stillwell, a handsome boy of about nineteen, with all the pluck and enthusiasm of an American frontier lad. A little after midnight he and Truedeau stole out quietly, walking backward in their stocking feet, and carrying their boots slung around their necks, that the impress of their feet in the sand might make a similar mark to that of a moccasin, and deceive the Indians, should they discover the sign." The Forsyth article had been illustrated by Zogbaum, Remington's only rival on the subject of the Indian-fighting army.

"A Failure of Justice" (*Harper's Monthly,* January 1900, *Men with the Bark On*) is a Remington romance with typically understated Western emotions expressed by prosaic protagonists.

"Mountain Lions in Yellowstone Park" (*Collier's,* March 17, 1900) is a far cry from "Bear-Chasing" in July 1895 where Remington bragged about the kill for *Harper's.* For *Collier's,* Remington is a conservationist.

Men with the Bark On was Remington's sixth book, an anthology published in 1900. It was advertised by Harper & Brothers as "Stories of the West and of Cuban Experiences," one of "The Best Books for Summer Reading." A modern criticism of the book would be that Remington's Indians and soldiers have become the victims of civilization, where helplessness replaces heroism. An example of the reason for this view is "They Bore a Hand" (*Harper's Monthly,* April 1900, *Men with the Bark On*), featuring "The Death of Oestreicher."

The origin of the title *Men with the Bark On* is hinted at in an exchange of letters between Remington and Harper. Remington wrote Harper December 28, 1899: "In re— to the book Men with the Bark On—I would add all the stories I have done up to date. The stories have no connection and will be in harmony."

Harper's questioning the title is implicit in

Remington's second letter: "I got the idea that the title was 'The Men with the Bark' because it was so written in the proofs which you are sending me to look over. What is the cover to look like and do you want to send me a contract." In Remington's third letter, January 19, 1900, he completes the matter: "The cover is all right— couldn't be better.—Also—please put the following where the dedication is usually placed/'Men with the bark on die/like the wild animals, un-/naturally—unmourned and even/unthought of mostly.'"

In *Western Words* "bark" is defined as "an old trapper's word meaning *to scalp.*" This would make *Men with the Bark On* the equivalent of "men with the hair on," the mountain men—perhaps a little different in meaning from Remington's dedication.

That is how "men with the bark on" appears to have grown as a phrase, from Remington's January 29, 1893, letter to Bigelow, to a reference in "When a Document," to a title, and then to a dedication. *Pony Tracks* had been dedicated to the "fellows," who would have been the punchers on the ponies. *Crooked Trails* were made by broncho Indians.

Men with the Bark On was the end of Remington's long relationship with the House of Harper. He wrote to Wister in October 1900: "As to Harpers—they are hard up and employ cheap men. Also Harpers wants new men. New and cheap let you out along with all the other old men. They dropped me out of the window over a year ago but I find a way to get printed."

Remington's primary "way" became *Collier's.* The relationship which began in 1898 produced works of importance by 1901. "A Gallant American Officer" (*Collier's,* April 7, 1900) was in the interim.

Remington also wrote for other publications. "A Shotgun Episode" (*Outing,* May 1900) was Remington's recollection of a hunt in 1896 when Captain Jack Summerhayes described an experience he had had in 1877. Remington had offered this story idea to Wister in his usual effort to promote Wister articles that would require illustrations: "Story told me by Army officer—Nevada—old Winnamucka going to break out—heard of job from friendly indian to murder him next day at ration issue —Capt. Summerhays rode with contract doctor in early morning right into old Winnie's camp—jumped right into wickeup— pulled down shot gun on Winnie-mucka— cowed old Winnemucka and no row—talk about your Mulligan Guards how can you beat that for desperate sand."

Like most of Remington's letters, this was undated. Wister's biographers see use of the facts in Wister's 1894 piece "The General's Bluff." In any event, Remington did get to illustrate both pieces, Wister's and his own. (The source is Vorpahl.)

Remington enjoyed the theater. His friends included actors like Joe Jefferson, Richard Mansfield, Otis Skinner, and his neighbor in New Rochelle, Francis Wilson. The reference to Mulligan Guards is explained in *Francis Wilson's Life of Himself* as of one of the old "Mulligan" series of plays with Ned Harrigan and Tony Hart. The series was a mix of farce and melodrama.

Remington's circle of correspondents was huge, too, and included many of the most celebrated painters, sculptors, writers, critics, military officers, politicians, bankers, and industrialists, as well as neighbors and relatives. Edward Kemeys, who was the one sculptor even Emerson Hough accepted as accurately Western, wrote: "After reading your 'Shotgun episode,' I felt it incumbent upon me to tell you how much I enjoyed it. You have handled Western slang in the most masterly manner. It is the most natural and unreserved 'bit' that I can remember, and I laughed until helpless when I read it."

"How a Trout Broke a Friendship" (*Outing,* September 1900) offers Remington as an outdoors humorist. Joel is Joel Burdick, the passenger traffic manager of the Delaware & Hudson Railroad, whose Albany office was the starting point for many Remington expeditions to the Adirondacks and Canada.

When Wister's volume of Western stories available for illustration seemed to dry up, Remington wrote to Wister in August 1900 praising a Grant biography that did not sell. As an inducement for Wister to get back to Westerns, Remington added: "Am never going to write any more—I have spread myself out too thin—I am going to begin to do the armadillo act."

Shortly thereafter, Remington wrote to his wife October 29, 1900, from Ignacio, Colorado: "I have 1 hide dresser—1 lance —1 beaded belt—1 Ute baby basket very fine—some cliffdweller pottery and expect to get more. Indian stuff simply cant be bought. The dealers lodge orders for all Indian stuff at any old price with post traders. I could get a great deal of money for my collection. I hope for some stories—I have only one so far but I have some good illustrations."

Again November 4, 1900: "Went over to Piedras—30 miles in wagon—Too cold to sketch. Came back here—have 10 color studies now—& two or three stories. The Utes are to far on the road to civilization to be distinctive."

"Natchez's Pass" (*Harper's Monthly,* February 1901) would have been an earlier purchase by *Harper's* rather than the result of Remington's Ignacio trip. The description of Marshall East as "a well-looking man, educated, and resourceful" elicited a February 2, 1901, letter from Edward Simmons, a member of The Ten Impressionist painters: "I have just read last night your 'Natchez Pass.' Damned good tale! How well & graphically told! And how damned good the two illustrations! At any age after calf-time it is dangerous to go on doing the same thing! So many fall by the way, but how you hold up your end! By-the bye—if with your mastery of clear cut 'American' language you ever say 'well-looking' again —so as to be pretty I'll make you less 'good looking' with a club! How many wells in a river of pedantry."

Every professional writer must have ended with some pieces that were unpublished. Remington had several he offered without success to various periodicals. His undated letter to Alden of *Harper's* read: "Well—here is the article on 'Taos' which McClure didnt take. I hope you will once it over." Judging by the story quality, it is likely that "Billy's Tearless Woe" (*McClure's Magazine,* March 1901) would have been rejected by *Harper's.*

Collier's on the other hand began to get its money's worth from Remington with "How the Worm Turned" (*Collier's,* May 4, 1901). The event described was real. Black troopers of Company D, Tenth Cavalry rode from Fort Concho into the town of San Angelo in 1878. Again in 1917, blacks of the 24th Infantry shot it out with whites in Houston. (The source is Katz.)

When Remington was visiting in Canton the summer of 1901, he admired a large black bearskin rug on a friend's floor. After receiving the skin as a present, he reciprocated by sending the original painting of the Worm Turning. This is typical of Remington's generosity with his work, although he usually related the subject to the recipient more appropriately. (The source is Manley.)

Remington's relationships with his editors at *Harper's* had been cool, sometimes cold. His May 1894 letter to Wister complained that "the duplicity of Harpers is very confusing." The August 10, 1894, letter was more pointed: "How much better red-blooded soldiers are than little stinking library upholstery such as Martin of Harpers is."

With *Collier's,* though, Remington found as editor his fellow artist George Wharton Edwards, who wrote in connection with "How the Worm Turned": "My dear Fred —No! do not print in the title—make a pen and ink heading (picture) to occupy the space. I'll put the title in type—*This* is *no* parody, but tis good advice! Be bold good Remington, and never fear/The carping critics or their pens severe!/Your art is young, the best is yet to be,/What is to come not even they foresee."

Remington's editor at *Century* in 1901 was another friend, the poet Robert Underwood Johnson, whose autobiography recalled: "Frederic Remington, the distinguished illustrator and sculptor, also possessed marked ability as a writer. Besides being an engaging companion, with an inexhaustible fund of adventure and anecdote, the delineator of the 'Bucking Broncho' had a remarkable faculty of visualizing his experiences in his verbal descriptions."

The title "A Desert Romance" (*Century,* February 1902) was negotiated. Johnson's October 12, 1901, letter to Remington asked: "Can you not give us a better title for your story, 'Ochoa Waters,' a title which will not attract a single reader. We want to get the *Southwest* in it somehow, though perhaps that could go into a sub-title, but we are sure you can do better than the title it now bears."

Remington wrote at the bottom: "I like 'Ochoa Waters' but you might call it 'A Desert Romance'—'The Romance of Ochoa Waters' or 'The Wooing of' giving her name which I can't remember. 'A Rough Wooing' 'A Old Tale of the South West' 'A wooing on horse-back'—Oh call it anything which suits your fancy."

Johnson wrote at the top: "Miss Bliss/ Make it A Desert Romance/A Tale of the Southwest."

In general, Remington's titles were catchy, like "The Strategy of the Blanket Pony" (*Collier's,* February 1, 1902). More prosaic was "Western Types" (*Scribner's Magazine,* October 1902) which consisted of captions for four full-page full-color illustrations. The pen decorations were not by Remington but by Will Crawford.

About 1901, according to Martha Summerhayes, "Remington was going to try his hand at a novel, a real romance. We talked a good deal about the little Indian boy, and I got to love White Weasel long before he appeared in print as John Ermine." The ermine is of course the white weasel that was John Ermine's Indian name.

In June 1902, when Remington wrote Wister from Ingleneuk that "the relaxation has come," Remington was really ready to start on what he considered his major story to that point, the novel *John Ermine of the Yellowstone* (Macmillan, 1902).

In the same letter to Wister, Remington's last sentence was: "The Kid says 'Virginian' out—will order a copy." This was of course a put-down of the Wister novel that issued in April 1902 and by June had been reprinted twice. It was reprinted, for example, four times in July, three times in August, and twice each in September, November, and December 1902, and so on. Remington would surely have read *The Virginian*. He would have considered it an inaccurate depiction of a cowboy's experience, and, if asked, would have repeated the criticism he gave Wister on another story in June 1895: It "is all right—I would make *more scenes* and less essay—if you can see your way to do it." Action is character.

Remington's life style while writing *John Ermine* was recounted by Edwin Wildman: "Remington is big, but he is a bundle of nervous energy that gives him the liveliness of a boy of ten. At Inglenook he was up by six o'clock and at work in his studio at eight. He works rapidly and permits nothing to interfere. Remington's play is taking to the water five times a day, a couple of hours at tennis, and common hospitality of cigar, nip, and heap talk. Remington wrote a book, a story of life of the plains in '76. I read several chapters. 'Come down here; I want to speak to you,' Remington called, one day. 'I've coined two words today. . . . T-h-e E-n-d!' "

The beginning of October 1902, Remington wrote Wister: "My little old story comes out soon but that wont interest you. However if you read it tell me what's what and spare not. I haven't seen you since you were a young man—I'm bald headed and one legged and the curves are more easily followed than ever."

John Ermine was published November 12, 1902. By December 2 Remington had heard from his friends. The simplistic Charles Dana Gibson wrote: "Your book is one of 'those things' and it puts you on history's pages in big fat letters. And I congratulate us all on having a man like you

about." The poetic George Wharton Edwards wrote: "I have been on the Plains with you and John Ermine for two hours—you have set up a character that will live with me as long as I have memory—A real man seems Ermine so great is your art. In the sunlit glare of the picture of yours the modern novel of the Boudoir seems as feeble as wax candle light—Your meat is too strong for Broadway but I am sure the plainsman will accept it as Good Medicine! You have soul—and your art lieth in the hollow of your hand! Vale!"

The attorney George M. Wright addressed his letter to "John Ermine Esq. You are all right and got yourself properly killed. I was afraid something would turn up to make you appear as a gentlemanly cowboy who should marry Katherine—but thank Heaven you respected the proprieties and died with your boots on—with your halfsavage breast all untamed. Shake, John."

Navy Captain J. D. Jerrold Kelley wrote: "Dont you worry, honey, about that book. Your friend Wister is, compared with what you have done, telling things at second hand in The Virginian. I was afraid for a moment you were going to fall down on the love making, and the girl—but it is all right. I am trying inadequately I know but honestly and admiringly to tell you just how your Greek Tragedy of the Plains strikes me. Oh but Wolf-Voice is a dandy—Do him over in another book."

More concretely, George Brett of The Macmillan Company wrote December 4, 1902: "You will be glad to hear that we are going to press with a second edition of 'John Ermine' to-day. I trust that this means that the book has now started on a long career of sale. The first edition is almost exhausted and will be quite sold out before we shall be able to get the second edition ready."

The book was reviewed in the New York *Times* December 12, 1902: "Ordinary human beings [were always surprised] when a man who has long done one thing superlatively well suddenly demonstrates that he has decided talents in another direction. It certainly does not seem quite fair that one who paints remarkably good pictures should also be able to write a remarkably good story. It has always been and always will be true that 'to him that hath shall be given.' It makes one think of The Virginian, and yet it is The Virginian with a thousand differences."

One of the differences was implicit in the Denver *Republican* January 11, 1905: "Remington has seemingly found a literary success with John Ermine. Critics are divided as to the strong points as a romance but none questions its fidelity to Western life. John Ermine is being compared to The Virginian."

Herbert Craly's January 1903 review in *The Reader* was thoughtful: "Ordinarily the illustrator is to the author very much as the actor is to the playwright . . . he almost necessarily changes. Apparently the only safe course is for the author to draw his own pictures, or for the artist to write—as Mr. Frederic Remington has begun to do. The story is a sketch with a development, a culmination, and a moral. The author is writing in a vernacular that he thoroughly knows; he is using a method that is as economical as veracious, and as carefully finished as that which produced his best figures in bronze. But it takes more than the companionship of white men to make John Ermine feel at home among his own people; it takes the love of a white woman. Just here Mr. Remington visibly flinches in the illustrating, as well as in the telling of his story. And, in working out his culmination, Mr. Remington's method or his patience fails him. His ending is pathetic, but it is nothing more."

In considering the abruptness of the ending, Craly might have recalled the dedication to *Men with the Bark On,* those kinsmen of John Ermine who "die like the wild animals, unnaturally—unmourned, and even unthought of mostly," as finally and cheaply as did Ermine, dead and gone.

Modern critics have seen *John Ermine* as conflict between two cultures, with the more admirable primitive culture yielding. In consequence, the wild man hero is destroyed by civilization. (The sources are Erisman and White.)

John Ermine could not, however, compare to *The Virginian* as a commercial success. Both novels were published in 1902, both were reprinted, both became plays that opened in New York City at the Manhattan Theater, but the duration in each medium was quite different. *The Virginian* has sold two million copies. As a play it ran for ten years and it was made into a movie four times. (The source is Rush.)

John Ermine as a play was tried out in Boston September 14, 1903, as "James K. Hackett produces Louis Evan Shipman's American Drama of Frontier Life/John Ermine of the Yellowstone/Founded on Frederic Remington's Story of the Far West."

Hackett was the producer and star. In 1901 *Harper's Weekly* had noted: "He is good to see, good to hear. But the next morning one remembers that Mr. Hackett laughed too much, swallowed many of his lines, and declaimed nasally."

Remington's contact was Shipman, the playwright. Remington's July 1903 letter to Shipman predated any difficulty: "Say—you indian—I am working like hell here so dont get me down to New York before August unless you have to. Have tried to answer your questions—in enclosure." By August Remington had doubts: "Do persuade Hackett to be a real John E and cut out the old world curves."

The beginning of September Remington participated in the revising of the Shipman script: "You d—— people nearly killed me —the Doctors are working but I fear the 'worst.'" By September 17 Remington was concerned: "Why don't you tell me what is happening—I should like to see the Boston notices &c. You are such a lobster Louis— it's out of sight out of mind with your frivolus nature."

Remington also wrote to Martha Summerhayes: "I fought for that long hair but the management said the audience has got to have some Hackett—why I could not see

—but he is a matinee idol and that long with the box office. I think the play will go —but we may have to save Ermine. The public is a funny old cat and won't stand for the mustard." Thus was Ermine's hair cropped and his life continued.

The notice of the New York opening was in *Harper's Weekly* November 21, 1903: "Mr. Hackett's new play, 'John Ermine of the Yellowstone,' was suggested by Remington's sketches of Western life. John Ermine, a white man, has lived from his childhood among the Indians. He is persuaded to become a scout in the United States service. He finds on the trail a photograph of a young girl whom he is told he may meet among the white army people. It turns out that the photograph was lost by the girl's lover. He demands it of Ermine, and during the quarrel which ensues is shot by the scout in self-defence. Ermine is accused of murder, but his innocence is finally established, and he wins the girl for his wife." By December 19, 1903, *Harper's Weekly* reported: "James K. Hackett in John Ermine of the Yellowstone failed to draw in New York."

According to Martha Summerhayes, Remington said a year afterward, "That sort of thing does not interest the public. What they want—here he began to mimic some funny old East Side person, and both hands gesticulating—is a back yard and babies' clothes. They don't want to know anything about the Indian or the half-breed, or what he thinks or believes."

The "East Side person" would have been from the "Mulligan" series.

One paradox was that Remington's severe critic Emerson Hough wrote under "Wild West Faking" that "James K. Hackett in John Ermine of the Yellowstone was cast for the poor but noble scout who married the Colonel's daughter. Why should so experienced an actor handicap himself by bad verities?" Thus Hough blamed Remington for the Shipman script and for the Hackett casting.

When Remington listed his books for Perriton Maxwell in 1907, he did not include *John Ermine* among his literary achievements, as he also omitted *Sundown Leflare*. Martha Summerhayes said Remington did not consider *John Ermine* to have been a success from a financial point of view, either. After more than fifty years, however, *Today's Art* in 1960 discovered "The Remington Revival," adding that "John Ermine is being readied for the movies as this is written." No such movie has been released.

But *John Ermine* may return as a more sophisticated public accepts veracity along with the unhappy ending the circumstances of the plot called for. This is the public that was being addressed directly by "A Few Words from Mr. Remington" (*Collier's*, March 18, 1905), Remington's most quoted autobiographical précis. "A Few Words" is the only account of Remington's first trip West in August 1881, apart from the bits that are sparsely dotted into other writings.

"Jefferson as a Painter" (*Harper's Weekly*, May 13, 1905) was an obituary based on an unprinted profile Remington had done for *Harper's* ten years earlier. When he saw the manuscript February 26, 1895, Jefferson had written to Remington: "I congratulate you on your article, and myself on my Biographer—I only wish that I deserved half of the good things you have said of me."

The last of Remington's writings was *The Way of an Indian,* which was serialized in *Cosmopolitan* beginning November 1905 and reprinted in hard cover 1906. This novel may have been at least begun years before.

As early as March 1900, Remington had told Wister: "I may write a short character story much like Sun-Down Leflare." Again, in the Watertown *Daily Times* for August 17, 1900, there was a feature article on what was Remington's first season at Ingleneuk, his island in the St. Lawrence River: "This summer he is engaged in writing a novel for serial publication in the magazine Hearst is about to launch with R. H. Russell as publisher. Remington says this will be his longest literary production, much longer than Sundown LeFlare. He has been engaged for some time in writing the story and it is nearing completion. He is spending a portion of his time on the illustrations for the novel." *The Way of an Indian* was written for serial publication.

In addition, when Remington provided his biographical data for the Metropolitan Museum of Art in July 1902, he listed himself as the author of *The Way of an Indian* more than three years before its publication. He did not list *John Ermine,* which he was in the course of writing.

Hearst did not own a popular magazine until 1905 when he bought *Cosmopolitan* and soon thereafter published *The Way of an Indian.* Remington's contact was R. H. Russell. Remington wired Russell from Ingleneuk July 24, no year given: "I am sending two drawings and MS by express today. A story called 'The Kites and Crows'—it being the fifth story of 'The Way of an Indian.' One is an upright and can be used as front or three quarter page, as you see fit."

The Way, written entirely from the viewpoint of the Indian, was peculiarly used by *Cosmopolitan.* Each installment was headed by a synopsis prepared not by Remington but rather by an antagonist: "White Otter sets forth to win the eagle-plume, which he does by the wanton murder of an Absaroke. Despite his cruelty, the young Indian shows a fine sense of honor in a deal. But the baser instincts again assert themselves when he steals a Minataroe girl, wife of the half-breed Papin." White Otter would have seen this as the scalping of an enemy and the rescue of a slave, both accomplished through a warrior's initiative.

Where Remington learned the detail of Indian genre in *The Way* is a question. Vestal claimed that one Remington informant on the Indians was the Sioux chief Rain-in-the-Face who spoke only after having been primed with whiskey: "He would not talk until he had emptied" the bottle, "and after he had emptied it he never told the truth."

The conclusion of *The Way,* pathetic through the eyes of the victims, is parallelled by General Custer's account of the battle at the Washita in 1868: "We had approached so near the village that from the dead silence which reigned I feared the lodges were deserted, the Indians having fled before we advanced. The entire command dashed rapidly into the village. The Indians were caught napping. Actual possession of the village and its lodges was ours within a few moments. Before engaging in the fight, orders had been given to prevent the killing of any but the fighting strength of the village; but in a struggle of this character it is impossible at all times to discriminate, particularly when, in a hand-to-hand conflict, the squaws are dangerous adversaries, while Indian boys were found expert in the use of the pistol and bow." Custer's use of the phrase "caught napping" could have been expanded to "caught napping while asleep," a gruesome pun.

After the battle, Custer was accused of having attacked a camp of peaceful Indians. His rejoinder was that he followed the trail of a war party. Remington recounts the mission of the war party in *The Way* to have been against the Absaroke, not the whites. Remington would have been familiar with Custer's account—the Custer book used Remington illustrations.

Theodore Roosevelt in a February 20, 1906, letter to Remington asked that Remington come to Washington to discuss appointments of Westerners and Indians to office. Roosevelt added, concerning *The Way:* "It may be true that no white man ever understood an Indian, but at any rate you convey the impression of understanding him." As was indicated in the Introduction, Roosevelt was referring to an old deprecation by Remington concerning the ability to know Indians.

A typical modern evaluation of *The Way* is to acknowledge that the novel is little remembered and to relate the events to Wounded Knee. *The Way* is then called a "sympathetic and deeply probing novelized study of the life of a chief habituated to the primitive ways and unable to cope with the inroads of the white men." It is pointed out that this is a "high spot" of American literature, that *The Way* is the best novel by a white man about Indian life, and that no one else has been able to look at these problems from the Indian viewpoint quite as well.

Alternately, it has been said that Remington's descriptions of the "boys in blue" are of the perfect life, and that *The Way* merely brings forth the savage foe necessary to permit the good fellows to demonstrate their heroics.

(The sources are Dippie, Dykes, Erisman, and Johnson.)

The Way of an Indian was the last of Remington's published writings. He told Perriton Maxwell in 1907: "I shall never write another word. I only wrote those books of mine to introduce people to the subjects I was trying to draw. Pony Tracks, Crooked Trails, The Way of an Indian were done with the deliberate view of educating men and women, who knew not the West, up to a certain standard of appreciation for its beauties, fascinations, and intrinsic worth."

Erisman indicates that Remington's task as a writer had become hopeless. Remington had believed in the superiority of the West over the East, and Remington's West had faded. Under the same conditions, though, Remington's art continued.

Augustus Thomas' observation was that in writing, Remington was self-taught. He abandoned writing because it was not as easy or as remunerative as painting.

It might also have been true that Remington had exhausted the primary outlets for his writing. He had been dropped from *Harper's* and from *Collier's*.

Under all circumstances, however, Remington could count on his friend Theodore Roosevelt for the last word. It was given in a letter on White House stationery July 17, 1907, to *Pearson's Magazine:* "It is no small thing for the nation that such an artist and man of letters should arise to make permanent record of certain of the most interesting features of our national life."

Remington died December 26, 1909, when he was forty-eight. The cause of his death was septic peritonitis resulting from appendicitis. The obituary was carried by the wire service and printed nationally. The headline on the front page of the New York *Times* the following morning was "Remington, Painter and Author, Dead."

AFTERWORD

The final question is, What is the relevance of Remington's writings today?

Remington was a major artist as well as a writer. Much of his writing was, and was expressly intended to be, an introduction to his art. Remington designed his writing to provide Western background for his Eastern art public. He said in interviews that appreciation of his paintings and sculpture would be enhanced by reading his writings.

Second, no biography in depth exists for Remington. In the course of preparing such a biography, it was found that not only are many of Remington's published pieces out of print, there is not any place even a complete listing of them. Yet the autobiographical elements which are substantial in Remington's writings remain the best source of published details on his life.

Third, 20 per cent of Remington's illustrations are for his own writings. The example of *The Cheyenne Camp* in the Introduction demonstrates that these writings explicitly describe some of the illustrations that were made for them. Each contributes to the other. The writing came before the art.

Fourth, Remington conceived of his own function as memorializing the West of his youth. Wister's foreword to *Drawings* granted that Remington "has made a page of American history his own." What Remington recorded in picture and text has become quite the most distinctive page of American history. In addition, Remington's West is the arena that clearly distinguishes America from the history of the rest of the world.

And, apart from this big tapestry, Remington accurately reported on the routine events and genre of his heyday, the turn of the twentieth century, thus providing the minutiae of a distinctive period.

As has been pointed out by McCracken, these historical details are of the little people of the West as well as the famous generals and chiefs. Remington sought for what the "white and red warriors thought and felt, both before and after their battles." That was for him "more important than any of the strategies or accomplishments involved."

When Remington's work is presented chronologically, as it is here, his progression from reporter to novelist demonstrably mirrors the movement from illustrator to painter and from craftsman to sculptor. It also reflects the changes in society during that period, in attitudes concerning war and concerning the Indian, for example.

As an incident of the writings, the illustrations are of course chronological too. One critical view is that Remington began as a pen-and-ink illustrator, poor at proportion, anatomy, and composition, that he continued as a romantic realist until challenged by Schreyvogel, and that he concluded with his personal brand of impressionism. The truth seems to be, Remington's published illustrations were almost immediately unique at a high plateau of action and truth. When viewed in black and white, there is little to distinguish the best of the early illustrations from the late. Remington's easel paintings are another matter.

As a consequence of these values, we must grant that Remington's writing is meaningful as Western history. How then does it rate as Western literature?

The "Western" began with the Leatherstocking Tales of the only major Western novelist, James Fenimore Cooper. The first tale was *The Pioneers* in 1823. These Cooper classics were bowdlerized in the four-penny weeklies about 1850 and in the dime novels that started about 1857. Biographies with popular appeal were circulated for heroes like Kit Carson and Buffalo Bill Cody.

After the Western frontier had disappeared in fact and the Indians had been subjugated, Owen Wister's *The Virginian* in 1902 launched the formula Western. This was the hero "Ivanhoe in chaps" resolving conflicts between the community and the savage. The plot was predictive, involving confrontation in the wilderness between a "transplanted WASP" and alien savages.

The happy ending to *The Virginian* was necessary, even supervening lynching and a gun duel. The cowboy hero protected society by killing outlaws in a conflict between justice and law.

The alternate growth to the "Western" is the more complex "Western novel" like *The Oxbow Incident* or *Shane*. It may involve a Hamlet hero, or even an antihero, to provide the "memorable difference." Encounter with Indians is usual. Indians and whites are irreconcilable, and the losing red culture may be depicted as morally superior.

There is now a susbstantial body of current analysis of Western literature, such as by Branch, Cawelti, Davis, Etulain, Folsom, Fiedler, and Keiser. In almost all such essays, Remington is a nonperson. After his death, as Remington's status as a major artist grew, his writings were equivalently overlooked.

In Remington's own mind, his validity as a writer was tied in a large measure to *John Ermine*. This is Remington's only work that was written directly for hard-cover publica-tion. Remington meant it as a challenge to Wister's talky and melodramatic *The Virginian*. Certainly the critics reviewed it that way.

John Ermine was a successful novel in 1902, but it soon went out of print. It did not meet the cultural requirements of the succeeding decades. The primary reason was that Westerns evolved into Wister's formula. The formula called for a happy ending, or at worst, a happy ending overlaid with melancholy. *John Ermine* was an inevitable tragedy.

On the modern scene, the formula Westerns continue. They appeal to those segments of society seeking entertainment and escape. Critical plaudits, however, are for the more complex "Western novel," for its inventive aspects. *The Virginian* was nostalgia when it was written and it still is, a cowboy opus without cows, a lament for a past that never was. *John Ermine* was a try at truth for its time, as Remington saw it. It approached the white-Indian conflict by having his protagonist split into both sides. It romanticized the Indian at the expense of the army.

Remington as a literary figure is thus a reversion to the origins of the novel of the West, the noble savage at odds with civilization and so destroyed. Ermine is a tragedian, equipped as a scout to handle the conventional conflicts between his community and the aliens, but devastated as a person by the internalized conflict he cannot resolve.

To have created a lasting Western on the formula level, Remington would have had to cause Ermine to accept that Katherine would not be permitted to marry a wild man such as he. Ermine would have had to ask her to wait while he went back to his mine for the wherewithal to secure an equivalency degree from Yale. To extend the plot into the complex contemporary Western, Ermine would then realize that for a well-to-do alumnus there are other available white women, more sincere signalers perhaps, and the conclusion to the book would be Katherine out there alone on the high plains, with only one glove.

BIBLIOGRAPHY

In the course of the Introduction and Notes, footnotes have been avoided. Where a reference to a work in the Bibliography is called for, the source is given in the text. Where an author or book is referred to in the text, it is listed in the Bibliography.

While the Bibliography is substantial, it is only that fraction of the body of existing work on Remington that relates to him as a writer. For brevity, some of the entries have been grouped; for example, a number of letters by the same hand in the same repository are made into one entry.

Where possible, quotations have been shortened by omitting matter not relative to the point.

The heading under which a bibliographic entry is alphabetized is judgmental. Where the usual form of entry might make that entry hard to find, for example a book by an unfamiliar author on a discussed subject, the name of the subject has been placed first, in parentheses; for example, the Heyneman·biography of Arthur Putnam is listed under Putnam as: (Putnam) Heyneman, Julie Helen, etc.

ADAMS, RAMON F. *Western Words/A Dictionary of the American West*. Norman: University of Oklahoma Press, 1968.

ALLEN, DOUGLAS. *Frederic Remington and the Spanish-American War*. New York: Crown Publishers, 1971.

———, ed. *Frederic Remington's Own Outdoors*. New York: The Dial Press, 1964.

———, comp. "Frederic Remington—Author and Illustrator/A List of His Contributions to American Periodicals." *Bulletin of the New York Public Library*, Vol. 49, No. 12 (Dec. 1945), p. 895.

ALLEN, TOM, and ROBERT CANTWELL. "Westward to the Long Forever," *Sports Illustrated*, Vol. 43, No. 6 (Aug. 11, 1975).

ALTER, JUDITH. "Frederic Remington's Major Novel John Ermine," *Southwestern American Literature*, Vol. 2 (Spring 1972), pp. 42–46.

American Art Annual, Vol. 8, 1910–11, p. 400.

ANDREWS, ROBERT HARDY. "Frederic Remington: The Man Who Invented John Wayne." "The Pickfair Remingtons," *Mankind*, Vol. 2, No. 10 (Nov. 1970).

BANGS, FRANCIS HYDE. *John Kendrick Bangs/Humorist of the Nineties.* New York: Alfred A. Knopf, 1941.

BIGELOW, POULTNEY. "Frederic Remington: With Extracts from Unpublished Letters," *Quarterly Journal,* New York State Historical Society. Cooperstown, 1929.

The Bookman/An Illustrated Magazine of Literature and Life, Vol. 30, Sept. 1909–Feb. 1910, p. 598. New York: Dodd, Mead and Company, 1910.

BOWERS MEMORIAL MUSEUM, CHARLES W. "Painters of the West." Santa Ana, Calif., Mar. 5–30, 1972.

BROWN, CHARLES H. *The Correspondents' War.* New York: Charles Scribner's Sons, 1967, p. 64 on.

BROWN, MYRA LOCKWOOD, and ROBERT TAFT. "Painter of the Rip-Roaring West," *Country Gentleman.* Vol. 117, No. 9 (Sept. 1947), p. 16.

CARD, H. L. *A Collector's Remington/Notes on Books by Him; Books Illustrated by Him; and Books Which Gossip About Him.* Woonsocket, R.I., n.d. [1946].

CARD, TERI. *Frederic Remington's Life Story.* MS, The Amon Carter Museum of Western Art, Nov. 1968.

(Clarke) "This Busy World," *Harper's Weekly,* June 10, 1893, p. 559.

(Clarke) "Waifs and Strays," *Harper's Weekly,* June 19, 1886, p. 395.

COFFIN, WILLIAM A. "The Bronco Buster," *The Century Illustrated Monthly Magazine,* Vol. 30 (May–Oct. 1896), p. 318.

CORTISSOZ, ROYAL. "Frederic Remington. A Painter of American Life," *Scribner's Magazine,* Vol. 47 (Jan.–June 1910), p. 181.

CRALY, HERBERT. "Frederic Remington as an Author," *The Reader,* Vol. 1 (Jan. 1903), p. 230.

CROOKER, ORIN EDSON. "A Page from the Boyhood of Frederic Remington," *Collier's,* Sept. 17, 1910, p. 28.

Current Literature. "Frederic Remington—A Painter of the Vanishing West." Vol. 43, No. 5 (Nov. 1907), p. 521.

(Custer) *Wild Life on the Plains and Horrors of Indian Warfare,* by a corps of competent authors and artists. St. Louis: Royal Publishing Co., 1891.

DARY, DAVID. "Frederic Remington in Kansas," *Westerners, Kansas Corral,* Vol. 1 (1973), pp. 79–84.

(Denver?) *Republican,* c. 1888. Cromwell Childe, "A Study of the Horse."

Denver *Republican,* Jan. 11, 1905. "Latest Picture of Frederick Remington, Maker of Western Pictures and Novels."

DIPPIE, BRIAN W. "Frederic Remington's Wild West," *American Heritage,* April 1975, p. 7.

DOBIE, J. FRANK. "A Summary Introduction to Frederic Remington," in *Pony Tracks.* Norman: University of Oklahoma Press, 1961.

———. "Titans of Western Art," *American Scene,* Vol. 5, No. 4 (1964), p. 4.

DYKES, JEFF C. "Frederic Remington—Western Historian," *American Scene,* Vol. 55, No. 2 (Summer 1961), p. 4.

EDGERTON, GILES. "Frederic Remington, Painter and Sculptor: A Pioneer in Distinctive American Art," *The Craftsman,* Vol. 15, No. 6, (Mar. 1909), p. 658.

ERISMAN, FRED. *Frederic Remington.* Boise: Boise State University, 1975.

EXMAN, EUGENE. *The House of Harper.* New York: Harper & Row, 1967.

GARLAND, HAMLIN. *The Captain of the Gray-Horse Troop.* New York: Grosset & Dunlap, 1902.

———. *Roadside Meetings.* New York: Macmillan, 1930, p. 394.

GARRATY, JOHN A. *The American Nation.* New York: Harper, 1966.

GILCREASE FOUNDATION, THOMAS. "An Exhibition of Paintings and Bronzes by Frederic Remington/Charles M. Russell/May–Oct. 1950."

Gund Collection of Western Art/A History and Pictorial Description of the American West, 1970, 1973.

HARPER, J. HENRY. *The House of Harper.* New York: Harper & Brothers, 1912.

HASSRICK, PETER H. *Frederic Remington.* Amon Carter Museum, 1972.

————. *Frederic Remington/An essay and catalogue to accompany a retrospective exhibition of the work.* Fort Worth: Amon Carter Museum, 1973.

————. "Frederic Remington at the Amon Carter Museum," *American Art Review,* Vol. 1, No. 1 (Sept.–Oct. 1973), p. 41.

————. *Frederic Remington/Paintings, Drawings, and Sculpture in the Amon Carter Museum and the Sid W. Richardson Foundation Collections.* New York: Harry N. Abrams, Inc., 1973.

HILLYER, V. M., and E. G. HUEY. *A Child's History of Art.* New York: D. Appleton-Century Company, 1940.

HOEBER, ARTHUR. "From Ink to Clay," *Harper's Weekly,* Oct. 19, 1895, p. 993.

HOUGH, EMERSON. "Wild West Faking," *Collier's,* Dec. 19, 1908, p. 18.

"Johnson, Harold B., Wrote in 1900 About Remington's Island," Watertown *Daily Times,* Sept. 28, 1961.

JOHNSON, MERLE. *High Spots of American Literature.* New York: Bennett Book Studios, Inc., 1929.

JOHNSON, ROBERT UNDERWOOD. *Remembered Yesterdays.* Boston: Little, Brown, 1923.

JOHNSON, ROSSITER, ed. *The Biographical Dictionary of America,* Vol. 9, not paged. Boston: American Biographical Society, 1906.

KATZ, WILLIAM LOREN. *The Black West.* Garden City: Doubleday & Company, Inc., 1973.

KNIGHT, OLIVER. *Following the Indian Wars/The Story of the Newspaper Correspondents Among the Indian Campaigners.* Norman: University of Oklahoma Press, 1960.

KRAKEL, DEAN. "Visions of Today," *American Scene,* Vol. 5, No. 4 (1964), p. 56.

KUNITZ, STANLEY J., and HOWARD HAYCRAFT, eds. *American Authors 1600–1900: A Biographical Dictionary of American Literature.* New York: The H. W. Wilson Company, 1938.

Letters from Brett, Buel, Clarke, Edwards, Forsyth, Gibson, Jefferson, Carter Johnson, Kelley, Kemeys, Miles, Pyle, Robertson, Simmons, Wister, and Wright to Remington, Archives of American Art.

Letter from Robert Johnson to Remington, New York Public Library.

Letter from Eva Remington to Horace Sackrider, Kansas State Historical Society.

Letters from Roosevelt to Remington, Archives of American Art, *Pearson's Magazine.*

Letter from Stevens to Remington, Library of Congress.

Letters Remington to Poultney Bigelow, New York State Historical Association.

Letter Remington to Mrs. Glentworth R. Butler, Addison Gallery of American Art.

Letter Remington to Caten, McKown.

Letter Remington to Gilder, New-York Historical Society.

Letters Remington to J. H. Harper and Harper Brothers, Denver Public Library, Amon Carter Museum, authors' collection.

Letters Remington to Ralph, Amon Carter Museum, Denver Public Library, Archives of American Art, authors' collection.

Letters Remington to Eva Remington, Kansas State Historical Society.

Letter Remington to R. H. Russell, Denver Public Library.

Letters Remington to Horace Sackrider, Kansas State Historical Society.

Letters Remington to Shipman, Amon Carter Museum.

Letter Remington to Turner, New-York Historical Society.

Letters Remington to Wales, Winterthur Estate Archives.

Letters Remington to Wister, Library of Congress.

Life, September 14, 1942, p. 72 on.

LUNDBERG, FERDINAND. *Imperial Hearst/A Social Biography.* New York: Equinox Cooperative Press, 1936.

MABIE, HAMILTON WRIGHT. "Indians, and Indians," *The Century Illustrated Monthly Magazine,* Vol. 38, No. 3 (July 1889), p. 472.

MANLEY, ATWOOD. *Some of Frederic Remington's North Country Associations.* Canton, 1961.

MAXWELL, PERRITON. "Frederic Remington—Most Typical of American Artists," *Pearson's Magazine,* Oct. 1907, p. 403.

McCRACKEN, HAROLD. "Chronicler of the Old West," *Arizona Highways,* Sept. 1950.

———. *Frederic Remington/Artist of the Old West.* Philadelphia: J. B. Lippincott Company, 1947.

———. *The Frederic Remington Book/A Pictorial History of the West.* Garden City: Doubleday & Company, Inc., 1966.

———. *Frederic Remington's Own West.* New York: The Dial Press, 1960.

———. "Frederic Remington—Writer." *The Westerners.* New York, Posse Brand Book, Vol. 3, No. 2 (1956).

McKOWN, ROBIN. *Painter of the Wild West/Frederic Remington.* New York: Julian Messner, Inc., 1959.

MECHEM, KIRKE. "Frederick Remington in Kansas/Kansas History Through the Years," *Kansas Teacher,* Vol. 60, No. 5 (Jan. 1952), p. 38.

Miles, General Nelson A., Personal Recollections and Observations of. Chicago: The Werner Company, 1897.

MILES, NELSON A. *Serving the Republic/Memoirs of the Civil and Military Life of.* New York: Harper & Brothers, 1911.

Modern Maturity, Feb.–Mar. 1964, p. 34. "Frederic Remington . . . the New Yorker who captured fame with a paint brush in the Old West."

Montana the magazine, Vol. 11, No. 4 (Autumn 1961). Cowboy and Cattleman's Issue.

Montana the magazine of Western History, Vol. 27, No. 1 (Winter 1977). Katherine M. Weist, "Ned Casey and His Cheyenne Scouts."

New York *Times,* Dec. 27, 1909, p. 1. "Remington, Painter/and Author, Dead."

PEABODY CENTENNIAL COMMITTEE. *Peabody the First 100 Years.* 1971, p. 55.

(Putnam) HEYNEMAN, JULIE HELEN. *Desert Cactus/The Portrait of a Sculptor.* London: Geoffrey Bles, 1934.

RALPH, JULIAN. "Frederic Remington," *Harper's Weekly,* Jan. 17, 1891, p. 43.

———. "Frederic Remington," *Harper's Weekly,* July 20, 1895, p. 688.

———. *The Making of a Journalist.* New York: Harper & Brothers, 1903.

REMINGTON, FREDERIC. *Crooked Trails.* New York: Harper & Brothers, 1898.

———. *John Ermine of the Yellowstone.* New York: The Macmillan Company, 1902.

(Remington) "John Ermine, James K. Hackett as." *Harper's Weekly,* Nov. 21, 1903, p. 1868.

(Remington, *Ermine*) New York *Times,* Dec. 13, 1902, review.

(Remington, *Ermine*) Programme, Globe Theatre/Boston, Mass/Week of Sep. 14 to 20 [1903].

(Remington) *Journal,* Kansas State Historical Society, 1886, 1888.

REMINGTON, FREDERIC. *Men with the Bark On.* New York: Harper & Brothers, 1900.

———. *Pony Tracks.* New York: Harper & Brothers, 1895.

———. *A Rogers Ranger in the French and Indian War.* New York: Harper & Brothers, 1897.

———. *Stories of Peace and War.* New York: Harper & Brothers, 1899.

———. *Sundown Leflare.* Harper & Brothers, 1899.

(Remington, Thackeray) Copy of Thackeray's *Vanity Fair* (New York, Harper & Brothers, 1868), signed S. P. Remington inside front cover (Hough collection).

REMINGTON, FREDERIC. *The Way of an Indian.* Fox Duffield & Company, 1906.

(Remington, Writings) MARTIN, E. S. "This Busy World." *Harper's Weekly,* June 23, 1894, p. 586.

ROGERS, W. A. *A World Worth While/A Record of "Auld Acquaintance."* New York: Harper, 1922.

ROOSEVELT, THEODORE. "An Appreciation of the Art of Frederic Remington." *Pearson's Magazine,* Oct. 1907, p. 403.

RUSH, N. ORWIN. *Frederic Remington and Owen Wister/The Story of a Friendship/1893–1909.* Tallahassee, 1961.

———. "Remington the Letter-Writer," *American Scene,* Vol. 5, No. 4 (1964), p. 28.

SMILEY, NIXON. *Yesterday's Florida.* Miami: E. A. Seemann Publishing, Inc., n.d.

SUMMERHAYES, MARTHA. *Vanished Arizona.* Salem, Mass.: The Salem Press Co., 1911.

SYDENHAM, LIEUT. ALVIN H., U.S.A. *Frederic Remington/A Supplement to "The Daily Journal of . . ."* The New York Public Library, 1940, p. 609.

———. "Tommy Atkins in the American Army." *Harper's Weekly,* Vol. 36 (Aug. 13, 1892), p. 780.

TAFT, ROBERT. *Artists and Illustrators of the Old West 1850–1900.* New York: Scribner's, 1953.

THOMAS, AUGUSTUS. *The Print of My Remembrance.* New York: Scribner's, 1922.

———. "Recollections of Frederic Remington," *The Century Magazine,* Vol. 86, No. 3 (July 1913), p. 354.

Today's Art, Vol. 8, No. 11 (Dec. 1960), p. 6. "Reputations Re-examined/The Remington Revival."

VAIL, R. W. G. *Frederic Remington/Chronicler of the Vanished West.* The New York Public Library, 1929.

VESTAL, STANLEY. *The Missouri.* New York: Farrar & Rinehart, 1945.

VORPAHL, BEN MERCHANT. *My dear Wister—/The Frederic Remington-Owen Wister Letters.* Palo Alto: American West Publishing Company, 1972.

WEBSTER, CLARENCE J. "Frederic Remington Was a Carefree Canton Youth." Watertown *Daily Times,* Aug. 9, 1932, p. A-10.

(Western Artists) JOHNSON, FRIDOLF. "Art Books," *American Artist,* Vol. 40, Issue 408 (July 1976).

(Western Literature) BRANCH, DOUGLAS. *The Cowboy and His Interpreters.* New York: Cooper Square Publishers, 1961.

(Western Literature) CAWELTI, JOHN G. *The Six-Gun Mystique.* Bowling Green: Bowling Green University Popular Press, n.d. [1975?].

(Western Literature) DAVIS, DAVID B. "Ten-Gallon Hero," *American Quarterly,* Summer 1954, p. 111.

(Western Literature) ETULAIN, RICHARD W., and MICHAEL T. MARSDEN. *The Popular Western.* Bowling Green: Bowling Green University Popular Press, 1974.

(Western Literature) FOLSOM, JAMES K. *The American Western Novel.* New Haven: College & University Press, 1966.

(Western Literature) FIEDLER, LESLIE A. *The Return of the Vanishing American.* New York: Stein and Day, 1968.

(Western Literature) KEISER, ALBERT. *The Indian in American Literature.* New York: Oxford University Press, 1933.

WHITE, G. EDWARD. *The Eastern Establishment and the Western Experience/The West of Frederic Remington, Theodore Roosevelt, and Owen Wister.* New Haven: Yale University Press, 1968.

WILDMAN, EDWIN. "Frederic Remington, the Man," *Outing, the Magazine,* Vol. 41, No. 6 (Mar. 1903), p. 712.

WILSON, FRANCIS. *Francis Wilson's Life of Himself.* Boston: Houghton Mifflin Company, 1924.

WISTER, OWEN. *Diary/Journal of Journies/World's Fair, Wyoming, Yellowstone/Arizona, San Francisco, Portland/June 14th–Dec. 31st, 1893.* Western History Research Center.

———. *Roosevelt/The Story of a Friendship/1880–1919.* New York: The Macmillan Company, 1930.

———. *The Virginian/A Horseman of the Plains.* New York: The Macmillan Company, 1902.

A CATALOGUE OF FREDERIC REMINGTON'S ILLUSTRATIONS FOR HIS WRITINGS

Illustration titles are Remington's own, except for those printed in italics, which are descriptive identifications by the Editors. Asterisks indicate illustrations reproduced in this book.

Ben. Clark, Interpreter
*A Cheyenne Camp
Cheyenne Agency
An Agency Policeman
*The Branding Chute at the Beef Issue (*also known as* The Beef Issue *and* The Branding Chute)
Waiting for the Beef Issue
Steer Hunting

Two Gallant Young Cavalrymen
Harper's Weekly, March 22, 1890, p. 219

Lieutenant James M. Watson, Tenth Cavalry
*Lieutenant Powhatan H. Clarke, Tenth Cavalry

Chasing a Major-General
Harper's Weekly, December 6, 1890, p. 946

Cheyenne Scout with Led-Horse
The Supply Train
General Miles and His Escort
*Troopers Singing the Indian Medicine Song

The Art of War and Newspaper Men
Harper's Weekly, December 6, 1890, p. 947

The Ambulances
Cavalry on the March
*Infantry on the March

Indians as Irregular Cavalry
Harper's Weekly, December 27, 1890, p. 1,004

*One of the Fort Keogh Cheyenne Scout Corps, Commanded by Lieut. Casey (*also known as* "The Cheyenne Scout")
Ideal Uniform for Indian Soldier
An Apache Scout
Lieutenant Casey's Scout Post at Fort Keogh
Fort Keogh Scout
Lieutenant S. C. Robertson, Chief of the Crow Scouts
Lieutenant Casey, Commandant of Cheyenne Scouts
Indian Soldier in the Crow Scout Corps

The Sioux Outbreak in South Dakota
Harper's Weekly, January 24, 1891, p. 57

In the Trenches at Pine Ridge
The Wounding of Lieutenant Hawthorne—The Hotchkiss Gun Playing on the Cave
A United States Infantry Soldier in Winter Uniform
*The Medicine-Man's Signal: Throwing Dust in the Air—Then the Firing Began
A United States Trooper in Winter Uniform
The Opening of the Fight at Wounded Knee

Lieutenant Casey's Last Scout: On the Hostile Flanks of the Chis-chis-chash
Harper's Weekly, January 31, 1891, p. 85

"Two Ghosts I Saw"
Chis-chis-chash Scout on the Flanks
A Cheyenne Scout in Winter Rig
Cheyenne Scout Eating a Beef Rib
*A Run to the Scout Camp
Watching the Dust of the Hostiles from the Bluffs of the Stronghold

General Miles's Review of the Mexican Army
Harper's Weekly, July 4, 1891, p. 495

*General Miles Reviewing the Mexican Army

A Day with the Seventh Regiment
Harper's Weekly, July 18, 1891, p. 536

Sentry full figure
Rub-down
The Colonel and His Orderly
The Call for Ammunition
Officer and Trumpeter
Off Duty
Adjutant
Stretcher Drill
*In Firing Position
Officer on Skirmish Line

Training Cavalry Horses to Jump Obstacles
Harper's Weekly, September 19, 1891, p. 710

*Training Horses to Leap Obstacles, Tenth United States Cavalry (*also known as* Nine Episodes at Cavalry School)

Coolies Coaling a Ward Liner—Havana
Harper's Weekly, November 7, 1891, p. 881

*Chinese Coolies Loading a Steamer at Havana

A Merry Christmas in a Sibley Tepee
Harper's Weekly, December 5, 1891, p. 976

*Merry Christmas in a Sibley Tepee (*also known as* Merry Christmas in a Sibley Tent, *also known as* The Toast: "Merry Christmas!")

The Galloping Sixth
Harper's Weekly, January 16, 1892, p. 57

*Cooking in Camp
United States Cavalry Officer
The Trooper Plan for Stuffing Holes in the Sibley

A Troop Picket Line of the Sixth United States Cavalry Camp at Rapid Creek
At the Mouth of Rapid Creek—General Carr Receiving the Report of a Scout

An Appeal for Justice
Harper's Weekly, July 9, 1892, p. 654

*An Appeal for Justice

Buffalo Bill in London
Harper's Weekly, September 3, 1892, p. 847

*Buffalo Bill's Wild West Show in London—The Cossacks and Guachos

Military Athletics at Aldershot
Harper's Weekly, September 10, 1892, p. 882

*An Athletic Tournament of the British Army at Aldershot

The Uprising in Chihuahua
Harper's Weekly, May 6, 1893, p. 419

*The Uprising in Chihuahua

Black Water and Shallows
Harper's Monthly, August, 1893, p. 449

The Portage
*Black Water
Breaking a Jam
The Fawn
Hung Up

The Advance-Guard, or the Military Sacrifice
Harper's Weekly, September 16, 1893, p. 886

*The Advance-Guard, or the Military Sacrifice (*also known as* The Advance-guard *and* The Ambush)

A Gallop Through the Midway
Harper's Weekly, October 7, 1893, p. 963

*Columbian Exposition—A Note from the Wild East in the Midway Plaisance

An Outpost of Civilization
Harper's Monthly, December, 1893, p. 71

Unknown—Killed by Apache
El Patron
*"Puncher Rope Man All Same Horse" (*also known as* Lassoing the Chinese Cook)
*A Hair-cut à la Puncher
The Administrator of San José de Bavicora
The Hacienda San José de Bavicora
Punchers Saddling in the Patio (*also known as* Vaqueros Saddling in the Patio)

The Puncher Costume
The Music at the "Baile" (*also known as* Mexican Cowboy Musicians)
Shoeing a Bronco

"Toro, Toro!"
Harper's Weekly, December 9, 1893, p. 77

*Toro Toro—An Old Time Californian Vaquero After a Wild Steer

The Rebellion in Northern Mexico
Harper's Weekly, December 30, 1893, p. 1,247

*The Revolution in Northern Mexico—Moving Regulars to the Front (*also known as* Mexican Cavalry Moving)

In the Sierra Madre with the Punchers
Harper's Monthly, February, 1894, p. 350

*Cowboy grabbing bull's horns (*also known as* Taking the Bull by the Horns)
My Comrade
Porphyry Rock
The Casa Camadra
Shooting in the Sierra Madre
*On the Mountains
The Indian's Story
The Cliff Dwellings

Julian Ralph
Harper's Weekly, February 24, 1894, p. 179

No illustration

A Rodeo at Los Ojos
Harper's Monthly, March, 1894, p. 515

Johnnie Bell's Ranch "Los Ojos"
Coming to the Rodeo
A Mexican Steer
Tailing a Bull
A Study of Action
Mounting a Wild One
*Waving Serape to Drive Cattle
Johnnie Bell of Los Ojos
A Modern Sancho Panza
William in Action

Troop A Athletics
Harper's Weekly, March 3, 1894, p. 210

A Note
The Mêlée
*Chasing the Ribbon
Potato Race
*Mounting Double
An Officer

A Model Squadron
Harper's Weekly, June 9, 1894, p. 539

Soldier with saber
General Guy V. Henry, Seventh United States Cavalry, Commandant at Fort Meyer
*Throwing a Horse
Riding Sitting on Legs
Over the Hurdle Back to Back
A Model Squadron—Over the Hurdles in Line

Troop A with the Dust On
Harper's Weekly, July 7, 1894, p. 631

A Trooper
Deployed as Infantry—Fourth Troopers in Charge of the Horses
On the Skirmish Line
*A Charge in Column of Fours

Chicago Under the Mob
Harper's Weekly, July 21, 1894, p. 680

*"Giving the Butt"—The Way the "Regular" Infantry Tackles a Mob
One of Capt. Capron's Battery-men
The Chicago Strikes—United States Cavalry in the Stock-yards
Illinois National Guards Picket in the Streets of Chicago at Night (*also known as* National Guard—Chicago at Night)
The Chicago Strikes—United States Infantry in the Stock-yards

Chicago Under the Law
Harper's Weekly, July 28, 1894, p. 703

Father Vattmann
*United States Cavalrymen Shaving
Deputies Bringing in a Prisoner
*Col. R. E. A. Crofton, 15th Infantry
*Major Wallace F. Randolph, 3d Artillery (*also known as* Major Wallace Randolph with his Troops)
Lieutenant Sherer, 7th Cavalry, Standing Off Mob at the Stock-yards
Captain Luther R. Hare, 7th Cavalry

Stubble and Slough in Dakota
Harper's Monthly, August, 1894, p. 452

A setter on buckboard seat
A Dakota Chicken-wagon
On the Edge of a Slough
A Conference in the Mud
"Don't Shoot!"
*"Mark—Left"

Trooping Homeward in the After-glow
"Mark!"

The Withdrawal of the U. S. Troops
Harper's Weekly, August 11, 1894, p. 748

A Detachment of the Fifteenth Infantry
*Watering the Texas Horses of the Third Cavalry in Lake Michigan

A New Infantry Equipment
Harper's Weekly, September 22, 1894, p. 905

Rice Equipment—As a Cape
*Rice Equipment—As Shoulder-belts

Policing the Yellowstone
Harper's Weekly, January 12, 1895, p. 35

Picking a Way Down
Working up the Divide
Burgess, Nearly Forty-five Years a Scout
Down the Mountain
*The Bell-mare Over a Bad Place
*On the Headwaters—Burgess Finding a Ford (*also known as* Burgess Finding a Ford)
Getting Grub (*also known as* Patrolling the Yellowstone)

The Affair of the –th of July
Harper's Weekly, February 2, 1895, p. 103

*"We Were Now Out of the Smoke."

Coaching in Chihuahua
Harper's Weekly, April 13, 1895, p. 347

*An Early Morning Bath (*also known as* Morning Toilet)
Grub
The Box of the Bavicora Coach
Harnessing in the Patio
All Off in a Bunch

Winter Shooting on the Gulf Coast of Florida
Harper's Weekly, May 11, 1895, p. 451

*Winter Shooting on the Gulf Coast of Florida

The Colonel of the First Cycle Infantry
Harper's Weekly, May 18, 1895, p. 468

*"I Began the Retreat as I Intended"
Officer and Men of the First Cycle Infantry

Bear-Chasing in the Rocky Mountains
Harper's Monthly, July, 1895, p. 240

"Gone Away"
*Crossing a Dangerous Place

The Soledad Girls
Harper's Round Table, May 4, 1897, p. 642

*The Half-wild Cattle Came Down from the Hills
Young woman with hands on hips

A Sergeant of the Orphan Troop
Harper's Monthly, August, 1897, p. 327

Aftermath of a battle (also known as The Battle of War Bonnet Creek)
"Mile After Mile Rushed the Little Column"
"The Horses Assembled in a Side Cañon"
"The Two Men Climbed Slowly"
*"The Brave Cheyennes Were Running Through the Frosty Hills"
"Through the Smoke Sprang the Daring Soldier"

The Great Medicine-Horse: An Indian Myth of the Thunder
Harper's Monthly, September, 1897, p. 512

The Mystery of the Thunder
Indian head
*"He Jumped from Hees Pony to Dees Red Horse"
The Going of the Medicine-horse

Joshua Goodenough's Old Letter
Harper's Monthly, November, 1897, p. 878

"I Did Not Conceive That They Were Much Fitted for Bush-ranging"
*The March of Rogers's Rangers
The Storming of Ticonderoga
*Paddling the Wounded British Officer
The Capture of the French Grenadier

Massai's Crooked Trail
Harper's Monthly, January, 1898, p. 240

Indian head
The Arrest of the Scout
The Chief of Scouts
Natastale
*Scouts

An Interesting Detail
Harper's Weekly, January 8, 1898, p. 43

No illustration

The Curse of the Wolves
Collier's, January 27, 1898, p. 11

The Curse of the Wolves in the Northwest

The Essentials at Fort Adobe
Harper's Monthly, April, 1898, p. 727

**Soldier in Form of Letter T*
*The Advance
A Tame Horse
Jumping on to a Horse
Horse Gymnastics
The Pursuit
The Attack on the Cossack Posts

The Training of Cavalry
Harper's Weekly, April 2, 1898, p. 321

*Hurdling on Three Horses (*also known as* Crack Drill)
*The Training of Cavalry—A Roman Race at the Riding-hall, Fort Myer, Virginia

How Order No. 6 Went Through: As Told by Sun-Down Leflare
Harper's Monthly, May, 1898, p. 846

"Un I Was Yell Terrible"
*"She Was Keep off Jus' Front of My Pony" (*also known as* How Order Number 6 Went Through)
*Sun-Down Leflare, Washed and Dressed Up

The War Dreams
Harper's Weekly, May 7, 1898, p. 454

No illustration

Wigwags from the Blockade
Harper's Weekly, May 14, 1898, p. 462

Naval officer
*Watching the Big Search-lights in Havana Wigwagging with a Dark Lantern—After deck

Soldiers Who Cry
Harper's Weekly, May 21, 1898, p. 502

*With the Regulars at Port Tampa, Florida —9th U. S. Cavalry (Colored) Skirmishing Through the Pines

The Spirit of Mahongui
Harper's Monthly, June, 1898, p. 53

*"This Was a Fatal Embarquation"
The Omen of the Little Blue Birds
"Ye Spirit Dogg Strode from Ye Darkness & Said It Was Time"

Sorrows of Don Tomas Pidal, Reconcentrado

Harper's Monthly, August, 1899, p. 393

   *"This Was the First I Felt of War"
   "And the Soldiers Fired Many Shots at Me"

Life in the Cattle Country

Collier's, August 26, 1899, p. 3

   *"The Round-up"

When a Document Is Official

Harper's Monthly, September, 1899, p. 608

   "No, I Am Not Loco"
   *"The Buffalo-hunters Knew by the 'Sign' on the Trail"

The Trouble Brothers: Bill and the Wolf

Harper's Monthly, November, 1899, p. 887

   *"This Is the Way It Began"

How Stilwell Sold Out

Collier's, December 16, 1899, p. 10

   Indian warriors watering horses
   Trudeau
   They Found Themselves in Close Proximity to the Lower End of the Sioux Village
   Jack Stilwell

A Failure of Justice

Harper's Monthly, January, 1900, p. 267

   *"The Captain Was a Gentleman and a Scholar, but He Didn't Look the Part"
   "Stop—Stop That, Dan!"

Mountain Lions in Yellowstone Park

Collier's, March 17, 1900, p. 14

   The Outlaw

They Bore a Hand

Harper's Monthly, April, 1900, p. 705

   *"Get Down!"
   "There Was Nothing to Do"
   "I Hope the Colonel Won't Get Mad—"
   The Death of Oestreicher

A Gallant American Officer

Collier's, April 7, 1900, p. 9

   *Colonel Luther R. Hare, Thirty-third Foot, Who Conducted the Pursuit of Aguinaldo's Forces in Northern Luzon and Rescued Lieutenant Gilmore

A Shotgun Episode

Outing, May, 1900, p. 117

   *"Todd Was to Sit on His Horse in Front of the Tepee, and Hold Mine While I Went In"
   "Then I Jumped to My Feet and Told the Visitors to Throw Off Their Blankets"

How a Trout Broke a Friendship

Outing, September, 1900, p. 651

   No illustration

Natchez's Pass

Harper's Monthly, February, 1901, p. 437

   *The Captain . . . Looked at the Moon
   Pushed Himself Back in His Chair Before the Horrible Sight

Billy's Tearless Woe

McClure's Magazine, March, 1901, p. 455

   Man and dog in front of tent
   *" 'Billy, I Find Him Dog . . .' "
   The Burial of Keno

How the Worm Turned

Collier's, May 4, 1901, p. 12

   *"Say, Boss, Ah Wasn't Thar—Ah Only Heared 'bout It from Men What Was" (*also known as* How the Worm Turned)

A Desert Romance: A Tale of the Southwest

The Century, February, 1902, p. 522

   The Old Texan
   Colonel Simms
   *The Trailer
   *In the Desert—Don Gomez and His Lancers at the Ochoa Spring (*also known as* Don Gomez and His Lancers at the Ochoa Spring)
   The Adobe Ranch Where the Fight Took Place

The Strategy of the Blanket Pony

Collier's, February 1, 1902, p. 12

   *"The Strategy of the Blanket Pony" (*also known as* Blanket Pony Strategy)

Western Types

Scribner's Magazine, October, 1902, p. 408

   *The Cow-boy
   *The Cossack Post (Cavalryman)
   *The Scout
   *The Half-breed

John Ermine of the Yellowstone
New York: Macmillan Company, 1902

Head of John Ermine
*John Ermine
Miner with a pick
*The Chairman
Indian head
*A Crow
*"In the Middle of the Bunch Sat Weasel"
Horse grazing
"He Called the Boy to Him and Put His Arm Around Him"
*Wolf-Voice
Rider with pack horse
*"Halt! Who Goes There."
Line of men's heads
Captain Lewis
A rifle
Major Ben Searles
*"Bullets Kicked up the Dust"
A soldier
A side-wheeler
*Katherine
*The Englishman
*"Will You Please Carry My Parasol for Me?'"
*Shockley
A magpie
*"He Bore the Limp Form to the Sands"
Man on horse
Man on galloping horse
*"A Tremendous Bang Roared Around the Room"
Buffalo skull
*Ramon
A playing card "club"

A Few Words from Mr. Remington
Collier's, March 18, 1905, p. 16

*The Map in the Sand

Jefferson as a Painter
Harper's Weekly, May 13, 1905, p. 684

No illustration

The Way of an Indian
Cosmopolitan, November, 1905, p. 37,
Chapters I and II

Two Indians on horseback

*He Looked on the Land of His People and He Hated All Vehemently (*also known as* White Otter)
The Wolves Sniffed Along the Trail, But Came No Nearer
*"O Gray Wolf of My Clan—Shall We Have Fortune?"
"Pretty Mother of the Night—White Otter Is No Longer a Boy"

The Way of an Indian
Cosmopolitan, December, 1905, p. 125,
Chapters III and IV

*The Ceremony of the Fastest Horse
*The Interpreter Waved at the Youth, Sitting There on His War-pony (*also known as* The Liar)
*"I Will Tell the White Man How He Can Have His Ponies Back"
*Nothing But Cheerful Looks Followed the Bat

The Way of an Indian
Cosmopolitan, January, 1906, p. 309,
Chapters V and VI

*The Fire Eater Raised His Arms
He Rushed the Pony Right to the Barricade
*The Fire Eater Slung His Victim Across His Pony, Taking His Scalp

The Way of an Indian
Cosmopolitan, February, 1906, p. 379,
Chapter VII

Indian chief on charging horse
*The Rushing Red Lodges Passed Through the Line of the Blue Soldiers

The Way of an Indian
Cosmopolitan, March, 1906, p. 563,
Chapter VIII

He Made His Magazine Gun Blaze Until Empty
*He Shouted His Harsh Pathos at a Wild and Lonely Wind, But There Was No Response

ACKNOWLEDGMENTS

We are at this writing in the course of a full biography of Frederic Remington and the compilation of a catalogue raisonné of his drawings and paintings, so it is difficult to acknowledge separately those who have helped us just with this book limited to Remington's writings.

Some of our correspondents and friends have gone to unusual efforts to make available to us their suggestions and materials. In alphabetical order, those persons include Peter H. Hassrick, Jack W. Traylor, Sandra Turner, and Nancy Wynne. The authors' photography was by Dennis Flynn.

Also, Christopher C. Cook, Addison Gallery of American Art; William K. Verner, The Adirondack Museum; Eugene B. Adkins; Marjorie Harvey, Akron Art Institute; Douglas G. Schultz, Albright-Knox Art Gallery; Richard N. Gregg, Allentown Art Museum; Hortense Zera, The American Academy of Arts and Letters; *American Art Review;* Dr. T. D. Nicholson, Nina J. Root, The American Museum of Natural History; Maxwell Desser, American Watercolor Society; Frances Gupton, Mr. Nancy G. Wynne, Amon Carter Museum of Western Art; George Schriever, The Anschutz Collection; R. Scudder Smith, *Antiques* and *The Arts Weekly;* Dennis Barrie, Marilyn Wheaton, Garnett McCoy, Margaret Roberts, Archives of American Art; Deborah Whitehurst, Arizona State University; Mrs. Marilyn Kelm, The University of Arizona; Mrs. Margaret Wickard, Arkansas Arts Center; Kenneth H. Lindquist, Arnot Art Museum; Milton Rhodes, The Arts Council; Vera Cross, Attleboro Museum; Alfred Bader; Betty Magill, Ball State University; Brenda Richardson, Susan Cumins, The Baltimore Museum of Art; Robert C. Woodward, Bangor Public Library; Rita Humphrey, Baylor University; Mrs. Betty W. Hirsch, Beaumont Art Museum; Archibald Hanna, The Beinecke Rare Book and Manuscript Library; Peter W. Cook, The Bennington Museum; John David Farmer, Ted Weeks, Birmingham Museum of Art; Stephen Rhodes, Blanden Art Gallery; Mary Brande, Book Collectors; R. Peter Mooz, Bowdoin College Museum of Art; Larry L. Bruns, The Bowers Museum; James T. Forrest, Ed Smyth, Bradford Brinton Memorial; Peter L. Myer, Brigham Young University; Patricia Janis Broder; Gary Reynolds, The Brooklyn Museum; John J. Whitlock, Brooks Memorial Art Gallery; Mel Brygut; Cole Heefter, Buffalo and Erie County Historical Society; Peter H. Hassrick, Buffalo Bill Historical Center; Richard P. LaGuardia, Buffalo Bill Memorial Museum; Charles E. Heilmann, Butler County Historical Society; Lorinda T. Butler, The Butler Institute of American Art; Frederick C. Cain; Gary F. Kirutz, Mrs. T. E. Whitesides, Jay Williar, California Historical Society; Marian Eber, University of California; Brooke Whiting, University of California, Los Angeles; Edward W. Lipoma, Canajoharie Library and Art Gallery; Paul F. Binai, Carnegie Institute; Prof. Walter K. Long, Cayuga Museum of History and Art; Stan H. Wiederspan, Cedar Rapids Art Center; Margaret Fish Rahill, Charles Allis Art Library; Mrs. Mary Black, Charleston Art Gallery; John Maxon, The Art Institute of Chicago; John S. Tris, Chicago Historical Society; Dennis R. Anderson, Chrysler Museum at Norfolk; Florence S. Jacobsen, The Church of Jesus Christ of Latter-day Saints; Millard F. Rogers, Jr., Mrs. Denny Carter, Kristin L. Spangenberg, Cincinnati Art Museum; Carmeletta Malora, The Cincinnati Historical Society; David Cass, Sterling and Francine Clark Art Institute; Joseph McCullogh, The Cleveland Institute of Art; Sherman E. Lee, William S. Talbot, The Cleveland Museum of Art; H. Gourley, Colby College Art Museum; Shelton Stanfill, Colorado State University Art Gallery; Joseph Morrow, The State Historical Society of Colorado; Peter Robinson, University of Colorado; John Richard Craft, Columbia Museum of Art; Kenneth A. Lohf, Columbia University; Edmund Kuehn, The Columbus Gallery of Fine Arts; C. Clay Aldridge, Columbus Museum of Arts and Crafts; Mrs. E. P. Freidland, The Connecticut Historical Society; Mary Kerr, Cooper-Hewitt Museum of Design; Dorothy W. Phillips, Corcoran Gallery of Art; Mary Riordan, Cranbrook Academy of Art; Roger D. Clisby, E. B. Crocker Art Gallery; Mrs. Melissa L. St. Cyr, Cumberland County Historical Society; John C. Mahy, Cummer Gallery of Art; David S. Brooke, The Currier Gallery of Art; Allen J. Clark, Custer Battlefield National Monument; Carol Robbins, Dallas Museum of Fine Arts; Beverly Chatham Crofoot, Linda Kastan, Jan van der Marck, Dartmouth College Galleries; Henry B. Davis, jr.; Richard S. Field, Davison Art Center; Bruce H. Evans, The Dayton Art Institute; Mrs. Phyllis J. Nixon, Delaware Art Museum; William I. Homer, University of Delaware; Georgianna Contiguglia, The Denver Art Museum; Eleanor M. Gehres, Sandra Turner, Denver Public Library; James T. Demetrion, Euphemia C. Conner, Des Moines Art Center; Holly B. Ulseth, Detroit Historical Museum; Kathleen A. Pyne, The Detroit Institute of Arts; Edward L. Daniel, Diocesan Center; Fairfax Downey; S. H. du Pont, Jr.; Jeff Dykes; Karl N. Ehricke; Mrs. George F. Martin, John W. Streetman III, The Evansville Museum of Arts and Science; Kathy Sullivan, Everson Museum of Art; Martin E. Petersen, Fine Arts Gallery of San Diego; D. Snowden, The Fine Arts Museums of San Francisco; Blaine E. Rieke, First Wisconsin Trust Company; Marjorie D. Zunder, Fletcher Free Library: Ann E. Reitz, Flint Institute of Arts; Deborah G. Harding, The Florida State Museum; Bonnie L. Ross, The Roswell P. Flower Memorial Library; Dennis Flynn; Ellen F. Clattenburg, Mrs. Phoebe Peebles, Fogg Art Museum; James E. Voirol, The Fort Wayne Museum of Art; Beatrice M. Grant, Fort Worth Public Library; Robert F. Looney, Free Library of Philadelphia; Mrs. Elsie Kronenberg, Freer Gallery of Art; Bernice Davidson, The Frick Collection; director, Charles and Emma Frye Art Museum; W. H. Leary, General Services Administration; Ethel Moore, Georgia Museum of Art; Mr. and Mrs. George F. Getz, Jr.; William C. Coleman, Gibbes Art Gallery; Carolyn Bradshaw, Thomas Gilcrease Institute; Andrew Oko, Glenbow-Alberta Institute; Fred A. Myers, Grand Rapids Art Museum; Walter E. Simmons II, Greenfield Village; Edith G. Walker, The Greenville Art Center; Enez Whipple, Guild Hall; Jack W. Warner, Gulf States Paper Corporation; Isabel B. Alexander, The Gund Collection of Western Art; Mrs. Ann Archambault, Hackley Art Gallery; Virginia M. Cline, George F. Harding Museum; Stephen R. Brogden, The Harwood Foundation; Peter H. Hassrick; Eva Ingersoll Gatling, The Heckscher Museum; Mildred M. Car, The Hickory Museum of Art Association; Mary Jo Saunders, The High Museum of Art; Gail Gilbert; Allen R. Hite Art Institute; James T. Holmes; Mrs. Jakie Tsarnas, Joseph Feher, Honolulu Academy of Arts; Mr. and Mrs. Edwin A. Hough; Donald M. Halley, Jr., The Hudson River Museum; Mary Alice Richardson, Huguenot-Thomas Paine Historical Association; William R.

Sargent, Huntington Galleries; Alan Jutzi, Huntington Library; Morton Raych, The Hyde Collection; Arthur A. Hart, Idaho State Historical Society; Betty I. Madden, Illinois State Museum; Tom Rumer, Indiana Historical Society Library; Diane Lazarus, Indianapolis Museum of Art; Mrs. Helen Noland, Carl H. Armstrong, Indiana State Museum; Linda J. Baden, Indiana University Art Museum; Gabor B. Inke; Gloria Sullivan, International Business Machines Corporation; Margaret W. M. Shaeffer, Jefferson County Historical Society; Thomas W. Leavitt, Herbert F. Johnson Museum of Art; Mrs. Kenneth A. Anderson, Miss Mildred Goosman, Joslyn Art Museum; Bertha Stauffenberg, Kalamazoo Institute of Arts; Jack W. Traylor, Forrest R. Blackburn, Mrs. George T. Hawley, Kansas State Historical Society; Charles C. Eldredge, The University of Kansas; William R. Buster, Kentucky Historical Society; A. Bruce MacLeish, Kentucky Library and Museum; Nancy Wolsk, University of Kentucky Art Gallery; Mrs. Muriel B. Christison, Krannert Art Museum; Joseph Ishikawa, Kresge Art Center Gallery; Mrs. Vi Kreutzer; Ruth S. Burton, Lafayette Art Center; Mr. Walter J. Laird, Jr.; Richard Armstrong, La Jolla Museum of Contemporary Art; Bridget Paddock, Lamont Gallery; Stuart Leech; Ricardo Viera, Lehigh University; Jerry L. Kearns, Robert H. Land, John C. Broderick, The Library of Congress; Harry Lockwood; Locust Valley Library; Jane E. Burrell, The Long Island Historical Society; Mrs. Rae Avrutin, Nancy Moure, Los Angeles County Museum of Art; John Dewar, Los Angeles County Museum of Natural History; Jay R. Broussard, (Louisiana) State Art Agency; Carol Hotchkiss, The Lowe Art Museum; Tom Mahoney; Marion Shepard, Lyman Allyn Museum; E. D. McGwire; Alice C. Simkins, John Palmer Leeper, Marion Koogler McNay Art Institute; G. C. Morris, Maine Historical Society; Vincent A. Hartgen, University of Maine; Dina G. Malgeri, Malden Public Library; Atwood Manley; Francis Martin, Jr.; Robert Campbell, Maryhill Museum of Fine Arts; Romaine Stec Somerville, Maryland Historical Society; Miss Winifred Collins, Massachusetts Historical Society; Sue Ruotolo, Massachusetts Institute of Technology; Mary Merwin, The Massillon Museum; Michael Matijevich; Sally Black, Maxwell Museum of Anthropology; Mrs. Anne R. Mannarino, Lewis A. Shepard, Mead Art Gallery; Lewis I. Sharp, The Metropolitan Museum of Art; Sterling Cook, MU Art Center; Jacquelynn Slee, The University of Michigan; Thomas E. Staicar, University of Michigan Library; Paul Tomidy, Mills College Art Gallery; Thomas Beckman, The New Milwaukee Art Center; Robert G. Carroon, Milwaukee County Historical Society; John W. Luedtke, Milwaukee Public Museum; Rosamond Hurrell, The Minneapolis Institute of Arts; Marlea R. Warren, Minneapolis Public Library; Lila J. Goff, Minnesota Historical Society; Sandra L. Lipshultz, Minnesota Museum of Art; Susan Brown, University of Minnesota; Julie Schiever, Mint Museum of Art; Robert L. Tettleton, The University of Mississippi; John H. Lindenbusch, Missouri Historical Society; Harry E. Hammer, Missouri Pacific Lines; Jim Duncan, Missouri State Museum; Priscilla A. Evans, The State Historical Society of Missouri; Mrs. Harriett C. Meloy, Ken Korte, Lory Morrow, Montana Historical Society; Mrs. Lorenson, Montclair Art Museum; Henry Flood Robert, Jr., Mrs. Elizabeth B. Brown, Montgomery Museum of Fine Arts; Janet Murrow, Mount Holyoke College; Bill Moyer; Muckenthaler Center; Virginia Kazor, Municipal Art Gallery; Edward H. Dwight, Munson-Williams-Proctor Institute; Frances Mawn, Museum of Art of Ogunquit; Mrs. Karin Peltz, Museum of Fine Arts, Boston; Susan Smith, Museum of Fine Arts, Houston; Mrs. Pauline M. Reynolds, Museum of Fine Arts, Springfield; Eric B. Rowlison, The Museum of Modern Art; Elvira V. Ogard, Museum of New Mexico; Mrs. Elizabeth Dobrinski, Museum of Northern Arizona; William F. Stiles, Museum of the American Indian; A. K. Baragwanath, Museum of the City of New York; R. G. Myers;

Phyllis Braff, Nassau County Museum; Germain G. Glidden, The National Art Museum of Sport; Abigail Booth, National Collection of Fine Arts; Dean Krakel, National Cowboy Hall of Fame; William P. Campbell, National Gallery of Art; Mrs. Andree Nehls, The National Gallery of Canada; Dick D. Grube, National Infantry Museum; Elaine E. Mann, National Museum of Racing; David H. Wallace, National Park Service; Robert C. Pettit, Nebraska State Historical Society; Norman A. Geske, The University of Nebraska; Beth Anctil, Nevada Art Gallery; Allen R. Neville; James W. Kreiter, Neville Public Museum; Mr. Robert J. Koenig, The Newark Museum; William J. Dane, The Newark Public Library; Charles B. Ferguson, The New Britain Museum of American Art; Susan C. Faxon, University of New Hampshire; Mrs. H. Worobec, New Haven Free Public Library; Howard W. Wiseman, The New Jersey Historical Society; Ed Grusheski, New Jersey State Museum; Cleta H. Downey, The University of New Mexico; William A. Fagaly, New Orleans Museum of Art; Mrs. Paul C. Rogers, The Art Association of Newport; Donald J. Gormley, Art Commission of the City of New York; Mary Alice Kennedy, Thomas Dunnings, The New-York Historical Society; J. R. McNiece, New York Public Library; Richard E. Slavin III, New York State Historical Association; Otto Noeding; Mrs. Gay M. Hertzman, The North Carolina Museum of Art; Joseph C. Sloane, The University of North Carolina; Norman Paulson, State Historical Society of North Dakota; Jerry M. Bloomer, The R. W. Norton Art Gallery; Christina Orr, Norton Gallery and School of Art; Peter M. Winkler, University of Notre Dame; John E. Peetz, Mrs. Marjorie Arkelian, The Oakland Museum; Linda S. Klinger, Oberlin College; Nicholas N. Smith, Ogdensburg Public Library; Douglas A. White, The Ohio Historical Society; Roger and Agnes Ohler; George F. Kuebler, Oklahoma Art Center; R. W. Jones, Oklahoma Historical Society; Judy Clothier, The University of Oklahoma; Bernie Rosenberg, Olana Gallery; Olga K. Melko, Old Mint; Janice Worden, Oregon Historical Society; Richard C. Paulin, University of Oregon; Arthur P. Pacheco; Jackie Wilson, Panhandle-Plains Historical Museum; Malcolm Parker, The Parthenon; Andrea Clark, Pasadena Art Museum; Mrs. Elinor Reichlin, Peabody Museum, Cambridge; Philip C. F. Smith, Peabody Museum, Salem; Elizabeth Kolowrat, Pennsylvania Academy of the Fine Arts; Donald A. Winer, Pennsylvania Collection of Fine Arts; Barbara Donley, The Pennsylvania State University; Lucy L. Hrivnak, Historical Society of Pennsylvania; Alan E. Morrison, University of Pennsylvania; Lois Pressman, Philadelphia Museum of Art; Linda F. Moore, Philbrook Art Center; James McLaughlin, The Phillips Collection; Lucinda Simmons, The Frank Phillips Foundation; James K. Ballinger, Charles P. Braendle, Phoenix Art Museum; Mrs. George H. Semler, Jr., Christine Stenstrom, Felice Stampfle, The Pierpont Morgan Library; Edwin Warfield III, Pikesville Military Reservation; Keith E. Dennison, Pioneer Museum & Haggin Galleries; L. A. Moore, Plainfield Public Library; Francis Newton, Diana Turner, Portland Art Museum; Kathryn Li, Portland Museum of Art; Franklin P. Bruns, Jr., Division of Postal History; Frances Follin Jones, Princeton University; Alfred L. Bush, Princeton University Library; Carl Pugliese; N. Richmond, Queens College; George M. Richard, Charles A. Wustum Museum of Fine Arts; Kent Ahrens, Randolph-Macon Woman's College; J. Daniel Selig, The Reading Public Museum and Art Gallery; Mildred B. Dillenbeck, Remington Art Museum; F. G. Renner; Mrs. Virginia Catton, The Rhode Island Historical Society; Mrs. Patricia M. Hurley, Rhode Island School of Design; Valleau Wilkie, Jr., Sid W. Richardson Foundation; Mrs. Ralph Whisenhunt, Art Association of Richmond; Mrs. Elizabeth S. Telford, John and Mable Ringling Museum of Art; Walter M. Hathaway, Roanoke Fine Arts Center; David B. Hartley, Robinson Museum; Patricia McDonough, Rochester Museum & Science Center; Alan Kusler, Rochester Public Library; Janet Otis, University of Rochester; John W. Pettibone, Rockport Art Association; Bob Rockwell, The Rockwell Gallery; Frances D. Cooper, Rollins College; William H. Hendrickson, Theodore Roosevelt Birthplace National Historic Site; Robert D. Powell, Theodore Roosevelt National Memorial Park; Suzanne Bolan, The Philip H. & A. S. W. Rosenbach Foundation; S. H. Rosenthal, Jr.; Wendell Ott, Roswell Museum and Art Center; Joseph Rubinfine; Ray W. Steele, C. M. Russell Museum; Phillip Dennis Cate, Rutgers University; John W. MacInnis, James L. Brown, Sagamore Hill National Historic Site; James Chase, The Saginaw Art Museum; C. I. Callim, St. Augustine Historical Society; John H. Dryfhout, Saint-Gaudens Museum; Rt. Rev. Robert G. Dodson, Saint Gregory's Abbey; Mahlon Peterson, Jennifer Bixby, Edward J. Blankman, Sarah E. Boehme, St. Lawrence University; Jo Ann Hayes, The St. Louis Art Museum; Frank A. Young, The St. Louis County Historical Society; Lydia Modi Vitale, de Saisset Art Gallery-Museum; Louis D. Liskin, Salmagundi Club Library; Joseph S. Sample; Mrs. Eric Steinfeldt, San Antonio Museum Association; Susan King, San Francisco Museum of Art; Laurel Vass, Terrell Hillebrand, Santa Barbara Museum of Art; Mark Winetrout, The Schenectady Museum; Anna Jane Moyer, Schmucker Memorial Library; George Schriever; Mrs. Elizabeth de Fato, Seattle Art Museum; Virginia Reich, Seattle Public Library; Thomas Seymour III; Doris J. Evans, Gilbert M. Simmons Library; Dr. Harold E. Simon; Peggy Parris, Sioux City Art Center; David Miller, Skidmore College: R. G. Jinks, Smith & Wesson; Donald O. Reichert, The George Walter Vincent Smith Art Museum; Deborah Chotner, Smith College Museum of Art; J. Roger Jobson, The Society of California Pioneers; John Moodie, The Society of Illustrators; Joan T. Washburn, Sotheby Parke Bernet; Vincenzo Mangione, (South Bend) Art Center; Joseph M. Stuart, South Dakota Memorial Art Center; Donald Brewer, University of Southern California; Helen Leath, *Southwestern American Literature;* Mrs. E. Clare Ulrich, Southwest Museum; C. J. Suckle, Southwest Texas State University; Addison Franklin Page, The J. B. Speed Art Museum; Mortimer Spiller; Darral A. Dishman, Spiva Art Center; L. Ross Johnson, Springville Museum of Art; Anita Moxley, Stanford University; Mrs. Anna Jean Caffey, Nelda C. and H. J. Lutcher Stark Foundation; Dr. Franz Stenzel; Susan Stitt, Stephanie K. Farrell, The Museums at Stony Brook; Ms. Merle M. Sanderson, Swain School of Design; Mary Ann Calo, Syracuse University; Jeanne Prine, Telfair Academy of Arts and Sciences; Alfred K. Guthe, The University of Tennessee; C. Sallander, Art Museum of South Texas; Colleen Kain, The Texas State Historical Association; Donald B. Goodall, The University of Texas at Austin; Donald E. Smith, Texas Woman's University; Dr. and Mrs. Oscar W. Thoeny; Otto Wittmann, Patricia J. Whitesides, The Toledo Museum of Art; Jessie Poesch, Tulane University; H. Peter Kriendler, "21" Club Art Collection; Matilda Carter, United States Army Military History Institute; Horace Mann, U.S.A. Quartermaster Museum; James R. Ketchum, The United States Capitol; Henry B. Davis, Jr., (previously) United States Cavalry Museum; Louis A. Ciotti, United States Department of the Interior; Dr. William W. Jeffries, James W. Cheeves, U. S. Naval Academy Museum; Ann Friedman, Everett L. Cooley, Utah Museum of Fine Arts; Mrs. Margaret D. Lester, Utah State Historical Society; Arley G. Curtz, Utah State Institute of Fine Arts; Lynne Ringwood, University of Utah Libraries; Mrs. Vera Costello, Valley National Bank; Peter Morrin, Vassar College; Robert L. Hagerman, Vermont Historical Society; Pinkney Near, Virginia Museum of Fine Arts; David B. Lawall, University of Virginia; Robert C. Vose, Jr., Vose Galleries; Mrs. Stuart Wade; Donna McKee Giunta, Wadsworth Atheneum; Gwen Bitz, Martin Friedman, Walker Art Center; Hal Wallis;

R. H. Randall, The Walters Art Gallery; Robert E. Preszler, Washington County Museum of Fine Arts; Delbert J. McBride, State Capitol Museum, Washington; Fred Dunagan, University of Washington; James E. Tucker, Weatherspoon Art Gallery; Merrilee Dowty, Wells Fargo Bank; June Witt, Jeff McDonald, Western History Collections; Gene M. Gressley, David Crosson, Western History Research Center; Marie Czach, Western Illinois University; Franklin P. Taplin, The Westfield Athenaeum; Paul A. Chase, Westmoreland County Museum of Art; Richard E. Kuehne, Michael E. Moss, Nancy Harlow, West Point Museum; Mary M. Jenkins, State of West Virginia; Susan Ewell Alexander, The White House; Lynn Herrmann, Whitney Museum of American Art; Mrs. Mary Lee Archer, The Wichita Art Museum; George L. McKenna, William Rockhill Nelson Gallery of Art; Mrs. Flora H. Bloedel, Williams College; Lucy McWilliams, William S. Hart Park; Jeffrey S. Blumberg, The Winnipeg Art Gallery; Karol A. Schmiegel, Charles Hummel, Sherry Fowble, Barbara Hearn, The Henry Francis du Pont Winterthur Museum; George Talbot, The State Historical Society of Wisconsin; Jan Marshall Fox, *The Wisconsin Union;* Paul Wolcott, Jr.; Mrs. Phyllis Clark, The College of Wooster; Timothy A. Riggs, Worcester Art Museum; Nancy E. Gaudette, Worcester Public Library; Mrs. Laura Hayes, Wyoming State Art Gallery; Lynne Silkman, Mrs. Nan Ross, Yale University Art Gallery; Barbara McCorkle, Yale University Library; Donna Forbes, Yellowstone Art Center; Albert K. Yohn; Jack Gyer, Yosemite Museum; Charles Dietz, Zanesville Art Center.